THE MAKING OF A TERRORIST

THE MAKING OF A TERRORIST

RECRUITMENT, TRAINING, AND ROOT CAUSES

Volume I: Recruitment

Edited by James J. F. Forest

PRAEGER SECURITY INTERNATIONAL
Westport, Connecticut · London

Library of Congress Cataloging-in-Publication Data

The making of a terrorist : recruitment, training, and root causes / edited by
James J. F. Forest.
    p. cm.
  Includes bibliographical references and index.
  ISBN 0–275–98543–1 ((set) : alk. paper)—ISBN 0–275–98544–X ((vol.
i) : alk. paper)—ISBN 0–275–98545–8 ((vol. ii) : alk. paper)—ISBN
0–275–98546–6 ((vol. iii) : alk. paper) 1. Terrorism. 2. Terrorists. I. Forest,
James J. F.
  HV6431.M353   2006
  303.6'25—dc22   2005016849

British Library Cataloguing in Publication Data is available.

Library of Congress Catalog Card Number: 2005016849
ISBN: 0-275-98543-1 (set)
        0-275-98544-X (vol. I)
        0-275-98545-8 (vol. II)
        0-275-98546-6 (vol. III)

First published in 2006

Praeger Security International, 88 Post Road West, Westport, CT 06881
An imprint of Greenwood Publishing Group, Inc.
www.praeger.com

Printed in the United States of America

The paper used in this book complies with the
Permanent Paper Standard issued by the National
Information Standards Organization (Z39.48-1984).

10 9 8 7 6 5 4 3 2 1

Contents

Editor's Note

Terrorism—a word which comes from the Latin *terrere*, "to cause to tremble"—has become a frightening global reality.[1] While there is no firm agreed-upon definition of the term, it is most commonly used in today's mainstream press to describe acts of politically motivated violence perpetrated against noncombatant targets by subnational groups or clandestine agents.[2] From New York to Bali to Madrid, ordinary citizens throughout the civilized world are under increasing fear of a deadly attack from unknown individuals, for reasons many of us do not fully understand. National and international security forces are on constant alert, desperate to prevent the next catastrophe, and yet many observers agree that our military and intelligence services are spread too thin and face insurmountable hurdles in the global war on terrorism. The situation calls for greater engagement with the public, as the necessary eyes and ears of the global antiterrorism coalition. However, to be effective the public must be equipped with the knowledge of how, why, and where an individual becomes a terrorist. This is the primary goal of this three-volume publication, *The Making of a Terrorist*.

The chapters of this publication revolve around one central question: What do we currently know about the transformation through which an individual becomes a terrorist? From decades of research on this question, a great deal has been learned about terrorism in general. Scholars have observed that terrorism is most often an action taken as part of a broad strategy, not a random act of violence by wild-eyed psychotic misfits as portrayed in the typical Hollywood film. Such a strategy is typically related to a group's desire for some form of political and/or social change. Islamic radicals in Egypt or Uzbekistan, for example, want to unite the global community of Muslims under a single Islamic authority, while in Russia and Sri Lanka, the violence is caused by groups (Chechens and Tamils respectively) who want to form their own independent state.

Based on historical studies of political and revolutionary violence, some scholars have suggested that individuals are drawn to terrorist organizations and violence primarily for pragmatic reasons of contributing to political or social change. Other experts in the field have focused their research on the conditions under which an individual might choose to join a terrorist organization, including socioeconomic status, family background, and religious orientation. In many cases, governments are overly oppressive, corrupt or outright illegitimate, while their citizens struggle with a severe lack of civil liberties and economic opportunities. The resulting climate of widespread social despair and humiliating powerlessness is ripe for recruitment by terrorist organizations.

Another body of research has examined the psychological aspects of terrorism, finding that since most terrorist attacks kill civilians indiscriminately, an individual must develop what Jerrold Post has termed a "psycho-logic," which involves the ability to dehumanize potential victims and moral disengagement from the act of murder.[3] Religious doctrines, public opinion, and the replacement of a personal identity with a powerful group identity are also contributing factors to the terrorist's mindset.

Overall, we have learned that the transformation through which an individual becomes a terrorist involves a variety of complex and intertwined issues. A single contributing factor—such as personal religious conviction, widespread poverty, or an oppressive government—is not likely to result in the formation of terrorist organizations. However, the current body of research on terrorism suggests that a combination of factors will, in most cases, result in some form of terrorism. This combination differs widely by region, and at a minimum involves motivations (political, social, and economic root causes), opportunities, contexts, processes (recruitment and training), personal disposition (psychological and religious orientation), and preparation (including family background, education, community history, and criminal record).

The Making of a Terrorist seeks to provide readers with a centralized and authoritative information source on the most essential topics of terrorist recruitment, training, and root causes. The chapters of this publication are organized in three volumes. Chapters in the first volume address central themes in the recruitment of terrorists, with special emphasis on the psychological and religious appeals of joining a terrorist organization. Chapters in the second volume provide a variety of insights on the training of terrorists (both how and where), and describe these actions within the context of specific terrorist groups. Contributors to the third volume focus on the political, social, and economic factors that contribute to terrorism both globally and within specific countries or regions. Each volume contains a preface and introductory chapter, describing the contributed essays and providing an intellectual background for the discussions that follow.

By examining in greater detail the processes and contexts that frame the transformation of an individual into a terrorist, we gain clarity in our understanding of terrorism—and how to combat it. Together, this collection of essays in *The Making of a Terrorist* will help us identify the direction of future developments in terrorism and counterterrorism. The volumes will equip the ordinary citizen with a more sophisticated understanding of terrorist recruitment, training and root causes, and as this knowledge comes to be shared by an increasing number of concerned observers, we can reasonably expect new and innovative strategies to address the short- and long-term causes of terrorism.

Preface

The chapters of this volume contribute to our knowledge of terrorist recruitment in a variety of dimensions. Some authors were asked to describe the types of recruitment activities that take place in prisons, criminal networks, and online. Others were asked to analyze the social, psychological, and ideological aspects of terrorist recruitment. As a collection, the chapters advance our understanding of terrorist recruitment, as well as raise important questions and issues for further research.

Part I: Places and Means of Terrorist Recruitment

The first section of the volume begins with a chapter by Madeleine Gruen, an intelligence analyst at the New York City Police Department's Counter Terrorism Division, in which she describes the ways in which extremist groups use American popular culture to introduce radical agendas to receptive youthful audiences. Her analysis illustrates how young Muslims are lured into association with radicalizing agents through traps set on the Internet and through seemingly sympathetic peer groups. By presenting their agendas to an American audience using vernacular and images recognizable to them, radical groups are winning acceptance of concepts with which their audience was not previously familiar. Already, groups such as Hizb ut-Tahrir (a political organization with a worldwide presence that seeks to overthrow Western governments through nonviolent means in order to install Islamic fundamentalist leadership) and Hizballah have used music and computer games to introduce their ideology and to engender anger and hatred against old enemies among a new generation. Young people who had never contemplated overthrowing their government are now listening to and singing songs about the establishment of an Islamic state. The examples given in Gruen's chapter demonstrate that Islamist radicalizing entities are intentionally crafting campaigns that do not violate U.S. laws, much less draw notice from authorities. The ultimate penalty for ignoring this burgeoning phenomenon will be an indigenous population sympathetic to the terrorist agenda that can be called upon to support operations, or worse, attack the U.S. from within.

In the next chapter in this section, Professor Michael Waller of the Institute of World Politics examines the relationship between prisons and terrorist recruitment in the United States. His analysis of white supremacist movements, religious extremists, and foreign-sponsored penetration of the U.S. prison system illustrates how these institutions have long been breeding grounds for terrorists of many ideologies. This chapter also demonstrates that prison recruitment is an age-old phenomenon in the United States and abroad, and that extremist organizations have the demonstrated capability to spot, recruit, indoctrinate, and materially support inmates as foot soldiers in the terrorists' army. In his conclusion, Waller warns that recruitment of prisoners could become an institutionalized, self-perpetuating process that, in the eyes of the terrorists and their allies, would ensure a steady supply of combatants in their war against civilization.

In the next chapter, Professor Brigitte Nacos of Columbia University notes how communication is a key factor in the recruitment of terrorists. Print and electronic media in general are important means to spread the terrorist "propaganda by deed" and inform, indoctrinate and prepare some individuals for recruitment. Further, terrorism has often been compared to theater because terrorist attacks are planned like stage productions. In both cases, the people in charge channel all efforts into one overriding objective: to manipulate the emotions of their audiences. While the theater metaphor remains instructive, it has given way to terrorism as television events that are watched by record audiences, transcending the boundaries of typical theatrical productions. And unlike even the most successful producers of theater, motion picture, and television entertainment, the perpetrators of the lethal 9/11 attacks on America affected all of their audiences in unprecedented ways. Among the spectators that the architects of 9/11 wanted to influence were undoubtedly the American public and public officials on all levels of the U.S. government. But equally important targets of their "propaganda by deed" were Muslims and Arabs in the Middle East and elsewhere around the globe, on whose behalf Osama bin Laden and al Qaeda claimed to act all along. The purpose of these communications, she argues, was multifaceted—including the desire to attract new recruits.

On a similar note, Professor Gabriel Weimann of the University of Haifa explores how terrorist organizations use the Internet to communicate with various audiences, including potential new recruits. Websites are only one of the Internet's services used by modern terrorism: There are other facilities on the Net—e-mail, chat rooms, e-groups, forums, virtual message boards—that are increasingly used by terrorists. Drawing on the findings of a recent study he and his colleagues conducted for the United States Institute of Peace, Weimann notes how the Internet can be used to recruit and mobilize supporters to play a more active role in support of terrorist activities or causes. In addition to seeking converts by using the full range of website technologies (audio, digital video, etc.) to enhance the presentation of their message, terrorist organizations capture information about the users who browse their websites. He concludes that the Internet has become a more popular apparatus for early stages of recruitment and mobilization, challenging governments, security agencies and counterterrorism services all over the world. Moreover, it also challenges the future of the Internet, since any attempt to limit or minimize the Net's use by terrorists implies imposing restrictions on the Internet's free flow of information, free speech and privacy.

In the next chapter, Professor Zachary Abuza of Simmons College explores the role of education-related dimensions of recruitment by Jemaah Islamiyah (JI), a terrorist group in Indonesia affiliated with al Qaeda. In the Muslim world of Southeast Asia, network-based recruitment is focused on four central factors: kinship, mosque, madrasa, and friendship. Education is the commonality between those and thus plays an important role in Islamist extremist recruitment throughout Southeast Asia. Abuza's chapter examines how JI has used Islamic educational networks and madrasas—called *pesantrens* in Indonesia or *pondoks* in Thailand and Cambodia—as centers of recruitment and the transmission of Wahhabi and Salafi principles. JI established these madrasas to be used as centers of recruitment and indoctrination, and the graduates of this school are a who's who of today's Southeast Asian terrorists. In his concluding remarks, Abuza reflects on the implications of U.S. foreign policy and the global war on terror, suggesting that new approaches are warranted, but unlikely.

Dr. Joe Felter, a Lieutenant Colonel in the U.S. Army, provides the final chapter of this section on places and means of terrorist recruitment with a case study of an insurgent movement in the Philippines. His analysis first explores some general theories about why some states and citizens are vulnerable to insurgency movements. He then examines data collected from former members of the Communist Terrorist Movement—an insurgency movement that has plagued the Philippines for over twenty years—and develops a profile of the typical recruit of this movement, covering issues of age, education, former occupation, propaganda, coercion, and grievances generated by abuses of the military, police, or local government. His chapter concludes by drawing lessons from this analysis for national security and counterterrorism policies—not just for the Philippines, but for countries around the world.

Part II: Social and Psychological Dimensions

In the first chapter of this section, Dr. P. W. Singer of the Brookings Institution addresses how terrorists recruit children. There are some 300,000 children under the age of eighteen (both boys and girls) presently serving as combatants, fighting in almost 75 percent of the world's conflicts and 80 percent of the conflicts where children are present include fighters under the age of fifteen.[1] Thus, he notes, it should be no surprise that children are also increasingly present in terrorist groups. Many of these groups have long had "youth wings" to provide broader support in the populace, but now youths are increasingly being used in actual operations to strike at targets behind the battle lines. This occurs for the same fundamental reasons that children are now on the battlefields: Children offer terrorist group leaders cheap and easy recruits, who provide new options to strike at their foes. He concludes that there are multiple reasons for children to become involved in terrorist groups, usually the result of the combination of a harsh environment that leaves children with no good choices and a deliberate mobilization strategy by the group itself to pull children into terrorism. Sometimes this process is enabled by the parents' approval. This may be the saddest aspect of children's involvement in such groups. When parents wish that their child grow up to be a suicide bomber instead of becoming a doctor or teacher and live to an old age, something is indeed wrong.

The next chapter of this section, by Dr. Matthew Levitt of the Washington Institute, addresses the social aspects of terrorist recruitment in Hamas—a group that is known not only for perpetrating suicide attacks in Israel but also for providing extensive and much-needed social services to Palestinians. Because of the notion that Hamas has independent "wings," its political and charitable fronts are allowed to operate openly in many European and Middle Eastern capitals. In these cities, Islamic social welfare groups tied to Hamas are given free passes for their support of terror simply because they also provide critical humanitarian support. Hamas logistical and financial support activity is often tolerated when conducted under the rubric of charitable or humanitarian assistance. However, he argues, Hamas grant making is largely determined by a cold cost-benefit analysis that links the amount of aid awarded to the extent of support that aid will buy. Individuals tied to Hamas receive more assistance than those unaffiliated with the organization, while members linked to terrorist activity receive even more. An Israeli government report notes that Hamas charitable organizations accord preference to those close to the movement and assure that they receive increased financial assistance. The results for Hamas recruitment are striking—according to an April 2001 survey conducted by the Islamic University in Gaza, while 49 percent of children aged nine to sixteen claimed to have participated in the *intifada*, 73 percent claimed they hoped to become martyrs.[2] Levitt argues that cracking down on terrorism is key both to meeting the social welfare needs of Palestinians in the West Bank and Gaza and for returning to negotiations over a viable political settlement. To do this, donor countries must not be distracted from debunking the myth that Hamas conducts legitimate charity work parallel but unrelated to its terrorist attacks. Further, cutting off the flow of funds to these groups, and replacing their largesse with an organized and regulated international aid effort to address the real and immediate needs of the Palestinian people, is now more urgent than ever.

A similar focus on the social welfare aspects of terrorist recruitment is offered in the next chapter, by independent researcher Keith Stanski, with a unique case study of women who join the Revolutionary Armed Forces of Colombia (FARC). Stanski draws from a combination of media accounts, human rights reports, and interviews with recently demobilized female FARC members to examine the role women play in the movement. Several key lessons emerge from his analysis. For potential recruits, the movement's political objectives may be secondary to the perceived opportunities of joining a terrorist movement. Further, even for young adolescents, joining a violent movement can be a calculated decision. While inflated expectations and recruitment rhetoric influence these decisions, some women may view terrorist movements as offering opportunities that are otherwise unattainable. In some cases, the difficulties and risks women face in civilian society may exceed those inherent in joining a terrorist movement. For others, terrorist organizations might be perceived as a relief from seemingly inescapable boredom. Additionally, the sense of purpose instilled by enlisting in a terrorist group may be heightened for women. As a distinct departure from civilian society, the training women receive—even when comparable to that of men—could elicit a special sense of importance for them. The physical and political training that terrorist movements provide may not only be the most sustained formal training women receive, but it also has immediate application for a cause greater than themselves; upon completing the training, women enter a political and social structure in which they have new, specific responsibilities and functions. In a way, a terrorist group validates the potential of a woman in a manner that civilian societies may not recognize. Overall, Stanski's analysis brings an important dimension to our understanding of terrorist recruitment.

The next chapter, co-authored by Ami Pedahzur and Arie Perliger of the University of Haifa, synthesizes information gained from different organizations to illustrate how suicide terrorists are recruited, prepared, and trained for their suicide missions. They argue that this phenomenon is a result of encouraging environmental and personal motivations, both of which are being used by terrorist organizations implementing suicide attacks. The conclusions they draw from their analysis highlight the differences in the recruitment and training process that exist between organizations operat-

ing internationally (al Qaeda) and organizations operating in a single territory (e.g., the Tamil Tigers in Sri Lanka or the Irish Republican Army in
the United Kingdom). Moreover, the operational resources of a particular
organization and their level of control over the population also influences
their recruitment and training methods. Further, in contrast to preparations
for other terrorist attacks, when recruiting a candidate for a suicide mission the recruitment process continues throughout the training stage and
until the suicide mission is perpetrated. When recruiting a candidate for a
suicide mission, it is necessary to reinforce his/her willingness and acceptance to participate in a suicide attack, and to continue this process up to
the final minutes. Finally, while some have argued that the phenomenon of
suicide terrorism is linked to one culture or religion, the opposite is true.
This can be seen clearly when analyzing the enlistment, training, and employment of the terrorists and particularly their emphasis on psychological
preparation. As with other chapters of this volume, their analysis offers important implications for our understanding of terrorism and counterterrorism policies.

The final chapter of this section on social and psychological dimensions
is authored by Raymond Hamden, a clinical and forensic psychologist
based in Dubai, United Arab Emirates. He describes how individuals who
reportedly have no emotional or social pathology in their psychological development, and no familial or social conditioning to any political or religious ideology, nonetheless turn to terrorism as a tactic towards extracting
retribution or vengeance against their enemies. In essence, he argues, some
individuals' motivation for violent acts can be understood as the result of
a major traumatic incident. As a member of a well-organized and capable
organization, the retributional terrorist is a daunting enemy. However, a
"lone wolf" retributional terrorist—like Oklahoma City bomber Timothy
McVeigh, for example[3]—may be even more dangerous than some groups.

Part III: Ideological Dimensions

The third and final section of this volume provides a diverse collection of
perspectives on ideologies that underscore terrorist recruitment, beginning
with University of Nevada Professor Leonard Weinberg's historical review
of various "call to arms" used by political and revolutionary movements
over time. His analysis reveals that throughout history, both left- and right-
wing ideologies have furnished small terrorist bands and their members with
an exaggerated sense of their own importance, which led them to commit
dramatic acts of violence in order to make their objectives known to wide
audiences. Further, these ideologies have offered these groups a perceived
pathway to power, through which terrorism was meant to raise the level of
awareness and trigger a violent uprising, from proletarian insurrection to

racial holy war, by a vast pool of supporters previously too victimized and too lacking the required audacity on their own. However, despite the pretensions and the damage—both physical and psychological—caused by the ideologically driven terrorist groups over the decades, none of the groups discussed in his chapter managed to bring their social revolutionary or counter-revolutionary campaigns to a successful conclusion. But, he notes, these failures have hardly been for want of trying.

In the second chapter of this section, Dr. J. P. Larsson (a researcher who works with the British government) explores the role of ideology in the recruitment of individuals by particularly violent religious groups. His analysis begins by explaining how many young people are "seekers" who are trying to find their own answers of how to make sense of the world around them. Religious ideologies, he argues, are often able to explain the state of the world, and in particular why believers are continuously persecuted, oppressed, or discriminated; further, they can also explain how and why violence may be condoned and necessary. Several dimensions of these ideologies are important to consider when examining terrorist recruitment: First, these ideologies are often *theologically supremacist*[4]—meaning that all believers assume superiority over nonbelievers, who are not privy to the truth of the religion. Second, most are *exclusivist*—believers are a chosen people or their territory is a holy land. Third, many are *absolutist*—it is not possible to be a half-hearted believer, and you are either totally within the system, or totally without it. Further, only the true believers are guaranteed salvation and victory, whereas the enemies and the unbelievers—as well as those who have taken no stance whatsoever—are condemned to some sort of eternal punishment or damnation, as well as death. Overall, religious ideologies help foster *polarizing values* in terms of right and wrong, good and evil, light and dark—values which can be co-opted by terrorist organizations to convert a "seeker" into a lethal killer.

Professor James Aho of Idaho State University highlights these polarizing values in the next chapter by examining the religious ideological components of the Christian Fundamentalist movement in the United States, with particular focus on individuals who are recruited into violent groups and militias within this movement. These religiously-oriented extremists engage in violent activities, from cross-burning to bank robberies and targeted assassinations, while believing that they are "God's battle-ax and weapons of war." Aho offers a multistep theory of recruitment to explain the process by which individuals become affiliated with Christian Fundamentalist militia groups. While ideology plays the most critical role in recruitment, he also notes that an individual's cognitive commitment to the group increases the more that they consider themselves to have voluntarily sacrificed to the group in terms of money, time, labor, personal freedom, and in rare cases, their physical well-being. His analysis sheds light on an important—yet insufficiently studied—dimension of terrorism in the United States.

In another chapter on religious ideology, Dr. Maha Azzam (of the Royal Institute of International Affairs in the United Kingdom) examines the rise of militant political Islam, with particular focus on the relationship between violence and Wahhabism—an interpretation of Islam which places its doctrinal emphasis on the absolute unity of God and a return to the pure and orthodox teachings of Islam according to the Koran. Islamist extremists breed on the politics and policies that are perceived by them as detrimental to Muslim interests, and which have remained unaltered for generations. A growing number among them believe they can influence this situation through a strategy of terror. Adherents of Wahhabism, with its anti-Jewish and anti-Christian overtones, have pressured their government leaders (for example, in Saudi Arabia) to maintain a puritanical and strict attitude towards any form of liberalization in either the social or political arenas, and they have been responsible for numerous acts of terrorism in pursuit of their ideological goals. Further, Wahhabism has played an essential role in the recruitment and training of members of al Qaeda because it frames the beliefs and values of the organization's leaders, including Osama bin Laden and Ayman al-Zawahri.

Professor Jarret Brachman, of the Combating Terrorism Center at West Point, continues this analysis of political Islam with a detailed look at the origins and differing interpretations of the term "jihad." For some, it has come to refer to the struggle to defend religious ideals against destructive forces. For others, jihad refers to a command by God to all Muslims to fight against the aggressors who seek to corrupt Islam—embodied and globally perpetuated by the West. Jihad has served as a rallying cry for those who see themselves suffering under the draconian policies of governments, for those in a struggle with corrupt imperial overlords for the right to establish a national homeland, and for those who see themselves fighting to stave off advanced stages of cultural corruption. Muslims both volunteered and were recruited from around the world to aid Osama bin Laden and the mujahideen in Afghanistan and were united under the call of jihad against foreign (Soviet) aggressors.[5] Clearly, while jihad remains a contested term, it does hold deep and powerful religious significance within Islam. Therefore, Brachman argues, whoever is able to wield the reigns of its meaning will have great power in drawing new recruits into that ideological abyss.

The final chapter of this volume, by nationally syndicated columnist Allan Brownfeld of the American Council for Judaism, offers insights into the origins and implications of an extremist ideology known as Zionism. Adherents of this ideology, nurtured within Israel's far-right religious institutions, have been responsible for several prominent acts of violence—including the assassination of Israel's Prime Minister Yitzhak Rabin on 4 November 1995, by Yigal Amir, an ultra-Orthodox religious zealot. Brownfeld notes that religious Zionists have adopted the notion that God demands not so much devotion to the Torah as to the land that Israel's army has conquered, and this emphasis on land—particularly the settlements in the West Bank and Gaza Strip—has underscored an extremist view toward any attempt at negotiating peace agreements with the Palestinians. He concludes by arguing that Zionist terrorism—as with terrorism by other groups, both religious and secular—is a form of traditional asymmetric warfare, an effort by a militant minority to impose itself upon an unwilling majority. Yet, because the majority has been hesitant to identify and isolate such extremists, their influence has been far out of proportion to their numbers. Operating under the cover of religion has been useful in expanding their following and muting criticism. If Israel and its neighbors are to move in the direction of a lasting peace, he argues, the majority of Israelis—particularly Israel's mainstream religious institutions—must act to neutralize those voices that have distorted Judaism's moral mandate and replaced it with worship of physical territory.

Conclusion

After digesting the offerings provided by these authors, readers will surely have a greater appreciation for the broad scope and diversity of factors behind terrorist recruitment. However, there are obviously other avenues to explore beyond what is covered in this volume. Thus, this collection will hopefully also stimulate the reader to pursue further research on their own, in order to expand our collective understanding of recruitment in the terrorist world. Only through broadening and deepening the intellectual energy devoted to such activity will we identify the means by which we can, over the long term, stem the flow of future terrorist recruitment.

Acknowledgments

The views expressed herein are those of the author and do not purport to reflect the position of the United States Military Academy, the Department of the Army, or the Department of Defense.

Acknowledgments

A massive endeavor such as this requires a great deal of support from one's colleagues, family and friends, as well as generous amounts of caffeine and hubris. Thankfully, I have not suffered for lack of any of these. For their continued support, I extend my sincere gratitude foremost to the faculty and staff of the Combating Terrorism Center (CTC) at West Point (Jarret, Kip, Bill, Brian, Lianne, Daniella, Thalia, Jeff, Janice, Jude, and Reid), from whom I continue to learn much every day. Two men in particular—General (R) Wayne Downing, Chair of the CTC, and Brigadier General (R) Russell Howard, former Head of the Department of Social Sciences at West Point and founding Director of the CTC—have inspired countless others with their leadership, counterterrorism expertise, and commitment to improving our nation's security, and I am grateful for the opportunity to learn from them. Guidance and suggestions from USMA Academy Professor (and Colonel) Cindy Jebb and Dr. Rohan Gunaratna (Senior Fellow at the CTC) were also very helpful in identifying themes and authors for this project. And my faculty colleagues throughout West Point—and particularly the Department of Social Sciences—have been a continual source of support and assistance.

Over the last few years, I have been intrigued and inspired by colleagues and friends who study terrorism and counterterrorism—many of whose words are represented in the pages of these volumes. Each of the chapters in these volumes is the product of thoughtful research and analysis, and I offer my heartfelt thanks to the authors for their hard work and commitment to excellence. It is my sincere hope that all the collective effort put into this project will inspire a new generation to pursue further research in the field of terrorism and counterterrorism studies.

Finally, and of course most importantly, I owe a great debt of gratitude to my wife Alicia, who provided an incredible amount of patience and understanding through long nights and weekends while I disappeared into the solitary world of editing. Her support during this process was particularly phenomenal given that while I was working to produce the final manuscript of these volumes, she was working on the final term of a demanding pregnancy. Book and baby are now being introduced to the world at roughly the same time; thus, with the appropriately optimistic and hopeful energy that newborns bring, I dedicate this book to my new daughter, Chloe Lynn. I pray that she and all those of her generation will grow up in a world where the scourge of terrorism is better understood, prevented, and defeated.

CHAPTER 1

Exploring the Recruitment of Terrorists: An Introduction

JAMES J. F. FOREST

What do we know about terrorist recruitment? Over several decades of research, we have come to understand terrorism as a product of many divergent factors. Studies have covered the role of religious and political ideologies, social motivators, psychological profiles, and economic benefits in explaining the phenomenon of terrorism. From these studies, we have learned a great deal about terrorism groups and their members. And yet, on an individual level, it is still difficult sometimes to explain why cousin Bobby is now a member of a violent Christian militia gang, why John Walker Lindh went off to Afghanistan to receive jihad military training at an al Qaeda camp, why a thirteen-year-old girl would willingly join a violent rebel group in Colombia, why a devout Muslim would join a militant organization that clearly violates the teachings of the Koran by murdering innocent civilians, or why a young woman with a law degree and a bright future would, within a very short span of time, join the Palestinian terrorist group Hamas, strap on an explosive belt, calmly walk into a busy café and destroy dozens of lives.

What appeal do terrorist organizations hold for the average individual? How do they reach out to potential new recruits? And how do they convert a potential recruit into a member of what Dana Dillon calls the "brotherhood of terrorism?"[1] A recent report examining the recruitment of jihadists in Europe asks similar questions: "Among Europe's millions of Muslims, who is susceptible to recruitment? Why do they join? How does one actually join the Jihad?"[2] In answering these questions, the report's author, Michael Taarnby, provides a definition of terms which may prove useful to those reading the chapters in this volume:[3]

Cell: A small group of terrorists. A closed unit but with one or more links.

Gatekeeper: [an individual] who is personally connected to a terrorist network.

Network: a number of cells interrelated through personal relationships.

Recruitment: understood as an activity that intends to enlist [individuals] in an existing terrorist cell. Recruitment is the bridge between a personal belief and violent activism.

While Taarnby's report (prepared for the Danish Ministry) is limited in scope to a singular focus on Islamic terrorism, these definitions can apply equally to ethnic separatists, Christian or Jewish extremists, insurgency movements and other organizations that use terrorism to achieve their objectives.

This introductory chapter of *Volume I: Recruitment* describes in general terms what the existing research literature tells us about some of the ways and means of terrorist recruitment, and offers some context for how this volume of essays contributes to the body of research on these topics. As a collection, the chapters address important questions of how, why, and where terrorist recruitment takes place. In terms of the latter question, the geographical diversity of terrorist recruitment is particularly salient in today's global war on terrorism. While conventional wisdom prior to 9/11 would have many of us believe that terrorists and potential terrorist recruits reside in some remote location, today it is much better understood that recruitment for terrorism can take place anywhere, from big cities like London, Hamburg and New York to the picturesque town of Cour d'Alene, Idaho, or the tranquil villages of Kamikushiki and Tomizawa, near Mount Fuji, Japan. Our understanding of terrorist recruitment must therefore encompass a global dimension—a goal that this volume seeks to achieve.

Understanding Terrorist Recruitment

At its very basic level, recruitment for terrorism requires communication and the sharing of information between two or more people. Recruitment-related communication typically takes place in oral, print and online formats, and largely deals in the realms of psychological, social, cultural, intellectual and emotional development. The predominant message of such communication is focused on developing an individual's *will to kill*, particularly in the service of the terrorist organization. Communication of this type can be found in a variety of social institutions, including colleges and universities, mosques, churches, temples, and prisons. These are places where significant political and religious indoctrination (and, by extension, terrorist recruitment) can take place.

Religious ideology is considered by many to be among the more power-ful motivating forces behind contemporary terrorism, and in recent years a number of best-selling authors have illustrated how matters of faith can lead to the murder of innocents. For example, Karen Armstrong's book *Battle for God* explores fundamentalist movements that have surfaced in Judaism, Christianity, and Islam (the three monotheistic faiths) and illus-trates how adherents of religious ideology—especially the demand for a re-turn of religion to a central role in daily life—have been responsible for many killings, assassinations, and other acts of terror over the past cen-tury.[4] In several of his publications, John Esposito highlights the various dimensions through which religious ideology has played a prominent role in a variety of modern conflicts—including Bosnia, Kosovo, Chechnya, Rwanda, Somalia, Sudan, and Sri Lanka—and gives particular attention to the importance of jihad (which incorporates warfare with an individual ef-fort to live a holy life) in contemporary Islamic movements.[5]

Another important book on this topic, authored by Daniel Benjamin and Steven Simon—two former members of the U.S. National Security Coun-cil—titled *The Age of Sacred Terror*, explores the forms of religious belief that drive adherents to commit violence, and the circumstances that give rise to what they call "the new terrorism."[6] While they began writing the book more than a year before the attacks of 9/11, and intended the book to be "a descriptive warning about the new terrorism," the authors added to their discussion substantial material about what the U.S. government has done to combat terrorism, observing that "our enemy has demonstrated a re-markable ability to turn assets—from Boeing jets to satellite phones to the open society itself—against us" and they caution us not to underestimate "an enemy unlike any seen in living memory—one with an extraordinary ability to detect weakness and exploit it, one with a determination to inflict catastrophic damage, one that will not be deterred."[7]

Mark Juergensmeyer's best-selling book, *Terror in the Mind of God*, ex-plores how and why the combination of religious conviction and hatred of secular society translates into the selection of potential terrorist targets. Al-though he illuminates the tenets of Islam that condone the use of violence, Juergensmeyer also highlights the ideological basis for Christian militant groups in the United States and shows that violent acts based on religious fervor are not the sole domain of Islamist terrorists.[8] And David Rapoport has published widely on the historical relationship between terrorism and religious ideology, noting that sacred terror has important differences from terrorism undertaken with secular intentions; terrorists undertaking action for religious means (whom he terms "sacred terrorists") always look to the past, at the beginning of a religious tradition, to justify their actions and dictate the means they shall use, while secular terrorists allow themselves to follow any and all successful paths.[9]

Secular terrorist groups—whose nonreligious ideology is geared more toward political goals, including ethnic separatism—offer their members an equally powerful motivation for taking up violent means to achieve their goals. From the Black Hand in Serbia before WWI to Marxist revolutionaries in Italy and radicals (both left-wing and right-wing) in Germany during the 1970s, a diverse mix of political ideologies has played an important role in European terrorist movements throughout the last century.[10] An array of ethnic separatist movements around the globe—from India and Mexico to Sri Lanka and Turkey—have also offered powerful ideological motivations for individuals to entertain the use of terrorist tactics.[11] However, it should be noted that few revolutionary, ideological, utopian, or apocalyptic groups are based solely on one type of motivation for using terrorism. For example, the political violence in Northern Ireland since the late 1960s was driven by a mixture of political ideology, ethnic nationalism, and cultural and religious convictions.[12]

From the social and psychological literature, a number of scholars have offered different, and sometimes even contradictory, descriptions of how a motivated "terrorist mindset" is formed. Robert Lifton, an expert on cults, notes that individuals come to see their chosen ideology—viewed as a set of emotionally-charged convictions about people and their relationship to the natural or supernatural world—as ultimately more valid, true, and real than any other aspect of actual human character or human experience, and thus one must subject one's experience to that "truth."[13] When this view of the world is put forth by a group with an absolute vision of truth, those who are not in the group are bound up in evil, are not enlightened, are not saved, and do not have the right to exist.[14] Psychologist Jerrold Post argues that terrorists have particular psychological natures that drive them to commit acts of violence, but admits that they are not psychopathic. He believes that terrorist actions stem from a need to satisfy this internal drive and that ideological belief and justifications are used to cover up their wholly personal acts of violence.[15]

Albert Bandura, a proponent of social cognitive theory, notes that in order for individuals to become lethal terrorists, they must acquire what he termed "moral disengagement"—an ability to sanctify harmful conduct as honorable and righteous, which is achieved by moral justification, exonerating comparison with graver inhumanities, sanitizing language, displacement of responsibility, and dehumanization.[16] In a similar vein, psychologist Anthony Stahelski's research led him to develop a model of social psychological conditioning through which individuals are transformed into terrorists—in essence, a group with extremist ideologies first eliminates a new recruit's old social and personal identities, and then reconditions them to identify the group's enemies as evil subhumans or nonhumans who should be killed.[17]

Sociologist Martha Crenshaw agrees with these other scholars in declining to ascribe abnormal pathology to terrorists, but argues that terrorists' actions are the product of a strategic, rational choice (often, but not always, fueled by a particularly powerful ideology).[18] Forensic psychiatrist Marc Sageman's research suggests that individuals are motivated to join terrorist organizations because of the social networks in which their loyalties to others develop. Indeed, he argues that "social bonds play a more important role in the emergence of the global Salafi jihad than ideology."[19]

For example, in January 2002, two Dutch young men of Moroccan origin living in Eindhoven were killed in suspicious circumstances in the Indian state of Kashmir.[20] An investigation by the AIVD (the intelligence agency of the Netherlands) revealed that they had been personally recruited in the Netherlands by radical Muslim acquaintances to participate in the violent jihad, which led them to take part in (and be killed during) terrorist attacks in the Muslim separatist region of Kashmir. According to one report, prior to September 11, 2001, recruitment for the global Islamic militant jihad most often necessitated an acquaintance who could arrange for training in Afghanistan, Bosnia, or some other location ripe with *mujahideen* camps.[21] However, as Sageman notes, "while many Muslims went to Afghanistan, less than 30 percent of the trainees were invited to join a terrorist organization,"[22] which indicates that terrorists are surprisingly selective in whom they allow to join their ranks. Indeed, despite the typical Hollywood portrayal of terrorists as wild-eyed fanatics, terrorist organizations actually tend to shy away from such individuals in reality—particularly because they bring a level of unpredictability and unreliability that could compromise the group's security and objectives.

In sum, a good deal of the literature in the study of terrorism agrees that a diverse combination of social, psychological, and ideological factors play a critical role in motivating an individual to become a terrorist (though there is some disagreement on the way in which this transformation takes place). There is also some agreement among researchers that recruitment for terrorism can take place at any one of a large variety of institutions and entities. Indeed, virtually anywhere that people gather—either physically or online—can potentially serve as a center for terrorist recruitment. There are, however, a few types of common locations where hatred of "the other" may be taught; these include places of education, worship, and incarceration. In the realm of education, for example, al-Azhar University in Cairo, Adbul Aziz University in Saudi Arabia, the Bandung Institute of Technology in Malaysia, and the Abu Bakar Islamic University in Pakistan have each earned a reputation as places of significant ideological indoctrination among potential recruits for Islamic extremist organizations.

Mosques can also serve as important centers of terrorist recruitment in the world of militant Islamism. Leaders of Islamist terrorist groups look for particularly devout Muslims—those who come not just to Friday prayers, but to prayers five times a day, every day—and work to develop their motivation for using violence to achieve social and political change. Mosques are important places where members of the Islamic community gather, and in most cases have nothing to do with terrorist indoctrination or recruitment. However, in more than a few cases, these institutions have been co-opted by firebrand leaders, spewing a message of hatred and violence that unfortunately appeals to the anti-Western sentiments of some Muslims.

For example, the Finsbury Park mosque in North London earned a reputation for its particularly radical brand of Islam. One of London's largest, this four-story mosque serves a diverse community of over 2,000 Pakistanis, Bengalis, Algerians, and Egyptians—most of whom simply come to worship and take part in classes in Muslim culture, Arabic, and the Koran. However, among those known to have worshipped at the mosque are alleged shoe bomber Richard Reid and Zacarias Moussaoui, the so-called "20th hijacker" of September 11.[23] Further, the mosque's leader—Sheikh Abu Hamza—was arrested in 2004 and charged with a variety of terror-related offenses.[24] A year earlier, the United Kingdom's Charity Commission, which oversees places of worship in Britain, banned Abu Hamza from preaching at the Finsbury Park mosque after he praised Osama bin Laden and declared—among other things—that the crew who died in the Columbia space shuttle disaster had been punished by Allah.[25] In another example, the al Muhadjirin and al Quds mosques in Hamburg, Germany, served to bring together and inspire several al Qaeda recruits, including Mohammad Atta, Ramzi Binalshibh, Said Bahaji, and Mounir Motassadeq—individuals who eventually took part in the deadly attacks of 9/11.[26] From Seattle, Washington (the Idris mosque and the now-closed Dar-es-Salaam mosque) to Albany, New York (the Masjid as-Salam mosque), U.S. authorities have launched investigations into allegations of extremist activities at mosques throughout the country. And the number of mosques that provide safe havens to Islamist extremists in the West pales in comparison to the vast array of mosques in Central and Southeast Asia, North Africa, and the Middle East.

In addition to these universities and mosques, a worldwide network of *madrasas* and *pesantren* (Muslim boarding schools)—many of which are Wahhabi-oriented[27] and funded by charities in Saudi Arabia and other Gulf countries—continues to play an important role in the growth of the jihadi terrorist network, at the very least by introducing students to radical Islamist ideology and activities.[28] For example, according to researcher Zachary Abuza, the Al Mukmin madrasa in Ngruki, Indonesia has played a central role in the development of the Islamic terrorist group Jemaah Islamiyah (JI). Established in 1972 by Abu Bakar Ba'asyir and Abdullah Sungkar, the founders of JI, the graduates of Ngruki are a who's who of Southeast Asian terrorists.[29]

According to research conducted by P. W. Singer, "around 10–15 percent of Pakistan's madrasas are affiliated with extremist religious/political groups, who have co-opted education for their own ends. These schools teach a distorted view of Islam. Hatred is permissible, jihad allows the murder of innocent civilians including other Muslim men, women and children, and the new heroes are terrorists."[30] Following a visit to Pakistan's al-Haqqania madrasa in 2002, an hour or so east of Peshawar, *New Yorker* foreign correspondent Mary Anne Weaver described a vast, fourteen-acre complex with "scores of classrooms, administrative buildings, mosques and dorms, and a state-of-the-art computer room."[31] Under the leadership of Maulana Sami ul-Haq—one of the most powerful and most anti-American of Pakistan's religious militants—students at this madrasa study a core curriculum of Arabic and Islam, memorize the Koran, and develop a commitment to fighting a jihad against the enemies of Islam. At institutions like these, militant education breeds militants; a curriculum oriented towards hatred and violence produces violent graduates.

Prisons can also serve as centers of terrorist-related indoctrination and recruitment. A variety of extremist organizations are active in prisons throughout the United States, from right-wing extremist groups like the Aryan Nations Church prison ministry (which preaches a violent flavor of Christian Identity ideology)[32] and the Confederate Knights of America, to religious organizations like the Islamic Society of North America (ISNA) and the Graduate School of Islamic and Social Sciences (GSISS).[33] As researcher Ian Cuthbertson recently observed, "The usefulness of prisons as universities for terrorists . . . has not escaped Islamic radicals [who are] free to recruit and train inmates they believe to be suited for work within a terrorist organization. . . . Local and immigrant, Muslim and non-Muslim, the bright, the dim, the violent: all are courted, all have a place in the network—provided they prove susceptible to indoctrination and radicalization."[34]

Similarly, criminal networks offer another source of potential recruits for terrorist organizations. The same networks used for trafficking in weapons, humans, and drugs can easily facilitate the logistical needs of a terrorist organization. As individuals within criminal networks and terrorist groups come into increasingly frequent contact with one another, and in some cases forge strategic alliances, observers would expect to see a gradual blurring of lines between the two entities. Indeed, the Spanish police had previously identified key members of the terrorist cell that carried out the 2004 Madrid bombings as drug dealers, while their other identity as terrorist operatives went undiscovered.[35] Thomas Sanderson, Deputy Director of the Transnational Threats Initiative at the Center for Strategic and International Studies, notes that "terrorism may serves as a 'tactic' for criminal groups, whereas criminal activity may become a permanent necessity for terror groups lacking sufficient sources of funding."[36] He warns of the likelihood that "terror groups would evolve into hybrid groups" and that "the world may face a number of transnational criminal-terrorist cartels that dwarf the Colombian cartels and al Qaedas of the 1990s and today."[37]

Finally, a growing amount of attention is being given to understanding how the Internet serves as a place where terrorist-oriented indoctrination and recruitment takes place. Hundreds of terrorist organizations of one kind or another currently have their own websites, marketing their ideologies and justifications for violence to a broad, global audience. Online discussion forums serve as meeting places where veteran terrorists can lure potential recruits deeper into an organization's philosophy and convince them to commit themselves to joining the group's cause.

Conclusion

In sum, this cursory review of the literature reveals that terrorist recruitment takes place at a significant variety of institutions and gathering places—both physical and virtual—as well as within existing social networks of family and friends. While many of these serve far more benign purposes than terrorist recruitment, they are still places of concern when developing an understanding of global terrorism. Their most important link to the spread of global terrorism is that they—or more accurately, individuals associated with these places—help produce the willingness to kill among potential terrorist recruits. This willingness to kill (and by extension, recruitment in the terrorist organization) is fostered through various forms of communication, including religious edicts announced at the pulpit, political manifestos posted to a website, and casual conversations among acquaintances and friends. From this brief overview of existing research, a portrait of terrorist recruitment begins to emerge—a portrait to which the chapters of this volume will now add color and depth.

Acknowledgments

The views expressed herein are those of the author and do not purport to reflect the position of the United States Military Academy, the Department of the Army, or the Department of Defense.

PART I

PLACES AND MEANS OF TERRORIST RECRUITMENT

CHAPTER 2

Innovative Recruitment and Indoctrination Tactics by Extremists: Video Games, Hip-Hop, and the World Wide Web

MADELEINE GRUEN

When a man lives in a country ruled by a corrupt government and has no money, no education, no job, and no promise of a better life for his children, it is easy to understand why he would join a militant extremist group that claims to have the power to create change. When he is taught to memorize religious texts and nothing else, then it is easy to understand how a terrorist group could manipulate him to kill in the name of God. But, what if he grows up financially comfortable, well-educated, and lives in a free democratic society? Then is his desire to join a terrorist organization as easily understood?

Militance is not a common consideration for a young man living in a Western democratic nation; more than likely, he has a solid roof over his head and his future success will not be impeded by a failing government. Even if he is religiously devout, he will have had a well-rounded education and therefore would not likely become a zealot. Nevertheless, Westerners do join terrorist groups and support their ambitions in increasing numbers. To explain why, this chapter describes the unorthodox ways in which several foreign-based political Islamist groups are deliberately targeting Americans for recruitment by using the Internet, video games, and hip hop music.

Defining the Enemy and Its Mission on the World Wide Web

Even though militant Islamists consider it a victory to kill Americans and their allies wherever they may be, it is still their ultimate goal to hit them at home. Watch lists, biometric screening, and better systems to detect fraudulent documents have made it harder for terrorist groups to smuggle operatives over U.S. borders. In order to facilitate operations, militant Islamists are now bound to recruit members with U.S. passports.

While militant Islamists still have access to American Muslims (and others with U.S. passports) when they travel abroad, it has become more difficult for them to reliably cultivate operatives in this way, since Western intelligence and law enforcement agencies have started to identify terrorist-associated mosques in countries of interest and have begun to watch travel patterns more closely. Therefore, in order for terrorists to be able to launch another spectacular attack in the United States or in Western Europe, they need to find an alternative way of radicalizing their target audience that does not require face-to-face interaction. A significant answer to their requirements is the Internet, which has quickly become the backbone of terrorist and extremist-group propaganda and recruitment programs. Through the Internet, extremists have been able to reach their target recruitment demographic in the United States by exploiting their love of pop culture and technology—ironically, the very aspects of American culture they loathe and eventually hope to eradicate. Political Islamists are developing computer games and promoting hip-hop artists in order to spread radical ideology and to reach sympathizers within adversarial populations.

The United States has learned that the enemy is more than just one organization called al Qaeda. Rather, the United States battles a loosely-tethered protean constellation of militant fundamentalist groups that embrace the same religious and political objectives as al Qaeda but are not necessarily affiliated with al Qaeda. This constellation includes ideological propagandists known as "radicalizing agents" or "support groups." One such group, which will be used as an illustrative example throughout this chapter, is Hizb ut-Tahrir (HT). HT is a political organization with a worldwide presence that seeks to overthrow Western governments through nonviolent means in order to install Islamic fundamentalist leadership. Although HT is not affiliated with al Qaeda, it is nevertheless motivated to realize the same objectives. While al Qaeda intends to smite its enemies through violence, HT uses propaganda as its weapon against the West. By exposing adversarial governments as corrupt to their victim population, HT holds that more people will unite with them; eventually, the sheer enormity of the will of HT's supporters will bring down the offending regime. HT is classified as radical not only for its seditious intentions but also because it is anti-Semitic and anti-American and it supports violence against all non-Muslim presence in the Middle East. However, its support of violent jihad is manifested only through its literature; customarily, HT does not encourage its own members to engage their enemies on the battlefield.

Many radical Islamic group leaders once belonged to the Muslim Brotherhood, through which they gained experience spreading sedition at a grassroots level. Now, they are applying their expertise online, making them the vanguards in the expansion of radical Islam in the West. Even though their leadership resides outside of U.S. borders, they are busy cultivating a fifth column that may be called upon to fight the United States from within.

How Extremists Overcome Physical and Cultural Barriers Using the Internet

Extremist groups that seek to spread their influence in the West focus their efforts on males between the approximate ages of sixteen and twenty-two, which happens to be the largest demographic population online in the West—10.5 million in the United States alone. These groups know that their target subject spends an average of thirty-two hours per month online, which is 17 percent more than any other age group. Most of their online time is spent instant messaging, playing computer games, and visiting sites where music can be downloaded. Therefore, extremists know exactly where their target recruitment demographic is, what their interests are, and how much time they spend indulging their interests. Although this is valuable intelligence to be exploited by Islamic extremist groups, they must first overcome three obstacles before they can successfully recruit Americans online.

First, extremists need to locate their target subject on the World Wide Web, which is not much easier than finding a needle in a haystack. They post messages on web boards and in chat rooms where individuals vulnerable to extremist ideology spend time, or they bait their targets by building attractive websites, taking care to not make the content of these sites so extreme that they draw unwanted attention.

Second, the extremists are at a disadvantage when they try to convince their young American audience to overthrow their government, which has ostensibly provided security and stability. It is far easier to convince an individual to fight the "far enemy" because it can be misrepresented through the murky lens of distance. In addition to asking the target subject to act without regard to the consequences of sedition, the extremists also ask them to work towards the establishment of a Caliphate. In other words, the subject must accept the entire agenda of overthrowing the secular government in order to replace it with Islamic leadership that would impose the strictest form of Islamic law. This would require the subject to renounce every standard and privilege he had been brought up to uphold, including the separation of religion and state, equality of the sexes, and the rewards associated with life in a meritocracy. Therefore, the extremist group needs to target someone who is not entirely enamored of American values, someone who is disaffected or marginalized.

Once the extremist group has identified a potential supporter, they need to isolate him from others who contradict the Islamist worldview. To separate him from their detractors, the extremists draw their target into a vast cyber universe with a built-in social network. The subject can reside within a "hostile" culture in the physical world without being dependent upon it for support or guidance. By operating a myriad of interconnecting websites, a virtual world is created that provides all the social support necessary to satisfy the prospective recruit's needs and to change his worldview.

Third, the prospective American recruit has almost nothing in common with the traditional mujahideen. He will not respond to the same motivators because of his social and cultural upbringing. If he is a typical young American in his late teens or early twenties, he is likely to be more concerned about his relationships with peers and family than with plots to overthrow the government. He grew up watching Tupac Shakur and Eminem on MTV, and he played "Super Mario" and "Doom" on his Playstation. To hold the target's attention, the radicalizing agent must present its corpus of doctrines with visuals and language that are consistent with American culture. Foreign extremists have studied the lingua franca of young America and its popular culture so that the language and visual styles can be replicated on their websites.

Propaganda on the Web

In their online propaganda campaigns, extremist groups have successfully overcome the aforementioned obstacles in order to begin the process of convincing their target to join a war against his own government. A website with its interactive features can be used to disseminate the same elements of a propaganda campaign that are employed in the physical world. Through audio and video streams, downloadable leaflets, discussion boards, and links to hundreds of other extremist sites, the Internet can be used to indoctrinate, fundraise, recruit, incite violence, and terrorize. Though not as effective as face-to-face interaction between recruiter and target, the Internet is a viable platform for peer interaction—particularly for those who do not have a solid support base in the physical world.

The comprehensive online propaganda campaign includes truth mixed with exaggeration and also some blatant deception. A steady stream of testimonials from well-known persons respected by the target subject, and from those he regards as peers, transforms his thinking about the world. Adversaries' positions are ridiculed. The target will be overwhelmed with literature that threatens grave consequences for not following the extremist's objectives. Finally, the target is bombarded with material that forces him to question his beliefs and persuades him that the radical's way of life is better for him and his loved ones.

One of the most potent aspects of extremist websites is the message board. The message board offers a 24-hour-a-day online community where people with similar interests can exchange ideas, a social network that may not exist for an individual in the physical world. The bonds developed online are just as deep as those developed among peers in the physical world, and the online peer group is equally influential in terms of shaping each others' ideological perspectives. Testimonials from other members of the board are used to manipulate potential recruits into perceiving themselves as marginal. Once they have been convinced of their marginal status, they are even more inclined to rely solely on the other members of the chat board for support and validation. The relief from alienation is a primary reason why people join irregular political organizations, and the communities found on boards often justify and give direction to people's sense of injustice.

HT uses message boards as a means to identify and indoctrinate Muslims who reside in vulnerable immigrant populations. They build boards as communities for people with common interests and backgrounds. For example, they have boards specifically devoted to second-generation Muslims who were brought up in the United States. A Muslim-American will find his way to the board either through a link posted on another board or by typing certain words associated with his interests into a search engine. Once he has found his way to the board he will be slowly introduced to the concept of joining HT. At first, participants who are already members of HT post testimonials that praise HT for the work that it is doing to make changes that will ultimately improve the lives of Muslims everywhere. Other posts discuss the benefits of joining the group, such as a sense of unity and empowerment. As the message board grows to become a full-fledged community, the postings are less varied in content. Eventually, the boards are entirely focused on HT, their ideology, and blatant pitches for chat board members to join a HT study circle. If there is an attempt to post a message with an opposing viewpoint, it is quickly taken down. The individual chat board member is left to believe that everyone on the board supports or intends to join HT, and when a critical mass of one's peers endorse a concept, it becomes more acceptable. An individual who previously had no inclination to join a politically extreme organization may do so because his online peer group—for whom he has developed respect—belongs.

Once the target has become more deeply involved with his online peer group, he will begin to receive e-mail directly from the sponsoring radicalizing agent. Messages point the way to other group-sponsored websites, keeping the subject exposed to an endless complex of similar propaganda. The e-mail messages will question his beliefs and will offer solutions to his problems. They will ridicule authority figures in his society and will introduce him to the radical group leader, who will appear wise and benevolent. Ultimately, the constant stream of messages that deconstruct everything he knew to be true will leave him confused. Then the radical group will offer him a position in a solid social structure and an objective, two things he may have lacked in life prior to his encounter with the radicalizing agent. In addition to these online communities, extremists groups also appeal to their target audience in the U.S. through music and computer games.

Music

The Neo-Nazis were pioneers in the exploitation of popular culture to enhance their recruitment efforts. They identified their target recruitment subject as male, in his mid- to late teens, who was angry and marginalized, and who had no constructive outlet for his frustration. Once they identified the target's interests, they then sought him out in the places where he went to enjoy these interests. One of the biggest recruitment booms for the racist right came in the mid-1980s, when a punk hybrid from Europe called Oi music became popular in the United States. With Oi music came Oi culture—shaved heads, leather jackets with chains, combat boots and tattoos. The Oi fans were referred to as Skinheads, although at the time they were not associated with racism. However, once the racist right began to recruit at Oi concerts the fan base transformed, which precipitated a change in the music itself. Within a span of only a few years, the Oi scene was saturated with "white power" rhetoric and became almost entirely associated with the racist right. Realizing the effective outcome of the white supremacist foray into the music scene, political Islamist groups are following their example.

In the United States, the type of music young people listen to is often their medium for self-expression; the lyrics put their feelings into words and validate their developing worldviews. In the United States, hip-hop culture influences clothing styles and vernaculars of young people. Several radical Islamist groups have harnessed the influence of hip-hop in American culture by producing their own bands, which are so successfully promoted on the web that they are becoming accepted by the mainstream. Muslim hip-hop clothing lines are sprouting up. One such line sells "jihad" bandannas, which are similar in style to traditional urban street gang identifiers.

Some songs composed by political Islamist groups are intended to encourage political awareness, while others intend to incite social change through insurgency. Hip-hop bands seek to grab the attention of Western teens and make them politically conscious, which enables extremists to steer the issues. For example, in the following song composed by *Arab Legion*,[1] a hip-hop band associated with HT, the lyrics express anger over U.S. military action in Muslim countries:

Baghdad Babies

As a third world traveler let me unravel the story
U.S. devilish glory, gulf war baloney
droppin bombs wit no qualms
cruise missiles droppin like rain
civilians feelin the pain, they dont tell you the numbas
aim to make ya wonder, the death toll
countless iraqis deceased, even worse
sanctions bring em down to their knees
Thoughtless policies, just victory by any means
Deceptive U.S. war goals
blindly supported in opinion polls
wake up people, if you only knew
what the few have planned for the many
power corrupts infinitely, tactical decisions made
secretly, to bring about a new world order
deception smells, brings a foul odor

This song is meant to raise political consciousness and shape the listeners' opinions, although the lyrics are not radical or seditious enough to draw unwanted inquiry from authorities; indeed, many in mainstream society would feel that the lyrics adequately express their own feelings about the war in Iraq.

The most extreme militant Islamic hip-hop is known as "Terror Rap." The video "Dirty Kuffar"[2] by the British hip-hop group *Soul Salah Crew*, features a masked "Sheikh Terra" dancing in front of the camera with the Koran in one hand and a gun in the other. The following verse is meant to glorify terrorist attacks and the inspiration derived from them:

Peace to Hamas and the Hizballah
OBL [bin-Laden] pulled me like a shiny star
Like the way we destroyed them two towers ha-ha
The minister Tony Blair, there my dirty Kuffar
The one Mr. Bush, there my dirty Kuffar . . .
Throw them on the fire

The words are simple and the tune catchy, making this song an effective tool for indoctrination; the lyrics can be easily memorized and are meant to be repeated like a mantra.

The identities of the members of *Soul Salah Crew* are unknown; therefore, it cannot be determined whether an organization is behind the production of the video or whether the individuals involved were inspired independently. Because "Dirty Kuffar" was released for free, exclusively over the Internet, the artists avoided interception of its quick and wide-spread dissemination by adversarial authorities. Another built-in advantage to Internet distribution of videos or MP3s is that it allows for unlimited accessibility.

Hizb ut-Tahrir's Hip-Hop Band

The creation of decoy or "honey-pot" sites is meant to expose unsuspecting individuals to radical ideology. Decoy sites will appear legitimate on the surface and will bear no indication of extremist group affiliation. For example, after HT was banned from university campuses in the United Kingdom for posting anti-Semitic fliers, the group launched a website called www.muslimstudent.org. The site could easily be found on a search engine by any Muslim student searching for a peer group or student activities. The site bore no mention of the group but was replete with group ideology. Only after a student participated in one of the activities advertised on the site would they realize that they were interacting with members of HT.

HT has been using honey-pot sites as one way to expand their presence in the United States. For example, an HT cell in the Los Angeles area assessed the interests of its target population, and as a result started a hip-hop band called Soldiers of Allah (SOA).[3] SOA had its own website, built to enable access to their potential supporters. www.soldiersofallah.com was easily found by typing the words "soldiers" or "Allah" into a search engine, or could be found by hip-hop fans who saw the band's URL posted on a hip-hop discussion board. The band's affiliation with HT was not apparent to website visitors because there was no mention of the group. Only after visitors were drawn into the band's fan community would they begin to see or hear the name Hizb ut-Tahrir.

The SOA website was professional and contemporary in appearance. Only two links from the home page led to additional pages; one to a page featuring song lyrics and the other to the registration page of their Yahoo! chat group. Likely, the lack of material was intended to steer visitors to view the information that SOA wanted to have viewed rather than distract them with superfluous material.

Visitors to the site could download MP3s of SOA songs or they could print out the lyrics that promoted HT's ideology. Listening to songs composed by extremists is a passive form of "studying" doctrines. The following song excerpts show how HT doctrines were expressed through the SOA lyrics:

Staring into Kafir's Eyes[4]

How many more
of our sisters do they have to rape!
How many more

of our brothers must they slaughter by hate!
Don't you know we have suffered too long without an Islamic State!
How much more can you take?

This verse presents the problems caused by the Kafirs (nonbelievers) in the Muslim world and then introduces the solution, which is the establishment of a Muslim state.

Sleeping Giant[5]

Governments who claim
They implementing Islam
like who??!
Like Taliban, Iran and Sudan.
All 52
So-called Muslim nations
Oppressing the masses
in the name of Islam
They are digging our graves
while we are asleep
over a billion
But ooh so weak
We need to rise up
And get back on our feet

This song highlights the oppression of Muslims under the rule of corrupt leadership and alerts listeners to the necessity of taking action. While the songs "Staring Into Kafir's Eyes" and "Sleeping Giant" clearly express HT's doctrines, they do not emphasize the nonviolent aspect of group ideology. Listeners are instructed to take a stand against leadership that oppresses Islam by establishing a Muslim state, but they are not told how. Thus, this method of propaganda dissemination raises the concern that the lyrics could be misinterpreted to mean that objectives should be achieved through violence.

Arab Legion has a website similar to SOA's in that there are very few pages of material. Like the SOA site, the Arab Legion site only has two functional links off the home page; one leads to the group's lyrics page and the other to their fan message board, where visitors interact directly with HT members and others who are contemplating group ideology. The aspect of the site that gives the most insight into group tactics is a video stream of the band giving a concert at a University of California campus. Posts to HT-affiliated chat boards indicate that all of the HT hip-hop bands perform at college campuses. HT likely realizes that college administrators do not pay much attention to which music groups are invited to the campus by student groups, and that they are not inclined to review the lyrics of the songs performed by those groups. Thus, concerts are a clever and effective way of promoting further exposure to group ideology; fans will attend more concerts, they will seek face-to-face interaction with band members, they will buy CDs, and they will visit fan websites.

Yet another HT-associated hip-hop group, An-Nasr Productions[6] (ANP), markets itself as the "Islamic carriers of *dawa* using the tool of hip-hop to convey the message of Al-Islam!" ANP's website revealed that the band sponsored a youth group called Muslim Youth Network (MYN). The sponsorship of community centers, youth retreats, and summer camps is a common HT front activity around the world. The community centers are most often established within immigrant communities that do not have many mosques or other facilities that provide proper Islamic education. HT assumes the role of spiritual guide for young people in communities that do not have legitimate alternatives. However, in reality the retreats and social events are forums for indoctrination to HT's radical ideology. The ANP site indicates that this tactic is now occurring in the United States. The cycle of promoting HT ideology through hip-hop bands and websites is perpetuated via retreats; councilors suggest starting hip-hop bands and they also teach participants skills to build websites. Graduates move to other Muslim immigrant communities and impart these skills and tactics to create a rapidly multiplying "army" of young people indoctrinated to the concept of overthrowing the government and replacing it with Islamic fundamentalist leadership.

Gaming

Like the burgeoning Islamist hip-hop world, the jihadi gaming industry also includes a range of extremes, from games that are designed to influence world views to games that are meant to incite violence. Electronic gaming has blossomed into an $11 billion-a-year industry.[7] It is a mainstream entertainment that is commonplace to teen and young-adult lifestyles. American teenagers now spend as much time playing games as they do watching television. However, gaming is participatory while television viewing is not, so the risk is greater that exposure to violent games will result in violent behavior, as many studies have proven.

White supremacists were among the first to exploit the popularity of computer games with their target recruitment demographic, laying foundations when the industry started to boom. Because white supremacists were the pioneers in the use of music and the Internet as a platform for their propaganda campaigns, it is likely that they will continue to set the standards for political Islamist groups in their recent foray into the development of games that will affect popular perception. White supremacist games are most often "first-person shooter" games with violent graphics, depicting real-life scenarios in which the player is the central character, killing Jews and other racial minorities. All the games developed by white supremacists can be downloaded from their websites. While some are available for a charge, most can be downloaded for free. Their strategy with the games is the same as it is with music—make them widely available on the web for free so that there can be no limit to the number of people exposed to the "white power" message.

For example, a website associated with the racist organization National Alliance offers game titles and descriptions such as:

"Shoot the Blacks"—Blast away the darkies as they appear.
"Nigger Hunt"—Safari in Africa: Kill all the Niggers you can.
"Rattenjagt"—Kill the Jewish rats!

The first computer game developed by a political Islamist group is "Special Force,"[8] which was launched in February 2003 by Hizballah. The game gives players a simulated experience of military operations against Israeli soldiers in battles re-created from actual encounters in the south of Lebanon, "real battles that humiliated the Zionist enemy, giving it a lesson. . . ." One feature of the programming allows players to sharpen their marksmanship skills using Israel's Prime Minister Ariel Sharon as a target.

The game was developed over a span of two years by the Hizballah Central Internet Bureau, whose intentions were to create a game that reversed the scenarios depicted in American computer games in which the Americans are the heroes and Arabs are the enemies. Top officials of Hizballah, who made the decision to produce the game, believe that resistance to the Israelis occurs not only through military operations but through the media as well. They hope that the game will introduce Israeli resistance to a new generation and that it will offer "a mental and personal training for those who play it, allowing them to feel that they are in the shoes of the resistance fighters." Hizballah has made it clear that the game is not intended to entertain, but to train children physically and mentally for military confrontation with their Israeli enemies.

By the end of May 2003, more than 10,000 copies had been sold in the United States, Australia, Lebanon, Syria, Iran, Bahrain, and United Arab Emirates. The game's content was so effective that in response to its launch in Australia, the Federal Labor Member of Parliament for Melbourne Ports issued a statement calling for its ban. "We don't need to encourage suicide bombers or people like that in Australia with things like this . . . particularly among vulnerable younger people who have a disposition to these kinds of political views. We have concerns about active terrorist cells and people being involved in making themselves into human bombs."[9] The MP's statement acknowledges the power of games to incite players to act on their political views using violence.

Games with violent themes, such as those distributed by the National Alliance and Hizballah, are intended to dehumanize the victim and to diminish the act of killing. Despite the many instances of legislators and concerned parents speaking out against the violence depicted in computer games, there have been no successful attempts to ban them in the United States. There are a number of websites that offer free games developed by amateurs. Developers from all over the world can post their games to these sites, which are entirely unregulated. Games with violent themes elicit violent tendencies. Extremist groups seeking to incite a lone actor residing in an adversarial country to attack a target will inevitably test the efficacy of computer games to stimulate the conversion of support into action.

Games marketed as educational may also be used to introduce Americanized Muslims to radical Islamist concepts. Such games may catch the attention of authorities, but would be difficult to ban because their intention to promote sedition or violence would be nearly impossible to prove.

Conclusions

This chapter has briefly described the ways in which extremist groups use American popular culture to introduce radical agendas to their target recruitment and support demographic. It has shown how young Muslims are lured into association with radicalizing agents through traps set on the Internet and through seemingly sympathetic peer groups. By presenting their agendas to an American audience using vernacular and images recognizable to them, radical groups are winning acceptance of concepts with which their audience was not previously familiar. Already, groups such as HT and Hizballah have used music and computer games to introduce their ideology and to engender anger and hatred against old enemies among a new generation. Young people who had never contemplated overthrowing their government are now listening to and singing songs about the establishment of an Islamic state. Those who never thought twice about Ariel Sharon are sharpening their shooting skills using his image as a target.

The examples given in this chapter show that Islamist radicalizing entities are intentionally crafting campaigns that do not violate U.S. laws, much less draw notice from authorities. The ultimate penalty for ignoring this burgeoning phenomenon will be an indigenous population sympathetic to the terrorist agenda that can be called upon to support operations, or worse, attack the United States from within.

CHAPTER 3

Prisons as Terrorist Breeding Grounds

J. MICHAEL WALLER

Prisons are age-old breeding grounds for political extremists of practically all ideologies and cultures. In the twentieth century, imprisoned radicals used the isolation from society to write their manifestos, plot their strategies, and make propaganda for their causes. They recruited the alienated and angry criminals to join their ranks, providing them with a cause to believe in, a special brotherhood to join, and a means to fight back at the society that locked them up. Today, prisons in the United States and around the world remain fertile breeding grounds for political extremists and terrorists. In examining the relationship between prisons and terrorist recruitment, this chapter will discuss

- the historical background of the subject;
- extremist recruitment in American prisons;
- the role of the terrorist lawyer and exploitation of "civil liberties";
- white supremacist movements;
- the new supernatural dimension of political warfare;
- the value of religious conversions to terrorists;
- the role of professional prison chaplains;
- extremist infiltration through religious programs;
- foreign-sponsored penetration of the U.S. prison system; and
- the strange alliance that has developed between various groups and networks.

Historical Background

Political and religious extremists' use of prisons as tools of warfare—recruitment bases, organizational headquarters, and propaganda centers—has been documented since antiquity. Some of the most powerful and violent political movements of the past century have been fueled and led by a hardened cadre who had been recruited, indoctrinated, and trained in prisons.

In the prisons of tsarist Russia, a renegade seminarian who would one day change his name to Josef Stalin enlisted and organized murderers and other criminals who, once freed, would lead the Bolsheviks and their ruthless Cheka secret police. As a young Italian antiwar activist in 1911, Benito Mussolini spent time in jail, where militant socialists recruited him as a propagandist—launching him into a political career that he would one day build into the Fascist party. Adolf Hitler, convicted in 1923 of treason, used his imprisonment as an opportunity to take a break from the day-to-day pressures and distractions of organizing his upstart Nazi party—a break which allowed him to develop his political ideology and strategy in *Mein Kampf*.

Less prominent radicals had similar experiences. Before the Soviet army conquered Poland, the Polish Communist Party recruited heavily among street criminals and prisoners, building an instant force of active robbers whose thefts funded party operations. Communist revolutionaries in Asia, Africa, and Latin America turned ordinary criminals into committed Marxist–Leninists who ultimately took power.

Some militants set their terrorist wars for political power in starkly religious terms. The Provisional Irish Republican Army, purporting to be fighting in the name of Catholics against the British Crown in Northern Ireland (but actually a nihilistic movement with a Marxist worldview), made use of prisons not only as places from which to recruit new terrorists but as centers of political warfare to inspire support and collaboration on the outside. During the 1970s, while the banned IRA was waging a terrorist campaign of urban bombings, it considered prisons as less of a punishment and more of an opportunity for its incarcerated members. Prisons, in the IRA's view, were "schools for the future."[1]

Extremist Recruitment in American Prisons

Extremist and terrorist recruitment within American prisons has taken place for decades. With the rise of New Left terrorism in the late 1960s and early 1970s—the Weathermen/Weather Underground, Black Panthers and Black Liberation Army, Puerto Rican Fuerzas Armadas Liberación Nacional (FALN) (Armed Forces of National Liberation) and Macheteros, and others—"public interest" law firms provided legal defense for the terrorists and litigated against the government, in order to eliminate or limit police powers in ways that helped keep the terrorists on the streets. A "prison reform" movement—led by groups with names like the Prison Law Project, the Prison Law Collective, and the Center for Constitutional Rights, and fought through litigation against the authorities—resulted in court decisions that literally aided extremist groups seeking to radicalize prison populations.

A major part of prison reform was the lifting of restrictions on extremist literature that incited violence. No sooner had the prison reforms been enacted when organized riots broke out in major prisons across the country, the most famous of which was the deadly four-day revolt in 1971 at the maximum-security Attica Correctional Facility in upstate New York. In a congressional investigation of extremist organizations within penal and correctional systems, prison officials noted how the "new policies allowing radical and militant-type reading materials have greatly contributed to the deterioration of inmate behavior, discipline and attitudes."[2] Russell G. Oswald, commissioner of New York State correctional facilities and a longtime advocate of prison reform, testified that "almost all inmate literature requests are for the more militant, radical kinds of reading materials."[3] Highly politicized prisoners, with propaganda help from outside organizations, were radicalizing other inmates.

"Prisons are a prime recruiting ground for causes that appeal to the discontented and dissatisfied," the commissioner said. "The growth of militant organizations, in numbers and size, presents new and different kinds of problems to correctional administrators."[4] While factions among inmates "have always been part of prison life," their nature had changed from cliques of prisoners from the same hometowns or neighborhoods: "A different kind of factional grouping has occurred, with active and brisk recruiting programs very much a part of the scene."[5] Prison officials found a sudden shift in the composition and nature of inmate factions: "Seemingly overnight, well-organized groups became established with accompanying and varying levels of militancy and ideology. Significantly, none of these groups indicate in any way the so-called establishment is other than repressive or that they could place any confidence in it or society. The ideology most common to all these groups is the destruction of the system through one means or another."[6]

Given the large numbers of inmates convicted of crimes of violence, these ideologies defeat the purpose of correction or rehabilitation and create new menaces to society. A congressional committee published excerpts of prisoners' letters to authorities describing conditions and warning about serious problems in the correctional system and implying that officials were not taking the developments seriously.[7] One letter read:

[I]t is positively amazing to this inmate that my neighbors in [name redacted] up & down the block are just considered "rowdy." I've learned just by listening to them how to wire a pig [police] squad car with a mixture of potassium chlorate & sulphur, how to put lye with gasoline for a Molotov Cocktail. How to file down a rear spring to make an automatic weapon, and listened to the debates on who should be put on the "list" of officials scheduled for execution after the "People's Revolution." I don't have to tell *you* your name is number 2 on the hit parade. Yet these characters are not considered "dangerous." But I don't think they are kidding one bit.[8]

A three-time Attica inmate agreed, testifying that "90 percent of those people in the prison are going to be back on the street, and it's more or less a training ground."[9]

Thirty years after the 1973 testimony, in October 2003, the Senate Subcommittee on Terrorism, Technology, and Homeland Security heard similar stories from new witnesses. "With over 2 million men and women incarcerated across the country, terrorist recruitment in prisons and jails is indeed a potentially serious concern for the country," said Paul E. Rogers, President of the American Correctional Chaplains Association.[10] While arguing that the situation was not as dire as others, including this author, had described, he agreed that the trend toward greater militant indoctrination was moving rapidly in a dangerous direction.

The Role of the Terrorist Lawyer

Radicalized inmates have two protected sanctuaries: the confidential client relationship with their attorneys and their penitential relationship with their chaplains or spiritual advisors. Local, regional, national, and international networks provide free legal support (including criminal defense and appeals), conduct litigation to change prison conditions or seek the overturn of convictions, and pursue litigation to expand prisoners' rights and privileges while restricting or crippling the counterterrorist functions of law enforcement and criminal investigative capabilities. The legal aid and solidarity groups pre-date World War II, but their explicit support for extremists dates to the mid-1960s, when New Left lawyers led by William Kunstler and Arthur Kinoy founded the Center for Constitutional Rights (CCR) explicitly to support violent political "activism." In Kunstler's words, "The thing I'm most interested in is keeping people on the street who will forever alter the character of this society: the revolutionaries."[11]

At first, those "revolutionaries" were on the radical left: members of the Weather Underground, Black Liberation Army, May 19 Communist Organization, and the Macheteros and FALN of Puerto Rico. During the 1980s, the CCR aided some of the more prominent euroterrorist groups, including the Baader–Meinhof Gang (Red Army Faction) of West Germany, as well as Soviet KGB agents. During the 1990s, it began its new and current approach: providing legal support for Islamist terrorist organizations and their members. By 2003, its client list had expanded to include members of the Taliban and al Qaeda being held as enemy combatants at the U.S. Naval Station in Guantanamo Bay, Cuba—actions directly hampering the war effort against the terrorists. A CCR lawsuit resulted in a landmark Supreme Court ruling that guaranteed American constitutional rights to al Qaeda terrorists who had been captured abroad and held at Guantanamo Bay. Notably the CCR has not defended white supremacist groups.

The CCR and other groups offer more than legal aid. They provide political platforms for the terrorists as individuals and for their movements as a whole, with experienced attorneys always on hand to offer skilled and spirited assistance. Though often characterized in the press as "civil rights" or "human rights" lawyers, they share a political belief system that is alien to both. CCR President Michael Rather admitted on a CNN program that he supports the Fidel Castro regime in Cuba.[12] One of his colleagues who represents the "Blind Sheik," Lynne Stewart, expresses similar beliefs: "I'm such a strange amalgam of old-line things and new-line things. I don't have any problem with Mao or Stalin or the Vietnamese leaders or certainly Fidel locking up people they see as dangerous. Because so often, dissidence has been used by the greater powers to undermine a people's revolution."[13] Her law partner Stanley Cohen, a Kunstler acolyte who represents several Islamist terrorists, noted that "most of my clients are involved with struggle, many of them armed struggle." He added, "If I can't support the politics of potential clients, I don't take the case."[14]

These types of lawyers can provide more than legal aid. They allegedly serve as clandestine couriers between the imprisoned terrorists and their lieutenants around the world. Stewart was convicted as one. They provide confidence and visibility, allowing the convict to know that he is taken care of, and more importantly, that he is far from alone.

The White Supremacists

Islamist extremism has eclipsed the small and fractious white supremacist movement. The movement is more complicated then it might appear: Diverse elements seek either to eliminate nonwhites and Jews from the country or to carve out an all-white "homeland" from part of the United States, follow either pagan Norse gods or a bizarre interpretation of "Christian identity," or manifest their white superiority in either a hateful Aryan style or simply a "love" for the "white race." Some factions call the United States "ZOG" for "Zionist-Occupied Government," believing that the country is under Jewish control. Parts of the movement are now so small that adherents have set aside their differences, and members of the Ku Klux Klan,

Identity Christians, pagan Odinists, and Aryans have now banded together for mutual support.[15] A general, amorphous global movement is loosely networked via the Internet. Though insignificant in their destructive power when compared to Islamist terrorists, the movement merits attention because continued Islamist terror, unchecked illegal immigration, and demographic trends point to a possible increased sense of alienation among some fringe sectors of white society, especially elements that feel threatened either by those developments or potentially by those who might make common cause with Islamism.

Some of the groups are minuscule in size. Imprisoned members of The Order, a group that at its peak in the early 1980s numbered about fifty, get out their message through a website, freetheorder.net, to keep their cause alive and to generate legal support for their appeals. The Order's goal is to establish a white separatist homeland in the Pacific Northwest of the United States, but one of its leaders, an inmate at the federal supermax prison in Florence, Colorado, admits that it is a failed cause.[16] Its members are in federal prisons for racketeering, robbery, and the murder of a Jewish radio host in Colorado. Supporters of The Order have their own small legal defense foundations operating under an innocuous-sounding Christian name. The remnants of The Order do not appear to recruit in prisons and are content just to get their word out, which includes messages of extreme sacrifice for their cause.

Other white supremacist groups do recruit actively in the penal and correctional system. Aryan Brotherhood recruits wear a tattoo with a stylized heart and crossed swords, with the initials "AB" in the center. Nazi skinhead gang members often bear a tattoo at the base of the shaved scalp. These groups have more adherents, but their exact sizes may be unknown.

The White Aryan Resistance (WAR) describes itself as "a network of highly motivated white racists. Each person is an individual leader in his or her own right." It says it "promotes the Lone Wolf tactical concept. Made up of individuals and small cells." This leaderless, horizontal, internetted structure is similar to other white supremacist groups, based on a "Leaderless Resistance" concept developed by an Aryan Nations leader in the early 1960s whereby "all individuals and groups operate independently of each other, and never report to a central headquarters or single leader for direction or instruction, as would those who belong to a typical pyramid organization."[17] Under the Leaderless Resistance idea, an organizational form that some Islamist terrorist groups appear to have embraced, supporters can set up their own cells and act autonomously without need to make contact with a central command structure. This concept allows adherents to draw inspiration from one another and take political, criminal, or violent action without fear of betrayal, infiltration, or unraveling by authorities. Individuals may identify themselves to one another by the tattoos they wore in prison.

The Supernatural Dimension of Political Warfare

Political violence, until recently, has been tempered by the human instinct of self-preservation that limited even the most fanatical revolutionaries. While committed people have for centuries been willing to die—that is, be killed—for a cause, they have been much less likely to kill themselves. The rise of Islamism, with its spiritual aspect that finds virtue and reward in the ultimate sacrifice, has changed that general rule.[18] On a similar note, some members of the Provisional Irish Republican Army (IRA) during the 1970s chose a drawn-out and agonizing method of suicide for propaganda purposes. Imprisoned IRA men staged hunger strikes lasting for weeks that received worldwide attention and inspired supporters both behind and beyond bars. However, these slow-motion suicides apparently had little supernatural aspect to them, as the self-starved prisoners neither exhibited nor inspired religious convictions. Indeed, although the IRA won support from Irish Catholics—especially among the large diaspora in the United States and around the world—by claiming to represent the Catholic cause against the Protestant British, the Catholic Church (with the exception of a few renegade priests and bishops) strongly condemned the IRA's suicidal and terrorist tactics, with the Bishop of Dublin going so far as to declare it a sin for a Christian to support the organization.

"Liberation theology," a mutation of Christianity that was popular in Latin America and other developing countries during the 1970s and 1980s, held that one could be liberated from worldly miseries by blending Christian faith with Marxist economic theory and Leninist political warfare. Adherents to liberation theology used their ideology to justify kidnapping, murder, and terrorist violence. One can draw a rough analogy today to certain strains of Islam, where the religion is perverted into a militant political ideology that can be called *Islamism*. Islamism is more political than religious, because its adherents seek political power to create an Islamic state.[19]

As a spiritual dimension of life, religion offers a detachment from the difficulties and hardships that human beings face daily. For others, it provides a means of sanctifying one's work and becoming closer to God. Religion can give meaning to suffering and offer hope to the afflicted. Ideally, it inspires changes of heart from sinner to saint. Improperly practiced, however, religion can be mutated into an ideological vehicle for channeling malaise, frustration, and anger, breeding not inner peace but rage and becoming a justification for political extremism and violence.

A congressional investigation of prison radicalism of the early 1970s found the schism most obvious among Muslim inmates. A militant national black Muslim group preaching that whites are a satanic race was found to be part of the organized Attica prison riots, while a Sunni Muslim group of Attica inmates said that its members practice their faith "to study and better themselves in order to be an asset to the community when they finish their sentences."[20]

It's easy to see how religion can be a powerful force, for good or for evil, in prisons. Captive populations—mainly of angry men whom society has banished behind bars—seek salvation or some other form of release. Missionaries and chaplains devote their lives to helping them. Christian teachings explicitly exhort the faithful to show mercy toward the prisoner—not necessarily by lenient sentencing, but by helping the prisoner to change his ways and open up his soul to be saved. Islamic traditions require a similar charity. Prison officials encourage missionary activity among the inmates because it helps lift prisoner morale and assists the corrections process of converting convicts into helpful and hopeful citizens.

Among those who respond to a call to prayer and conversion, prisoners have two basic choices. One is to embrace a faith and practice that will help them become better fathers, sons, spouses, and citizens (once they have done their time and returned to civil society). This is the path preached by mainstream Christians and Muslims. The other is to follow a spiritual path that alienates them further from civil society and encourages them, figuratively or literally, to continue their conflict with the world at large. This is the path offered by political extremists and religious fanatics—most notably Islamists—who promise earthly emotional gratifications and materialistic or sensual spiritual rewards. For some convicts attracted to religion, Islamism is the more attractive of the two choices because it is, in a strange sense, the easiest. True religious conversion is hard work: It requires a true change of heart and a constant and conscious battle against the evils of one's own nature. By contrast, conversion to religious teachings that merely feed on hostility and resentment is more emotionally gratifying because of its immediacy (no need to fight the evils of one's own nature) and its supportiveness (it reaffirms the prisoner's sense of victimhood, encouraging attitudes that civil society is the enemy and must be taken down). Such teachings allow the convict to shift blame away from himself and toward the society that never accepted him (and indeed, put him away). This sense can be particularly profound if the convict is of a particular ethnic or racial minority that has real or imagined grievances against "the system."

The prisoner mindset that makes inmates vulnerable to extremist organized rhetoric is as true today as it was more than three decades ago when the New York State Prisons Commissioner told Congress:

> When one is discontented and feels that the world is against him and society is against him and he gets the kind of literature we are talking about as a steady diet of reading, talking about the advantages which the people have taken of them, it seems to me it can have a very deleterious effect on the individual's attitudes.[21]

The individuals and organizations that sponsor extremist religious teachings in prisons provide an automatic support system of like-minded people, both within the prison and in society at large. Adherents become members of a fraternity that offers a special camaraderie, friendship, and brotherhood (much as street gangs offer to troubled kids) while they serve their time and that will be there for them once they are freed. Like a sports club, the peer pressure and encouragement help the newcomer maintain the rigors of spiritual and political training.

The religious context encourages personal discipline and a new sense of purpose. Inmates indoctrinated in peaceful religious teachings find peace with themselves and with fellow human beings, according to Sheik Muhammad Hisham Kabbani, head of the moderate Islamic Supreme Council of America and one of the foremost Islamic scholars in the United States. Inmates indoctrinated in militant and violent teachings find satisfaction in a new sense of empowerment that will allow them to fight back. Civil society, for such adherents, is the malignant evildoer. If an embittered and fanatically indoctrinated convict is convinced that he as a religious person cannot coexist with evil—indeed, if his religious instructors or spiritual leaders demand that he not coexist with evil, or worse, if they declare that God wills it—he finds himself at a spiritual rubicon. What is his next step?

Value of Religious Conversions to Terrorists

For the Islamist terrorist leaders of the early twenty-first century, conversions of non-Muslims to Islamism are vital to their political strategy. Europeans, Asians, and Americans from non-Muslim backgrounds do not fit the terrorist profile that many are accustomed to seeing. They know their societies far better than immigrant terrorists, and they blend in seamlessly. They also have valuable passports. Some analysts view the conversions as a new generation of political and social protest against the West and in support of the "Third World," with Islamism being adopted as a political and cultural statement more than as a religion. Recently, young Europeans from non-Muslim backgrounds have been increasingly surfacing as Islamist militants. To Olivier Roy, Director of the National Center for Scientific Research in Paris, these are "protest conversions" not unlike the Marxist fanaticism of Europe's left-wing terrorist groups of the 1970s and 1980s, and are not true expressions of religious faith. "The young people in working-class urban areas are against the system, and converting to Islam is the ultimate way to challenge the system," according to Roy, who told the *Los Angeles Times*, "They convert to stick it to their parents, to their principal. . . . They convert in the same way people in the 1970s went to Bolivia or Vietnam. I see a very European tradition of identifying with a Third World cause."[22]

Perhaps so, but few Marxist revolutionaries would blow themselves up as suicide bombers, and not even the most radical terrorists of that era attempted to blow up a civilian airliner loaded with people. European intelligence services say that al Qaeda views European converts as vital to keeping the network functioning and moving forward, as the converts do not fit the generally understood cultural and racial profiles of Arab terrorists. Terrorist groups like al Qaeda find converts to be important tools in their war. The converts are useful to a new al Qaeda strategy of "training the trainers," a method that the increasingly decentralized organization used to export terrorism to other countries in quick-moving, internetted international networks that are difficult for authorities to detect, let alone penetrate or counter.

The Role of Professional Prison Chaplains

Chaplains are a vital part of correctional life, and until 9/11 they have been above reproach. While the U.S. federal prison system, the fifty states, and thousands of regional, county, and local jurisdictions do not always agree on the definition of chaplaincy or the professional requirements for prison chaplains, the American Correctional Association (ACA) has concrete standards:[23]

> Much like our colleagues in the military and at hospitals, correctional chaplains provide pastoral care to those who are disconnected from the general community by certain circumstances—in this case to those who are imprisoned, as well as to correctional facility staff and their families when requested. Where permitted, we also minister to the families of prisoners.
>
> Each correctional chaplain is also a representative of his or her faith community and is required to be endorsed by their denominational body in order to qualify as a chaplain. Correctional chaplains are professionals, with specialized training in the unique dynamics of the corrections world. Most serve as full-time correctional facility employees or part-time contract employees.

The "vast majority" of prison chaplains, including Islamic chaplains, are supportive of homeland security and national security priorities, according to U.S. prison officials. "Regarding reports of prisons being infiltrated by terrorists or terrorist organizations via prison religious programs, these have been blown way out of proportion," American Correctional Chaplains Association President Paul E. Rogers told a Senate terrorism subcommittee in 2003.[24] "Nonetheless, what should concern us are conditions that can allow these kinds of things to happen," such as:[25]

- Unqualified chaplains and/or inadequate supervision of programs and volunteers, who allow opportunities for abuse of religious programs.

When these conditions are present, there is significant potential for problems;

- A lack of commitment to employing certified correctional chaplains to administer religious programs;
- Budget cutbacks that reduce or eliminate the numbers of professional correctional chaplains; and
- Replacement of professional chaplains with noncertified volunteers.

Rogers also warned that "having unqualified volunteers operate in prisons without proper supervision can possibly lead to terrorist infiltration."[26] Here, he agreed with the critics, including this author, that the problem looms large on the horizon. Professional correctional chaplains know the faith groups of the prison community and personally know the volunteers and the resources (such as literature) that outside groups bring into the prisons. Furthermore, "properly trained chaplains can distinguish between things that may be done in houses of worship in the community but are not appropriate in a correctional setting. If a correctional chaplain observes or witnesses anything in a worship service or a religious study that in any way appears to be a threat to the institution, he or she is obligated to report it. Unfortunately, however, this is not the case in facilities that utilize unqualified chaplains or volunteers to oversee religious programs."[27] The state of Colorado illustrates the problem at its most extreme. In 1993, it did away with its $500,000-a-year corps of nineteen professional chaplains and replaced it with twenty-seven volunteers.

Referring to the problem of terrorist recruitment in prisons, Rogers told senators that professional chaplains can help "fight terrorism" and "be vigilant against our enemies wherever they might be." He offered to be an "effective partner with all jurisdictions." The American Correctional Chaplains Association subsequently announced that it was ready to promote certification of all prison chaplains in the United States.

Extremist Infiltration through Religious Programs

Since the mid-1990s, mainstream Muslim prison chaplains and distributors of classical Islamic literature warned of a disturbing trend. Sheik Kabbani calls it the "hijacking" of their prison programs by extreme Islamist organizations. He reports that prison libraries and religious centers were purged of traditional Islamic books, pamphlets, tapes, video, and other media, and replaced with militant, fundamentalist literature. Moderate Muslim inmates feared protesting because of what they described as intense intimidation from the Islamists.[28]

"In these prisons it is hard to come across authentic Islamic books," another inmate wrote in 2001, "because the Wahhabism dominates the prisons with their possenous [*sic*] books." Wahhabism is an extreme fundamentalist sect that has been sweeping Muslim chaplaincies in American federal prisons. Like other fundamentalist strains of Islam it projects an expression of political action that both its proponents and detractors claim is justified according to their reading of Islam.[29] The Wahhabism is the official state religion of Saudi Arabia, as it was of the Taliban regime in Afghanistan. Osama bin Laden is an adherent to Wahhabism. Extremist adherents to the Wahhabi (and Salafi) interpretation of Islam teach a Taliban-like intense hatred toward the United States, democratic civil society in general, and other Muslims who fail to comply with its primitive and violent views.

Sheik Kabbani found that after a 1999 speech he made in Washington, where he warned about the Wahhabi infiltration of Islam in America, prisoners began writing to his organization "asking what's going on, and telling us that our books are being confiscated by chaplains and by the officers. We were surprised—prison officers confiscating our books."[30] According to Kabbani, Muslim chaplains "accredited by a certain overseas country" that he would not identify (but which is understood to be Saudi Arabia) were behind the confiscations. "Prisoners wrote us letters: 'We don't have the literature to fight their extremism. Please send us books,'" Kabbani said.[31] "We sent books, but the prison authorities throw them away. They won't let our material in the prison because the chaplains confiscate them." The sheik said he complained to the U.S. Bureau of Prisons, but the response was "nothing."[32]

The shift in literature made available to prisoners tracks with what the New York Corrections Commissioner reported in 1973: a growing appeal to extremism and violence that justifies the inmates' crimes and deepens their alienation against society—in the more recent Wahhabi case, attempts to expunge prisons nonviolent Islamic literature. The commissioner testified at the time:

> For years and years, such literature was not allowed into prison systems for the seemingly logical reason that this material would add to the discontent of already discontented men and that the espoused philosophy of militancy or revolution reaching men who were already bitter, frustrated, and often dangerous would be an added ingredient to an already volatile situation.[33]

During the 1960s and 1970s, the controversial material available in prisons was mainly Marxist, anarchistic, or nihilistic in ideological content, and often race-based, particularly among blacks and Hispanics. Muslim material ranged from the ascetical and purely spiritual to the militant, but was seldom seen as a threat to society. Today, by contrast, the extremist material of most concern is militant Islamist in orientation. Just as spiritual Muslim prisoners report intimidation that prevents them from asking for nonmilitant religious literature, inmates in 1973 spoke of being afraid to complain about the radicalized books and pamphlets then flooding the prisons. Commissioner Oswald testified, "I have received many letters from prisoners who object to the proselytizing and the threatened actions which would be taken against them if they don't get along with these groups."[34] Prison officials also reported how, in contrast to the Sunnis, the Black Muslims used coercion to recruit new inmates:

> The NOI [Nation of Islam] was found to be the largest and best organized of the inmate groups within the New York State prison system. Its membership is recruited from the new black inmates entering prison. They are subjected to constant pressure to join. Discipline is strict, and the membership is generally neat in appearance. They often wear white shirts and black ties even with their prison garb. A prison chaplain of the Christian faith revealed that NOI had made concerted efforts to block black inmates from attending a Christian church by claiming that Christianity was a white man's religion.[35]

As a parallel trend, one finds that some of the most prominent radical organizers themselves, such as black separatist H. Rap Brown, switched from a secular revolutionary ideology and in 1971 converted to Islamist beliefs. These conversions are anything but temporary fads of rebellion. Brown re-emerged as Imam Jamil Abdullah al-Amin, and is serving life in prison for murdering a Georgia deputy sheriff. "Imam Jamil"—a cause célèbre in certain sectors of society, with a gaggle of admiring Websites—also has a strong following in the prison system, where he propounds his revolutionary Islamist views. His shooting to death of the Georgia officer, who happened to be black, is often excused as a necessary or even heroic act of resistance against the system. As an imam, or theological teacher, Jamil leads an Islamist movement that recruits alienated convicts, particularly African Americans, as his followers. A similar propaganda effort exists for convicted murderer Mumia Abu-Jamal, the revolutionary murderer turned self-styled poet, in Pennsylvania.

As the Senate Subcommittee on Terrorism and Homeland Security heard in 2003, radical Islamist groups—most tied to Saudi-sponsored Wahhabi organizations suspected by the U.S. government of being closely linked to terrorist financing activity—dominate Muslim recruitment in the United States and seek to create a radicalized cadre of felons who will support their political efforts. Estimates place the number of Muslim prison recruits at between 15 and 20 percent of the prison population. This group is overwhelmingly African American with a small but growing Hispanic minority. It appears that in many prison systems, including the federal system, Islamist imams have demanded and been granted the exclusive franchise for Muslim proselytization to the forceful exclusion of moderates.

As of this writing, two organizations dominate the training and selection of Muslim prison chaplains in the United States. The Graduate School of Islamic and Social Sciences (GSISS) trains the chaplains, while the Islamic Society of North America (ISNA) refers Muslim clerics to the Bureau of Prisons. According to testimony before the Senate Subcommittee on Terrorism and Homeland Security, ISNA "is an influential front for the promotion of the Wahhabi political, ideological, and theological infrastructure in the United States and Canada. . . . ISNA seeks to marginalize leaders of the Muslim faith who do not support its ideological goals. Through sponsorship of propaganda, doctrinal material and mosques, it is pursuing a strategic objective of dominating Islam in North America."[36]

The best-known graduate of this system is Imam Umar, whom the Bureau of Prisons fired after his post-September 11 extremist rhetoric appeared in the *Wall Street Journal*. Another public case was Aminah Akbarin, a Muslim chaplain at the Albion Correctional Facility in New York, who was put on paid administrative leave two weeks after the 9/11 attacks for calling Osama bin Laden "a hero to all Muslims."[37]

According to an investigative press report in 2002, "For many disaffected young people, their first contact with Islam comes in jail. Over the past 30 years, Islam has become a powerful force in America's correctional system. In New York State, it's estimated that between 17 and 20 percent of all inmates are Muslims—a number that experts say holds nationally."[38] "Currently, there are approximately 350,000 Muslims in federal, state and local prisons, with 30,000–40,000 being added to that number each year," writes Siraj Mufti, a writer for an online Muslim journal.[39] "These inmates mostly came into prison as non-Muslims. But, so it happens that once inside the prison a majority turn to Islam for the fulfillment of spiritual needs. . . . It is estimated that of those who seek faith while imprisoned, about 80 percent come to Islam. This fact alone is a major contributor to the phenomenal growth of Islam in the U.S."[40]

While those numbers may be inflated, they indicate a large and growing Muslim prison population in the United States and an aggressive proselytization offensive. It is among this mass of alienated converts—converts who receive a steady diet of militant political and spiritual rhetoric that further alienates them from society—where the terrorists find their recruits. In the United States, al Qaeda has found prisons and jails "a key area of recruitment" of "men who have already been convicted of violent crimes and have little or no loyalty to the United States. . . . It's literally a captive audience, and many inmates are anxious to hear how they can attack the institutions of America" according to a federal corrections official.[41]

The prison recruitment trend is occurring worldwide. Prominent British prison psychiatrist Theodore Dalrymple says that Islamism is attractive to inmates not only because it answers their need for transcendence, but because "it does more than that: it revenges them upon the whole of society.

For whatever official apologists of multiculturalism might say, everyone knows that Western society has long felt uneasy about the growing number of Muslims in its midst. By converting to Islam, the prisoner is therefore expressing his enmity towards the society in which he lives and by which he believes himself to have been grossly maltreated."[42]

Some prominent examples of prison converts-turned-terrorists:

- Aqil, a convert to Islam while serving time in California's boot-camp detainment system. After being released he went to a training camp in Taliban-ruled Afghanistan with one of the men accused of kidnapping and murdering *Wall Street Journal* reporter Daniel Pearl.

- José Padilla, a Puerto Rican who changed his name to Abdullah al-Mujahir. Padilla was exposed to radical Islam while a convict in U.S. prisons, and al Qaeda recruited him allegedly to detonate a radiological or "dirty" bomb. United States authorities arrested him in May 2002 upon his return from Switzerland. Padilla had connections among other converts to Islam who were part of the al Qaeda network in Europe.

- Richard Reid, the "Shoe Bomber." While an inmate in a British prison, Reid converted to Islam under a radical imam at the suggestion of his father. A Jamaica-born career criminal, Reid converted to Islam before trying to blow up a civilian jetliner full of people over the Atlantic.

Foreign-Sponsored Penetration of U.S. Prisons

Foreign governments and organizations backed by them have been producing or subsidizing large quantities of inflammatory literature for prisoners over the past three decades or more. Congressional investigators in 1973 found extremist literature covertly funded by the Soviet Union and the People's Republic of China, including a now-defunct weekly paper called the *Guardian*, which was subsequently revealed as having received covert funding from the KGB.[43] They also cited political agitation and literature produced by the Workers World Party, which is identified with the government of North Korea.

Foreign states and movements have been financing the promotion of Islamism within America's armed forces and prisons. Most of the money has come from the Wahhabi states of Saudi Arabia and Qatar, though some is believed to have come from other Persian Gulf states and Libya. Abdurahman Alamoudi, the locus of Islamist political organizing at the national level in the United States, is a Yemeni–Ethiopian immigrant with a talent for raising money from Saudi banks for his American political warfare operations. On 16 October 2004 Alamoudi was sentenced to 23 years in prison for money-laundering Libyan money and for his involvement in a plot to assassinate the Crown Prince of Saudi Arabia, a personal rival to Libyan dictator Muammar Qaddafi.[44] During the 1990s, Alamoudi persuaded the Pentagon and U.S. prison officials to set up chaplaincies whose imams were vetted, trained, and credentialed by other Alamoudi-affiliated entities.

In addition to cash contributions, the Saudi Embassy provides religious literature and theopolitical propaganda. The "Islamic Affairs Department of [the Saudi Arabian] Washington embassy ships out hundreds of copies of the Quran each month, as well as religious pamphlets and videos, to prison chaplains and Islamic groups who then pass them along to inmates," the *Wall Street Journal* reported in 2003.[45] "The Saudi government also pays for prison chaplains, along with many other American Muslims, to travel to Saudi Arabia for worship and study during the hajj, the traditional winter pilgrimage to Mecca that all Muslims are supposed to make at least once in their lives. The trips typically cost $3,000 a person and last several weeks, says Mr. Al-Jubeir, the Saudi spokesman."[46]

While some Saudi-funded Muslim charities provide legitimate humanitarian services to Muslim inmates and their families, others prey on prisoners' disaffection. Some do both. The Chicago-based Institute of Islamic Information & Education (III&E), whose leaders claim to have received support from Saudi government front organizations like the World Assembly of Muslim Youth (WAMY), says it reaches "more than 20,000 individuals a year in the prison system" through its literature.[47] III&E officials make little attempt to conceal their beliefs. Shortly after the 9/11 attacks, III&E Managing Director Amir Ali gave the benefit of the doubt to the al Qaeda leader: "I know that Osama bin Laden is a true Muslim with in-depth knowledge of the Qu'ran and teachings of the Prophet. I would never suspect that he would do anything against the teachings of Islam and harm anyone who is a civilian, and has not taken up arms against Islam or Muslims."[48] Concerning the attackers specifically, he said, "I would absolve the Taliban from any part of the air crashes at the WTC [World Trade Center], the Pentagon and other place." He declared that "it would be wrong" for Pakistan, Afghanistan, and Arabs to cooperate with the Americans.

Strange Alliance

As a final comment on prisons as terrorist recruiting grounds, one should note that extremists of varying—even opposing—ideologies often cooperate closely. Marxist or nihilistic groups whose worldviews clash with the disciplines of Islam, and whom Islamists generally consider infidels, have nonetheless worked closely with Islamic militants for decades. Court cases since 9/11 have shown that Islamic fundamentalist terrorists are comfortable working with individuals considered among their archenemies, including Jews and radical feminists, as long as they are fighting a common foe.

One sees the relationship most visibly in the enthusiasm that overtly Marxist lawyers from the Center for Constitutional Rights and National Lawyers Guild show for their Islamist clients, be they al Qaeda terrorists detained at the U.S. Navy base at Guantanamo Bay, Cuba, or Sheik Omar Abdel Rahman (a.k.a. Umar Abd al-Rahman), the Egyptian Islamic Jihad figure known as the "Blind Sheik" who was the spiritual leader of the 1993 World Trade Center bombers.

The 1973 hearings produced evidence that New Left militants forged the alliances among the Marxists, black and Puerto Rican separatists, Black Muslims, Sunni Muslims, and Islamists to bring about the organized prison violence of that period. An Attica prisoner testified, "Probably the Weathermen had the greatest outside contact through lawyers, through visitors, through the grapevine. . . . the Weathermen were probably the catalyst among the revolutionary groups. I think they were probably the ones that brought everything together and brought it to a head."[49]

Lynne Stewart, the avowedly Marxist lawyer representing the Blind Sheik, sees the Islamists as comrades-in-arms against a common enemy. She objected to an interviewer with the *Monthly Review*, a small, radical journal, who commented that left-wingers "are conflated in the government's eyes with right-wing Moslem fundamentalists."[50] Stewart said that the Islamic Jihad and other terrorist groups should be viewed as progressive forces. "I don't think it's quite fair to say right-wing," Stewart corrected, "because they are basically forces of national liberation. And I think that we, as persons who are committed to the liberation of oppressed people, should fasten on the need for self-determination. . . . To denigrate them as right-wing, I don't think is proper. My own sense is that, were the Islamists to be empowered, there would be movements within their own countries, such as occurs in Iran, to liberate."[51]

Conclusion

Prisons have long been breeding grounds for terrorists of many ideologies, so the awareness of prison-based terrorist support activity today should not be considered the discovery of something new, but the rediscovery of something old. This chapter has attempted to demonstrate that prison recruitment is an age-old phenomenon in the United States and abroad, that terrorist inmates now have a near-automatic legal and political support system, and that the enemy has the demonstrated capability to spot, recruit, indoctrinate, and materially support inmates as foot soldiers in the terrorists' army.

The spiritual dimension of Islamist prison recruitment adds a new factor to the conventional terrorism and political warfare of the past, because the enlistee can be persuaded and conditioned to override all natural self-defense impulses and to seek out and glorify his own death in martyrdom.[52] Cultivating this supernatural dimension requires constant close access to the inmate, a steady supply of literature and media to fuel anger and justify political violence, personal spiritual counseling and group support to reinforce the conversion to the terrorist side, and the elevation of inspirational leaders within the correction and penal systems. These operations to penetrate the prisons require and receive significant foreign funding and ideological guidance, sufficient also to overwhelm the civil and moderate Muslim presence among the inmates. They also require either a breakdown or reduction in the professional corps of chaplains who might provide alternative moral leadership and assist with uplifting inmates on the path of correction, as opposed to creating public menaces once the sentences are served. Along with the weakening of the traditional professional chaplaincies, the terrorists and their allies seek to create their own body of chaplains under their direction (if not control).

All of this is dependent on ready access to aggressive and committed attorneys with the knowledge and experience to manipulate the legal system in ways that weaken the official authorities and benefit the terrorists. Thus recruitment of prisoners becomes an institutionalized, self-perpetuating process that, in the eyes of the terrorists and their allies, would ensure a steady supply of combatants in their war against civilization.

Acknowledgments

Portions of this chapter are based on testimony I delivered before the Senate Subcommittee on Terrorism, Technology and Homeland Security in October, 2003. I wish to acknowledge the staff of the Center for Security Policy for assistance with that testimony.

CHAPTER 4

Communication and Recruitment of Terrorists

BRIGITTE L. NACOS

Assessing the violent anti-Vietnam protests of the 1960s and early 1970s, Jerry Rubin, a leader of the Yippie movement, observed, "Every revolutionary needs a color TV. Walter Cronkite is SDS's [Student for a Democratic Society] best organizer. Uncle Walter brings out the map of the United States with circles around campuses that blew up today. The battle reports. Every kid out there is thinking, 'Wow! I wanna see *my* campus on that map.' "[1]

Actually, the "Uncle Walters" of television and the rest of the news media did not organize anti-Vietnam radicals and certainly did not recruit their violent offspring in the Weather Underground and Black Power movements. Terrorists in particular, whether from the right or left, have at all times enlisted the bulk of their new comrades through person-to-person contacts. In a study of left-wing terrorism in Italy, for example, Donatella della Porta found that 88 percent of Italian terrorists with known recruitment ties were drafted by relatives, friends, colleagues, and other acquaintances.[2] More recently, al Qaeda operatives, too, have been recruited through personal contacts, as the 9/11 Commission learned with respect to the team that carried out the attacks on New York and Washington. But the mass media play a crucial role as well: By paying extraordinary attention to terrorist strikes and to the motives of the perpetrators of terrorism the news disseminates, unwittingly as it may be, what nineteenth-century anarchists and radical social reformers called "propaganda by deed." This news content is one of the factors that condition certain individuals to become terrorists for the sake of a cause they support to begin with.

How can one equate an act of political violence with propaganda? In their book, *Age of Propaganda: The Everyday Use and Abuse of Persuasion*, researchers Anthony Pratkanis and Elliot Aronson point out that modern men are permanently bombarded with persuasive communications—"not through the give-and-take of argument and debate but through the manipulation of symbols and of our most basic emotions."[3] Nothing surpasses carefully orchestrated acts of terrorism, especially if they reach the level of spectaculars, in the exploitation and manipulation of symbols and emotions. The events of 9/11 serve as a perfect example. Within a span of 82 minutes the United States suffered a series of synchronized attacks as terrorists flew hijacked commercial airplanes into the two towers of the World Trade Center in New York and into the Pentagon outside of Washington, DC. Americans and people around the globe watched the attacks live and in endless replays. Unable to receive television in the mountains of Afghanistan, Osama bin Laden and his associates listened to the radio. The breaking news all the time described it again and again: the symbol of America's economic and financial power toppled in New York, the symbol of America's military might partially destroyed in Washington, and a symbol of political power, most likely the White House or Capitol, believed spared by courageous citizens aboard another jetliner that crashed near Pittsburgh, Pennsylvania. From the terrorists' point of view the "attack on America" was a perfectly choreographed production aimed at American and international audiences—among them potential recruits to bin Laden's declared jihad against all Americans.

Terrorism has often been compared to theater because terrorist attacks are planned like stage productions. In both cases, the people in charge channel all efforts into one overriding objective: to get to the emotions of their audiences. While the theater metaphor remains instructive, it has given way to terrorism as television event that is watched by record audiences and transcends by far the boundaries of theatrical productions. And unlike even the most successful producers of theater, motion picture, and television entertainment, the perpetrators of the lethal attacks on America affected all of their audiences in unprecedented ways. Among the spectators that the architects of 9/11 wanted to influence were undoubtedly the American public and public officials on all levels of the U.S. government. But equally important targets of their "propaganda by deed" were Muslims and Arabs in the Middle East and elsewhere around the globe, on whose behalf Osama bin Laden and al Qaeda claimed to act all along. Muslims and Arabs learned of the 9/11 attacks and the motives of the perpetrators through Western-controlled global TV networks, such as CNN and the BBC, and a number of relatively new Arab TV Channels, such as al Jazeera and al-Manar. As a result, bin Laden became a hero for many—not just temporarily. Opinion surveys conducted in early 2004 by the Pew Research Center for the People and the Press revealed that Osama bin Laden was still an immensely popular figure in the

Muslim world some two and a half years after 9/11. Sixty-five percent of Pakistanis, 55 percent of Jordanians, and 45 percent of Moroccans viewed the Al Qaeda leader favorably. A year earlier, 71 percent of Palestinian residents of Gaza and the West Bank, 58 percent of Indonesians, 55 percent of Jordanians, and 49 percent of Moroccans expressed confidence in the "world figure" bin Laden "to do the right thing." The notion that the defeat of al Qaeda in Afghanistan had dampened pro–bin Laden sentiments in the Muslim world was simply not born out by these and other polls.

Impressed by the success of the 9/11 operation and by bin Laden's repeated appeals for Muslims to join his jihad, young Muslims were eager to fight in his holy war. In an interview with a Portuguese daily, Omar Bakri Muhammad, a suspected member of al Qaeda, explained this post-9/11 pull when he stated,

> September 11 made Muslims understand that they have power. A new chapter of history has begun. That's why we have initiated a new calendar. We are now in Year Three of the al Qaeda era. *Many youths dream of joining al Qaeda, and there are many freelance groups ready to launch operations similar to al Qaeda's* [emphasis added].[4]

Many of the young Muslims that Muhammad referred to did not just dream. Thousands of volunteers joined the al Qaeda–led international web of terrorism.

While particularly instructive in the case of a terrorist movement that has specialized in staging catastrophic spectaculars, small bands of extremists can also exploit the media for spreading their "propaganda by deed." Thus, after the news media overcovered the insignificant violence by a few hundred self-proclaimed anarchists at the 1999 World Trade Organization summit in Seattle, a large number of radicals joined the violent core of the international antiglobalization movement. Similarly, overblown media reports about arson attacks on new housing developments or gas-guzzling sports utility vehicles by the Earth Liberation Front familiarized the American public with the motives of this by and large negligible "eco-terrorist" movement. More importantly, information in the mainstream media helped interested persons to find the group's Internet site that serves as a recruitment tool and a how-to-commit-terrorism resource. For example, an article in the *New York Times* about the sentencing of a young arsonist contained the following passage:

> At the time of the sentencing Mr. McIntyre was 17 and a member of the Earth Liberation Front, an organization that aims to "inflict economic damage on those profiting from the destruction and exploitation of the natural environment," its Web site (www.earthliberationfront.com) says.[5]

Whether hostile, neutral, or supportive of a terrorist cause, media organizations help terrorists to further their propaganda goals—simply by discharging their primary responsibility of covering important events and developments. To be sure, some media outlets accommodate terrorist groups more than others. Terrorists, in return, make themselves and their communications available to friendly media organizations. Bin Laden gave several interviews to Western and Arab news organizations before 9/11 and talked to an al Jazeera reporter after the attacks on New York and Washington. The religious edicts or *fatwa* that the al Qaeda founder and other religious leaders issued jointly in 1996 and 1998 were first published by an Arab-language newspaper in London. While explaining their grievances against the American-led crusaders and Zionists, these tracts—like bin Laden's interviews—were also appeals to Muslims everywhere to join the jihad against infidels. For years, al Qaeda's faxes, audio- and videotapes have been typically delivered to al Jazeera television. The purpose of these communications was multifaceted—including the desire to attract new recruits.

Counterterrorism as Motivation to Join the Terrorist Cause

Military responses to terrorism that attract an extraordinary volume of news reporting and result in shocking mass-mediated images of death and destruction are just as potent as terrorist acts for creating favorable recruiting conditions. The American-led invasion of Iraq was a case in point. While it was justified by the United States, the United Kingdom, and other coalition partners as part of the "war on terrorism," Muslims and Arabs in particular were not buying this explanation after watching the visual media images of killed Iraqi civilians and destroyed neighborhoods in Baghdad and elsewhere. It did not help that al Jazeera and other Arab TV networks highlighted these scenes. As a result, a vast majority of Muslims opposed not just the invasion of Iraq but America's "war on terrorism" altogether. For example, a year after the invasion of Iraq the majority of Jordanians (71%), Turks (64%), Moroccans (63%), and Pakistanis (53%) thought the "war on terrorism" was fought by the United States to control oil in the Middle East and to dominate the world. Counterterrorism experts identified this widespread reaction among Muslims and Arabs as the main reason for a significant jump in the recruitment of new terrorists by al Qaeda and like-minded cells and groups. The recruitment surge was not limited to the Middle East and elsewhere in Muslim countries but occurred in the Muslim diaspora of Western Europe as well. Conditioned by the mass-mediated images from Iraq, young Muslims were eager to join the fight against the United States and its allies. According to a team of *New York Times* reporters:

The call to jihad is rising in the streets of Europe, and it is being answered. The team found that Iraq dramatically strengthened their [al Qaeda's] recruitment efforts, one counterterrorism official said. He added that some mosques now display photos of American soldiers fighting in Iraq alongside bloody scenes of bombed out Iraqi neighborhoods.[6]

The horrifying scenes of Iraqi detainees tortured by their American guards at the Abu Ghraib prison, shown and replayed many times in TV newscasts, had equally strong, perhaps even stronger effects.

While Abu Ghraib was an extreme case, the point here is that mass-mediated descriptions and images of Muslim suffering as a result of infidels' actions, whether in Afghanistan, Iraq, the West Bank, or elsewhere, have been potent motivators for young Muslims to join terrorist groups.

Stories and visual evidence of police brutality against the participants of political protests also have the capacity to move predisposed persons towards violence. This was the case in the making of the Baader–Meinhof terrorist group in Germany. The killing of Benno Ohnesorg, a student demonstrator shot to death by a police officer in 1967, the nearly fatal attempt on Rudi Dutschke, a leader in the Socialist Student Association in 1968, and subsequent clashes between police and protesters provided left-wing radicals in West Germany with powerful images. These powerful "pictures in their heads" of police brutality backed by the government were among the factors that led to the establishment of the Red Army Faction.

Textbooks and Educational Video Clips as Recruitment Tools

When the political authorities provide or condone textbooks and other classroom media that glorify terrorism—along with like-minded instructors—impressionable youngsters are conditioned to admire and even become terrorists. In the early years of the twenty-first century, one-third of all Pakistani children were educated in religious schools (*madrasas*), many of which prepare them for joining the jihad against nonbelievers. Because these Islamic schools enjoyed strong support in the population, the secular authorities have not been able to regulate the "jihad factories" or "nurseries of terror."

The textbooks and video clips used in schools on the West Bank and in Gaza were approved and produced by the Palestinian Authority (PA). In her study of educational tools to indoctrinate Palestinian children to join the jihad against Israel, Daphne Burdman examined official textbooks, specifically developed teachers' training guides, and PA television campaigns that celebrated violence and urged boys and girls to become martyrs for Palestine and for Allah. After reviewing these textbooks and teachers' guides Burdman concluded,

> In summary, the teaching program conveys that the Zionists must be expelled from the land (that is, Israel). The Jew/Israel is the conqueror, thief, enemy. The Jew wants to rule the world. You should hate and kill the enemy. We must take back our land of Palestine. Jihad is our duty. Death as a martyr is glorious. The Martyr will be rewarded in heaven.[7]

Burdman found furthermore that the Palestinian Authority produced TV programs designed to indoctrinate children. Beginning with appeals to second- and third-graders to throw away their toys and pick up stones, the reviewed clips escalated to promoting more violent involvement and ended with the glorification of a young martyr who wrote in his farewell letter, "For my country, martyrdom! How sweet is martyrdom and I embrace you, oh my land. My beloved, my mother, my most dear. Be joyous over my blood and do not cry for me."[8] The letter writer was not an exception. In the summer of 2004 a Palestinian trauma specialist reported that 25 percent of Palestine children in Gaza "would like to be martyrs."[9]

The Written Word

If at all possible, terrorists—just like actors in the nonviolent, legitimate political process—like to control their propaganda and recruitment pitches. To this end, terrorists have utilized pamphlets, manifestos, articles, and books for some 150 years. If anyone questioned the power of the printed word in the recruitment of terrorists, those doubts were laid to rest after the assassination of President William McKinley in 1901. The assassin was Leon Czolgosz of Cleveland, a self-described anarchist. John Most, the founder of the anarchist newspaper *Freiheit*, was eventually convicted for publishing an article and thereby "endangering the peace and outraging public decency." The material in question was a reprint of Karl Heinzen's fifty-year-old essay "Murder" that justifies terrorism for the just political cause. Although the defense claimed that no copy had been sold before the president was assassinated, the judge stated in his ruling against Most:

> It is in the power of words that is the potent force to commit crimes and offenses in certain cases. No more striking illustration of the criminal power of words could be given, if we are to believe the murderer of our President, than that event presents.
>
> It is impossible to read the whole article without deducting from it the doctrine that all rulers are enemies of mankind, and are to be hunted and destroyed through "blood and iron, poison and dynamite."
>
> It [the article] shows a deliberate intent to inculcate and promulgate the doctrine of the article. This we hold to be a criminal act.[10]

This was a remarkable decision in that it made a direct connection between the inflammatory written word and the indoctrination of readers. Since the case arose in the context of the assassination of a president, it implied the power of words to recruit terrorists as well. But this linkage did not deter subsequent generations of terrorists from using the presses and the power of their words as effective recruiting tools.

In the *Mini-Manual of the Urban Guerrilla*, Carlos Marighella wrote about a two-fold approach to the terrorist propaganda scheme and suggested that the "[m]odern mass media, simply by announcing what the revolutionaries are doing, are important instruments of propaganda. However, their existence does not dispense fighters from setting up their own secret presses and having their own copying machine."[11]

Modern-day terrorists, too, author their own political statements, tracts, and books in order to find new supporters and recruits. Although he and his associates utilized literally all advanced media to enlist participants in their holy war against what they called the enemies of Islam, bin Laden was reportedly eager to write and publish a book. Before 9/11 he actually worked on a book that he hoped to turn into a bestseller in the Muslim world. Terrorism researcher Simon Reeve learned that bin Laden chose "America and the Third World War" as a working title. According to those who read the draft, the manuscript "consisted of a lengthy exhortation to Muslims to rise up and destroy the United States."[12] Perhaps because of 9/11 and al Qaeda's flight from Afghanistan, bin Laden's book was not published as planned.

Even by writing novels that advocate terrorism, preachers of extremism and hate can disguise their intention to indoctrinate and recruit followers. William Pierce is probably the best example. The former physics professor was a member of the American Nazi Party before he founded in 1974 his own organization, the National Alliance, and formulated a white supremacy ideology as hateful as that of his idol Adolf Hitler. But it was especially his novel *The Turner Diaries* (published under the pseudonym Andrew MacDonald) that influenced a whole generation of extremists in radical right-wing circles, from Christian Identity adherents to Neo-Nazis, Klansmen, militia, and survivalist activists. The book describes a civil war in the United States in which white Aryans fight what the author and other right-wing extremists call the Zionist Occupation Government (ZOG), killing blacks and Jews indiscriminately. The dramatic highlights are the ruthless destruction of American cities to pave the way for the dream of a white America and a white world come true. Even before Pierce's death in 2002, it was clear that he would be best remembered as the author of *The Turner Diaries* and his second book, *Hunter*. Popular for many years among right-wing extremists, these books have inspired some people in this milieu to follow the path of Pierce's heroic terrorists. *The Turner Diaries* was the favorite book of Oklahoma City bomber Timothy McVeigh, who used the description of the FBI headquarters' destruction as a blueprint for his real-life terror attack. His accomplice Terry Nichols preferred *Hunter*. One of the three white men who in 1998 beat and decapitated James Byrd Jr., an African-American citizen of Jaspers, Texas, as he was dragged on a chain by their pickup truck, told his accomplices during the killing, "We're starting *The Turner Diaries* early."

For many years, fans of Pierce have celebrated his books in customer reviews posted on the web sites of online booksellers. In one typical posting, a reader gave *The Turner Diaries* five stars, the best grade. He began and ended his review with the white supremacist greeting RAHOWA (for Racial Holy War) and praised Pierce for "a brilliant book that graphically captures the inevitable race-war we'll soon face." Obviously, Pierce's fans have embraced the content of his books as reality, not fiction— precisely as intended by the author.

From Telephone to Radio Transmitters

Today's terrorists have the luxury of utilizing more media and communication technologies to publicize their propaganda and make their recruiting pitches. They can choose between the oldest and the newest means of communication. When personal meetings are not feasible, terrorists communicate via telephone with attractive prospects for recruitment as the following case demonstrates: Before arresting Rabei Osman Sayed Ahmed as the suspected ringleader of the Madrid train bombings in March 2004, the Italian police recorded the Egyptian national's phone conversations. In one of the wiretaps, Ahmed tries to persuade twenty-one-year-old fellow Egyptian Yahia Payumi to become a suicide bomber. After telling the young man that one must be ready if one has the desire to sacrifice oneself in the name of God, Ahmed pushes on. "It is a shame," he says, "we young people must be the first to sacrifice ourselves. There is one solution, join al Qaeda. We see death every day, let us hope that God gives us the courage to win. The reward for those who choose death has no limit." Payumi responds, "Stay at my side and you will see how I rise, with the power of God I will finish there." At one point, Ahmed urges the young man to listen to particular cassettes and CDs in preparation to become a martyr. This seems to do the trick. "I am ready to sacrifice myself," Payumi says. Ahmed is delighted. "Consider yourself in paradise," he says.[13]

While telephone conversations may be as effective as face-to-face meetings, they are subject to wiretaps and thus risky. But there are plenty of other tools and methods to win new recruits, namely cassettes, CDs, videotapes, and DVDs, that terrorist groups and their supporters produce themselves. These electronic products are put into the hands of persons who seem most likely to respond positively to recruiting pitches. For example, in the spring of 2004, Islamic militants poised to fight Pakistan's military and U.S. Special Forces along the mountainous frontier between Pakistan and Afghanistan began to hand out sophisticated DVDs in a recruiting drive. Typically, the DVDs depicted compelling images of Americans mistreating Iraqis, Israelis abusing Palestinians, and Pakistani soldiers attacking their civilian countrymen. In one case, the presentation ended with the narrator's appeal: "Let's wage jihad!"

Reportedly, al Qaeda hired a production company to videotape bin Laden's declarations and to produce videotapes to be used as recruiting tools. A 100-minute tape that surfaced after al Qaeda's flight from Afghanistan featured the terrorist attack of the USS *Cole* prominently and was obviously produced several months before 9/11. In one scene bin Laden, wearing a traditional Yemini dagger on his belt, makes a direct connection between his organization and the attack on the *Cole* and celebrates the courage of the Muslim destroyers of the U.S. Navy's warship. Inspired recruits fire at the image of former President Bill Clinton and dive through a fiery hoop. Young boys, dressed in camouflage, shout and cheer in support of the jihad. There is no doubt that these kinds of tapes were produced with one objective in mind—to attract new recruits.

While Marighela recommended that "revolutionaries" should tape messages and find radio stations willing to broadcast the revolutionary propaganda, some contemporary terrorist groups in Latin America and Asia have their own clandestine radio broadcasts. Thus, members of the Revolutionary Armed Forces of Colombia (FARC), the longest surviving Marxist terror movement that controls large parts of the country, do part of their fighting on the air waves by broadcasting its "Voice of Resistance" over half a dozen mobile transmitters. According to FARC leaders in charge of communication, their air war is about propaganda. Claiming that they do their shooting from the radio, disk jockeys play traditional Colombian hit songs with one twist: In FARC's adaptation the songs have more radical lyrics and revolutionary titles such as "We Will Conquer," "Ambush Rap," and "Guerrilla Girls." Nobody knows for sure the size of FARC radio's audience—mostly impoverished peasants, many of whom cultivate illegal coca leaf, the raw material for the production of cocaine, but in the rugged terrain that is controlled by the group, commercial radio is difficult to receive. Thus, the "Voice of Resistance" fills a void and, at the same time, exploits the airwaves for propaganda messages and recruiting pitches. By and large, however, terrorist groups that operate their own radio stations are the exception, not the rule.

Hizballah and Al-Manar Television

The Lebanese Hizballah, closely tied to and supported by the Islamic Republic of Iran and listed by the U.S. Department of State as a terrorist organization, is the only movement with a distinct terrorist track record that operates its own television station. Al-Manar (the Arabic word for beacon) grew from a small local station that serviced part of Beirut to a regional broadcaster and, after switching to satellite broadcasting in 2000, to a global television channel that offers its own programs around-the-clock. Although getting less attention than rival Arab stations, such as al Jazeera and al Arabiya, al-Manar became a major global player following the events of 9/11.

In his article "Religious Terrorism, the Media, and International Is-lamization Terrorism: Justifying the Unjustifiable" Ayla Schbley wrote that al-Manar "has been steadily gaining audiences throughout the Islamic world, Europe, Australia, and the United States."[14] Millions of Muslims watch al-Manar's one-sided programs regularly, consume the station's tra-ditional anti-Israel propaganda and, more recently, watch an equally ag-gressive anti-American campaign. The regular features devoted to showing tapes of terrorist attacks, the constant glorification of terrorists as martyrs, and the cleverly packaged justification of killing innocents as expression of God's wrath add up to a diet of powerful indoctrination. Researcher Avi Jorisch noted in his recent article that

> the most blatant propagandizing takes place between programs in music videos that serve as fillers. These video packages constitute up to 30 percent of al-Manar's satellite programming. According to officials in the art graph-ics department, the videos are meant to "help people on the way to com-mitting what you in the West call suicide mission. It is meant to be the first step in the process of a freedom fighter operation."[15]

More important, al-Manar has been very successful in indoctrinating and mobilizing Muslims far beyond the Middle East, as Schbley's survey of 2,619 Arab and Muslim men in eight cities (Berlin, Bern, Copenhagen, The Hague, London, Paris, Rome, and Diekirch) of eight European Union coun-tries revealed. Establishing that the respondents recalled and were affected by the content of CNN and the European media (e.g., by information about bomb making), the research found, too, that "Hizballah and its TV sta-tion . . . yielded the strongest impact on the psyche of this study's sample population."[16]

While al-Manar, like other terrorist media, are not directly recruiting members for Hizballah and other terror organizations, its programs cer-tainly condition Muslim and Arab audiences at home and abroad to sup-port terrorism against Israelis and Americans and, perhaps, become terrorists themselves. As Schbley noted,

> The overwhelming majority of this population of 2,619 Arabs and Muslims have self-reported a strong willingness to accept and justify terrorism, a strong affinity for martyrdom, a strong propensity for violence, considerable

religious commitment and preference for theocracy, considerable membership in religious organizations, high susceptibility to media broadcasts, perception of unity among Muslims, and favorable support for Osama bin Laden.[17]

The respondents, all members of the Muslim diaspora in Europe, characterized the media as the "minarets of Islamic jihad," and thereby underlined the importance of al-Manar TV in particular and other media organizations in general for the highly successful recruiting process. While al-Manar TV seems perhaps the strongest media influence on the Muslim diaspora with respect to indoctrination and recruitment, it shares this sort of impact with other broadcasters in the Middle East. Take the following discussion on recruitment and training of Palestinian suicide terrorists between the Hamas spokesman in Gaza, Sami Abu Zuhri, and an expert on Palestinian matters, Faraj Shalhoub, that was broadcast in June 2004 on al-Majd TV, a channel in the United Arab Emerites:

> (*Shalhoub*): "The volunteers are those who initiate and accept upon themselves to commit a martyrdom operation. There is a widespread misconception, propagated by the Zionist enemy, that there are recruiters among the Palestinian fighters who look for martyrdom bombers. The opposite is true. The martyrdom bombers are the ones looking for the resistance factions in order to commit martyrdom operations. We are talking about hundreds of martyrdom bombers waiting in line to commit martyrdom operations."
>
> (*Abu Zuhri*): "There are hundreds of female martyrdom bombers, who stream en masse and insist on participating in martyrdom operations. This is a unique phenomenon, reflecting the live spirit of jihad among this people. . . . We see this stream of young men and women seeking martyrdom. This people emphasizes its adherence to the option of martyrdom, especially in light of the models of female martyrdom bombers."[18]

Whether or not whole armies of volunteers lined up to serve as suicide terrorists does not really matter. What mattered was the use of broadcast media to praise "martyrdom" and thereby condition men and women for recruitment. Moreover, the Arab media carry outright recruitment pitches regularly as well. On the Iranian television channel al-'Alam, for example, Sheik Muhammad al-Zein told his audience in the summer of 2004,

> I call to our brothers, the Intifada youth, whether from Hamas, Jihad, or al-Aqsa Martyr's Brigades to rise above internal conflict and raise the banner of Jihad and martyrdom for the sake of Allah. . . . We cannot confront this entity [Israel] in familiar politics and negotiation, calling for peace and other conventional ways. The struggle should be through resistance and martyrdom.[19]

Communication, Media, and the Recruitment of Terrorists

No doubt, then, communication is the key factor in the recruitment of terrorists. As mentioned at the outset, the vast majority of persons are convinced by relatives, friends, colleagues, or acquaintances to join a terrorist group. This sort of recruitment occurs in personal meetings and in communications via telephone and e-mail. But the print and electronic media in general are important means to spread the terrorist "propaganda by deed" and inform, indoctrinate and prepare some individuals for recruitment.

CHAPTER 5

Terrorist Dot Com: Using the Internet for Terrorist Recruitment and Mobilization

GABRIEL WEIMANN

"The Internet has become the new Afghanistan for terrorist training, recruitment, and fundraising. . . . Terrorist groups are exploiting the accessibility, vast audience, and anonymity of the Internet to raise money and recruit new members."[1]

—*PC World, July 7, 2004*

Without recruitment terrorism cannot prevail, survive and develop.[2] Recruitment provides the killers, the suicide bombers, the kidnappers, the executioners, the engineers, the soldiers—the armies of modern terrorism. As RAND's Bruce Hoffman argues:

Al Qaeda's resiliency and longevity are predicated not on the total number of Jihadists that it might have trained in the past but on its continued ability to recruit, to mobilize, and to animate both actual and would-be fighters, supporters, and sympathizers.[3]

In a recent study, Marc Sageman examined the background, recruitment, and motivations of more than 150 members of four specific terrorist networks: the Central Staff around Osama bin Laden, the Core Arabs, the Maghreb Arabs, and the Southeast Asians.[4] His book, *Understanding Terror Networks*, highlights the role of social networks in the recruitment of modern terrorism. The study documents the role of kinship and social networking as means of recruiting, of providing social and psychological security, and of radicalizing and mobilizing supporters. For example, he found that 68 percent of his sample of terrorists had friends in the jihad or joined as groups. An additional 20 percent had close relatives who were already members. Sageman argues that recruitment is a bottom-up self-selected process rather than a top-down "seek out and recruit" process. Thus, his findings emphasize the war for the hearts and minds of these hundreds of thousands of prospective terrorists.

Following the American campaign in Iraq, al Qaeda and other terror organizations have intensified their efforts to recruit young Muslim men, directing the rising anger about the American presence in the Middle East. According to *The Military Balance*—the annual report of the London-based International Institute for Strategic Studies—the war in Iraq has swollen the ranks of al Qaeda and "galvanized its will" by increasing radical passions among Muslims. The Institute believes the network is present in more than sixty countries, has a rump leadership intact, and that there are more than 18,000 potential terrorists at large, with al Qaeda recruitment continuing daily. Today, governments throughout Mexico and Central America are on alert as evidence grows that al Qaeda members are looking for recruits to carry out attacks in Latin America—the potential last frontier for international terrorism. The territory could be a perfect staging ground for Osama bin Laden's militants, with homegrown rebel groups, drug and people smugglers, and corrupt governments. As Hoffman argues, al Qaeda's resiliency (and longevity) is predicated on its continued ability to recruit and mobilize actual and would-be fighters, supporters, and sympathizers.[5]

Despite the attacks on al Qaeda over the last several years, the arrests and personnel losses, and the dismantling of its operational bases and training camps in Afghanistan, al Qaeda has managed to maintain an efficient campaign of propaganda. A professionally produced al Qaeda recruitment video, for example, was recently circulated around various foreign Muslim communities in hopes of attracting new martyrs to bin Laden's cause. The seven-minute videotape openly extolled the virtues of martyrdom and solicited new recruits to bin Laden's cause. It presented various scenes of jihadists in combat, followed by the images of twenty-seven martyrs shown in rapid succession with the name of each listed, where they came from, and where they died. Twelve of the martyrs were then featured in a concluding segment accompanied by the voiceover: "They rejoice in the bounty provided by Allah: And with regard to those left behind who have not yet joined them in their bliss, the martyrs glory in the fact that on them is no fear, nor have they cause to grieve." Abu Ghaith, the group's chief spokesman, argued: "Those youths that destroyed Americans with their planes, they did a good deed. There are thousands more young followers who look forward to death like Americans look forward to living." According to U.S. government officials, al Qaeda now uses chat rooms to recruit Latino Muslims with U.S. passports, in the belief that they will arouse less suspicion as operatives than would Arab-Americans.

Since the outbreak of the "al-Aqsa Intifada" in 2001, there has been a growing trend in the use of Palestinian children aged eleven to seventeen who are recruited by terrorist organizations to perpetrate suicide attacks in Israel. Female terrorists have also been recruited to carry out suicide bombing attacks—at least forty in the last three years. Salah Shehadeh, one of the former leaders of Hamas in the Gaza Strip, discussed the use of children for terrorist attacks during an interview on the *Islam Online* website (26 May 2002). He said that the children must be trained well prior to perpetrating terrorist attacks and are recruited into a special branch within the organization's military apparatus in order to instill the jihad culture and teach them right from wrong. Expressions such as these represent one of the primary elements in convincing parents to send their children to perpetrate terrorist attacks. In many countries wracked by ethnic, political, or religious violence in the developing world—such as Algeria, Colombia, and Sri Lanka—new members of terrorist organizations are recruited at younger and younger ages. Adolescents and teenagers in these countries are often receptive to terrorist recruitment because they have witnessed killings firsthand and thus see violence as the only way to deal with grievances and problems. Militant groups in Jammu and Kashmir are increasingly recruiting children of Gujjar and Bakerwal tribes in the hills of Udhampur and using them in operations against security forces. Most of these children are between nine and fifteen years old, belong to the higher reaches of the Pir Panjal, and are soft targets for terrorist groups. Recruitment of children is particularly important in the information age. As discussed later in this chapter, the Internet has become an increasingly prominent tool for recruiting a younger generation of terrorists, in large part because these younger generations are more tech savvy than their elders.

Recruitment Practices

The oldest example of recruitment by a terrorist organization comes from a thousand years ago, and carried out by those who gave us the word *assassin*.[6] They were members of a secret Islamic order active in Persia, Iraq, and Syria about 1090–1272, who believed it was a religious duty to harass and murder their enemies. The most important members of the order were those who actually did the killing. Having been promised paradise in return for dying in action, the killers, it is said, were made to yearn for paradise by being given a life of pleasure that included the use of hashish. From this came the name for the secret order as a whole, "ashishin" or "hashish users." In the thirteenth century, Mongol and Arab armies went after the "assassins," destroying their castles and killing their leaders.

At the beginning, religion, sex, and drugs were used to persuade young men to join the group of the "Assassins." Indeed, both then and now, it takes a combination of factors to recruit new terrorists. First, one needs a cause to attract and motivate recruits. Very often the target population is poverty-stricken, feeling oppressed, deprived, and hopeless. Religion is another recruitment tool and motivational dimension, but not a necessary condition. For example, the Tamil terrorists in Sri Lanka rely more on patriotic and social motives. However, oppression and a well-run organization which can channel the resentment into action are essential. Sometimes the attractions to join a terrorist group are material—for example, the family of the terrorist may be rewarded with money and public praise after the family member successfully conducts an attack. This factor is most important among the poor, the young, and the economically dispossessed. Thus, poverty, anger, resentment, religious and nationalistic zeal, and even the desire to take revenge for a relative killed by the enemy are all used to successfully attract and recruit new terrorists. Sageman argues that poverty, religious belief, and political frustration are "necessary but not sufficient" to explain how a few angry young Muslim men—but not many, many others—decide to embrace jihadist violence. More important, he notes, are "social bonds" among the young volunteers, the sense of clandestine belonging they develop, and their ability to make reinforcing contact with al Qaeda leaders or trainers. Groups of young men become effective terrorist cells "through mutual emotional and social support, development of a common identity, and encouragement to adopt a new faith."[7] These internal group ties are more significant, Sageman argues, than external factors "such as common hatred for an outside group."[8]

Personal problems are also exploited by recruiters; often, people with mental problems are targeted, as long as their disability does not make them incapable of terrorist operations. Widows or unmarried women who have lost their parents are another source of recruits. In Chechen culture, for example, such women face bleak prospects for a happy future. People who have been condemned to death by religious courts may be given the option of becoming a suicide bomber to atone for their crime, and some are provided cash for their families. Men who have lost many family members to Russian troops and are keenly aware of the Chechen tradition of revenge comprise another source of volunteers.

Al Qaeda uses the most advanced headhunting methods to recruit terrorist agents. It advertises by using recorded videos on Internet websites, CD-ROMs, recorded cassettes, and blast faxes. Osama bin Laden and his subordinates also offer interviews to sympathetic radical Muslim newspapers and television and radio stations. Abdullah Azzam, bin Laden's mentor, inspired many al Qaeda volunteers with his fiery preaching. Bin Laden and his al Qaeda aides emulate him by persuading Muslim preachers around the world to help with recruiting. The many thousands of Afghan Arabs whom he trained and fought with against the Soviets in Afghanistan still take their lead from al Qaeda. The network recruits terrorists worldwide, including from immigrant communities in the United States and Western Europe as well as Australia, the Philippines, Indonesia, and Malaysia. Its agents seek new human talent in all six inhabited continents. Even far-off South America and Australia now host al Qaeda members and recruiters.

Modern Recruitment Methods

Adam Gadahn was an average American boy who loved watching television and listening to music, raised by parents who farmed goats in Riverside County, California. However, at the age of seventeen he discovered Islam on the web and soon started a conversion process that led to his joining al Qaeda. In 2003, U.S. federal authorities labeled him an enemy, saying he was one of seven individuals suspected of being al Qaeda operatives who may be working to mount a terrorist attack in the United States. Gadahn, now twenty-five, has attended al Qaeda training camps and worked as a translator for the terrorist group, the FBI said. Authorities said he may be using the names Adam Pearlman or Abu Suhayb al-Amriki. In his own words, Gadahn described how the Internet was the gate for his recruitment:

> The turning point, perhaps, was when I moved in with my grandparents here in Santa Ana, the county seat of Orange, California. My grandmother, a computer whiz, is hooked up to America Online and I have been scooting the information superhighway since January. But when I moved in, with the intent of finding a job (easier said than done), I began to visit the religion folders on AOL and the Usenet newsgroups, where I found discussions on Islam to be the most intriguing. You see, I discovered that the beliefs and practices of this religion fit my personal theology and intellect as well as basic human logic.[9]

In October 2004, a videotape in which a masked man claims to be American and warns of coming attacks in the United States has drawn the scrutiny of federal intelligence agencies. They concluded that the person was Adam Gadahn. The speaker identifies himself as "Assam the American" and refers to Osama bin Laden and his top deputy as "our leaders." In some respects, Gadhan's case is reminiscent of that of John Walker Lindh, the "American Taliban" from Marin County, who embraced Islam, traveled to Afghanistan, met Osama bin Laden, and was captured by U.S. forces in December 2001.

Many other modern recruitment operations have emerged on the web. For example, in June 2004, the magazine *Insight Online* obtained a recruitment appeal seeking Iranians who would commit suicide in deadly attacks on American and coalition forces in Iraq, on Israel, and on U.S. citizens around the world.[10] It was posted on the Internet by an Iranian recruiting group. Reuters news agency reported (on 5 June 2004) that the group is known as the Committee for the Commemoration of Martyrs of the Global Islamic Campaign. It quoted the group's spokesman, Mohammad Ali Samadi, as saying, "Some 10,000 people have registered their names to carry out martyrdom operations on our defined targets." Ali Samadi, according to Reuters, says the alleged independent group's targets include "mainly the occupying American and British forces in the holy Iraqi cities, all the Zionists in Palestine, and Salman Rushdie—the only nonmilitary target for us, because we believe his attack against Islam was much worse than a military assault." The recruitment application was translated from Farsi as follows:

In the Name of God
Preliminary Registration for Martyrdom Operations

I _____, child of _____, born 13_____ [Islamic calendar], the City of: _____ proclaim my preparedness for carrying out martyrdom operations:

____ against the occupiers of the holy sites [referring to Najaf, Karbala, and other places in Iraq].

____ against the occupiers of [Jerusalem].

____ for carrying out the death sentence of the infidel Salman Rushdie.

Also, I would like to become an active member of the Army of Martyrs of the International Islamic Movement. Yes ____, No ____

Contact telephone:

Applicant's address:

Applicant's signature:

In October 2004, *Intelwire* presented an al Qaeda recruiting video showing young boys training in terrorist techniques.[11] The video includes a statement read in Arabic by a young son of Osama bin Laden. The video was hosted on an Arabic-language website connected to Tawhid Wal Jihad, the terror organization led by Abu Musab al-Zarqawi. The video, titled "Hamza Laden," appears to show young boys between the ages of ten and fourteen engaged in commando training, including marching in formation, running a military-style obstacle course, rappelling, and reading written statements in Arabic. All these examples show how modern terrorists are using advanced communication technologies to attract and seduce potential followers, recruits, supporters and would-be terrorists.

When Terrorism Met the Net

The great virtues of the Internet—ease of access, lack of regulation, vast potential audiences, fast flow of information, and so forth—have been turned to the advantage of groups committed to terrorizing societies in order to achieve their goals. Today, as recent studies have revealed, almost all active terrorist groups have established their presence on the Internet.[12] The following analysis draws from a more general research project hosted and funded by United States Institute of Peace that summarized seven years of monitoring terrorist presence on the Net.[13] The population for this study was defined as the Internet sites of terrorist movements as they appeared in the period between January 1998 and July 2004. The study used U.S. State Department's list of terrorist organizations, which meets the accepted definition of terror.[14] Our scan of the Internet revealed thousands of websites serving terrorists and their supporters. Websites are only one of the Internet's services used by modern terrorism: There are other facilities in the Net—e-mail, chat rooms, e-groups, forums, virtual message boards— that are used more and more by terrorists. Terrorism on the Internet is a very dynamic phenomenon; websites suddenly emerge, frequently modify their formats, and then swiftly disappear—or, in many cases, seem to disappear by changing their online address but retaining much the same content. To locate the terrorists' sites, numerous systematic scans of the Internet were conducted, feeding an enormous variety of names and terms into search engines, entering chat rooms and forums of supporters and sympathizers, and surveying the links on other organizations' websites to create and update a comprehensive set of lists. This is often a Herculean effort, especially because in some cases (e.g., al Qaeda's websites) the locations and contents of websites change almost daily.

This study identified different (albeit sometimes overlapping) ways in which contemporary terrorists use the Internet. Some of these parallel the uses to which everyone puts the Internet—information gathering, for instance. Some resemble the uses made of the medium by traditional political organizations—for example, raising funds and disseminating propaganda. Others, however, are much more unusual and distinctive—recruiting terrorists, instructing terrorists, and mobilizing terrorists using the Net. The following section of this chapter will focus on the use of the Internet as a terrorist apparatus of recruitment and mobilization.

Recruitment on the Net

The Internet can be used to recruit and mobilize supporters to play a more active role in support of terrorist activities or causes. In addition to seeking converts by using the full range of website technologies (audio, digital video, etc.) to enhance the presentation of their message, terrorist organizations capture information about the users who browse their websites. Users who seem most interested in the organization's cause or well suited to carrying out its work are then contacted. Sophisticated methods are used by terrorists to refine or customize recruiting techniques on the Net: "Using some of the same marketing techniques employed by commercial enterprises, terrorist servers could capture information about the users who browse their websites, and then later contact those who seem most interested. Recruiters may also use more interactive Internet technology to roam online chat rooms and cyber cafes, looking for receptive members of the public—particularly young people. Electronic bulletin boards and Usenet discussion forums can also serve as vehicles for reaching out to potential recruits. Interested computer users around the world can be engaged in long-term 'cyber relationships' that could lead to friendship and eventual membership."[15] However, it should be noted that modern terrorists do not recruit directly online; they use the Net only to identify, profile, and select potential candidates for recruitment. Afraid of having their groups infiltrated by security agencies and counterterrorism forces, they will use the Internet only for the early stages of the recruitment process.

Thomas Hegghammer, a Norwegian researcher, divides the jihadi Internet community into three categories.[16] First, there are the message boards where one finds the political and religious discussions among the sympathizers and potential recruits. Among the most important message boards for al Qaeda sympathizers are al Qal'ah (the Fortress), al Sahat (the Fields), and al Islah (Reform). These message boards, Hegghammer argues, provide links to the second type, the "information hubs," where new radical-Islamist texts, declarations, and recordings are posted. These sites are often posted in the "communities" sections of popular Western sites such as Yahoo!, Lycos, and others. Among these, the most important one is the "Global Islamic Media." Finally, there is the third type of sites, the "mother sites," which are run by people who get their material directly from the ideologues or operatives.

The Internet also provides a useful tool to reach the "conventional" media (television, radio, press). The wave of hostages' beheadings in Iraq was followed by posting gruesome footage of the killings on websites. These were picked up, sometimes within minutes, by television networks and news agencies all over the world. This creates a new type of symbiosis between terrorists, the Internet, and some television networks, allowing publicity seeking terrorists like al-Zarqawi to stage cruel executions that will be channeled to world media through Internet websites, carrying his manifestos, declarations and calls for action.

In addition, some would-be recruits use the Internet to advertise themselves to terrorist organizations. In 1995, as reported by Verton in *Black Ice*, Ziyad Khalil enrolled as a computer science major at Columbia College in Missouri. He also became a Muslim activist on the campus, developing links to several radical groups and operating a website that supported Hamas. Thanks in large part to his Internet activities, he came to the attention of bin Laden and his lieutenants. Khalil became al Qaeda's procurement officer in the United States, arranging purchases of satellite telephones, computers, and other electronic surveillance technologies and helping bin Laden communicate with his followers and officers. In February 2004, a U.S. National Guardsman was arrested and accused of trying to provide information to the al Qaeda terrorist network. U.S. Army Specialist Ryan G. Anderson was being held at Fort Lewis, charged of "aiding the enemy by wrongfully attempting to communicate and give intelligence to the al Qaeda terrorist network."[17] Anderson had converted to Islam five years before his arrest. The National Guardsman was held after allegedly offering military information through an Internet chat room. He thought the people he was contacting were Muslim terrorists, but in fact they were FBI agents running a "sting" operation. CNN reported that the information the suspect was trying to sell concerned protective equipment for armored vehicles deployed in Iraq. An investigation of Usenet discussion forums, conducted by *National Review Online* reporter Michelle Malkin, yielded some interesting clues about Anderson:

> Using the e-mail address wensler@wsunix.wsu.edu, Anderson posted prolifically to a strange and volatile variety of Internet newsgroups, including forums for gun enthusiasts, skinheads, cinema, games, Islam, and Arabic culture. He offered opinions on everything from the movie *Starship Troopers* to sniping weapons and presidential politics. Putting aside the chronic misspellings, the 154 messages are an instructive glimpse into the mind of an immature American youth with a potentially dangerous longing to belong. . . . On September 26, 1997, Anderson—now with a new, adopted Muslim name, Amir, posted to soc.culture.arabic: "Salaam Alaaykum all, I am a Muslim convert studying at Washington State University for an Asian History Major, my focus is on Arabic nations. . . . In October, 1997 . . . Anderson offered a conspiracy theory posted to soc.culture.somalia, soc.culture.palestine, alt.religion.islam and alt.culture.somalia: "Is it possible Mossad replaced the Sheik entirely? With the amount of knowledge they have on people, I wouldn't put it entirely beyond them to be able to substitute an imposter."[18]

In September 2004, Anderson was found guilty on all five counts of trying to help the al Qaeda terrorist network. More typically, however, terrorist organizations go looking for recruits rather than waiting for them to present themselves. The SITE Institute, a Washington, D.C.–based terrorism research group that monitors al Qaeda's Internet communications, has provided chilling details of a high-tech recruitment drive launched in 2003 to recruit fighters to travel to Iraq and attack U.S. and coalition forces there.

Potential recruits are bombarded with religious decrees and anti-U.S. propaganda, provided with training manuals on how to be a terrorist, and—as they are led through a maze of secret chat rooms—given specific instructions on how to make the journey to Iraq.[19] Rita Katz, the SITE Institute's director, argues that "al Qaeda's use of the Internet is amazing. We know from past cases—from captured al Qaeda fighters who say they joined up through the Internet—that this is one of the principal ways they recruit fighters and suicide bombers."[20]

On 6 June 2003, Abu Thur, a computer programmer in Malaysia, posted a message to the Arabic-language "himmame" message board, hosted by Lycos in the United Kingdom. The message read:

> Dear Brothers,
> I have already succeeded with the grace of Allah and his help, to go to Kurdistan for jihad through one of the brothers in this forum. Praise be to Allah, I have fought there, by the grace of God and his bounty. But martyrdom was not granted to me, and therefore I ask Allah to give me more lifetime and to make my deeds good. I ask anyone who has the capacity to organize for me to go to another jihad front to correspond with me.[21]

Asad Allah, an Egyptian based in Malaysia, posted a similar message, asking for help from forum members:

> I told myself that if I am already here (in Malaysia), I might as well fulfill my jihad, far away from the Egyptian authorities. . . . I failed to contact or get to know someone who might help me with fulfilling jihad here. Should I go back [to Egypt]?[22]

In one particularly graphic exchange in a secret al Qaeda chat room in early September 2003, an unknown Islamic fanatic, with the user name "Redemption is Close," wrote, "Brothers, how do I go to Iraq for jihad? Are there any army camps and is there someone who commands there?" Four days later he received a reply from "Merciless Terrorist," who wrote: "Dear Brother, the road is wide open for you—there are many groups, go look for someone you trust, join him, he will be the protector of the Iraqi regions and with the help of Allah you will become one of the Mujahidin." "Redemption is Close" then pressed for more specific information on how he can wage jihad in Iraq. "Merciless Terrorist" sent him a propaganda video and instructed him to download software called Pal Talk, which enables users to speak to each other on the Internet without fear of being monitored.[23]

Many terrorist websites stop short of enlisting recruits for violent action, but they do encourage supporters to show their commitment to the cause in other tangible ways. "How can I help the struggle: A few suggestions," runs a heading on the Kahane Lives website; "Action alert: What you can do" is a feature on the Shining Path's website. The power of the Internet to mobilize activists is illustrated by the response to the arrest of Abdullah Ocalan, leader of the Kurdish terrorist group the PKK. When Turkish forces arrested Ocalan, tens of thousands of Kurds around the world responded with demonstrations within a matter of hours—thanks to sympathetic websites urging supporters to protest.

In the summer of 2002, Israeli police arrested three Jerusalem Arabs linked to Hamas who allegedly planned to carry out a mass poisoning of patrons in a Jerusalem café. One of the three, Othman Kiania, was employed as a chef at the restaurant, and planned to mix poison in the drinks. His partners were Sufian Abdo and Mussa Nasser, who ran a Hamas Internet forum. According to the *Jerusalem Post*, "Abdo had contacted various members of Hamas via e-mail early this year, expressing his willingness to take part in terrorist activities. For the next eight months, he and Nasser kept in contact with Hamas officials, by providing them with the name of an Egyptian engineer who could help them develop Kassem rockets and raise funds for Hamas. In July, Abdo told them he wanted to carry out a suicide bombing to avenge the death of Salah Shehadeh [a well-known Hamas leader]. They suggested he carry out a mass poisoning at a large Jerusalem café, and he agreed."[24] They were tracked down and arrested by Israeli security agents just a day before executing the plan.

The use of the Internet by radical Muslim terrorists was formally sanctioned by Sheikh Abdul Aziz al-Alshaikh, the Grand Mufti of Saudi Arabia and the highest official cleric in the country. In December 2002, the Saudi Information Agency obtained a *fatwa* issued by the Grand Mufti regarding cyberterrorism. This special *fatwa* appeared in the religious magazine *Al-Dawa*, published in Riyadh. The *fatwa*, in the form of question–answer, is:

> **Question:** If there were websites on the Internet that are hostile to Islam, and broadcasting immoral materials, is it permissible for me to send it viruses to disable and destroy these websites? *Abdul Aziz Saleh Al-Morashid Erqa.*
>
> **Answer:** If these websites are hostile to Islam and you could encounter its evilness with goodness; and to respond to it, refute its falsehood, and show its void content; that would be the best option. But if you are unable to respond to it, and you wanted to destroy it and you have the ability to do so, it's ok to destroy it because it is an evil website.[25]

Following the publication of this *fatwa*, Saudi hackers began to attack FBI and Pentagon websites. In an interview with one of these hackers, published in the *al-Riyadh* newspaper on 5 September 2001, he reported attacking over 1,000 websites in the United States, including many official government websites.

Targeting Children

The Internet is very popular among children and youth. Terrorists know this, and are increasingly using the Internet to target children. One of Hamas's websites, al-Fateh ("The Conqueror"), appears every other week and is clearly meant for children, with its cartoon-style design and colorful children stories. The website's title promises "pages discussing jihad, scientific pages, the best stories, not be found elsewhere, and unequalled tales of heroism." The al-Fateh site has a link to the official Hamas site, www.palestine-info.com. Among its attractive graphics, drawings, children's songs, and stories (including "The Thrush" and "The Troubles of Fahman the Donkey," as well as texts written by children themselves), the site posts messages promoting suicide terrorists. Thus, in October 2004, the website presented the picture of a decapitated head of a young female, Zaynab Abu Salem, a female suicide bomber. On 22 September 2004, she detonated an explosive belt at a soldiers' hitchhiking stop at in Jerusalem, killing two Border Patrol policemen and wounding seventeen civilians. The text accompanying the horrible picture praises the act arguing that she is now in paradise, a "shaheeda" like her male comrades. The caption reads: "The perpetrator of the suicide bombing attack, Zaynab Abu Salem. Her head was severed from her pure body and her headscarf remained to decorate [her face]. Your place is in heaven in the upper skies, oh, Zaynab, sister [raised to the status of heroic] men."[26]

The same website, among its cartoons and children's stories, posted the last will of a Hamas suicide bomber, who in 1 June 2001, perpetrated a suicide bombing attack at the Dolphinarium in Tel Aviv, a club frequented by teenagers. The attack resulted in the deaths of twenty-one Israeli civilians, most of them teenagers, and wounded eighty-three. In his online will, the suicide bomber writes to "the Engineer, Yahya Ayyash" (a Hamas terrorist who was an expert in constructing bombs and explosive belts until he was killed by the Israelis): "You taught us . . . that the true heroes are those who write the history of their people in blood. . . . I will turn my body into shrapnel and bombs, which will chase the children of Zion, will blow them up and will burn what is left of them. . . . There is nothing greater than killing oneself on the land of Palestine, for the sake of Allah."[27]

Hizballah also targets children and adolescents use of the Internet. In 2003, Hizballah began online marketing of a computer game simulating terrorist attacks on Israeli targets. The computer game, called "Special Force," was developed by the Hizballah Central Internet Bureau, and its development—according to a report in Lebanon's *Daily Star*—took two years.[28] The game places the player in different Hizballah operations against Israelis. The producers of "Special Force" argue that it is based on actual Hizballah battles with Israeli forces. "Special Force" can be played in Arabic, English, French, and Farsi, and is available on one of the Hizballah websites. The violent game also features a training mode where players can practice their shooting skills on targets such as Israeli Prime Minister Sharon and other Israeli political and military figures. A good performance earns a certificate presented by Hizballah leader Sheikh Hassan Nasrallah in a "cyberceremony." The game ends with an exhibit of Hizballah "martyrs"—fighters killed by Israel. On the game's cover and in the online version, there is a message to users that says, "The designers of Special Force are very proud to provide you with this special product, which embodies objectively the defeat of the Israeli enemy and the heroic actions taken by heroes of the Islamic Resistance in Lebanon. Be a partner in the victory. Fight, resist and destroy your enemy in the game of force and victory." Mahmoud Rayya, a member of Hizballah, noted in an interview for the *Daily Star* that the decision to produce the game was made by leaders of Hizballah, and that "In a way, "Special Force" offers a mental and personal training for those who play it, allowing them to feel that they are in the shoes of the resistance fighters."[29]

Conclusion

The future of terrorism relies more on future recruitment than on any other factor. Although terrorists do not use the Internet for direct recruitment but only to identify and profile potential candidates for recruitment, this use of the Net is alarming. The fact that the Internet has become a more popular apparatus for early stages of recruitment and mobilization is challenging governments, security agencies, and counterterrorism services all over the world. Moreover, it also challenges the future of the Internet, since any attempt to limit or minimize the Net's use by terrorists implies imposing restrictions on the Internet's free flow of information, free speech, and privacy. Thus, any step or measure to fight the terrorists' use of the Net should involve a careful examination of the costs in terms of civil liberties; we need to find a "golden way" that will minimize the abuse of the Internet by both terrorism and counterterrorism. A failure to find compromises and best trade-offs between security and civil liberties when it comes to the Internet may have disastrous consequences—terrorist use of the Internet will grow and will become more sophisticated and more manipulative. This, in turn, may lead to harsher counterterrorism measures enforced by terror-stricken governments and security agencies.

CHAPTER 6

Education and Radicalization: Jemaah Islamiyah Recruitment in Southeast Asia

ZACHARY ABUZA

There are contending views on what drives terrorist recruitment. Some studies focus on political factors—for example, individuals cross the line and engage in violence because there are no legal means for them to try to address their grievances. Other studies focus on economic factors—for example, people experience relative depravity leading to frustration and aggression. Economic factors can be exacerbated by demographics, such as youth bulges in the population. Yet all of these explanations—which focus on the "push" towards joining militant groups—are lacking. They explain what makes these people angry and psychologically predisposed to violence, but do not explain the actual process of joining a terrorist organization, which by its very nature is an elite organization. The single most important determinant in terrorist recruitment is "pull," which is achieved through organizational and social networks. In the Muslim world of Southeast Asia, network-based recruitment is focused on four central factors: kinship, mosque, madrasa, and friendship. Education is the commonality between those.

The superb analysis of Sidney Jones and the International Crisis Group has concluded that kinship ties, including marital ties, are the single most important determinant of membership in Jemaah Islamiyah (JI), the regional affiliate of al Qaeda.[1] JI, according to Jones, is held together "by a complicated web of marriage alliances that at times makes it seem like one large extended family." Malaysian intelligence concluded that "over 100 marriages involving families of key Jemaah Islamiyah or JI leaders" comprises the core of the organization's membership. Indonesian investigators, however, think that JI is larger: "The figure is just the tip of the iceberg. We believe the number of marriages involved is certainly much higher judging from the information we have continued to gather."[2] These marriages were arranged to forge bonds between Malaysian and Indonesian JI members. In the 1980s and 1990s many of JI's members were in Malaysia, seeking refuge from the Suharto regime. Researchers and security officials alike have been astounded at the degree to which JI has been built upon the Darul Islam movement of the 1940s–1950s. Most JI members were recruited by other family members. Yet education plays a role here as well, as there are familial ties rooted in mosques and madrasas, very much family-run affairs in Southeast Asia.

While there are no central mosques that have been epicenters of JI recruitment, the mosque remains key to recruitment. JI "talent scouts" look for pious Muslims of a certain age, who come not just to Friday prayers but to prayers five times a day, every day. They are then invited to private "study sessions," in which they are slowly indoctrinated. This is a multistage process over the course of a year in which their commitment and religious understanding is tested and appraised. The "mosque" is important in understanding JI recruitment, because religiosity is the paramount trait that the JI leaders look for in their recruits.

Recruitment is often based on friendship with JI members. This seems to be the weakest explanation, as religiosity is not necessarily a factor. Friendship seems to be a very important variable in understanding the recruitment into JI's two former paramilitary arms, the Laskar Jundullah and the Laskar Mujahideen. Membership in those organizations, and participation in the jihad in the Malukus and Sulawesi, is not the same as membership in JI, but it is clearly an important recruitment pool that JI draws from. There is some indication—though there is little available evidence—of peer pressure being used in the recruitment process. In general, it seems to be a greater desire to conform with the "in group." This is a very common phenomenon in terrorist organizations, and the literature is rich with analysis based on small group dynamics that focus on pressure for conformity and consensus, which tends to result in groupthink and a Manichean worldview—a socialization process that forges a sense of belonging to a community and how the group becomes a surrogate family.[3]

The fourth network-based form of recruitment is madrasa and educational institutions, the subject of this chapter. JI has used Islamic educational networks run by its own members and supporters, as well as secular institutions. These madrasas, called *pesantrens* in Indonesia or *pondoks* in Thailand and Cambodia, have been established slowly and methodically and serve as centers of recruitment and the transmission of Wahhabi and Salafi principles.

Background on Jemaah Islamiyah[4]

Jemaah Islamiyah is an al Qaeda—linked organization whose stated goals are to turn Indonesia into an Islamic state and then to create a pan-Islamic state that would also include Malaysia, Southern Thailand, Brunei, and the Philippines. It was founded between 1992 and 1993 by two Indonesian clerics living in exile in Malaysia, Abdullah Sungkar and Abu Bakar Ba'asyir. Sungkar met with Osama bin Laden around that time and received support for the establishment of the organization. The organization itself was put together and administered by an al Qaeda member and Afghan veteran Riduan Isamudin, better known as Hambali. Hambali spent the remainder of the decade patiently building up a network of cells, establishing madrasas that would serve as centers of recruitment, training new members, and dispatching them to al Qaeda training camps in Afghanistan and later to Moro Islamic Liberation Front (MILF) camps in the southern Philippines. Hambali divided JI into four different *mantiqis* or regions, each seemingly focused on a specific task or function. Each *mantiqi* was divided into *wakalah* (sub regions) and then *fiah* (autonomous cells).

Throughout this period, Jemaah Islamiyah was at al Qaeda's disposal and served as an important back office for the terror organization, including establishing front companies and bank accounts, forging documents, procuring weapons, running meetings, and laundering money. In 1999, Hambali threw his efforts into waging jihad in the Malukus and later Central Sulawesi, where sectarian violence had erupted. Jemaah Islamiyah established two paramilitary organizations, the Laskar Mujahideen and the Laskar Jundullah, financed by money diverted from Saudi charities, to wage jihad. The Maluku conflict also integrated JI into the broader global jihadist network. More than 200 radical Islamists from around the Muslim world came to fight alongside their Indonesian counterparts. Abu Abdul Aziz and one other bin Laden lieutenant, Rashid, were dispatched to Ambon at the height of the crisis, and Mohammed Attef visited the Malukus in June 2000. In 2000, JI cells began their first actual terrorist operations, including the August 2000 bombing cum assassination attempt of the Philippine ambassador to Indonesia, the Christmas church bombings across Indonesia, the Light Rail Transit bombing in Manila, the train station and hotel attacks in Southern Thailand, and the May 2002 attacks on Medan churches. At the time, investigators were unaware of the existence of Jemaah Islamiya, and did not connect the bombings. JI operatives assisted in the 1995 plot to blow up eleven American jetliners over the Pacific. They later surveilled the U.S. embassy in Jakarta for a planned al Qaeda attack. JI and al Qaeda operatives were in the final stages of launching a major attack on U.S. targets in Singapore in late 2001, when their cell was uncovered by Singapore and Malaysian investigators.

Following the U.S. invasion of Afghanistan and the assault on the al Qaeda leadership, Hambali was given money and ordered to execute a major attack in Southeast Asia. This resulted in the 12 October 2002 attack on the Bali nightclubs. The al Qaeda leadership was so pleased with the results of the attack that they transferred another $100,000 to Hambali to launch further attacks, the first of which was the 5 August 2003, attack on the J. W. Marriott hotel in Jakarta. On 9 September 2004 JI detonated another truck bomb in front of the Australian embassy in Jakarta, killing ten and wounding hundreds. Despite more than 300 arrests around the region, JI remains a tactile and resilient organization capable of launching major terrorist attacks.

JI-linked Madrasas

There are approximately 25,000–35,000 madrasas in Southeast Asia, more than 14,000 in Indonesia alone. Most are benign. Though they may be theologically conservative, they are not churning out jihadists and terrorists. Almost 20–25 percent of Indonesian school children attend Islamic boarding schools, and in some regions, such as East Java, it is as high as 40 percent.[5] While we can question the value of the education provided at these institutions, based on rote memorization of the Koran, we cannot assert that they are all a problem. Indeed, many of the moderate Nahdlatul Ulama (NU) *pesantren* have a diverse curriculum that includes general education and vocational skills as well as religion.[6] Moreover, it would be nearly impossible for the government to do anything about the sheer number of them. "We won't let a wayward few destroy tens of thousands of *pesantrens* that have brought peace to this country for ages," said Mohammed Irfan, director of Islamic religious schools at Indonesia's Ministry of Religious Affairs. "We do not see any worrying sign. We will not intervene because intervention will only breed distrust."[7]

However, some *pesantren* do pose problems, and we must disaggregate them. JI's madrasas have two commonalities: They were founded by Southeast Asian veterans of the anti-Soviet Mujahideen and/or by graduates of the al Mukmin madrasa in Ngruki, Solo, Indonesia. This madrasa (in Ngruki) was founded in 1972 by Abu Bakar Ba'asyir and Abdullah Sungkar, the founders of Jemaah Islamiyah. JI itself established these madrasas to be used as centers of recruitment and indoctrination, and the graduates of this school are a who's who of today's Southeast Asian terrorists.

The origins of the Jemaah Islamiya network are found in Indonesia. During the 1960s, Sungkar and Ba'asyir, both of Yemeni descent, established a pirate radio station that advocated the imposition of *sharia* (Islamic law), which got them into trouble with the Suharto regime. The two considered themselves the ideological heirs of Sekarmadji Maridjan Kartosuwirjo—the founder of the Darul Islam. The two met when they were both leaders of the Geragan Pemuda Islam Indonesia, an Islamic youth movement. In 1972, Ba'asyir and Sungkar established an Islamic boarding school in Solo, al Mukmin. The land was donated by Kiai Haji Abu Amman, an *ulama* (a religious leader in Islamic communities) in Solo who was notable in the 1960s for his fervor to create an Islamic state. The school, which opened with thirty students, grew rapidly and in 1976 moved to a four hectare compound outside of the city; it now has approximately 900–1,000 students, with plans to double in size with the construction of a girl's campus.[8]

On 19 November 1978, Ba'asyir and Sungkar were arrested by the Suharto regime and were sentenced to nine years for violating a 1963 subversion law. A second court upheld the conviction but lessened the sentence to four years, and they were released in 1982. Ba'asyir saw the September 1984 massacre of Muslim protestors by the army in Tanjong Priok as a declaration of war and stepped up his vitriolic attacks of the New Order regime; he allegedly encouraged a series of bombings in 1984–1985. In 1985, the Supreme Court overturned the appeals court's conviction and reimposed the original nine-year sentence; both Ba'asyir and Sungkar immediately fled to Malaysia. Sidney Jones noted that "the government's case against the two men rests far more on the content of statements urging disobedience to secular authority than on any evidence of an underground organization."[9] Government authorities remained suspect. Although their school was allowed to reopen, one of its masters, Abdul Qadir Baraja, was arrested for writing the *Jihad Guide Book* for his students that urged *jihad* against all opponents of *sharia* law.[10] The two JI leaders—Abu Bakar Ba'asyir and Abdullah Sungkar—found a safe haven in Malaysia, where they lived and preached openly for several decades and built up a large following of radical Indonesians who had fled the Suharto regime, as well as radical Malays.[11] Even with Ba'asyir and Sungkar's flight to Malaysia in the 1980s, al Mukmin remained open, as it does to this day.

Indonesian intelligence and police officials are studying the entire network of graduates of Abu Bakar Ba'asyir's al Mukmin madrasa. When a JI safehouse was raided in November 2002, Indonesian police found a list of 141 madrasas that JI had determined would be susceptible to recruitment. While they were not successful in penetrating all of them, there is a network of some 60–100 madrasas that Indonesian security forces believe are centers of JI recruitment, most of which are run or staffed by Ngruki alumni.[12] These madrasas include Mutaqin Jabarah in Central Java, Darul Syahadin and the Madrasa Luqmanul Hakiem in Kelantan, and the Hidyatullah network throughout East Kalimantan and South Sulawesi, which is where many of the Bali bombers were hiding when they were arrested. Malaysian authorities have shut down the two JI-linked madrasas in their country, Tarbiyah Luqmanul Hakiem in Johor and Sekolah Menengah Arab Darul Anuar in Kota Baru. Both schools had several hundred students enrolled. However, madrasa-style recruitment still takes place at schools throughout Pakistan, Yemen, and Egypt, as well as at one particular madrasa in Medina, Saudi Arabia, discussed later in this chapter.

The curriculum in these schools is based entirely on Arabic language training and Koranic study. Rote memorization and recitation are the academic norm. But the interpretation of religion that is taught at these schools is decidedly militant and depicts a stark Manichean world view between the Darul Islam (House of Islam) and the Darul al Harb (House of War). Wall posters at al Mukmin, for example, exhorted students to jihad, to fight in defense of their religion. Al Mukmin, however, did have new computer labs when this author last visited in 2002, and clearly the faculty is cognizant of the use of technology in *dawa* (proselytizing) activities.

Wahhabism–Salafism and the Saudi Influence

At the broader societal level, there has been both a growth in the number of madrasas and a more doctrinaire interpretation of Islam due to exogenous factors. This is part of a trend in the past two decades of creeping "Arabization" of Islam in Southeast Asia. Traditional Sufism is losing ground as Salafism and Wahhabism begin to take root in a region where they were never at all strong. Islam came to Southeast Asia through traders and was superimposed on a rich indigenous religious culture. The spread of Salafism is the result of both Saudi–Gulf funding for mosques, madrasas, and scholarships, and a critical mass of Southeast Asians who have returned from studying in Middle Eastern and South Asian Islamic institutions.

Saudi charities such as the International Islamic Relief Organization (IIRO) and al Haramain were active in funding the construction of mosques and madrasas that were pressured to conform to Wahhabi dictates. Both funded scholarships, as did the World Assembly of Muslim Youth that exposed many Southeast Asians to the greater Islamic world through scholarships and exchanges.

But influence also came directly. The Office of Religious Affairs in Saudi embassies around the region was also active in distributing textbooks. The embassy in Jakarta is estimated to distribute some one million religious texts to Indonesian educational institutions per year.

In Indonesia, officials of the largest mass-based Muslim organization in the world—the Nahdlatul Ulama, which runs a network of small madrasas around the archipelago—express great concern over the Saudi influence. Leaders of the NU are alarmed that the condition for accepting Saudi scholarships or receiving Gulf financial assistance is the renouncing of the moderate NU's values and leadership.[13] Yet, students and leaders of the NU's rival, the Muhammadiyah, which has a tradition of a more literal interpretation of the Koran, are willing and able to accept these conditions. This is allowing Salafi principles to make inroads into mainstream Islamic institutions.

The Om al-Qura (OAQ) Foundation in Phnom Penh, Cambodia, was ostensibly established to address the needs of Cambodia's small Cham Muslim population, which had fallen by 75 percent from 300,000 to 70,000 under the Khmer Rouge between 1975 and 1978. To support this aggrieved community, there has been a steady inflow of Gulf money and outflow of students to study in foreign madrasas. Middle Eastern charities funded the construction of more than 120 mosques; there are now 150 (up from twenty at the time of the UN intervention in the early 1990s). Annually, eighty Cambodian students study in Middle Eastern and Pakistani madrasas, where they are taught in the doctrinaire Wahhabism. Some 400 students study in neighboring Malaysia and Indonesia on scholarships funded both from Gulf-based charities and the host governments (who hope to counter some of the Saudi influence). OAQ provided full funding for a school in Kendal province for grades 7 through 10, enrolling approximately 580 students. The school and foundation were also used to launder significant amounts of al Qaeda funding each month.[14]

The role of Saudi–Gulf charities cannot be overstated. Though they are maintaining a lower profile now, they are still active in the region. They are one of the prime transmission vehicles for a more austere and intolerant version of Islam than is traditionally found in the region. This is occurring in a region where there has been an Islamic revival and manifestations of Islamic identity are growing rapidly. Individual piousness is being matched by state piousness: In Indonesia and Malaysia right now, religious (read Islamic) education is now mandatory, even in secular institutions. Secularism is being steadily eroded. Islamic education, the study of Arabic, the veiling of women, mosque attendance, and hajj pilgrimages are all on the increase. This plays into the radical's desire to move Southeast Asia from the "Islamic periphery" and to identify with the "Islamic core."

There has not been an honest debate over Koranic education. Are madrasas the problem? Defenders of Koranic education always assert that Islam is a religion of peace. Critics assert that merely a Koranic education, based on rote memorization, does not teach critical thinking. Nor does a madrasa education prepare people for the workforce. Thus, frustrated young men with only a Koran to justify their actions are easily swayed by respected and charismatic masters.

Indonesia alone has 14,000 *pesantren*. Most of these are run by the moderate Nahdlatul Ulama and are not the immediate problem. Whereas the NU tends to be more moderate, and based in jurisprudential interpretations of the Koran and *Hadiths* (the collected traditions, teachings, and stories of the Prophet Muhammed), there is greater concern over the schizophrenic Muhammadiyah that has increasing ties to Saudi charities and educational institutions. There has been a steady increase in Saudi funding and support for Indonesian Islamic institutions as well as provision of scholarships. While NU officials express concern over the conditions for accepting those scholarships (as mentioned earlier), students and leaders of Muhammadiyah madrasas are willing and able to accept these conditions.

Indeed, the Muhammadiyah is a schizophrenic organization. Committed to a literal interpretation of the Koran, it has both a modernist wing and a group of hard-core Islamists. Most militants in Indonesia come from the Muhammadiyah tradition. Following the 1965 coup by Major General Suharto, Muslims were politically emasculated. The Muhammadiyah adopted a "policy of non-cooperation with the government."[15] Its senior members, such as Mohammad Natsir, never abandoned their pro-*sharia* stance, but retreated to academia or focused on *dakwah* (appeal). In 1967, they founded the Dewan Dakwah Islamiyah Indonesia (DDII), which, Robert Heffner notes, "made no effort to hide the fact that their central ambition was to create a conservative Islamic constituency capable of challenging the Suharto regime."[16] Political repression hardened groups such as the DDII, and created a cadre of hard-core Islamists who railed against secularism and the role of Christians and Chinese. The DDII was active in funding scholarships for young radical students to study in Saudi Arabia and Pakistan. One such scholarship recipient was Umar Jafar Thalib, the founder of the Laskar Jihad, which waged sectarian violence in certain parts of the archipelago from 2000 to 2002 that claimed the lives of some 9,000 people.

It is not clear where the DDII gets all of its funding. A large part does come from contributions by Indonesians, but how much foreign assistance comes in is unknown. DDII established a charitable arm in 2000—the Committee to Overcome Crisis, or KOMPAK—that was the executive agency to al Haramain, World Assembly of Muslim Youth (WAMY) and the IIRO. Of KOMPAK's thirteen regional officers, three were also regional officers for Saudi charities. Moreover, three and possibly four of KOMPAK's officers were JI members, who diverted KOMPAK and Saudi funds to militant activities.[17]

Pondoks in Thailand

We have also seen Islamic militancy in Southern Thailand in recent years, emerging directly from the pondok (religious boarding school) networks. In the 1970s to early 1990s there were a number of armed separatist groups; the largest and best known was Patani United Liberation Organization (PULO), fighting the government in Bangkok. The insurgency, however, died in the 1990s for several reasons, and Bangkok assumed that the Muslims in the south had been pacified. However, since 2000, and especially since January 2004, the insurgency has renewed. This has caught the Thai government completely by surprise, and at first Thailand's Prime Minister Thaksin downplayed the issue, but the insurgency escalated. There were a number of very well-executed raids on police and military bases, and large arsenals were stolen. Thaksin blamed it on drugged-out teenagers, but the raids were too well executed. Violence raged in October 2004, when Thai security forces inadvertently killed more than sixty Muslim protestors.

No one thoroughly understood who is behind the attacks, and often the label "New PULO" is used by Thai officials, but it has been narrowed down to a few tiny groups of militants, including the Guragon Mujahidin and Wae Kah Rah. Both were founded by veterans of the anti-Soviet war and are hard-core Wahhabis. For much of the 1980s and 1990s, they ran guns for other Muslim insurgents (the MILF in the Philippines and Free Aceh Movement (GAM) in Aceh). In 2000–2001 they were approached by JI to become Thai arms of the organization. No one really knows how far that went, as JI became caught up in other events and went on the run. A lot of JI members fled to southern Thailand in the fall of 2001 where they clearly have relatives and social networks. Thai intelligence officials now speak of the insurgency as being a "pondok-based" movement. According to one official, in the 1980s people spoke of "Pattani liberation" and "Siamese hegemonism."[18] Now they speak of "Islamist jihadism." The discourse has shifted from ethno-nationalist liberation to Islamic Jihad, and it has all come through a network of Islamic schools.

Nonetheless, there are limits to what these groups are willing to do. The Rector of Yala State University and one of the leading Wahhabi clerics in Southeast Asia, Ismael Lufti, was approached by Hambali, JI's operations chief and a senior al Qaeda member arrested in August 2003, to recruit a cadre of bombers for an attack on the J. W. Marriott hotel in Bangkok, which Lufti refused to get involved in, though he supported grassroots militancy. Yet, the *pondok*-based network, of which he is a spiritual leader, has been implicated in the radicalization of Southern Thai youth.

Foreign Madrasas

Tens of thousands of Southeast Asian Muslims have traveled to the Middle East and South Asia to study in madrasas and Islamic universities, including those in Egypt, Syria, Yemen, Pakistan, and Saudi Arabia. In the 1990s, the CIA tried to keep track of some 700–1,500 Indonesian students who went to Egypt, Syria, and Iran for study. According to a retired CIA officer, "We figured 30–40 percent of them never showed up. We don't know where they went."[19] None of the countries in Southeast Asia has an accurate fix on how many of their nationals studied in madrasas in the past or are currently studying now. There are an unknown number of Malaysian students studying in other Islamic universities and madrasas in Pakistan, as the government keeps no records on privately-funded students studying abroad.[20] One Malaysian official noted that its embassy in Islamabad, Pakistan, believed there were five–ten Malaysians studying at a certain madrasa in Pakistan; there turned out to be 150.[21] In the Philippines, some 1,600 madrasas have been established, unsupervised by state educational authorities, and almost entirely funded by contributions from the Middle East.[22] Forty-four Indonesian students were expelled from Yemeni madrasas in February 2002 alone.

The Indonesian government has no idea how many Indonesians are studying in Egypt, Pakistan, or elsewhere. In addition to the Pakistani madrasas, many Southeast Asians have attended Egypt's al-Azhar University and Yemen's al-Imam University, both of which teach very rigid Wahhabi interpretations of Islam and have produced the most radical firebrands in the Muslim world—such as Abdel Meguid al Zindani—and have been key recruiting grounds for al Qaeda. At Egypt's al-Azhar University, the foremost Islamic university in the world, there are some 6,000 Malaysian students alone. Each of the nine state governments on the Malaysian peninsula rents a block of apartments for the students that it sponsors. While most of these students will return and join the government's Islamic bureaucracy, and not turn militant, some students return committed to turning Malaysia into an Islamic state. This was brought to the government's attention in February to March 2002, when some twelve Malaysian students were arrested in Yemen in a crackdown on radical Islamic madrasas. Though released after they were found to not have "terrorist connections," Malaysia agreed to repatriate the 250–300 privately funded students in Yemen.[23]

Perhaps the most important school is the Islamic University of Medina, in Saudia Arabia. The school has become an important center for international networking as 85 percent of IUM's student body is non-Saudi. It is a huge academic melting pot and "an important tool for spreading Wahhabi Islam internationally."[24]

As part of a crackdown on Islamic militants, Pakistan's president, General Pervez Musharraf, announced new measures in early 2002 to rein in the estimated 6,000 to 8,000 madrasas, especially those schools that "propagate hatred and violence" and produce only "semiliterate religious scholars." Pakistan more recently pledged to reduce the number of foreign students attending Pakistani madrasas by 60 percent.[25] However, to date these policies have been only half-heartedly implemented.

Al Ghuraba in Pakistan

In the fall of 2003, Pakistani officials arrested a nineteen-member cell of JI members, known as Al Ghuraba, who were living in a Lashkar-e-Toiba (LET) madrasa; some studied there while others attended the Abu

Bakar Islamic University in Karachi.[26] The group was led first by Abdul Rahim, Abu Bakar Ba'asyir's son, and later by Hambali's brother Rusman Gunawan, who also handled some finances for his brother. According to the Singapore government: "The cell was set up in 1999 by Indonesian JI operations commander, Hambali, for the purpose of developing young JI members to become trained operatives and future leaders."[27] Of the nineteen members, six were Indonesian and thirteen were Malaysian, though two resided in Singapore. Fifteen are currently in jail in their home countries of Singapore, Malaysia, and Indonesia,[28] while two each have been released from Malaysian and Indonesian custody. Thirteen of the nineteen have family ties to JI. The two Singaporeans are the sons of members of Jemaah Islamiyah and the Moro Islamic Liberation Front; in Malaysia, three of the five detained students' fathers are JI members.[29] Six of the Malaysians are graduates of JI's Luqmanul Hakiem school.

They were to be the core of the next generation of JI's leadership and were sent to Pakistan for advanced religious training. JI did not send their future leaders to combat zones, to gain "jihad" experience in fighting America and infidels. Although there is evidence that Hambali called on them to provide operational assistance to JI and al Qaeda, it was primarily a religious study group.[30] Only a few received combat training at LET or al Qaeda camps. Abdul Rahim, in a recent interview, said "al Ghuraba was formed purely for religious study and discussion." Syaifudin said senior Jemaah Islamiyah members "saw the urgency of regeneration in the movement and sent their sons and their students to Pakistan to study to become *ulamas*."[31] They focused on religion to rebuild their depleted ranks. The most respected people within JI, as in al Qaeda, are not the Afghan Mujahideen or operatives with "street credibility," but highly esteemed religious leaders. This is not surprising, as members of terrorist groups tend to subordinate their own judgment and turn to an omnipotent leader who is lionized as a hero within a group and pilloried by "out groups" for direction.[32]

Western analysts of terrorism tend to discount the "religious" nature of terrorists' struggle. We cannot make this mistake; we need to bring the religion back in. This will be all the more difficult because political and security analysts have little religious understanding or training. But groups like JI base their membership on religious conviction. They will want their leaders not only to have technical or operational know-how, but also to be steeped in religious understanding.

JI requires its membership to be well grounded in religious training and to be highly devout individuals. The *Pedoman Umum Perjuangan al-Jama'ah al-Islamiyyah* (The General Guidebook for the Struggle of Jemaah Islamiyah) or PUPJI, a 1996 document that codified the authority structure and ordering principles and philosophy of JI, is exceptionally religious in nature. It is no surprise that it was written by two of the organization's most militant clerics, Ali Ghufron (Muchlas) and Abu Rusdan, who succeeded Abu Bakar Ba'asyir as the organization's *amir*, or spiritual leader.[33] Although it also includes the *General Manual for Operations*, the PUPJI is far more Koranic than the al Qaeda training manual that was found in the Manchester (England) house in 2002.[34] It is not necessarily a practical guide on conducting terrorist operations, but a document steeped in Islamic principles and teachings.[35] The document makes very clear that the cornerstone of JI, its membership and goals, is a deepened understanding and practice of Islam. There is almost nothing about violent jihad. The PUPJI is broken down into four main sections: Preamble, the General Manual for Operations, the *Nidhom Asasi*—which outlines the organization's hierarchy, rules and procedures—and a section on explanations and clarifications. The document begins by outlining the ten core principles of the organization:

> First Principle: Our aim is only to seek Allah's blessings by means which had been determined by Allah and his apostle.
>
> Second Principle: Our belief is the belief of a *Sunnah Wal Jama'ah 'Ala Minjis Salsfish Shalih* Specialist.
>
> Third Principle: Our understanding about Islam is *Sumul* following the understanding of *As-Salifish Shalih*.
>
> Fourth Principle: The goal of our struggle is for men to serve only God by re-erecting *Khalifah* on earth.
>
> Fifth Principle: Our road is creed, *Hijrah* and *Jihad Fie Sabilillah*.
>
> Sixth Principle: Our provisions are knowledge and piety, conviction and trust in Allah, gratitude and patience, simple life and preference for a life hereafter, love for *Jihad Fie Sabilillah* and a *Syahid* [martyr's] death.
>
> Seventh Principle: Our *Wala* to Allah and his Apostle and faithful people.
>
> Eighth Principle: Our enemy is the Devil's evil spirit and human devils.
>
> Ninth Principle: The ties of our *jama'ah* based upon the similarity of goals, faith, and understanding of *Ad-Dien*.
>
> Tenth Principle: Our Islam charity is in a pure way and *Kaffah* with the *Jama'ah* system then the *Daulah* and then the *Khalifah*.

The writings of JI members, including the three volumes written by Ali Ghufron (Mukhlas) while in jail, were not simplistic interpretations of Islam, but rather very well argued and displayed a nuanced understanding of the Koran. Indeed, U.S.-based experts on Indonesian Islam who have reviewed the manuscripts in detail have found the writings to be relatively sophisticated. Moreover, the writings put the movement ideologically within the historical trajectory linking Darul Islam to al Qaeda.

State Universities and Secular Institutions

Many scholars tend to be overly focused on Islamic institutions and this may be misguided. Much Islamist activity is conducted at state universities and secular institutions. From one account, the most checked-out book at the University of Malaysia is Sayyid Qutb's seminal *Milestones*, written in 1965 while on death row after being convicted for treason by Egyptian leader Col. Gamal Abdul Nasser.[36] Like many al Qaeda operatives, Qutb had studied in the United States, where he became disgusted with Western materialism and sexuality and advocated a strict and literal implementation of *sharia* to protect Muslim values.

One aspect of JI that is so impressive is their ability to recruit across the board, irrespective of education or class. Their recruits are not just students from the madrasa of the region, but young technical students and disenfranchised youth with little prospects. They are younger, angrier, and technically savvy. JI members pride themselves on being computer literate. JI members also include many technical faculty members, including architects, engineers, geophysicists, chemists, and robotics engineers. JI has actively recruited in leading technical institutes, including the University of Technology of Malaysia, Universitas Semerang, and Bandung Institute of Technology. The surviving leadership of JI today is divided between people with nothing more than a Koranic education and field experience in Afghanistan (e.g., Zulkarnaen and Mustopha) and middle-class, secularly educated individuals (e.g., Dr. Azahari bin Husin, Noordin Mohammed Top, and Zulkifli Marzuki).

Some of JI's most important leaders, indeed the three leading suspects in the September 2004 bombing of the Australian Embassy in Jakarta, have scientific backgrounds in addition to their radical Islamist beliefs. Dr. Azahari bin Husin, believed to be the lead bombmaker, studied for four years at Adelaide University in the late 1970s and later at Reading University in England in the 1980s; in 1990, he received his doctorate in engineering. Soon after returning to Malaysia in the early 1990s, Azahari and his wife received well-paid jobs at the Universiti Teknologi Malaysia at Skudai. Though he still showed little sign of being the strict Muslim he was later to become, he was active in student Islamic study groups. He was also very active in the Taribyah Luqmanul Hakiem school that Abdullah Sungkar established in the 1980s. He was a visiting lecturer sometime in the 1990s at Gajah Mahda University in Indonesia and returned to Malaysia a changed man. Azahari abandoned his wife in the mid-1990s as she lay in bed suffering from throat cancer shortly after giving birth to their second child. At the time he told her, "I have a greater cause in life. It is to serve God." He went on to Afghanistan where he trained in an al Qaeda camp. He is believed to have honed his skills in Mindanao in the Muslim separatist southern Philippines in 1999.

Noordin Mohammed Top came to science from a madrasa education. Like Azahari, he is also a Malaysian, born on 11 August 1968. He attended JI's Sekolah Islam Luqmanul Hakiem, where the Bali mastermind Muchlas was the master. He has only a bachelor's degree (B.Sci.) from UTM. He has always been close to Azahari and was probably recruited by him.

The third suspect, Dulmatin, was also responsible for the Bali attack and has significant bomb-making and electronic skills. Dulmatin was a student activist on his Central Javanese university campus. Coming from a well-to-do family, he dropped out of the university after being drawn into extremist teachings at religious boarding schools. With his keenness for electronics, it was only natural that he developed an interest for making bombs and forging a natural affiliation with Azahari, whom he saw as "a father figure." On a side note, an associate of this cell—Shamsul Bahari Hussein, another Malaysian lecturer at UTM—was arrested in Indonesia in August 2003.

There has not been a thorough sociological study as to why al Qaeda, JI, and other Islamist radical groups have been so successful in recruiting from the secular middle class. Singaporean authorities noted that JI members in their custody were very middle class. The products of secular public schools, "these men were not ignorant, destitute, or disenfranchised. Like many of their counterparts in militant Islamic organizations in the region, they held normal, respectable jobs."[37] These findings are supported by the general terrorism literature. Al Qaeda itself was split between madrasa-educated foot soldiers and well-educated leaders, such as Osama bin Laden, an engineer; Dr. Ayman al-Zawahiri, a surgeon; Khalid Sheikh Mohammed, an engineer; and Mohammed Atef, the leader of the 9/11 hijackers, who was an urban planner. Al Qaeda detainees in Guantanamo Bay—especially the Saudi-born operatives—are "educated above reasonable employment level [and] a surprising number have graduate degrees and come from high-status families."[38] In Palestine, rather than impoverished and dispossessed youth, researchers have found that "the majority of Palestinian suicide bombers have a college education (versus 15 percent of the population of comparable age) and that less than 15 percent come from poor families (although about one-third of the population lives in poverty)."[39]

There are some general hypotheses as to why people from the seemingly secular middle class—and specifically scientists and people in technological fields—are driven to militant Islam. Islam fills a spiritual need in their lives, dominated by scientific inquiry and reason. As the Singapore *White Paper* stated, what drove them was their religiosity: "Most detainees regarded religion as their most important personal value."[40] Other hypotheses suggest that being computer savvy, they "learn their Islam online" and are drawn to jihadist websites. Some of the most technically proficient sites offer Koranic interpretations, video clips from jihads in far-flung corners of the world, and ample evidence of egregious and violent persecution of fellow

Muslims. The Internet creates a virtual community for Muslims that allows alienated Muslim youth to find a "responsive and compassionate forum."[41] As the French scholar Gilles Keppel said about the Internet, "It erases the frontiers between the *dar al-Islam* (House of Islam or Peace) and the *dar al-Kufr* (House of the Unbeliever). It allows the propagation of a universal norm, with an Internet *sharia* and *fatwa* system."[42]

Another hypothesis focuses on opportunity structure, turning the Gary Becker hypothesis on crime (1968) on its head. Becker theorized that the greater the amount of human capital—such as education, experience, and wealth—that a person has, the less likely he or she will engage in crime.[43] Islamic jihadists, however, include people who have high amounts of human capital and yet are willing to sacrifice themselves, a sign of their true devotion to their faith.[44] In many ways it is incumbent upon them to be leaders in their community, and to martyr themselves to inspire others. Indeed, much of the cult status of bin Laden is that he forsook his wealth and privilege to live in Afghan caves and fight on behalf of his religion. Finally, militant Islam tends to be very anticlerical, and therefore is an empowering ideology, a strong force for disgruntled youth.

Radical Islamist activity is divided into three general categories at state institutions in Southeast Asia: Islamic study groups, known as *dak'wah*, formal organizations, and overt political groups. *Dak'wah* groups are found at educational institutions throughout Southeast Asia, but it was really in Malaysia where they had the greatest impact. In a political culture that stifled and repressed dissent, Islam was one of the only ways to challenge the state. Islamic study groups emerged and spread rapidly as—in the context of a fairly authoritarian political regime—they were one of the few channels through which students could air their views and protest government policies. The first and most prominent *dak'wah* was the Muslim Youth Movement of Malaysia (ABIM), co-founded in 1972 by a young student activist Anwar Ibrahim, who would go on to be the country's deputy premier. Many others emerged during the 1980s. The largest, the Islamic Republic Group, has close institutional ties to the Islamist opposition party PAS. It was estimated that by the 1980s, 60–70 percent of students had ties to a *dak'wah*.[45] *Dak'wah* groups are also found in Indonesia, Thailand, and the Philippines.

The *dak'wah* groups were ostensibly Islamic study groups that delved into the role of political Islam and served as a forum to challenge the state. In addition to these are a number of formal organizations involved in militant activities. In Indonesia, there are a number of such groups that espouse a militant Wahhabism and whose goal is to establish an Islamic state governed by *sharia*. Other Islamic groups include the Islamic Youth Movement (GPI), the Defenders of Islam (FPI), Indonesian Committee for Solidarity of the Islamic World (KISDI), Anti-Zionist Movement (GAZA), Indonesian Muslim Students Action Front (KAMMI), and the Muhammadiyah Students Association (MMI). The FPI, formed in 1998, is now the largest radical Muslim group in the country, and was able to organize demonstrations of over 10,000 people in Jakarta in October 2001 and then again in the spring of 2003. These groups were also active in leading demonstrations and mobilizing popular support during the debate over the Jakarta Charter in the fall of 2002. They have been active in leading anti-American demonstrations, and, most troubling, they have become a pool of recruits for Jemaah Islamiyah. All of these groups in some way are the progeny of the Tarbiyah movement, which rose to prominence in Indonesia mainly among students at the major state universities during the late 1980s, though whose roots go back to the 1930s. The Tarbiyah movement is the oldest and most established Wahhabi vehicle in Indonesia, and has always reflected the interests of the Arab minority. The Al Irsyad Foundation, which runs Islamic boarding schools across the country, is the most important foundation (*yayasan*) in this movement. Two of the board members of the Al Irsyad foundation are close relatives of Fuad Bawazir, Finance Minister in Suharto's last cabinet and are believed to act in his interest. Bawazir is believed to be a key financial patron. Financial support for the Tarbiyah movement—as well as other groups, such as the Laskar Jihad—tends to reflect its Arab origins, specifically through Indonesian Arabic groupings.

The goal of the Tarbiyah movement was the creation of an Islamic state. In addition to its network of *pesantren*, the movement was very active on university campuses in Jakarta and Bandung, beginning in the 1980s. It has since extended its network to other universities throughout Java and on other islands. Tarbiyah established a strong following among students linked to the Association of Inter-Campus Muslim Student Action (HAMMAS) and the Indonesian Muslim Students Action Front (KAMMI).[46] Most of the movement's activists have joined the Prosperous Justice Party (PKS) led by Hidayat Nur Wahid, though some are active with Vice President Hamzah Haz's *Partai Persatuan Pembangunan* (PPP). An increasing number have studied in the Middle East. Individuals, such as Fuad Bawazir, are suspected of using the Komite Indonesia Untuk Solidaritas Dunia Islam (the Indonesian Committee for Solidarity of the Muslim World, or KISDI) and KAMMI (of which Bawazir is the chairman)[47] as vehicles to transfer large amounts of elite Indonesian money to small radical groups, such as Dwikarna's Laskar Jundullah. Bawazir has been implicated in funding the Laskar Jihad as well.[48] There is no evidence to suggest that Fuad Bawazir is a member of Jemaah Islamiyah, but there is evidence that he has channeled funds to groups and organizations that do have ties with the terrorist group.

Perhaps the most active and militant group on campuses is the Islamic Youth Movement (*Gerakan Pemuda Islam*, or GPI). The Western media tends to discount the Islamic Youth Movement as a bunch of grandstanding and marauding students. The GPI made headlines in the fall of 2001 when it recruited and dispatched 300 members to go to Afghanistan to fight alongside the Taliban against the Americans. They got as far as Pakistan. The GPI also threatened to conduct "sweeps" in Solo throughout 2002–2003 and was at the forefront of anti-American demonstrations in the run-up to the Iraq war in early 2003. Muhammad Iqbal Siregar, Chairman of the Jakarta branch of the GPI, was arrested and sentenced on 16 June 2003, to five months imprisonment for defacing a picture of the President during an antigovernment protest on 15 January 2003, raising the ire of some human rights groups. The GPI's leader Syuaib Didu has ties to both Vice President Hamzah Haz and the PKS's Hidayat Nur Wahid.

Indonesian intelligence and police are more suspect about the GPI and its activities.[49] First, they believe that it is a very important recruiting mechanism and in a way serves as a talent scout for JI. Second, it has been active in recruiting people for foreign jihads dating back to the late 1980s, including those in Afghanistan and Chechnya. The funding for these operations has come from the Saudi-based charity, World Assembly for Muslim Youth (WAMY), which has long been suspected of involvement in diverting funds for al Qaeda.

The third way that Islamists organize on campuses is through political party activism. In Malaysia, PAS has been very active on university campuses. But perhaps there is no better example of this type of activity than the Prosperous Justice Party (PKS),[50] which won a surprise 7 percent of the vote nationally—as well as the largest number of votes in metro Jakarta, with 22.9 percent of the total—in the April 2004 parliamentary elections in Indonesia. The PKS's success is due in large part to its formidable grassroots organization, with a core of dedicated supporters throughout Indonesia's universities. Members of PKS tend to be young (twenty to forty years old) and have a high level of education. Many are members or former members of the university-based KAMMI network of Muslim activists. The party, which began with only 200,000 members, was able to win 1.4 million votes in the 1999 election and now has 8 million voters. Its supporters, however, are concentrated in urban areas, and primarily on the island of Java. It polled especially well in precincts that included major state universities, indicating that the party remains popular with idealistic students. PKS supporters are instructed to either recruit or at least persuade between five and ten people to vote for the PKS.[51] PKS now has 400,000 core members who are obliged to attend small weekly "learning circles," or party cells.[52] One "learning circle" led by thirty-two-year-old senior party leader Zulkieflimansyah, asserts that nine of ten members hold doctorates.[53] Party leaders are hoping to expand the membership to over two million in the next five years through more grassroots activism. Yet at the same time, the PKS does not want to rush and become a mass-based party, for fear of losing its Islamic core and becoming filled with members who are unwilling to abide by strict Islamic principles. Thus PKS membership is based on a network of cells where members meet for Koran reading and discussion.

Conclusion and Policy Implications for the United States

In sum, educational institutions play an important role in Islamist extremist recruitment throughout Southeast Asia. There is very little the United States will do to alleviate this situation. First, although President Bush announced, during his two-one-half-hour stopover in Bali following the APEC summit in Bali, $157 million in educational aid to shore up Indonesia's secular and nonsecular schools (much of the aid had already been pledged and committed), it is a paltry amount; further, it focuses on one country alone. Educational assistance is worthy, but there needs to be significantly more over a long period of time before any impact is made. Clearly, the United States should not engage in educational engineering and try to tinker with their curricula. What would be more constructive is to finance the publication of texts written by groups such as the NU. Such aid will do little to diminish anti-American sentiment unless there are concurrent steps to increase trade and investment and lower tariffs and import quotas on Southeast Asian goods. A key component of our counterterrorism strategy must be job creation, though this is unlikely.

Second, the U.S. visa policy is counterproductive. Malaysians and Indonesians in particular are seething and consider the policy abjectly racist. Now that it is harder to get into the United States, more students will be studying elsewhere, including the Middle East.

We also need to address "push factors" such as demographics. The U.S. Agency for International Development recently announced it was ceasing all family planning in the Philippines, which is already experiencing unsustainable and skyrocketing birth rates. USAID argues that the government should fund this initiative, despite the fact that the country is wracked with soaring budget deficits and constrained by the political pressure of the Catholic church.

Finally, U.S. foreign policy will continue to anger Muslims in Southeast Asia, who believe that the war on terror is patently anti-Muslim. Anti-Americanism is not going to diminish until America starts to live up to the ideals upon which it was founded.

CHAPTER 7

Recruitment for Rebellion and Terrorism in the Philippines

JOSEPH FELTER

Individuals join rebel and terrorist groups around the world for a multitude of reasons. Some argue that these decisions are rooted in severe economic and identity-based grievances, while others claim that criminal predation and the opportunity to profit provide the strongest motives to rebel. Ultimately, the ranks of these subversive groups swell because, at some level, the state fails to prevent or effectively interdict rebellion. Prevention and interdiction require a combination of incentives and disincentives tailored to the unique circumstances of individual cases of rebellion. The optimal mix and nature of these carrots and sticks will reflect an appreciation of common rebel characteristics and the factors initially responsible for driving them across the threshold into rebellion.

This chapter examines the case of the Communist Terrorist Movement (CTM)[1] in the Philippines to describe one particular process of rebel and terrorist recruitment and to highlight the challenges states face in trying to limit the accession of their citizens into rebel organizations in general. The discussion begins with a brief review of several prominent theories explaining a state's risk of rebellion and how these are relevant to our understanding of rebel recruitment. Next, the Philippines' communist insurgency case is used to describe the profile of the typical rebels that are recruited and the reasons they joined. The chapter discusses a number of the Philippine government's initiatives to deter recruitment, emphasizing their particular challenges, and concludes with some lessons from the case appropriate for states striving to prevent their citizens from joining the ranks of rebellion.

Why Do Individuals Join Rebel Groups and Initiate Violence against the State?

"Why do men rebel?"[2] What drives citizens to choose a life outside the fold of the law, fraught with the risks associated with insurgency and terrorism? Identifying the rationale behind these decisions fuels an enduring debate among policy makers and academics alike. Several broad explanations emerging from the literature explaining state's risk of rebellion and civil war provide a useful framework for understanding the problem of rebel recruitment.

Grievance and Deprivation

Relating the attraction of rebellion to social–psychological factors—such as politicized ethnic and religious cleavages and manifestation of discontent among marginalized groups in society—seems to support explanations for many cases of rebellion against the state. An early champion of this theory is Ted Robert Gurr, who in *Why Men Rebel* (1971) explains the propensity of individuals and groups to rebel as a function of the severity of perceived grievances and the strength of their sense of identity. Gurr's well-known term *relative deprivation* is defined as actors' perceptions of discrepancy between their value expectations and their value capabilities. According to grievance-based theories, differences in this perception provide the best explanation for popular support of rebellion.[3] Grievance-oriented theories suggest that recruitment will be most successful when individuals see rebellion as the most viable way to redress intolerable inequities and oppressive nature of their situation.[4]

Greed and Opportunity

More recent scholarship indicates that grievances are far less important predictors of an individual's likelihood of joining a rebellion than are conditions that provide rebels greater relative opportunities to *profit* from rebellion. These conditions include the presence of natural resources that lend themselves to being "looted," as well as other opportunities for extortion by rebels/quasi-criminals motivated by the prospect of profit and not ideology or grievances.[5] Rebellion is more of an organized criminal enterprise, according to this theory, and its participants use grievances merely to buttress the legitimacy of their decision to take part in what amounts to organized criminal activity.[6] The decision to "rebel," according to this model, is made by comparing the perceived gains—potential for profit—versus the opportunity costs of rebellion. If the net assessment is that rebellion is more attractive than not, then we see individuals join and engage in this criminally rooted enterprise. States reduce the pool of willing recruits by diminishing rebellion's relative appeal—for example, by increasing opportunities available for those living within the law.

"Because They Can": State Capacity and Conditions Favorable to Insurgency

The grievances and greed described above are quite common among groups around the world, but do not always lead those afflicted to join rebel groups and perpetrate violence against the state. Support for rebellion occurs selectively from among the many cases where portions of a state's population are oppressed or opportunities to engage in criminal predation are present. James Fearon and David Laitin explain this irregularity with another leading theory relating a state's risk of civil war with *conditions* that allow insurgency to fester. These include financially, organizationally, and politically weak central governments, the presence of rural base areas, rough inaccessible terrain, and rebels with superior local knowledge and external support.[7] The Fearon–Laitin study demonstrates that a state's level of development—measured by gross domestic product per capita—offers the most significant prediction of a state's risk of rebellion. Their theory points out that political, cultural, and economic grievances or ethnic or religious fractionalization are common around the world and are not statistically significant predictors of participation in rebellion and the violence that comes with it. The most important determinants of the prospects of an insurgency, according to the Fearon–Laitin 2003 study, are most likely the *police and military capabilities and competences of the government and the reach of government institutions into rural areas.*[8] This theory supports an argument that the world is full of oppressed and/or criminally motivated would-be recruits, but the discriminating predictors of whether they actually join in rebellion are found in a state's opportunity structures for rebellion.[9]

The Puzzle of Rebel Recruitment: Why Do States Fail to Prevent It?

Whatever combination of grievance, greed, or insurgency-friendly conditions are present, individuals join rebel groups because at some level the state fails to prevent them from doing so.[10] A puzzling question, certainly from a theoretical perspective, is why states ever *allow* their citizens to join subversive groups that commit crimes and acts of violence. In theory, states will develop and implement practices within their military and police forces that generate the most effective capabilities possible relative to their available resources. Failure to do so results in weaker states that are less competitive in the international system and more vulnerable to external threats and exploitation.[11] A rational state with superior resources should choose to implement effective internal security operations that bring their capabilities decisively to bear on nascent rebel threats. In reality, however, rebel groups are able to recruit individuals in states whose resources vastly outnumber those of the rebels taking up arms against it. Rebel organizations are often able to mature and gain strength without aggressive interdiction by the government. Despite power and resource asymmetries, rebels in many instances grow in numbers, avoid defeat, and even prevail against stronger government internal security forces.[12]

The Communist Terrorist Movement (CTM) in the Philippines[13]

Armed with an appreciation of these broad theories predicting risks of internal conflict, this discussion turns to focus on a specific case of rebellion and terrorism for context. The following section provides a brief history of the Philippines' experience with communist insurgency along with a synopsis of the evolution of the group now officially called the Communist Terrorist Movement. The chapter, then, outlines the general strategies and techniques used by the Communist Terrorist Movement cadres to garner support and recruit new members into its ranks and offers lessons we can learn from this analysis.

History of the Movement[14]

Communist insurgency in the Philippines traces its roots back to 1930, when the desire for social and agrarian reforms exacerbated by global economic depression led to the formal establishment of the *Partido Komunista ng Pilipinas* (Communist Party of the Philippines). When the Japanese invaded at the beginning of World War II, the armed wing of the party—the *Hukbong Bayan Laban sa Hapon*—was employed in a campaign to resist them. After the war, these experienced former guerrillas formed the core group that launched the *Hukbalahap*, or Huk Rebellion, ostensibly to rectify long festering grievances of the rural peasantry over land tenancy in Central Luzon. Support for the insurgency grew to over 15,000 men and women in arms by 1950, but was ultimately suppressed four years later after a successful U.S.-assisted counterinsurgency campaign by the Philippine government.[15]

In 1968, former members of the *Partido Komunista ng Pilipinas*, led by José Maria Sison, created the Communist Party of the Philippines (CPP) along with the New People's Army (NPA) as its armed component. Sison, a former English professor at the University of the Philippines, endeavored to launch a nationwide struggle based on the dictums and principles of

Maoist people's war. With only 155 members and thirty-five firearms at its inception, the NPA's ranks grew to a high of 25,200 militant rebels by 1987, with nearly 8,500 villages affected by the organizing efforts of the movement (see Figure 7.1). The strength of the communist insurgency declined considerably in the early 1990s, bottoming out in 1995 with 6,025 active CPP–NPA members and only 445 villages considered affected by communist organizing efforts.[16] With the communist insurgency appearing on the verge of being eliminated, the government drastically reduced the number of territorial militia members deployed throughout the country, transferred primary responsibility for internal security operations from the armed forces to the police, and made plans to reorient the military towards external defense. The resulting security vacuum permitted the CPP–NPA to retake lost villages and recruit members into its ranks with less aggressive intervention by the military.[17]

By 2000, the CPP–NPA was making an aggressive comeback. Following the Second Rectification Campaign in the early 1990s, the CPP–NPA party cadre called for a new emphasis on "widespread and intensified guerrilla warfare with ever-widening and deepening mass base."[18] Today, the CPP–NPA is officially called the Communist Terrorist Movement by the gov-

Figure 7.1
Communist Terrorist Movement Strength 1968–2004

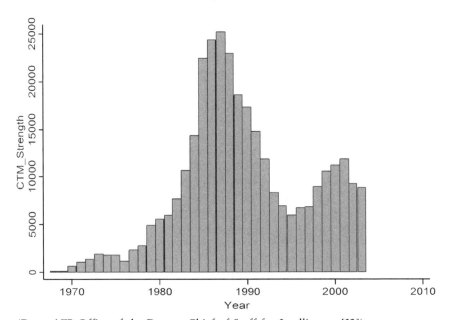

(Data: AFP Office of the Deputy Chief of Staff for Intelligence [J2])

ernment, and is estimated to include close to 9,000 combatants affecting nearly 2,500 villages around the country.[19] While maintaining its ideological *raison d'être* of the revolutionary overthrow of the government, many of the actual activities the CTM take part in, however, are geared more towards criminality than ideological ends.[20]

Techniques of Recruitment and Expanding Mass Base Support[21]

According to researcher Ying-Mao Kao, "Evidence shows that Communist movements never occurred due to the 'systemic frustrations' of poverty and deprivation alone without a well-organized and determined Communist leadership. The ability of insurgents to formulate new ideologies, creative leadership techniques, and effective strategies of mobilization is treated as the determinant of revolution."[22] The Communist Terrorist Movement of the Philippines bases its strategies and techniques of recruitment on the same classic Maoist principles successfully employed in support of the communist revolutionary triumphs in China and Vietnam. Mobilizing the support of the poverty-stricken masses in the countryside and recruiting rebel fighters into the armed components of the rebel organization is achieved through a systematic and proven process.

Once a village is selected for infiltration, small groups of trained communist cadre members make contact with residents and begin a clandestine progression of community organizing activities using tested methods of propaganda and coercion. These efforts strive to undermine the traditional role of the family and other bonds of social cohesion and replace them with alternate communist party structures. Their goal is to shift the loyalties of the people away from the government and establish an environment conducive to supporting communist activities in the future.

Active measures to organize and recruit support in rural villages start with a team of party workers called *Sendatahang Yunit Pampropoganda* (or SYPs) consisting of approximately seven to nine personnel. The SYP members are selected by the CTM party leadership for their communication skills, and are specially trained in community organizing techniques.[23] Organizing a village begins when a three-person element of an SYP team known as a Semi-Legal Team (SLT) establishes contact with a resident of the village and befriends them.[24] This provides the cover needed to enter the village and conduct an initial social investigation and class analysis of the village population. The residents are classified by the SLT as part of either the *Revolutionary Classes*—the poor peasants and farm workers—or the *Reactionary Class*, which in the case of the rural Philippines is made up of the land owners.[25] The SYP members use this analysis and initial reports from the SLT to identify the most contentious issues among the residents and determine how best to exploit the prevailing grievances and agitate the population.

The SYP coordinates with their village contacts to find candidates they believe would be suitable to attend a program of lectures and classes where they begin a systematic compartmentalized effort to agitate the residents through carefully scripted means of propaganda. This focuses on the contradictions of the "feudal struggle" and develops sympathies and support for the insurgency, stressing that revolution is the only way to improve the situation. After these initial contacts are made within the village, the CTM cadres begin formal efforts to infiltrate the village and recruit its members into the movement. The following four steps are followed systematically to achieve these ends:[26]

1. Organizing the *Grupong Tiglambigit* (Village Liaison Group). This group facilitates the interaction of the organizing cadre with village residents deemed most likely to support their efforts. The group dissolves once sufficient liaisons between the cadre and local populace have been established.

2. Forming the *Grupong Tig-Organisa* (Organizing Group). This small compartmented group is recruited based on their reliability assessed during the early social investigation of the village. The group disseminates propaganda provided by the SYP, allowing the party members to avoid exposure in the village. The Organizing Group conducts "teach-ins" and begins the carefully scripted process of breaking the social divisions of the village down into sectoral leagues of farmers, women, and children.

3. Establishing the *Komitemg Tid-Organisa* (Organizing Committee). The CTM party cadre forms an Organizing Committee to help supervise the activities of multiple Organizing Groups. This marks the consolidation of the CTM political infrastructure within the village and frees up the SYPs to begin the infiltration and recruitment process in other villages.

4. Organizing formal mass organizations known locally as the *Hingpit na Katipunan ng Masa* (Solid Mass Organization) and establishing the following three Sectoral Organizations: *Samahang Makabayang Magsasaka* (Farmers), *Malayang Kilusan ng Bagong Kababaihan* (Women), and *Kabataang Makabayan* (Youth).

The secret recruitment of village militias begins concurrently with step two of the mobilization process described above. The CTM party cadres select individuals deemed to possess sufficient commitment level, motivation, and physical attributes for this role and organize them into the *Yunit Milisya* (Village Militia). Eventually, each infiltrated village will maintain a squad-sized militia unit composed of part-time guerrilla fighters.[27] These militias are tasked with "liquidating the enemies of the people" and other limited military actions.

Figure 7.2
Structures of Authority in CTM-Infiltrated Villages

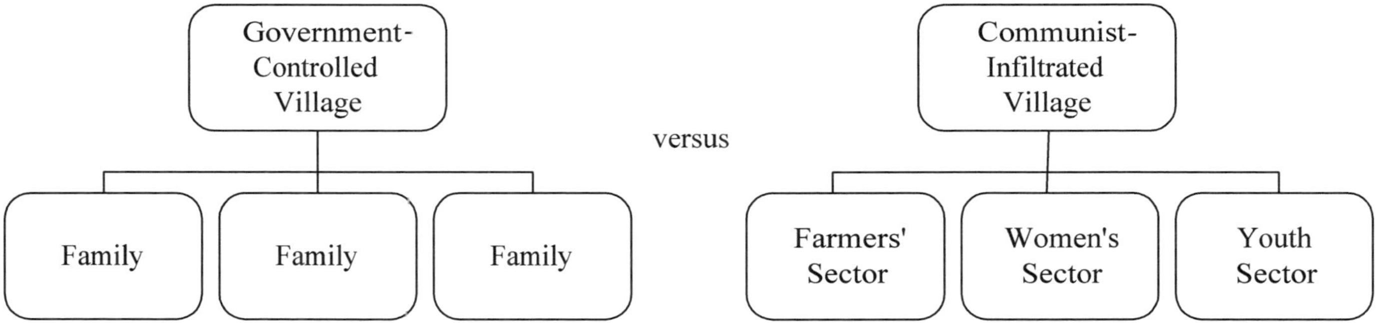

Figure 7.3

Communist Terrorist Movement Affected Villages 1981–2004

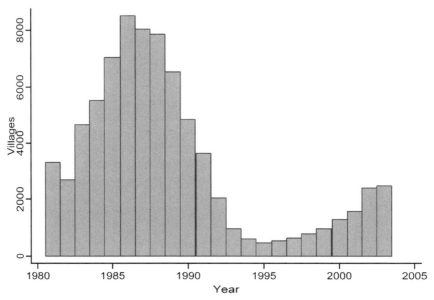

(Data: AFP Office of the Deputy Chief of Staff for Intelligence [J2])

As reflected in Figure 7.2, the net effect of these organizing efforts is to disrupt the natural ties of kinship and friendship—which normally are the most cohesive social forces within the village—and replace them with new structures of authority that challenge the legitimacy of the government. The political infrastructure established through this organizational process institutionalizes the CTM's presence in these villages and makes it very difficult to dismantle. The peak years of this village-based recruitment took place between 1980 and 1991, as shown in Figure 7.3.

Profiles of Former Rebels from the Communist Terrorist Movement

The historic experience of the CTM's organizing efforts demonstrates that it can be highly effective infiltrating villages and recruiting members into its ranks. A critical early step in developing plans to prevent rebel recruitment is identifying what types of individuals are being recruited and the factors increasing the odds of individual recruitment. The next section of this chapter helps accomplish this by developing a profile of a former rebel from the Communist Terrorist Movement.

The sample used to generate this profile includes former rebels that surrendered to the government during the years 2000–2003. This profile is developed from an analysis of Tactical Interrogation Records and Psychological Profiling Reports collected from the field by the Armed Forces of the Philippines' Office of the Deputy Chief of Staff for Civil Military Operations (J7) between 2000 and 2003. A total of 767 rebels completed reports describing their background and circumstances of their recruitment. Of these, a random sample of 30 percent of the reports—230 in all—were analyzed in detail by the Armed Forces of the Philippines Special Operations Team Center, in an effort to develop a profile of the typical Communist Terrorist Rebel.[28]

Gender, Marital Status and Age at Joining

Out of 230 former rebels in this sample, only twenty-one were females. Nearly 59 percent of both the men and women identified themselves as married, with the remainder either single, cohabitating, or widowed/widower. The average age upon joining the rebel group was 23.6 years, with women joining slightly younger on average than men, at 22.0 years.

Education

One hundred and ninety responses in the sample contained data on level of education attained by the former rebels. The large majority indicated they had an elementary level of formal education or lower, with 77 percent of respondents claiming to have spent some time in grades one through six. A total of eight individuals, all of them male, reported no formal education and were classified as illiterate. Over 23 percent attended secondary school, and a total of five reported attending some college before joining the rebel group. Overall, male rebels reported a mean level of education of grade 5; while women had somewhat more formal education on average reporting a mean of two years of high school (see Table 7.1).

Occupation

Almost 80 percent of the 190 former rebels listed some form of agricultural-related work when asked about their primary occupation prior to joining the Communist Terrorist Movement (see Table 7.1). Skilled workers accounted for 8 percent of the responses and unskilled totaled nearly 6 percent. The most commonly reported occupational background for men was "farmer," at 82 percent of the male responses, and women declared "unskilled worker" most frequently, with 29 percent of the female responses coded in this way.

Table 7.1
Select Demographics of CTM Recruits

	Men	Women	All
EDUCATION LEVEL			
Minimal/Illiterate	11%	0	5%
Some Primary School	*53%*	*12%*	*54%*
Completed Primary School	22%	25%	23%
Some High School	11%	25%	12%
High School Graduate	2%	25%	2%
Some College	3%	12%	3%
College Graduate	1%	0%	1%
Total Responses	174	16	
FORMER OCCUPATION			
Agricultural Worker	*82%*	*14%*	*79%*
Skilled Worker	8%	0%	8%
Unskilled Laborer	5%	29%	6%
Student	3%	29%	4%
Other	2%	29%	3%
Total Responses	183	7	

Sample: 190 former CTM rebels. (Percentages are rounded to nearest whole number.)

Reasons for Joining Communist Terrorist Movement

Nearly all respondents identified at least one reason for joining the rebel group, with 224 of the 230 field reports including responses to this question. Multiple answers were permitted for this open-ended question. Three-quarters of the responses, 169 in all, claimed to have been persuaded to join the rebel group to some degree by the CTM propaganda efforts described earlier. Fifteen percent claimed they were disillusioned with the government and were convinced that joining the rebel movement held the promise of a better life. Over 8 percent of the responses identified abuses committed by the military, police, or local politicians as the catalyst for crossing over to the rebel camp. Another 8 percent blamed close relatives who were already members of the rebel group for convincing them to join. Another sixteen respondents claimed they were forced or coerced into join-

Figure 7.4

Reasons Joined Communist Terrorist Movement

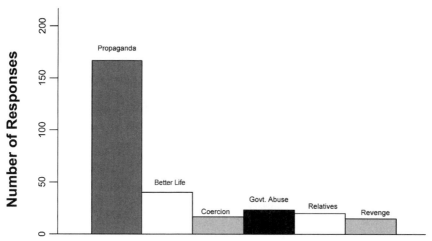

Sample: 190 Former Rebels—Multiple Responses Allowed

ing, while thirteen former rebels admitted they joined as a means of seeking revenge (see Figure 7.4).

Summary: A Profile of the Communist Terrorist Movement Rebel

Based on the data analyzed from this random sample, we can paint a picture of the typical former rebel and why he or she joined the group. Young men approximately twenty-four years old with a 3rd-grade education and a farming background are the typical new recruits for the Communist Terrorist Movement.[29] They are persuaded to join the rebel group most often as a result of concerted propaganda efforts of the CTM as well as by real disillusionment with the ability and sincerity of the government to provide for a better future. Other contributing factors include coercion by the rebels; grievances generated by abuses of the military, police, or local government; encouragement from relatives already part of the rebel group; and the desire to use rebel status to exact revenge.

Curbing Recruitment: Current Initiatives and Challenges

Joining a rebellion is ultimately a very personal decision with considerable individual variation in rationale. However, the profile developed here, along with select theories of rebellion described earlier, combine to offer insights into what types of activities can be effective in reducing the pool of rebel enlistees in general. Described below are some of the current programs and initiatives the Philippine government is implementing to address issues of rebel and terrorist recruitment. These are assessed within the context of what we know theoretically about rebellion and specifically about the profile of today's Communist Terrorist Movement rebel.

Addressing Grievances Driving Rebel Recruitment

The profile of the former rebel developed above indicates that propaganda efforts of the village organizers from the Communist Terrorist Movement are effective catalysts for recruitment. CTM propaganda focuses on securing the sympathy and support of the local populace, largely by discrediting the sincerity and commitment of the government. Effective responses to such propaganda turn on a state's ability to satisfy expectations generated by the hearts and minds of the population. This competition manifests itself in an intense struggle for legitimacy between the government and rebels as they vie for the loyalty of the local populace, down to the village level. The Philippine government recognizes this and has implemented comprehensive state-sponsored development programs targeting the grievances of the population.

One example is the government's current flagship effort to address poverty—the biggest grievance of the population—called the *Kapit-bisig Laban sa Kahirapan* (KALAHI) program.[30] KALAHI's goals are to improve governance, empower communities, and reduce the incidence of poverty at the grassroots level, with the government working in close partnership with local communities. KALAHI targets the poorest villages considered most vulnerable to insurgent influence, designating them as *convergence zones*. In these areas, the government initiates focused and accelerated interagency efforts to address the immediate needs and most pressing grievances of their residents.

Initiatives such as KALAHI respond directly to the grievances that manifest into risk factors for rebel recruitment. The propaganda the CTM cadres get their most leverage out of are rooted in poverty and lack of government efforts to improve local conditions, both of which are countered by targeted development programs such as KALAHI and its predecessors. KALAHI not only provides needed livelihood assistance, it boosts the legitimacy in the hearts and minds of the residents of these remote underdeveloped villages as well.

Given resource constraints, only select villages are able to receive the benefits of such intensive government-sponsored development efforts. The residents of these fortunate few villages may be less vulnerable to the propaganda the CTM uses to encourage defection. However, such selective development efforts can serve to exacerbate the grievances in neighboring villages, as they ask the government, "You helped them, what about us?" Residents of villages not at risk of being infiltrated by the communists might conclude that the government is essentially *rewarding* failure and not success in suppressing insurgent threats. The unintended consequences of such well-intended initiatives could overshadow the real benefits to its select recipients. CTM propaganda will merely shift its efforts and target the much larger number of villages that have not benefited from additional targeted aid from the government.

Undermining Recruitment by Raising the Risks and Opportunity Costs of Rebellion

This case lends considerable support to theories that stress the significance of natural resource predation and other criminal opportunities in explaining rebellion. Despite the movement's professed ideological goals and the "people friendly" image the party cadre strive to project, the truth is the CTM engages in widespread criminality, banditry, and looting to sustain their activities. The euphemism "collecting revolutionary taxes" is used by CTM rebels to extort money from businesses and citizens under the threat of violent retaliation. One indication that natural resource predation contributes to support for the CTM is the increased number of CTM-related incidents recorded in areas rich in natural resources such as timber and minerals. In these and other areas, the distinctions between insurgent activities and criminality are often blurred or even indistinguishable.[31] Many former CTM rebels identified the desire for a better life as a reason for joining the insurgency. Those who believe this "better life" can be secured in the near term through criminality, and who have few attractive alternatives available, are at greater risk for recruitment, as they will associate life as a rebel with the near-term rewards possible through looting and extortion.

The government can modify individual cost–benefit calculations of joining a rebellion by either increasing the risks associated with recruitment or providing more viable alternatives to life as a rebel and terrorist, or combinations of both. The Philippine government's current National Internal Security Plan and the Armed Forces of the Philippines' internal security operations plan, *Bantay Laya*, recognize the importance of both the "left hand" (economic development) and "right hand" (security) components of successful campaigns to combat insurgency and terrorism.[32]

The military prioritizes the most active and advanced CTM Guerrilla Fronts[33] around the country for combat operations. These "right hand" efforts, when carried out discriminately, are an important element in deterring recruitment. Young men, attracted by the adventure, prestige, and profit they associate with armed rebellion confront a harsh wake-up call if their peers are killed during encounters with state internal security forces.

If taking up arms against the state is not associated with a credible risk of death in combat, the opportunities provided by rebellion remain that much more attractive in any rational decision calculus.[34]

The military's efforts to clear villages of communist influence are challenged over the long term, however, if an improvement in the livelihood of the residents does not follow shortly behind. The axiom that the center of gravity in counterinsurgency is not defined in terms of occupying villages or seizing key terrain but by securing the hearts, minds, and perceptions of the populace applies in this case. Military action to clear one village of CTM influence often results in the CTM presence melting away into the countryside and finding new potential recruits to prey on elsewhere, or simply returning to the same village once the government troops move on. Synchronizing efforts to develop villages once they have been cleared by the military is critical and an often mentioned challenge to government-sponsored interagency peace and development initiatives.[35]

On the "left hand," the survey of former rebels reveals they have an average 3rd-grade education level. This profile strongly suggests that individuals on the margins of support for joining the CTM are less likely to cross the threshold if they are educated. Improving the quality and participation in formal education in remote rural areas is thus tantamount to counterinsurgency and counterterrorism, as it reduces the pool of recruits who have fewer alternatives to rebellion because they are illiterate or uneducated. Appreciating this, the Philippine government has a number of campaigns to boost education in the remote rural areas, and even the military contributes to this effort through the Army Literacy Patrol (ALPS) program.

Unfortunately, it is not just the rebels that prosper from the looting of natural resources and criminality. The best-laid plans of the central government and senior military planners are often derailed by endemic corruption at local levels. The challenge the government faces in reducing opportunities to profit from rebellion applies to a broader audience than just prospective rebel recruits, and real progress to reduce such opportunities must account for the difficulties posed by local level corruption.

Encouraging Conditions Favoring Counterinsurgency

The Fearon–Laitin theory described earlier argues that the greed and grievances which some believe are the driving factors behind rebellion are ubiquitous, and the real catalyst for this behavior is generated by external conditions—namely, those favorable to the technology of insurgency.[36] The geography and economic conditions in the Philippines provide classic breeding grounds for insurgency to fester. The government cannot physically "move mountains," which provide sanctuary for rebels in many provinces, or build roads to the far-flung islands of this archipelago. A developing country, the Philippines is confronted with major constraints on its ability to project the capacities of the state into the hinterlands where rebels are most often recruited. For example, many remote villages do not have any law enforcement personnel available to enforce order.[37]

Given that deploying larger full-time police or military personnel to all the far-flung villages is not feasible, the government relies on territorial militias and volunteer law enforcement organizations—as part of its Integrated Territorial Defense System—to establish its presence in the remote areas so often targeted by the organizing and recruiting efforts of the CTM. The organization and employment of locally recruited forces into Citizens Armed Forces Geographical Units (CAFGUs) is an excellent example of measures the government is taking to reduce the risk of insurgent infiltration by providing greater government presence in remote villages at risk of communist infiltration. With over 3,000 detachments deployed throughout the country, CAFGUs along with law enforcement–oriented Civilian Volunteer Organizations (CVOs) play a critical role in the "Hold" phase of the government's Clear-Hold-Support[38] methodology used to combat insurgency. While active military units move around to address threats as they arise, the CAFGUs are a permanent presence, with the tremendous advantage of local knowledge and the ability to tap information sources much more readily. A native of the village, a CAFGU member can spot CTM organizing teams far more effectively than a regular soldier recently assigned to the area.

However, supervision and control of these far-flung CAFGU detachments are hard to provide, with only a small number of regular army cadre available to supervise their training and employment. Some cases of CAFGU detachments becoming sympathetic to the rebel cause—or at least tolerant of their activities—have been reported. Also, CAFGUs are killed at much higher rates by the CTM than soldiers from regular army units.[39] While these territorial militias are critical to the projection of state capacity in remote areas, deploying them has its risks and limitations.

Lessons from the Philippines' Experience

The government of the Philippines strives to address both the symptoms of rebellion—through "right hand" efforts of the military and police—and its roots, by employing comprehensive interagency development responses in underdeveloped insurgency-prone areas. Despite the government's superior resources and support of holistic peace and development initiatives, however, the Communist Terrorist Movement in the Philippines has recruited Philippine citizens into its ranks with varying success for the last thirty-five years. Government competition with the communists for legitimacy and control of the population is hampered by long-standing grievances, the relative appeal of criminality, and conditions that make it difficult for the government to intervene. Despite these challenges, it remains a puzzle why the government with its superior resources has not achieved greater success in deterring recruitment into the rebel's ranks. This chapter concludes with a few general lessons learned from the conflict theories and case study details presented here.

All Recruitment Is Local: Deterring a Rebel "Army of One"[40]

Profiles of typical rebels and the reasons they joined indicate that a variety of factors contribute to each individual decision to defect to the rebel side. Grievances and motives mentioned by former rebels such as desire for a better life, revenge, or family pressure are generated at local levels and can illicit a range of responses beyond simply joining the rebellion or not. For example, some individuals may be comfortable only with providing passive support for rebel militia, while others are willing to leave their village and join mobile guerilla forces fighting the government. The propensity of individuals to join an insurgency or terrorist group and the degree of support they are willing to provide can vary greatly from village to village, neighborhood to neighborhood, and even among family members living in the same dwelling.[41] Importantly, it is the *perception* of grievances and of what options are available to redress them that drives recruitment efforts, and not necessarily grievances measured in real terms. Sun Tzu warns that "What is of supreme importance in war is to attack the enemy's strategy"; government efforts to deter recruitment should heed this maxim. Grievance intensity, responsibility, and options to deal with them are all manipulated by communist party cadre in deliberate efforts to infiltrate villages and recruit individual members into their ranks. Successful efforts to combat the communist propaganda efforts will address perceptions of grievances at the lowest level possible and complement measures to improve actual livelihoods for all citizens.

The Logic of Collective Action May Favor Rebellion

Rebels can recruit effectively using propaganda and selective incentives.[42] Joining the Communist Terrorist Movement offers the prospect of greater economic and social opportunities for many potential recruits. Immediate payoffs gained through criminal predation appeal to some, while the distant prospect of greater prosperity through agrarian reform may appeal to a subset of the more idealistic.[43] Poor agricultural workers make up three-fourths of the pool of former rebels. Neglected, powerless, and disenfranchised for generations, some farmers also have social incentives to participate in the CTM, as it represents a chance for prestige and a greater sense of self-worth.[44] Communist party cadres are able to enlist the support of recruits by offering such selective rewards. The cousin of a rebel may be drawn to join the group because he is envious of her improved status in the community or the occasional "revolutionary subsidies" she secures through participation in rebel activities.

The government, by contrast, is obliged to "produce" in more consistent and tangible ways. Maintaining loyalty and support from village residents requires greater accountability (as the incumbent authority) in comparison to the option of a "vote for change" or the prospect of rewards offered by supporting the rebels. Selective government incentives such as targeted development projects risk serving as disincentives for government support from the nonbeneficiaries of these resources.

Capacity *and* Commitment

Curbing rebel recruitment in the Philippines is particularly challenging given its physical characteristics, which provide protection for rebels, combined with the limited resources the state has to employ in the effort to suppress the communist insurgency. Enhancing state capacity to interdict the rebel and terrorist groups responsible for recruiting citizens is a necessary but insufficient step in addressing this threat. A state's ability to protect its citizens from rebels and discriminately interdict belligerents threatening to take up arms against it is a critical component of any successful campaign to limit support for rebellion. This capability means little, however, in the absence of consistent government commitment to employ it. It is difficult for a developing country to proactively allocate resources to combat threats to its security *before* they are visible. Unfortunately, by the time the first CTM rebel conducts a raid or ambush against the government, it is possible that his entire village has already been infiltrated and organized by the communists.[45] Sufficient capacity *and* proactive commitment are both essential to address such an insidious threat. Commitment at the village level is especially difficult when select local government, police, or military members have incentives not to fully eradicate the communist presence.[46]

Collectively, the Philippines' population is much better off eliminating support for the communist insurgency. The symbiotic relationship between conflict and poverty make this especially challenging to achieve. Recruiting citizens into rebel and terrorist organizations will never be fully eliminated until individual citizens at the margins of recruitment are convinced, for reasons real and perceived, they are better off remaining loyal to the government.

PART II

SOCIAL AND PSYCHOLOGICAL DIMENSIONS

CHAPTER 8

The New Children of Terror

P. W. SINGER

I will make my body a bomb that will blast the flesh of Zionists, the sons of pigs and monkeys. I will tear their bodies into little pieces and cause them more pain than they will ever know.

A., age 11[1]

Terrorism, it is said, is the "weapon of the weak." But while our conception of warfare is often an assumption of men in uniform fighting for the political cause of their nation–states, it is a misnomer. The reality of contemporary conflict is that increasingly it has pulled in the "weak" of society, most specifically children, both as targets and participants. Although there is global consensus (based on moral grounds) against sending children into battle, this terrible practice is now a regular facet of contemporary wars. There are some 300,000 children (both boys and girls) under the age of 18 presently serving as combatants, fighting in almost 75 percent of the world's conflicts; 80 percent of these conflicts where children are present include fighters under the age of fifteen.[2]

Thus, while it may be disturbing, it should be no surprise that children are also present in the dark terrorist domain of modern global conflict. As on the world's battlefields, children are increasingly present in terrorist groups. Many of these groups have long had "youth wings" to provide broader support in the populace, but now youths are increasingly being used in actual operations to strike at targets behind the battle lines. This occurs for the same fundamental reasons that children are now on the battlefields: Children offer terrorist group leaders cheap and easy recruits, who provide new options to strike at their foes.

With the global war on terrorism, children's role in this aspect of war should take on added importance to Americans. Captured al Qaeda training videos reveal young boys receiving instruction in the manufacturing of bombs and the setting of explosive booby traps. The very first U.S. serviceman to die in Afghanistan was shot by a fourteen-year-old sniper. At least six young boys between the ages of thirteen and sixteen have been captured by U.S. forces in Afghanistan and taken to the detainee facility at Guantanamo Bay, Cuba.[3] They were housed in a special wing entitled "Camp Iguana."[4] In addition, several more combatants in the sixteen–eighteen-year range are thought to be held in the regular facility for adult detainees at "Camp X-ray." U.S. soldiers continue to report facing child soldiers in Afghanistan, with the youngest on public record being a twelve-year-old boy. He was captured in 2004 after being wounded during a Taliban ambush of a convoy.[5]

U.S. forces in Iraq have also had to contend with the challenge posed by children's new involvement in conflict. Iraq, under Saddam Hussein, built up an entire apparatus in the 1990s designed to pull children into his military. This included the noted *Ashbal Saddam* ("Saddam's Lion Cubs"), a paramilitary force of boys between the ages of ten–fifteen that was formed after the first Gulf War and whose members received training in small arms and light infantry tactics. They were the feeder organization of the paramilitary *Saddam Fedayeen* force that troubled U.S. forces far more than the Iraqi Army. Over 8,000 young Iraqis were members of this group in Baghdad alone.[6] During the recent war that ended Saddam Hussein's regime, American forces engaged with Iraqi child soldiers in the fighting in at least three cities (Nasariya, Mosul, and Karbala).[7] This is in addition to the many instances of children being used as human shields by Saddam Hussein loyalists during the fighting.[8]

The implications of this training and involvement in military activities by large numbers of Iraqi youth were soon felt in the guerilla war that followed. Beaten on the battlefield, insurgent leaders sought to mobilize this cohort of trained and indoctrinated young fighters. A typical incident in the contentious city of Mosul provides a worrisome indicator of the threat posed to U.S. forces by child soldiers. Here, in the same week that President Bush made his infamous aircraft carrier landing, heralding the end to the fighting, an Iraqi twelve-year-old boy fired on U.S. Marines with an AK-47 rifle.[9] Over the next weeks, incidents between U.S. forces and armed Iraqi children began to grow, to the extent that U.S. military intelligence briefings began to highlight the role of Iraqi children as attackers and spotters for ambushes. Incidents with child soldiers ranged from child snipers to a fifteen-year-old who tossed a grenade into an American truck, blowing off the leg of a U.S. Army trooper.[10]

In the summer of 2004, radical cleric Muqtada al Sadr directed a revolt that consumed the primarily Shia south of Iraq, with the fighting in the holy city of Najaf being particularly fierce. Observers noted many child soldiers, some as young as twelve years old, serving in Sadr's "Mahdi" Army that fought U.S. forces. Indeed, Sheikh Ahmad al-Shebani, al Sadr's spokesman, defended the use of children, stating, "This shows that the Mahdi are a popular resistance movement against the occupiers. The old men and the young men are on the same field of battle."[11] A twelve-year-old-fighter commented, "Last night I fired a rocket-propelled grenade against a tank. The Americans are weak. They fight for money and status and squeal like pigs when they die. But we will kill the unbelievers because faith is the most powerful weapon."[12] Fighting in the radical Sunni hotbed of Falluja also involved child soldiers. During the November 2004 offensive into the city, Marines reported being fired at by "twelve-year-old children with assault rifles."

The overall numbers of Iraqi children involved in the fighting are not yet know. But the indicators are that they do play a significant role in the insurgency. For example, British forces have detained more than sixty juveniles during their operations in Iraq, while U.S. forces have detained 107 Iraqi juveniles in the year after the invasion, holding most at Abu Ghraib prison.[13] The U.S. military considered these children "high risk" security threats, stating that they were captured while "actively engaged in activities against U.S. forces."[14]

Perhaps the most disturbing aspect of contemporary terrorism is the growth in suicide bombing, particularly emanating from the Middle East. Here, too, children are present. Radical Islamic groups like Palestinian Islamic Jihad and Hamas have recruited children as young as thirteen to be suicide bombers and children as young as eleven to smuggle explosives and weapons. At least thirty suicide bombing attacks have been carried out by youths since the Israel-Palestine conflict sparked up again in 2000.[15] Possibly the most tragic example was a semi-retarded sixteen-year-old, who was convinced by Hamas to strap himself with explosives. He was caught by Israeli police in the town of Nablus, just before he was to blow himself up at a checkpoint.[16]

But Palestine is not the only locale to see this practice emerge. In Morocco, a pair of thirteen-year-old twin sisters, who had been recruited by al Qaeda-linked groups, were caught during the summer of 2003 in the process of trying to suicide-bomb Western businesses and local government buildings.[17] Likewise, U.S. Army intelligence reports claimed that in late summer 2003, the insurgent forces in Iraq began to copy this tactic and give young children explosive vests to suicide-bomb Coalition forces.[18]

It is important to note, though, that neither terrorism nor children's roles in it are a uniquely Muslim phenomena. Just as there are a variety of terrorist groups across the world, whose members represent nearly all the world's religions, so too is there a broader set of terrorist groups that seek to mobilize children. For example, the "Real IRA," a coalition of dissident IRA terrorists in Northern Ireland, began to recruit boys in the four-teen–sixteen-year-old range in the late 1990s.[19] The youngest reported terrorist was a nine-year-old boy in Colombia, sent by the National Liberation Army to bomb a polling station in 1997; a ten-year-old was later used by the FARC to bomb a military checkpoint in 2003.[20] Likewise, when radical Muslim groups began to use child suicide bombers, they were not actually breaking any new ground. Instead, they were following the lead of the Tamil Liberation Tigers of Tamil Eelam in Sri Lanka, which has consistently been one of the most innovative of terrorist groups. The LTTE, which has utilized suicide bombers to kill both a former Indian prime minister and a Sri Lankan president, is a master of this technique. It has even manufactured specialized denim jackets designed to conceal explosives. Some are specially tailored in smaller sizes for child suicide bombers.[21]

Why Terrorists Recruit Children

Terrorist groups choose to utilize children for reasons that mimic those of the myriad other armies, warlords, and rebel groups that recruit and use children (40 percent of the armed organizations around the world—157 of 366—use child soldiers). Children are a relatively low-cost way to build out their forces, whose youth also brings certain distinct advantages in operations.

The thinking behind using children derives from both tactical and strategic reasons. For example, the Real IRA began to pull in children at the low point of its recruiting efforts in the late 1990s. The group faced a recruiting decline due to the emerging peace process, as well as opposition from other competing Irish nationalist groups, and thus had a strategic rationale to expand its recruiting base. Additionally, many of its activists were also well known to the British authorities. The recruitment of young "clean skins" (as they were called by British intelligence) was thus an operational response by the group as well. These boys had no records and allowed the group to raise its membership numbers with less fear of infiltration.[22]

Similarly, two factors have led Palestinian groups to use children during the two *Intifadas*. The first motivating factor was strategic, in that having children take part in the violence (whether it be burning tires or throwing Molotov cocktails) was a way to attract the television cameras needed to keep the Palestinian cause on the world's screens. The second factor was tactical. Israeli troops had a standing order to not shoot live ammunition against children under the age of twelve. So Palestinian gunmen began to work in tandem with the children, using their efforts to draw out Israeli troops as well as provide a screen for their sniping.[23]

This same rationale also holds for why groups recruit children for suicide bombing. Suicide bombing is an efficient method for weaker forces to strike at an otherwise well-prepared opposition. Even if they lack the technology for guided missiles or other "smart bombs," the inclusion of the human element allows groups to create a thinking bomb that can adjust to changing circumstances. As one leader of Hamas commented, "We do not have tanks or rockets, but we have something superior—our exploding Islamic human bombs. In place of a nuclear arsenal, we are proud of our arsenal of believers."[24]

By the standards of typical costs of guided weaponry, the human bomb is stunningly cheap. All that is needed to make an effective bomb suit for the terrorist is a nine-volt battery, a light switch, a short cable, mercury (readily obtainable from thermometers), acetone, gunpowder, and some form of homemade shrapnel such as nails or screws. Palestinian experts note that the total cost of a typical operation is about $150, with the most expensive part often being the bus fare to transport the bomber to his/her target. Add in a young terrorist, and the bomb is then able to kill or wound all individuals within a 25–50-meter area.[25]

The suicide bomb is also an effective attempt to sidestep or wear down the common means of defense. Deterrence plans fail, as the terrorists do not care about the consequences. Likewise, guards have greater difficulties in screening, particularly if the terrorists are willing to die and take the guard with them. By including children among the set of potential attackers, the scope of defenses must be even wider. As the mother of one suicide bomber in Palestine commented, "This is a girl who would never appear on a wanted list. She sat at home. She was not active in anything political. [Israeli President] Sharon can chase all the ones he says organize these operations, but he cannot chase away the will of young people to carry out these things."[26]

There is thus an additional, distinctly psychological, element to using child terrorists. The use of suicide bombers spreads wider fear than conventional terrorism. It presents the image of an unbending foe who will seek victory at any cost, including its own destruction. A child in this role heightens the hysteria that terrorists seek to cause. If even children are a potential threat, then everyone is.

Why Children Join Terrorist Organizations

While it is easy to see why terrorist group leaders would see the appeal of children as operatives, it is more complex why children would join terrorist groups, and be willing to sacrifice their lives in suicide bomb attacks. The information is far from complete, and certainly varies across cases. There are, however, some common threads that lead children into this pernicious form of violence. As with conventional child soldiers, many of these factors center on the combination of youth's inherent susceptibility to powerful influences and the harsh environments which can shape them.

The first factor that might lead children to join terrorist groups is the potential of warped religious motivation. While most religions are decidedly against suicide, most also tend to laud the concept of martyrdom, of dying for one's faith. As one fourteen-year-old fighter in Najaf commented, "My parents encouraged me to come here [to Najaf, the site of a battle against U.S. forces during the summer of 2004]. I would prefer to live and taste victory, but if not my death will be rewarded with spiritual gifts in heaven."[27] This trend is particularly poignant in many Islamic regions, where the concept of jihad, a personal battle to improve one's faith, has been warped and expanded by radicals to declare holy wars against nonbelievers. They cite passages from the Koran claiming that a *shaheed*, or martyr, will be immediately forgiven all his sins and will even be married to seventy-two beautiful virgins in paradise. Additionally, martyrs are given the ability to admit seventy of their relatives to paradise, perhaps adding an element of motivation for family support of the faithful. For children who have known nothing but poverty and hopelessness, such visions for the future are highly enticing. As one Palestinian psychiatrist in Gaza noted, "an important factor in suicide bombers is their sense of frustration with their surroundings, connected to the desire to go to heaven."[28] However, it is noteworthy that not only radical, religiously-motivated groups use suicide attacks. As the appeal of the operations grew in Palestine, for example, the Fatah and Popular Front for the Liberation of Palestine—which are both highly secular militant groups—adopted the tactics.[29]

There is also the potential of economic motivations. While the majority of terrorist group leaders—such as Osama bin Laden of al Qaeda or Carlos Castaño of the AUC—come from relatively privileged backgrounds, they often target the youngest and the very poorest for their foot soldiers.[30] As one extremist leader in Pakistan explicitly notes, "We want their children."[31] The head of Laskar Jihad in Indonesia admits that he even likes to recruit "children as young as eight" to train in terrorist and suicide operations.[32]

The financial inducements that these groups are able to offer vary. One particularly powerful element for children are rewards that flow to the family. In this recruitment tactic, a group is able to promise poor youngsters that their family will be better taken care of in their absence. In Palestine, for example, suicide bombers' families were offered up to $25,000 from the Iraqi government of Saddam Hussein and by private Saudi donors to the "Martyr's Fund." The rate from Hamas was about $5,000, along with such staples as flour, sugar, and clothing.[33] Other groups, such as the LTTE in Sri Lanka and the Jamiat Islami in Pakistan, move young suicide bomber's families into nicer homes or provide them with first access to better jobs. Thus, their sacrifice is portrayed to the children as a means to be selfless and raise their family's lot in life. To do otherwise, then, when there are no better options, can be spun as an act of selfishness.[34] These offers particularly resound with children growing up in conflict zones and refugee camps, who can visualize no other way to help their families out of their fate.

The institutions that a child interacts with, most particularly educational, might also play a role. In a number of areas, militant groups that use child terrorists actually run schools themselves. These institutions are then used as recruiting and training grounds for future terrorists. For example, LTTE-run orphanages in Sri Lanka even have shrines set up to honor suicide bombers.[35] In the border regions of Pakistan, approximately 15 percent of madrasas provide some sort of training that prepares children for militant groups.[36] In the occupied territories of Palestine, Hamas has set up a series of schools that are highly politicized, even down to the preschool level. The walls in these schools are labeled with posters such as, "The children of the kindergarten are the *shaheeds* of tomorrow," and classes similarly teach hatred along with reading skills.[37] As one Hamas leader—Sheikh Hasan Yusef in Ramallah—commented of the bombers his group had trained, "We like to grow them from kindergarten through college."[38]

Sheik 'Ikrimi Sabri, the Mufti of Jerusalem, appointed by the Palestinian Authority, expressed a similar sentiment in an October 2000 interview:

Question: What do you feel when you pray [for the souls of the martyrs]?

Sabri: I feel the martyr is lucky because the angels usher him to his wedding in heaven. . . .

Question: Is it different when the martyr is a child?

Sabri: Yes, it is. It's hard to express it in words. There is no doubt that a child [martyr] suggests that the new generation will carry on the mission with determination. The younger the martyr, the greater and the more I respect him. . . .

Question: Is this why the mothers cry with joy when they hear about their sons' death?

Sabri: They willingly sacrifice their offspring for the sake of freedom. It is a great display of the power of belief. The mother is participating in the great reward of the jihad to liberate Al-Aqsa.[39]

Other related institutions with which children have a deep contact can also motivate. For example, the Palestinian Authority ran a series of summer camps in 2000 that had a distinctly violent aspect. More than 25,000 campers learned everything from infiltration techniques and assembling AK-47s to the art of ambushing units and kidnapping leaders.[40] Similar camps were run in Iraq under Saddam Hussein and likely added to the capacity and the potential for the subsequent attacks and terrorist strikes at U.S. forces in a post-Saddam Iraq.[41]

Social motivations may also play a powerful role in inducing children to join these groups, often with their parents' approval. It is no coincidence that the majority of suicide bombings take place in what anthropologists call "shame societies." In such settings, young people are taught from birth that the acquisition of honor and avoidance of shame are the critical motivators of behavior. These beliefs take on an added power in settings that entail humiliation and subservience. Any act of retaliation, even one that has no realistic chance of recompense, can still be interpreted as heroic and cancels out the shame. Violence thus becomes viewed as what psychiatrist Franz Fanon described as a "cleansing force," which releases the youth to become fearless in their actions and use bloodshed to drive out their feelings of "inferiority," "despair," or "inaction."[42]

This can take place at the level of the individual or family unit or at the greater societal level. For example, one of the more tragic incidents in the U.S. operations in Afghanistan was when a Special Forces medic, Sergeant First Class Christopher Speer, was killed by a fifteen-year-old al Qaeda member while operating in the Khost province. The young boy, who was originally from Canada, was the sole survivor of a group of al Qaeda fighters who had ambushed a combined U.S.-Afghan force. This led to a five-hour firefight involving massive air strikes. When U.S. forces went to sift through the rubble, the young boy popped up, with pistol in hand, and threw a grenade which seriously wounded Speer. The young boy was shot down by Speer's comrades, but survived his wounds. A few months later, he spent his sixteenth birthday at the U.S. detention facility at Guantanamo Bay. By this time, however, Speer had died from his injuries. In a sad irony, Speer had risked his life just two days earlier by going into a minefield to save two injured Afghan children.[43]

Most believe that the young fifteen-year-old al Qaeda member was brought into the realm of terrorism at such a young age by his family. Not only was his father a noted terrorist financier, but his two older brothers were also members of the organization. As one cleric—who knew the family while they were in Canada—noted, "Ahmed Khadr made his boys into his own image—a fanatic driven by hate for the West and wrong ideas of Islam."[44]

The challenges faced by Palestinian society during the present conflict may be the best current example of how this individual-level phenomenon can build up to a broader national-level concern. In Gaza City, the heartland of Hamas, some 1.3 million refugees live in a 140-square-mile enclave of semi-permanent shelters; 70 percent are unemployed, and 80 percent live in abject poverty.[45] Thus, the occupation, with its the treatment of two generations of Palestinians as second-class refugees, followed by the nearly complete decimation of Palestinian civil society through the violence over the last decade, has arguably backfired on the Israelis. Rather than creating a cowed populace, its product has instead been broad youth rage expressing itself through the violence of the *Intifada* and suicide bombers. Participating in violence has given many youths a sense of mission and control over their lives that they otherwise lacked while growing up in squalid—and seemingly permanent—refugee camps.[46] As one Hamas leader notes, he finds no shortage of willing recruits for suicide operations from this pool. "Our biggest problem is the hordes of young men who beat on our doors, clamoring to be sent. It is difficult to select only a few. Those whom we turn away return again and again, pestering us, pleading to be accepted."[47]

These social motivations can also be directed through the family. Some groups, such as the LTTE in Sri Lanka and the Jamiat Islami in Pakistan, give young suicide bombers' families special recognition and honors in the community. Hamas in Palestine even celebrates the child's "martyrdom" with festivities, treating the event as if it were a wedding. The death notice will take the form of a wedding announcement in the newspaper.[48] Hundreds of guests congregate at the family's house to offer congratulations. Sweet desserts and juices that the youth chose in their will are served. These joyful scenes and the idea that they might achieve similar notoriety in their home village resonate to other potential recruits and their families.

Many parents whose children have died in the operations take it as a point of pride. Mothers have been seen to dance with joy at the occasion.[49] As one Kashmiri father noted, "Everyone treats me with more respect now that I have a martyred son. And when there is a martyr in the village, it encourages more children to join the jihad. It raises the spirit of the entire village."[50] In turn, those parents who demur from providing their children can expect anything ranging from low-level harassment to condemnation in the local newspaper.[51]

The broader social environment can also help construct children's identity in ways intended to reinforce these tendencies. For instance, if martyrdom is taught as being a good and honorable deed on national TV, then it is more likely to become an unfortunate part of a national consciousness. Palestinian television, for example, even once had a Sesame Street–like television program called the "Children's Club." With its puppet shows, songs, and a Mickey Mouse character, the show definitively had a children's audience in mind. However, the substance of it was very adult and pernicious, celebrating violence. Its shows even included songs with such lyrics as "When I wander into Jerusalem, I will become a suicide bomber." Another song sung by a seven-year-old girl expressed, "I finished practicing on the submachine gun. . . . I trained my friends from among the children and the youths. We swore to take vengeful blood from our enemies for our killed and wounded."[52]

Likewise, many worry about the effect that the repeated images of civilian casualties in Iraq will have in the Islamic world. The concern is that repeated airings of civilian casualties in the Arab media will motivate Arab youngsters to join groups like al Qaeda that target the United States. As one seventeen-year-old in Syria noted of his response, "I was watching what was happening and I found myself cursing for the first time in my life. I felt I wanted to kill, not only curse."[53]

These influences of society, family, and so on, may not be the only environmental factors that are sufficient to lead a child into terrorist activity or its support. Further personal experiences might play a role. These include the loss of a relative or friend, or some other form of direct suffering from violence. A common experience is jailing or brutalization from local security forces. Rather than deterring the youths from radicalization, it often places them under the influence of radical groups' leaders while in custody. Such children then want to use violence even more when they get out and are better prepared to do so.

It is important to note that while all these factors may provide an explanation for why children might join a terrorist group, they do not combine to offer any sort of justification. Terrorism is typically a highly communitarian, unspontaneous enterprise. The suicide bomber is, as terrorism expert Walter Laqueur describes, "only the last link in the chain."[54] Few terrorist attacks, and no suicide bombings we have seen so far, are the result of freelancing individuals. Instead, most are the result of careful planning by groups that recruit, indoctrinate, and train specifically for the purpose of killing defenseless civilians. In some cases, they are doing so with children in mind as both perpetrators and potential victims, making their actions even more distasteful.

Thus, while the motivations may vary by individual recruit, the underlying success of an effort by terrorist groups to recruit children is dependent on their having a recruiting pool at hand. This pool is shaped by both its environment and the permissiveness that society may or may not give to the group to access it. When children are disillusioned, humiliated, lack proper schooling, and see themselves with no viable future, they are more likely to take refuge in radicalism. For many, then, even killing themselves becomes interpreted as relief from a present life that they see as intolerable. In turn, society's willingness to sacrifice their youth may be generated by external political actions, such as an occupation, or by internal societal causes, such as an ethic of revenge.

In any case, the outcome is that it is children who bear the costs of society's failures. It is particularly disturbing that an increasing number of radical Muslim clerics preach that Islam permits suicide bombings and that the child bombers are martyrs to be lauded. Their view is that Islam may forbid suicide, but that these cases are different because of the adversary. As one cleric in Kashmir put it, "If jihad is undertaken according to the strict interpretations of the Koran, suicide missions can be allowed if they offer military or strategic advantage to the Muslim army."[55] Such individuals are then described as not taking their own lives, but rather as sacrificing themselves for the good of the community. These are highly controversial assertions—and, as many respected Muslim clerics and scholars would argue, they lack any merit in religious texts.[56] However, in the present context, such beliefs too often go unchallenged, and popular support for the practice is especially high among Muslim populations that see no other options available to them. For example, over 70 percent of Palestinians approve of suicide bombings.[57]

That this practice is tolerated, let alone celebrated, is a terrible indictment of political and religious leaders. As one Arab journalist put it, "What kind of independence is built on the blood of children while the leaders are safe and so are their children and grandchildren? Are only the miserable destined to die in the spring of their lives? Those children who are killed may not, in their short lives, have enjoyed a fresh piece of bread, sleeping in a warm bed, the happiness of putting on a new piece of clothes, or carrying books with no torn pages to school."[58]

Training and Action

The training of children in terrorist actions varies as much as the techniques for recruitment. Indeed, it is a process that is undergoing constant refinement. The training process begins with the selection of children. In addition to their intelligence and enthusiasm, appearance in relation to potential targets is highly important. The ability to blend in or otherwise not raise suspicions among security forces allows the attackers to get closer to their targets. Thus, groups are careful to keep this in mind in selecting their operatives. For example, the LTTE uses cute young girls that are less likely to look suspect; Palestinian Islamic Jihad often selects those who can pass for Israeli Jews.[59]

Once selected, the terrorist often goes through an intense period of mental preparation. For suicide bombers, this often takes place in small cells, made up of a training leader and two or three candidate bombers. This compartmentalization not only makes it harder for security forces to crack the organization, but also increases the intimacy and hold of the leader over the new recruits.[60] The cells are sometimes named for resounding events or subjects, to increase their impact on motivation. Hamas suicide bombing cells, for instance, are usually given a name taken from a Koranic text or event in Islamic history. There is also the use of pledges among the new members. For example, some radical Islamic groups pledge the *bayt al ridwan* (named after the garden in Paradise), which seeks to lock the group further together in a shared fate.

The training often includes concentrated study of texts that reinforce the notion of sacrifice, as well as tasks of memorization and visualization. Other indoctrination strategies include carrying out re-enactments of past successful operations. Repetition is used to drive points home. A focus is also made on the ease of death. Its pleasures are extolled in contrast to a future life of sadness, sickness, and continued humiliation. Hamas, for example, has its recruits rest in empty graves, in order to see how "peaceful" death will be. In turn, LTTE survivors tell of training drills in which they would rehearse what they would do if captured or wounded. Their coaches would instruct them how to bite into the cyanide capsules that they would wear in necklaces during operations. As one fourteen-year-old trainee tells, "It mixes with our blood, and within one second, we die."[61]

Rather than sadness at their coming fate, potential suicide bombers often describe this training and indoctrination as a period of great anticipation and happiness at their selection. As one young member of Hamas (who survived his intended suicide attack and woke up from a coma a month later) describes, "We were in a constant state of worship. We told each other that if the Israelis only knew how joyful we were they would whip us to death! Those were the happiest days of my life."[62] Trainers reinforce these feelings by extolling the coming triumph and celebration at their success. The candidates are even referred to by new honored titles, such as *al shaheed al hayy* (the living martyr) that afford them special status.

The final hours are often spent in prayer and making wills or farewell messages that are recorded on video or audiocassettes. These farewell videos and tapes not only are used for future recruiting, but help make it harder for the bombers to back out, and thus risk public humiliation.[63] In the LTTE, young suicide bombers were given the honor of spending their last meal in camp with the leader of the Tigers.[64]

Once trained and indoctrinated, the terrorists are sent into action. Again, the intersection of the group's needs and the target's responses determine their use. Some operations may be highly targeted, such as the LTTE strategy of aiming at individual leaders, and thus require complex planning. They may even involve layers of infiltration to get the bomber as close to their target as possible. Others, whose intent is simply to strike wider fear in the opposition's public, may be aimed at collateral damage and thus less tightly designed. Hamas, for example, has a more ad hoc approach and typically lets the bomber choose the target themselves. As one trainer describes, "We told them 'blow yourselves up any place where there are people.' They went wherever they knew to go."[65] These might include buses or former workplaces.

After the operation is carried out, groups are usually quick to claim credit. This is both an achievement of their wider goals to spread fear, as well as an aid in their recruiting strategy. For example, Hamas and Palestinian Islamic Jihad typically notify the local media right after attacks and distribute copies of their attacker's final video or audio message. This is followed up by extolling the action in local organizations affiliated with the group, such as mosques or schools. They also might praise the heroism of the youth through posted leaflets and graffiti (usually depicting the bomber in Paradise under a flock of green birds, referring to a belief that the soul of a martyr is carried to Allah upon the wings of a green bird of Paradise). Calendars are even distributed that have illustrations of the "martyr of the month."

Conclusions and Policy Responses

While there are multiple reasons for children to become involved in terrorist groups, none are simply coincidental or beyond the control of the groups themselves. Instead, they are usually the result of the combination of a harsh environment that leaves children with no good choices and a deliberate mobilization strategy by the group itself to pull children into terrorism. Sometimes, this process is enabled by the parents' approval. This may be the saddest aspect of children's involvement in such groups. When a parent wishes that their child grow up to be a suicide bomber instead of becoming a doctor or teacher and live to an old age, something is indeed wrong.

In attempting to defeat this practice, the key is to influence both the recruiting pool and the groups' willingness and ability to access it. A focus should be made on the underlying problem of hopelessness that often leads children (and/or their parents) to believe that they have no better future than involvement in terrorism and a likely early death. An essential problem to deal with is the surroundings of violence, humiliation, and lack of opportunity that underlie this desperation. As Charles Stith, the former U.S. Ambassador to Tanzania (who served in the wake the 1998 al Qaeda attack there), noted, "People who have hope tend not to be inclined to strap 100 pounds of explosives on their bodies and go into a crowd and blow themselves up."[66]

Some counter such claims by asserting that terrorism is an affair of the well-off elite from rich, stable countries; they usually point to those who perpetrated the 9/11 attacks as evidence. However, in doing so, they focus on the leadership (Osama bin Laden or Mohammad Atta) rather than the membership of the wider organization and the troops who make the operations possible. For instance, if we look at all of those who seized the planes on 9/11—an event that was also rare in involving a crosscontinental infiltration rather than the mass of attacks that occur within the local environs—prosperity was not one of their hallmarks. Indeed, a number of the hijackers were "alghamdi"—a name that indicates that they did not even have a respectable tribal origin, and thus were accorded a low social status within their countries. Equally, all—even the Saudis—came from countries with growing poverty, steeply declining standards of living, and declining job prospects. Aside from the 9/11 example, the youth involved in suicide bombings typically fit the profile laid out above.

Focusing solely on the leadership of terrorist organizations also misses the larger socioeconomic context of radicalism and terrorism, as well as how and where terrorists thrive. Successful terrorist groups are based in (and thrive in) zones of chaos, poor governance, and lawlessness. Indeed, it is the context that surrounds, nurtures, and protects a group like al Qaeda that makes it such a magnified and continuing threat, as compared to a group like Germany's Baader–Meinhof Gang or the Oklahoma City bombers, who enjoyed no societal resonance and thus never became a magnified threat. Likewise, effective extremist groups rely on a division of labor between young and uneducated "foot soldiers" and ideologically trained and well funded elite operatives.[67] Al Qaeda's use of this structure was further illustrated by the 2003 Morocco bombings. The operatives in these attacks were young men, some as young as 17, who were recruited from local slums. In short, elites certainly play a role in terrorism, but it is a broader, communal affair.

Two particular issues must then be resolved to undercut the present terrorist threat. The first is to affect the context. The seemingly permanent status of conflict and its dispossessed refugees in a number of war zones (including Israel-Palestine and Kashmir) is an obvious driving force behind children's participation in violence. This is heightened by failing educational systems and economic stagnation that hold back the realization of human potential across many regions. As Fadl Abu Hein, a psychology lecturer from Gaza, notes, "Martyrdom has become an ambition for our children. If they had a proper education in a normal environment, they won't have looked for a value in death."[68]

The second facet is to undercut the institutions that assist terrorist groups in the mobilization and recruitment of children. Possible options to do so range from enlisting religious leaders to speak out against the use of children—specifically by noting that the use of children and involvement in terrorism is counter to the true intent of religious texts—to establishing campaigns designed to reverse the social and economic rewards that accrue. Shutting down payment plans and punishing families for the actions of their children are other strategies. The overall key is to weaken the high regard that such terrorists are too often given by embattled societies.

Finally, the cost-benefit analysis of terrorist groups must be altered. Presently, the downside for groups to use children is minimal. They have created a context in which neither local nor international support has been harmed by such a decision. Those who use children must be convinced that it is no longer in their best interest. When the institutions that influence children are controlled by groups that can be identified, such as organization-linked media or schools that extol attacks by children, costs must be extracted. Not only must the programs be shut down, but the group that enabled and planned them should be made to fear the loss of something it values more, such as recognition by and interaction with international authorities. The ultimate intent of the pressure is to force the group into the realization that recruiting and using children for violence is not just an illegal and immoral strategy, but also that it will detract from its long-term goals.

In battling terrorist groups, and particularly those that use children to carry out violence, we cannot simply hope to shame the shameless. But we can begin to alter their methods, gains, and ultimately, their strategies.

CHAPTER 9

Hamas Social Welfare: In the Service of Terror[1]

MATTHEW A. LEVITT

It is a painful reality that Palestinians living in the West Bank and Gaza have endured a deplorably low standard of living for years. The Palestinian community not only suffered from living under occupation, but from the neglect of a corrupt Palestinian leadership as well. As a result, the economic, social, and health conditions in the West Bank and Gaza are truly miserable. Making the situation more complicated yet, Hamas (The Islamic Resistance Movement) capitalizes on this humanitarian crisis to build grassroots support, radicalize youth and recruit future recruits, and fund and facilitate suicide bombings and other acts of terrorism.

Palestinians suffer from extensive economic hardship. The West Bank and Gaza economies are in crisis, as evidenced by an unemployment rate as high as 33.5 percent in 2003.[2] With a struggling economy and limited employment opportunities, it is not surprising that approximately three-fourths of the Palestinian population living in the West Bank and Gaza falls below the poverty line of $2/day.[3] Health conditions in the West Bank, and especially Gaza, are very poor. As of 2003, 30 percent of Palestinian children under age five suffered from chronic malnutrition and 21 percent from acute malnutrition.[4] In 2001, Palestinian Ministry of Health officials estimated that the infant mortality rate in Gaza was at forty deaths per 1,000 live births.[5]

Clearly, the vast majority of Palestinians are in desperate need of assistance, ranging from unemployment compensation to food and medicine handouts of income to access to proper medical care. Both the Israeli government and Palestinian leadership have consistently failed to provide these essential services to the Palestinian community, thus leaving a void that groups like Hamas are all too eager to fill.

As a result of the heightened focus on exposing terrorist networks in the post–9/11 global environment, it has become undoubtedly clear how terrorist groups systematically conceal their activities behind charitable, social, and political fronts. Investigators, faced with the threat posed by al Qaeda and its many affiliates, have come to appreciate the crucial role played by charities, foundations, and individual donors who support terrorist groups through social service organizations. These same organizations effectively provide recruits, logistics, and cover for terrorists; part of the battle against terror has been an international effort to shut them down. Few experts are misled anymore by the fictitious entities established by terrorist groups. Indeed, many of these fronts have seen their officials arrested, their assets seized, and their offices closed down by authorities.

Yet al Qaeda is not the only terrorist group that has used social services to conceal and support its terrorist activity. Hamas is known not only for perpetrating suicide attacks in Israel, but for providing extensive and much-needed social services to Palestinians. Hamas benefits from an ostensible distinction drawn by some analysts between its "military" and "political" or "social" wings. Analysts who make such a distinction regularly dwell on the "good works" of Hamas, as though these activities had no connection whatsoever with the attacks on civilians and the suicide bombings that are the trademark of the organization. Because of the notion that Hamas has independent "wings," its political and charitable fronts are allowed to operate openly in many European and Middle Eastern capitals. In these cities, Islamic social welfare groups tied to Hamas are given free passes for their support of terror simply because they also provide critical humanitarian support. Hamas logistical and financial support activity is often tolerated when conducted under the rubric of charitable or humanitarian assistance.

While convenient for Hamas and its radical Islamist supporters, this distinction is contradicted by the consistent if scattered findings of investigators, journalists, and analysts. A review of the evidence regarding the integration of social services and terrorism in Hamas demonstrates the centrality of these services to the organization's ability to recruit, indoctrinate, train, fund and dispatch suicide bombers to attack civilian targets.

The Founding of Hamas

Though Sheikh Ahmed Yassin and several colleagues officially founded Hamas in December 1987, the group had been active since the 1960s as the Yassin-led Palestinian branch of the Muslim Brotherhood. Under Yassin's leadership, longtime Muslim Brotherhood activists were simply redirected from promoting Islamic observance to engaging in violent anti-Israel activities. Khaled Mishaal, a senior Hamas official, noted that in 1983—four years before the group's official founding—Yassin and other internal and external Hamas leaders gathered at a meeting at which "the decision to found the Palestinian Islamic project for the cause and preparing the requirements for its success was taken."[6]

Yassin's history of leading terrorist attacks against Israeli targets far precedes the official founding of the Hamas organization. As Mishaal recounts: "In 1983, we carried out our first military experience under the leadership of Sheikh Ahmed Yassin."[7] Palestinian author Khaled Hroub also notes that various attacks against Israeli interests from 1985 to 1987 were conducted by Yassin's group, including military cells such as the Yahya al-Ghuoul's Mujahideen of Mifraqa Group, Salah Shehadah's Group Number 44, and Muhammad Sharathah's Group Number 101.[8]

Yassin is also credited with founding the Hamas *dawa* network. Yassin originally set up the Hamas *dawa*—its "call" to Islam, conducted among Palestinian Muslims with the objective of recruiting and mobilizing them—to mirror the structure he helped perfect as a Muslim Brotherhood activist.[9] The Hamas *dawa* provides desperately needed social services to needy Palestinians and serves as a de facto Islamist opposition to the Palestinian Authority (PA).

The importance of the Hamas *dawa* network Yassin founded was highlighted at a 1993 Hamas meeting in Philadelphia, which the FBI surreptitiously monitored. In a presentation on "the situation in Palestine" and the status of "Islamic works" tied to Hamas, Muin Kamel Mohammed Shabib, an identified Izz al Din al Qassam operative, described the institutions tied to Hamas as falling under the following classifications: educational (schools, universities), social and charitable (refugees, orphans, relief), cultural, health institutions (clinics, medical centers), public syndicates, technical institutions, sports clubs, media, religious institutions, and women's institutions.[10]

Shabib then proceeded to list specific institutions tied to Hamas, which he described as "our institutions." In the Gaza Strip alone these included the Islamic University, the Islamic Complex [Society], the Islamic Association, al-Salah Association, the Young Woman Association, al-Wafa Association for the Elderly, the Orphans Center, some of al-Zakah committees, and some general service committees that received new licenses, such as the organization of the Truth and the Law.[11] Today, these and other Hamas *dawa* organizations actively radicalize Palestinian society, recruit new members, provide operatives with day jobs, launder funds for Qassam Brigade terrorist cells, provide logistical support for their terrorist attacks, and incite Palestinian society to violence.

Debunking the Myth of "Wings"

Though some analysts do distinguish between the military wing of Hamas and its political or social wings, the most convincing denial of this distinction comes from Hamas's former leader Sheikh Yassin. Yassin rejected the idea that Hamas has uncoordinated wings: "We cannot separate the wing from the body. If we do so, the body will not be able to fly. Hamas is one body."[12]

Hamas leaders themselves frequently acknowledge the central role that their "political" leaders play in the group's operational decision-making. Hamas military commander Salah Shehadeh put it this way: "The political apparatus is sovereign over the military apparatus, and a decision of the political [echelon] takes precedence over the decision of the military [echelon], without intervening in military operations."[13]

Another Hamas leader, Abdel-Aziz al-Rantisi, pointed precisely to the primacy of the political echelon in July 2001 when he told Reuters, "The [Hamas] political leadership has freed the hand of the [Izz al Din al Qassam] brigades to do whatever they want against the brothers of monkeys and pigs [i.e., Jews]." According to the Reuters article, "Hamas's political wing determines overall policy for the movement."[14]

Moreover, Hamas itself sees the social services it provides as a jihadist extension of its terror attacks. For example, in July 2002, Hamas's "Islam-online" website featured a special page glorifying suicide attacks and stressing the need not only to support Palestinian armed struggle but also youth education, social activity, and economic assistance as a means of fighting what it defined as the "economic jihad."[15] The site provided a long list of European, American, South African, and Arabic social organizations which serve, according to the site, as a channel to transfer funds to charitable associations Hamas recommends. Needless to say, these organizations are tied to Hamas.[16]

Indeed, the activities of the group's political, social, and military "wings" are so intertwined that even Palestinian security officials themselves see them as one and the same. In the words of Palestinian Brigadier General Nizar Ammar, "The difference between the [political, social and military] wings [of Hamas] is often a fiction."[17]

For years, the Israeli government has understood the coordination of Hamas's political leaders with its military activities. According to court documents filed by the government of Israel in the 1995 extradition case of Hamas leader Musa Abu Marzook from the United States, "The [political] bureau operates as the highest ranking leadership body in the Hamas organization, setting policies and guidelines respecting Hamas' activities. In addition to its other functions, this bureau has responsibility for directing and coordinating terrorist acts by Hamas against soldiers and civilians in Israel and the territories."[18]

The United States government has also come to share this view. In the Treasury Department's August 2003 announcement designating six senior Hamas political leaders and five charities as terrorist entities, it asserted that "the political leadership of Hamas directs its terrorist networks just as they oversee their other activities."[19]

Even a Human Rights Watch report has concluded that Hamas functions as a unified entity, with the military operatives subservient to the political leadership: "In the case of Hamas, there is abundant evidence that the military wing is accountable to a political steering committee that included Shaikh Ahmad Yassin, the group's former acknowledged 'spiritual leader,' as well as Ismail Abu Shanab, 'Abd al-'Aziz al-Rantissi, and Mahmud Zahar. Yassin himself, as well as Salah Shehadah, the late founder and commander of the 'Izz al-Din al-Qassam Brigades, have confirmed in public remarks that the military wing implements the policies that are set by the political wing."[20]

The social welfare organizations of Hamas, supported by numerous charities, answer to precisely the same "political leaders." Yet some observers have determined that these institutions bear no relationship to the terrorist campaigns authorized by those same leaders. In some cases, the mere existence of these institutions is invoked to classify Hamas as a social welfare organization, rather than a terrorist organization.

Thus, *The Washington Post* ombudsman wrote a column explaining that, since Hamas is a "nationalist movement" engaged in "some social work," the perpetrators of Palestinian suicide and other attacks should be described in the press as "militants" or "gunmen," as opposed to the "terrorists" of al Qaeda.[21] The *Boston Globe* ombudsman wrote much the same, arguing that to "tag Hamas, for example, as a terrorist organization is to ignore its far more complex role in the Middle East drama."[22]

To debunk these specious assumptions, it is necessary to fully expose what Hamas calls the *dawa*. This is sometimes difficult because, as one U.S. official recently testified, "Hamas is loosely structured, with some elements working clandestinely and others working openly through mosques and social service institutions to recruit members, raise money, organize activities, and distribute propaganda."[23]

Nevertheless, there is ample evidence for the role of Hamas social institutions in the terror activities directed and authorized by Hamas leaders and commanders. Inside the Palestinian territories, the battery of mosques, schools, orphanages, summer camps, and sports leagues sponsored by Hamas are integral parts of an overarching apparatus of terror. These Hamas entities engage in incitement and radicalize society, and undertake recruitment efforts to socialize even the youngest children to aspire to die as martyrs. They provide logistical and operational support for weapons smuggling, reconnaissance, and suicide bombings. They provide day jobs for field commanders and shelter fugitive operatives.

Dawa as the Backbone of Hamas

The Hamas *dawa* serves as an ideal logistical support network. By its very nature the *dawa* operates overtly, offering an extensive and entrenched network of charities, social service organizations, mosques, employees, members, and donors available to support Hamas activities. Many support Hamas operations knowingly and willingly, while others do so unwittingly or out of a sense of obligation for charity or services they receive from Hamas.

Sports clubs, mosque classes, universities, charity committees, and other organizations run by Hamas all serve as places where Hamas recruiters—usually themselves *dawa* activists—recruit Palestinian youth for positions in the Hamas *dawa*, for terrorist training courses in Syria or Iran, or for suicide and other terror attacks. The *dawa* network also serves as the group's spotting and recruitment pool. *Dawa* operatives recruit at the organization's social-service institutions, as in the case of Ahmed Saltana, head of the Jenin Charity Committee, who recruited young men working for the charity committee into Hamas.[24]

The Jihad mosque in Hebron has its own soccer team. While not particularly known for athletic talent, the team's claim to fame is striking: It produced several Hamas terrorists responsible for a string of attacks conducted over the first six months of 2003, five of which were suicide bombings executed by team members. The team's jersey bore a picture of a hand holding an axe with an inscription reading, "Prepare for the enemy and to fight the occupation."[25] Another such sports club has the notorious reputation of serving as the recruitment grounds for six different suicide bombers.[26]

In their analysis of interviews with jailed terrorists, including Hamas members and others, Jerrold Post, Ehud Sprinzak, and Laurita Denny found that the "prerecruitment" social environment for members of Islamist groups like Hamas "was dominated by the mosque, religious organizations and religious instruction."[27] This trend was also confirmed by Palestinian security officials. The PA's General Ammar explains how Hamas spots potential recruits at local mosques:

> Hamas members are there and notice him looking anxious, worried and depressed and that he's coming every day. It's a small society here—people tend to know each other. They will ask about him, discover his situation. Gradually they will begin to recruit him. They talk to him about the afterlife and tell him that paradise awaits him if he dies in the jihad. They explain to him that if he volunteers for a suicide bombing, his family name will be held in the highest respect. He'll be remembered as a *shadhid* (martyr, hero). He'll become a martyr and Hamas will give his family about $5,000, wheat, flour, sugar, other staples, and clothing. The most important thing is that the family's status will be raised significantly—they too will be treated as heroes. The condition for all this: he is not allowed to tell anyone.[28]

Hamas spotters also recruit new members on university campuses. In his statement to Israeli police in January 1993, Hamas Qassam Brigades member Salah Arouri noted that he, like so many others, was first recruited into Hamas on the campus of Palestinian universities, in his case at Hebron University.[29]

A key component of the *dawa* network is the group's reliance on charity (*zakat*) committees. These charities and social service organizations— which fund and facilitate Hamas attacks—form the backbone of the group's operational capacity. Consider the following examples cited by the FBI:

- Fadil Muhammad Salah Hamdan, a member of the Ramallah charity committee, was "directly connected with the planning of suicide attacks and the spiritual preparation of those about to commit suicide attacks, including the Mahane Yehuda attack in July 1997."

- Ahmed Saltana, head of the Jenin charity committee, was involved in transferring bomb-making materials for the preparation of explosives in 1992 and participated in a car bombing in 1993.

- Khalil 'Ali Rashad Dar Rashad, an associated member of the Orphan Care Association in Bethlehem, was known to provide shelter and assistance to Hamas fugitives, including Hamas bomb maker Muhi ad-Din ash-Sharif and Hasan Salamah, the commander behind the string of suicide bus bombings in February–March 1996.

- Nur ad-Din Kamal Asad Tahayna was in charge of the Jenin *zakat* committee computer. Tahayna was imprisoned from July to December 1994 for " 'aiding' one of the suicide bombers in the 1994 terrorist attack against an Israeli bus in Afula" and again from January 1995 to January 1996 "for conducting Hamas activities."

- Nasir Khalid Ibrahim Jarrar, another member of the Jenin *zakat* committee, was detained for three months in April 1994 "for recruiting young men to the Hamas terrorist wing" and again in January 1998 "for his connection to one of the suicide bombers in the 1994 terrorist attack against an Israeli bus in Afula, as well as his assistance to other Hamas operatives."

- 'Abd al-Jabir Muhammad Ahmad Jarrar, also a member of the Jenin *zakat* committee, was arrested in May 1993 "for transferring weapons to Hamas recruits who subsequently conducted terrorist attacks."

- 'Adnan 'Abd al-Hafiz Musbah Maswada, directorate co-chairman of the Islamic Charity Association (the Islamic Charitable Society in Hebron), was detained for several months in 1989 and again in 1994 "for Hamas activity." According to the government of Israel, "Maswada is a member of Hamas headquarters in Hebron and is connected to Hamas terrorist activities against settlers." Maswada was therefore included among the Hamas and Islamic Jihad leaders Israel deported to Lebanon in 1992.[30]

Medical institutions, such as hospitals and clinics, are also used by Hamas operatives as part of their logistical support network. Hamas is known to use the hospitals it supports to secure recruits, medical supplies, and chemicals.

In one case, Hamas recruited Mustafa Amjad, a doctor at al-Ghazi Hospital in Jenin, to help infiltrate suicide bombers into Israel from the Jenin area. After his arrest in June 2002, Amjad confessed to helping Hamas terrorists enter Israel while delivering medicines in his professional capacity.[31] In another case, Nasser Nazal, a senior Hamas operative in Qalqilya, took advantage of the fact that his brother Nidal enjoyed "freedom of passage" rights as a Palestinian Red Crescent ambulance driver. Nidal transferred weapons and messages in his ambulance from one cell to another across the West Bank.[32] Fawaz Hamdan, active in both the Hamas-funded al-Ghazi Hospital in Jenin and the *zakat* committee there, "was imprisoned for his activities in connection with Hamas, which included aiding fugitives and funding weapons purchases."[33]

In an additional case, Hamas commanders Khaled Abu Hamed and Said Kutab recruited Rashed Tarek al-Nimr, a chemist employed at hospitals in Nablus and Bethlehem, to procure chemicals for Hamas bomb making. Al-Nimr first met these and other Hamas fugitives when they hid inside hospitals where he worked to evade arrest. Over a period of months, al-Nimr provided Hamed with six containers of hydrogen peroxide, a precursor ingredient used in the production of the TATP explosive favored by Hamas. In at least one instance, Hamed specifically informed al-Nimr upon receiving the chemicals that "there would be a large explosion in Israel in the near future." Al-Nimr agreed to help find a safe place to store the chemicals, and offered to covertly transfer them to Hamas in a Palestinian ambulance. In their later request, made just days before his arrest in November 2003, al-Nimr's handlers tasked him with procuring nitrous acid and hydrogen sulfide, chemicals used to make nitroglycerine explosives.[34]

There have even been instances in which Hamas has used institutions of learning such as schools and libraries as fronts for terrorist activity. In March 2000, Palestinian security officials arrested several Hamas members and found explosives, intended for an attack against Israel, hidden in a kindergarten in Gaza's Shati refugee camp. The arrests followed a raid by Israeli commandos on a Hamas safe house in the Israeli Arab town of Taibeh. That raid and the Palestinian arrests foiled a major terrorist attack plotted by five Hamas suicide bombers.[35]

In an additional case, a Nablus homeowner rented an apartment to someone who claimed to be a schoolteacher. In fact, the schoolteacher proved to be a Hamas fugitive bomb maker who used the apartment as a safe house and bomb production lab. This became self-evident when the explosives he was handling detonated prematurely, wrecking the apartment and killing the tenant.[36]

At one point, Hamas operatives in Gaza were in need of a place to safely photocopy Hamas leaflets (claims of responsibility for attacks, political messages, propaganda) they received from the West Bank cell that produced them. The Gaza cell commander recounted photocopying the materials himself "in the library on 'Umar al-Muranawi Street beside the court house of appeals through a fellow named Nazim who works as a caretaker there as a cover for his Hamas activity." Hamas so valued its access to the library, and the services Nazim provided, that it contributed to the library. "We helped him buy books for four hundred dinars" for the library and "bought a photocopying machine for 4,000 [Israeli] shekels and saw to it that it was taken to the library."[37]

As early as 1996, Israeli authorities identified Hamas logistical support networks as critically important support structures facilitating Hamas attacks. In the wake of a series of suicide attacks in February and March 1996, then–prime minister Shimon Peres told the Israeli Knesset (parliament): "Hamas has established charitable organizations in order to camouflage its true nature. These charitable organizations raise funds abroad, supposedly to aid orphans, but in fact they use the contributions to purchase explosives."[38]

The *dawa*'s logistical role in the attacks of early 1996 is among the most fully documented examples available in unclassified sources. Hamas military commander Hasan Salamah openly acknowledged the support he received from Hamas facilitators, "from contacts to recruiting, to locating the places, and all these matters."[39] After sneaking into Israel from Gaza, Hamas *dawa* facilitators ferried Salamah across Israel's midsection into the West Bank, avoiding Israeli checkpoints as they traveled from town to town in the West Bank before arriving in Jerusalem. According to Salamah, Hamas operatives provided him with safe houses, scouts to identify targets, and recruiters to find the individual suicide bombers.

The operatives came from West Bank colleges and vocational schools, and the safe houses included private homes and, in at least one case, a Ramallah mosque where Salamah met a potential suicide bomber for final vetting and assignment. Hamas logistical operatives drove Majdi Abu Wardah, one of the suicide bombers, to a Jerusalem safe house where others shaved his beard and dressed him to look like an Israeli. The following morning, Abu Wardah boarded the number 18 bus on Jerusalem's Jaffa Road and detonated his explosive vest killing twenty civilians, including three Americans, and wounding ten,[40] including another American.[41]

Dawa activists frequently play tactical roles in Hamas terrorism. *Dawa* activists are often used to collect preoperational intelligence on potential targets, to lead suicide bombers to their target sites, and to bolster the cover identity of suicide bombers on route to their attacks. For example, Ahlam Tamimi, a Jordanian woman working as a journalist in Ramallah, confessed after her capture that she led a Hamas suicide bomber to the Sbarro restaurant in Jerusalem on 9 August 2001. On 30 June 2001, just weeks after being recruited into Hamas, Tamimi played an even more direct role in a Hamas attack by personally placing a bomb hidden in a beer bottle at a Jerusalem supermarket.[42]

Today, Hamas leaders openly call for civilian support for Hamas terrorists wanted by authorities. In August 2003, Hamas leader Rantisi urged average Palestinians to help Hamas fugitives, writing that "protecting the fighters and to offer them support is part of our religion, is part of the holy war."[43]

Hamas operatives frequently hold day jobs working within the group's *dawa* system, which provides both a salary to live on and cover for planning and carrying out terror attacks. For example, documents seized from the offices of the Islamic Relief Agency (IRA) revealed that the charity had been paying the salaries of ten West Bank Hamas activists.[44] Additionally, the placement of battle-hardened operatives in key *dawa* positions, especially on charity committees, streamlines the organization's ability to deftly skim and launder funds from its charities and social service organizations.

According to a Federal Bureau of Investigation (FBI) report on the Holy Land Foundation, a Hamas charity that funds many *zakat* committees, the funded committees "are controlled by Hamas. GOI [government of Israel] analysis has also determined that Hamas activists have been elected or appointed to senior leadership positions on these *zakat* committees."[45] The Hamas social welfare activists running these organizations in the West Bank and Gaza are often closely tied to the group's terror cells or may even be current or former members of such cells.

Buying Support

Hamas aid buys the support of those who benefit from the group's largesse. Palestinians dependent on Hamas charity are likely to actively assist Hamas by ferrying fugitives, serving as couriers for funds or weapons, storing and maintaining explosives, and more. Recipients of Hamas aid know better than to ask questions when asked for a favor by Hamas *dawa* activists. Hamas capitalizes on this passive support, employing "unsuspecting" Palestinians to unknowingly launder and transfer funds on behalf of the group.[46]

Sheikh Yassin himself proudly noted, "We don't go looking for people, they come to us." Citing one of the many examples of people won over by Hamas financial support, Yassin talked of a family of ten living in one room: "We gave them 1,200 shekels ($300). Sometimes it's a sack of flour, or at very least the taxi fare home" from visiting Yassin.[47] As the mother of ten children and a recipient of Hamas aid told a reporter, "All we know is they [Hamas] are the ones who bring us food."[48] However, in the words of an Israeli defense official, "In the territories, there are no free lunches:

those who receive help from the Islamic associations pay with support for Hamas."[49]

Ibrahim al-Yazuri, an original participant in the founding of Hamas, offered this description of Hamas' all-strings-attached philosophy regarding charitable giving:

> Everyone knows that the Islamic Resistance Movement, Hamas, is a Palestinian jihad movement that strives for the liberation of all Palestine, from the [Mediterranean] sea to the [Jordan] river, from the north to the south, from the tyrannical Israeli occupation, and this is the main part of its concern. Social work is carried out in support of this aim, and it is considered to be part of the Hamas movement's strategy. . . . The Hamas movement is concerned about its individuals and its elements, especially those who engage in the blessed jihad against the hateful Israeli occupation, since they are subjected to detention or martyrdom. The movement takes care of their families and their children and provides them with as much material and moral support as it can. This is one of the fundamental truths of Islamic work and thus represents the duties of the Islamic state. . . . The movement provides this aid through the support and assistance it gives to the *zakat* committees and the Islamic associations and institutions in the Gaza Strip.[50]

Hamas grant making is largely determined by a cold cost–benefit analysis that links the amount of aid awarded to the extent of support that aid will buy. According to Yassin, Hamas distributes $2 to $3 million in monthly handouts to the relatives of Palestinian suicide bombers, "martyrs" killed in attacks on Israelis, and prisoners in Israeli jails.[51] According to the FBI, "evidence strongly suggests that the Holy Land Foundation has provided crucial financial support for families of Hamas suicide bombers, as well as the Palestinians who adhere to the Hamas movement."[52] By providing these annuities to families of Hamas members, the FBI concludes, "Hamas provides a constant flow of suicide volunteers and buttresses a terrorist infrastructure heavily reliant on moral support of the Palestinian populace."[53]

Individuals tied to Hamas receive more assistance than those unaffiliated with the organization, while members linked to terrorist activity receive even more. An Israeli government report notes that Hamas charitable organizations accord preference to those close to the movement and assure that they receive increased financial assistance. According to the report, families of Hamas activists killed or wounded while carrying out terror attacks and those imprisoned for their involvement in such attacks "typically receive an initial, one-time grant of between $500–$5,000, as well as a monthly allowance of approximately $100." Significantly, "the families of Hamas terrorists usually receive larger payments than those of non-Hamas terrorists."[54]

This finding was reinforced by materials confiscated in a 1995 raid of the Holy Land Foundation's office in Beit Hanina outside Jerusalem. Israeli authorities seized financial records of fund transfers from the Holy Land Foundation to the Islamic Aid Committee (also known as the Islamic Relief Agency, or IRA) and lists of people supported by those funds. Analysis of this material revealed that individuals unaffiliated with Hamas received relatively small monthly payments. In contrast, families of Hamas terrorists killed or detained in the process of conducting terror attacks received the largest stipends. Examples include the family of Yasir Hajjaj, "a Hamas activist serving a life sentence for placing an explosive charge on a Tel Aviv beach on July 28, 1990, killing a Jewish tourist from Canada"; the brother of Ra'id Zakarna, a Hamas terrorist who committed a suicide bombing in Afula in April 1994; and the family of Sulayman Idan, killed during a car-bomb attack in Beit-El in October 1993.[55]

Similar evidence was found in searches of the IRA offices in Nazareth on 27 July and 8 November 1995. Records seized there revealed that "the IRA transferred funds to, among others, the families of Hamas activists who carried out several terrorist attacks, including kidnapping and murder of civilians, policemen, and soldiers" as well as families of prisoners, deportees, and Hamas terrorists killed during attacks. According to IRA documents, the agency paid salaries to ten Hamas activists in the West Bank who were imprisoned or deported in the past and were acting as IRA representatives. Investigators uncovered forms seeking financial support for the families of "the fallen," which reported details of the attack in which the terrorist was killed, his former activities in Hamas, and a description of the special circumstances of the family of "the fallen."[56] U.S. Secretary of State Colin Powell highlighted the twisted nature of such benevolence, saying, "I think it's a real problem when you incentivize in any way suicide bombings."[57]

Organized Radicalization

In its effort to Islamize the Palestinian national struggle, Hamas invests significant resources in molding Palestinian culture. Experts have noted that giving the Palestinian cause an Islamic flavor is part of Hamas's effort "to link the particular Palestinian struggle with the wider Islamic wave in the Muslim world."[58]

To this end, Hamas charities, social service organizations, hospitals, schools, and mosques openly laud suicide bombing, teach hate, and incite even the youngest and most impressionable of Palestinians to violence. For example, the graduation ceremony at a kindergarten run by al-Jam'iya al-Islamiya, a Hamas charitable association run by Sheikh Ahmad Bahar, featured 1,600 preschool-aged children wearing uniforms and carrying pretend rifles. A five-year-old girl reenacted attacks on Israelis by dipping her hands in red paint, mimicking the bloodied hands Palestinians proudly displayed after the lynching of two Israelis in Ramallah.[59]

The Hamas radicalization and incitement campaign continues through the course of a Palestinian student's academic career. The Hamas Islamic Student Movement in the Bethlehem area distributed instruction cards bearing the pictures of Hamas suicide bombers and others killed carrying out terrorist attacks and encouraging Palestinian youth to follow in their footsteps.[60] Other educational material produced by Hamas *dawa* activists and distributed by the Hamas charity committees includes collectible postcards featuring Hamas and Islamic Jihad suicide bombers with rhythmic Arabic inscriptions such as, "Oh, Mother, the time for leaving [this world] is quickly approaching," and, "Oh, Mother, do not speak of me should I fall and lie dead on the ground."[61] In the al-Fawwar refugee camp, key rings and children's trading cards also feature suicide bombers, and teenage singing groups, such as "The Martyrs," sing their praises.[62]

Radicalization is no less prominent at Palestinian institutions of higher education. Hamas incitement material appears on university campuses, including pamphlets, posters, and a printed timetable for university lectures featuring pictures of Hamas suicide bombers. One class schedule featured Karim Nimr Mafarja, a Qassam Brigade member, with the inscription, "The *shaheeds* [martyrs] are with their Lord and light shines from them."[63]

Hamas members on college campuses, however, not only support the group's attacks but actively participate in them. Campaigning at Bir Zeit University student elections, Hamas candidates reenacted suicide bombings by blowing up models of Israeli buses and wore sample models of Hamas's homemade Qassam rockets on their shoulders. In a campus debate, a Hamas candidate taunted his Fatah challenger, asking, "Hamas activists in this University killed 135 Zionists. How many did Fatah activists from Bir Zeit kill?"[64]

According to Sheikh Bahar, Hamas summer camps are especially successful in indoctrinating religious and secular youth alike. Bahar explained that by teaching children the history of Islam and surrounding them with pictures of Hamas suicide bombers, the camps instill "seeds of hate against Israel."[65] Children socialized in this environment make willing and supple recruits.

In one case, Hamas military commander Muhammad Zakarna recruited a twelve-year-old Palestinian boy to take small arms to Hamas terrorists across the West Bank, to shoot at Israelis traveling West Bank roads, and to carry out a "sacrificial terror attack" targeting the West Bank settlement of Maale Adumim. The boy, in his statement to police, expressed no remorse, stating instead, "I have no heart, like the Jews have no heart," and adding, "I hate Jews, and at any opportunity I have, I will kill Jews. I am a *shaheed* [martyr]."[66] At the child's hearing, the judge commented, "From everything taken together, there emerges a picture that in the heart of a young child influenced by the adults around him is aroused a hatred that leads him to carry out actions that are among the gravest in the law books."[67]

According to press reports, moderate Palestinian parents find it increasingly difficult to shelter their children from Hamas recruiters seeking to breed future suicide bombers. One mother recounted how her son's behavior changed when he started going to the mosque regularly:

> At first I thought it was normal when my son Muhammad, who is eighteen, started going to the mosque frequently. But when I found out he was watching films about suicide attacks, I was worried. . . . My son was going to the mosque late at night and early in the morning, adding to our fears. . . . His behavior changed. He became introverted, which made his father and me search his room and spy on his comings and goings. . . . We even locked the door to stop him going out. . . . We later found out that those in charge of the mosque are members of Hamas, which teaches children about jihad and shows them documentaries about suicide bombings.[68]

The father of fifteen-year-old Hamas recruit Musa Ziadah told a similar tale. Originally pleased with his son's growing faith, the father did not realize Hamas had begun radicalizing his son when the boy was just ten years old and sweeping the mosque floors. Musa would later tell reporters that Hamas "taught me about the heroes of Islam who were killed as saints and how they are now in heaven beside God. . . . I also learned that the Jews have no right to exist on this land, which belongs to Muslims."[69]

By all accounts, polling data corroborates the anecdotal evidence of Hamas' successful radicalization efforts. According to an April 2001 survey conducted by the Islamic University in Gaza—itself intimately tied to Hamas—while 49 percent of children aged nine to sixteen claimed to have participated in the *intifada*, a terrifying 73 percent claimed they hoped to become martyrs.[70]

Indeed, the Palestinian Authority (PA) grew concerned about Hamas's successful penetration of its Ministry of Education and the group's radicalization of Palestinian youth in PA schools. According to a PA intelligence report, "The Hamas movement has begun to constitute a real threat to the PA's political vision, its interests, presence, and influence. The influence of the Hamas movement through its teachers in the [PA] schools is absolutely clear."[71]

Supporting Aid, Not Terror

David Aufhauser, the former counsel to the Treasury Department and chair of the National Security Council's policy coordinating committee on terrorist financing, described the drawing of distinctions between terrorist groups' charitable and military wings as "sophistry" and maintains that "the idea that there's a firewall between the two defies common sense."[72] He adds,

> No one is at war with the idea of building hospitals or orphanages or taking care of people who are displaced. But the same people that govern how to apply the money to hospitals govern how to apply the money to killing people, and you cannot abdicate responsibility for one and celebrate what you're doing on the other: it remains blood money.[73]

The State Department concurs: "As long as Hamas continues to rely on terrorism to achieve its political ends, we should not draw a distinction between its military and humanitarian arms, since funds provided to one can be used to support the other."[74] For any renewed peace initiative to take hold, the international community must endorse this basic principle. Recognizing this, President Bush issued a call on 25 June 2003 for "swift, decisive action against [Palestinian] terror groups such as Hamas, to cut off their funding and support."[75] Such cooperation, however, remains elusive largely due to the veil of legitimacy Hamas charitable work provides for its terror attacks.

Islamic social welfare groups must not be given a free pass simply because they provide humanitarian support alongside their support role for terrorism. Instead, the international community must insist that humanitarian support for Palestinians be divorced from support for terrorist activity. To do otherwise is to be complicit in the Hamas campaign to destroy any prospect of Israeli–Palestinian reconciliation. It is essential that Europe, the Gulf states, and other countries strictly regulate which Palestinian charities receive international aid and shut down front organizations raising funds for Hamas and other terrorist groups.

To be sure, Palestinians face dire social welfare needs not addressed by the PA, creating an opportunity Hamas eagerly exploits. Tolerating this exploitation is neither in the interest of Israeli–Palestinian peace nor Palestinian humanitarian assistance. Islamic social welfare groups that contaminate their benevolent activities with support for terrorism muddy the waters of charitable giving and good works, making the job that much harder for those genuinely trying to better conditions in the West Bank and Gaza.

Shutting down the Hamas *dawa* must be accompanied by a cooperative effort by the international donor community to fill the gap and provide organized humanitarian aid for needy Palestinians in a way that does not support terrorists, facilitate their attacks, fill their ranks with new recruits, and incite society. Cutting off the flow of funds to Hamas and replacing its terror-spawning social network with an organized and regulated international aid effort are now more urgent than ever.

Conclusion

In the wake of continued Hamas attacks, White House spokeswoman Claire Buchan called dismantling Palestinian terror networks "the highest priority."[76] And in an interview on Egyptian television, Secretary of State Powell criticized Hamas for stressing the temporary nature of the short-lived cease-fire. Powell continued, "It is time to end the use of terror as a way of achieving a political objective. It's part of the solution for the Middle East. It's also part of the global campaign against terrorism."[77]

Indeed, cracking down on terrorism is key both to meeting the social welfare needs of Palestinians in the West Bank and Gaza and for returning to negotiations over a viable political settlement. To do this, donor countries must not be distracted from debunking the myth that Hamas conducts legitimate charity work parallel but unrelated to its terrorist attacks. It is worth recounting, as noted above, that Hamas activists meeting in 1994 feared that American and Israeli investment in Palestinian territories would undercut "the Palestinian anger, desperation, revolution by raising the standards of living of the Palestinians" and hoped "the failure of the self rule administration to solve the problems of the Palestinian population and providing the needed services to them will be detrimental to the peace accord."[78] Therefore, they concluded, "to defeat the [Oslo] accord we [Hamas] should make services available to the population."[79] Indeed, Hamas social welfare support is both tactical (as a financial and logistical support network) and strategic (as a means of undermining the PA and thwarting the peace process).

Moreover, the continued suicide bombings perpetrated by groups like Hamas, Islamic Jihad, and al-Aqsa Martyrs Brigades demonstrate that such groups cannot be co-opted, nor can they be eliminated through military tactics alone. While Israeli forces have killed several key leaders (including Yassin, Shehada, and Rantisi) and arrested many more, the group remains capable of executing deadly attacks. Indeed, between the money they receive from "charitable" donations and the assistance of state sponsors like Iran, Palestinian terrorist groups are if anything better funded and more capable now than ever before. Cutting off the flow of funds to these groups, and replacing their largesse with an organized and regulated international aid effort to address the real and immediate needs of the Palestinian people, is now more urgent than ever.

CHAPTER 10

Terrorism, Gender, and Ideology: A Case Study of Women who Join the Revolutionary Armed Forces of Colombia (FARC)

KEITH STANSKI

For all the attention terrorism receives from policymakers, media outlets, and the public, women's involvement in terrorist activities remains widely overlooked. As Jean Bethke Elshtain reflects, "Certainly when most of us think 'terrorists' we do not *see* 'woman.' The perpetrators, or the alleged perpetrators, who have flashed across our television screens in recent years are pretty much a youthful male lot."[1] Prevailing understandings of men as the primary perpetrators of violence, frequently augmented by the media's portrayal of terrorism, disassociates women with terrorism. Terrorists are too often profiled as wild-eyed male fanatics.

When women are identified as terrorists, often it is as a result of their participation in violent, and hence dramatic, acts. Analysts especially scrutinized the 2002 suicide attack by Wafa Idris, as it defied the conventional wisdom that Palestinian militants employed only male suicide bombers. Similarly, the Tamil Tigers received special attention in 1991 when a young Tamil woman detonated explosives as she knelt at the feet of Rajiv Gandhi, killing the former Indian prime minister. Chechen women implicated in several acts of terror—including the Beslan school takeover in 2004—have been dubbed "black widows."[2] Overall, relatively little is known about female terrorists beyond their involvement in violent acts.

Fixating on dramatic acts of violence reveals little about why and how women participate in terrorist movements. As terrorism continues to strain international relations, the consequence of having inaccurate understandings of who perpetrates political violence and how they become involved in organized campaigns only grows. In order to develop a more complete understanding of women's involvement in terrorist activities, researchers and policymakers should look beyond violent acts and analyze factors that shape women's enlistment in terrorist movements. Examining the social conditions and ideology that influence women's recruitment into and involvement in terrorist movements can reveal the more subtle origins, nature, and complexities of women's participation. With these insights, policymakers, the media, and the public may be more likely to approach and address terrorism not only as a violent political strategy, but as the product of interrelated social, cultural, political, and economic elements.

This chapter explores how women enter and function in the Revolutionary Armed Forces of Colombia (FARC)—Colombia's largest terrorist movement. After outlining the history and ideology (or political vision) of the FARC movement, the chapter draws from a combination of media accounts, human rights reports, and interviews with recently demobilized female FARC members to examine the role women play in the movement. Overall, focusing on how social conditions and ideology facilitate women's involvement in the FARC reveals the ways in which ideology allows substantial and substantive contradictions to pass unexamined, as described in the chapter's conclusion.

History and Early Ideology of the FARC

A legacy of socioeconomic inequality, sustained political violence, and Cold War tensions fueled the formation of the FARC in 1964. Beginning in the 1920s and 1930s, peasants and their reformist allies fought land-owning elites over harsh working and living conditions, disputed property rights, and limited land access for smaller agrarians.[3] This class conflict mimicked the political divide between the Liberal Party, which was comprised of reform-minded peasants and their supporters, and the Conservative Party, which was composed of landowners, their peasants, and the hierarchy of the Catholic Church. Decades of political violence and dispute escalated when Jorge Eliécer Gaitán, a charismatic Liberal and land-reform movement leader, was assassinated in Bogotá in 1948. A period of violence known simply as *La Violencia* pitted supporters of the two major parties against each other. More than 300,000 deaths mark this period as one of the bloodiest in Colombian history.

As violence marred the countryside, squatters and poor peasants formed self-defense organizations in an effort to defend their land parcels from state and large landowners. Under the protection of these armed groups, peasant movements formed "independent republics"—plots of land organized, occupied, and cultivated by peasants. Predominantly in the southern and central regions of the country, these enclaves became centers of Liberal and Communist supporters. According to Dennis Rempe, U.S. intelligence estimated that roughly forty self-defense groups, comprised of more than 6,000 men, defended the independent republics.[4]

In 1958, Liberal and Conservative parties officially ended *La Violencia* by agreeing to share public offices and alternate the presidency in a plan known as the National Front. In an effort to rebuild the country and quell continued violence in the countryside, the government invited self-defense groups to lay down their arms, disband independent republics, and reintegrate into civilian society. Groups that refused were violently removed. State military campaigns to subdue independent republics, however, yielded only mixed results, as individuals displaced by the state largely fled to the safety of other independent republics.

In 1964, the Colombian army undertook what would be the most notorious and disastrous attack on the independent republics—the Battle of Marquetalia. According to the FARC, more than 16,000 soldiers attacked and captured the holdout of Manuel Marulanda Velez and Jacobo Arenas, two infamous peasant leaders, only to find that it had been abandoned; Marulanda and forty-seven other combatants had fled.[5] No longer able to remain in fixed localities, Marulanda and his followers regrouped as the FARC and decided to shed their defensive posture in favor of a mobile guerrilla war strategy. The group describes the Battle of Marquetalia as the "seed" of their struggle for a "New Colombia."[6]

The FARC's leaders explained their early struggle as a revolutionary effort on behalf of all marginalized Colombians. In moving from a defense organization to a mobile fighting movement, the group's goal of self-preservation and land reform, as embodied by the independent republics, evolved into a broader political strategy to capture state power. The FARC, by their own account, "arose in the course of the [Marquetalia] confrontation with a revolutionary program calling together all the citizens who dream of a Colombia for Colombians, with equality of opportunities and equitable distribution of wealth, and where among us we all can build peace with social equality and sovereignty."[7]

The FARC's call for "a Colombia for Colombians" reflects the movement's rural origins and its close ties with the Colombian Communist Party (PCC). Initially comprised of and led by agrarians fleeing violence, the FARC understood and presented itself as a telluric movement; the purpose and legitimacy of the FARC emanated from Colombia's legacy of inequality. Similar to the PCC, the FARC pushed a highly nationalistic, Marxist-Leninist platform of massive redistribution of land and wealth, state control of natural resources, and a substantial increase in social welfare. While scholars debate the exact influence the PCC had on the FARC, the group was founded on the principle that they would have to take up arms and combat the state in order to realize their revolutionary vision.

The FARC's Current Mission and Composition

After more than forty years of combat and the end of the Cold War, the FARC has drifted away from its strict nationalist, Marxist-Leninist ideol-

ogy. The movement has adopted a more elastic ideology, labeled "Bolivarianism" in reference to Simon Bolivar's independence campaigns in the
early nineteenth century. The FARC uses the term to encompass their vision for better social protection for lower classes, sweeping agricultural reform, and local autonomy. During negotiations with the government
between 1999 and 2002, FARC demands included "development and economic modernization with social justice" and "democratic participation in
national, regional and municipal decisions."[8] These proposals reflect a recent incorporation of liberal and nationalist ideas into the FARC's political platform. While Bolivarianism may not depart completely from classical
socialist platforms, it does demonstrate an ideological flexibility unseen earlier in the FARC's history.

The group's ideological evolution has also altered how the FARC presents itself relative to the Colombian government. Román Ortiz notes that
instead of continuing to question the legitimacy of the Colombian government, the FARC has "heightened their critique of the government's incom-
petence in dealing with the country's biggest problems (social inequality,
crime, and deficient public services), while increasingly presenting themselves as a credible alternative for 'good government.'"[9] Portraying the
movement as an alternate public administrator has ameliorated their message of political change, particularly in remote, rural regions of Colombia
where government services do not reach. In some cases, the FARC is the
primary provider of social services, conflict mediation, and public order in
these areas.

In establishing a more flexible ideology and new political profile, the
FARC has come to embrace women in their cause. The group depicts
women as vulnerable to the same inequality, exploitation, and injustice that
the movement is combating. FARC publications about women regularly
reference statistics about poverty, forced displacement, and violence dis-
proportionately affecting women. In an undated article detailing women's
exploitation and suffering in capitalist systems, the FARC cite statistics
about homicide being the leading cause of violent death for women, sexual violence being perpetrated against women and young girls, and women
heading the majority of displaced households.[10] These statistics are treated
as evidence of how Colombian women—regardless of their class, ethnicity,
or age—are oppressed. This portrayal is captured in a FARC leader's explanation of why women join the FARC: "A woman perceives injustice
through every pore in her body; from the moment she is born, she is discriminated against."[11]

In light of the systematic hardships women face, the FARC presents itself as a relief from everyday discrimination and a solution for women committed to solving inequality. The group describes its political project as a
means for women to fight for equal treatment and the protection of their
rights. In a statement denouncing the discrimination women face, the FARC
"invites [all women] to participate in our just revolutionary fight for the

New Colombia with social justice, for better living, dignity and independence."[12] Emblematic of its vision of equality, the FARC bills itself as a community where men and women are equal. A press release marking the International Day for Women (8 May) explains, "In our organization, women and men acquire the same duties and rights in the fight to take political power for the people."[13] The FARC's ideology of equality between men and women is consistently marshaled when the FARC discusses women's involvement in the movement.

The development of an ideology of equality coincides with a noticeable shift in the FARC's composition. In 1964, only two women were among the last 48 fighters resisting government forces at the Battle of Marquetalia. This group would later form the nucleus of the FARC. While noted historian Arturo Alape has documented women's involvement in the early forms of the FARC, recent growth in the movement has seen women's participation reach unprecedented levels. Several estimates suggest that upwards of 40 percent of the 18,000-member movement are women, with some units approaching 50 percent.[14] Although it is uncertain how the development of a political platform about women influenced the increase in women's enlistment, it is reasonable to believe that the two are closely related. The agenda likely facilitates women's enlistment by asserting that, as members, women can and do contribute to achieving the FARC's vision of a "New Colombia."

With this review of FARC's history, ideology, and demographics in mind, it is useful to focus on the experiences of women in FARC. Media accounts, human rights reports, and interviews with recently demobilized female combatants reveal four inter-related dimensions of activity—recruitment, training, discipline, and relationships—that illustrate how social conditions and ideology shape women's recruitment and involvement in the FARC.[15] In particular, interviews with women indicate that FARC offered them a life of adventure and meaning, as well as a sense of gender equality (in both training and the enforcement of discipline), that could not be found in civilian society. However, as discussed toward the end of this chapter, it is important to recognize how terrorist movements' ideologies allow these promises to pass unquestioned and unfulfilled.

Recruitment

At age thirteen, Laura[16] left her home in a rural region of the Department of Arauca to join the FARC. After describing her childhood as boring and uneventful, she recalls the moment when a contact in the community told her and her sister about the opportunities that awaited:

> [A]n older man told us about a uniformed man, that would give us schooling and all this other stuff. Since we were in my mother's house and she didn't

give us education or anything else, I joined the group with my sister, but she died there.[17]

It is not certain what Laura's contact promised her when she joined, or whether Laura faulted her mother for her lack of education, but she clearly perceived that joining an armed group—despite the accompanying uncertainties and inherent dangers—offered more opportunities than she could find by staying in her community. Human Rights Watch points out that the voluntary decision to join irregular military forces may be more of a reflection of the dismal opportunities available to children in rural Colombia than an exercise of free will.[18] Together with her sister, Laura decided to pursue the promises of a recruiter.

The recruiter's pledges were bolstered by his persistence and selective message. While Laura only described him in vague terms, the recruiter's attempts to enlist Laura and her sister seem sustained:

> Well, then every time he came to our house he asked us whether we would go [to join the movement]. We decided to go because he said it would give us an education that staying at home wouldn't. So we left.[19]

The regular recruiting pitch and community presence seems to have reinforced the potential benefits of joining the group. But sustained recruiting did not completely familiarize Laura with the movement. Interestingly, Laura initially did not know what group she was joining and only learned that she was a new member of the FARC when she arrived for training.

The recruiter's continued and choice presentation did not convince everyone that joining the movement was the best option for Laura and her sister. Laura acknowledges that her mother did not share her daughters' excitement, and disapproved of their enlistment:

> The day [sister] and I told our mother that we were joining she cried and told us that we should not go to the [movement] because it was a very harsh life, but we did not listen to her. We said no, that we would go [to the movement] because they would give us an education . . . and well, she did not say anything else. Mom would come looking for us but the group would deny that we were there.[20]

In trying to prevent her daughters' recruitment, and in her subsequent attempts to convince them to return home, Laura's mother demonstrates the relative nature of the FARC's glamour. Perhaps because they are more impressionable and desperate for opportunities than older people, young women appear to be more exposed to the FARC's message, while those more familiar with the legacy of Colombia's armed movements may be more likely to discount the benefits of taking up arms. Part of the mother's disapproval could also stem from her knowledge and understanding of the group. Knowing with whom to speak or where to reach them in order to bring her daughters home suggests some familiarity with the FARC's local presence. Subtly, Laura's description also speaks to the movement's determination to retain its recruits. In addition to deflecting pleas from parents such as those of Laura's mother, according to several reports the FARC issues dire warning to any combatant caught deserting.[21]

For some young women, joining the FARC may be less an issue of recruitment and more about flight. After growing up with her grandmother and serving as an informant for the FARC, María Clara joined the movement when she was thirteen. When asked why she joined, María Clara is clear about her difficulties with her grandmother:

> I left because I wasn't raised by my mother, but by my grandmother. She locked me up often and told me that she didn't want me around. And one day my grandmother gave me a real beating so I left there and entered [the FARC].[22]

María Clara portrays joining the FARC as a deliberate, if not calculated, decision. She identified the FARC as an escape from the hostility and abuse she regularly suffered while living with her grandmother. Like María Clara, some potential recruits—especially those in rural villages—might consider joining the FARC as a way to ensure their safety. The uncertainty and risk that accompanies an armed movement, for some, may not compare to the constant violence at home.

The FARC's appeal provides more than a potential for escape and new opportunities. The perception of danger and violence that surrounds the movement may deter some potential recruits, while attracting others with a mystique not found in rural life. After having some connection with the movement, María Clara still saw the FARC as a vehicle for achieving her dreams. María Clara was resolute about her aspirations, and saw the FARC as the best way to achieve them:

> I wanted to be a doctor. But I was not able to because I didn't have the means. I did not have a mother and because of this, I made the decision to leave [for the FARC]. When I was there everything seemed cool.[23]

María Clara realized that staying in her community would not allow her to achieve her dream of becoming a doctor. While the FARC may not lead directly to medicine, joining the group did depart from her seemingly certain fate of a life of poverty. As María Clara clearly states, at least in the FARC she could lead an exciting or "cool" life. No accounts have yet been published about how young girls perceive FARC members;[24] however, one can speculate that girls may be attracted to the movement's lifestyle, particularly if they experience boredom or abuse at home. When recruiting young girls, the FARC likely exploits the monotony of domestic life in rural settings by embellishing the image and ideology of the movement to fulfill their recruits' desires.

Training

Training appears to be one of the first contexts shaped by the notion of the FARC being a space of equality between men and women. Both sexes receive the same basic training upon entering the movement. In their interviews, the women emphasized the arms training they received in preparation for combat. Laura explains the training as an accelerated process:

> When I entered, they gave me little training because, for example, they often put a six month training course into three months. It also depends on your intelligence, because if one learns quickly like that you finish. But no, I [received] about three months and then I was off to combat.[25]

Some may attribute men and women sharing training to the equal demands the FARC claims to place on both genders. It should not be assumed, however, that men and women have equal opportunities to receive advanced training. As Laura mentioned, training "depends on your intelligence." However, it is not clear how prepared trainers are to recognize a woman's excellence and recommend her entrance into more advanced leadership positions. While training may be presented as one early example of equality in the FARC, the rigor of advanced training may sustain a tradition of men filling most leadership positions.

The consequences of training extend beyond the actual instruction. Training involves imparting authority, prestige, and identity upon new recruits. Laura's description of training focuses on arms and tactics: "They show you, for example, how to handle arms, a way of chasing, how to maneuver when in combat . . . how to throw grenades, how to shoot a rifle, everything."[26] According to Serena, a friend of Laura who also recently left the FARC, the training taught new recruits "how you have to take it out on the enemy in combat so they don't kill you . . . [and] how to defend ourselves."[27] The effect of receiving training in weapons, tactics, and self-defense should not be underestimated nor considered the same for all women. In the case of Laura and Serena, their arms training may have been the first formal vocational training that they shared with men. While accelerated, FARC training provides a certain responsibility and authority. For many new recruits, a "military uniform" can help reverse a loss of self-esteem and, for some, can even serve as a form of empowerment. The specific knowledge imparted during training is part of a greater induction into the movement and exposure to the movement's beliefs.

Training also raises issues of physical capacity. Men and women are expected to fulfill the same physical demands during training. Women interviewed for this study expressed a mixture of pride and disbelief when describing their ability to withstand the rigors of military training. Serena surmised that life in the countryside pales in comparison to the movement. She concludes, "[The FARC] is worse I say. It is harder [in the movement] than the work one does in the country; they work one much harder in the [FARC]."[28] She noted that even though she was fourteen upon joining FARC, she was expected to keep pace with the training, marching, and other strenuous activity. The physical demands of the FARC surprised some of the interviewees. María Clara recalls,

> I spent three months in one [location], and three months in another and this was very hard on me. [The training] cut my feet until they bled, like open flesh. I slept without blankets or anything else.[29]

The physical demands faced by men and women are closely linked to an understanding of equality among FARC combatants. Although combatants' strength varies biologically (according to sex), these women's testimonies suggest that performance expectations are the same for men and women.[30] Part of the women's sense that performance expectations do not vary may be due to the inherently physical nature of the lifestyle. The level of self-sufficiency in carrying one's gear, keeping pace with the group, and maintaining order may contribute to the impression that training demonstrated a level of gender equality in the movement.

Discipline

In reflecting on the differences between civilian and FARC life, the women interviewed for this research identified a slight, but important, difference relative to discipline. Although they noted that they were subject to "orders," the penalties they faced for disobedience at home did not compare to those in the FARC. Serena explains the difference in a realistic generalization:

> [When] one is at home and your mother tells you [to do something], then one might be brave and leave ... but when one arrives [at the movement] they force you to submit to everything they say, it is an order. For example, they order you to make a hole and if you don't do it, the first time to their satisfaction, [or] if you do not fulfill more than five orders, they beat you [to the point of death] and bury you in a polyester bag.[31]

Serena seems to trust that punishment that accompanies disobeying an order—or not fulfilling it to a commander's satisfaction—acts as a measure against impunity. Unlike many areas of civilian society, both public and private, all combatants could expect an immediate consequence for breaking established rules. The discipline of the FARC may be understood as helping to ease, or perhaps even erase, the notion of male superiority found in civilian society by maintaining a sense of equality among all men and women in the basic functioning of the movement.[32] By extension, perhaps the FARC's emphasis on the equality of discipline enforcement, regardless of gender, helps women find a greater sense of self as equal to their male counterparts—an unusual experience, considering the male-dominated culture found in much of Latin America.

Living under a military hierarchy, however, is not without sacrifices. Many of the simple freedoms of civilian society are absent in the FARC. From his research on FARC, Arturo Alape quotes a woman named Rubiela as she explains having sacrificed civilian freedoms:

> Here [in the FARC] everything is different, even going to the bathroom or any other place—you have to ask permission for everything. There is an internal order that must be followed and it's for everyone; you start to butt heads, you know? Because you can't go wherever you want when you want and come back when you want . . . no, you have limited time and you have to follow the rules. From the time you join they explain these norms to you, and if you promise to follow the norms and statutes that guide it, then you have to do it.[33]

The regimen of the FARC is an abrupt change from civilian society. As a collective of combatants—one in which order is integral for the survival and success of the group—members must relinquish part of their individuality and subscribe to shared rules. Strictly read in these terms, the disciplinary mechanisms present a picture of equality in the movement.

Relationships in the FARC

To mitigate the impact of sexual relationships on the organization and on combat readiness, FARC attempts to regulate intimate relationships between men and women. According to a number of personal and journalistic accounts, commanders must approve all intimate relationships.[34] Laura explicitly mentioned the commanders' oversight as a primary difference between relationships in the FARC and civilian society:

> [T]he difference is, for example, if you are my partner, and I leave for the front, I ask [a commander] to stay the night with you. But [I could only stay] Sundays and Wednesdays.[35]

Regimenting combatants' sexual relationships is not inconsequential. In effect, the commanders' supervision serves as a median between combatants as revolutionaries and combatants as individuals. Overseeing relationships provides some assurance that relationships do not detract from (or perhaps complicate) combatants' involvement in the FARC's revolutionary struggle, while also helping combatants manage their relationships. Although it is not clear how vigilant commanders are in supervising relationships, it is reasonable to presume that in order to ensure healthy relationships, their presence and potential intervention exceeds what might be found in civilian society.

For many women, the FARC's oversight of relationships may be a welcomed change from civilian society. In his research on women in the FARC, Alape notes that the treatment of relationships allows women a certain level of agency in their relationships that could not be found in the civilian society.[36] When asked whether she "feels like a fulfilled women in the [FARC]," Sonia (a woman identified as a commander) replies,

> I do because you have what you need, they give you what you want, you have your rights. If you want to have a partner, you get one, then in that sense you feel fulfilled. Plus, you don't have to take orders from your partner. In the [movement] love is secondary, the struggle is primary.[37]

Sonia's assessment of relationships in the FARC presents an interesting comparison to civilian society. While female FARC members may not have to follow their partners' rules in the FARC, they do have to follow the FARC's orders. As Sonia infers in her comments, however, the FARC's orders are issued under the auspices of the greater "struggle" for revolutionary change, which includes a better status for women. The overarching understanding of the social and intimate relationships of men and women belonging to a revolutionary struggle furthers the notion of equality in the FARC. Contrary to civilian society, where men and women are treated differently, in the FARC (as Sonia explains), "We treat each other like brothers and sisters in arms."[38]

The ideology of equality between men and women is central to the recruitment, training, and deployment of women in the FARC. However, despite the FARC's stated commitment to gender equality, incongruities between ideology and practice are apparent. Examining the more insidious sides of the FARC's activities reveals how its ideology of gender equality allows these incongruities to pass unquestioned.

Ideology Shrouding Reality

Contrary to the FARC's assertions of men and women enjoying equal status in the movement, many women are exploited by the same power structure that purports to maintain equality. In her account of women's lives in the FARC, Sandra Jordan observed that "foot soldiers must lead blameless, disciplined lives, while their leaders get drunk, gamble and kill indiscriminately."[39] Within the FARC's military structure, the hierarchy of power and authority (e.g., commanders being the superiors of combatants) may not always respect the ideology of equality between men and women. Studies support claims that the incongruence between combatants and commanders may be as dramatic as Jordan suggests.[40] Human Rights Watch reports that male commanders used their authority to arrange "sexual liaisons with under-age girls."[41] In the same report, Andrea, a sixteen-year-old, testified that "her relationship with an older commander saved her from being killed when she was suspected of collaborating with the army."[42] While the other accused girl was put to death for the offense of "robbing the movement," Andrea was sentenced to three months of digging trenches.[43] In many ways, women may join the FARC in order to escape violence in civilian society, only to encounter similar manifestations in the group itself. The power dynamic between commanders and combatants can quickly replicate unequal power relations found in civilian society. With the majority of higher-level positions filled by men, it is likely that sexual exploitation of women continues, but is omitted from discussions about equality in the FARC.

While arguably less troubling than being complicit with sexual exploitation, the FARC's oversight of relationships raises complex questions about their understanding of healthy relationships. In the name of their revolutionary mission, the FARC mandates that all women use birth control. Human Rights Watch reports that Norplant contraceptive implants, contraceptive injections, birth control pills, and condoms are most frequently used.[44] The organization also reports that even young girls are required to use contraception, often by having an intrauterine device (IUD) inserted by FARC nurses.[45] Although compulsory use of birth control may be interpreted as the prioritization of "the struggle" before relationships between combatants, testimonies of young women suggests a grimmer picture. In an interview with Human Rights Watch, a young woman identified as Angela explains that when she joined at age twelve, "They put in an IUD the day I arrived. That was the only birth control I ever used."[46] The use of IUDs is not simply a single event in women's adjustment to the FARC but a regular part of women's lives in the FARC. Another young woman in a Human Rights Watch study claims that she had an IUD inserted eight days after she arrived, and a nurse regularly checked the contraceptive.[47]

In the event that women do become pregnant, abortions—whether by choice or by force—are common. Laura and Serena felt that the FARC does not waver in denying women the opportunity to have children while in the movement. In her interview with Human Rights Watch, Angela flatly states, "If you get pregnant, you have to have an abortion. Lots of women get pregnant. I had two friends who got pregnant and had to have abortions.

They cried and cried. They didn't want to lose the baby."[48] The FARC may even employ deception in order to exercise authority over the women's reproductive health. An unidentified woman admits to Human Rights Watch, "The worst thing is that you can't have a baby. Two years ago, in 2000, I got pregnant. They gave me an abortion but they didn't tell me in advance that they were going to do it. They told me they were checking on it. I wanted to have the baby."[49] In many ways, the inclusion of women in FARC is predicated on intervening in women's biological capacity for reproduction, either through forced contraceptives and abortions. Controlling pregnancies within the movement allows FARC leaders to maintain some control over the actions and decisions of their fighters. This control, however, comes at the expense of women's autonomy over their bodies. Although as combatants women place their bodies and lives at risk, the FARC lays a greater claim on women's bodies by forcefully employing contraceptives and abortions. Instead of recognizing women's capacity to make responsible (or at least informed) decisions, the FARC pre-empts the issue in order to maintain the notion of equality within the revolutionary movement. Forcefully preventing wanted or unwanted births does not create equality within the movement. This practice is a control exercised exclusively over women, while the consequences for men are only incidental.

Contradictions within the ideology of the FARC as a place of equality are not limited to sexual politics. Beneath the questions of sexual harassment, forced contraception, and abortion lie fundamental questions, such as whether positions of authority are equally accessible to men and women, how authorities conceptualize healthy relationships between men and women, and whether roles from civilian society are selectively reproduced in the movement. These broader questions are largely left unaddressed by analyses and policies that do not consider the social and ideological forces behind women's involvement in the FARC.

Conclusion

Several interrelated factors hamper our understanding of women's involvement in terrorist movements. Men are overwhelmingly presented as the only perpetrator of political violence. When women are recognized as terrorists, it is largely only as a result of their participation in violent and dramatic acts. While these acts are scrutinized, particularly because of their deplorable nature, they reveal little about why and how women join terrorist movements. This chapter argues that understanding the origins, nature, and complexities of women's participation requires that researchers and policymakers look beyond women's involvement in perpetrating political violence. Instead, we must examine the social situations that women leave behind and the ideology of the movement they join, as these can reveal important subtleties of women's involvement and can inform future policy decisions. However, only through more research, particularly of a regional and comparative nature, can researchers better understand how and why women participate in terrorist organizations worldwide.

Several key lessons emerged from examining women's participation in the FARC. For potential recruits, the movement's political objectives may be secondary to the perceived opportunities of joining a terrorist movement. This investigation revealed that, even for young adolescents, joining a violent movement can be a calculated decision. While inflated expectations and recruitment rhetoric influence these decisions, some women may view terrorist movements as offering opportunities that are otherwise unattainable. In some cases, the difficulties and risks women face in civilian society may exceed those inherent in joining a terrorist movement. For others, terrorist organizations might be perceived as a relief from seemingly inescapable boredom. Further study of women's involvement in terrorist movements can expose how broader social issues are intimately linked to success of these organizations.

Additionally, the sense of purpose instilled by enlisting in a terrorist group may be heightened for women. As a distinct departure from civilian society, the training women receive—even when comparable to that of men—could elicit a special sense of importance for them. The physical and political training that terrorist movements provide may not only be the most sustained formal training women receive, but it also has immediate application for a cause greater than themselves; upon completing the training, women enter a political and social structure in which they have new, specific responsibilities and functions. In a way, a terrorist group validates the potential of a woman in a manner that civilian societies may not recognize.

Lastly, ideology is integral in concealing contradictions between recruitment rhetoric and reality. Developing compelling interpretations of society, values, and symbols that claim to address the concerns of women aids and legitimizes terrorist organizations' efforts to incorporate women into their activities. Creating and sustaining an ideology that appeals to women is particularly important given that prevailing understandings do not associate women with violent projects. Simultaneously, employing ideological visions allows terrorist leaders to deflect (or at least suspend) questions about whether the recruits' expectations are met or recruiting promises fulfilled. Recognizing the manner in which ideology influences women's participation in terrorist movements is vital to understanding terrorist movements and reducing their ranks.

The policy implications for these conclusions are considerable. Stemming the recruitment of women by the FARC requires the Colombian government to adopt a multifaceted strategy, one that addresses the complex conditions that contribute to women's recruitment and combats the FARC's political message. Addressing the interrelated factors that contribute to women's entrance into the FARC requires a concerted effort to generate new educational and professional opportunities, especially for women in rural and impoverished areas. Local mentorship or federally funded scholarship programs could support women as they pursue their studies or return to school to complete their degrees. Vocational training and microlending programs that reach out to women could generate rewarding entrepreneurial opportunities. Entirely new programs may not be necessary; ensuring that women have access to (and are adequately served by) existing state-sponsored social services could prove effective. Additionally, it is important that the Colombian government commit resources to reducing domestic abuse against girls and women. Ensuring the safety of girls and women is central to reducing flight to the FARC. Recognizing and responding to the conditions from which women are recruited into the FARC should be a primary focus of any attempt to reduce women's entrance into the FARC.

Besides providing otherwise unattainable opportunities, social and political programs can complement efforts to combat the FARC's political message. This chapter highlights cases in which women studied the benefits, for themselves and possibly their communities, of entering the FARC. While it is impossible to understand all the factors influencing their decisions, presumably, the women could also have chosen to not enter the group and pursue other engagements. The Colombian government needs to highlight, perhaps through public awareness campaigns, how its citizens, particularly women and young people, have the potential to make valuable, constructive contributions to their communities. Without compromising individuals' safety, the government could recognize and even support these efforts to underscore the choice individuals have to not take up arms. Affirming that Colombian citizens even in the most desperate conditions have a choice powerfully undermines the allure of the FARC's political message.

In conclusion, the Colombian government should strive to formulate and implement policies that relieve the lack of opportunity for women that the FARC's ideology preys upon. This attainable, albeit ambitious, goal is key to reducing the involvement of women in the FARC and certainly integral to building a lasting peace in Colombia.

Acknowledgments

I would like to thank Chris Amirault, Chuck Call, and Annick Wibben for their guidance and encouragement throughout this project, and its predecessors. I am also indebted to Lila Cruikshank, Kate Ogden, and Angela Robertson for their careful readings and valuable suggestions.

CHAPTER 11

The Making of Suicide Bombers: A Comparative Perspective

AMI PEDAHZUR AND ARIE PERLIGER

Suicide terrorism is nothing new in human history; it first appeared long before modern times. This phenomenon was already seen among the Jewish Sicaris as early as the first century, among the Muslim Hashishiyun in the eleventh century and among the Asians in the eighteenth century.[1] However, in the late twentieth century, and especially during the last two decades, suicide terrorism has become one of the most prominent types of terrorism, globally widespread, and especially dominant in countries such as Lebanon, Egypt, Israel, Turkey, and Sri Lanka.

The first organization in modern times that used suicide terrorism consistently was Hizballah in Lebanon, conducting several attacks during the 1980s, mostly against the Israeli army in South Lebanon. This was followed by the LTTE (Liberation Tigers of Tamil Eelam), an organization that was formed in Sri Lanka as part of the struggle for the independence of the Tamil minority on the island. During the 1990s, the Kurds in Turkey (the Kurdistan Workers' Party, or PKK), the Palestinians in Israel (Hamas, Fatah, and Palestinian Islamic Jihad), and of course al Qaeda (and other Muslim organizations worldwide) also adopted suicide tactics in their terrorist campaigns.

In contrast to other terrorist attacks, even the most dangerous ones, the suicide attack is an "operational method in which the very act of the attack is dependent upon the death of the perpetrator."[2] The terrorist is fully aware that if he does not kill himself, the planned attack will not be successful. Hence, because suicide terrorism obligates the perpetrator to make the biggest sacrifice of all—his life—understanding and exploring how such an individual has been recruited, trained and convinced to undertake such an act has become one of the most intriguing features of this phenomenon as well as a key to understanding its growing prominence all over the world.

How does a terrorist recruit transform into a live bomb? To begin with, the story of Zarema Muzhakhoeva is instructive. Muzhakhoeva was a twenty-three-year-old single parent when she was recruited for a suicide attack by a group of Chechen rebels. Her main incentive to join the "black widows" (the name by which the female Chechen suicide bombers were known) was financial. Shortly after her husband was killed during the course of a business dispute, the dead husband's family took away Muzhakhoeva's newborn baby girl, and she was prevented from seeing her child. Spurred on by her distress, Muzhakhoeva stole her grandmother's jewels, sold them for $600, and made her way to her mother-in-law's house. She asked for permission to spend some time with her daughter, yet her real plan was to run away with the baby to Moscow. Members of her late husband's family kept a close watch on her the whole time and when Muzhakhoeva tried boarding an aircraft, they took her child away. Muzhakhoeva was heartbroken; not only had she stolen her grandmother's jewels, she had also lost her daughter.[3]

After that, she joined the Shamil Basayev faction of the Chechen rebel movement. Her only incentive in doing so was financial. She learned that the family of a suicide bomber received $1,000 for carrying out a mission for this faction. Muzhakhoeva, who did not see much point in continuing life without her daughter, thought that with her death, at least her grandmother would be compensated for the stolen jewels.

After she joined the "black widows" group, she was trained for two weeks in a training camp and was then sent to carry and detonate a bomb inside a military bus at a Russian military base. However, as revealed later in her statement after she was caught, Muzhakhoeva did not really want to sacrifice her life, so she told her operators that she had missed the bus. Shortly thereafter, she was sent to Moscow and taken on a tour of the city, where she was introduced to various potential targets. The next day, she was dressed in black and given a text to read in front of a video camera. She was told that the tape would be sent to her family. Two days later, on the 9 July 2003, she was given an explosive belt to wear, and sent to Red Square; from there, she took a taxi to the coffee shop where she was supposed to detonate her explosives. However, she panicked again, told a guard in the area that she had been sent to blow herself up, and was immediately arrested.[4]

Economic deprivation, however, is just one of the various motives used by terrorist organizations to recruit suicide bombers. For example, Hanadi Jaradat–a twenty-nine-year-old female Palestinian suicide bomber who exploded on October 2003 in a restaurant in the city of Haifa, killing nineteen people and injuring more than sixty—was recruited into the Palestinian Islamic Jihad (PIJ) organization after her fiancé and her brother were killed by Israeli security forces. In this case, the PIJ activists who recruited her used her strong urge for revenge. In another recruitment by the PIJ, a young Palestinian named Rasan Satiti was enlisted to detonate explosives in Tel Aviv. He accepted the task after more than six months of religious studies in a mosque in Ramallah and after he was persuaded that it was one of the greatest and superior religious acts available to every Palestinian Muslim.

Such stories illuminate the intriguing process of recruiting and training these human bombs. In the following sections, this chapter will describe the recruitment and training processes of suicide bombers and argue that this phenomenon is a result of encouraging environmental and personal motivations, both of which are being used by terrorist organizations implementing suicide attacks. The first part of the chapter will explore the recruitment processes of potential suicide terrorists, and the second part provides a comparative analysis of the training process of suicide bombers. Finally, the discussion examines how the interactions between the organizations and the surrounding environment influence the process of recruiting and training suicide bombers.

Processes of Recruitment

The ability to locate the right candidate for a suicide attack is the most important element in the preparations stage of the attack, since all the success of the attack is virtually dependent on the abilities, skills, and loyalty of the suicide bomber. Moreover, the recruiting process demands that the organization overcomes a basic contradiction. On one hand, there is a need to verify that the candidate has the skills, ability, and loyalty to execute a successful suicide attack, and on the other hand, in most cases the organizations cannot afford to use suicide bombers who are well trained, valuable activists who could be of more use in other, long-term projects. Hence, there is a need to recruit a candidate that the organization can spare, but still demonstrate the appropriate skills and loyalty for the organization.

In order to tackle this complicated mission, in most cases the suicide terrorist has been recruited directly to the suicide mission from other sections of the organization or from outside its personnel. However, in some cases, the training process could be very long and sometimes the recruited activists are unaware that they have been recruited to conduct a suicide mission.

In general, recruitment procedures can be classified into two main categories. The first category includes cases in which the candidates approach the organization on their own initiative, volunteering to participate in suicide attacks, while the second category encompasses those individuals who are recruited directly by an organization that feels they could be persuaded to become suicide bombers because they show great identification with its goals.

Voluntary Recruitments

Individuals who volunteer to become suicide bombers are in most cases people who find themselves in a certain state of personal crisis, and they perceive the suicide act as a way to overcome this crisis. When they approach the organizations, the members they speak to foster in their minds the idea that martyrdom will solve their crisis.

Several cases illustrate this type of recruitment, beginning with the example of Faiza Amal Jumuah from the Askar refugee camp near Nablus. Faiza was subject to mockery all her life because she was built and looked like a man. When she was a teenager she decided to go for a gender-change operation, but could not afford it. Her mother died of cancer when she was fifteen years old, and soon afterwards she went to work for several years in Israel to help her family, which was in a difficult economic situation. In 2002, when she was thirty-five years old, after her father died and the surrounding environment pressed her to finally get married, she decided that she wanted to volunteer for a suicide mission. She approached a PIJ activist, who sent her to Sayyid Qutb, a Hamas activist who had engineered many earlier suicide attacks. He questioned her about her motives and promised her that after the attack Hamas would look after her family. He also gave her 400 NIS (New Israeli Shekel), roughly equivalent to US$92, and asked her to find a person who knew how to bypass Israeli Defense Force (IDF) roadblocks. A few weeks later, in early June 2004, she was sent to the "Carmel" Open Market in Tel Aviv to blow herself up. However, on her way to central Tel Aviv, she was caught by Israeli security forces with the explosive belt on her body and arrested.[5]

The story of Hanadi Jaradat, mentioned earlier, also reveals how mental crises can push a very educated person with a nonviolent record to volunteer for a suicide attack. After she finished her high school studies, Jaradat went to Jordan where she began studying for a law degree. In 1995, when she was twenty-one years old, her fiancé was killed by IDF troops. However, her eventual decision to join the PIJ was a result of the killing of her brother Fadi by IDF soldiers. Fadi had always supported her desire for higher education and helped her financially during her stay in Jordan (the father of the family suffered from cancer and could not work). More traumatic for Jaradat, however, was the fact that after her brother was shot in front of her, the IDF soldiers did not let her approach and help him. Shortly afterwards, during the funeral, she declared that she wanted to revenge her family by participating in a suicide mission. From that moment, the road to becoming a PIJ bomber was short. On 4 October 2003, she entered a restaurant in the city of Haifa in Northern Israel, exploding and killing twenty-one people, many of them families with young children.[6]

These and other stories of Palestinian suicide terrorists emphasize the contention that the combination of a crisis situation in one's personal life or in the community to which the prospective bombers belongs, along with a strong sympathetic culture, can lead a person to volunteer for a suicide mission. However, it should be mentioned that this kind of recruitment for suicide attacks is not exclusive to the Palestinian case, as shown also in the case of Zarema Muzhakhoeva, the Chechen widow who volunteered for suicide attacks because of a personal economic crisis.

One can also find this type of suicide terrorist recruitment, for example, in the case of the Amal movement in Lebanon. Mohammed Mahmoud Berro was sixteen years old when he was sent by Amal to detonate a car bomb near the IDF headquarters at the village of Nabatia on 23 February 1985. Berro grew up in the slums of Beirut. In the fifth grade he left school and, in order to help support his family, started to work as a phone installer. However, in 1984, the phone infrastructure in Beirut collapsed and he was left unemployed. At this time, the economic status of the family became more difficult, and after his father had a traffic accident, the family had to borrow money from the Amal movement in order to meet their financial needs. Soon, the Amal members demanded that the family repay their debt, and that was when Berro, who knew that the family was unable to do this, volunteered for the suicide mission in order to pay back the Amal organization.[7]

Active Recruitment

Another method of suicide mission recruitment involves instances where an organization contacts certain individuals who show great potential for identification with its goals. In such cases, the movement's leaders feel that they can convince this new recruit to sacrifice his or her life for the organization's goals. In many cases of active recruitment, the organization also uses its influence over the local community to mobilize candidates for suicide missions.

Al Qaeda is a good example of this aggressive method of recruitment. Its leaders have been especially interested in enlisting young people (Muslims) in the West or Arab countries to fight for Islam. The organization finds its candidates mainly among lonely, rootless young men who congregate in the mosques for company. Often a group of these far-from-home youngsters share an apartment and become like a family. Some are more politically extreme than others, but through proximity they are able to influence their moderate colleagues and usually succeed in recruiting them to join the movement.[8]

Al Qaeda also has a network of experienced fighters, who were trained in camps throughout Afghanistan. Many of them returned home after the anti-Soviet jihad, but some went to a Western country, where they are encouraged to marry local women, find jobs in mosques, familiarize themselves with the local communities, and identify suitable young men for enlistment and training in the organization.[9] Following the U.S. invasion of Afghanistan, the al Qaeda organization lost its bases in that country, contributing to a reduction in terrorist activity. This has further emphasized the importance of individuals and groups living in other countries, which are now al Qaeda's main source of active terrorists. Many of the recent attacks have been carried out by local cells, only loosely connected to the main organization.[10]

Similar recruitment processes are also evident in other places. Sana Mheidleh was the first woman to conduct a suicide attack in Lebanon, which took place on 9 April 1985 against an IDF roadblock in south Lebanon. A year before she executed her attack, she joined the Nationalist Social Syrian party and identified closely with Syrian interests in Lebanon. Before she went on her suicide mission, she declared in a videotape that she wanted to sacrifice her life in order to fulfill her national duty and that she was glad that she could give her life for the Syrian president Assad. In this case, the strong convictions of this young female were used in order to convince her to sacrifice her life.[11]

As mentioned above, sometimes the organization's influence over local communities and societies has been used to recruit young people. In Sri Lanka, the LTTE used its power among the Tamil community to recruit school dropouts, aged twelve–sixteen, whose families were usually in financial straits. The LTTE went even further, becoming very involved in civilian life and infiltrating the education system, thus gaining access to schools and ultimately to students. The teachers were forced to indoctrinate the children in Tamil history and the role of the LTTE. Later, LTTE members themselves lectured the children, explained the organization's motives and methods, and generally succeeded to a large extent in causing many of the children to enlist. There were also cases where some youngsters were forced to join up.[12]

Similar recruitment techniques were also employed by leaders of the Chechen rebels. Aside from Arab and Muslim fighters who perceived the Chechen fight against the Russians as another chapter in the mujahideen struggle which began in Afghanistan, and thus voluntarily joined the Chechen forces, rebel groups also relied on local manpower. Once again, unemployed young persons were the most vulnerable group for recruitment. The main incentive for joining the rebel forces was the salary offered by recruiters. Other reasons included fear of the Russian forces and the desire to avenge the death of a friend or relative who was killed by the Russians.[13] In sum, terrorist recruitment involves many dimensions, some of which are unique to suicide attacks. Training for suicide terrorism is also a unique subcategory within the broader discussion of terrorist organizations.

The Training Process of Suicide Bombers

A comparative analysis of different terrorist organizations reveals that the training process is conducted in two separate dimensions. The first dimension of the training process is focused on giving the suicide bomber the basic operational skills for executing his attack. This includes an introduction to basic military techniques and knowledge on how to penetrate security, approach the target, operate the explosives, and avoid being detected, as well as protocols of operation for specific situations that might be encountered during the attack. The second dimension of the training process is focused on developing the appropriate mental mindset of the perpetrator—an ideological perspective which guarantees that at the right moment he or she will not hesitate to die for the success of the attack. The organization's main concern is to make sure that the potential bomber does not back down, a move that would not only jeopardize the specific mission but could also disclose organization members and tactics.

However, although all the organizations employ this two-dimensional training process, two types of implementation can be detected. The first is a rapid one, when the entire process takes place in a matter of weeks, while the second one consists of months and sometimes years of preparation. In most cases, these differences are due to the specific operational capabilities and character of an organization. For example, while the LTTE and Hizballah are actually vast paramilitary organizations that control large territories (and thus have the ability to construct training camps where a long-term training process can take place), the Palestinian organizations—as well as their Chechen counterparts—are more oriented toward short but intense training processes because of their limited operational sources.

It must also be mentioned that in order to ensure that the suicide bomber will be focused solely on the mission, many organizations release him or her from other duties, such as gathering intelligence or tactical preparations. Moreover, in most cases, the potential suicide bomber is escorted by the organization's operatives almost until reaching the target, and he or she receives instructions up to the very last stage. This reinforces the importance of mental preparation. In order to complete the mission, the suicide bomber must reach his or her target calm, confident, and focused.

Whether the organization uses a short and suicide-oriented training process or a military-type long-term training process, a comparative examination reveals important similarities. To begin with, the training process in Hamas includes three phases. In the first, the potential suicide bombers go through long sessions with recruiters who talk to them about the religious importance of their acts and also try to remove the fear of dying. In some cases, this includes taking the recruits to a cemetery and placing them inside a grave.[14] The second stage includes technical and operational preparations. The final stage includes a public demonstration of the potential suicide bomber's commitment to the Palestinian cause, most of the time through a videotape, in which the bomber reads a prepared testament, declaring that the decision to go on the suicide mission was made willingly and no compulsion was involved. A day before the mission, the candidate will be shown the tape over and over again, will ask for mercy for all his or her sins, and will check that all the equipment is ready. All three stages of this process take only a matter of days to complete. For example, Muhammad Habishy, who perpetrated a suicide attack on the Naharia Rail station, disappeared from his home just ten days before he exploded on 9 September 2001. There are also some known cases where this whole process lasted no longer than a few hours, in which the candidate was praised for choosing this path and given basic technical instructions regarding the activation of the device.[15]

Another important feature of the training process is that the perpetrator is not left alone in the days before the suicidal act, in order to prevent regrets or misgivings. He or she is always escorted by one of the Hamas activists. Fatah, which is a non religious Palestinian group, also favors a very short, intense training period, usually preparing for an attack only a few days before it is due to take place.

In the Chechen organizations, the training process is also relatively short. The majority of Chechen suicide bombers have been women, and the period of preparing these females for suicide missions has been minimal, lasting only a few weeks, during which they become acquainted with basic terrorist tactics.[16] However, in contrast to the emphasis put by the organizations mentioned above on the mental preparations of the potential suicide bomber, in the Chechen case this dimension of the training process seems to be very primitive. From the limited knowledge existing about this process in several Chechen organizations—such as the "Arbi Barayev" (Shamil Basyev organization)—it has been learned that some women have been drugged during the mental preparation process, while other women were whipped up into an ecstatic frenzy. Some of them were taken into large rooms where they were ordered to repeat a sentence over and over again and move their bodies in monotonous motions until they lost control.[17] It seems that the introduction of drugs in the training process of Chechen women has made an impression on other organizations. There are many indications that since the American invasion of Iraq, the use of drugs as part of the preparation of suicide bombers has increased. Suicide bombers under the patronage of Abu Musab al-Zarqawi have been reported to have taken antipsychotic pills during the training process and before setting out on their mission.[18]

In contrast to the Palestinian and Chechen organizations, the LTTE and

Hizballah have maintained a more sophisticated training process, with less focus on the specific mission for which the suicide bomber is recruited. This is mainly because the Palestinian organizations lack the resources held by Hizballah and the LTTE and also because they did not succeed, in contrast again to the latter organizations, in gaining full control over part of the territories; instead, their activities have been closely monitored by the Israeli army. Moreover, the Palestinian suicide attacks were mostly against easy civilian targets, thus the military training needed to infiltrate these targets was minimal, in contrast to what was needed from the suicide bombers of the LTTE and the Hizballah, who attacked mostly well-guarded military and political targets.

Hizballah, a Shiite Muslim organization which was formed in the early 1980s in Lebanon by special units of the Iranian revolutionary guard brigades, launched its campaign of suicide attacks first against Western military forces in Lebanon and afterwards against the Israeli Defense Forces. This organization was also the first to develop a two-stage training program for suicide missions. With the help of Iranian officers, the Hizballah established its own training camps in the Baqa Valley (a Shiite-populated area) in Lebanon. The first phase of the training process included the introduction of guerrilla tactics, which consisted of (among other assignments) laying landmines, infiltrating enemy camps, using automatic weapons and rockets, and mastering techniques of self-defense. During the operational training, the trainers selected trainees who showed an exceptionally strong commitment to the cause and a willingness to die for Islam. These trainees then proceeded to the second stage, which included religious indoctrination (hence, all the Hizballah camps were equipped with mosques) and preparation for highly sophisticated guerrilla attacks, as well as suicide missions.[19]

The LTTE has also used the same two-dimensional training system developed by Hizballah. In the first stage, all recruits (many of them children between twelve and sixteen years of age) undergo several years of nonmilitary training, focused on the history of the Tamil people and the horrors they have suffered as a national minority in Sri Lanka. When they reach the age of sixteen, the candidates are moved to special training camps, where they go through a basic training period of four months. This basic training includes an introduction to military tactics and of course, continuation of the indoctrination to the organization's ideology. At this stage, much emphasis has also been given to glorifying and idolizing the organization's leader, Prabhakaran.

In a typical day at the LTTE camps, the children conduct physical training in the jungle, followed by lessons in the martial arts and classes where they are introduced to the history of the organization. At later stages, they study intelligence gathering and the handling of explosive devices. Only after the basic training period does the selection process for the suicide squad—the Black Tigers—begin. Prospective suicide bombers are selected according to their achievements during the initial training period.[20] Specific training for suicide missions lasts for a few more weeks, during which trainees learned suicide tactics in greater detail. However, in the eyes of LTTE, mental preparation is even more important. The instructors' objective is to get the recruit to fully commit to the mission and make sure he or she would not have second thoughts.[21] The training process of the PKK is quite similar; in the PKK training program, the suicide bomber undergoes lengthy training programs in camps that are located in Syria, Lebanon, and the northern Kurdish part of Iraq.[22]

Unlike these and other terrorist organizations, al Qaeda is a multinational entity, which presents challenges for efficient coordination of recruitment and training. Prior to September 11, the main al Qaeda training camps were in Afghanistan, and the terrorists were recruited from Muslim and Western countries. After being approved by the al Qaeda leaders, recruits were supplied with money and documents for the journey to Afghanistan. There they were trained and thoroughly indoctrinated and then returned to their own countries to establish new groups. Some stayed on in Afghanistan for further military training—a very select few were chosen for suicide missions,[23] receiving general military training, but with more emphasis on the psychological process entailed in terror. Through indoctrination, the recruits were brought into a mental state of total commitment to the organization and a readiness to sacrifice everything, even their own lives. This was accomplished by means of a constant emphasis on the role of Islam, its superiority, and the overwhelming importance of countering the infiltration of the "infidels" into Muslim lives.

This brainwashing continued right up to the attack. The "Hamburg group," which carried out the 9/11 attack, lived together before the mission, presumably to encourage and help each other emotionally and psychologically. Actual preparations for the mission were short-lived.[24] Al Qaeda officials seemed to feel that the success of the operation depended more on the mental and emotional stability of the perpetrators, rather than their skills.[25]

After 9/11 all this changed. The training camps in Afghanistan were destroyed by the American invasion, and al Qaeda had to change its procedures. The training process shifted to the countries of recruitment.[26] The organization began to depend much more on modern technology, and first and foremost on the Internet. Over the Internet, al Qaeda has put out its ideology through propaganda, and gained support for its cause. It provides relevant literature to groups around the world, including intelligence and tactical information, as well as special orders before an attack.[27]

The Role of Society in the Recruitment and Training Processes

Terrorist organizations attempt to create a supportive social environment and political culture for their aims, as do other political organizations such as parties and special interest groups. Moreover, organizations using suicide tactics will try to mobilize the society and political culture to support those acts. Achieving this goal will facilitate their ability to mobilize and recruit suicide bombers. Suicide terrorism is widespread throughout the world, but in different societies, even with different histories and culture, we can still find several elements that are common to many or most of them.

First, suicide terrorist recruitment is rare in affluent and prosperous societies. Hence, we can argue that one of the factors facilitating the emergence of suicide terrorism is economic deprivation. As can be drawn from the examples of the Palestinian arena, as long as the economic situation in the Palestinian territories continued to deteriorate, more and more suicide terrorists have volunteered for these operations for economic reasons. This has also been the case in other places, especially in Chechnya.

However, suicide terrorism is also not present in some poorer societies or places where life is considered to be no more than a path that must be taken before death. So in what conditions will economic deprivation lead to the emergence of suicide terrorism? In general, this analysis suggests four important factors which, when combined with economic deprivation, facilitate the emergence of suicide terrorism:

1. A review of the countries in the world where suicide terrorism has emerged shows that economic deprivation, when combined with violent conflict against a stronger adversary, has been the cause of much suffering, a predicament that generates frustration and results in the dehumanization of the enemy. This dehumanization, together with the long period of suffering from the conflict, facilitates the emergence of people seeking mainly to harm members of the opposition, to get revenge and use the suicide mission as a way out from ongoing political frustration. All over the world, economic distress—together with ongoing conflict with a stronger power—leads to the phenomenon of suicide terrorism, a direct result of dehumanization and frustration. People who have lived for a long time in such circumstances seek revenge upon those who they designate as "persecutors." The suicide mission is thus seen as an escape from an unacceptable political situation.

2. Another important factor is the feeling among the suffering society that political resolution is unobtainable not just for a short while, but also in the long-term. In these situations, the feeling that there is a need to intensify the violence could emerge. In this situation, the society could perceive the struggle as a zero sum game where restrictions on violence should be put aside. The cases of the LTTE and the Chechen rebels exemplify this factor.

3. Societies that perceive themselves as weak, and feel hopeless and oppressed by a powerful enemy, have seen suicide terrorism a tool to empower that society—or more exactly, the image of society—in the eyes of its members.

4. Suicide terrorism is encouraged by the terrorist organizations through disseminating a "culture of death." One notable case was that of Ahmad Qasir, who blew up the Israeli military headquarters in Tyre, Lebanon, on 11 November 1982.[28] His identity was kept secret for two years, but when his picture was finally released he became a hero and celebrity in Lebanon and in Iran, due to the efforts of both the Hizballah and Iran to present him as such.[29] They placed large posters of him in southern Lebanon, along roads and in villages, and dozens of young people announced their willingness to follow in his footsteps and become martyrs for the cause.[30] Although Hizballah had stopped its suicide missions, Sheikh Naim Kassem (one of its leaders) asserted that there were still many volunteers, who were swayed by the "death culture," offering themselves as martyrs. It was just a question of choosing the best people for the job.[31] The Palestinian organizations of Hamas and the Islamic Jihad has also adopted this "culture of death," glorifying martyrdom and self-sacrifice, and this approach has resulted in an increase of volunteers for suicide missions. During the 1990s, the terrorist organizations were furious with Israel for not implementing the Oslo Accords, and with the Palestinian Authority for not improving the lot of the average man in the street. These two facts went a long way towards propagating the "death culture" and acquiring volunteers. The *shaheeds* (martyrs) were praised at every opportunity, with posters depicting them and plays, poems, and Internet sites all telling of their bravery and self-sacrifice. These efforts were highly successful, and the idea of *istishad* (martyrdom) became an overriding factor in the daily lives of the Palestinians. Mock suicide attacks were acted out by young children, and public support for this type of terrorism increased by leaps and bounds. Instead of being looked upon as a sign of despair, the Palestinian *shaheed* was (and by many accounts, continues to be) seen as a powerful symbol of hope.[32]

Discussion

Terrorism and death have always been closely intertwined. However, from the first appearance of modern terrorism, most acts were directed at taking people's lives, and death was typically the fate of only the victims of terrorism. But suicide has not been entirely unknown in the history of modern terrorism. For example, Ulrike Meinhof, leader of the German Red Army Faction, committed suicide by hanging herself in prison in 1976, as did four of her colleagues, after it was evident that they stood no chance of being liberated from prison. In addition, in the famous hunger strike of 1981, the Irish Republican Army men starved themselves to death in their prison cells in Belfast after learning that their petition to be recognized as political, instead of criminal, prisoners had been rejected by the British authorities. Nevertheless, until the last three decades, terrorists generally abstained from killing themselves in the very act of terror they implemented. This has changed since the 1980s, and the number of terrorists setting out on suicide missions is definitely increasing, a tendency that poses a genuine challenge for social scientists.

This chapter has synthesized information gained from different organizations to illustrate how suicide terrorists are recruited, prepared, and trained for their suicide missions. What conclusions can be drawn from this analysis? First, although there are several similarities in the training and recruiting processes of all organizations, one can still find disparities that stem from the varied character of every organization. For example, differences in the recruitment and training process exist between organizations operating internationally (al Qaeda) and organizations operating in a single territory (e.g., LTTE or Hamas). Moreover, the operational resources of the organization and their level of control over the population also influenced their recruitment and training methods.

Second, in contrast to preparations for other terrorist attacks, when recruiting a candidate for a suicide mission the recruitment process continues throughout the training stage and until the suicide mission is perpetrated. When recruiting a candidate for a suicide mission, it is necessary to reinforce his or her willingness and acceptance to participate in a suicide attack, and to continue this process up to the final minutes.

Third, while there are a variety of recruiting methods, it would seem that the first necessity must be that of feelings of hopelessness on the part of the recruits, which are then countered by the understanding and supportive environment established by their mentors. The recruits are then offered a way out of despair through their ultimate sacrifice, thus facilitating the enlistment process. Finally, while some have argued that this phenomenon is necessarily linked to one culture or religion, the opposite is true. This can be seen clearly when analyzing the enlistment, training, and employment of the terrorists, and particularly their emphasis on psychological preparation. The idea is to hit the "soft spot" in the prospective *shaheed*, whether through religious, nationalistic, or other means of indoctrination.

How does this knowledge on the process of producing a suicide terrorist assist us in developing ideas that can help us defend and fight this phenomenon? The first conclusion that can be drawn from the chapter is that in order to diminish the number of suicide bombers there is a need to create an unsupportive environment and not just fight the infrastructure of the organizations. The success of the Turkish authorities against the PKK was partly because they succeeded in creating divisions between the Kurdish population in Turkey and the organization by initiating extensive economic reforms for this deprived community. Hence, in order to confront the roots of suicide terrorism, there is no alternative but to explore the needs of the organizations' constituencies and see what can be done to meet some of their demands, in order to reduce their support for terrorist actions. Moreover, the example of the LTTE during the late 1990s shows that even when the organizational infrastructure has been damaged, the organization can still perpetrate suicide attacks, as long as there is a supportive environment. The suicide attacks of the Palestinians during 2003–2004 also illustrate this argument.

The Turkish success also reflects the important role of undermining the activity of the leaders of the organizations. After they caught the PKK leader Abdullah Ocalan in Kenya, the suicide attacks stopped completely. In the Palestinian case as well, after Israel began to launch small-scale operations which were aimed directly at the leaders and the members of the organization who are responsible for planning and launching the perpetrators, the number of Palestinian suicide acts was reduced dramatically. The prevailing reason was that the leaders needed to focus most of their time on survival, rather than on planning future attacks. Hence, the leaders need to be kept under constant surveillance and their activities undermined in almost any possible way, starting with ongoing arrests and ending with the freezing of assets and bank accounts. This will not diminish the organizations' capabilities to carry out suicide missions, but it will shift the focus of the elite's energy from initiating attacks to protecting their own existence.

Finally, understanding that such attacks cannot be completely prevented, we should think of ways to minimize their consequences by developing civilian and security infrastructures that will help us to adapt to this relatively new type of terrorism. In the Israeli case, such infrastructure proved to be effective. By building the separation wall, creating special public transportation guard units, establishing routine prevention procedures and mechanisms for the treatment and rehabilitation of attack victims and their families (including medical, psychological, and social aspects), rebuilding the areas damaged in the attack, and restoring the activity within the territories to normality, Israel has sought to minimize the direct and indirect damage of most suicide attacks. However, as implied in this and other chapters of this volume, curbing the rise of suicide terrorism requires addressing underlying social, political, and economic factors which facilitate the recruitment and training of individuals for these kinds of attacks.

CHAPTER 12

Unresolved Trauma and the Thirst for Revenge: The Retributional Terrorist

RAYMOND H. HAMDEN

When people think of terrorism and terrorists, the conjured picture is typically of a psychopathic, political, or religious nature; often all terrorists are rigidly placed into one general category. However, from research on terrorism, hostage situations, and fundamentalism, there is evidence to suggest that professionals must be more flexible in examining particular types of international terrorists and aggressors. Political and religious terrorists often refer to themselves as "freedom fighters," a manipulation of semantics that seems to give psychological justification and warranted responsibility for their atrocities. The political and religious "fighters" have ethnogeographic concerns; they are generally leery of psychopathic terrorists because of their seemingly nondirected goal behavior as well as their obvious narcissistic style of conduct. Members of political or religious terror groups are convinced that they seek to achieve a goal for the "common good," while the psychopathic type of terrorist has a self-as-the-center-of-the-world perspective and no goals in common with others.

There is, however, a fourth category of terrorists—the Retributional Type—comprised of individuals who reportedly have no emotional or social pathology in their psychological development and no familial or social conditioning to any political or religious ideology. The term *retribution* is generally defined as a justly deserved penalty; the act of correcting for wrongdoing.[1] Vengeance is defined as the act of taking revenge (harming someone in retaliation for something harmful that they have done). Both retribution and vengeance are often used interchangeably in describing an individual's motivation for violent acts, typically understood to be the result of a major traumatic incident. For example, these individuals may have witnessed the slaying of family members while hiding during a massacre, or they may have arrived home to discover the bodies of loved ones and friends after a mass execution. From such trauma, the desire for revenge can emerge, along with feelings of hopelessness, helplessness, and a sense of life with no foundation (i.e., the family loss) and no destiny, goals, or future aspirations.

These individuals, purely and discriminately, seek retribution as a self-guided response to the trauma they suffered. Especially when the surviving victim was not directly or indirectly involved with the conflict or dispute, the vital question is whether the trauma of losing loved ones to war or militia activities can be psychological or socially resolved. Further, one must consider the environmental dimensions that may facilitate or support retributional violence. Examining such questions allows us to better understand The Retributional Terrorist.

The Psychological Profile of the Retributional Terrorist

From studies of war victims and individuals who fought in "third world" crises, and who may have engaged in acts of international violence and crime,[2] a general psychological profile can be offered. This profile encompasses an array of developmental aspects and contributes to our understanding of what motivates a retributional terrorist.

Developmental History and Adjustment

The psychological and medical history of interviewees revealed no pathology (in other words, the person seemed normal). The usual childhood illnesses were experienced with no complications. Developmental milestones (walking, talking, bladder control) were reportedly met within usual age ranges. Childhood emotional and behavioral patterns were indicated (or were reported) as uneventful. The individuals may admit to substance use (alcohol, drugs, and cigarettes) at a social level, but considered themselves nonabusive.

Born into "close-knit" families and raised by both parents, they usually had several brothers and sisters. Some siblings were as young as preschool age at the time of the traumatic incidence. Typically, an extended family of grandparents, aunts and uncles, and cousins lived in the same community. There were several gatherings during each week for socials events—family, community, or both. The extended family embraced relatives and the community at large.

Educated through secondary schools and possibly a few years of university, some individuals could speak three languages fluently and performed well in science and literature courses. Social adjustments in school were evident of a large number of friends and acquaintances. They reported no disciplinary problems.

Resulting from a war or a crisis, severe economic loss was experienced and some financial assistance came from a cultural welfare system. This was personally humiliating for the individual and surviving family members.

Some were married and had financial and emotional responsibilities to a spouse and children, while others were never married and had no children, thus having no responsibilities to any significant others. In either case, surviving parents and siblings would constitute mutual support and the quest of provisions for basic survival.

Mental Status Evaluation

The participants interviewed for this study were alert but guarded. There were no peculiar mannerisms, tics, or tremors. They looked clean and neat. Height and weight varied from individual to individual. Speech patterns were relevant, coherent, and appropriate to the conversation (in their language of origin and in English). Their manner of speaking was appreciatively dramatic, and their range of intelligence seemed to vary. There were no signs of psychosis or neurological deficit. The prevailing mood was blunted. Emotional swings and anxiety symptoms were attributed to the significant family trauma experienced. Clinical signs of depression were observed. They were oriented to person, place, and time. Memory was intact, insight was good, and rational judgment was not impaired.

Sleep patterns were reportedly marked by sporadic insomnia. Nightmares were reported and related to the massacre of their family and friends. Feelings of guilt were associated with the individuals' feelings of social impotence in not being able to stop the unjust crime against significant others. Trends of paranoia were reported in relation to a general anxiety about the enemy, concerns of further attacks, and political paranoia about the nation/state.

Summary of the Retributional Terrorist Characteristics

In sum, the individuals interviewed in these studies exemplified the following characteristics:

- There were males and females of various ages, with no unusual developmental history other than suffering a significant personal trauma in early life.
- They were sociable and disciplined and observed moral codes.
- They lacked self-control in vengeance but would discriminate between the innocent victims and the sought target(s).
- They were bright and intelligent, formally educated, with very close family ties.

- They demonstrated appropriate adaptation and use of ego defense mechanisms.
- Their socioeconomic status varied.
- They felt alienated and discriminated against.
- They articulated no future goals (lacking aspiration and in some cases exhibiting a total loss sensation).
- Their adolescent patterns were interrupted by war and necessary undertaking of militia roles for economic/cultural survival; their young adulthood process discontinued with little or no aspirations for marriage or family (hopelessness).
- Even though they first pursued individual retribution, they later joined and adopted ethnogeographic groups (political or religious) for support (as a result of feeling helplessness).
- They exhibited frustration from conflict between conditioned motivation and unconditioned economic and political restraints.
- They knew that terrorism was a crime, but believed in no other way to avenge their loved ones' unjustified and unwarranted death and the loss of their own future aspirations.

A Lack of Forgiveness

Survivor guilt may override one's cognitive restructuring of reasoning and earthly mission. Resentment is usually fuelled by guilt. Rather than live with the guilt of having not protected one's family, friends, and community, one may fixate on the resentment and anger (usually fuelled by psychological hurt), bypassing the process of forgiveness. The retributional terrorist may not want compassion and understanding or respect when offered by sympathizers. Yet history gives examples of horrendous offenses and heroic forgiveness. For example, noted author Corrie Ten Boom lost her family in the Holocaust and was able to forgive.[3] Can one forgive the kidnapping and murder of a child, or an automobile accident killing innocent bystanders caused by a deliberate reckless driver who was drag racing, intoxicated, or both? Forgiveness is a choice, says Robert D. Enright in his book by the same title.[4]

One may never forget, but one can muster forgiveness. It is unnatural not to be angry at the brutal death of a loved one. Yet, psychologically speaking, no act is unforgivable. However, some choose not to forgive. Professionals seeking an understanding of the retributional terrorist need to respect the right of choice to forgive or not forgive or to appreciate that the process of forgiveness has not begun.

Unpardonable, Therefore Unforgivable

The atrocity experience—a loss of family, friends, community, or any combination—can mean the total destruction of life's purpose to the retributional terrorist. He or she faces an absolute, unrepentant, unredeemable aggressor. Thus, the avenger perceives no wrong in pursuing equal retaliation in the form of physical destruction and loss of life. Annihilation is a deserved reaction, one that is justified and warranted in the eyes of the retributional terrorist.

A Comparison of Profiles

One goal of the study of terrorism and terrorists is to establish a useful categorization and diagnostic differentiation of terrorist types for effective profiling and negotiating with the different styles. To curtail or even negate international terrorism, professionals must understand the type of terrorist with whom we are dealing whether engagement is preventive or defensive action. Not only will this strategy aid in recognizing recruitment styles, but it will also assist in recognizing negotiation tactics that should vary with the personality types. Table 12.1 provides a brief summary of some of the most salient characteristics of various terrorist types.

The psychopathic terrorists may be the easiest with whom to deal. Although they may recklessly and indiscriminately harm and murder others, their narcissistic quality lends itself to self-survival, so personalizing the negotiations can be considered. The ethnogeographic (political or religious) terrorists are demonstrative and have specific goals that are basically unrealistic for making a deal. These persons usually want the land of their forefathers returned and they want this area to be governed only by their ideological system. Also, martyrdom or suicide missions seem more likely to be related to this type of terrorism.

In contrast, the retributional terrorist may be the most difficult to negotiate with. Although hostages may be just instrumental victims (leverage for negotiating), little or no harm may come to the captives. These terrorists have a very specific target—the individual or group responsible for the trauma they experienced. They seek only that person or group. This type will discriminate harm from nonsignificant others as opposed to demonstrative random killings. They may be suicidal, but do not necessarily wish harm to innocent people. Also, they may be explosive for purposes of controlling a situation when they are not carefully approached. Possible negotiations may center on an emotional approach regarding the innocent victims and hostages, just as the recruitment may have been an emotional approach.

Post-Traumatic Stress Disorder

Many of the characteristic features of the retributional terrorist are similar to the diagnostic symptoms of Post-Traumatic Stress Disorder (PTSD). In

Table 12.1
Terrorist Types and Characteristics

Psychopathic	Ethnogeographic (political/religious)	Retributional
Amoral	Ideological	Moral
Manipulative	Seeks control	Social
Exploitive	Rigid, inflexible	Educable/intelligent
No goals	Displaces the word "wrong doing" with the word "war"	Ethical
Intelligent		Significant early-life trauma onset
Personality disorder	Egocentric	
Nondiscriminative targeting	Emotional priority for the cause	Discriminates targets
		Object relative
Narcissistic	Possibly suicidal martyr	Hopelessness
Unethical (lacks superego)	External superego	Age varies
	Educable/intelligent	Male or female
Age varies	Specific goals set	Close family ties
May kill for money (secondary gain)	Adolescent/young adult	No premorbid characteristics leading to disorders
	Male or female	No familial conditioning or loyalty to a particular group
	Close family ties	
	Familial conditioning and loyalty to the group	
	Ambivalence target discrimination	Good use of psychological defense mechanisms but possibly explosive
	Believes that death for the cause is rewarded in Heaven and others (hostages) who die during the act will also be rewarded in kind	May later join a support group
		Suicidal
		Death is not a threat for them but they do not want others to die necessarily
		Hostages are instrumental victims or third party leverage for negotiations

Note: This categorization was developed in 1986 by Raymond H. Hamden while serving as a Visiting Fellow in the Center for International Development and Conflict Management, University of Maryland, College Park, 1986. It is the product of research and consulting in political psychology, with an emphasis on the psychology of terrorists, hostage situations, and fundamentalism.

clinical terms, PTSD[5] results when an individual has been exposed to a traumatic event in which two elements are present: 1) the person experienced, witnessed, or was confronted with an event or events that involved actual or threatened death or serious injury, or a threat to the physical integrity of self or others; and 2) the person's response involved intense fear, helplessness, or horror (it is important to note that in children, this may be expressed instead by disorganized or agitated behavior). These traumatic events can be persistently re-experienced in several ways:

1. recurrent and intrusive distressing recollections of the event, including images, thoughts, or perceptions (in young children, repetitive play may occur in which themes or aspects of the trauma are expressed);

2. recurrent distressing dreams of the event (in children, there may be frightening dreams without recognizable content);

3. acting or feeling as if the traumatic event were recurring, which may include a sense of reliving the experience, illusions, hallucinations, and dissociative flashback episodes, such as those that occur upon awakening or when intoxicated (in young children, trauma-specific re-enactment may also occur);

4. intense psychological distress at exposure to internal or external cues that symbolize or resemble an aspect of the traumatic event; and

5. physiological reactivity upon exposure to internal or external cues that symbolize or resemble an aspect of the traumatic event.

An individual with Post-Traumatic Stress Disorder will typically seek to persistently avoid stimuli associated with the trauma and will demonstrate a numbing of general responsiveness, as indicated by three (or more) of the following: efforts to avoid thoughts, feelings, or conversations associated with the trauma; efforts to avoid activities, places, or people that arouse recollections of the trauma; an inability to recall an important aspect of the trauma; markedly diminished interest or participation in significant activities; a feeling of detachment or estrangement from others; a restricted range of affect (e.g., unable to have loving feelings); and a sense of a foreshortened future (e.g., he or she does not expect to have a career, marriage, children, or a normal life span). Individuals will also exhibit persistent symptoms of increased arousal (not present before the trauma), as indicated by two (or more) of the following: difficulty falling or staying asleep; irritability or outbursts of anger; difficulty concentrating; hypervigilance; and exaggerated startle response.

Individuals exhibiting signs of Post-Traumatic Stress Disorder (often represented by clinically significant distress or impairment in social, occupational, or other important areas of functioning) require professional treatment. Perhaps the same can be said for individuals who demonstrate an unusual concern for retribution or vengeance, given the reality that both are rooted in the realm of psychological forces, and require an understanding of how psychological defense mechanisms may dictate a person's behavior.

Psychological Defense Mechanisms to Traumatic Experiences

The justification of retribution is critical to the psychology of the retributional terrorist. To this individual, a crime of terror has cost him or her every purpose in life (family, friends, community, or all), even when the crime was an act against the state, a violation of a law, or an abstract idea that originally had nothing to do with the individual. The avenger may realize or perceive that the criminal justice system was not able (or simply did not) control this and other similar crimes against him or her. Yet the offender must be held accountable and must be punished, and if the state is not doing so, then this individual feels he must avenge his family, friends, and community.

When the crime is an individual act, then the individual is held responsible; when the crime is a state act, then the state is held responsible. The retributional terrorists view innocent victims as peripheral to the process of obtaining vengeance and may use hostages as instrumental victims or third party leverage for negotiations. They typically have no direct intention to harm the guiltless, as well as members of their own family, friends, and community. Their focus on establishing blame and guilt is emphasized in their adversarial relationship with an aggressor, individual or state, and their responses are focused on the offender's past behavior. When individuals fail at their attempts at extracting vengeance on their own, their typical next step is to join a group—most commonly, an ethnogeographic organization—that is both committed and able to carry out the overall goal of retribution.

Our understanding of psychological defense mechanisms to traumatic experiences comes from the integration of contrasting coping models—social support, conscious cognitive strategies, and unconscious defense mechanisms—that have been developed by various social psychology and personality theorists. A synthesis of these models of human psychology can help us better understand the retributional terrorist.[6]

Early contributions to human psychology include Dr. Sigmund Freud's hypothesis that unconscious defense mechanisms protect the individual from painful emotions, ideas, and drives. However, among the professional psychology community, there is disagreement about the nature of defense mechanisms. Some believe that discrete defense mechanisms can be understood both as building blocks of psychopathology and as stepping-stones of ego development. Others consider defenses to be obscure: The more closely one looks at them, the more difficult it is to study and verify such individualized psychological defense mechanisms.[7] Freud discovered most of the defenses mechanisms that we refer to today and identified five important properties:

1. Defenses are a major means of managing instinct and affect.
2. They are unconscious.
3. They are discrete.
4. Defenses are dynamic and reversible.
5. They can be adaptive as well as pathological.

The likely defense mechanisms found with the retributional terrorist are

- *controlling*—an excessive attempt to manage or regulate events or objects in the environment in the interest of minimizing anxiety and solving internal conflicts;
- *rationalization*—the justification of attitudes, beliefs, or behavior that may otherwise be unacceptable by an incorrect application of justifying reasons or the invention of a convincing fallacy;
- *anticipation*—a realistic anticipation of, or planning for, future inner discomfort; and
- *intellectualization*—dealing with emotional conflicts (or internal or external stressors) by the excessive use of abstract thinking or generalizing, in order to avoid experiencing disturbing feelings.

These defense mechanisms can be categorized as anxiety defenses, disavowal defenses, and mature defenses. Other defense mechanisms that may apply are displacement, dissociation, and possibly sublimation. *Displacement* refers to the purposeful redirection of feelings towards a safer or less important object than the person or situation arousing the feelings or impulses. The feelings remain the same, but the object is changed. Displacement involves the discharge of emotions, often anger, onto a person perceived as less dangerous by the individual than those with whom the feelings were originally evoked. *Dissociation* is a temporary yet drastic modification of character or sense of personal identity to avoid emotional distress. While *sublimation* is considered a mature defense, it is defined as gratification of an impulse whose goal is retained but whose aim or object is changed from a socially objectionable one to a socially valued one.

When investigating the status of defense mechanisms and their scientific application, there are three questions that must be answered in the affirmative. First, can defenses be reliably identified? Second, do they have predictive reliability? And third, can maturity of defenses be demonstrated to be independent of the environment? An effective way to alter a person's choice of defensive style under stress is to make their social milieu more predictable and supportive. This serves to stabilize the external environment. Altering the internal environment is equally important. Facilitating internal as well as external safety may be the cornerstone to the process of modifying the individual's behavior.[8] Most psychologists believe that people are better at sublimation and reaction formation when basic needs (food, water, shelter) are met.

Environmental Influences that Support Retributional Terrorism

Communities reinforce the psychological aspects of retributional terrorism identified earlier. In many cases, they may offer verbal and nonverbal social pressures to pursue revenge. An individual's family, surrounding peer group, or community may reinforce their view that pursuit of vengeance is absolutely necessary. This may be seen mostly in organized communities who have a political or religious mission, but there are other factors to consider as well, such as the rule of law (or lack thereof).

A Community of Violence

In many instances, violent communities are hotbeds of retributional terrorists. Places where disagreements or feuds are settled through violence—as opposed to the rule of law—serve to further support the worldview of the retributional terrorist. Easy access to weapons, and in many cases weapons training, aids the retributional terrorist in developing the ability to achieve his or her goal of extracting vengeance upon the enemy. Areas of high crime and personal insecurity reinforce the "us against them" mentality of the retributional terrorist. And government oppression of civil liberties creates an environment with great potential for retributional terrorism.

As described earlier in this chapter, there are several psychological dimensions which may lead to retributional terrorism at the individual level. There are also a number of environmental dimensions which may lead to retributional terrorism at the community level. For example, ethnic cleansing or other forms of widespread atrocities can easily lead to the types of bloodshed seen in recent history: in Rwanda, the Hutus and Tutsis; in the former Yugoslavia, the Serbs, Bosnians, Croats, and Albanians; in Chechnya, the Russians and Chechens; and in the Middle East, the Palestinians and Israelis. In each of these cases, horrific examples can be found of violence that was pursued as retribution for perceived injustices.

Human populations are targets of terrorism because of the vulnerability of people. Some possible terrorist agendas involve more or less direct assaults on human life as a primary objective. These can include bombings of human assemblies at sporting events and other mass gatherings; attacks using nuclear weapons on large cities; assaults on toxic/explosive storage and production sites; assaults on water systems; bombing of mass-transit systems, particularly at rush hour; bombing of hospitals and day-care centers; and biological, chemical, and radiological contamination. Attacks such as these—where mass casualties are seen as the necessary step towards achieving a particular terrorist group's goal—blend into attacks that involve the *possibility* of human deaths but whose primary objective is to disrupt institutional functions and social processes. In many cases, these attacks upon populations and social processes are driven by a desire to extract retribution for perceived injustices. As such, individuals committed to such retribution are perhaps one of the most lethal—and most motivated—type of terrorists the world has ever seen.

Recruiting the Retributional Terrorist

Psychological and environmental factors combine to develop opportunities for terrorist recruitment. Organized terrorist regimes typically have some form of personnel vetting system, through which they scrutinize individuals seeking group membership. In nations of poverty, a potential recruit may be seeking financial benefits by joining a terrorist organization, some recruits may be conditioned by family and community sociopolitical values, others may be persuaded to become heroes for the welfare of their community, and there are those who seek Heavenly reward by fighting for a cause. As for the retributional terrorist, recruitment may only come after the individual has sought vengeance alone. This individual usually begins the quest for vengeance as a "lone wolf." Successful accomplishment of retaliation against the "enemy" has been limited or has failed. Since little is left in life for the individual to pursue, he or she will tirelessly chase the foe. Recognizing that the quest requires support, the retributional terrorist will consider or seek attachment to a group which shares the same enemy.

Therefore, enlisting the retributional terrorist in a terrorist group is fairly easy when the goals of both are aligned—that is, where a common enemy is identified. Recruitment of individuals by such groups, given their shared objectives of retributional violence, is fairly straightforward and easy to understand. The potential of a long-term relationship with a religious or political group is dependent upon a sense of belonging and purpose with the organization. The group or organization may become the "family, friend, and community."

As evidenced by the diversity of chapters in this volume, there are many strategies with which terrorist groups will seek recruits, including radical interpretations of religious texts or teaching radical ideas to young impressionable boys and girls who are seeking a purpose in their respective lives. Islamic fundamentalists use religious, economic, and political themes to convince potential recruits that they are acting heroically to save "their kind (of people)" from the satanic Americans, with particular focus on Western military presence in Saudi Arabia and Iraq. With the strength of this argument focused on the stereotype of the West as "evil" and immoral, relatives and friends influence the potential recruits as hopeful heroes who will save the world from Western demise. This can also satisfy the recruits' Survival Guilt Syndrome—men and women feeling guilty that their friends, family, and relatives have died for "the cause" but they are living the benefits of the martyrs sacrifice.

Examples abound in the Middle East of individuals seeking revenge, through violence and terror, against an enemy (Hamas, Hizballah, the al-Aqsa Martyrs Brigades, the Israeli military, etc.) because of some incident or another. For example, the story of Hanadi Jaradat reveals how mental crises can push a very educated person with a nonviolent record to volunteer for a suicide attack.[9] After finishing her high school studies, Hanadi went to Jordan where she began studying for a law degree. In 1995, when she was twenty-one years old, her fiancé was killed by Israeli Defense Forces (IDF) troops. Years later, in 2003, she witnessed the killing of her brother Fadi by IDF soldiers. Further, after her brother was shot in front of her, the IDF soldiers did not let her approach and help him. Fadi had always supported Hanadi's desire for higher education and helped her financially during her stay in Jordan (the father of the family suffered from cancer and could not work). Shortly after this traumatic event, during her brother's funeral, she declared that she wanted to revenge her family. She was almost immediately recruited by the Palestinian Islamic Jihad (PIJ) organization to become a suicide bomber, and on 4 October 2003, she entered a restaurant in the city of Haifa in Northern Israel and detonated her explosives, killing nineteen Israelis and injuring more than sixty—many of them families with young children.[10] Clearly, the PIJ activists who recruited Hanadi used her strong urge for revenge.

Any number of dimensions can have a role in recruiting the retributional terrorist. However, whether online or in physical form, the most likely scenario is that a retributional terrorist would join a group not only for ideological or economic considerations, but because that group is perceived as helping the retributional terrorist achieve his or her goal of extracting vengeance upon their sworn enemy. In situations where an individual seeking retribution or vengeance may not have access to a local group with a shared goal, he or she may then join groups with more broadly defined violence goals and targets, simply as a means to an end. Of course, some terrorist organizations may not want to be "used" by the retributional terrorist in this fashion. As other chapters in this volume have indicated, alignment of goals between the individual and group plays an important role in terrorist recruitment.

Conclusion

Terrorist recruiting reaches across the globe, facilitated by the rapid spread of modern communications and transportation. Potential terrorist recruits typically need goals and purpose in their life; they seek a life of fairness, freedom of expression, economic security, and health. Terrorist groups can attract the recruit with financial security, while offering them the right to be heard and be treated with respect, as well as an heroic purpose for the common good of his and her people.

An additional set of factors are found among the retributional terrorist, both at the individual/psychological level as well as the environmental/community support level. As a member of a well-organized and capable organization, the retributional terrorist is a daunting enemy. However, a "lone-wolf" retributional terrorist may be even more dangerous than some groups. Timothy McVeigh, for example, is considered by some to have bombed the Alfred P. Murrah federal building in Oklahoma City—killing 168 and injuring hundreds more—in retribution for the government's actions against David Koresh and the Davidians in Waco, Texas, two years earlier.[11]

What are the implications of understanding the retributional terrorist? For one, a government's actions must be examined in terms of potential for creating a community of future retributional terrorists. In recent years, Osama bin Laden and other Islamic terrorist leaders have done much to spread the idea that a violent jihad is needed against Western nations as retribution for the sufferings of the Palestinians and others in the Muslim world.

One psychological interpretation of the reasons that a person resorts to terrorism involves the concept of frustration—particularly economic or political frustration. Extreme frustration may be the result of deprivation—for example, when communities experience work and income deprivation, there is little or no sense of productivity. This can lead low self-esteem or a perceived lack of belonging to a society, particularly if the individual perceives that he or she is not contributing to the welfare of the family and the community. In such instances, it is not money that alleviates frustration. Frustration equals expectations minus attainment. Of course, while money does not "buy happiness," we can observe that a little more money could make some people a little happier. Yet, when employees of companies go on strike "for more money," and they are successful on obtaining concessions from the company's management, the same outcry can be heard just a few months later. Analysts thus realize that money is not the answer. Instead, money is symbolic of the ability to provide and protect one's family, and gives a false sense of importance. In actuality, the demands of the employees were based more on a need to be respected and trusted, treated with dignity, appreciated for their contributions to the workplace, and have the ability to live with pride and integrity.

Although there are similar psychological explanations for acts of terror, there is no excuse. The purpose of terrorism, of course, is to terrorize. And terror is, above all, a response on the part of people whose fear (the terrorist hopes) will alter policy or behavior in some way which the terrorist desires. This definitional truth, however, is only partial. The effects of terrorist activities, like the individual and collective motives for such activities, can be multiple—political, economic, military, and symbolic.

It is thus exceedingly difficult to foresee and plan to cope with any specific terrorist act. Each nation must make efforts to deter such acts and, when that is not possible, to counter and minimize terrorists' actions. Since good intelligence may be difficult to acquire, it is useful for the academic community to study terrorist recruitment techniques, organizational modes, and methods of operations (such as choice of targets and weapons). This is only one of the areas in which social science research can make a useful contribution. Given that terrorists may arise from many cultures and be motivated by a range of attitudes, studying the phenomenon of terrorism from a social and behavioral perspective could help to interpret fragments of intelligence information, to broaden understanding of terrorists' modes of actions, and perhaps ultimately could tell us how to curtail such actions.

PART III

IDEOLOGICAL DIMENSIONS

CHAPTER 13

Political and Revolutionary Ideologies

LEONARD WEINBERG

The purpose of this chapter is to investigate the relationship between political and revolutionary ideologies and terrorism. The overall project is aimed at explaining how and why people become terrorists. The working assumption is that the acquisition of certain kinds of ideologies has played an important role in the making of terrorists, or at least certain kinds of terrorists. In order to pursue the investigation it is necessary to answer two preliminary questions. First, what is meant by the term "ideology"? Second, how does an ideology lead to the making of terrorists, if it does? After responding to these questions, this chapter then investigates the contents of the ideologies themselves, by analyzing both left- and right-wing versions of the "philosophy of the bomb."

Ideology and Terrorism: Structure and Function

The temptation is very strong, at least at first, to identify the term "ideology" with the various "isms"—such as socialism, communism, fascism, or Nazism—that emerged during the nineteenth century and early decades of the twentieth. From this perspective, "ideology" comes to mean a complex set of linked ideas which purport to explain current social and political conditions by reference to the past and which also have a predictive quality: If such and such is done, the future will be bright and glorious. In other words, the "isms" were, but for most are no longer, secular religions which replaced the real thing in Europe and elsewhere in the decades following the French Revolution.[1] This definition is not wrong so much as it is limited.

Many years ago David Apter argued that "ideology" refers to more than doctrine. He maintained that ideology "links particular actions and mundane practices with a wider set of meanings and, by doing so, lends a more honorable and dignified complexion to social conduct. From another vantage point, ideology may be viewed as a cloak for shabby motives and appearances."[2] The message that Apter sought to convey is that in addition to their status as doctrines, ideologies function as rationalizations which justify certain courses of action, usually in the name of some general principle(s). Thus, when the nineteenth-century utopian socialist Pierre Proudhon wrote that private "property is theft" he was providing a justification for stealing it.

Another commentary from the 1960s that also has an important bearing on this discussion was offered by Neil Smelser. In seeking to explain the bases of "collective behavior," including violent behavior, Smelser stresses the power of generalized beliefs in mobilizing groups of people to take action.[3] In other words, such objective social conditions as poverty and racial or religious discrimination are insufficient in themselves to cause those so afflicted to engage in collective action. What is required is a set of ideas, an ideology that explains the situation in such a way that groups become ready to act against those people and institutions the ideology identifies as responsible for their circumstances. Then when an event occurs that crystallizes the situation for the deprived, they will be prepared to act.

Based on the above account, one should think of ideologies as sets of ideas that 1) purport to explain general social and political conditions; which 2) perform the function of justifying or rationalizing certain actions; and consequently 3) serve to mobilize people into seizing whatever opportunities for change they may confront.

Now, how do ideologies contribute to the making of terrorists? The best way of answering this question is to distinguish between the personal and the collective. In regard to the personal, Albert Bandura's work on "moral disengagement" is particularly salient.[4]

Most people, most of the time, find it difficult to kill individuals with whom they have had no previous contact. If terrorism involves just such an activity, killing unsuspecting strangers, non combatants, plane or train passengers, largely on a random basis in order to achieve some psychological effect, how do the perpetrators of such acts justify their behavior to themselves and others? What is the rationale for their murderous conduct? How do they evade responsibility?

For more than a century now the perpetrators of terrorist acts have sought to distance themselves from their own deeds based upon nationalist, religious, or ideological formulations. What these formulations have in common is the idea of a transcendent cause which may be employed to justify virtually anything. Thus, it is really God that directs the suicide bomber to detonate his explosive (and himself) in the middle of a crowded bus. The achievement of national independence for a particular people—e.g., Tamils or Algerians—is of such significance that leaving time bombs in bus station waiting rooms or the departure lounges of airports seem trivial measures.

By the end of the twentieth and during the first years of the twenty-first centuries, the world has become accustomed to terrorist attacks justified in religious and nationalist terms: God and the nation have become the dominant rationalizations for terrorism. It was not all that long ago, however, that revolutionary ideologies played a similar role for those Dostoevsky called "The Possessed." For those drawn to the revolutionary "isms," the transcendent cause—on the basis of which terrorism becomes justifiable—is that of a social class or social classes: workers and peasants, or the proletariat. These are the groups in the population whose sufferings are so great at the hands of capitalist exploiters that any form of violence and self-sacrifice becomes justifiable if it can be linked to their redemption.

What should be understood about fascism in this context? The revolutionary or reactionary nature of fascist ideas has been extensively debated by scholars for decades.[5] That fascism provided a justification for the use of terrorist violence in Europe and elsewhere largely during the interwar era is beyond dispute. But was its idea(s) transcendent? In the case of the Nazis and the various groups inspired by them, the main idea was race. To them, the Nordic or Aryan race represented the sole source of human advancement and creativity, and the future of this race was threatened by Jews and inferior races. The defense of the race then offered a rationale for terrorism. The second and more commonly articulated justification for fascist terrorism is the "red" threat. Communists or "reds" were engaged in a murderous struggle to undermine the very bases of European or American civilization on behalf of plotters in the Kremlin, Havana, or Beijing. Any means available were therefore appropriate to defeat this "red menace."

As rationalization and justification for the use of terrorist violence, ideologies have certain properties in common with religious and nationalist ideas. Their common function is to absolve the terrorist and the terrorist group of responsibility for their acts by establishing distance between the perpetrator and the deed or by deflecting responsibility onto to others. The violence is defensive in character because the other side initiated the conflict and is responsible for far more suffering than the terrorists are prepared to inflict to achieve their transcendent cause. The enemy is responsible for their own demise. All peaceful remedies have either been exhausted or were nonexistent in the first place; violence is the only option remaining. The other side is not really human. Rather, the other side constitutes an objective and inherently "criminal" category in the population, so that acts of terrorism carried out against members of the category are not equivalent to attacking human beings. For bearers of revolutionary ideologies, such categories as "bourgeoisie," "capitalist exploiter," "imperialist agent," or "communist" are every bit as dehumanizing and self-justifying as "infidel," "apostate," and "godless" for religiously motivated terrorists.

The willingness to sacrifice the self also seems to be a common theme for religious and nationalist as well as ideologically motivated terrorists. If the terrorist presents himself or herself as prepared to die in the course of staging an attack, that willingness in and of itself constitutes a justification for the deed. The use of martyrdom and self-sacrifice are by no means restricted, for example, to members of the al-Aqsa Martyrs Brigade or Hamas. Revolutionaries may offer to sacrifice themselves as well. The members of the Russian People's Will organization that assassinated the Czar in 1881 justified their act, in part, on the basis of their willingness to die in order to achieve it.[6] The distinction between religious and ideological martyrdom blurs when considering the Russian nihilist Sergey Nechaev's 1869 "Catechism of the Revolutionist:" "The revolutionary is a doomed man. He has no interests of his own, no affairs, no feelings, no attachments, no belongings, not even a name. Everything in him is absorbed by a single exclusive interest, a single thought, a single passion—the revolution. . . . Hard towards himself, he must be hard towards others also."[7]

Revolutionary ideologies also contribute to the making of terrorists collectively as well as individually. If a focus on the individual highlights ideological justification or rationalization for terrorism, analysis of the role of ideology on the collective or group level should focus on the mobilization for terrorism. In the nineteenth and twentieth centuries, the various groups that waged terrorist campaigns in order to make a social revolution (or to prevent one from occurring, for that matter) were typically very small. During the 1970s, for example, such West European revolutionary bands as the Italian Red Brigades and the West German Red Army Fraction consisted of some hundreds of members at the height of their operations. In the United States, the Weather Underground and the Symbionese Liberation Army had a few dozen adherents during the course of their revolutionary activities. How can such aggregations hope to make a mass revolution, given the vast gap between the small size of the group and the large numbers required to topple the existing order?

The answer, in part, is that the members of the groups involved learn that they constitute an elite of the "enlightened" who possess a kind of special knowledge that gives them a unique understanding of the way in which events are destined to unfold. It is the possession of this revolutionary ideology that gives the group strength and mobilizes its members for violent action against the prevailing order. Thus at the beginning of the twentieth century, Russia's small Socialist Revolutionary Party (SR) embarked on a terrorist campaign against the Czarist autocracy based upon its "scientific" socialist ideology, a set of ideas which provided a road map to revolution.[8]

The other way in which the revolutionary ideology serves to mobilize the group's members is the belief that the terrorism will have a ripple effect.

For the anarchists, terrorism was propaganda by deed. A spectacular terrorist attack itself, for example, the assassination of a monarch, served to mobilize the masses for revolutionary insurrection.

Then there is the matter of target selection. Not only does ideology affect mobilization for attack, it also influences the targets of attack. There is evidence suggesting that the type of ideology expressed by the group largely determines who or what it will attack.[9] Revolutionary socialist or anarchist groups tend to attack banks, corporations, business executives, monarchs, and other heads of state. Fascist or racist groups, by contrast, tend to attack "communists" and other "reds" along with their self-defined racial or ethnic enemies.

In what sense does ideology make terrorists? In many cases those recruited by or who seek out a terrorist organization do not possess a clear understanding of the latter's ideological perspective. In fact, terrorists or would-be terrorists may be individuals who have grown tired of talk and fancy phrases. Instead, they are typically individuals who crave action, not rhetoric. Since this is often the case, the role of a full-blown ideology in the recruitment of terrorists is quite limited. Rather, the teaching and learning of ideology usually occurs after the individual joins the organization. Understanding the ideology helps to socialize the recruit and reinforce his or her commitments to the aims of the group and its need to use terrorism to achieve them.

Philosophy of the Bomb: Left-Wing Version

Since its modern origins in the last third of the nineteenth century, two waves of terrorism have been based upon what Walter Laqueur labels the "philosophy of the bomb."[10] Terrorism based upon and justified in terms of left-wing revolutionary ideas (almost all involving the destruction of capitalism and the repressive state) appeared at first in Europe and the Russian Empire following the defeat of the Paris Commune in 1871. The latter had been the largest mass urban insurrection of the nineteenth century and the one that produced the bloodiest repression. In the years following the Commune until the outbreak of World War I, Europe, Russia, and, to some extent, the Americas experienced the first of these revolutionary terrorist waves. The second wave may be traced to the Vietnam War era of the 1960s and early 1970s. In geographic terms, the second wave was more far ranging than the first. In addition to a significant presence in Latin America, revolutionary terrorist activity was seen in virtually all the industrialized democracies, including both the United States and Japan, in the years following the American military buildup in Southeast Asia.

Violent, right-wing, racist organizations willing to use terrorism as a means of repressing their racial or ethnic enemies have been present at least as long as their left-wing revolutionary counterparts. For example, in the American South the Ku Klux Klan waged a terrorist campaign to prevent African Americans from exercising their citizenship rights in the decade following the end of Civil War in 1865. In Czarist Russia, the Black Hundreds staged terrorist attacks on Jewish communities at the end of the nineteenth century. Similarly, in the early to mid-1990s, Serb militia bands carried out a terrorist campaign aimed at ethnically cleansing Bosnian Muslims and Croats from parts of former Yugoslavia. In these and many other cases, the perpetrators of the terrorism possessed little by way of an ideology. When limiting one's inquiry to right-wing groups which conduct their violent operations based upon a complex ideology, it is necessary to focus particular attention on the "fascist epoch" of interwar Europe, on the serious outbreak of neo-Fascist violence that broke out in Italy during the 1970s, and, finally, on the ongoing terrorism associated with far right-wing groups and individuals in the United States beginning in the early 1980s and including the bombing of the Murrah Federal Building in Oklahoma City in 1995—the most lethal act of domestic terrorism in American history.

Between the 1870s and the outbreak of World War I in 1914, social revolutionary terrorism manifested itself in two forms: First, there were efforts to bring down the Russian autocracy by a succession of groups, the most significant of which were the People's Will (*Narodnaya Volya*) and the Socialist Revolutionaries (SRs). The former case involves a small, student-centered band that turned to individual assassination (including that of the Czar in March 1881) after its members' attempts in the 1870s to convert Russia's peasantry to the cause of revolution failed. In ideological terms, the People's Will sought to replace the Czarist regime with popular government. But it did not incorporate in its program a coherent rationale for the use of terrorist violence.[11] Rather, the party turned to terrorism, meaning the killing of single individuals, in reaction to efforts by the police to repress Russia's broader revolutionary movement. The first shot was fired in 1878 by Vera Zasulich at the commander of the police in St. Petersburg in reaction to the fact he had ordered the flogging of a student radical. More than anything else it was revenge or retaliation that led the People's Will to launch its campaign of targeted assassinations, rather than a set of ideas deriving from a revolutionary doctrine.

The SR presents us with a different case. Formed in 1901, the Socialist Revolutionaries Party proved to be the principal rival of the Bolsheviks before the 1917 revolution. The SR shared with the latter a commitment to Marxism, but interpreted the ideology somewhat differently; it sought to win over the entire Russian working class, not merely the urban proletariat. The SR leadership justified the extensive wave of terrorist killings carried out by the Party's Combat Organization in terms of its revolutionary aspirations. Terrorism, the SR argued, was both necessary and inevitable in the Russian context. It performed three essential functions. First, it provided a means for the masses to defend themselves against a police state armed with the most up-to-date weapons and repressive techniques. Second, terrorism performed a propaganda function; it drew attention to the cause, publicizing it particularly among the potentially revolutionary working class. Third, terrorism instilled fear and promoted disorganization among Russia's rulers. The SR, though, emphasized the view that terrorism worked best when it was incorporated with other revolutionary tactics. It had to be part and parcel of the broader revolutionary struggle.[12]

But this was precisely the critique that the Bolsheviks, Lenin and Trotsky in particular, leveled at the SR's tactics. Lenin, with considerable insight, referred to SR terrorism as "revolutionary adventurism" carried out and directed by members of the Russian intelligentsia divorced from the revolutionary movement of the toiling masses.[13] Trotsky was even more scathing: "Conceived in the absence of a revolutionary class, born as a consequence of lack of faith in the revolutionary masses, terrorism can best support its own existence only by exploiting the weakness and disorganized state of the masses by belittling their achievements and magnifying their defeats."[14] In other words, the founders of the modern communist movement dismissed the reputed benefits of terrorism and defined it as a tactic employed largely by middle-class adventurers lacking any authentic ties to Russia's potentially revolutionary working classes. One czarist functionary more or less did not make a difference. The entire system needed to be replaced, and that could only be accomplished by carefully preparing the workers and peasants for their historic revolutionary task. (However, despite their ideological objections, the Bolsheviks themselves were not above engaging in a certain amount of terrorist violence—such as armed bank robberies, or "proletarian expropriations"—in their ascent to power.)

The most explicit case for the use of terrorism expressed by European revolutionaries in the decades between the end of the Paris Commune in 1871 and the outbreak of World War I in 1914 was made by writers identified with the anarchist movement. Anarchism is an ideology which grew out of the ideas of the French utopian socialist Pierre Proudhon and the Russian revolutionary Mikhail Bakunin. As it developed in the 1860s and 1870s, anarchism came to be defined as an ideology which advocated a society of voluntary associations among free individuals for both economic and social activity. The state or government was an inherent barrier to the achievement of such a free society. There is nothing inherently violent about such an outlook. In fact, most anarchists (including the writer Leo Tolstoy), were explicitly opposed to the use of violence to achieve their objectives.

But, if this is true, how can one explain the following? Between 1892 and 1901 individual anarchists assassinated President Carnot of France, Prime Minister Canovas of Spain, Empress Elizabeth of Austria-Hungary, King Umberto of Italy, and President William McKinley of the United

States. Less prominent figures were also targeted during the 1890s. Among other acts, anarchists threw bombs into crowded cafes and theatres, religious processions, and the French chamber of deputies.[15] How are these deeds to be explained?

At the most general level, the answer is that there was another, violent strand in anarchist thought that played an important role in the development of a revolutionary movement that took root in Italy, France, and Spain. This strand emphasized the need to physically destroy the state and bring about the elimination of oppressive economic conditions caused by capitalism. The German writer Karl Heinzen's 1849 essay "Murder" set the tone: "The greatest benefactor of mankind will be he who makes it possible for a few men to wipe out thousands. So when we hear that trainloads of murderers' accomplices have been hurled from the track by a thimble full of fulminating silver under the rails; . . . or that, perhaps, containers filled with poison, which burst in the air, can rain down ruin on entire regiments; or that underground rooms full of fulminating silver can blow whole towns into the air. . . . Then in such methods we shall perceive only to what desperate measures the party of freedom has been driven by the mass party of the barbarians."[16] Writing in the 1880s, another German revolutionary, Johann Most, called attention to the benefits of dynamite. This new invention had made it possible for a few individuals to set a revolution in motion on a modern scientific basis by, among other things, hurling bombs from hot-air balloons down on dignitaries assembled on reviewing stands to witness important state ceremonies. In 1880, the Russian anarchist Kropotkin struck another note: "When a revolutionary situation arises in a country, before the spirit of revolt is sufficiently awakened in the masses to express itself in violent demonstrations in the streets or by rebellions and uprisings, it is through *action* that minorities succeed in awakening that feeling of independence and that spirit of audacity without which no revolution can come to a head."[17]

This leads us naturally to consider the concept of "propaganda by deed." Historians differ over which revolutionary figure was the first to coin the term. The Italians Carlo Piscane, Carlo Cafiero, and Enrico Malatesta— along with the Frenchman Paul Brousse—are the leading contenders. Suffice it to say that at the 1876 and 1881 meetings of the Anarchist wing of the First International, there were repeated calls for the "insurrectionary deed." What its advocates, Cafiero and Malatesta, had in mind was a popular revolt in various Italian localities as a way of showing the masses the way to general revolution. Attempts were made along these lines but failed. These failures led Brousse and other Anarchists to the view that small groups of revolutionaries and even single individuals were capable of making revolutionary propaganda by carrying out spectacular acts of violence against highly visible targets. The new mass circulation newspapers would take care of the rest. The seed would be planted.

The principle, then, that these nineteenth-century anarchists bequeathed to the ideology of revolutionary socialism is this: A small band of the enlightened, or even sufficiently fanatical individuals, can by staging violent actions against selected targets of capitalist exploitation achieve enough publicity to show the working classes the way to revolution. Orthodox Marxists, including Marx himself, had little faith in propaganda by deed. The animosity was often reciprocated. Many of those in France, Germany, Italy, and Spain drawn to anarchist violence at the end of the nineteenth century had come to believe that the orthodox socialist or social democratic political parties and trade unions, though Marxist, were becoming too bureaucratized, their leaders too bourgeois, to be serious in promoting a revolution against the prevailing order. They had become too much a part of that order themselves.

This leads us to the second wave of revolutionary terrorism in modern times, the period of the 1960s and mass protests against the Vietnam War, and what the French writer Regis Debray referred to as the "revolution within the revolution." At the time this new wave of revolutionary terrorism appeared in the mid- to late 1960s, there had also emerged a New Left in both Latin America and Western Europe that was highly critical of the Old Left's evident abandonment of the revolutionary cause. Admirers and followers of Leon Trotsky, Mao Tse-tung and, at least to a certain extent, Fidel Castro asserted that the Soviet Union and the numerous and increasingly bureaucratized Communist Parties around the world that expressed their loyalty to Moscow had abandoned the goal of revolution in favor of reaching an accommodation with the United States and the other capitalist countries—that is, détente—and with the political status quo domestically, that is, euro-communism. "Revisionism," to quote Abimael Guzman, the founder of Peru's Shining Path, "is a cancer that must be totally removed in order to advance the revolution."[18] In a sense then, the ideological dispute between the Old Left and the New Left during the 1960s bore a resemblance to the nineteenth-century conflict between anarchists and Marxists or the early twentieth-century one between Socialist Revolutionaries and Bolsheviks over how to make a revolution or over how a revolution was likely to come about. It was from the New Left or from those seeking to make a "revolution within the revolution" that this new wave of revolutionary terrorism appeared.

The most serious outbreaks of this new wave of leftist terrorism were in Latin America and Western Europe. The former case involves, by and large, groups whose aims were to trigger revolutionary changes in their own countries: Argentina, Brazil, Uruguay, and Colombia. In Western Europe, on the other hand, the terrorist groups were substantially weaker but more ambitious. They hoped to topple the capitalist/imperialist system on a worldwide basis.

The Latin American "urban guerrilla" groups emerged in the wake of

Che Guevara's defeat in Bolivia in 1967. Guevara had hoped to apply techniques from Fidel Castro's successful Cuban revolution, based on a rural guerrilla insurgency launched from the Sierra Maestra Mountains, to all the Andean countries of South America. But these tactics did not work; the Bolivian authorities managed to kill Che and destroy his band of *guerrilleros*. This failure, along with the defeat of a few less ambitious insurgencies, led at least two Latin American revolutionaries to rethink the problem.

In his *Mini-Manual of the Urban Guerrilla*, the Brazilian Communist Carlos Marighella developed an argument in favor of using the city as a base of operations for the revolutionary struggle; only after success had been achieved in the country's vast urban areas should an attempt be made to initiate operations in the countryside.[19] The final stages of the revolutionary conflict would involve the transformation of these guerrilla forces into a conventional army capable of defeating the by-then-demoralized defenders of the corrupt state. Marighella reasoned that the slums of Brazilian and other Latin American cities had become home to millions of the poor and desperate, recently arrived from the countryside. Furthermore, the cities were where the mass media were headquartered. Put these two elements together and you had, Marighella believed, the appropriate conditions for launching revolutionary action. "Terrorism is a weapon the revolution cannot do without. . . . Armed propaganda is an integral part of coordinated urban guerrilla operations. Each individual urban guerrilla operation is in itself a form of armed propaganda. . . . Inevitably all armed actions serve as propaganda vehicles that are fed into the mass communications system. Bank assaults, ambushes, desertions, the diversion of weapons, the rescue of prisoners, executions, kidnappings, sabotage, terrorism . . . are cases in point."[20]

Writing in a similar vein, Abraham Guillen (a Spanish refugee) stressed the importance of small-scale actions to be carried out by clandestine cells operating largely independently of one another and without receiving instructions from a central command. He advised the Tupamaros in Uruguay and the People's Revolutionary Army in Argentina against engaging in large-scale "Homeric" battles with the police and armed forces, confrontations the urban guerrillas could not hope to win.

Marighella, Guillen, and other Latin American revolutionary thinkers were also advocates of "provocation." They believed that acts of terrorism would provoke the police or the armed forces in Brazil, Uruguay, Argentina, and elsewhere into carrying out indiscriminate counterattacks on elements in the population thought to sympathize with the urban guerrilla's revolutionary ambitions. The effect of these reprisals would be to so antagonize these elements that they would become converts to the cause and constitute a growing pool of supporters from which new urban guerrillas could be drawn. The government, in other words, would help to defeat itself. In practice however, when the authorities were sufficiently provoked, they managed to virtually destroy the organizations that had hoped to benefit from this strategy.

The situation in Western Europe in the late 1960s and throughout the 1970s was vastly different from that in Latin America. The latter abounded with millions of the desperately poor, people for whom finding or maintaining enough food, clothing, and shelter was a constant struggle. Most of the countries of Western Europe, on the other hand, were among the wealthiest on earth. The social bases for mass-based social revolution, so obviously present in Latin America, were very limited in such countries as West Germany and Italy. Though both countries suffered serious bouts of left-wing terrorism during the 1970s and beyond, the ideological statements of the relevant groups were significantly different than those active in Brazil, Argentina, Uruguay, Colombia, and similar places.

Leaders of the Italian Red Brigades as well as the German Red Army Fraction expressed admiration for the Latin American revolutionaries, the Tupamaros in particular. And to some extent they sought to emulate their tactics, at least during the early phases of their terrorist campaigns. Early on, for instance, the Red Brigades kidnapped Italian business executives and subjected them to "People's Tribunals" at which they were shown looking forlorn, wearing dunce caps and compelled to confess their "crimes" against the working class. The technique was borrowed from the Tupamaros. Given the differences in both social circumstances and geography however, there were limits to what the European terrorists could take from the experiences of their Latin American counterparts.

The revolutionary ideology was also adjusted accordingly, both in terms of friends and enemies. Both the Latin American and European revolutionary terrorist organizations almost always defined themselves as Marxist in a general sense. The West European bands, however, declared themselves to be at war with capitalist imperialism on a worldwide basis, not simply its local manifestation. In its "manifestos" the Red Brigades' Strategic Direction proclaimed itself to be at war with "SIM," the Imperialist State of the Multinationals. They argued that using such instruments as the Trilateral Commission, NATO, and the European Economic Community, multinational corporations had conspired to bring Italy under their control.[21] The Italian state was simply the weak link in the chain, the one that would prove the easiest to break.

In addition to confronting global enemies, the West European revolutionary terrorist organizations also saw themselves as acting as agents for allies and friends on a worldwide basis. To quote Walter Laqueur on the German groups: "Their policy was not to fight for the 'oppressed and exploited' in their own country [i.e., the metropolitan proletariat] but 'to destroy the islands of wealth in Europe,' to act as agents of the Third World."[22] In practical terms this usually meant collaboration with the Popular Front for the Liberation of Palestine, the Popular Democratic Front for the Liberation of Palestine, and other Third-World terrorist bands attempting to adapt Marxist ideas to what were essentially nationalist struggles.

Philosophy of the Bomb: Right-Wing Version

Fascism was a latecomer in the constellation of "isms" that appeared in Europe in the century following the French Revolution. Though analysts stress that its intellectual origins are in the late nineteenth-century revolt against positivism and liberalism, science and individualism, the movement that first adopted the name, Mussolini's *Fasci Italiani di Combattimento*, appeared following the end of World War I in 1919.[23] In the succeeding years, fascist movements came to power in Italy and Germany. But virtually all the countries of Europe—from Great Britain (the British Union of Fascists) to Finland (the Lapua movement) to Romania (Iron Guard)—witnessed the formation of Fascist movements within their own borders during the interwar period. Like their Italian and German models, all the various movements developed paramilitary organizations designed to engage in street combat against their left-wing opponents and, through public marches and other displays, leave the impression they possessed copious doses of power and dynamism.

Street violence is one thing, terrorism something else. Did the various nonruling fascist movements also carry out the kind of small-scale, premeditated acts of violence normally associated with terrorism? The answer is yes, at least to a certain extent. In Romania, for example, the Iron Guard (or Order of the Archangel Michael) set up small Death Squads that assassinated a long list of politicians including two prime ministers. Also during the 1930s, French fascists belonging to a Secret Action Committee killed—among others—the Rosselli brothers, anti-Mussolini émigrés. And most spectacularly of all, members of the fascist Croat group, the Ustasha, assassinated the king of Yugoslavia and the French foreign minister in Marseilles while the monarch was on a state visit to France in 1936. (This event prompted the League of Nations to draft the first international conventions concerning terrorist attacks on heads of state.)

Beyond its obviously violent anticommunism and antisocialism, important components of fascist ideology provided justification for the use of terrorism. According to virtually all its advocates and observers, fascism is a doctrine that celebrates a life of action and self-sacrifice. As compared against the drab life of individual material acquisition linked to capitalism or the equally degrading world of socialist collectivism, fascism stresses lives of adventure, heroism, and violence in the service of a noble idea, to be lived by small élite orders of the most spiritually elevated and physically gifted elements in the population.[24] While the left-wing version of the philosophy of the bomb tended to regard terrorism as instrumental—a means to the end of revolution—the fascist version sees terrorist violence as an existentially beneficial activity.

Italy, the same country that gave birth to the original Fascist movement, was also the locale for Europe's most significant wave of neo-Fascist violence during the 1960s and 1970s. The context for its expression was a growing wave of extraparliamentary Left agitation and protest in which hundreds of thousands of students and industrial workers participated in 1968 and 1969.[25] On the Far Right the belief became widespread that the mass street demonstrations and the growth in electoral support achieved by Italy's large Communist Party was part of a general scheme to transform the country into an East European–style people's republic.

As a result of this view various violent anticommunist groups emerged. The most attention getting, during Italy's "years of lead," were the New Order, the National Vanguard, and the Nuclei of Revolutionary Action. The quintessential acts of terrorism carried out by members of these neo-Fascist bands over the years were the anonymous bombings of public places. The first episode of its kind was the bombing of the National Agricultural Bank branch in Milan on 12 December 1969, an attack that killed 16 bank customers. The last, at least to date, was the explosion within the waiting room of the Bologna railroad station on 2 August 1980, which killed eighty-five vacation-bound travelers.

The initial purpose behind the neo-Fascist terrorism was to create an atmosphere in which Italians would tolerate a coup d'état by elements within the country's military/police leadership. Accordingly, under the label "strategy of tensions," neo-Fascists and their sympathizers staged the initial anonymous bombings to make it appear as if they had been carried out by left-wing revolutionaries. Eventually this scheme was discovered by the press and defeated by the Italian government, judicial investigators in particular. By the end of the decade the neo-Fascist groups had turned to "armed spontaneity" in the hope that the Italian state could be "disarticulated." At this point the neo-Fascist terrorists committed to a course of armed spontaneity appeared less interested in toppling the Italian government than in acting as "holy warriors," achieving a kind of self-fulfillment by attacking the drab institutions of bourgeois society.

The ideologue most responsible for this line of reasoning was Julius Evola (1898–1974). A minor figure during the Mussolini era, Evola became revered among neo-Fascists in the decades following the World War II. He believed that Italy—and indeed the Western world more generally—had entered a period of almost irretrievable decline, the result of the impact of materialism, Marxism, liberalism, and Zionism (he was a "spiritual" anti-Semite).[26] Evola thought that some hope might rest in the efforts of a handful of dedicated, self-sacrificing elites, such as the Waffen SS, engaged in the near hopeless task of stopping the advance of Bolshevism into the middle of Europe during the closing phases of World War II. Élites of "heroes," spiritually advanced men, might through the use of exemplary violence, rest control of the state from the corrupt politicians who presently control it allegedly on behalf of an equally corrupt public. What is called for, Evola believed, was a strong, virile state capable of dominating the economy and the slothful masses. These antidemocratic views were music to the ears of the New Order, National Vanguard, and other neo-Fascist terrorist bands that defined themselves as élites of heroes out to slay the dragons in control of Italian public life.

Since the early 1980s, the United States has also been the locale for significant campaigns of terrorism waged by groups and individuals belonging to the far right end of the political spectrum.[27] Lest one forget, it was Timothy McVeigh—an individual who emerged from this milieu—who was responsible for the worst single act of domestic terrorism in American history: the 19 April 1995 bombing of the Murrah Federal Building in Oklahoma City. The Far Right groups responsible for the terrorist violence may be classified in a number of ways.[28] There are neo-Nazi groups that venerate the memory of (and express the ideology of) Adolph Hitler, and there are Ku Klux Klan groups, whose stock in trade is straightforward racism. But there are also a significant number of right-wing extremist organizations that articulate complex ideological understandings of why the United States is the way it is and what needs to be done to change things. These groups on occasion have spun off terrorist bands, such as the Silent Brotherhood and such "lone wolves" as McVeigh.

What these groups have in common is a view that the Nordic or Aryan race, which was intended by God or nature to rule the United States, is now in great peril. This race has become dispossessed. Inferior races, aka "mud people" or "beasts of the field," now populate America's cities. The government in Washington has fallen under the control of ZOG or JOG, the Zionist or Jewish Occupation Government. Jewish control means that the government promotes such policies as race-mixing and abortion for white women, aimed at destroying Aryan racial purity. What should be done to reverse these developments?

A work of fiction by the late National Alliance leader William Pierce offers popular answers, at least among white racists. In *The Turner Diaries*, Pierce tells the story of Earl Turner a white "yeoman" who joins a band of racial revolutionaries, the Order, that wages a successful terrorist campaign, which includes the destruction of FBI headquarters in Washington, culminating in nuclear war that ends Jewish control (and the Jews themselves along with it) and restores Aryans to their rightful place of domination. The novel's ideas clearly inspired Robert J. Mathews, a member of the Idaho-based Aryan Nation, to form his own real-life Order in 1983 which proceeded to carry out a series of terrorist attacks before federal and local authorities put an end to its operations the following year.[29] Timothy McVeigh, the Oklahoma City bomber, found *The Turner Diaries* so inspiring he sold copies at a financial loss at gun shows throughout the United States.

Louis Beam, a long-time Far Right activist and ex–Klan leader, reached the conclusion that terrorist groups such as the Order are likely to fail in their efforts to ignite a racist revolution because of their vulnerability to infiltration by police informers. Instead, Beam has become the leading advocate of "leaderless resistance." According to his view, single individuals, "lone wolves," or small bands without central direction or control stand a better chance of triggering an Aryan uprising by staging relatively spontaneous acts of terrorism, such as murdering mixed-race couples or highly visible antiracist figures. The goal in this case is RAHOWA, or racial holy war. The hope is that African Americans or Hispanics will be provoked into violent retaliation against the terrorist murders and thereby elicit a violent backlash by enraged whites.

Conclusions

What do these various philosophies of the bomb, both left- and right-wing, have in common with one other? Despite substantial differences in the long-term goals and the range of social settings of the terrorist groups articulating them, these ideological expressions share at least three attributes. First, the ideologies furnish small terrorist bands and their members with an exaggerated sense of their own importance. To observers on the outside, the groups and the individuals belonging to them may appear inconsequential and virtually powerless. But those who come to learn the ideology come to know as a matter of certainty that they possess the means for achieving great things. As a result, the terrorist groups are able to achieve a kind of élitist esprit de corps.

Second, the philosophies of the bomb provide a magic formula by which the groups involved can get their way. Dramatic acts of violence, given sufficient publicity by the mass media, will make the groups' objectives known to wide audiences. Neither enemies nor potential friends can ignore these objectives when they are advertised through dramatic and repeated terrorist attacks. The big talk and the big deed have the effect, then, of placing the terrorist groups at center stage.

Third, and finally, the ideologies offer a pathway to power. The terrorism will raise the level of awareness and trigger a violent uprising, from proletarian insurrection to racial holy war, by a vast pool of supporters previously too victimized and too lacking the required audacity (Order leader Robert Mathews often referred to Americans as "sheeple") to take the initiative.

Despite the pretensions and the damage—both physical and psychological—caused by the ideologically driven terrorist groups over the decades, the formula does not seem to work. None of the groups discussed in this chapter managed to bring their social revolutionary or counter-revolutionary campaigns to a successful conclusion. But these failures have hardly been for want of trying.

CHAPTER 14

The Role of Religious Ideology in Modern Terrorist Recruitment

J. P. LARSSON

A long time ago in a galaxy far, far away a disillusioned young man wanted to follow in his martyred father's footsteps and join a rebellion against an oppressive power. Orphaned by a longstanding struggle, and now left alone as his friends went to join a terrorist recruitment and training camp far away from home, he was poor and dabbled in petty crime. After meeting a charismatic leader of a mystical religion aligned with the rebellion, who employed all the tricks of the trade to recruit him, this young man needed only to see his sole remaining family (his uncle and aunt) killed by oppressive troops, and his recruitment into the terrorist insurgency was complete. He converted to the mystical religious sect of his newfound mentor, and over time became one of its most powerful figures. This young man was, of course, Luke Skywalker, and already after a half-hour of the original *Star Wars* film, we have been shown several of the most important elements effecting recruitment into terrorist groups.

We may surprise ourselves that no matter how abhorrent we find terrorism, we, too, may condone it at times, although we may need a fictional example to illustrate this, as reality is often harder to understand. With very little persuasion, and some good cinematography, most of us are undoubtedly on the side of the terrorists that young Skywalker joined. Even without being an expert in the expanding phenomenon that is George Lucas's *Star Wars*, we must recognize that whatever else they were, Luke Skywalker and Princess Leia and the other rebels were certainly terrorists, as were the cute and furry Ewoks. Han Solo, with his hairy, mercenary sidekick, does not of course start off as a terrorist but as a common criminal whose primary motivation is money. However, as fascinating and enlightening an intergalactic tangent of comparing *Star Wars* and contemporary terrorism may be, it does provide some excellent examples not only of the terrorist/freedom fighter contrast but also of recruitment into terrorist organizations.

With *Star Wars* in mind, it is useful to remember the oft-quoted mantra that "one man's terrorist is another man's freedom fighter." Or, better still, a terrorist is a freedom fighter who attacks you; a freedom fighter is a terrorist who attacks someone else. Though this statement is well-worn it is true inasmuch as very few—if any—violent groups perceive themselves as terrorists. It is a negative and pejorative label. It is also one that inhibits our understanding of the phenomena associated with it, for it would be difficult to perceive of someone *wanting* to join such a group. If, however, observers and researchers recognize that the perpetrators of violent acts (in legal terms, perhaps, acts of terrorism) may not perceive their acts as terrorism, it makes it easier to conclude why some individuals may join such groups voluntarily. They may, for example, see themselves, as "religious warriors" rather than "religious terrorists."[1]

This distinction is important to understand before examining a number of religious elements instrumental in terrorist recruitment. Although many scholars have an intellectual problem with the term "terrorism" as such, there can be little difficulty in defining many violent religious groups as terrorists, in the legal sense, at least.

There are, of course, many reasons why religion is so adept at mobilizing its followers and inspiring them to fight, to the death if necessary. Religion persuades individuals that it is worth both killing and dying for.[2] These are the very ideologies that play a part in terrorist recruitment today, as they have for thousands of years, throughout the history of the religious traditions.[3] Fundamentally, they also tend to be the elements that are conducive to violence within the religious framework. This chapter will not focus on religious violence in general, or religious terrorism in particular; that has been done elsewhere, in this volume and in earlier publications.[4] Instead, this chapter will investigate what sort of individuals may join terrorist groups for religious reasons, and why.

Terrorist groups, much like religions, have no shortage of recruits. While mainstream religions are faced with falling numbers of worshippers, many young people who are angry with society, disillusioned, or under stress tend to turn to more alternative groups that are more in line with their own rebellious thinking. Instead of adopting a liberal and mainstream perspective on life, they therefore turn to a more radical view, with the result that "fundamentalist" groups, "sects," and "cults" gain more followers. These groups, frequently on the margins of society and mainstream beliefs, are often those that espouse violence or provide justifications of violence rather than condemning it. Thus, groups that are in effect "offshoots" from mainstream religions (e.g., Christian Identity, race/religious-supremacy groups, "fundamentalist" groups, etc.) have seen an increase in membership, as have both syncretic groups ("new age" or new religious movements, as well as traditional religions such as Santería, Voodoo, Palo Mayombe, Brujería, etc.) and other nonmainstream groups (e.g., Satanism, Vampirism, etc.).[5] Though greatly different, what the large number of these alternative religious movements typically tend to show is that they are more radical—and more prone to violence—than their mainstream counterparts. However, it is important to emphasize that such groups are by no means always violent, though their approach to religion is often more conducive to such interpretations. Particularly concerning recruitment, it is useful to draw a parallel between "cults" and "religious terrorist groups," as they often have the same organizational structure and function along the same lines. (Although "cults" are not necessarily religious terrorist groups, it may be argued that religious terrorist groups are always "cults.")[6]

Who Joins Religious Terrorist Groups?

There is no single predictable profile of a potential recruit into terrorist organizations, which has made both law enforcement and research very difficult. However, as this chapter describes, various religious ideologies may be conducive of recruitment appeal (and apply) to different types of potential recruits. For example, a well-educated and materially well-off individual may renounce these riches and whole family structures for more spiritual attainment or self-fulfillment (as was the case with many recruits of the Aum Shinrikyō religious terrorist organization in Japan).[7] For others, it may be the exact lack of these riches and families that turn them towards a system which offers a viable alternative and gives them a new family (like, for example, young Tamils joining the LTTE in Sri Lanka or Palestinians joining Hamas in the Middle East). It is the latter group of individuals that are more easily and directly recruited into terrorist groups by a charismatic leader or his lieutenants, whereas the former are more likely to voluntarily seek out the group.

Somewhere between these two camps is a potent mix of the most common form of potential recruit: one that is neither exclusively sought out and recruited, nor joins entirely voluntarily (or not knowing, perhaps, the true extent of the group's beliefs or goals). In these cases, a variety of ideologies, such as fear of punishment or exclusion, play a part in ensuring allegiance.

There is a range of religious ideologies active in recruitment (as explored below), from those that appeal to the voluntary recruits—who actively seek out a group that may express their own beliefs and sentiments—to ideologies that recruiters use to target especially vulnerable individuals, hook them and reel them into the folds of the organization. In between, there are ideologies that ensure allegiance to the group and prevent betrayal and distrust, as well as those that may enhance the violence-conducive elements of religion, turning new recruits more and more towards a path of violence, and ultimately perhaps, terrorism.

In the same way as there are three main types of religious ideologies playing a part in terrorist recruitment, there are also arguably three corresponding types of individuals. While a single profile of the potential recruit may be impossible to establish,[8] it may be possible to suggest that as various religious ideologies appeal to different sets of individuals, types of potential recruit profiles may be established. Although this chapter will not attempt any such profiling in detail, a few observations may be useful.

Despite thorough scholarship to the contrary, the most common misperception—both in cult and terrorist research—is that only weak-minded, irrational, and illogical people join these violent-prone groups.[9] While it is certainly true, as some writers have observed, that the individual religious terrorist is often psychologically damaged, such an argument seems to be proving the exception rather than the rule, as most religious terrorists are highly intelligent and emotionally stable. Indeed, in reality, there is no simple profile of a recruit. While it may be true that many young and disillusioned people turn to religion in times of distress or anxiety, this may be an entirely voluntary choice, as many young people are "seekers" who are trying to find their own answers of how to make sense of the world around them. For some, it is even a "higher calling," with instances where people feel they were "born" to join a certain group. It is often, however, these young and often disillusioned people that are targeted by existing groups, both mainstream and "alternative."

Today, rather than weak-minded, poorly informed individuals on the margins of society, turning to terrorism is more often the conscious decision of educated and strong-willed people who want to make a difference and effect change in society. Often, they have tried other methods before turning to violence, and when they do, religion offers everything they need, from justifications to legitimate targets, tactics, and methods. It is true, however, that they are often marginalized in mainstream society. That is to say, their religious beliefs or social, economical, or political views may not be taken seriously. They may, as a result, feel oppressed, frustrated and disillusioned.[10]

While recruits may be intelligent and strong, it is often when these feelings of frustration and disillusionment are roused that they are more likely to be targeted for recruitment to terrorist groups at these times, as they are seen as vulnerable, naïve and in need of dependency. Schools and colleges, as well as churches and mosques, are perfect places for recruiters to target young people who show these characteristics, as research into "cults" and new religious movements has shown. Before the potential recruit has joined the group, they are often being coached in the beliefs of the group. The group leader, or the recruiter, is very capable at picking up on the sentiments of the individual, and backs that up with arguments from the group's ideology. This is a common feature of all violent religious groups around the world, and echoes true from the Middle East—where views of Israel's occupation are given to young people who feel oppressed—to angry white men who are targeted by white supremacist religions in America, enforcing their thoughts on why they are in seemingly meaningless jobs and so forth. The recruit is therefore given a place in a system that seems to mirror his or her own beliefs.[11]

Scholars and observers from every conceivable discipline have offered reasons for why individuals become terrorists.[12] There are feminist views, psychological perspectives, economic standpoints, and political angles. Some scholars claim that it is young men's sexual failure which leads them to terrorism;[13] others, that it is their allegiance to a "cult of violence," where they become a terrorist because they want to be a terrorist and commit acts of terror.[14] Anthropologists, sociologists, theologians, and jurists offer viable and often very interesting approaches to why an individual turns to the kind of behavior often described as terrorism. In short, although there may not be a single profile of the potential terrorist "recruit," it is clear that there are often "family resemblances" in the type of individual most likely to join terrorist groups (or, indeed, freedom fighters). Of course, while some ideologies are exclusivist to a certain race or creed, taken as an entire phenomenon, members of terrorist groups can come from all nationalities, races, social status, or (former) religion. Indeed, the most striking observation may be that terrorists are so "normal" and so like "us." In many instances, religion features—but often not, and rightly so. Religion does, however, have a fundamental capacity to bind people together in common creed, code, and community organization.

Why Join Religious Terrorist Groups?

The range of religious ideologies that play a role in modern terrorist recruitment can be arranged in three categories, according to the appeal they may have to various individuals as mentioned earlier. One category would include "purely" religious ideologies, which are either by divine mandate or which only serve to benefit the religion directly. Another contains the elements that are focused on the individual; that is, what he or she may be likely to gain, both spiritually and materially. The last category includes the social or societal ideologies, which may benefit the group, society, or community. This last group of ideologies may be the most goal-oriented, and either appeals to, or can be used for, purposes that are not entirely religious, such as a political goal.

The individual may, of course, be influenced either by the religious or societal ideologies. For the very pious, there is little doubt that the religious elements will be more important than secular (or at least not purely religious) considerations. For less pious or religious individuals, considerations such as status or empowerment may prove to be the most central. Either interpretation is, however, without doubt simplistic.

Without trivializing the specific religious ideologies that play a part in modern terrorist recruitment, this chapter seeks to illustrate them within the larger context of a more general exploration of all ideologies. In essence, these can be grouped beneath three categories: religiously focused ideologies, individually focused ideologies, and socially focused ideologies. Although there is considerable overlap between the three categories, they are not exhaustive and are not presented in any order in relevance to importance or rank. It should also be remembered that not all of these categories of ideologies may be valid for all terrorist groups at any one time, but merely that they may influence the recruit as well as being useful for the recruiter. Finally, as discussed later in this chapter, it is important to remember that in addition to playing a role in terrorist recruitment, ideologies are the elements of religion that are most often violence-conducive.

Religiously Focused Ideologies

All religions are *theologically supremacist.*[15] This means that all believers assume superiority over nonbelievers, who are not privy to the truth of the religion. Being allowed the privilege of knowing the truth, by joining the group to whom it is exclusive, gives the individual a certain sense of status, far removed from anything that could be granted in the "normal," secular world. In addition, religion inspires a feeling of ecstasy and enthusiasm not possible through perceivably "lesser" systems, leading those close to new recruits of religious groups to report that he or she initially seems much happier and more content than had been the norm. Other systems may be allowed to exist ("religious tolerance"), as these do not know the truth, they are harmless, or may need to be annihilated (there can be only one truth).

Theological superiority also extends to the physical realities that individuals are faced with in their normal life, as *religious truth is exclusivist.* However, if this exclusivity includes physical promises, such as the believers being a chosen people, or their territory being a holy land, it means that both are given by God to be defended. The individual faced with oppression by a secular enemy will find a religious ideology affirming that his is a holy land given to his people by God, legitimizing violence against his enemy who has thus become a religious enemy. If God chose the people, and their land was similarly given to them by divine mandate, the cause must be just and fighting on the side of God both permissible and obligatory. The potential recruit will be told that his are the chosen people (whether that be according to race, religion, ethnicity, or class) and that God is on his side, thus affirming his place in the group.[16]

As well as being theologically supremacist, and exclusivist, *religious traditions are invariably absolutist*. It is not possible to be a half-hearted believer. You are either totally within the system, or totally without it. There is no possibility of choosing when you are part of the group, or what part of it you chose.[17] Of course, newer systems, such as new religious movements, or "new age" religions, offer a greater choice. Believers of more fundamentalist, or traditional, religions believe that such "marketplace religion" undermines the very essence of religion, and absolute commitment is required. There is only one way to the father, says Jesus, and that is through the son, affirming the argument that monotheistic religions are on the whole more absolutist than other systems. Many mystical religions, or mystical branches of mainstream religions, affirm that personal belief is more important than scriptural belief, and that there are many ways to the same goal (and all religions are thus true for someone). This in itself is an absolutist standpoint, as it negates exclusivist belief in one path and therefore assumes that its truth (that of many paths to the same goal) is uniquely superior.[18] Hence you cannot be a true "liberal" mystical believer and believe that all religions are equally true, as that would include the monotheistic religions with their singular path to salvation. The potential recruit is made well aware of the absolute nature of truth and that the group offers the only way to attain it.

By thus being exclusivist and absolutist, religion affirms that since it is right (and the only holder of the truth), someone else is wrong. It is therefore invariably polarizing values in terms of right and wrong, good and evil, light and dark. While another religion may be tolerated it can never be accepted completely on the same level, as that would compromise its uniqueness beyond possibility. Compromise is impossible, as this would mean accepting that the other may be right too, which it cannot be if there is only one truth. The very *raison d'être* of religion is that it is unique. This polarizes the world into believers and unbelievers. As it is also absolutist, it is not possible to be neither or a bit of both. The potential recruit is drawn towards this both by a sense of belonging, and for fear of being excluded.[19]

Having established that there is only one valid truth, or path, most religious systems entail some provision for mission or proselytizing. There are, obviously, those who are less well off since they have not grasped the true faith. This may not be through any fault of their own, as they may be children or savages. They should therefore be taught the right path, and converted onto it. An individual may see it as his or her duty to embark on such a mission, in the family home, in the local society or beyond. As the crusades and other missionary excursions have proven through the ages, although the mission is to spread a peaceful and loving religion to those less fortunate, the process is very rarely peaceful and loving in itself.

Frustrated teenagers may in vain try to convert their parents and siblings to their newfound faith. This may be prompted by a profound compassion for them—they need to be saved from the error of their ways, or they will perish by the wrath of God, for example. There is also evidence, however, that compassion may take a somewhat more sinister form. By killing an unbeliever (and thus adversary) who does not (cannot or will not) accept the truth, the true believer is saving the unbeliever from the error of his ways. By this reckoning, killing an unbeliever is an act of good (a mercy killing), though this may come as a surprise to the "victim." (A religious fundamentalist once told me that at the outset of the next world war—which, according to him, would be religious—he would kill me first to spare me any further suffering.)

True religion offers the only path to truth, and therefore the only path to *salvation*. This is, of course, related to the aforementioned ideologies of religious supremacy, exclusivity, and absolutism as well as the thoughts on mission and compassion. Most religious traditions affiliate with some kind of final-day scenario, be it a judgment day, doomsday, or rapture. For some it may even be a final battle between good and evil (on the battlefield at Armageddon, for example). Only the true believers are guaranteed salvation and victory, whereas the enemies and the unbelievers—as well as those who have taken no stance whatsoever—are condemned to some sort of eternal punishment or damnation, as well as death. These are powerful images, and allow for easy recruitment of those who fear their fate on this final day. Some groups, of course, believe that actively advancing these events is in their best interests, and violence may be a necessary element in this.

In this coming and ultimately final war, religious truth will reign supreme; Fundamentally, religious ideology affirms that the *cause is transcendental*. It ensures the eventual victory of good against the enemy and the end of oppression.[20] Victory as such is not for the individual, and may not occur in the individual's lifetime, but it will come one day, as the believers are on the side of God. It may, indeed, be impossible to win against the enemy in this lifetime, as the enemy may have far superior military might or a larger number of supporters, but if the cause is religious, the struggle continues through generations of believers, ultimately to triumph over the evil enemy. This gives the individual (the potential recruit) a sense of purpose and importance that may not be there if victory was necessary within one generation (as, for example, may be perceived in the cases of nationalism, anticolonialism, self-determination, etc.). Ultimately, religious (cosmic) dualism is temporary, because truth will eventually win, be it on the battlefield at Armageddon or elsewhere. Each generation may lose their particular battle, but in the end those of the true faith will win the war, thus making the struggle worthwhile.[21]

In the coming battles, as in the final war, the allies of God (the true believers) may be called upon to protect the faith, and defend it from the enemies of God. As the unbelievers—who are often openly hostile towards the believers and their faith—are out to annihilate them, it may prove necessary either to initiate or join a defensive war for the sake of the religion. Even if the religion espouses nothing but true love, compassion, and truth, it may be necessary to employ violence to protect it against perversion, unbelief, and extinction. This is especially the case if it is felt that the religion is cornered and, much like a wounded animal, the only way to survive is to fight.[22] For many individuals, certain religious concepts like this may force them to consider a path of violence and terrorism if they see this as an obligation or a neglected duty of the religion.[23] While this is usually the case in more fundamentalist readings of the scriptures, young people are, as mentioned earlier, on the whole more likely to take such an approach to the belief. The scripture may call for every true believer to rise up from the normalcy of everyday life and fight the unbelievers "wherever ye shall meet them." This realization is often portrayed and perceived as a duty they have neglected, and once it has been pointed out to them they often pursue this newfound purpose with the greatest zeal and are thus likely to not only join terrorist groups who espouse similar views, but will often volunteer for "front-line" duty.[24]

As individual life may not be important in a cause that knows no limits as to time or place, believers may be willing to resort to sacrifice. Although sacrifice in itself is one of the most researched violence-conducive elements of religion, very little has been written on the relation it has with recruitment into religious groups. It is likely that the appeal it has for a potential recruit may be related to the idea of finding a scapegoat onto which the suffering of the believers can be placed. Alternatively, the instant relief promised by the pleased divinity having accepted the sacrifice may affect recruitment.

While these ideologies may seem overly "Western" in their theology, other ideologies are decidedly "Eastern," like *karmic retribution*. Certain religious terrorist groups have been known to justify violent actions against nonbelievers by claiming that it was the bad karma of the "victims" that entitled the believers to use violence against them.[25] It would, as such, be a righteous killing, not unlike killing for compassionate reasons, as noted earlier. Rather than the unbeliever living any longer in this lifetime and accumulating more bad karma, it would be both righteous and compassionate to kill them now. The potential recruit may both be worried about his or her own karma, and therefore do the good deed of killing the adversary, or worried about the other's bad karma, and therefore feel compassionate to kill them. Though karmic thinking is generally found mostly in eastern religions, such as Buddhism, similar justifications for violence (and thus recruitment into violent groups) have been found elsewhere, including in the West, where the "victim" of violence or terrorism is believed to have brought it upon him or herself.

Theological justifications of violence often include some concept of the insignificance of ordinary life, for example that it is impossible for a human being to kill any other human being, as only God can give and take life. While this may mean that it is impossible to kill an adversary in battle (God does the actual killing), it also means that it is impossible to be killed in such a battle (God decides the time and place of death). Normal, secular questions of life and death become futile. Indeed, ordinary life may be completely devalued and an individual may be seen as fatalistic. For the potential recruit, knowing that the enemy cannot kill him or her may come as a huge relief. It also ensures allegiance to the end, as God decides when it is the time to leave this world. Any responsibility is removed from the potential recruit, and any amount of violence may be condoned.

Individually Focused Ideologies

Where an individual is emotionally stable and has support from family and friends, as well as material well-being and, for example, a solid career, they may still feel that something is missing from their lives. They may be *seeking something (spiritually) higher*, or for a sense of belonging. While it is often mostly teenagers that show such feelings, but later "grow out of" them as they become more settled into their identity, another large group are those facing a "mid-life crisis" or a realization that it is not about how many cars are parked on the drive, or how many holidays one can afford every year. Such individuals may turn to religion, and it is often the religions that are more alternative, fundamental or nonmainstream (as highlighted earlier) that receive them with open arms and offer an alternative to the secular, material way of life. These groups may also be more violent than others, as they are more "fundamental" in their approach to life. The pious individual, or the seeker, may be attracted by the clear and concise answers offered, or feel that their concerns are extremely well addressed by the group. Religion offers the potential recruit a chance of self-fulfillment that may not have a secular alternative.

Being empowered through joining a religious terrorist group has the added benefit of giving the individual a *new, and much acclaimed, status*, proving his or her worth as a person. This newfound status is often twofold: first, among his or her peers and family, and second, in society in general, where martyrs, for example, may be revered as heroes. The status of being a member of a terrorist group shows the individual as being truly religious, not just in word but also in deed. On a personal note, the individual feels this increased sense of status by being part of an "élite" group, much like membership to a "secret society," or being an alumni of a prestigious university. Religious ideologies thus also provide a role for individuals whose life otherwise seems to have no meaning or purpose. This role may be to fight the infidel, or change the state of the oppressive world, or (through violence) end the cause of suffering.

For a marginalized individual, the feeling of *empowerment* that can result from membership of a (particularly religious) group is one of the most commonly cited reasons for individuals joining religious terrorist groups.[26] No longer is the person an outsider, a nobody, a failure or unwanted, but as recruiters point out early on in the process they are now given power to "be" somebody and achieve something. The potential new recruit, having been marginalized in society, feels empowered with a new status and a feeling of belonging. They may have suffered tragedy in their lives, such as family death, or grapple with lack of love or worthwhile employment. The religious group offers a solution to this by giving the recruit a new "family" and, fundamentally, a sense of importance and being valued. Psychologically, this is one of the most potent reasons why individuals join terrorist organizations, and as it often plays an extremely important part in this process, religion may be thought to provide the ultimate form of empowerment. In days gone by, joining a religious order or group was seen as so important and empowering that it was not only the prerogative of the eldest son of a family, but also of noblemen, knights, and kings.

At the same time as religion asserts the *identity* of the believers, it also affirms that there are those who do not believe. They do not have access to the truth, and are therefore unbelievers or infidels. Worse yet, perhaps, is that they are hostile towards the truth and the guardians of the truth (the believers). This hostility may be threatening the very existence of the believers and their faith. But although such an enemy is undoubtedly a threat, it is also a promise, for it clarifies the identity of the true believers. Indeed, to an extent the existence of the enemy ensures the existence of the believers, due to a negative definition: "We" are what "they" are not, and since "they" are evil, "we" must undoubtedly be good.[27] For many individuals with the kind of characteristics described previously, this may fit nicely into their beliefs of who they are, or even give them an identity. In return, they are willing to fight this eschatological enemy, to the end if necessary.

As highlighted in the earlier discussion on religion, one of the most potent religious ideologies at work in violence and terrorism is the exclusivity of the belief. In terms of the individual, this may be interpreted as being an issue of self-preservation. Religious rhetoric reaffirms this with statements such as "you are either with us or against us" or that "there is only one way to the goal." It is not possible to be a bystander, or an innocent, in a religious conflict.[28] In order not to be perceived as the enemy, and hence possibly subjected to violence or death, individuals may join religious terrorist groups in order to be on the right side of that exclusivist ideology. That is, the ideology provides the individual with a choice: Either join the group or be castigated as an enemy and face the consequences. Of old, this was a common practice ("convert or die") but it is still very actively the case today around the world, even in the most liberal of societies, as outcast academics, politicians and journalists can vouch for. There is no other choice than to join the ranks and toe the party line. Indeed, the group may provide the only source of information, confirmation, and security, which the new recruit desperately needs.

Having seen religious truth, the pious individual may be ready to *renounce the world*, its material riches and its chaos. The religious ideologies offered by the group, and perhaps the comforting answers from a charismatic leader, make this possible. Religion has, throughout its history, been able to offer renunciation for ascetics, hermits, priests, and monks, as well as for a host of other ranks. This might be what the potential recruit is seeking, and thus he or she joins a group where either such sentiments are the norm, or where they are welcomed as truly religious.

In most religious systems, there is the promise of salvation, as highlighted earlier. For the individual, this may take the form of some kind of *enlightenment*. Being promised a place in paradise, or the key to all knowledge, or simply the escape from the otherwise endless cycle of rebirth is a powerful ideology in effecting recruitment into a religious group. The type of contemporary group that usually offers these all-encompassing final solutions is often fundamental. Complete commitment is required and expected. The potential recruit may be offered the seventy-two virgins in paradise, but only if something—usually violent—is carried out to prove his or her commitment, faith, and loyalty.

There are, of course, other "ranks of attainment" within the hierarchy of religious systems, each with their own access to the truth. As only the highest level (or enlightenment) would offer complete truth, the potential recruit is charmed with the possibility of rising through the hierarchical ranks of the group attaining various rights and privileges. This works to ensure loyalty, much like a corporation or military system would offer the incentive of promotion and pay-increase. The potential recruit may expect to join the organization higher up the ranks, but finds him- or herself on the lowest rung. To gain knowledge, which comes with a higher rank, means having to stay put in the organization or risk exclusion or punishment.

Religious ideologies affirm that almost anyone who is pious and committed to the cause can attain *some form of immortality*, while only the highest ranks may offer complete immortality. This may be true religious immortality of ever-lasting life (in paradise) or it may be a more "secular" version where the memory of the person lives on forever (and thus also the person), as is the case with saints and martyrs. As with the hierarchy, however, attaining immortality usually means proving one's faith and commitment, for example by carrying out a mission that will lead to the sacrifice of one's mortal self with the reward of immortality.

To show his or her ultimate belief and gain the favor of God, an individual may choose to sacrifice his or her own life. There is a school of thought which observes that religious terrorism is for God, without any need for a human audience. There are no human rewards or benefits, only divine ones. For individuals who are very pious, the only option may be to make the ultimate sacrifice to show one's faith to God. Indeed, the very word "martyr" comes from the Greek word meaning "witness."[29] To be a martyr would be to become the ultimate witness to the faith and God. Extremely religious individuals may thus seek out groups where such extremist views are held so that they may get organizational and logistical support for the act of proving their faith. Of course, the group may not be as pious as the individual, but in a mutually beneficial relationship the martyr may take his or her own life only to prove witness to God, which at the same time furthers another cause. Sometimes, therefore, the families of martyrs have been known to become heroes, or to receive monetary "remuneration" for the life of the martyr, as well as the group and cause getting publicity.

Where an individual has led a particularly sinful or nonreligious life, joining a religious terrorist group to fight for the cause and religious ideologies may be seen as the *ultimate purification for the sins committed*. Research indicates that many terrorists swing like a pendulum from one extreme to another—for example, from sexual overindulgence, alcohol, and drugs, to fundamentalist religion. The latter is often violent, and the individual—in the course of seeking penitence, forgiveness, and reconciliation with god—will often pursue a path of violence and terrorism against his or her former life.

If, as some eminent psychologists have observed, terrorism may be a phenomenon for itself,[30] meaning that individuals join terrorist groups in order to become terrorists and pursue a path of terrorism, religious ideology may *provide the moral justification needed to allow for such violence*.[31] It is, in short, a way out of the moral impediments that would otherwise make the transition from individual to terrorist impossible. The religious justifications for violence are foolproof and indubitable for those who believe in them. When mandated by God, any amount of violence is allowed. Also, religious ideologies provide justifications for what otherwise would be regarded as crime, and there are many links between recruitment into organized crime syndicates and into terrorist groups.

One of the clearest religious ideologies at work in recruitment into terrorist organizations is that of *reward and punishment*. The warrior in the cause of God and good is guaranteed a place in paradise, especially if losing his or her life in the struggle. On the other hand, one that refuses this obligation and duty may be punished by eternal damnation in hell. Throughout the history of religion this has been a strong enough influence on people to guarantee their allegiance and commitment to the cause whatever the consequences may be. According to fundamentalist religions, nonbelief leads to damnation while belief leads to salvation. This is the kind of exclusivity described earlier, where religious terrorist groups will use the dualistic rhetoric of "us" and "them" to ensure that potential recruits make the right choice. While the rewards and punishments are after death (in the case of heaven and hell) there are also implications in the believer's lifetime, as inclusion in the group will be a reward and exclusion, conversely, will be the punishment.

Socially Focused Ideologies

Religious cosmology offers an explanation of the world not only as it is, but also how it was and will be. As such, it makes sense of the world in a way that secular systems cannot. The oppression, disillusionment, and fear felt by certain individuals may not be satisfactorily explained—in their mind—by theories of economic globalization, geopolitics, or resource mismanagement. Instead, religion offers a viable alternative to why the world is as it is. Religious myths of persecution through the ages, an original sin, or a fall from grace may all explain to the potential recruit that a better world order is worth fighting for. To restore the glorious past, or ensure a sustainable future, any tactic might be allowed. As such, the religious group affirms the ideology that provides the sole definition of the world.[32]

In addition to making sense of the world, religions also make sense of time. If the present is a time of upheaval, or of revolution, violence may be allowed or even necessary. Similarly, the coming (or return) of a prophet may both explain and require violence. Natural or manmade omens are interpreted as heralding a significant event or action. Individuals may at these times be drawn towards millenarian or apocalyptic groups, as these are very skilful in explaining such omens as signs from God, and so forth.

Not only does a religious system offer explanations to potential recruits of how and why the world is as it is, many religious terrorist groups also show a high level of complex organization. This appeals to many individuals who feel that the world is in chaos. Everything not only makes sense, but there are rituals and structures, scriptures, symbols, flags, and sometimes even uniforms. This is the complete opposite of the chaos of the world, and research (particularly of white supremacist groups)[33] has shown that many individuals are drawn by the almost militaristic structures and thus join the group primarily to be a part of that structure, to be able to wear the uniforms, carry the flags and participate in the rituals. Indeed, the religious organization of ideology and belief also provides groups with one of the best recruitment tools available, as religious symbols and narratives allow for very easy mobilization. In almost every conflict, such symbols and narratives have been invoked to justify, fuel, and sustain violence. The ideologies may be sound and coupled with the power of religious symbolism almost all obstacles can be overcome. In terms of their organizational structure, religious groups also provide the sole source of support for their members by undermining every other system.

While religious ideologies may be able to explain the state of the world, and in particular why believers are continuously persecuted, oppressed, or discriminated, they can also explain how and why violence may be condoned and necessary. That is, religions can explain manifestations of violence. For example, victimization is an extremely powerful recruiting and mobilizing concept, as it condones feelings and actions of vengeance and revenge. It is easy to wonder how a religion that is normally the epitome of peace, love, and compassion can adopt a course of violence and terrorism. The answer is similarly easy: These are not normal times. Many traditions justify violence where society is immoral or decadent. Even Buddhism, for example, which in Western eyes is often seen as the archetypal nonviolent religion, justifies violence in times of *mlecca* (savage).[34] On the other hand, religious ideologies may also explain terrorism and violence as something completely natural and normal, as is the case, for example, in caste systems. If an individual belongs to a warrior caste, like *kshatriya*, he may be required to carry out acts of violence, as this is a duty.[35] Although the caste system (and similar, or tribal, systems) is often thought to be completely extinct in the modern world, millions of people still abide by its rules, and there are even reports of it being on the increase, much like "cults" or nonmainstream religions.

Where believers perceive society to be immoral, decadent, in decline or secular, religious ideology may justify violence to bring about a better world, ultimately built on religious foundations. This would mean returning to a religious "golden age," before the corruption of savages, ignorance, or secularism. The return to the golden age (which may be mythical) gives disillusioned individuals hope of an ideal, and the terrorist group that espouses such ideals provides the methods to get there. At best, the desire to return to this golden age may signify a revival of religious behavior in schools and society, and at worst it may lead to a holy war against those who do not support this perception of pure faith.

Where an individual is faced with difficult choices, religious ideologies explain what is and is not permissible. Indeed, religious ideologies provide the potential recruit with clear guidelines of what methods and tactics are both allowed and expected—for example, when deceit is to be used to facilitate violence against the enemy. For individuals struggling with day-to-day life, and not being sure of when it would be beneficial to oppose the enemy or how, religious terrorist groups provide the answer. All terrorists perceive themselves, on the whole, as altruists, in that they want to make the world a better place. As the goal is thus invariably good, it is often assumed that this end justifies the means, and any violence is therefore condoned.[36]

Religious belief offers an antidote to secularism. In some cases, the "secular project" is deemed to have failed, and religious leaders are quick to step in and explain why this is so, and why religion offers a better (and only) way of life. In many places around the world, individuals may feel that the hardship, suffering, and oppression they face is due to "westoxification"—that is, imported secularism from the West, with its debauchery, drink, drugs, pornography, brash music, and revealing clothing. Though the abhorrence of these "Western" vices is not unique to non-Western societies, religious groups in the West tend to have assimilated more with such a culture, though they may not approve of it. Where "westoxification," or antisecularism, is seen as an issue it may lead to individuals joining groups that vow to rid their country of such foreign influences and re-establish a pure, religious society. This task may not be simple, and may require significant levels of violence. In many ways, these are the wars of independence of the present world, where instead of colonial powers and territorial claims, the imperialism is about ideas and behavior.

In the individual category, discussed earlier, rewards and punishments were highlighted as extremely important in an individual's decision to join and stay in a terrorist group. When applied to the societal sector it becomes more a tool for direct recruitment. That is, threats of punishments and promises of rewards are proffered to the potential recruit. The punishments and rewards that religion provides are very good at ensuring loyalty, as they appeal to the most basic individual fears and hopes. Nonallegiance may not only mean exclusion from the group, and possible subsequent violence or death, but also punishments after death, for example by bad karma or some kind of hell-state. Conversely, commitment and loyalty to the group and cause not only yields rewards in this lifetime, but in subsequent lives (by accumulating good karma) or in paradise. The choice is easy and is usually defined as "you are either with us or against us."

As religion contains the fundamental tenets needed to make proclamations concerning not only the present but also the past and future, it has a strong psychic power of prophecy.[37] By declaring what is happening in the world, what has happened, and what will ultimately happen, it asserts a hold on its followers and a powerful magnetism to potential recruits. It is able to confidently assert the truth and provide all the answers, at the same time as it is explaining the signs and omens from everyday life that enforces these statements. This is prophecy at its most vibrant. It is easy to see how the clear and concise answers that are provided by groups who have mastered this particular religious ideology appeal to many individuals who are perhaps anxious or disillusioned about the world. Prophecy, or perceived prophecy, has a psychic hold on people. Potential recruits may feel they have finally stumbled upon what they have been searching for. With little, if any, manipulation, prophetic statements can be tailor-made to suit a particular audience, to ensure loyalty, or hasten recruitment.

As well as containing the possibility of offering truths as prophecy, religion contains provisions for a charismatic leader.[38] This can be a messiah or a prophet, or a lesser messenger, or "simply" a teacher or guru. In any case, religion affirms that this person is to be followed, and what he (usually, this role is male-dominated) says is tantamount to religious law. In addition to this, as noted earlier, obedience to this leader is compulsory, or members of his group will be punished. It is, however, a religious ideology that directly appeals in the recruitment of young men, as they will invariably see the charismatic leader as a father figure (perhaps where one is lacking from "normal" life). The leader is seen as all-powerful and absolute, much like in a military system. Obedience to this leader is compulsory, and any members harboring doubt or rebellious attitudes are soon weeded out, leaving a hard core of loyal followers. In addition to this, many of these leaders use various other religious ideologies to claim multiple wives (by whom he will father many children), or various forms of abuse.

An interesting tangent to this last point may be to highlight one final religious ideology that plays a part in terrorist recruitment now, as it has for millennia. By fathering many children himself, and encouraging others to procreate, the leader of the group continues the most proven recruitment technique that both alternative religious groups and (religious) terrorist groups use: being born into the organization. Breeding a new generation of religious terrorists, of whatever religious belief, has always proved to be the most effective way of ensuring the continuation of the group and a steady stream of recruits.[39] This is also the best way for religion in general to ensure a continued following, as each new generation is brought up into the wider family of the believers.

Like most issues concerned with religion, as with the ideologies briefly outlined in this chapter, it must be remembered that religious belief is complex. It is likely, for example, that while most of these elements may affect recruitment into terrorist groups, taken together with the various religious elements that may be conducive to violence, the individual believers may not be able to separate them and there is substantial scope for overlapping and expansion. Also, while some may do so, it is unlikely that the average terrorist (or potential recruit) harbors such philosophical thoughts or rationalizations, or pursues intellectual investigations to this degree.

As Easy as ABC?

To conclude this chapter on the role of religious ideology in modern terrorist recruitment, it might be useful to draw all these ideologies into one further argument that some scholars have found helpful in their efforts to understand religious violence: Although a simplified argument, religious violence may really be as easy as ABC. To avoid overly academic language or procedure, it is possible to reduce terrorism to its lowest common denominators without trivializing the phenomenon. This analysis indicates that there are three constants in religious-oriented terrorism, based involving the elements of ideology explored in this chapter, and these constants can be labeled by the first letters of the alphabet.

"A" is for "Another," which represents the always-present concept faced by all groups that take to violence and "terrorism"—namely the existence of an enemy, or "an Other," in the paradigm of the groups. As noted earlier, the religiously defined enemy may not only legitimize the very existence of the group, but the threat of the Other may also justify both the threat and use of violence. This notion of Another is often portrayed as the conflict between the "in-group" and the "out-group," or between "us" and "them."

"B" represents "Blasphemy," and shows us how "terrorism" and political violence may be a prescribed mode of conduct for the group and thus makes it necessary. Not following such a precept (of "terrorism") would be regarded as blasphemous against oneself, the group, and ultimately against God. Although such a term undoubtedly has religious connotations, the concept works equally well with secular groups and ideologies, because a member of the group who does not conform to the standard (of violence, in this case) will often be regarded as not quite true to the cause and often be rejected, becoming an outcast from the "in-group."

"C" is for "Commitment" and illustrates how in order to be entirely accepted as part of the "in-group" (in the sense of "Another") and for fear of not becoming an outcast (as in "Blasphemy") it may be necessary for the "true believer" to show his or her genuine commitment to the cause. Usually this involves compromising any other ideals or principles in favor of those supporting the cause. This may, for example, mean that to show true and genuine commitment, one may be asked to sacrifice the lives of others as well as of oneself for the (perceived) benefit of the cause or that any means of violence may be employed to defend and protect the cause (and the "in-group" of its followers).

Combined with the points raised throughout the chapter, this somewhat simplistic overview of terrorism shows how recruitment into particularly violent religious groups works on the most base and fundamental levels of the human psyche. However, when faced with a belief system that may take to violence and terrorism to further its beliefs or goals, the results may be devastating. Like the original juggernaut, under which people threw themselves—and others—during the Hindu festivals in Jagannath (India), modern religious ideologies may have the power to inspire recruitment into violent terrorist groups around the world. These are what can be called the "juggernaut religions," not because of their size, but because they represent notions for which people are willing to sacrifice both themselves and others.

Acknowledgments

Among the scholars, colleagues, and friends I have used to bounce ideas off, I would especially like to thank three: Greg Barker for helping me see more clearly what drives religious fundamentalists, Lee Harkin for helping me in my attempt to get my head around *Star Wars* (although I did not end up using it—as an example—as much as initially imagined), and—as always—for putting up with my ramblings, Lisa.

CHAPTER 15

Christian Fundamentalism and Militia Movements in the United States

JAMES AHO

Fundamentalist terrorism is on the march worldwide, in Hinduism, Judaism, Islam, and Christianity. Of course, not every orthodox Jew is a potential assassin; only a small minority of Muslim Wahhabis—members of Osama bin Laden's faith—relish the thought of massacring Americans; most Christian fundamentalists would prefer to raise their children in peace. Nevertheless, given the technology of modern violence, it takes only a few bigots to wreak great havoc. Not counting the 169 children and government clerks who died at the hand of Timothy McVeigh in 1995—a per capita murder rate comparable to that of the 9/11 terrorist attack—several scores of people were killed by various types of self-proclaimed American Christian Fundamentalists in the last two decades of the twentieth century, most of them during the first six years after 1980. This does not count the twenty-one McDonald's restaurant customers in San Ysidro, California, shot to death by an alleged Mid-America Aryan Nations member in 1984, the fatal shootout between a renegade Utah Mormon polygamist and police in 1988, or the deaths two years earlier of a married couple who took an entire rural Wyoming grade school hostage to extort ransom from Congress to underwrite the founding of a racially pure utopian society. Because of this, the *who, what, where,* and *why* of Christian fundamentalist terrorism have evolved from matters of idle curiosity into urgent questions of public policy.

This chapter begins by defining what the phrase "Christian Fundamentalism" means, followed with a survey of its appearance throughout American history, briefly describing some of its more notorious recent manifestations. These preliminaries position me to address the pivotal question concerning Christian fundamentalist terror: Why? Here, critical review

is provided of the major social—psychological explanations of the phenomenon. The chapter concludes on a hopeful note, by entertaining suggestions about how to deter bigotry or at least rechannel its energies into
more constructive directions.

Definitions

Although the two overlap, as discussed (see later in this chapter), there is an
important distinction between Fundamentalist Christianity and lower case
Christian fundamentalism. The first term refers to a sectarian movement in
American Protestantism whose origins can be traced to a 12-volume series
of pamphlets issued in 1919 by two Los Angeles businessmen, entitled *The
Fundamentals*. These assert the six basic tenets of Christian orthodoxy:
Christ's virgin birth, the deity of Christ, Christ's substitutionary atonement,
Christ's bodily resurrection, Christ's future return, and Biblical inerrancy.

Originally, Fundamentalist Christianity abjured politics and military life
because they involve compromises with the world of power and violence.
Instead, it encouraged believers to "separate themselves out from the
world," to quote a biblical maxim, and patiently await the Rapture. This
is the moment when they would be bodily assumed into Heaven to sit at
the right hand of God the Father. After the founding of the Moral Majority and the Christian Coalition in the 1980s, many Fundamentalist
Christians renounced their earlier squeamishness concerning power and
violence and began participating in anti-gay, anti-abortion, home-
schooling, and related political campaigns. In other words, they became
assimilated into the larger tradition of what can be called Christian fundamentalism.

Christian fundamentalism (CF) refers to any form of Christian millenarian theology, or to any movement preoccupied with events surrounding the
prophesied thousand-year reign of Christ on earth (the Millennium). It is
especially concerned with the culminating event of Tribulations, the war of
Armageddon between the sons of Darkness and Light. Far from fleeing the
world, CF activists vigorously enter into it—either to reorder it according
to God's precepts, thus preparing it for Christ's Second Coming, or (what
amounts to the same thing) to defend it from the forces of Satan.

The earliest manifestations of CF in history occurred not in American
Protestantism, but in Europe prior to the Reformation. The first notable
case concerned a Christian guerrilla militia known as the Taborites who
flourished in present-day Bohemia. Other non-American examples of the
same phenomenon are the English revolutionaries known as Levellers; the
Dutch theocratic tyrant, Jan Bockelson; the military prophet Jan Zizka; and
Thomas Muntzer's rainbow flag-bedecked League of the Elect.[1] All of these
cases confirm what has subsequently become a general principle in regard

to CF: Wherever and whenever it arises, it is associated with shrill words, smoking ruins, and bloodshed.

Like its Jewish, Muslim, and Hindu counterparts, CF is rooted in social dislocation, a subject covered again later in this chapter. In the modern era, the primary source of dislocation has been modernization, or as it used to be honored, "progress." Indeed, contemporary CF is inconceivable without its alter-ego, modernization. But here, a second distinction is helpful, that between modernity and modernism. By modernity is meant the material instrumentality of the modern world: the cell phone, World Wide Web, palm pilot, satellite TV, video camera, and modern weaponry—the AK-47, the Uzi machine gun, plastic explosives, and fertilizer bombs. Like fundamentalisms elsewhere, CF enthusiastically adopts these tools to promote its mission of world redemption.

Modernism, in contrast, points to a particular kind of intellectual and moral sensibility; one mirrored in notions like individual rights, equality, rational law, pluralism, separation of church and state, and scientific doubt. To CFs these represent "secular humanism." This is a catchphrase referring to liberal judges who rule in favor of (for example) equal rights for racial minorities, gay marriage, and abortion "on demand." *Martin Luther King: His Dream, Our Nightmare* is the revealing title of a CF pamphlet published by the Laporte, Colorado, Church of Christ in the 1990s; *Death Penalty for Homosexuals is Prescribed in the Bible* is another.

Secular humanism stands for "pointy-headed intellectuals" who are said to ridicule Creationism while advocating a nonliteralist, allegorical understanding of Bible stories. It symbolizes socialized medicine and public vaccinations (*Warning: Vaccinations are Dangerous!* another pamphlets reads). It is government control of the commons (like the Forest Service and the Bureau of Land Management). Secular humanism means Godless flag pledges, prayerless schools, moral relativism, and multicultural curricula. It represents public welfare, rap music, and rock 'n' roll; witchcrafters and Eastern philosophy; the ATF, the IRS, and OSHA. In short, secular humanism is ZOG (Zionist Occupation Government), or as it has traditionally been known, the Book of Revelation's Whore of Babylon. This is the hideous specter against which CF takes a stand.

Fascism is the second of the two great reactions of the last century against modernism. In fact, fundamentalisms of all faiths not only share just a superficial affinity with fascism. According to Roger Griffin, the two display "a substantive kinship," for both revile modernism's open-minded tolerance of difference, its alleged promotion of moral decay, and its presumed weak-kneed timidity in the face of evil. Above all, both fundamentalism and fascism espouse notions of rebirth to a new kind of manhood.[2]

To be sure, fascism has temporal, terrestrial aspirations; its martyrs are gallant military heroes, rarely humble religious saints. In this way fascism is a unique species of reactionary ideology. Nevertheless, when fundamentalisms are conflated with notions of racist, ethnic, gender, or national destiny, fascist–fundamentalist hybridization is possible. Recent non-Christian examples of this are (Meier) Kahani Zionism, pan-Arabic Wahhabism (e.g., the Taliban and al Qaeda), and Hinduvata. During the twentieth century, virtually every European country experienced its own brand of fascistic-fundamentalism, including the (Nazi) German Evangelical Church, the Spanish Falange, the Belgian Rex, the French National Alliance, the Finnish Lapua Party, the Romanian Iron Guard, the Russian Pamyak movement, and the Croation Ustasha, to name just a few.

American Fundamentalist–Fascist Hybridization: A Brief History

American culture has always comprised a promiscuous mix of Biblical icons and civic myths. Because of this, the potential for fundamentalist–fascist hybridization has existed in American political discourse from the days of the Revolution.

America is popularly viewed in explicit Old Testament terms as a New Jerusalem, a Shining City on a Hill; like ancient Israel, it is said to have entered into its own sacred covenant with the Lord, the Constitution of the United States. With its elaborate system of checks and balances this holy compact reflects a pessimistic Calvinist ontology of Original Sin. American history, furthermore, is routinely pictured as a divine theophany of sorts, a realization of God's will on earth. This "Manifest Destiny" in turn is said to be played out through various "crusades" to "spread" or "save" democracy from "evil empires" and "axes of evil." In the course of these quasi-sacred enterprises, "Judases" (Benedict Arnold) are exposed, "martyrs" (Abraham Lincoln) are created, and national saints (George Washington) made, their sacrifices subsequently memorialized on hol(i)days (the Fourth of July) and celebrated at holy sites (Arlington Cemetery).

This repository of imagery and legend has been available for appropriation by any American citizen, and has probably been employed with mercenary fervor by every group in the country at one time or another, from used-car salesmen and clothiers to drug manufacturers and food retailers. Throughout American history, however, CFs have seized upon it with especial enthusiasm.

Without giving the impression of a kind of social mechanics, upsurges of CF militancy have occurred approximately every 30 years in American history since 1800, a cyclical pattern that bears little connection to periods of economic boom and bust.[3] The Ku Klux Klansmen (who enjoyed their greatest popularity during the 1920s) and McCarthyism of the 1950s both flourished during times of unprecedented prosperity. On the other hand, the white American Nativist movement of the 1890s and the New Christian Right of the 1980s both exploded onto the scene during economic recessions. What evidence there is suggests that what is at work here is something on the lines of a generational process. As each generation comes to political maturity, assuming the time is propitious, its own brand of CF is welcomed by a significant portion of the American populace, either as one final chance to cleanse the earth in preparation for the Second Coming or as the last chance to stop Satan's spawn before it is too late. Each in turn invariably culminates in rumors of sexual scandal, exposures of deception, financial fraud, prosecutions for terrorism, and ridicule. Thereafter, like an irritating cicada, its erstwhile members burrow underground, only to have their children reemerge into the light of day three decades later.

The first outbreak of CF enthusiasm in America occurred soon after ratification of the Constitution, when Federalist Party activists—led by Presbyterian and Congregationalist preachers—took up arms against a mythical anti-Christian cabal they called the Illuminati (literally, bringers of light, hence Luciferians). The most significant outcome of anti-Illuminati fervor was what became popularly known as the "Reign of Terror": passage of the Alien and Sedition Acts (1798), whose edicts ironically presaged the Patriot Act of 2002. They included registration of "alien immigrants" to America and (where deemed appropriate) their forced deportations back to their homelands—the reputed birthplaces of Illuminatism, Ireland and France. The acts also lengthened the time it took immigrants to become naturalized citizens and censored "subversive" speech and newspapers (i.e., those promoting republican, Jeffersonian sentiments).

The names of the various "children of Lucifer" selected as foils for successive generations of American "freemen" and "patriots" have changed over time, reflecting alterations in historical circumstances. In the 1830s they were called Freemasons; in the 1860s, they were Southern slaveholders and polygamous Mormons. (The published depictions of chattel slavery and the sexual intrigues of the polygamous Mormon "seraglio" are interchangeable; in fact, some of the exposés were authored by the same persons.) In the 1890s, the sons of Darkness had evolved into Papists and Jesuits, expressing the terror American Protestants had of mass immigration of Roman Catholics from Italy and eastern Europe. (*Awful Disclosures of the Hotel Dieu Nunnery* was only the most widely read of the scores of period exposés of alleged convent crimes.) By the 1920s Negroes had become the primary domestic enemy of CF, in the 1950s attention shifted to Communists, and in the 1980s Satan's minions had transformed into liberal residents of "Jew York City," "Jew York University," and "Kosher Valley" (Hollywood)—hirelings of the so-called "Jews' media."

Changing titles aside, however, the libel against this succession of internal foes has remained uncannily stable over time. Except for details, the charges first leveled against the Illuminati in *Proofs of A Conspiracy Against All the Religions and Governments of Europe Carried on the Se-*

cret Meetings of . . . Illuminati (1798) are found essentially unchanged a century later in the anti-Jewish pamphlet, *Protocols of the Learned Elders of Zion* (1897), and sixty years after that, in the John Birch Society's *None Dare Call It Conspiracy.* As the second Christian millennium drew to a close, literally hundreds of books by CFs on the impending Apocalypse repeated many of the same themes. Each satanic cabal, so the story line goes, is merely one finger on a "Hidden Hand," a secret order devised by Satan to establish a reign of evil (modernism, as defined above) on earth. It constitutes an archenemy against whom all good Christians are duty-bound to resist.

The Rise of Contemporary CF Organizations

So, thirty years after the anti-Illuminatist hysteria of the early 1800s, the Anti-Masonic Party came into existence, then thirty years later, the Party of the Star Spangled Banner (the so-called Know-Nothings, who were ordered to say they "know nothing" if asked about the group's inner workings). Then in 1890 came the anti-Catholic American Protection Association, followed by the modern Ku Klux Klan (which at its height during the 1920s boasted several million members). Following this in the 1950s were groups such as Reverend Fred Schwarz's Christian Anti-Communist Crusade and Reverend G. L. K. Smith's Cross and Flag. Finally, in the 1980s the New Christian Right was born. It is tellingly ironic that all of these groups, without exception, evolved into secret societies in their own right, with arcane passwords, handshakes, and (occasionally) garish vestments, who plotted campaigns of resistance behind closed doors. In other words, they came to mirror the fantasy enemies against whom they presumed to fight.

The most notable, dangerous expressions of the New Christian Right in the 1980s were represented by members of the Idaho-based Church of Jesus Christ Christian–Aryan Nations. This was home of "the Order" or *Bruders Schweigen* (Secret Brotherhood), American history's most deadly terrorist group, ten of whose twenty-three cadres received federal prison sentences ranging from forty to 100 years. The closely-related Covenant, Sword and the Arm of the Lord, headquartered on the Missouri-Arkansas border, was another of the most fearsome CF groups. It amassed one of the largest private arms caches ever uncovered in American history on its 224-acre base, Zarepath-Horeb. It consisted of a 30-gallon oil drum of arsenic, at least one improvised armored vehicle, facilities for retooling machine guns out of semiautomatic weapons, grenades, RPGs, silencers, and thousands of rounds of ammunition. A third organization, the Army of God—or Phineas Priesthood—was implicated in a number of anti-gay bar bombings and abortion clinic murders. This group honored the name of a biblical hero who slew the Jew, Zimri, and his alien Midianite wife, after Zimri brought her into the camp and enraged the racially sensitive Lord, Yahweh. Finally, another of these most dangerous CF organizations was the Christian Patriot's Defense League (CPDL), which established a perimeter of armed encampments around the American heartland to protect it from a planned incursion of troops from Africa, allegedly stationed on America's borders awaiting orders from the UN to invade. ("Black helicopters in our skies, Russian troops on our soil," warned one CPDL alert.)

All of these associations, as well as a number of terrorist spin-offs—such as the Bob Matthews Brigade, the Christian Posse Comitatus, and the Order Strike Force II—espoused a peculiar brand of CF known as Christian Identity. Christian Identity is so named because its theology maintains that the populations of various European countries and white America have descended from one or more of the Lost Tribes of Israel.[4] Timothy McVeigh, who instigated the murderous attack on the Murrah Federal Building in Oklahoma City in 1995 was a frequent visitor to Elohim City (literally, the City of God), a CI enclave located nearby.

Causes

The question of why people affiliate with CF groups, thus at least indirectly abetting collective violence, has led to a library of speculation and a variety of informative conclusions. To begin with, all serious researchers agree: The popular nostrum that CF activists are somehow mentally deficient is patently untrue. Clinical examinations of even the most heinous CF terrorists indicates that psychologically they lie well within the bounds of normality, irrespective of how bizarre their beliefs may be. Three cases in point: David Rice, who bludgeoned to death an entire Jewish family of four in Seattle (1985) to avert what he feared was the impending invasion of UN troops (a CPDL belief, as mentioned in the previous section); Frank Spisak Jr., who (from 1980–83) wandered the back streets of Cleveland dressed as an old woman, carrying a .22-caliber pistol in a hollowed-out copy of *Mein Kampf* on "search and destroy" missions "to exterminate as many niggers and Jews as possible"; and Joseph P. Franklin, who is alleged to have shot to death thirteen members of mixed-race couples in Utah, Wisconsin, and elsewhere (from 1980–82). All of these men were found capable of standing trial and eventually were found guilty of first-degree murder.

Related to this, there is no evidence that CF activists are less intelligent than more moderate Americans, or that they have fewer years of formal education. The author of *The Turner Diaries*, the cookbook novel that Timothy McVeigh used to devise his bloody meal of vengeance, earned a Ph.D. in physics from the University of Colorado. At the time, he was leader of the National Alliance, a crypto-Nazi group. Stories like his are not uncommon. The membership rolls of the Order (a.k.a. the Secret Brotherhood) included two graduates of Florida State University, one each from the universities of Wyoming, Utah, Arkansas, and Georgia, as well as Eastern Washington and Boise State. Research on radical CFs residing in the greater Idaho area during the 1980s found that 23 percent of them reported having graduated from college, as compared to only 17 percent of white Americans over the age of twenty-five nationwide.[5] Most of them majored in arts and sciences, education, business, and religion.

These facts being true, attention today increasingly is being directed away from psychopathological and idiocy explanations of CF and toward considerations of social causality. Several theories have been developed, including social disorganization, economic deprivation (or exploitation), status displacement, socialization, and (the most plausible) the multistep theory of recruitment. What follows is a brief summary of (and critical commentary on) each.

Social Disorganization

Human beings are naturally social animals. They have a need to belong, if for no other reason than personal survival. When traditional family and community bonds are loosened, due primarily to rapid social change, those left in its wake search for something with which to replace them—a new "family" of sorts, a different kind of "community." They sometimes find these in gangs, cults, or in radical religio-political movements such as fascism or fundamentalism. Entities like these offer the emotional succor, the moral guidance, and the security they so desperately crave. Sociologist Robert Nisbet has expressed the principle this way: "Where there is widespread conviction that community has been lost, there will be a conscious quest for community in the form of association that seems to provide the greatest moral refuge."[6] He goes on to write that the "eager acceptance" of Nazism by "otherwise intelligent Germans" is "inexplicable" without this quest for community. For all its benefits, modernization is a juggernaut of unending change. Wherever it alights, old customs lose legitimacy, ancient moral precepts are thrown into doubt, and once reliable group affiliations begin to disintegrate—in essence, social disorganization ensues. This is one reason why developing nations (and developing areas of advanced nations—namely, rural districts) become hotbeds of religious fundamentalism of all kinds, including Islamic, Jewish, Hindu, and Christian.

Economic Deprivation

Fundamentalisms flourish primarily in rural regions undergoing transition from farming to some other land use. According to the theory of economic deprivation, this is not because an impersonal force like modernization magically causes them to fall apart. Instead, it is because rural areas are perennially subject to exploitation by specific agents—namely, urban banks, railroad shipping companies, and food brokerage firms. Exploitation contributes to the social disorganization discussed earlier. Farm foreclosures on indebted tillers of the soil shatter families, and the local towns and villages that were once patronized by them collapse and die—schools are consolidated and shut, storefronts go vacant, houses crumble. As the bucolic rural world turns to dust, its denizens frantically search for remedies, and not without irony, these remedies are readily supplied by urban-dwelling CF intelligentsia. It is they who frame the situation as the End Times and assign blame. "It's godless Communism," they proclaim. "It's seed of Satan Jews who sacrifice people in darkness," "sodomite homosexuals waiting in their lusts to rape," "negro beasts who eat the flesh of men at night." "It's liberals who fight for the 'rights' of these 'minorities'!" (All of these phrases are from *Prepare War!*, published in the 1980s by the Covenant, Sword and Arm of the Lord.) These become the emotionally satisfying, imaginary targets against whom the rural victims of exploitation fight—not the corporations, credit agencies, and transportation companies who have actually dispossessed them.[7]

Status Displacement

Historically, urban intellectuals and artists tend toward liberalism. In Europe and America, furthermore, many are Jewish. Some, however, gravitate toward conspiracy-mongering, End Times fantasies, and defamation of groups like those listed above. According to the theory of status displacement, this is not because they are usually deprived economically. Rather, it is because as typically older, white, Protestant, straight, and male, they fear that their traditional status privileges are threatened by newly rising groups.[8] Among these privileges are the exclusive right to vote and to hold office, to join exclusive country clubs, to live in gated communities, and to send their children to élite finishing schools and Ivy League colleges. They get a renewed (if symbolic) sense of pride by rhetorically inflicting their religious beliefs and moral convictions on those who threaten their position—youth, people of color, non-Europeans, homosexuals, non-Protestants, non-Christians, and female activists. Most often, they do this through lectures, radio talk shows, pamphleteering, video documentaries, and books (e.g., Rev. Wesley Swift's *The Mystery of [Jewish] Iniquity*, lay-preacher Jack Mohr's *Exploding the "Chosen People" Myth*, or Reverend Pete Peters' *John Lennon Imagined a New World Order*). In other words, they become spokespeople for CF—a role in which they labor to enlist economically deprived, falsely conscious, rural discontents in the cause against equality, pluralism, and democracy (which is to say, modernism).

Socialization

Each of the previous theories offers a compelling account of Christian Fundamentalism. Indeed, as presented here they constitute an overarching macroparadigm that appears to take into consideration most of the complexities of the CF phenomenon. Yet on closer examination they are still not completely satisfying, for they fail to explain (or predict) who in particular is more likely to join a CF group. After all, most residents of socially disorganized, economically depressed rural towns do not enlist in the CF movement; even fewer straight, white, male, Protestant, urban denizens become CF leaders. Socialization theories attempt to overcome this weakness. They begin by assuming that men are not born with hatred in their blood. The infection, so to say, is usually acquired by contact; it may be injected deliberately or unconsciously, by parents, preachers, and teachers. There are two types of socialization theories. The first focuses on the *content* of information used in the socialization process, and the second on the *form* by which it is conveyed.

Regarding the content of socialization, Christian Fundamentalists are neither crazier than their neighbors nor are they less educated, as observed earlier. However, their religious upbringing and present religious affiliations are decidedly different from most. Specifically, a greater proportion of CF activists are from independent Fundamentalist Christian churches (as defined in the first paragraph), from the Presbyterian Church, and from Southern Baptist congregations than would be expected given their numbers in the general population. There are also fewer Methodists, Congregationalists, and Unitarians.[9] Evidently, the reason for this is that Sunday school teachings, Bible study courses, and sermons heard in Fundamentalist, Presbyterian, and Baptist churches contain themes that make CF ideology palatable to believers. Without being exhaustive, these include the notion of Godly transcendence and the utter depravity of man and the world; the attribution of sin to Woman and to their "girlie men" allies who are used by Satan as unconscious dupes to secure hegemony over the world; the necessity to resist Satan by assuming an obsessively cautious attitude toward all bodily appetites, especially sexuality; and millenarian prophesying, emphasizing the struggle for control of earth between God and Satan.

An additional theme found in Fundamentalist Christian theology is anti-Semitism. Although pagan Greece and Rome were critical of Jewry, anti-Jewish hatred reaches unparalleled heights in the Christian gospels where it becomes (according to theologian Rosemary Ruether) the "left-hand of Christianity." In Matthew, the "unbelieving" and "hypocritical" Pharisees are described as "plotting" to "kill Christ" out of "jealousy": "You serpents, you brood of vipers." In John's bitter polemic, the idea of Satan as "father" of the Jews is made explicit. These notions are absorbed as literal truths by many Fundamentalist Christians, which makes them susceptible for mobilization by CF apostles of discord during times of crisis.[10]

The recent support given by CF pastors to the in-gathering of Jews in Israel appears to contradict the observation just made. A closer reading of this support, however, reveals an attitude of ambivalent condescension toward Jewry on the part of these pastors. They see the return of Jews to the Promised Land, the rebuilding of the Temple (on the present-day site of an important mosque) and their prophezied conversion to Christianity as but necessary preludes to Christ's Second Coming. This is far from acknowledging Judaism as a distinct religion worthy of respect in its own right. As the president of the Southern Baptist Convention announced in 1980, "God Almighty does not hear the prayer of a Jew." Without Jesus, he continued, Jews "are lost."[11]

In terms of the form by which socialization proceeds, the following quote is apropos: "The presence or absence of extreme[ly] . . . prejudice[d] . . . individuals . . . tends to be related to a complex network of attitudes . . . relating to the family."[12] Specifically, if one has been traumatized by physically painful or emotionally cold child-rearing practices (regardless of the content of the lessons the parents are trying to instill), they will acquire an Authoritarian (fascist) Personality as a "defense mechanism" to protect the integrity of their ego. This is characterized by paranoia, moral rigidity, an admiration of physical power, and a contempt for weakness, apocalypticism, and an obsession with bodily orifice deviation. Such individuals will be drawn to fundamentalist ideologies, which typically espouse all these themes.

The Multistep Theory

The multistep theory of recruitment examines the actual process by which people, perhaps already predisposed by socialization to join CF, actually become affiliated with it. The theory begins with a simple, powerful assumption: Extreme effects do not necessarily have extreme causes. On the contrary, the way in which people join (or are recruited to) CF is analogous to how others become vegetarians, pacifists, Moonies, or for that matter, purchasers of commodities, including doctors and political candidates.[13] On pain of oversimplification, the process consists of five steps. Each is represented by a single letter: S (Seeker), I (Invitation), P (Pull), P (Push), (E) Engulfment—SIPPE. No suggestion is made that the five steps necessarily follow in this particular order.

(S)eeker. All CFs were once active seekers. They were never passive victims of group forces—such as social disorganization, status displacement, or exploitation—that moved them willy-nilly this way or that independent of their own personal inclinations. On the contrary, they were (and remain) relatively rational pursuers of their own emotional, material, intellectual,

and moral interests. And they actively choose to join CF, when they do so, as a way to satisfy, if not to maximize, those interests. As the term suggests, the ordinary seeker is on the lookout for a group and/or belief system promising a better payoff than the one they presently enjoy. Perhaps they are discontented with their present personal relations, have doubts about the pre-given answers they have to existential questions (e.g., "What is the meaning of my life?"), or they are profoundly upset about a recent local crime, a political scandal, or an ongoing social problem. Any of these alone or in combination makes them available for becoming a CF.

(I)nvitation. Most seekers do not affiliate with CF for the simple reason that they are never proffered an invitation to do so. This, in turn, is because they do not have access to the CF "opportunity structure": they chance to live in locales where there are no functioning CF groups (e.g., in university towns or coastal cities); their friends, co-workers, and colleagues are not members (they are, say, Democrats, peace activists, environmentalists, or the like); or their families know nothing about the movement (perhaps they are Congregationalists, Jews, Muslims, agnostics, or New Agers). Invitations to join CF are meted out in a variety of ways, including by pamphlets or videos to "take home for the weekend"; by offers to attend a retreat with or a new church with "people just met" (who have not revealed their theology); or by offers to date a "good Christian man" (who has hidden the darker side of his identity). Occasionally, CF recruiters, invitations at hand, strategically position themselves where there is a good likelihood of "accidentally" bumping into seekers: guns shows, Christian book stores, Adventist revival meetings, Fundamentalist Christian Sunday schools, and Bible study groups.

(P)ull. If the invitation is accepted—most often, it is not—a relationship between the seeker and the recruiter becomes concretized. The seeker is then positioned to convert to CF. The basic proposition is this: People do not join because they first believe; they come to believe because they first join—with a recruiter. At first perhaps dumbstruck, outraged, or simply amused by CF doctrine—such as, the idea that Jesus was not a Jew, but an Aryan; that the ancestors of the Danes were the ancient tribesmen of Dan; that the Saxons are the sons of Sac, Isaac, hence they are God's chosen people; or that "British" comes from the Hebraic words *b'rith* (covenant) plus *ish* (men)—the seeker begins to convert themselves in order to nourish and sustain the now treasured relationship with the recruiter. They begin rehearsing the newly received CF vocabulary, begin trying on the newly introduced costumery (such as, camouflage trousers, combat boots, and T-shirts emblazoned with "Kill 'em all; let God sort 'em out," "White pride worldwide," or "RAHOWA" [Racial Holy War]). They begin cultivating an appetite for novel CF foods and intoxicants.

(P)ush. As this happens old acquaintances, co-workers, and family members who are not in the movement begin to avoid them. Even if the

intention in their dissociation is to discourage the new recruit from conversion, their gestures often have the opposite effect. The recruit comes more fully to embrace the only people "who truly understand them," namely, movement activists. "I've never known such love and affection." Full engulfment in CF is the predictable result.

(E)ngulfment. Full commitment to CF is relatively rare, but when it occurs, it proceeds at three levels: cognitive, emotional, and moral.

The recruit's cognitive commitment increases the more that they consider themselves to have voluntarily sacrificed to a CF group in terms of money, time, labor, personal freedom, and in rare cases, their physical well-being. This rather paradoxical fact is accounted for by the human propensity to avoid holding "dissonant" (inconsistent) thoughts, feelings: "I am experiencing pain" (from giving group X my money, time, and the like); "I am doing so voluntarily." One way to alleviate the evident dissonance in this example is by devising good reasons for one's actions, namely, "Group X is so wonderful."[14] Or, to say it more plainly: The more one pays for something, the more value it comes to have for them.

The moral commitment of the recruit increases the more that the group in question claims to have an exclusive monopoly over truth or salvation— a common attribute of CF—and the more that it practices rituals of group confession and mandatory self-abasement.

Finally, emotional commitment to the group increases the more that recruits' ties to the conventional world are shut off and the more they become exclusively involved with other in-group members. CF groups accomplish this by isolating themselves in wilderness enclaves and by staging elaborate Freedom Festivals, Family Bible Retreats, and Aryan Conferences. Included among the social activities at such annual convocations are relatively passive practices such as being entertained by CF musicians and cloggers, and attendance at lectures by self-proclaimed experts on income tax avoidance, race, the "Jewish question," and "the betrayal of America." Workshops are another big draw. They provide advice on everything from natural childbirth, naturopathic medicine, yarn-making, and weaving, to nuclear survival, martial arts, rappelling, candle-making, and first aid. Joint meals are consumed of supposed Aryan and Christian foods, camp markets held, sacred texts jointly studied, Aryan games played: the caber toss and stone toss, the "man of steel" contest, the competition for title of "woman of grace." There are standard Protestant baptisms, marriages, and worship services. There are even Christian patriot telephone calling cards ("15 cents per minute"), and dating rites "for the older singles" using lunch-box auctions.

The most powerful social activities of CF groups have a darker resonance. One is the notorious cross-burning, a quasi-sacrament at which congregants are required to don garish white, green, or purple silk robes and hoods with black eye holes. The flaming cross is said to be "a light to guide the white in the darkness of these times." Another frequently seen activity is the "nigger shoot." ("Nigger hunting licenses" and "official 'Runnin' Nigger' targets available for purchase," reads an Aryan Nations advertisement.) One more activity is training in guerrilla warfare with live ammunition in mock urban arenas like "Silhouette City," wearing camouflage and blackface. Finally, there is battle with the enemy itself: street fights, bank robberies, arson attacks, graveyard and synagogue vandalisms, and targeted assassinations. Through participation in these kinds of events, CFs recognize who they are, namely, "God's battle axe and weapons of war." Their mutual bond is renewed.

A Case Study of Movement Activism

The following anecdote is presented here to illustrate three of the theories just recounted: social disorganization, socialization, and the multistep theory. The element of economic deprivation is probably implied. Readers should attend to the complex ways in which the theories interpenetrate. Hopefully, this will underscore the difficulty, if not impossibility, of framing Christian Fundamentalism in any simple or linear way.

Steve and Gary Yarbrough are two of the red-headed sons of a family of five who were driven from the dust bowl of Bible Belt Oklahoma to the Southwest during the early 1950s. Like many so-called Okies, they eventually wound up in Arizona where Red, the father, worked off and on in construction and mining. His strong-jawed wife, Rusty, tended bar and waited tables.

It did not take long for the Yarbroughs to catch the attention of local law enforcement officials. "We have about 400 deputies," one of them told reporters later, "and I'll bet if you mention the Yarbroughs, you'll get a reaction from every one." Charges against the clan ranged from burglary and strong armed robbery à la James Dellinger, to military desertion and witness intimidation.

Domestic violence was not a stranger to the Yarbrough household. Rumors have it that the parents had "at least one fight per month which normally resulted in them striking each other." In one incident, an enraged Rusty stabbed Red, landing him in the hospital. Red in turn inflicted "a heavy hand" on the sons, "severely" punishing them for the slightest infraction of the family regime. When added to this, the fact that the boys "did not get very good schooling," their sad end was perhaps predictable.

While still teens, Gary and Steve broke into the mobile home of a vacationing retired couple. With the stolen money, they purchased beer illegally, got drunk, vandalized a local junior high school, and slashed the office furniture. Evidently blind to the possibility of that her sons might break the law, Rusty was outraged by their subsequent arrest, and "jumped over the bar" to attack one of the investigating detectives. She later threatened an eyewitness to the crime spree with the words, "You're dead, you're dead."

As it turns out, Rusty's bluff and swagger was to no avail; Gary and Steve were both found guilty of burglary and sentenced to prison. It was there that Gary received an invitation from the Aryan Nations Church prison ministry to learn more about Christian Identity. Gary was the kind of man the Church was looking for: malleable, fearless, sentimental, tough. Intrigued, immediately after his release, he headed straight to Idaho with his wife and infant daughter, taking up temporary residence inside the Church's 20-acre, gated fortress with guard tower.

With other ex-cons and fellow seekers, Gary donned the requisite blue twill pants and postman's shirt of an Aryan warrior, together with Nazi lightning pins, Sam Browne holster belt, and a 9mm semiautomatic pistol. At long last, he had found his calling: working with like-minded souls in the name of Christ to protect God's chosen people, the white race, from mongrelization. He was appointed to head the security detail, guarding church leaders at public appearances.

It all came to a summary end one afternoon when federal agents posing as Forest Service officials, looking for his probation-violating brother, Steve, arrived at Gary's cabin. Gary shot at the intruders and fled into the woods. Several months later, he was arrested climbing out the back window of a Portland, Oregon, motel, clad only in pants.

It seems that Gary had grown bored with the routine of guarding the compound from aliens who never arrived. Others in the congregation shared his impatience. Together one evening deep in the pine woods of north Idaho, over the napping figure of one of the member's infant children, they founded the Order (or *Bruders Schweigen*), swearing together an oath to war against what they were the first to identify as ZOG.[15] The search of Gary's cabin disclosed an arsenal of explosives and firearms. Included among them was the machine gun used to kill a prominent Jewish talk show host from Denver earlier that year.

At the trial of the Order—the prosecution of which involved more than a quarter of the FBI's total manpower and millions of dollars—it was learned that Gary had been assigned to the group's assassination unit. Eventually, he was also implicated in bank robberies and in armored-car heists in Washington and in California—at the time, the largest ever recorded in American history.

Conclusion

It is fortunate indeed that the career trajectory of the typical CF activist is not inevitably like Gary Yarbrough's, toward totalistic engulfment, imprisonment, and possible death. One of the consoling discoveries of recent research on the movement has been the phenomenon of apostasies from it: people renouncing their former commitments and in some cases actually working on behalf of their one-time enemies.

The temptation has been to explain such dramatic conversions by means of pop psychology: Like Paul of Tarsus, "they've finally 'seen the light'." But as is the case for joining CF, this too would be mistaken. All evidence points to the fact that apostasy is a mirror image of initial affiliation. Briefly put, a dissatisfied seeker within the movement receives an invitation from an outsider, perhaps under the guise of friendship, love, aid, or a new job, to disaffiliate from the CF organization. If they accept the invitation, they are slowly insinuated back into the conventional world, changing their dress, their diet, and most importantly, their outlook. This deepens the newly valued relationship with the recruiting agent, and as this occurs, former movement colleagues push the apostate away, not uncommonly with death threats, assaults, and acts of vandalism. This, of course, confirms the wisdom of the apostate's suspicions concerning the undesirability of further radicalism. Engulfment in the conventional world now becomes virtually unavoidable. Once more, a seeker is "born again."

True, the new commitment to convention is theoretically just as unstable as the old one to CF, but knowledge about how apostasy proceeds suggests guidelines for intervention by human-rights workers. Specifically, the ultimate precipitant of reconversion is not altered beliefs as such; it is altered relationships. Successful intervention therefore requires two things: First, relations within CF groups must be weakened. The most vulnerable point of attack in this regard are relationships between the sexes.[16] When given the choice between protecting their children or staying loyal to the cause, most CF mothers are susceptible to inducements to safety by outsiders. Second, ties between members and outside agents—social workers, health-care officials, and educators—must be strengthened. However, this cannot be in the form of what Christians might call "unconditional love." Rather, acceptance of the apostate by human-rights workers must be made contingent upon their demonstrating a sincere willingness to repudiate hateful language and violent acts. How precisely these tasks are to be accomplished in individual cases remains one of the great intellectual and moral challenges of the twenty-first century.

CHAPTER 16

Political Islam: Violence and the Wahhabi Connection

MAHA AZZAM

Political Islam has become increasingly associated with violence. This is due primarily to the legitimization of violence and an increased resort to the use of terror by some of the groups and individuals working to bring about the establishment of an Islamic political order. They have done so partly because they have been unable to effect political change in Muslim countries and partly to counter the perceived political, military, and cultural onslaught on Muslim societies by the West. Further, the explanation by the public (as well as experts) of the resort to violence by Islamist groups is often based on and associated with the teachings of Islam or an interpretation of it, such as Wahhabism. Before venturing into a discussion of the Wahhabi connection it is important to make some observations about political Islam.

The term "political Islam" is used to denote politics that adhere to Islamic law (the *sharia*) and tends to refer, particularly in the contemporary environment, to a radical interpretation of Islamic teachings and dogma. For most Muslims, the idea that Islam encompasses all aspects of life, including the political, is perceived as a basic tenet of the religion. What is new is that increasingly, throughout the twentieth century and into this century, this has been emphasized because of an ensuing struggle with secularism and Westernization.

There have been an array of terms that have emerged over the past few decades to refer to an extremist interpretation of Islam. They include Islamic fundamentalist, Islamist, Jihadi, Salafi, and Wahhabi. They are all attempts to make sense of the violent expression of political action that both its proponents and detractors claim is justified according to their reading of Islam.

The struggle for a political system of government based on Islam has been taken up by different groups and factions in the modern history of Muslim states. Although states as diverse as Saudi Arabia and Iran uphold the *sharia* (albeit each with a different emphasis and interpretation), nevertheless, the main feature of contemporary radical Islam is opposition to the regimes in power in the various Muslim states and particularly those of the Arab Middle East. This is combined with anger at the United States and Western policies towards the Muslim world. The failure of most Arab and Muslim governments to deliver on the political and economic fronts, coupled with their repressive policies and the absence of the rule of law, has given rise to anger and frustration at the existing political order that has managed to survive in most instances since the second half of the twentieth century. This inability to bring about change on the domestic front or to influence regional and international policy has resulted in the resort to terror by different political elements, be they secular Palestinian forces during the 1970s in the Middle East, or the militant Islamists whose terrorist activities picked up momentum from the late 1970s onwards.

Nationalism, in conjunction with a strong assertion of religiosity and cultural identity in the face of foreign encroachment, is not new to the Muslim world. It has precedents in the colonial period and is not unique to it. Other groups and societies throughout history have resorted to violence as a means of empowerment. The use of religion as a means of justifying violence is powerful in the context of Muslim societies, where Islam continues to make progress as the dominant ideology and culture.

This has happened gradually throughout the Muslim world, where the attraction of religious subjects and debates now penetrates a once more secular environment. The increasing adherence to religious teachings and the expression of piety have helped change the face of many Muslim states that were previously set on a path that appeared more secular. This societal and cultural transformation continues to battle with Westernization and globalization while absorbing some aspects of it and rejecting others. The line between cultural definition and political commitment to an ideology that claims to emanate from the same source is an easy one to cross. Therefore, the increasing Islamization of different societies brings with it a greater acceptance of those calling for an Islamic political order as a reflection of society. That is not to say that the state has to express a violent or anti-Western ideology, but given the nature of politics and crises in the Muslim world today, the resort to extremism will initially be more appealing as a means of defense and as a channel for anger.

The most violent and challenging manifestation of political Islam at present is al Qaeda and those groups that espouse its tactics. It is therefore important to clarify the political and religious parameters, so often blurred by the rhetoric of both bin Laden and his opponents, which in turn is critical for the United States and its allies in defining policy towards states such as Saudi Arabia and Iran—and increasingly towards Muslims within their own societies—as well as distinguishing between those Islamist groups which espouse violence and those which do not.

Wahhabism

The teachings of Muhammed Ibn 'Abd al-Wahhab (1703–1791), the founder of what later came to be referred to as Wahhabism, are a very particular response to Arabian society during the eighteenth century. He emphasized the oneness of God in the face of a growing veneration of saints and excessive visits to shrines, and called for an unembellished and strict adherence to the Koran. He sought to rid Islam of these mystical customs that he believed were polluting it and to return it to its original purity, which he believed to be unadulterated with mysticism.

The key to understanding the different schools of Islamic interpretation is to realize that Islam is not like modern Christianity with a variety of churches. If there is a division in Islam, it is one between Sunni and Shii Islam, and even that is denied by many theologians. Within Sunni Islam there is a broad division into "four schools," a division which is not so much about fundamental disagreement on the basics of the religion, but merely on small variations of interpretation—for example, the detail of how to hold your hands when standing in prayer. Also, none of the four schools claims to be exclusively right in its interpretation. Hence, there is a powerful concept in Islamic theological law which states that no interpretation of one of the four imams may negate that of any of the others. For most practicing Muslims, the "school" they belong to is neither important nor emphasized. However, in interpreting the ways in which a Muslim must put into practice God's commands, some are stricter than others, with the Hanafis being the most liberal and the Hanbalis the strictest.

Wahhabism is derived from the Hanbali school of thought, and places its doctrinal emphasis on the absolute unity of God and a return to the pure and orthodox teachings of Islam according to the Koran and the Sunna (the way) of the Prophet Muhammed. Ibn 'Abd al-Wahhab was an adherent of the Hanbali school, and contrary to what many believe, his campaign against the cult of saints is within the main corpus of Islamic theology. His campaign to remove all innovation after the establishment of the four schools and outside the Koran and Sunna, might be seen as zealous, but theologically mainstream. Where Ibn 'Abd al-Wahhab seriously diverged from Ibn Hanbal and the rest of the mainstream was in stating that the mere utterance of the Islamic creed is not sufficient to make a man a believer, and in waging war on those who followed the various cults of saints or holy objects as if they were polytheists rather than erring Muslims. It is the willingness to declare a Muslim a polytheist (Mushrik) or nonbeliever (Kafir) which makes mainstream Muslims very uncomfortable. Muhammad Ibn 'Abd al-Wahhab expounded his thoughts in ten main texts, key among which are *al-Tawhid*, *Kashf al-Shubuhat*, *Tathir al-I'tiqad*, and *al-Risalah al-Mufida*.[1]

The Wahhabi tradition has remained strong, particularly in Arabia, and its followers have historically formed an important and influential force that formed an alliance with the founders of the Saudi state, the al-Sauds. It is this alliance that helped give legitimacy to the al-Sauds and has formed an essential cornerstone of the Saudi state since its inception. The Wahhabi version of Hanbali thought also spread beyond Arabia—as early as the 1820s, Saiyed Ahmad was spreading it in India, which is partly why there is an established tradition of Wahhabism in Bangladesh as well as in Pakistan. Saudi money did not instill a new interpretation of Islamic doctrine in these regions, it merely financed a consolidation of what was already there. More recently, as Muslims from the Arabian peninsula spread either as Du'a (missionaries) or as political activists, they have naturally tended to take their interpretation of Islam with them into the CIS, the Balkans, and elsewhere. That is why observers started noticing Wahhabi fighters in Kosovo, Afghanistan, and Chechnya. However, the center of the movement theologically is clearly Saudi Arabia.

Much is made in the West of Wahhabism's anti-Jewish and anti-Christian emphases. It is viewed by non-Muslims—and by many Muslims as well—as representing a strict and narrow-minded interpretation of Islam in many fields including, for example, women's role in Islamic society. Its followers resist innovation and change, and have pressured the Saudi state to maintain a puritanical and strict attitude towards any form of liberalization in either the social or political arenas. The role of the Mutawwa—the moral police force that patrols the streets of Saudi Arabia, maintaining a strict adherence to what it sees as an Islamic moral code—is viewed as part of the strong Wahhabi influence on society. However, these attitudes are endorsed by many in Saudi society who, while accepting a puritanical social agenda, are likely in the same instance to reject the resort to terrorism and object to al Qaeda.

While all these features represent an ultraconservative interpretation of Islam, they do not fully explain the resort to violence in recent years from those individuals and groups defined as Wahhabi. The Saudi state has faced previous challenges to its authority on the basis of religion, most notably with the siege of the Grand Mosque in Mecca in November 1979. However, when an authoritarian state is faced with a challenge from within, it is not unusual for that challenge to be violent and for the language and ideology of that challenge to be a familiar one that its opponents claim has been discredited. It appears that those who have resorted to violence and who have been brought up in the Wahhabi tradition, such as the fifteen Saudis involved in the September 11th attacks, may have been motivated by a different set of considerations, mainly political in nature, as well as motivations that are shared by those from non-Wahhabi traditions.

The Salafi Dimension

The term Salafi has been frequently used interchangeably with Wahhabi to describe the militant and puritanical interpretation of Islam. Salafi adherents are viewed as potential supporters of global terror. Salafism is essentially a reference to a return to the teachings of Islam as practiced and understood by the early followers of the Prophet. Most practicing Muslims will refer to the Salaf al-Salah (the pious predecessors) as neither radical nor controversial but with awe and admiration. The Azhar, the bastion of traditional "moderate" Islam today in the Muslim world, would refer to Salafism by saying that all good Muslims would seek to be Salafi, that is, to be true to the tenets and practice of the early fathers. The overlap with Wahabbism lies in the shared stress on the essential components of the faith and practice, untarnished by later practices and interpretations.

These are the traditions that have become increasingly appealing throughout the world—particularly to Muslim youth—partly because they offer a clear alternative in terms of worldview and lifestyle to what is perceived as the materialistic and decadent alternative offered by a dominant Western secular culture. The strict observance of rules and regulations as regards daily life and conduct and the segregation of the sexes appeals in a world that is viewed as allowing freedoms that offer little direction.

This social and cultural worldview is shared by nonpoliticized and politicized Muslims alike. The driving force behind the advocacy for terror is not doctrinal, but rather it is the issue of injustice. There is a widespread belief among politicized Muslims that the political order in Muslim countries is essentially unjust and that the international system, led by the United States, is also unjust; that both these manifestations of injustice have to be resisted; and that given the weakness of the Muslims, the resort to violence is therefore legitimate.

Influences beyond Saudi Arabia

In the search for an explanation for the rise in Islamist militancy and the source of violence, attention has been drawn to the madrasas (literally schools, but in this context, the religious schools) in the Muslim world, particularly in Pakistan, and to Saudi funding of these schools and other charitable organizations. These schools which exist in many countries—including Pakistan, Bangladesh, Indonesia, Uzbekistan, and Bosnia—offer education, albeit a religious one, to many who would otherwise perhaps receive no education at all due to economic hardship.

The fact that many of the Taliban (literally students) were educated in madrasas, many of them Saudi-funded, on the Afghan–Pakistani border has lent weight to the connection between Saudi-funded Wahhabism and militancy. According to a report by USAID, the links between the madrasas and radical Islamist groups "is rare but worrisome."[2] In noting that the linkage is rare, this report undermines the argument that Wahhabism encourages the resort to violence. Indeed, one should note that many of the extremists that make up the various Islamist groups at present come from differing educational backgrounds and religious traditions.

Other Muslim countries, namely Iran and Egypt (through the institution of al-Azhar) have also played a role in promoting Islam through their own traditions. Potentially all *dawa* (spreading of the faith) offers a danger of being politicized and interpreted in extreme form.

Attempting to interfere in the madrasa system and the educational curriculum in Muslim countries in order to divest it of religious references that are believed to encourage militancy and violence—and in the case of Qatar, cutting back on the teaching of Islam and Arabic in the general school curriculum, so as to allow more time for technical subjects—is likely to be viewed by many as yet another onslaught on Islam and its value system.

As regards Muslim youth in the West who are viewed as being potentially attracted to militancy and violence through various mosques and religious leaders, the failure to integrate fully for many (partly because of discrimination and partly because many are still fairly new immigrants) has allowed for their continued association with Muslim causes. The freedom of expression found in the West has allowed Muslims living there a channel for opposition that they would be denied in Muslim states and therefore has partly allowed them to bring the domestic battles of their countries of origin to their newly adopted countries.

The Development of an Ideology of Violence

There has been a gradual radicalization of modern Islamist political thought over the last century. The most extreme manifestation of this radicalization became apparent with the attacks of September 11th. This is best illustrated through the ideology of al Qaeda which has been emulated by, and which has inspired, other groups.

At different historical junctures, a particular Islamist group would appear as the most radical development that could possibly emerge, only to be later superseded by more extreme elements. The recent history of political Islam is punctuated with various attempts to develop a theory of radical opposition to those in power. Ideologically, the ground was prepared from the time of Sayyid Qutb, the leading ideologue of the Muslim Brotherhood who was writing during the repressive Nasser era of the 1950s and 1960s. His description of modern day Muslim society as Jahili (unbelieving, barbaric, and ignorant) and his call on Islamic activists to prepare themselves to replace the existing political order[3] was to be followed in the 1970s with the less sophisticated but nonetheless poignant arguments of Abdel Salam Faraj in his pamphlet *al-Farida al-Ghaiba* (The Missing Pillar), which set out the need to pursue jihad as one of the essential pillars of Islam in order to bring about change. By the 1990s and at the turn of the century, al Qaeda leader Ayman al-Zawahiri was openly justifying the resort to violence not only against regimes in power but against the "enemies of Islam" in general.

Underlying the progressive radicalization of Islamist activism is the opposition to mainstream Islamic theological thought as expounded by the main clerics, because these clerics are perceived as the tools of regimes and therefore, their pronouncements are viewed as suspect. The radicals seek out alternative interpretations through other nonmainstream *ulama* (theologians), various historical texts, and increasingly, through individual theorizing (with scant knowledge of "fiqh" or theological training) in order to justify their politics.

Wahhabism and al Qaeda

Much is made of the influence of Wahhabism on bin Laden and al Qaeda. However, many al Qaeda members have also been members of the Muslim Brotherhood, which is not a Wahhabi-oriented organization.[4] For example, in his early years bin Laden joined forces with Abdullah Azzam, a legendary Arab fighter who fought the Soviets in Afghanistan and was a member of the Brotherhood. The Muslim Brotherhood broke off its links with bin Laden in the mid-1980s when he established al Qaeda, not because of religious disagreement but because politically he had gone his own way.

An essential component in the recruitment and training of members of al Qaeda and new arrivals in Afghanistan was *Ilm al-sharia* (knowledge of Islamic law). Recruits had to attend lectures given by Osama bin Laden and Ayman al-Zawahiri (widely acknowledged to be the ideologue of the group). One of the main textual sources used in these lectures were the writings of a twelfth-century Muslim theologian, Ibn Taymiyya, who wrote at the time of the Mogul occupation and who professed the necessity for Muslims to oppose tyrannical rule by force.[5] Ibn Taymiyya has long been a favorite with many in the Islamist movement, especially in Egypt, partly because they find in his writings a response to what they see as closer parallels to the modern political situation in the Muslim countries and partly because, unlike much of the theological works favored by the mainstream, Ibn Taymiyya seems to encourage direct action.

The nature of the recruits also offers little clues as to ideology. Those who joined bin Laden were an array of nationalities, some of whom came as committed Muslims while others needed basic instruction in Islamic dogma and practice. It seems therefore that the connection between bin Laden, the Taliban, and Mullah Omar was one of collusion of interests and of defiance in the face of a common enemy, rather than a confederation of "Wahhabi"-influenced Islamists.

The idea behind al Qaeda was the establishment of a "base" which would bring together the different Islamist groups and coordinate their activities. Many of those who were attracted to al Qaeda were non-Arab. The aim was for the different Islamist groups to remain independent while receiving funding from bin Laden. However, at its inception, the new organization failed to attract the mainstream of the radical Islamist movement in Arab countries. In a meeting in 1988 in Afghanistan, two of the main Arab Islamist groups, the Egyptian Jihad and the Jama'a al-Islamiyya, refused to join al Qaeda.[6] This refusal seemed to be based on two objections. First, the members had no wish to relinquish leadership to bin Laden, who at the time had no particular claim to fame among Islamists. Secondly, and probably of greater significance, was a key disagreement about the scope of Islamist action. With few exceptions (notably the Hizb ut-Tahrir, with its pan-Islamist emphasis), most Islamist groups took the view that revolutionary Islamist action should be confined within each group's nation–state and that they should not interfere in each other's territory, beyond moral support. It seems, however, that some of the key Islamist figures started to change their outlook toward a more internationalist revolutionary movement. Crucially for al Qaeda, Ayman al-Zawahiri—a leader of the Egyptian Islamic Jihad movement, and close associate of Osama bin Laden—seemed to have had such a conversion. The shift made by al-Zawahiri lay in the premise that the Islamist groups within each state were hemmed in and that, although the enemy lay within, there was nevertheless a common external enemy that represented an obstacle to any radical change on the domestic front.

Thus, the new movement brought together Islamists who had proven their revolutionary credentials in several ways—by having joined the Afghan jihad and by having employed the tactics of terror against their own regimes—and who espoused strong religious sentiment (even though recognized by many as misdirected). This band succeeded in capturing the imagination of many who saw in their actions a much needed act of defiance against "the enemy," the amorphous mass accused of being the source of all the ills affecting the Muslim world, especially the United States because of its support of Israel and the corrupt dictatorships of the Middle East. The majority in the Muslim world would not join the few who make up al Qaeda, but many would find justification for their actions.

A "New" Theory of Violence

It is also becoming clearer that while bin Laden provided the front and the finance, the political theory of al Qaeda was developed by al-Zawahiri.[7] The original strands for the political theory of al Qaeda can be found in a treatise which al-Zawahiri published after the bombing of the Egyptian Embassy in Islamabad in 1996, entitled *Shifa' Sudur al-Mu'minin* [The Cure for Believers Hearts].[8] This document illustrates the shift from takfir (declaring a Muslim as a nonbeliever) made in the 1970s by the Takfir wa'l Hijra[9] group in Egypt and others—and which provided the justification of Sadat's assassination—to the more explicit legitimization of suicide bombings and attacks on innocents that had its precedents in the jihad group's attacks on tourists in Luxor.

The Takfir wa'l Hijra movement started in Egypt in the late 1970s. By 1977 it was led by one Shukri Mustafa who took Qutb's view that society was Jahili to its extreme conclusion. He declared that since the world was in a phase of Jahiliyya (pre-Islamic ignorance) there were no true Muslims other than his own disciples. There are parallels with the Wahhabi movement, which also declared saint venerators as Mushrikeen (polytheists) and saw war against them as theologically a jihad, but the Takfir wa'l Hijra movement was unrelated to Wahhabi thought in that it was a product of the post-Sadat period in Egypt with its shift in political allegiances and the disruptions deriving from economic liberalisation. It was also much more extreme in that it declared *everybody* outside it to be a nonbeliever (kafir).

Shukri then ordered his followers to flee from Jahili society, in an imitation of the immigration of the Prophet to Medina, and moved them from Cairo to caves in Upper Egypt or into communal apartments. His plan was to build up the numbers and strength of his followers until he was able to take over the country in a holy war. His followers were mostly from the lower economic strata, and his vision offered them a community life that severed all links with Egyptian culture. Their first brush with the law was when families whose daughters, sisters, or wives were enticed away tried to get the government to intervene. At the time, the government refused to interfere because it saw the movement as a marginal one. The movement then came to the notice of the main theological community, who found its views abhorrent. The group was condemned by a prominent Azharite, Sheikh Dhahabi. It was the kidnapping and murder of Dhahabi that finally led to the arrest and trial of Shukri.

While this group cannot be seen as a truly political movement, and was more properly a sect that developed in parallel with the emergence of the new Islamist groupings, it—and not the Wahhabi doctrine—introduced the concept of takfir into the modern political discourse of the Islamist movements. As articulated in al-Zawahiri's justification for the 1996 attack on the Egyptian Embassy, takfir and other concepts of the group (along with the tenets of Wahhabism) are components of what would later develop into the politics and methodology of al Qaeda.

First, and clearly most importantly, is the view ranking the main issues facing the Islamist movement in order of priorities. At the very top of this list is the issue of Palestine. The view expressed is that all Arab and Islamic regimes, including the Palestinian Liberation Organization (PLO) had sold out by the mere fact that they accept the authority of the United Nations and the very idea that any Jew may remain in any part of Palestine. One should remember that al-Zawahiri is very much part of the Nasser generation, and this rejectionism echoes the rejectionist front of the 1960s.

This main issue of Palestine then defines the way in which al-Zawahiri views the various governments and regimes he comes into contact with. For example, he sees the Saudi regime as traitorous because of its ties with the U.S. government which supports Israel. Hitherto, the assumption has been that the Islamists rank the application of Islamic law (*sharia*) at the top of their list of priorities; however, by invoking the Palestine issue, al-Zawahiri can justify declaring the Saudis who apply *sharia* law as outside the fold of Islam. Furthermore, he sees Saudi and U.S. support for the mujahideen movement in Afghanistan as a ploy to distract the Arab mujahideen from their real goal of change in the Muslim world. He then stated that the mujahideen saw clearly through this ploy and established the base (al Qaeda) of their operations in Afghanistan, from where they could undertake their worldwide struggle.

Subservient to that first point is the struggle against the oppressive regimes that fight the Muslims (i.e., Islamists) through physical and intellectual means. It is secondary because he sees these regimes as clients of the infidels, Christians and Jews, which is clearly prohibited in Islamic Law (a view he recently reiterated in another treatise serialized in *al-Quds* newspaper in London) and which therefore places them outside the fold of Islam.[10]

Secondly, he expounds his views of personal responsibility in Islamic law. In essence, he argues that members of the rank and file of these regimes cannot take refuge in their claim that they were merely following orders, but that they must accept personal responsibility for their actions. He includes not only members of the security apparatus but all supporters of the government, including the media. However, the crucial point is that in discussing the victims of the bombing in Islamabad, he dismisses their description as innocent civilians in the Egyptian media by saying that the fact that they worked for the Egyptian government makes them party to the crimes of that government and therefore a legitimate target. He then goes further and expounds the view that there is a contradiction between being a Muslim and serving in such a regime in any capacity (a view reiterated in the recent *al-Quds* publication). In essence, he is reviving the extreme ideology of the al-Takfir wa'l Hijra group of the 1970s in Egypt.

As al-Zawahiri became the theorist for the new al Qaeda movement he translated that concept of personal liability to the group's view of Western governments. This theory can be presented as follows: Civilians in the West elect and pay for their governments; they are therefore responsible for the actions of these governments; they thus negate their status under Islamic law of being innocent noncombatants and become a legitimate target because they are in essence the decision makers—a view reiterated by bin Laden in his message to the American people during the 2004 presidential election.

Thirdly, al-Zawahiri propounds the twin ideas of the greater good and the need to react to exceptional circumstances. Ideologically, he is grappling with two major problems. First, he tries to counter the clear and absolute prohibition of suicide under Islamic law. As this is one of the strongest taboos in Islam, he cannot find any theological backing except for the idea of martyrdom in the Christian sense.

Suicide bombing has developed into a cult that partly attracts recruits on the basis of exclusivity and association with heroism in the name of a sacred cause. The main corpus of Islamic theology prohibits such acts, which have been condemned by leading religious authorities, such as the Mufti of Saudi Arabia and the Sheikh of the Azhar. However, the religious dimension does not explain why this cult has spread in the occupied territories from the Islamist Hamas movement to the secular al-Aqsa Brigade movement which occasionally recruits female volunteers.

The examples al-Zawahiri uses to support his case are instances in early Islam when some Muslims were captured by the "idolaters." They were asked to recant on pain of death. Despite this threat, they refused. He views their refusal as an act of suicide for the glory of God. Since these early martyrs were not condemned for their actions by the early Muslims and great theologians, he argues that an Islamist can commit suicide for the greater good. That provides the movement with the legitimacy for suicide attacks, which 1,500 years of Islamic theology would view as heretical. Secondly, al-Zawahiri needs to justify collateral damage. Having dismissed the innocence of non-Muslim civilians, he tries to tackle the possible collateral death of Muslims and children who might be unintentional victims of these attacks. Again, he is struggling against the main corpus of Islamic theology, which is clear in its rejection of such collateral damage. To counter this, he invokes the fact that Muslims are facing exceptional circumstances, with an overpowering enemy and weak resources. These exceptional circumstances allow for a more lax interpretation of the law.

It was this political theory that formed the basis and justification for the

attacks on the Twin Towers. The United States supports Israel and is therefore the enemy. No U.S. civilians can be deemed innocent because they elect
and pay for their government, and, while killing children and Muslims is
normally not acceptable, the exceptional circumstance of the current situation where the Muslims (i.e., Islamists) are fighting superior forces allow
for an exception to these rules. Finally, because these attacks are for the
greater good of Islam, there can be premeditated suicides, which would
otherwise be deemed heretical.

The implication of this theory is a complete separation between the Islamists and the "enemy" which now includes all Muslims who are in any
way connected to non-Islamist regimes in the Muslim world as well as all
citizens of Western countries that recognize the state of Israel, even if at
times they support Muslim causes in Afghanistan or Bosnia.

It is important to note that this is a new departure for the Islamist movement. This theory is based neither on the main schools of Islamic theology
nor on the often-misunderstood Ibn Taymiyya. Indeed, al-Zawahiri presents his views as equivalent to those of the founders of the four main
schools of Islamic thought. Although theologically questionable, these arguments nevertheless provided al Qaeda—and those Islamists who wish to
follow their example—with a theoretical legitimization for violence.

The Reaction of the Mainstream

This new ruthless form of confrontation has found fertile grounds for recruits. In many ways, al Qaeda is echoing the rejectionist views prevalent
in the region during the 1960s and 1970s. Palestine remains a core issue
in the Muslim world (as any casual observation of the content of the news
broadcasts of the al Jazeera satellite TV channel would reveal), with support for the Palestinians heightened by blanket coverage of the intifada and
the subsequent suicide bombings in Israel in the Muslim media. At the same
time, there is a shared antipathy toward what are seen as undemocratic
and corrupt regimes in Muslim states.

At present, al Qaeda remains a revolutionary group with an ideology
that greatly diverges from the mainstream, but whose actions find general
popularity by feeding on long-standing feelings of despair and impotence
on the Muslim street. Given that al Qaeda has presented itself as the champion of anti-imperialism (in the Arab 1960s understanding of the term), it
will inevitably benefit, in terms of popularity, from the actions of any group
that emulates its tactics.

The next move that al Qaeda is trying to make is to export its political
theory to a wider arena, hence the various video tapes sent to the al-Jazeera
satellite station and the serialization of al-Zawahiri's most recent book in
al-Quds, a leading Arabic newspaper. In trying to win over converts from

the mainstream to his political theory, al-Zawahiri is hoping for a galvanization of the Muslim ummah (nation of believers). He is translating the ideology that the jihad formed in Egypt to a wider Muslim arena. It is worth noting that radical Islamist activity in Egypt, while resulting in a general move away from a secular to a religious world view, still failed to result in a revolution. However, an increasingly angry mood within Muslim societies has opened the door to a greater number turning to extremist politics.

Conclusion

Militant political Islam has emerged in societies that have a tradition of expressing a moderate form of Islam—for example, in Egypt since the 1970s and more recently in Morocco and Indonesia, where there has been local support for al Qaeda. It is therefore not surprising that Saudi Arabia, given that it is home to Islam's holiest places and given the state and society's stress on its Islamic identity, became entangled in the global battle over the definition of political Islam.

Specifically, in Saudi Arabia the Wahhabi voice that so far had been involved with social issues has begun to voice its opinion directly on political and security issues (as can be seen most recently in the open letter sent by several Saudi theologians opposing the U.S. Army attack on Fallujah in November 2004). The breakdown in the Saudi consensus was triggered by the presence of United States and other foreign troops on Saudi soil during the 1990–91 Gulf War. Regional and international politics had forced the al-Sauds to cross the line that would make their alliance with the United States unacceptable to many, and therefore the extremists in their society responded. Combined with this was the growing discontent with the deteriorating economic situation (shared by many in the Muslim world) and of population expansion, poor rates of economic growth and development, and high levels of corruption. On the political level, the lack of accountability and respect for the rule of law became a source of despair and frustration across classes and especially among the young.

Some of those who want to diffuse this situation believe that they need to tackle the ideological and cultural source and expression of the phenomenon of Islamist extremism. This ranges from legislation against the hijab in France to changing the educational curriculum of schools that are perceived as encouraging militancy. The hope is that Islam will be expressed in a more moderate way and that it will mirror values that are more in tune with Western values. Underlying this is the desire to establish a more conducive political environment for Western interests as well as greater stability and prosperity for Muslim states. Similarly, there is the argument that improving the economic situation in Muslim states will undermine the appeal of the Islamists. However, both these arguments fail to recognize that the struggle in Muslim societies has been largely over the restoration of lost political power and dignity and that the resort to violence and terror is a desperate attempt to achieve empowerment.

Islamist extremists breed on the politics and policies that are perceived by them as detrimental to Muslim interests and which have remained unaltered for generations. A growing number among them believe they can influence this situation through a strategy of terror. Counterstrategies that involve, for example, changing certain textbooks and curricula are likely to give rise to a renewed rhetoric and literature of resistance. An increasing encroachment, either military or cultural, into Muslim territories or way of life will further justify the resort to violence in order to defend what is viewed as sacred.

CHAPTER 17

Jihad Doctrine and Radical Islam

JARRET BRACHMAN

"We remind that victory comes only from God and all we have to do is prepare and motivate for jihad."

—*Osama bin Laden*[1]

"In essence we are calling for a jihad—a battle for hearts and minds—to persuade people through our conduct and good deeds that Islam is all about peace."

—*Rafiq Ahmed Hayat*[2]

While teaching an international relations seminar recently, a student of mine used the term "McJihad," merging the notions of McWorld and Jihad.[3] This insightful West Point cadet had captured in a single word what had taken me an hour to explain—namely, how today's extremist Islamic ideologies have found such global resonance by globalizing the notion of militant struggle. "McJihad" imaginatively highlights how the universalistic ideology advanced by extremists like Osama bin Laden and Ayman al-Zawahiri has become so readily applicable within diverse local contexts, thanks in large part to their skillful grounding of their ideology in the guise of transcendental religious obligations, like that of jihad.

The face of jihad has changed dramatically over the past century. For some, it has come to refer to the struggle to defend religious ideals against destructive forces. For others, jihad refers to a command by God to all Muslims to fight against the aggressors who seek to corrupt Islam—embodied and globally perpetuated by the West.

There are two broad arguments within the Islamic community regarding what to do with this contested jihad concept. The first consists of those advocating the use of violence against infidels, who justify it as a religious duty either for the individual or the broader community of Islamic believers—referred to as the ummah. Those advocating this martial understanding and conduct of jihad do, however, vary widely across the spectrum; whereas some focus on limited, qualified, and targeted violence—such as in fostering the overthrow of un-Islamic Arab governments—others adopt methods, such as terrorism, that focus on killing civilians.

The second, diametrically opposing line of argument contests this equation of jihad with holy war. Rejecting the notion that Islam is a violent religion, advocates in this group argue that jihad refers to the internal struggle more than the external struggle. Referred to as "apologists," "modernists," or "reformers" in some bodies of literature, those advancing this argument point to particular Koranic passages that emphasize the use of violence only for self-defense from unsolicited aggressors. This moderate line of reasoning is, however, a sharp reversal from the centuries of Islamic interpretation of jihad as being primarily associated with war and therefore is clearly not the dominant interpretation of jihad within either the non-Muslim or the extremist Muslim camps.

Jihad has served as a rallying cry for those who see themselves suffering under the draconian policies of governments; for those in a struggle with corrupt imperial overlords for the right to establish a national homeland; for those who see themselves fighting to stave off advanced stages of cultural corruption; and for a host of others. Even Saddam Hussein employed the term in an attempt to garner international Islamic support against the "wicked Americans" should they attack him. However, from as early as 1877, American popular media have consistently discussed and understood jihad as being synonymous with "holy war."[4] In short, jihad has come to mean many things to many people. Due to the criminal genius of a handful of modern Islamic ideological promoters, diverse grievances are being tied together into a singular coherent agenda, that of the already persuasive Islamic concept of the "struggle" or jihad. While jihad and warfare are intimately interwoven concepts within Islam, jihad does not necessarily equal violence. Equally true is that warfare need not be grounded in jihad. A civil war can be said to be ongoing within Islam over how to understand the meanings of foundational concepts, like that of jihad.[5]

Defining such a fluid concept may at first seem like an impossible task. But as this chapter will highlight, audiences worldwide can and must understand what jihad is and determine for themselves whether a particular usage of the concept is a religious term or an extremist ideological call to violent war. This chapter will seek to disentangle these complexly intertwined and often blurry distinctions between religion and ideology.

This chapter is organized around very basic questions. First, what is jihad? This section will explore the doctrinal foundations of the concept, looking at its usage in the Koran, the *Hadith*, and other written interpretations. Importantly, one must ask: When is jihad acceptable according to Islamic doctrine? When is it considered obligatory? And perhaps most importantly, how should the jihad be conducted?

The chapter then works forward through sociopolitical history, exploring how the term *jihad* has been leveraged by local groups on behalf of this global ideology. Readers should pay particular attention to the way that jihad evolves from a relatively hard concept into a loose symbol that is used to justify a broad range of activities—especially recent terrorist attacks— anywhere in the world. The final section tracks the employment of certain arguments to justify the conduct of martial jihad in the form of several terrorist acts since September 11th, 2001.

What Is Jihad?

Contemporary disputes over the dominant interpretation of jihad have been shaped by over 1,400 years of both thought and action. Those seeking to make their interpretation of jihad dominant tend to look as far back in Islamic thought as possible for justification. Therefore, this chapter begins by exploring the doctrinal prescriptions and proscriptions cited within Islam about what, when, and how Muslims should strive to achieve with their lives

Believers of Islam accept that the literal word of God, as reflected in the Koran, was revealed to the Prophet Muhammad in the year 570 A.D. This message, taken together with centuries of Islamic scholarship, interpretation, and example, informs how practicing Muslims ought to live their daily lives. A common trend among extremist Islamic ideologies is the demand that followers interpret the Koran literally. This is not particular to Islam, however; the call for literal interpretation or authentic understandings of holy texts can be found at that nexus of religion and political ideology worldwide. One can locate many appearances of the term jihad (or its close derivatives) within the Koran, some of which speak to that sense of internal struggle, but most appear within the context of warfare. But the reader will likely notice that various Koranic references to obligatory warfare are qualified and even contradictory. The current consensus that seems to have emerged, equating jihad with warfare, has developed in the post-Koranic centuries of Islamic history, jurisprudence, and scholarly interpretation.

Within the Koran, various passages discuss the idea of waging jihad or struggling on behalf of God within the context of self-defense. One passage states, "To those against whom war is made, permission is given [to defend themselves], because they are wronged—and verily, Allah is Most Powerful to give them victory."[6] This statement, understood by practicing Muslims as the literal word of God, discusses the need for the sanction to fight when being attacked directly; however, other statements are not so clear. It is not difficult to see how these open-ended types of passages can be subject to various interpretations.

A different Koranic passage commands believers to "exert (also translated as "strive") yourself in the way of God as is His right."[7] Referring to this jihad-based concept of exhausting oneself in the pursuit of religious purity, this phrase in no way implicates warfare in that pursuit, but rather internal struggle to live as according to the example of the Prophet. Other passages in the Koran indicate that a critical distinction must be drawn between fighting and aggression. Muslims are instructed to "fight in the path of God those who fight you, but do not aggress. Surely God does not love the aggressors. And fight them where you come upon them, and send them out from where they have sent you out, for persecution is a worse thing than fighting."[8] This theme of limited but divinely sanctioned combat when it is self-defense in the face of aggressors pervades most militant and radical texts, especially in their claims of responsibility for attacks. And by identifying certain stipulations on methods and appropriate places at which to engage in that fight against aggressors, readers are left interpreting the struggle in terms of actual combat.

What is clear is that Islam provides us with a text, the holy Koran, and volumes of subsequent interpretations by theological experts, biased partisans, and even demagogic hacks. But what we lack is the historical context in which these original statements were written. We do not know, nor can we find out, just what was meant by the word "fight." It is left as a matter of opinion, and therefore, can be wielded by those who most persuasively frame arguments. The centuries of interpretation are, however, crucial in better understanding the evolution of how jihad has been perceived and implemented.[9]

Historical Precedence

The debate over whether Islam is inherently a "violent religion" continues to rage throughout many corners of the world. This question, however, is problematic for several reasons. Most important to understand is that the religion of Islam, like Judaism, emerged in times of intense competition among Semitic tribes for resources, land, kinship ties, tradition, and honor. That struggle to survive in the face of societal conflict is embedded in Islamic history and must be recognized as such. While this is not to say that Islam is necessarily predicated on violence, a student of Islamic history must candidly acknowledge the bellicose events that are critical components shaping early Islamic history. This section of the chapter explores the use of religiously justified violence in early Islamic history by Muhammad and his followers.

As the central historical figure in the religion of Islam, the Prophet

Muhammad and his actions establish important precedence for both interpretation and application of Koranic injunctions on action. As Islamic and non-Islamic scholars have widely stated, Muhammad preached about the religious duty to defend Islam, using military force if necessary, when it is under attack. And as a statesman, Muhammad did call his troops to war under the banner of a united Islam. It is therefore critical, given the extent to which today's extremist Islamic ideologues cite the Prophet Muhammad's own example, to understand what Islamic texts say about that time within the context of jihad.

Struggling to unite the warring Arabian tribes under the rule of Allah, the Prophet Muhammad consistently employed the use of force to regulate the interactions of his population. Throughout his tenure, Muhammad secured new lands and new subjects. Noted Islamic scholar Mulla ʿAli al-Qari, discussing received histories from the time of the Prophet in his book *al-Mawduʿat al-kubra*, noted,

> The Prophet came back from one of his campaigns saying: "You have come forth in the best way of coming forth: you have come from the smaller jihad to the greater jihad." They said: "And what is the greater jihad?" He replied: "The striving (mujahadat) of Allah's servants against their idle desires."

If one accepts this story as instructive, one will conclude that the smaller jihad refers to rejection of desire in thought, while the greater jihad refers to the struggle in action. But again, the bounds of that struggle—whether violence must be included in the active struggle—is a conclusion left as a matter of interpretation.

While the notion of jihad is an important one for practitioners of Islam, only a minority extremist Islamic sect, that of the Kharijites, places it on par with the five foundational pillars of Islam—those of *zakat* (charity), prayer, the hajj (or pilgrimage to Mecca), fasting (during ritual periods), and the belief in one God, Allah. The overwhelming majority of Muslims understand jihad as a nonviolent recognition of the struggle to avoid Earthly temptations and their destructive consequences. They place a premium on the notion of social justice and purity in thought and action, as do many world religions.

But as numerous scholars have already made clear, the association of jihad with violence quickly came to dominate understandings of the concept, even within Islam. In subsequent examinations of jihad by Islamic scholars and jurists, the concept assumed a legal understanding that was thoroughly developed, in the vein of equating it with warfare. Even these deeply thoughtful and erudite interpretations are nonetheless problematic given that they are just that—interpretations.

The intellectual roots of the more popular strains of today's militant Islamic ideologies have evolved over the twentieth century through the writings of three primary ideologues: Egyptians Hassan al-Banna and Sayyid Qutb and Pakistani Sayyid Abul Ala Maududi. While there are countless other thinkers who have participated in advancing this ideology, these three authors pioneered the particular articulation of today's radical forms of Islam.

The early twentieth century bore witness to the unfolding of two parallel movements, one in Egypt and one in Pakistan, which both criticized the existing state of affairs for the Islamic world. Egyptian Hassan al-Banna's *Muslim Brotherhood* and Pakistani Sayyid Abul Ala Maududi's group, Jamaat Islami (a.k.a. Jamaat-e-Islami), rejected the perceived Western idea of splitting religion and politics. They cited those types of cultural influences as corrupting the ideals of Islamic civilization.

Both movements also advanced similar solutions: to return to a more traditional understanding and practice of Islam, where the Koran was interpreted literally and where social activity was regulated under a strict code of Islamic religious law.

After a brief visit to the United States during the 1950s, Sayyid Qutb returned to his home country of Egypt on a mission to advance the arguments of al-Banna and Maududi even further. Disgusted with the cultural corruption he saw in America, Qutb began feverishly writing about the need for Islam to return to its roots, as he understood them, in order to achieve the original ideals of the religion—social justice and belief in one God, Allah. For his outspoken participation in the Muslim Brotherhood against the Egyptian government, which Maududi viewed as Kafir, or apostates, Egyptian President Gamal Abdel Nasser had Qutb executed in 1966. But killing Qutb did not end the power of his ideas, especially regarding the need for Muslims to wage jihad—understood as violent overthrow of the oppressive regimes in Middle East states that conspire with corrupt influences of the West and, by maintaining the false separation between religion and politics, reject the Islamic obligation to serve only the laws of Allah.

Why Does Jihad Resonate?

The notion of jihad is clearly more than just an intellectual concept. The term, given its multifaceted uses, now triggers a collection of emotions, memories, and understandings for people—ranging from the most positive to the most negative. Like other symbols, jihad can evoke visceral feelings of duty, honor, connectedness, obligation, and justice for those who employ it. This section of the chapter will highlight the ways in which jihad is used in radical Islamic propaganda and will seek to answer why it has been such a successful mobilizing device.

The contemporary mainstreaming of jihad may be usefully compared with efforts by global consumer branding techniques. Similar to multinational corporations who market products across cultures and countries, promoters of jihad associate carefully selected logos, personalities, and collective memories with their product. The green flag with inscribed Arabic lettering, the pairing of the holy Koran and the deadly Kalishnikov, the bandana-masked militant—all of these provide the accoutrements of today's "Jihad, Inc." Whether they appear in Jakarta, Cairo, Manila, London, or New York, these symbols receive instant recognition—much like any other global franchise.

Importantly, each individual and group that promotes this particular branding of jihad does so in a different fashion. Again, as global franchises seek to make a single product appeal to a wide variety of local tastes, a jihad in one part of the world may actually be towards a completely different goal than it might be in another.

Jihad is an evolutionary term. It has been effectively applied to a wide range of perceived challenges in any number of areas. So what makes extremist understandings of jihad appealing? This is a complex question that lacks a single answer. Rather, a multitude of factors, including societal, economic, political, and even psychological reasons contribute to the degree of resonance that radical interpretations of the jihad concept have for individuals. It is possible, however, to identify broader trends in the way extremist jihadist arguments are promoted.

Terrorist mastermind Osama bin Laden has seemingly become the poster child for the most violent understandings of jihad. He has specifically discussed jihad on multiple occasions in his public statements, with the goal of co-opting broader understandings of the concept. In his 1996 *Declaration of Jihad Against the United States*, bin Laden states, "Our youths knew that the humiliation suffered by the Muslims as a result of the occupation of their sanctities can not be kicked and removed except by explosions and Jihad."[10] The association of destruction with this notion of jihad could not be any clearer for bin Laden in this statement. Again, readers must recognize that jihad retains few objective qualities after centuries of manipulation, and is now the source of competition by any number of idea entrepreneurs attempting to convince others that their understanding of jihad is correct. In bin Laden's understanding, jihad primarily involves the conduct of violent activities against a particularly defined set of enemies, which he commonly describes as the "Zionist–Crusader" alliance—an alliance that, he argues, is seeking to attack and even eliminate Islam.

Bin Laden's call for all practicing Muslims to wage jihad by taking up arms against the infidels, or nonbelievers—whom he argues are corrupting Islam—is by no means new. In fact, citing the example of the Prophet—who fled his hometown of Mecca when he came under assault, only to rally his forces in Medina and return to conquer his former oppressors—

Islamic entrepreneurs have been quite successful drawing on the symbol of jihad in wartime recruitment efforts. Perhaps the most important example of this is seen in the case of the Soviet Union's 1979 invasion of Afghanistan.

The Soviet Union invaded the sovereign state of Afghanistan on 24 December 1979. Against vocal international protest, including a United Nations Resolution calling for their immediate withdrawal, Soviet troops continued their assault in order to support the perceived nascent move toward communism within Afghanistan, as well as out of fear that an extremist Islamic government might emerge in the region.[11]

To counter the Soviet advance and to stem the risk of losing another country to communism, a broad coalition of countries—spearheaded by the United States, Pakistan, and Saudi Arabia—began funding a movement of both foreign and indigenous fighters, who would fight the Soviets under the unified banner of Islam. Those Muslims who joined the fight against the Soviets became known as "mujahideen," or "mujahid" in the singular. Literally meaning "one who struggles" in Arabic, the term mujahid contains the same three-letter root in Arabic, or the equivalent of "J-H-D," as the term jihad.

These "holy warriors" or mujahideen, received tremendous financial and material resources from involved countries and were upheld as heroes. U.S. President Ronald Reagan called these mujahideen "freedom fighters . . . defending principles of independence and freedom that form the basis of global security and stability."[12]

Among the number of mujahideen organizers involved in the resistance against the Soviets was Osama bin Laden. Working closely with Abdullah Azzam—a prominent Palestinian extremist and Islamic ideologue—bin Laden launched the Makhtab al-Khidmat (MAK), an organization that focused on coordinating the global movement of funds, resources, and Muslim fighters. Muslims both volunteered and were recruited from around the world to aid in Afghanistan and were united under the call of jihad against foreign aggressors.[13]

After the Soviets withdrew their forces in 1989, these well-trained and combat-hardened mujahideen literally roamed the world—facilitated by men like bin Laden—to fight in places like Bosnia and Chechnya.[14] Jihad became their calling. And jihad for them meant war.

There are lasting consequences, however, of using the concept of jihad to mobilize Muslims for combat. In both Muslim and non-Muslim communities, it has become quite difficult to disentangle those memories of war conducted on behalf of God from the other elements of jihad. As described in the next section of this chapter, jihad is being used as a rallying flag today for both extremist Muslim groups (advocating violence) and moderate Muslim groups (advocating peace).

Discussions about what is and what is not jihad, though, are further complicated by how we use the term in our own descriptions of violence. For instance, in the wake of the gruesome murder of Dutch filmmaker Theo Van Gogh, a high-ranking Dutch government official stated that, "The jihad has come to the Netherlands and a small group of jihadist terrorists is attacking the principles of our country." He went on to say that "these people don't want to change our society, they want to destroy it."[15] When the term jihad is employed by non-Muslims to describe such events, and furthermore equated with intended destruction of a society, it only serves to further legitimize the use of that term by radical militants and terrorists in their own distorted justifications of such behavior.

In its broadest conception, jihad literally means "to strive" or "to struggle." Viewed as a religious duty for practicing Muslims, the concept is derived from the idea of "effort, exhaustion, exertion, strain."[16] The struggle can be within oneself or can be manifested between two parties; one of those parties has, at least in later Islamic writings, been understood to include Satan. And the Koran does not explicitly link the struggle of jihad between practicing Muslims and believers from other faiths. As discussed below, Muslims may face challenges—which may actually be tests sent from God—where their belief and ability to practice freely comes under constraint. In that sense, believers must respond with jihad—to include warfare if necessary. Islam, like Judaism, consists of a coherent body of mandatory laws and ritual practices that are rooted in a particular faith.

Knowing when and how to engage in jihad is, however, neither a straightforward nor agreed-upon process for Muslims. Beyond its basic translation, little consensus seems to exist—both within and outside of the Islamic community—as to what it includes. One often hears that there are actually two understandings of jihad, referred to as the greater one and the lesser one. Within the Islamic world, the greater jihad, *jihad-i-akbar*, has come to refer to the internal struggle that believers must conduct in order to overcome destructive temptations; this understanding has seemingly become the less popular among the two in broader public discourse. The lesser jihad, *jihad-i-asghar*, has come to mean the active defense (often militarily) by Muslims against aggressors. Even these characterizations, however, are contested across Islam.

Looking through an average newspaper, one will almost invariably see the word jihad in some form. Militant organizations use jihad in their names, including bin Laden's own mid-1990's creation, *The International Islamic Front for the Jihad Against Jews and Crusaders*, al-Zarqawi's group in Iraq, *Attawhid wal Jihad*, as well as *Salafia Jihadia*, *Egyptian Islamic Jihad*, and *Harkat-ul-Jihad-al-Islami*, among others. Does this mean that their understanding of jihad as violence against civilians is divinely sanctioned? Because there is no single arbiter about what constitutes jihad, there has been a proliferation of voices seeking to influence the debate.

Jihadist Violence Today

Today's terrorist threats are rooted in a selective reading and recounting of history by a particular group of people. No longer is the generation of mujahideen fighters from Afghanistan and Bosnia the most dangerous to global order. Rather, a new breed of ruthless and militant fighters, one embodied by men like Abu Musab al-Zarqawi in Iraq, promote an understanding of jihad that is more unrestrained than perhaps ever before. Those who accept this purely lethal demarcation of jihad employ it instrumentally to rationalize, justify, and recruit for nefarious purposes, most often associated with terrorism. It is possible to identify a general process by which young men from a variety of socioeconomic backgrounds move into more extremist forms of Islam and see themselves as necessarily bound by this particular mutation of understanding jihad. For any number of reasons, potential terrorist recruits—mostly young men—become dislocated from the traditional ties that bind them to mainstream society. This dislocation increases their susceptibility to any number of temptations—however, given that most of them are schooled in Islam, more radical forms of Islam become the drug of choice.

Through a variety of pathways, these young men become increasingly radicalized through reading gradually more extremist literature, engaging in increasingly radical discussions, and surrounding themselves with like-minded and similarly socially positioned young men. It becomes a mutually reinforcing process, within which they develop meaning both in buying into these radical ideas, and having others to share these views with. Finally, they feel part of something greater than themselves, and they are willing to devote their lives to defending its propositions.[17]

The readings and discussions in which militant ideologues engage are rooted in a long-developed historical process. Drawing on historical parallels, these ideologues have been able to paint a very compelling picture of the world to their followers, and, more importantly, to their audience—the Muslim world. It is not a war on terror that is being waged, but rather a global war against a virulent ideology—one that interprets jihad as unrestrained bloodletting, where terrorism is an important methodology

Two primary trends keep violent understandings of jihad in the public spotlight. First, by conducting, coordinating, sponsoring, and supporting multiple terrorist attacks under the justification of jihad, Osama bin Laden and the al Qaeda organization have popularized their formation of the concept on a level greater than ever before. And second, the continued resistance to Coalition presence in Iraq, being waged by both domestic and foreign elements who often describe themselves as mujahideen, harkens back to the holy fighters in Afghanistan—who at the time were publicly supported by the United States, leaving many to question why they were wholly against one superpower but illegitimate when targeting another.

But while these may be the motors driving international conversations about what jihad is and how it should be conducted, there are a multitude of other ongoing debates over these questions. Perhaps among the most relevant are conversations related to the motivations of militant Islamic extremists. We are seeing continued production of young, disaffected Muslim males who have bought wholesale into these militant interpretations of jihad, the kind advanced by al Qaeda, as being a divinely mandated call to war against the infidels. The next section of this chapter explores the recent trends of militant jihadist terrorism.

Jihad and Post-9/11 Attacks

Since the tragic events of September 11, 2001, populations worldwide have suffered a number of smaller-scale attacks waged by groups not necessarily affiliated with any broader network or organization. Importantly, the perpetrators of these attacks all share an understanding of their mission as being a religious duty, one that will be rewarded in the afterlife by God and framed using the language of jihad. Simply by tracking the statements associated with these attacks, one can quickly identify a pattern of justification based on a supposed religious duty to defend against aggressors, colonizers, and imperialists.

On 11 April 2002, terrorist attacks against a synagogue on the resort island of Djerba, Tunisia, killed nineteen people. Shortly after the attacks, the *al Quds* newspaper cited a copy of the suicide bomber's will, dated 5 July 2000, where the bomber called on his surviving family to contribute to a holy war "with their souls and money."[18]

The bombings of nightclubs on the Indonesian island of Bali on 12 October 2002 by a remotely triggered bomb killed 202 civilians (many of them Australian), primarily disco-goers and Balinese employees. The alleged field commander of the Bali bombings, Imam Samudra, stated in his trial that "as a Muslim I have a conviction that I have to defend oppressed Muslims, as stipulated by the Koran."[19] This type of justification, grounded in a sense of religious duty, further shifts public understandings of how Muslims understand both what jihad is and how it is conducted.

The 28 November 2002 attacks in the Kenya city of Mombasa were brutally directed at Jewish and Israeli targets. Driving a car filled with explosives into the lobby of a primarily Israeli tourist hotel, terrorists killed fifteen. At the same time, militants unsuccessfully sought to bring down an Israeli airliner during by launching a surface-to-air missile at it during take-off from the nearby Mombasa airport. A statement was subsequently posted on the website www.azfalrasas.com, attributed to *The Political Office of al-Qaeda Jihad Organization*. Pledging to continue operations, the statement argued that "it is a war between faith and the infidel, between truth and fallacy, between justice and injustice."[20]

Using camouflaged cars to avoid detection, a group of terrorists managed to shoot their way into a housing compound in Saudi Arabia and detonate explosives killing twenty-three on 12 May 2003. Soon thereafter, an article was published in a magazine commonly associated with al Qaeda, likely written by alleged terrorist plotter Abu Hajjer, stating that "Jihad members and lovers of Mujahideen were split. . . . There were those who said we must attack the invading forces that defile the land of the two holy places, and that we must turn the Americans' concerns to themselves and their bases, so they would not take off from there to crush Muslim lands and countries, one by one."[21] Construing the impetus for their attacks as part of a more universalistic theme—one where defense of the land, people, and religion of Islam is seen as a religious duty or jihad—Abu Hajjer seeks to make a very local attack take on global significance.

On 5 August 2003, a suicide bombing in Jakarta's business district killed thirteen people and wounded 149, setting cars afire and scattering glass shards for blocks. An unconfirmed, anonymous statement made by someone claiming to be from the group Jemaah Islamiyah in Singapore's *Straits Times* newspaper was released after the attack: "This is a message for . . . all our enemies that, if they execute any of our Muslim brothers, we will continue this campaign of terror."[22] Again, notice how the responsibility is grounded in violence construed as defense of Islam against aggressors.

On 15 November 2003, two car bombs exploded outside synagogues in central Istanbul, killing thirty people and injuring 300. The *al-Quds al-Arabi* newspaper subsequently published a statement from the group, the *Brigades of the Martyr Abu Hafz al-Masri*, which claimed responsibility for the attacks in Istanbul, and included the following text: "O nation of Islam: You should support those fighting for the cause of God, each according to his ability. Those who can support them by waging jihad, thus sacrificing their own souls, let them do so."[23]

While no claims of responsibility have been made for the 16 May 2003 attacks in Casablanca, Morocco, which killed forty-four bystanders and wounded sixty more, it is critical to recognize how it fits into this broader militant understanding of the jihad concept. Prior to those attacks, Osama bin Laden stated in one of his audio letters sent to al-Jazeera that Morocco was among the countries cooperating with the West and hence was the enemy of Islam.[24]

In an assault on a government building in Riyadh, Saudi Arabia, a suicide bomber managed to kill five people, including two senior police officers and an eleven-year-old girl, and wound approximately 145. An Islamic militant group, the *al-Haramain Brigades*, claimed responsibility and followed the pattern of grounding their violence in religious duty by stating, "If the brave mujahideen of the al-Qaeda network of Osama bin Laden, for whom God has assured victory . . . stops attacking you . . . (in favor of) the occupier war by the crusaders . . . we will devote ourselves to inflicting on you the price for apostasy, crime and corruption."[25]

At least thirty people were killed and approximately 120 wounded when car bombs exploded on 7 October 2004 at multiple resorts on the Red Sea coast of Egypt's Sinai Desert. A group calling itself *Brigades of the Martyr Abdullah Azzam* and claiming to be affiliated with al Qaeda claimed responsibility, posting an Internet statement that read, "The Brigades of the Martyr Abdullah Azzam give our Arab and Islamic nation the good news of the heroic martyrdom operations in Egypt, through which our sons in the squad of the leader martyr cleansed the land of Taba from the filth of the Jews."[26]

Since 9/11 many of the terrorist attacks we have seen involved participants who had seemingly been fully integrated into their respective countries. One could say that the new trend in terrorism is to draw on "homegrown" individuals, greatly complicating counterterrorism expectations of who and how terrorism is conducted. But while the term "homegrown" is accurate territorially speaking, it fails to capture the reality that many of these individuals see themselves as culturally homeless—disconnected from traditional understandings of society. A crucial question not yet being widely asked is "Why are these second- and third-generation young men feeling culturally isolated and therefore taking up arms against their home countries?"

In the case of recent terrorist attacks, those involved who were ideologically motivated understand their identity as rooted in an idea of what is wrong with the world, and how their participation in militant Islam will move toward a solution. These "re-born" believers, for any number of reasons, moved through a process whereby they became removed from their immediate worlds. While they may retain the behavior typically associated with the trappings of Western culture, the trend seems to be a psychological dislocation from that society while selectively participating in it. They have rejected the components that they perceive to be corrupt in their worlds, selectively filling in those gaps with the culture of militant jihad, informed by the body of radical Islamic literature and understandings detailed above.

Through a process of transformation, these individuals come to view the world through the lens of a universal and ahistorical ideology—but one that allows them to persuasively understand their local and even personal grievances through a predefined and coherent body of terms, symbols, and historical parallels, all grounded in the notion of a transcendental authority. The jihadist doctrine packaged and promoted by people like bin Laden and al-Zawahiri devolves religious interpretive authority to the individual level. No longer do those interested in this form of radicalism necessarily need the rigorous religious study that seemed a prerequisite for entrée into such groups, nor do they need to outwardly demonstrate their commitment to an austere Islamic lifestyle. Individuals can access these universal ideals and connect with like-minded individuals worldwide without altering their behavior or even leaving their immediate contexts.

Conclusion

This chapter investigated the notion of jihad and the body of radical Islamic doctrine seeking to dominate public understanding, both within and outside of the global Islamic community. It is important to understand the challenges posed by extremist martial jihad and the broader radical Islamic ideologies informing them has only recently been recognized as important. The chapter sought to emphasize that while jihad remains a contested term, it does hold deep and powerful religious significance within Islam. Therefore, whoever is able to wield the reigns of its meaning, as we have seen in the aftermath of September 11, will have great power in drawing new recruits into that ideological abyss.

Extremist ideologues have only further refined their ability to persuade young dislocated men to take part in this particular jihad. Making their universal messages applicable to very local and even individual grievances, extremist Islamic ideologues have franchised their virulent ideas to all parts of the world. These attempts are only bolstered through misuse and glamorization of the concept in the broader non-Islamic media. Descriptions of terrorist attacks as being waged as part of a perceived jihad against a society runs roughshod over necessary distinctions between religion and ideology. While the jihad concept has developed part and parcel with war and violence, the struggle or exertion it refers does not have to be interpreted as solely or necessarily violent. That doctrine must be understood as being strategically promoted by those employing violence for political and ideological reasons to line their actions with a religious veneer. The campaign to interpret jihad within Islam as being a peaceful process of striving must therefore be equally dedicated in its scope and persuasiveness.

Acknowledgments

The views expressed herein are those of the authors and do not purport to reflect the position of the United States Military Academy, the Department of the Army, or the Department of Defense.

CHAPTER 18

Zionism and the Pursuit of West Bank Settlements

ALLAN C. BROWNFELD

All too often, when terrorism in the Middle East is discussed, it is that perpetrated by Islamic fundamentalists and Palestinian groups unwilling to achieve some form of reconciliation with Israel. That such terrorism has been a dangerous and often deadly phenomenon is, of course, clear to all. It remains a serious threat, not only to Israel but also to the United States, other Western targets, and Arab governments which some Islamic groups bitterly oppose and seek to overthrow. Often under-reported, and also a serious threat to the prospects of peace in the Middle East, is Jewish/Zionist terrorism, which has a long but less well-known history.

The assassination of Prime Minister Yitzhak Rabin of Israel on 4 November 1995 by an ultra-Orthodox religious zealot, Yigal Amir, brought the world of Israel's religious extremists under public scrutiny. The assassin was not a lone psychotic gunman, but a young man nurtured within Israel's far-right religious institutions. After the murder, he was hailed as a hero by many, not only in Israel but also by kindred spirits in the United States.

Two weeks before the assassination, Victor Cygielman, Tel Aviv correspondent of the French weekly *Le Nouvel Observateur*, wrote an article describing the visceral hostility towards Rabin among certain groups of Israeli Jews. He told of a ceremony in which religious fundamentalists had stood outside Rabin's house on the eve of Yom Kippur and intoned the mystical *pulsa da-nura*, a kabbalistic curse of death. He wrote of rabbis who invoked against Rabin the Talmudic concept of *din rodef*, the death sentence pronounced on a Jewish traitor. Cygielman also cited the handbill passed out at a mass demonstration in Jerusalem on 5 October 1995 showing Rabin in an SS uniform. "The stage was set for the murder of the prime minister," he said. Unfortunately, technical problems delayed the publica-

tion of Cygielman's piece until Thursday, 2 November, just two days before Rabin's assassination.[1]

In their study of the Rabin assassination, Michael Karpin and Ina Friedman note that Yigal Amir believes

> there is only one guideline for fixing the borders of the Land of Israel—the
> Divine Promise made to the Patriarch Abraham: "To your descendants I give
> this land, from the river of Egypt to the great river, the river Euphrates" (Gen.
> 15:17). Today these borders embrace most of the Middle East, from Egypt
> to Iraq . . . zealots read this passage as God's Will, and God's Will must be
> obeyed, whatever the cost. No mortal has the right to settle for borders nar-
> rower than these. Thus negotiating a peace settlement with Israel's neighbors
> is unthinkable.[2]

The assassination of Rabin was just one of many acts carried out by individuals whose beliefs closely mirror those of Yigal Amir. And yet, there
has been insufficient attention in the mainstream media about such individuals or what motivates their deadly terrorist agendas. This chapter thus
seeks to illuminate the primary sources and implications of religious extremists in Israel, with particular attention to Jewish/Zionist terrorism.
After a brief historical review, the chapter discusses the importance of land
to the Zionist extremist, and provides an account of some of the key players in the story of Zionism—including Abraham Isaac Kook, Baruch Goldstein, Yigal Amir, Meir Kahane, and Zvi Yehuda Kook. Finally, the chapter
examines the role of Zionist extremism in contemporary Israel and argues
that the country's citizens and mainstream religious institutions must act
to thwart the efforts of those who have hijacked Judaism's moral mandate
in their quest to secure permanent ownership of land.

Religious Zionism: A Brief History

The philosophy of "Religious Zionism" has been growing in Israel since
the 1967 Six-Day War. This philosophy holds that God gave all of the historic "Land of Israel" to the Jewish people, that the victory in 1967 was
a "miracle" which would usher in the messianic era, and that it would be
sinful to return a "single inch" to the Palestinians. Christian Fundamentalists share this view, for they believe that the return of the Jews to the
Holy Land is a prelude to the second coming of Christ, the Battle of Armageddon, and the end of the world.

The growth of religious Zionism is a relatively new phenomenon. Traditionally, Orthodox Judaism held that only the Messiah could bestow Jewish sovereignty on Palestine. Religious Jews firmly opposed the Zionist
movement based on what they argued were legitimate religious reasons.

The conventional rabbinic doctrine maintained that Jews had a duty to wait patiently until the Messiah led them back to Palestine. The return, they said, would be at the end of days. According to this view, since God sent the Jews into exile to punish them for their sins, only God had the power to lead them back.

Rabbi Hayyim Eleazor Shapira, a Hungarian Hasidic leader, argued that migration to the Holy Land, in abandoning "faith in miraculous redemption from heaven," pre-empted the Messiah. Zionism, he declared, violated Halacha, or Orthodox Jewish law. Rabbi Shapira called the Zionists "evil forces who have become stronger in our Holy Land and they undermine its very foundation through their ploughshares and agricultural colonies." Efforts at "forcing the End," he maintained, were a "sacrilege."[3] Rabbi Joel Teitelbaum, a celebrated leader of the Satmar sect, called the founding of the Jewish state a terrible crime. It was the Jews' untimely return to the Holy Land, he wrote, that was to blame for the deaths in Hitler's crematoria.[4]

The Basel Meeting

Theodor Herzl convened the first Zionist Congress in 1897 in Basel, Switzerland, the German Rabbinical Association having successfully opposed Herzl's original plan to hold it in Munich. Both the Association's Orthodox and Reform wings had their own reason for opposition. The Orthodox said, "The aspirations of the so-called Zionists . . . contradict the messianic promises of Judaism as enunciated in the holy scriptures and later religious canons."[5] According to the Reform group, "Judaism obliges its adherents to serve the fatherland to which they belong with utmost devotion and to further its national interest with all their heart and strength."[6] Indeed, the two factions' only area of agreement seemed to be their opposition to Zionism. The Zionist leaders, on the other hand, were largely secular, and sought to create for Jews what they hoped would be a "normal nation." Among the Zionist slogans was, "Israel has no messiah, get to work."[7]

At the Basel meeting's closing session, the chief rabbi of that city tested Herzl's intentions by offering to abandon his opposition to Zionism in exchange for assurance that any future state would keep Judaism's tenets, starting with the Sabbath. Herzl answered that, though the rabbis had nothing to fear, Orthodoxy was only one of Judaism's schools of thought. His words indicated his backing for religious tolerance, and the audience applauded. Orthodox Judaism, however, withheld any support.[8]

The Evolution of Zionism from the 1967 War to the 1993 Oslo Accords

Originally, those religious Jews who embraced Zionism did not share the Orthodox disdain for the secular state, but rather esteemed it as an agent of Jewish power. While they sought to make the state as hospitable as possible to Orthodox practice, there was little messianic fervor about their efforts or their worldview.

The 1967 war, however, changed all of that. In a thoughtful book, *What Shall I do with This People? The Jews and the Fractious Politics of Judaism*, author Milton Viorst—who has worked for three decades as a journalist covering the Middle East—notes that "Religious Zionism . . . saw the victory as an opportunity. Religious Zionism's position . . . long at the margins of Jewish mysticism, held that Zionism, however secular, was God's way of preparing the land for the Messiah's arrival. To the rabbis, the victory was a message from God to seize the land for all time."[9]

Rabbi Zvi Yehuda Kook (son of Abraham Isaac Kook), who spearheaded the religious Zionist movement, said, "Under heavenly command, we have just returned home in the elevations of holiness and our holy city. We shall never move out of here. We are living in the middle of redemption. The entire Israeli army is holy. The Kingdom of Israel is being rebuilt. It symbolizes the rule of the [Jewish] people on its land."[10]

According to Viorst,

> Kook and his followers reshaped Halacha, religious law, to serve their political ideology. Not only did they insist that the law required permanent Jewish rule in the territories but they proclaimed its supremacy over secular law. . . . Religious Zionism was not alone . . . in urging Jewish hegemony over all Palestine. Since the 1920s, Zionism had contained a minority wing known as Revisionism, progenitor of the present-day Likud Party, which promoted the kind of territorial nationalism that pervaded Europe in the nineteenth and early twentieth centuries. Religious Zionism's role was to sanctify this nationalism, imparting new energy to it by characterizing it as God's command. Religious Zionism after 1967 sparked the Jewish settlement movement in the occupied territories. . . . Every stake driven into the soil, it maintained, served God's will.[11]

When Yitzhak Rabin signed the Oslo accords with Yasser Arafat in 1993, the settlers' wrath shifted from the Arabs to the "traitors" they perceived in their own society. "Rabin's proposal to evacuate a small settler enclave in Hebron, considered especially vulnerable to Arab attack, provoked a defining crisis," reports Viorst.

> Hebron, where Abraham is said to be buried and David made his first capital, is sacred to Judaism. . . . Rabin's plan to remove the settlers signaled to religious Zionism the defeat of its holy mission, and its forces mobilized to fight. Led by a former chief rabbi of Israel, religious Zionists issued a Halachic ruling. Not only did God command the settlers to resist evacuation, it said, but He instructed Israeli soldiers to disobey any orders to withdraw.

The ruling pitted Halachic judgments against democratic legitimacy. Rabin, facing civil war, backed off, and the Hebron settlements remain to this day.[12]

The Increasing Devotion to Land

After Oslo, some rabbis circulated charges through their network of religious schools that Rabin, in surrendering Jewish territory, was a religious outlaw. Orthodox circles debated whether, under religious law, he was guilty of capital crimes. In New York, hundreds of Orthodox rabbis signed a statement declaring that Rabin deserved to die. On 4 November 1995, Yigal Amir, an Orthodox student, killed Rabin with two pistol shots in the back. Competent rabbis, he said, had convinced him of his Halachic duty to commit the murder. In killing Rabin, Amir was convinced he was doing God's work.

In Viorst's view, such religious extremism has been an element in Judaism from the beginning, and has frequently led to disaster: "Jewish history shows that when a stiff-necked nature manifests itself in persistent defiance of reality, its consequences can be catastrophic." He cites

> defeat in two wars against Rome, the superpower of the age, which the Jews, being a tiny nation, should never have waged. These wars resulted in the annihilation of the state, the destruction of the holy Temple and the scattering of the people to the ends of the earth . . . The Jews lost their homeland and spent two thousand years in exile, dreaming of a way back. In our own era, they have regained their state, but it is still tiny and with limited resources and its inherent fragility raises the question of whether their stiff-necked nature does not again place their national life in peril.[13]

Israeli historian Yehoshafat Harkabi, a retired general, points out that historians regard Hadrian as Rome's wisest emperor and that Jews alone of his subjects made trouble for him.[14] Harkabi calculates the Jewish population worldwide on the eve of the Bar Kokhba rebellion at 1.3 million and estimates that only half that number survived the war. Since, under Roman law, Jews and others were permitted to practice their religion, Harkabi maintains that it was nationalism, not religion, which motivated the war. He now fears that Israelis might one day be imprudent enough to repeat this disaster. Harkabi is particularly alarmed at Israel's present day habit of resurrecting not just the Bar Kokhba revolt but the mass suicide at Masada, transforming them into a mythology of national glory. He calls this phenomenon the "Bar Kokhba Syndrome," enticing Jews into foolish, perhaps deadly, misadventures.[15]

Today, religious Zionists have adopted the notion that God demands not so much devotion to the Torah as to the land that Israel's army has conquered. Their theology comes from Rabbi Abraham Isaac Kook, who taught that by settling the land the Jews would hasten the Messiah's arrival. This doctrine was largely overlooked until the Six-Day War, when it became religious Zionism's ideology.

Shortly after the 1967 war, seventy-two noted intellectuals, many of them mainstream Zionists, founded the Land of Israel movement. In a highly publicized manifesto, they put aside historical differences to proclaim a nationalism based on divine imperative: "The Israeli army's victory in the Six-Day War located the people and the state within a new and fateful period. The whole of the Land of Israel is now in the hands of the Jewish people. Just as we are not allowed to give up the State of Israel, so we are ordered to keep what we received there from the army's hands: the Land of Israel."[16]

Religious Zionism's rabbis spoke of the victory as a "miracle" and said that it meant the messianic process was reaching fruition, even if the Messiah himself was absent. The 1967 war was called the War of Redemption and the victory God's sign that every inch of the land was holy. Mainstream Zionism, while in theory continuing to favor exchanging territory for peace, found it difficult, once the land was in Israel's hands, to give it up. As time passed and settlements continued to grow, religious Zionism became Israel's most dynamic political force.

Some observers argue that religious Zionism has produced a fanaticism such as Judaism has not seen since the Second Temple days. Securing territory became a divine commandment equal to traditional piety. On Israel's 27th anniversary, Rabbi Kook declared,

> The principal overall thing is the state. It is inherently holy and without blemish. All the rest is details, trivia, minor problems and complications. . . . Not only must there be no retreat from a single kilometer of the Land of Israel, God forbid, but on the contrary, we shall conquer and liberate more and more. . . . In our divine, world-encompassing undertaking, there is no room for retreat.[17]

Kook went so far as to describe the Holocaust as a blessing in disguise. The settler movement, Gush Emunim, became the vanguard of territorialism and held a mystical concept of the Jewish state. It was a resurrection of David's kingdom, which God entrusted to reestablish Jewish rule over holy soil. To pursue its goals, terrorism was permissible. In 1980, the Jewish Underground—a secret society of Gush Emunim militants—boobytrapped the cars of several mayors of Arab towns, leaving two of them severely maimed. In 1983, gunmen killed three students and wounded thirty at Hebron's Islamic college. Disciples of Rabbi Kook openly applauded the attacks. In the synagogues of religious Zionism, worshippers debated whether "Thou shalt not kill" applied to Arabs at all.

Zionism and the Jewish Defense League

Among the activists Yigal Amir, Rabin's assassin, holds in high esteem is Baruch Goldstein, the physician from the settlement of Kiryat Arba adjoining Hebron, who gunned down twenty-nine Palestinians at morning prayer in the Cave of the Patriarchs on 25 February 1994. Among the ideologues Amir especially admires is Noam Livnat of the Od Yosef Chai (Joseph Still Lives) yeshiva—a religious school—in Nablus. The yeshiva's patron, Rabbi Yitzhak Ginzburg, repeatedly expressed a doctrine of racism, declaring that "Jewish blood and Gentile blood are not the same."[18] He defended the act of one of the yeshiva's students who opened fire indiscriminately on Arab laborers standing alongside a highway near Tel Aviv in 1993, and he subsequently lauded Baruch Goldstein for massacring Arabs in Hebron. Ginzburg explains that he differentiates between the murder of a Gentile and that of a Jew because the Torah places a "light prohibition" on the former and a "grave" one on the latter.

The case of Goldstein highlights the connection between Jewish extremism in the United States and in Israel. Goldstein, a militant Zionist from New York, had been a member of the Jewish Defense League (JDL), founded in May 1969 by the late Meir Kahane, who urged his followers to emigrate to Israel and called for the removal of all Arabs from the West Bank. After the mass murder at Hebron, Goldstein was viewed as a hero by many of the Israeli settlers. At his funeral, Rabbi Yaacov Perrin declared that "one million Arabs are not worth a Jewish fingernail."[19] Shmuel Hacohen, a teacher in a Jerusalem college, said: "Baruch Goldstein was the greatest Jew alive, not in one way but in every way. . . . There are no innocent Arabs here. . . . He was no crazy. . . . Killing isn't nice, but sometimes it is necessary."[20]

The JDL's stated goal was to combat anti-Semitism and to support agencies of government charged with the responsibility for maintaining law and order. Its street patrols soon gave way to violence and vandalism. By January 1972, the JDL chose to attack eighty-three-year-old Jewish impresario Sol Hurok, who was completing preparations for the premiere of a Russian balalaika troupe. They bombed Hurok's building in midtown Manhattan, and Iris Kones, a twenty-seven-year-old Jewish woman who worked in accounting, was killed.

The ostensible aim of the JDL campaign was to call attention to the 2.1 million Jews living in the Soviet Union. Author Donald Neff notes that

Unknown to the public was the fact that the anti-Soviet actions were being orchestrated by several militant Israelis, including the Mossad spy agency; Yitzhak Shamir, later Israel's prime minister; and Guelah Cohen, a leader of the extremist Tehiya Party and member of the Knesset. The Israelis persuaded Kahane to wage the anti-Soviet campaign. The goal was to strain U.S.–Soviet relations, calculating Moscow would ease the strain by allowing increased numbers of Soviet Jews to emigrate to Israel.[21]

A 1985 Federal Bureau of Investigation study of terrorist acts in the United States since 1981 found 18 incidents initiated by Jews, 15 of which were by the JDL.[22] In a 1986 study of domestic terrorism, the U.S. Department of Energy concluded: "For more than a decade, the JDL has been one of the most active terrorist groups in the United States. . . . Since 1968, JDL operations have killed seven persons and wounded at least twenty-two."[23]

In 1985, Alex Odeh, regional director of the American-Arab Anti-Discrimination Committee (ADC) in Santa Ana, California, was killed by a bomb planted at his office. Donald Neff writes,

> Odeh had appeared the previous night on a television show and called Yasser Arafat 'a man of peace.' The JDL praised the bombing but denied involvement, its usual practice in such incidents. One of the suspects was Robert Manning . . . a JDL member. He and his wife, Rochelle, moved to Israel, where he joined the Israel Defense Forces. FBI agents said Manning and others were also suspected of being involved in a year-long series of violent incidents in 1985. . . . Israeli police finally arrested the Mannings on March 24, 1991. Although strongly suspected in the Odeh murder, they were charged in a separate suit involving the 1980 letter-bomb murder of California secretary Patricia Wilkerson. . . . Robert Manning was eventually extradited to the U.S. on July 18, 1993, and was found guilty on October 14, 1993. . . . He was sentenced to life in prison.[24]

Meir Kahane's Blend of Racism and Separatism

Two years after founding the JDL, Rabbi Meir Kahane moved from the United States to Israel in 1971, and by 1984 he had become popular enough to win a seat in the Knesset under the banner of his Kach Party. He developed legislation for "The Prevention of Assimilation between Jews and Non-Jews and for the Security of the Jewish People." Among the provisions it demanded were separate beaches for Jews and non-Jews and an end to mixed summer camps and community centers. Kahane's legislation declared that "Jews are forbidden to marry non-Jews . . . mixed marriages will not be recognized even if recognized in the countries in which they were held. . . . Jews are forbidden to have sexual relations of any sort with non-Jews. . . . Transgressors will be punished with two years imprisonment."[25] A member of the Knesset from the Likud Party, Michael Eitan, likened Kahane's proposed legislation to the anti-Semitic Nuremburg laws enacted in Nazi Germany on 15 September 1935, the "Reich Citizenship Law" and the "Law for the Protection of German Blood and Honor."[26]

In his study of Israeli fratricidal violence, Ehud Sprinzak of the Hebrew University in Jerusalem describes how Kahane celebrated winning his Knesset seat in 1984: "A day after the elections, Kahane and his supporters held a victory parade to Old Jerusalem's Western Wall. Marching defiantly through the Arab section of the Old City, Kahane's followers smashed through the market, overturning vegetable stalls, attacking bystanders . . . and telling frightened residents that the end of their stay in the Holy Land was near."[27]

A new subculture of violence was rapidly growing in Israel, and on 27 April 1984 another event shook the country. A plot was uncovered to blow up five buses full of Arab passengers during the rush hour. Within days, twenty-seven suspected members of an anti-Arab terrorist group were arrested. Soon it was learned that the suspects had been responsible for an unsolved 1980 terror bombing in which two West Bank Arab mayors were crippled and three others were saved only because of a last minute failure to booby trap their cars. Several members of the group also admitted responsibility for numerous acts of anti-Arab terrorism, including a 1983 attack on the Islamic College in Hebron that killed three students and wounded thirty-three.

The emergence of the militant Jewish settler movement on the occupied West Bank slowly revealed the new philosophy of messianism and fundamentalism which fuelled much of the terror. Rabbi Zvi Yehuda Kook, who became a leader of the fundamentalist movement, defined the state of Israel as the Halakhic (Jewish law) Kingdom of Israel, and the Kingdom of Israel as the Kingdom of Heaven on Earth. Every Jew living in Israel was holy.

Ehud Sprinzak explains that

> the single most important conclusion of the new theology had to do with Eretz Israel, the land of Israel. . . . The land—every grain of its soil—was declared holy in a fundamental sense. The conquered territories of Judea and Samaria (the West Bank) had become inalienable and nonnegotiable, not as a result of political or security concern but because God had promised them to Abraham four thousand years earlier, and because the identity of the nation was shaped by this promise. Redemption could take place only in the context of greater Eretz Israel, and territorial withdrawal meant forfeiting redemption.[28]

The most extreme reaction to the September 1978 Camp David accords between Israel and Egypt can be seen in the establishment of the "Jewish underground." Originally, it was considered an ad hoc terror team whose purpose was to avenge terrorism by the Palestinian Liberation Organization. But the chief item on its original agenda was blowing up what it called "the abomination"—Jerusalem's Dome of the Rock, one of Islam's holiest shrines and believed to be located almost exactly on the site of the Jewish Temple that was destroyed nearly two thousand years ago.[29]

The idea of blowing up the Dome of the Rock was raised by two fundamentalist religious Zionists, Yeshua Ben Shoshan and Yehuda Etzion. They sought the restoration of the biblical Kingdom of Israel and the building of the Third Temple, both these goals necessitating destruction of the Dome of the Rock. In 1980, Etzion convened a secret meeting at which the operation was spelled out in great detail. The conspirators had the necessary technical expertise to carry out their plan. But they felt obliged to suspend it because they could not find a rabbi willing to bless their venture. It was only after the arrest in 1984 of Etzion and other Jewish underground members in connection with the attempt to blow up the five Arab buses that the Dome of the Rock plot was discovered. Had it been effected, the consequences would have been catastrophic—at the very least, a war between Israel and a Muslim world united in outrage, with the additional danger of a U.S.—Soviet nuclear confrontation as the superpowers backed their respective clients in the Middle East conflict.

Contempt for non-Jews is inherent in the Zionist terrorist mindset, as evinced by Yehuda Etzion: "For the Gentiles, life is mainly a life of existence, while ours is a life of destiny, the life of a kingdom of priests and a holy people. We exist in the world in order to actualize destiny."[30] With contempt goes hostility. Rabbi Kahane openly sought revenge against Gentiles for centuries of anti-Semitic persecution: "A Jewish fist in the face of an astonished Gentile world that had not seen it for two millennia, this is *Kiddush Hashem* (sanctification of the name of God). Jewish dominion over the Christian holy places while the Church sucked our blood vomits its rage and frustration. This is *Kiddush Hashem*. A Jewish Air Force that is better than any other and that forces a Lebanese airliner dawn so that we can imprison murderers of Jews rather than having to repeat the centuries-old pattern of begging the Gentile world to do it for us. This is *Kiddush Hashem*."[31] Kahane concluded that "Jewish violence in defense of Jewish interests is never bad." He urged the expulsion of Israel's Arab citizens and of the Palestinians in the occupied territories.

Baruch Goldstein was a personal student of Kahane, who in 1983 placed him as a third candidate on Kach's Knesset list. After the Oslo Accords, which he perceived as a disaster for Israel, Goldstein came to believe that only an extreme act of *Kiddush Hashem* could return the Jewish state on the path of its messianic destiny. The result was the Hebron massacre.

Israeli journalist Yossi Melman notes that

> Dr. Baruch Goldstein was no exception. . . . He was preceded by Elliott Goodman and Craig Latner. In April 1982, Goodman—of Tenafly, New Jersey—stormed into the El Omar mosque on Temple Mount in Jerusalem and fired into a Palestinian crowd. Miraculously, "only" two worshippers were

killed and eleven wounded. . . . Two years later, Latner and three colleagues, all from Jewish neighborhoods in New York, opened fire on a bus carrying Palestinian workers near the same city. Five were injured. . . . Successive Israeli governments regarded these incidents as isolated, refusing to admit they were products of a larger psychological environment—the Jewish settlers' movement that had nourished Palestinian hatred.[32]

The Assassination of Yitzhak Rabin

In what is perhaps the landmark example of Jewish terrorism in Israel, the assassination of Prime Minister Yitzhak Rabin, all of the various ultranationalist elements and philosophies came into play. According to Sprinzak, Rabin's assassination did not take place in a vacuum. Although Amir acted alone, his act should be viewed as the culmination of a process of delegitimation of the Israeli government by Israel's ultranationalists. The 1993 Oslo Accords triggered the renewed radicalization of the right, but "the final countdown to the assassination had begun in the aftermath of the 1994 Hebron massacre."[33]

When Rabin held office, the ultra-Orthodox weekly *Hashavna* ("The Week") was used by its publisher Asher Zuckerman to wage a vicious crusade against the prime minister. The magazine regularly called Rabin "a kapo," "an anti-Semite," and "a pathological liar." The weekly, which was read by close to 20 percent of the ultra-Orthodox community, published a symposium on the question of whether Rabin deserved to die and on the appropriate means of executing him. By the critical summer of 1995, *Hashavna* went so far as to charge that Rabin and his foreign minister Shimon Peres were "leading the state and its citizens to annihilation and must be placed before a firing squad."[34]

A group of Orthodox rabbis gave religious sanction to the murder of Yitzhak Rabin. These rabbis, both in Israel and abroad, revived two obsolete concepts—*din rodef* (the duty to kill a Jew who imperils the life and property of another Jew) and *din moser* (the duty to eliminate a Jew who intends to turn in another Jew to non-Jewish authorities). By relinquishing rule over parts of the biblical Land of Israel to the Palestinian authorities, these rabbis argued, the head of the Israeli government had become a moser (informer, collaborator with Gentiles). They thus effectively declared Rabin a legitimate target for Jewish extremists.

In a meeting with Samuel Hollander, Israel's Orthodox cabinet secretary who visited New York over the High Holy Days in 1995, a group of rabbis told the stunned official that his boss was a moser and rodef. Rabbi Abraham Hecht, the head of New York City's large Sharei Zion synagogue, did not hesitate to say in public what many of his colleagues had been saying privately. In a 9 October 1995 interview with *New York* magazine, he maintained,

Rabin is not a Jew any longer. . . . According to Jewish law, any one person who willfully, consciously, intentionally hands over human bodies or human property or the human wealth of the Jewish people to an alien people is guilty of the sin for which the penalty is death. And according to Maimonides . . . it says very clearly, *if a man kills him, he has done a good deed.*[35]

In 1995, the Purim holiday was an occasion for a special radical right ceremony, the anniversary of the Hebron massacre and the death of Baruch Goldstein. A Goldstein cult had emerged, and his memory became the rallying point of the disbanded Kahane movement, A 550-page edited memorial was published in March 1995, the Hebrew title of which translates as *Baruch, the Man: A Memorial Volume for Dr. Baruch Goldstein, the Saint, May God Avenge His Blood.* Edited by Michael Ben Horin, a Golan settler, the major theme of the book was conceived by Rabbi Yitzhak Ginzburg, head of the radical Tomb of Yoseph yeshiva in Balus. Ginzburg made headlines in 1988 by providing Halakhic support for several of his students who had unilaterally shot Palestinian civilians. It was fully legitimate, he declared, to kill noncombatant Palestinians. Goldstein, he believed, was not a criminal and mass murderer but a man of piety and deep religious conviction. Ginzburg wrote: "About the value of Israel's life, it simply seems that the life of Israel is worth more than the life of the Gentile and even if the Gentile does not intend to hurt Israel it is permissible to hurt him in order to save Israel." He called the Hebron massacre "a shining moment."[36]

Amir, Rabin's assassin, avidly read *Baruch The Man*. He explained the assassination to his interrogators by saying that, "If not for a Halakhic ruling of *din rodef*, made against Rabin by a few rabbis I knew about, it would have been very difficult for me to murder. Such a murder must be backed up. If I did not get the backing and I had not been representing many more people, I would not have acted."[37]

A Pattern of Zionist Terrorism

Amir's actions were certainly dramatic—but not isolated—representations of Zionist terrorism, which is hardly a new phenomenon. Indeed, the history of pre-Israel Palestine gives ample evidence of the terrorist mindset of many Zionist activists, a mindset that produced acts of violence which took the lives of fellow Jews, Arabs, and others who involved themselves in the political debates over the creation of Israel. Consider some of the major examples:

- In 1933, Chaim Arlosoroff, a young Labor politician seemingly destined to be the first prime minister of a future Jewish state, was shot dead while walking on a Tel Aviv beach. His murder came at the height of a campaign of personal denunciation conducted by a small group of right-wing Zionists known as B'rith Habirionim ("Covenant of Terrorists"—the original "Habirionim" had been vigilantes who targeted collaborators during the Jewish revolt against ancient Rome). Arlosoroff attracted the wrath of the extreme right because of his attempts to negotiate with Nazi Germany for freedom for wealthy German Jews to leave with their money provided they used it to buy German goods and bring them to Palestine. The murder was never proved in court, but it blackened the image of the Revisionist movement, causing it to be widely seen as fascist and terrorist.

- During the darkest days of World War II, when Great Britain stood alone against Nazi Germany, Lehi (Israel's Freedom Fighters)—a group launched in 1940 by Abraham Stern—fought the British. When all other Jewish groups in Palestine declared a cease-fire with the British and prayed that the Allied forces would survive the 1940–42 Nazi offensive, Lehi fighters planted bombs in British installations and killed British soldiers. Their leaders even sent messages of support to the Nazis and offered their cooperation in the future Nazi world order.

- On 6 November 1944, Lehi members murdered Lord Moyne, a member of the British war cabinet who served as state minister for the Middle East, in Cairo. The reason for his murder? He was thought to be responsible for blocking the entrance to Palestine of Jewish refugees.

- On 22 July 1946 members of the Zionist terror group Irgun blew up Jerusalem's King David Hotel, which served as the headquarters of the British administration in Palestine. More than eighty civilians were killed, including many Jews.

- On 9 April 1948 the Irgun and Lehi launched an attack on the Palestinian village of Deir Yassin. Situated in the hills on the outskirts of Jerusalem, Deir Yassin was of no immediate threat to Zionist forces. Its residents were considered passive, and its leaders had agreed with those of an adjacent Jewish neighborhood, Givat Shaul, that each side would prevent its own people from attacking the other. It was the Muslim Sabbath when the attack by the Irgun and Lehi—with the reluctant acquiescence of the mainstream Jewish defense organization, the Haganah—took place. All the inhabitants of the village were ordered out into a square, where they were lined up against the wall and shot. More than 100 civilians were killed. News of the massacre spread rapidly and helped prompt a panic flight of hundreds of thousands of Palestinians from their homes. Most of the victims of the Deir Yassin massacre were women, children, and older people. The men of the village were absent because they worked in Jerusalem. Irgun leader

Menachem Begin issued this euphoric message to his troops after the attack. "Accept my congratulations on this splendid act of conquest. . . . As in Deir Yassin, so everywhere, we will attack and smite the enemy. God, God, Thou hast chosen us for conquest."[38]

David Shipler, Jerusalem' bureau chief for the *New York Times* from 1979 to 1984, reports that

> The Jewish fighters who planned the attack on Deir Yassin also had a larger purpose, apparently. A Jerusalem woman and her son, who gave some of the men coffee in the predawn hours before their mission, recall the guerrillas' talking excitedly of the prospect of terrifying Arabs far beyond the village of Deir Yassin so that they would run away. Perhaps this explains why the Jewish guerrillas did not bury the Arabs they had killed, but left their bodies to be seen, and why they paraded surviving prisoners, blindfolded and with hands bound, in the backs of trucks through the streets of Jerusalem, a scene still remembered with a shudder by Jews who saw it.[39]

There were other massacres of Arabs as well. One occurred on 29 October 1956 the eve of Israel's Suez campaign, when the army ordered all Israeli–Arab villages near the Jordanian border to be placed under a wartime curfew that was to run from 5 P.M. to 6 A.M. the next day. Any Arab on the streets would be shot. No arrests were to be made. But the order was given to Israeli border police units only at 3:30 P.M., without time to communicate it to the Arabs affected, many of whom were at work or in their fields. In Kfar Kassem, Israeli border troops took up positions at various points and slaughtered villagers as they came home, unaware that a curfew had been imposed. The troops fired into one truck carrying fourteen women and four men. Villagers were hauled out of trucks, lined up and shot. In all, forty-seven Arabs, all of them Israeli citizens, were killed during the early hours of the curfew at Kfar Kassem. Lance Corporal Shalom Ofer, deputy squad leader, ordered that all women and children should be shot repeatedly until none remained alive.[40]

Contemporary Zionism and Extremist Violence

There is too little understanding of the nature of the Jewish religious extremism which continues to be so much a part of Israel's political life. In his study of the similarities between terrorist groups motivated by religion, be they Jewish, Christian, Muslim, Hindu, Buddhist, or Sikh, Mark Juergensmeyer of the University of California tells of a conversation he had with Yoel Lerner, an activist leader who served time in prison for his part in the attempt to blow up the Dome of the Rock:

Yoel Lerner . . . believes in a form of Messianic Zionism. In his view the prophesied Messiah will come to earth only after the temple is rebuilt and made ready for him. . . . [T]he issue of the temple was not only a matter of cultural nostalgia but also one of pressing religious importance. . . . In Lerner's view the redemption of the whole world depends upon the actions of Jews in creating the conditions necessary for messianic salvation. . . . [He] told me that there had been a great deal of discussion in the months before Rabin's death about the religious justification for the political assassination— or 'execution,' as Lerner called it—of Jewish leaders who were felt to be dangerously irresponsible and were *de facto* enemies of Judaism. Thus it was "no surprise" to Lerner that someone like Yigal Amir was successful in killing Rabin. The only thing that puzzled him, he said, was that "no one had done it earlier."[41]

The growth in Israel of a form of "messianic Zionism" makes control over all of the biblical Land of Israel a religious mandate. According to Rabbi Yitzhak Kook, the chief rabbi of pre-Israel Palestine, the secular state of Israel is the precursor of the religious Israel to come. Juergensmeyer points out that

This messianic Zionism was greatly enhanced by Israel's successes in the 1967 Six-Day War. . . . Jewish nationalists impressed with Kook's theology felt strongly that history was quickly leading to the moment of divine redemption and the re-creation of the biblical state of Israel. Kahane deviated from Kook's version of messianic Zionism in that he saw nothing of religious significance in the establishment of a secular Jewish state. According to Kahane, the true creation of a religious Israel was yet to come. . . . However, he felt that . . . he and his partisans could help bring about this messianic act. This is where Kahane's notion of *Kiddush Hashem* was vital: insofar as Jews were exalted and their enemies humiliated, God was glorified and the Messiah's coming was more likely.[42]

Jewish extremists, according to Juergensmeyer, are convinced that their violent acts have been authorized as weapons in a "divine warfare sanctioned by God." Goldstein's massacre in Hebron in 1994 was thus described as a military act.

In recent years, the threat of Jewish terrorism has continued. The *Jewish Telegraphic Agency* reported in June 2000 that

threatening letters arrive regularly at the premier's office. One recently sent anonymously to Moledet Knesset Member Benny Elon read, "To the best of my judgment, one should prepare a shelf plan to assassinate Ehud Barak. Just like the Oslo Accord process was slowed down after the annihilation of Yitzhak Rabin, one can prevent withdrawal in the Golan by annihilating

Ehud Barak." Settler preparations for the "final battle" are strongest in the areas where radicalism is usually most pronounced—Hebron, Beit-El and Kedumum.[43]

Shimon Riklin, leader of a group of young militant settlers, warned. "If Barak evacuates settlements, he might be murdered."[44] Rabbi Daniel Shilo declared in his settlement's newsletter that "the transfer of parts of Eretz Israel amounts to treason."[45] In June 2000, Benny Katzover, a leader in the West Bank settlement movement, called Education Minister Yossie Sarid, head of the dovish Meretz Party, "an executioner among executioners" because he is "ready to transfer tens of thousands of Jews to the enlightened regime of his Excellency Yasser Arafat." Katzover suggested that those protesting against the peace process not stick to the "law book" in their demonstrations.[46]

In his book, *A Little Too Close to God*, David Horovitz, editor of the *Jerusalem Report*, recalls the atmosphere at anti-Rabin rallies sponsored by Benjamin Netanyahu's Likud Party. "I felt as if I were among wild animals, vicious, angry predators craving flesh and scenting blood. There was elation in the anger, elation bred of the certainty of eventual success."[47] This extremism, he fears, remains very much a part of Israel's political life.

In June 2000 a Conservative synagogue was set on fire in Jerusalem. Yonathan Liebowitz, a spokesman for the Conservative movement, said witnesses reported seeing apparently Orthodox men, wearing black velvet skullcaps, fleeing as the flames raged. The synagogue had previously been defaced with graffiti that labeled it a place unworthy for worship. The refusal to permit genuine religious freedom for non-Orthodox forms of Judaism surely plays a part in such actions.

The response to such religious violence has been minimal in Israeli religious and governmental circles. Barbara Sofer points out that when three synagogues were burned in Sacramento, California, the city's entire religious community—of Protestants, Catholics, Jews, and Muslims—as well as the civic leadership, came together to show solidarity in the face of such a brutal assault. Law-enforcement authorities quickly apprehended the guilty parties. In Israel, she laments, "Where is our religious establishment? Rabbis cannot remain silent. . . . I'm just one observant Jewish Jerusalemite. I condemn violence against any synagogue, any church and any mosque."[48]

Synagogue president Hilary Herzberger said that "if the chief rabbi had come out against such behavior, maybe it could have been prevented."[49] Rabbi Ehud Brandel, president of the Masorti, the Conservative movement in Israel, said that the lack of a strong response by authorities the last time a synagogue was attacked "sent a message of encouragement to those radical groups."[50] Legislator Meir Porush of the ultra-Orthodox United Torah Judaism bloc accused the Conservative movement of being responsible for burning its own synagogue. This charge led Naomi Hazan of the secular

Meretz Party to charge Porush with making "anti-Semitic statements" by blaming the victim for the crime.[51]

Rabbi Andrew Sacks, director of the Conservative movement's Rabbinical Assembly in Israel, said the key to change lies as much with the ultra-Orthodox establishment as with the police, who did not make any arrests after past attacks on Reform and Conservative synagogues. "I have no reason to think that the arson will change anything," he said. "As long as there is no punishment meted out, then what incentive is there for an individual not to do this?"[52]

Israel's reluctance to take action against Jewish terrorism has a long history. Ehud Sprinzak points out that following the 1948 assassination by Lehi terrorists of United Nations mediator Count Folke Bernadotte, talks were held between Shaul Avigur, aide to Prime Minister David Ben-Gurion, and the leaders of Lehi (including future prime minister Yitzhak Shamir), who were then in hiding.

> An agreement of the latter to stop all subversive operations if Lehi's members would not be discriminated against in the army was achieved. Avigur asked Shamir the names of the assassins, promising that nothing would happen to them, but Shamir refused to give them. Not one member of the hit team would ever spend a night in jail or face a court of justice. For years there was a conspiracy of silence about the Bernadotte assassination. . . . In 1960, the most talkative of all former Lehi commanders, Israel Eldad, approached Gideon Hausner, the state attorney general, and offered to tell the truth about the assassination. "God forbid," was Hausner's response. "Do you know the problems you will create for your country?"[53]

In 2004, Israeli opposition leader Shimon Peres said that he feared Israeli extremists might try to assassinate Prime Minister Ariel Sharon, who became the target of growing right-wing fury over a planned withdrawal from the Gaza Strip. Peres said the divisive atmosphere recalled the climate when Prime Minister Rabin was killed by an ultranationalist opposed to his peace deals with the Palestinians. "I am very fearful of the incitement, of the harsh things that are being said," Peres declared.[54]

In October 2004 some sixty leading rabbis issued an unprecedented call for Israeli settlers to defy any orders to evacuate Jewish settlers from the Gaza Strip and the West Bank.[55] The rabbis, many of them heads of religious academies, or yeshivas, declared that the soldiers have a higher duty to preserve Jewish control of the Holy Land than to obey "immoral" orders from the army. This declaration was stimulated by National Religious Party mentor and former chief rabbi Avraham Shapira.

According to Avi Dichter, director of the Shin Bet security service, right-wing opposition to Prime Minister Ariel Sharon's Gaza disengagement plan "is becoming more extreme and more dangerous."[56] In a closed-door session of the Knesset's Defense and Foreign Affairs Committee in July 2004, Dichter reported that 150 to 200 extremist settlers were speaking and writing in violent terms and wanted to see Ariel Sharon dead because of his plan to dismantle settlements in the Gaza Strip and West Bank.

These warnings came after a series of declarations by rabbis forbidding the evacuation of settlements as a violation of religious law. One respected rabbi, Svigdor Nebenzahl, chief rabbi of the Old City of Jerusalem, declared in July 2004 that withdrawing from the territories might incur the so-called *din rodef*, or "verdict of the pursuer," the Talmudic concept of Jewish treason traditionally punished by death. "Whoever gives away parts of the land of Israel to others should be considered according to this verdict," he told a rabbinical gathering in Jerusalem.[57]

Such sentiments remain very much alive. Yossi Alpher, a former director of the Jaffee Center for Strategic Studies and former senior adviser to Prime Minister Ehud Barak, recently observed: "Israel's most ideologically committed and politically skilled minority knows it is in a fight for its life. If Sharon succeeds in removing even a single settlement, a fateful precedent will have been set, one that puts Israel on the road to a Jewish and democratic state in part of Eretz Yisrael, rather than a Jewish but undemocratic state—a mini South Africa really—in all of Eretz Yisrael."[58]

If Ariel Sharon were murdered by right-wing extremists, Alpher argues,

> the assassination of a second Israeli leader seemingly bent on rolling back the settlement movement probably would mark the end of attempts to remove settlements or otherwise restrict Israel's territorial agenda and its ethnopolitical nature. . . . Why aren't the rabbis and settlers who threaten violence and murder against their fellow Jews—or for that matter, against anybody—in jail? . . . Because not only do their inciters' fellow ideological settlers condone their remarks . . . but the pragmatic secular mainstream seemingly fears to touch the extremists, ostensibly lest it trigger the very escalation of violence that is already being visited upon its leaders. . . . Virtually everyone on the political, legal and security scene seems to back off when it is a rabbi who is invoking religious law to justify political murder.[59]

In a report from the occupied territories, Jeffrey Goldberg notes that

> A brigade of soldiers, coils of razor wire, and hundreds of concrete barriers stand between Hebron's fewer than 800 Jewish settlers and its 150,000 Arab residents. Across from Hadassah House is a school for Arab girls, called Cordoba, after the once-Muslim Spanish city. On one of its doors someone had drawn a blue star of David. On another door a yellowing bumper sticker read "Dr. Goldstein Cures the Ills of Israel." The reference is to Baruch Goldstein [described earlier in this chapter], a physician from Brooklyn who killed twenty-nine Muslims in 1994 while they were praying in the Tomb of the Pa-

triarchs just down the road. Across the closed door of a Palestinian shop someone had written, in English, "Arabs are Sand Niggers."[60]

Goldberg interviewed many West Bank residents, including Rabbi Moshe Levinger, Hebron's first Jewish settler, who in 1988 killed a Palestinian shoe-store owner. He served thirteen weeks in jail for the killing. He said, "I'm not happy when any living creature dies—an Arab, a fly, a donkey." Levinger told Goldberg, "All my ideas are formed from the Torah. It's not complex. This land is ours. God gave it to us. We're the owners of the land."[61]

Many of the settler leaders have contempt for democracy and would like to create in Israel the kind of theocracy which exists in a country such as Iran. As Goldberg reports,

> Some of the leading ideologues of the settlements, far from supporting the idea of Jewish democracy, hope to establish a Jewish theocracy in Israel, ruled by a Sanhedrin and governed by Jewish law. Moshe Feiglin, a Likud activist who lives in a West Bank settlement and heads the Jewish Leadership bloc within the Party . . . believes that the Bible, interpreted literally, should form the basis of Israel's legal system. "Why should non-Jews have a say in the policy of a Jewish state?" Feiglin said to me. "For two thousand years, Jews dreamed of a Jewish state, not a democratic state. Democracy should serve the values of the state, not destroy them." In any case, Feiglin said, "You can't teach a monkey to speak and you can't teach an Arab to be democratic. You're dealing with a culture of thieves and robbers. Muhammad, their prophet, was a robber and a killer and a liar. The Arab destroys everything he touches."[62]

The most hard-core settlers, in Goldberg's view, "are impatient messianists, who profess indifference, even scorn for the state; a faith in vigilantism; and loathing for the Arabs. . . . The settlers, if they have their way, would build an apartheid state ruled by councils of revanchist rabbis."[63]

Of continuing concern is the fear of an attempt to blow up the Dome of the Rock and al-Aqsa Mosque on Jerusalem's Temple Mount. In July 2004 Tzachi Hanegbi, Israel's Minister of Internal Security, said that intelligence services fear the threat could grow as right-wingers seek to block Prime Minister Ariel Sharon's disengagement plan. "There is a real danger that they will want to make use of this most sensitive, most explosive and most sacred site to the Muslims to stage a terrorist attack on the site, whether in a mosque or against worshipers, and then hope that a chain reaction will lead to the collapse of the political process," Hanegbi said.[64]

According to one report,

> right-wing radicals plan to stage a mega-attack on the Temple Mount, possibly by flying an airplane into Muslim worshipers during prayers. The buildings on the mount—al-Aqsa Mosque and the gold-topped Dome of the Rock—have attracted Jewish extremists since the early 1980s, and blowing

up these landmarks was one of the grand designs of the "Jewish underground" that operated during that period.[65]

The *Jewish Telegraphic Agency* reported that

Most of the Jewish groups who dream of rebuilding the Holy Temple say they would not resort to violence but would wait for the Messiah to destroy the Muslim shrines. Some fringe groups, however, could be more inclined to take matters into their own hands. Aryeh Amit, former commander of the Jerusalem police, warned . . . that this was exactly the scenario security forces fear. "The problem does not necessarily lie in all those potential terrorists known to the security forces," he said, "but rather in the single anonymous terrorist, unknown to the security forces." Some thirty-five years ago, an Australian Christian, Michael Dennis Rohan, set fire to part of al-Aqsa. In 1982, Alan Goodman, an American tourist, burst onto the mount and shot at Muslim worshipers.[66]

While Israel's Shin Bet is carefully following known extremists, it is also

deeply worried about another "profile" of extremists: veterans of elite combat units who have taken a cold, considered decision to use violence to prevent withdrawal. That description recalls the 1980s Jewish underground, whose members—prominent and respected settlement activists—aimed instead to prevent any accommodation with the Palestinians by blowing up the Dome of the Rock. A decade later, the same kind of thinking propelled Baruch Goldstein to open fire on Palestinian worshipers in Hebron—which, indeed, almost derailed negotiations over the Gaza and Jericho Agreement. When that course failed, Yigal Amir, an admirer of Goldstein's, targeted Rabin. It's precisely due to the Amir precedent . . . that the Shin Bet has been alerting the public to its concerns about extremism. Amir was regarded as a "normative" citizen—an army vet and law student who lived in Herzliyah, in the heart of mainstream Israel. He expressed radical views, but few who heard him suspected he'd really kill the prime minister.[67]

A key ingredient in molding Jewish terrorism is a fundamentalist religious vision of a greater Israel encompassing all of the Biblical Israel which, advocates of this view argue, was given to the Jewish people by God for eternity. Much of the terrorism we face in today's world is motivated by similar, often conflicting, religious visions. Professor Mark Juergensmeyer, in his book *Terror in the Mind of God*, provides this overview:

Terrorism is meant to terrify. The word comes from the Latin *terrere*, "to cause to tremble," and came into common usage in the political sense, as an assault on civil order during the Reign of Terror in the French Revolution. The fear often turns into anger when we discover the other characteristic that frequently attends these acts of violence [including] their justification by religion. . . . In many cases, religion has supplied not only the ideology but also the motivation and the organizational structure for the perpetrators. It is true that some terrorist acts are committed by public officials invoking a sort of "state terrorism" in order to subjugate the populace. The pogroms of Stalin, the government-supported death squads in El Salvador, the genocidal killings of the Khmer Rouge in Cambodia, ethnic cleansing in Bosnia and Kosovo, and government-spurred violence of the Hutus and Tutsis in Central Africa all come to mind.[68]

The term "terrorism," however, has more frequently been associated with violence committed by disenfranchised groups attempting to gain a shred of power or influence. Some have been inspired by purely secular causes. They have been motivated by leftist ideologies, as in the cases of the Shining Path and Tupac Amaru in Peru, and the Red Army in Japan; and they have been propelled by a desire for ethnic or regional separatism, as in the cases of Basque militants in Spain and the Kurdish nationalists in the Middle East. But more often, it has been religion—sometimes in combination with these other factors, sometimes as the primary motivation—that has incited terrorist acts.[69]

For those engaged in terror on behalf of a religious vision of a Greater Israel, an apocalyptic worldview is common. Yochay Roy, a Jewish activist in Hebron, said that the war with the Arabs did not begin with the intifada in the 1980s or even with the establishment of the state of Israel. It goes back to "biblical times," indicating that the present-day Arabs are simply the modern descendents of the enemies of Israel described in the Bible for whom God has unleashed wars of revenge.[70] Another Hebron activist, Sarah Nachshon, says. "It's written in the Bible, that until the Messiah comes there will be a big war, and the war will be in Jerusalem."[71]

"There is no such thing as coexistence," Jewish activist Yoel Lerner states, explaining that there is a biblical requirement for Jews to possess and live on biblical land. Militant leaders on the other side share this view.[72] Dr. Abdel-Aziz al-Rantisi, a Hamas leader, argued that it is necessary for Arab Muslims to occupy what he regards as their homeland, while Sheik Yassin, Hamas' spiritual leader, described the conflict as "the combat between good and evil."[73] A communiqué issued by Hamas, when the United States sent troops to the Saudi Arabian desert following Saddam Hussein's invasion of Kuwait in 1990, declared it to be "another episode in the fight between good and evil" and "a hateful Christian plot against our religion, our civilization, our land."[74]

Conclusion

There is every indication that the overwhelming majority of both Israelis and Palestinians seek a negotiated peace settlement and the establishment of a Palestinian state on the bulk of the West Bank. How well these majorities are able to isolate the militant advocates of terror, who believe that God is on their side, will determine the future of the region. Thus far, terrorism has managed to prevent a settlement, with leaders on both sides hesitant to take the steps necessary to bring extremism under control. Whether the future will learn from the past is yet to be determined. Sadly for all, the appeals of religion-based terrorism do not yet appear to be in decline.

However slowly, more and more Jewish voices are rising in criticism of the extremists in their ranks. Reuven Firestone, professor of medieval Judaism and Islam at Hebrew Union College in Los Angeles and author of, among other works, *Children of Abraham: An Introduction to Judaism for Muslims*, observes:

> Before dismissing the appalling behaviors of our Muslim cousins engaged in holy war, let us put our own house in order. Holy war has been revived among Israel the people and within Israel the state. . . . After the Mishnah, Jewish holy war ideas lay virtually dormant . . . though they were discussed briefly by certain medieval thinkers and appear in some of our apocalyptic and messianic writings. But holy war has been revived in contemporary Israel, especially among ultranationalist Orthodox settlers in Judea and Samaria (the West Bank) and their many supporters. The war—and it may now be accurately called a war between Israel and the Palestinians—is defined by many religiously observant settlers and their supporters as a divine obligation to reclaim the whole of the Land of Israel as either a prelude to or actually part of the messianic awakening.[75]

Dr. Firestone writes that

> Many in this camp cite *ad nauseum* the now famous statement of Nahmanides in his gloss on Maimonides' Book of Commandments (Positive Commandment 4), who teaches that the conquest and settlement of the Land of Israel lies in the category of obligatory war (*milhemet mitzah*). "It is a positive commandment for all generations obligating every individual even during the period of exile." As Jewish holy war has entered religious and political discourse in relation to the Israel–Palestine conflict, so has the increase of Jewish atrocities in the name of a higher cause. It reached its peak in the mid-1980s to mid-1990s with the maiming and murdering of Muslim noncombatants by the Jewish underground, the massacre of Muslims in prayer by Baruch Goldstein, and Yigal Amir's assassination of Prime Minister Yitzhak Rabin. Holy war ideas continue to inform the behavior of many religious settlers to this day.[76]

While there has been much attention paid to the advocates of "holy war" within the Islamic community—as well there should be—insufficient attention has been paid to similar movements within Judaism. Reuven Firestone concludes:

Holy war is a dangerous reality. We have now felt its sting. Let us, therefore, before we try vainly and patronizingly to intervene in another religious community, put our own house in order. We must neutralize if not eradicate the ugly and gravely dangerous revival of holy war within Judaism. The first step is to acknowledge its existence. The next is to engage in public discussion within *our own* community, especially among the spectrum of religious leaders, to mitigate the inherently self-destructive and ultimately immoral efforts to define our fighting with Palestinians as holy war.[77]

As with terrorism by other groups, both religious and secular, Zionist terrorism is a form of traditional asymmetric warfare, an effort by a militant minority to impose itself upon an unwilling majority. Yet, because the majority has been hesitant to identify and isolate such extremists, their influence has been far out of proportion to their numbers. Operating under the cover of religion has been useful in expanding their following and muting criticism. If Israel and its neighbors are to move in the direction of a lasting peace, the majority of Israelis, particularly Israel's mainstream religious institutions, must act to neutralize those voices which have distorted Judaism's moral mandate and replaced it with worship of physical territory, surely a form of idolatry that Judaism has always condemned.

Profiles of Terrorist Organizations

The following descriptions of terrorists and terrorist organizations are adapted from open source materials in the public domain, including the 2003 *Patterns of Global Terrorism Report* (Appendix B and Appendix C), published by the U.S. State Department (online at http://www.state.gov/s/ct/rls/pgtrpt/2003/c12108.htm) and the Council on Foreign Relations "Terrorism: Questions & Answers" website (http://cfrterrorism.org/home). Several of the groups listed here are described at length in one or more chapters of this 3-volume set—including the Abu Nidal Organization, Abu Sayyaf Group, al Qaeda, Ansar al-Islam, Jemaah Islamiyah, al-Aqsa Martyrs Brigade, Armed Islamic Group, Aum Shinrikyō, Basque Fatherland and Liberty, HAMAS, Hizballah, Islamic Movement of Uzbekistan, Irish Republican Army, Jaish-e-Mohammed, Japanese Red Army, Liberation Tigers of Tamil Eelam, Moro Islamic Liberation Front, Irish Republican Army, Palestinian Islamic Jihad, Popular Front for the Liberation of Palestine (PFLP), Posse Comitatus, Revolutionary Armed Forces of Colombia (FARC), and the Salafist Group for Call and Combat (GSPC). Please see the volume Index for more information.

Abu Nidal Organization (ANO)

a.k.a. Fatah—the Revolutionary Council, Arab Revolutionary Brigades, Black September, and Revolutionary Organization of Socialist Muslims

Description

International terrorist organization founded by Sabri al-Banna (a.k.a. Abu Nidal). Split from PLO in 1974. Made up of various functional committees, including political, military, and financial. In November 2002, Abu Nidal died in Baghdad; the new leadership of the organization is unclear. First designated in October 1997.

Activities

Has carried out terrorist attacks in 20 countries, killing or injuring almost 900 persons. Targets include the United States, the United Kingdom, France, Israel, moderate Palestinians, the PLO, and various Arab countries. Major attacks included the Rome and Vienna airports in December 1985, the Neve Shalom synagogue in Istanbul and the Pan Am Flight 73 hijacking in Karachi in September 1986, and the City of Poros day-excursion ship attack in Greece in July 1988. Suspected of assassinating PLO deputy chief Abu Iyad and PLO security chief Abu Hul in Tunis in January 1991. ANO assassinated a Jordanian diplomat in Lebanon in January 1994 and has been linked to the killing of the PLO representative there. Has not staged a major attack against Western targets since the late 1980s.

Abu Sayyaf Group (ASG)

Description

The ASG is a small, brutally violent Muslim separatist group operating in the southern Philippines. Some ASG leaders allegedly fought in Afghanistan during the Soviet war and are students and proponents of radical Islamic teachings. The group split from the much larger Moro National Liberation Front in the early 1990s under the leadership of Abdurajak Abubakar Janjalani, who was killed in a clash with Philippine police on 18 December 1998. His younger brother, Khadaffy Janjalani, has replaced him as the nominal leader of the group, which is composed of several semiautonomous factions. First designated in October 1997.

Activities

Engages in kidnappings for ransom, bombings, beheadings, assassinations, and extortion. Although from time to time it claims that its motivation is to promote an independent Islamic state in western Mindanao and the Sulu Archipelago—areas in the southern Philippines heavily populated by Muslims—the ASG has primarily used terror for financial profit. Recent bombings may herald a return to a more radical, politicized agenda, at least among the factions. The group's first large-scale action was a raid on the town of Ipil in Mindanao in April 1995. In April of 2000, an ASG faction kidnapped 21 persons—including 10 Western tourists—from a resort in Malaysia. Separately in 2000, the group briefly abducted several foreign journalists, three Malaysians, and a U.S. citizen. On 27 May 2001, the ASG kidnapped three U.S. citizens and 17 Filipinos from a tourist resort in Palawan, Philippines. Several of the hostages, including one U.S. citizen, were murdered. During a Philippine military hostage rescue operation on 7 June 2002, U.S. hostage Gracia Burnham was wounded but rescued, and her husband Martin Burnham and Filipina Deborah Yap were killed during the operation. Philippine authorities say that the ASG had a role in the bombing near a Philippine military base in Zamboanga on 2 October that killed three Filipinos and one U.S. serviceman and wounded 20 others. It is unclear what role ASG has played in subsequent bombing attacks in Mindanao.

Al-Aqsa Martyrs Brigade (al-Aqsa)

Description

The al-Aqsa Martyrs Brigades consists of an unknown number of small cells of Fatah-affiliated terrorists that emerged at the outset of the current *intifada* to attack Israeli targets. It aims to drive the Israeli military and settlers from the West Bank, Gaza Strip, and Jerusalem and to establish a Palestinian state. First designated in March 2002.

Activities

Al-Aqsa has carried out shootings and suicide operations against Israeli civilians and military personnel and has killed Palestinians suspected of collaborating with Israel. At least five U.S. citizens—four of them dual U.S.-Israeli citizens—were killed in al-Aqsa's attacks. In January 2002, al-Aqsa claimed responsibility for the first suicide bombing carried out by a female.

Al-Badhr Mujahidin (al-Badr)

Description

Split from Hizb ul-Mujahidin (HM) in 1998. Traces its origins to 1971 when a group of the same name attacked Bengalis in East Pakistan. Later operated as part of Gulbuddin Hekmatyar's Hizb-I-Islami (HIG) in Afghanistan and from 1990 as a unit of HM in Kashmir.

Activities

Has conducted a number of operations against Indian military targets in Jammu and Kashmir.

Al-Gama'a al-Islamiyya (Islamic Group, IG)

Description

Egypt's largest militant group, active since the late 1970s, appears to be loosely organized. Has an external wing with supporters in several countries worldwide. The group issued a cease-fire in March 1999, but its spiritual leader, Shaykh Umar Abd al-Rahman—sentenced to life in prison in January 1996 for his involvement in the World Trade Center bombing of 1993 and incarcerated in the United States—rescinded his support for the cease-fire in June 2000. The IG has not conducted an attack inside Egypt since August 1998. Senior member signed Osama bin Laden's *fatwa* in February 1998 calling for attacks against the United States.

Unofficially split in two factions: one that supports the cease-fire led by Mustafa Hamza, and one led by Rifa'i Taha Musa, calling for a return to armed operations. Taha Musa in early 2001 published a book in which he attempted to justify terrorist attacks that would cause mass casualties. Musa disappeared several months thereafter, and there are conflicting reports as to his current whereabouts. In March 2002, members of the group's historic leadership in Egypt declared use of violence misguided and renounced its future use, prompting denunciations by much of the leadership abroad. In 2003, the Egyptian government released more than 900 former IG members from prison.

For members still dedicated to violent jihad, the primary goal is to overthrow the Egyptian government and replace it with an Islamic state. Disaffected IG members, such as those potentially inspired by Taha Musa or Abd al-Rahman, may be interested in carrying out attacks against U.S. interests. First designated October 1997.

Activities

Group conducted armed attacks against Egyptian security and other government officials, Coptic Christians, and Egyptian opponents of Islamic extremism before the cease-fire. From 1993 until the cease-fire, IG launched attacks on tourists in Egypt—most notably the attack in November 1997 at Luxor that killed 58 foreign tourists. Also claimed responsibility for the attempt in June 1995 to assassinate Egyptian President Hosni Mubarak in Addis Ababa, Ethiopia. The IG never has specifically attacked a U.S. citizen or facility but has threatened U.S. interests.

Al-Ittihad al-Islami (AIAI)

Description

AIAI rose to power in the early 1990s following the collapse of the Siad Barre regime. Some members of AIAI maintain ties to al Qaeda.

Activities

The group is believed to be responsible for a series of bomb attacks in public places in Addis Ababa in 1996 and 1997 as well as the kidnapping of several relief workers in 1998. AIAI sponsors Islamic social programs, such as orphanages and schools, and provides pockets of security in Somalia.

Al-Jihad

a.k.a. Jihad Group, Egyptian Islamic Jihad (EIJ)

Description

This Egyptian Islamic extremist group merged with Osama bin Laden's al Qaeda organization in June 2001. Active since the 1970s, the EIJ's primary goals traditionally have been to overthrow the Egyptian government and replace it with an Islamic state and to attack U.S. and Israeli interests in Egypt and abroad. EIJ members who did not join al Qaeda retain the capability to conduct independent operations. First designated in October 1997.

Activities

Historically specialized in armed attacks against high-level Egyptian government personnel, including cabinet ministers, and car bombings against official U.S. and Egyptian facilities. The original Jihad was responsible for the assassination in 1981 of Egyptian President Anwar Sadat. Claimed responsibility for the attempted assassinations of Interior Minister Hassan al-Alfi in August 1993 and Prime Minister Atef Sedky in November 1993. Has not conducted an attack inside Egypt since 1993 and has never successfully targeted foreign tourists there. Responsible for Egyptian embassy bombing in Islamabad in 1995, and in 1998 an attack against U.S. embassy in Albania was thwarted.

Al-Qaida (al Qaeda)
a.k.a. Qa'idat al-Jihad

Description

Established by Osama bin Laden in the late 1980s to bring together Arabs who fought in Afghanistan against the Soviet Union. Helped finance, recruit, transport, and train Sunni Islamic extremists for the Afghan resistance. Current goal is to establish a pan-Islamic Caliphate throughout the world by working with allied Islamic extremist groups to overthrow regimes it deems "non-Islamic" and expelling Westerners and non-Muslims from Muslim countries—particularly Saudi Arabia. Issued statement under banner of "the World Islamic Front for Jihad Against the Jews and Crusaders" in February 1998, saying it was the duty of all Muslims to kill U.S. citizens—civilian or military—and their allies everywhere. Merged with Egyptian Islamic Jihad (al-Jihad) in June 2001. First designated in October 1999.

Activities

In 2003, carried out the assault and bombing on 12 May of three expatriate housing complexes in Riyadh, Saudi Arabia, that killed 20 and injured 139. Assisted in carrying out the bombings on 16 May in Casablanca, Morocco, of a Jewish center, restaurant, nightclub, and hotel that killed 41 and injured 101. Probably supported the bombing of the J. W. Marriott Hotel in Jakarta, Indonesia, on

5 August that killed 17 and injured 137. Responsible for the assault and bombing on 9 November of
a housing complex in Riyadh, Saudi Arabia, that
killed 17 and injured 100. Conducted the bombings of two synagogues in Istanbul, Turkey, on 15
November that killed 23 and injured 200 and the
bombings in Istanbul of the British Consulate and
HSBC Bank on 20 November that resulted in 27
dead and 455 injured. Has been involved in some
attacks in Afghanistan and Iraq.

In 2002, carried out bombing on 28 November
of hotel in Mombasa, Kenya, killing 15 and injuring 40. Probably supported a nightclub bombing in
Bali, Indonesia, on 12 October that killed about
180. Responsible for an attack on U.S. military
personnel in Kuwait, on 8 October, that killed one
U.S. soldier and injured another. Directed a suicide
attack on the MV *Limburg* off the coast of Yemen,
on 6 October that killed one and injured four. Carried out a firebombing of a synagogue in Tunisia
on 11 April that killed 19 and injured 22. On 11
September 2001, 19 al Qaeda suicide attackers hijacked and crashed four U.S. commercial jets—two
into the World Trade Center in New York City,
one into the Pentagon near Washington, DC, and a
fourth into a field in Shanksville, Pennsylvania,
leaving about 3,000 individuals dead or missing.
Directed the attack on the USS *Cole* in the port of
Aden, Yemen, on 12 October 2000 killing 17 U.S.
Navy members and injuring another 39.

Conducted the bombings in August 1998 of the
U.S. embassies in Nairobi, Kenya, and Dar es
Salaam, Tanzania, that killed at least 301 individuals and injured more than 5,000 others. Claims to
have shot down U.S. helicopters and killed U.S.
servicemen in Somalia in 1993 and to have conducted three bombings that targeted U.S. troops in
Aden, Yemen, in December 1992.

Al Qaeda is linked to the following plans that
were disrupted or not carried out: to assassinate
Pope John Paul II during his visit to Manila in late
1994, to kill President Clinton during a visit to the
Philippines in early 1995, to bomb in midair a
dozen U.S. transpacific flights in 1995, and to set

off a bomb at Los Angeles International Airport in 1999. Also plotted to carry out terrorist operations against U.S. and Israeli tourists visiting Jordan for millennial celebrations in late 1999. (Jordanian authorities thwarted the planned attacks and put 28 suspects on trial.) In December 2001, suspected al Qaeda associate Richard Colvin Reid attempted to ignite a shoe bomb on a transatlantic flight from Paris to Miami. Attempted to shoot down an Israeli chartered plane with a surface-to-air missile as it departed the Mombasa airport in November 2002.

Alex Boncayao Brigade (ABB)

Description

The ABB, the breakaway urban hit squad of the Communist Party of the Philippines/New People's Army, was formed in the mid-1980s. The ABB was added to the Terrorist Exclusion list in December 2001.

Activities

Responsible for more than 100 murders, including the murder in 1989 of U.S. Army Col. James Rowe in the Philippines. In March 1997, the group announced it had formed an alliance with another armed group, the Revolutionary Proletarian Army (RPA). In March 2000, the group claimed credit for a rifle grenade attack against the Department of Energy building in Manila and strafed Shell Oil offices in the central Philippines to protest rising oil prices.

Ansar al-Islam (AI)

a.k.a. Partisans of Islam, Helpers of Islam, Supporters of Islam, Jund al-Islam, Jaish Ansar al-Sunna

Description

Ansar al-Islam is a radical Islamist group of Iraqi Kurds and Arabs who have vowed to establish an independent Islamic state in Iraq. It was formed in December 2001 and is closely allied with al Qaeda. Some of its members trained in al Qaeda camps in Afghanistan, and the group provided safehaven to al Qaeda fighters before Operation Iraqi Freedom (OIF). Since OIF, it has been one of the leading groups engaged in anti-Coalition attacks.

Activities

The group has primarily fought against one of the two main Kurdish political factions—the Patriotic Union of Kurdistan (PUK)—and has mounted ambushes and attacks in PUK areas. AI members have been implicated in assassinations and assassination attempts against PUK officials and work closely with both al Qaeda operatives and associates in Abu Mus'ab al-Zarqawi's network. Before OIF, some AI members claimed to have produced cyanide-based toxins, ricin, and alfatoxin.

Anti-Imperialist Territorial Nuclei (NTA)

a.k.a. Anti-Imperialist Territorial Units

Description

Clandestine leftist extremist group that first appeared in the Friuli region in Italy in 1995. Adopted the class-struggle ideology of the Red Brigades of the 1970s and 1980s and a similar logo—an encircled five-point star—for their declarations. Seeks the formation of an "anti-imperialist fighting front" with other Italian leftist terrorist groups including Revolutionary Proletarian Initiative Nuclei and the New Red Brigades. Opposes what it perceives as U.S. and NATO imperialism and condemns Italy's foreign and labor polices. Identified experts in four Italian government sectors—federalism, privatizations, justice reform, and jobs and pensions—as potential targets in a leaflet dated January 2002.

Activities

To date, the group has conducted attacks against property rather than persons. This pattern continued in 2003 when NTA claimed responsibility for the arson attacks against three vehicles belonging to U.S. troops serving at the Ederle and Aviano bases in Italy. In January 2002, police thwarted an attempt by four NTA members to enter the Rivolto Military Air Base. It claimed responsibility for a bomb attack in September 2000 against the Central European Initiative office in Trieste and a bomb attack in August 2001 against the Venice Tribunal building. During the NATO intervention in Kosovo, NTA members threw gasoline bombs at the Venice and Rome headquarters of the then-ruling party, Democrats of the Left.

**Armed Islamic Group
(GIA)**

Description

An Islamic extremist group, the GIA aims to overthrow the secular Algerian regime and replace it
with an Islamic state. The GIA began its violent
activity in 1992 after the military government suspended legislative elections in anticipation of an
overwhelming victory by the Islamic Salvation
Front, the largest Islamic opposition party. First
designated in October 1997.

Activities

Frequent attacks against civilians and government
workers. Since 1992, the GIA has conducted a terrorist campaign of civilian massacres, sometimes wiping
out entire villages in its area of operation, although
the group's dwindling numbers have caused a de-
crease in the number of attacks. Since announcing its
campaign against foreigners living in Algeria in 1993,
the GIA has killed more than 100 expatriate men
and women—mostly Europeans—in the country. The
group uses assassinations and bombings, including
car bombs, and it is known to favor kidnapping victims. The GIA highjacked an Air France flight to Al-
giers in December 1994. In 2002, a French court
sentenced two GIA members to life in prison for conducting a series of bombings in France in 1995.

**Army for the Liberation of
Rwanda (ALIR)**

a.k.a. Ex-FAR/
Interahamwe, (formerly
Armed Forces of Rwanda)

Description

The Armed Forces of Rwanda (FAR) was the army
of the ethnic Hutu-dominated Rwandan regime
that carried out the genocide of 500,000 or more
Tutsis and regime opponents in 1994. The Interahamwe was the civilian militia force that carried
out much of the killing. The groups merged and
recruited additional fighters after they were forced
from Rwanda into the Democratic Republic of
Congo (DRC; then Zaire) in 1994. They became
known as the Army for the Liberation of Rwanda
(ALIR), which is the armed branch of the PALIR
or Party for the Liberation of Rwanda. In 2001,
ALIR—while not formally disbanded—was sup-
planted by the Democratic Front for the Liberation
of Rwanda (FDLR). Though directly descended
from those who organized and carried out the

genocide, identified FDLR leaders are not thought to have played a role in the killing. They have worked to build bridges to other opponents of the Kigali regime, including ethnic Tutsis.

Activities

ALIR sought to topple Rwanda's Tutsi-dominated government, reinstitute Hutu domination, and, possibly, complete the genocide. In 1996, a message—allegedly from the ALIR—threatened to kill the U.S. ambassador to Rwanda and other U.S. citizens. In 1999, ALIR guerrillas critical of alleged U.S.-UK support for the Rwandan regime kidnapped and killed eight foreign tourists, including two U.S. citizens, in a game park on the Democratic Republic of Congo–Uganda border. In the 1998–2002 Congolese war, the ALIR/FDLR was allied with Kinshasa against the Rwandan invaders. FDLR's political wing has mainly sought to topple the Kigali regime via alliance with Tutsi regime opponents. They established the ADRN Igihango alliance in 2002, but it has not resonated politically in Rwanda.

'Asbat al-Ansar

Description

'Asbat al-Ansar—the League of the Followers or Partisans' League—is a Lebanon-based, Sunni extremist group, composed primarily of Palestinians and associated with Osama bin Laden's al Qaeda organization. The group follows an extremist interpretation of Islam that justifies violence against civilian targets to achieve political ends. Some of those goals include overthrowing the Lebanese Government and thwarting perceived anti-Islamic and pro-Western influences in the country. First designated in March 2002.

Activities

'Asbat al-Ansar has carried out multiple terrorist attacks in Lebanon since it first emerged in the early 1990s. The group assassinated Lebanese religious leaders and bombed nightclubs, theaters, and liquor stores in the mid-1990s. The group raised its operational profile in 2000 with two attacks against Lebanese and international targets. It was involved in clashes in northern Lebanon in December 1999 and carried out a rocket-propelled grenade attack on the Russian embassy in Beirut in January 2000. 'Asbat al-Ansar's leader, Abu Muhjin, remains at large despite being sentenced to death in absentia for the murder in 1994 of a Muslim cleric.

In 2003, suspected 'Asbat al-Ansar elements were responsible for the attempt in April to use a car bomb against a McDonald's in a Beirut suburb. By October, Lebanese security forces arrested Ibn al-Shahid, who is believed to be associated with 'Asbat al-Ansar, and charged him with masterminding the bombing of three fast-food restaurants in 2002 and the attempted attack in April 2003 on the McDonald's. 'Asbat forces were involved in other violence in Lebanon in 2003, including clashes with members of Yassir Arafat's Fatah movement in the 'Ayn al-Hilwah refugee camp and a rocket attack in June on the Future TV Building in Beirut.

Aum Supreme Truth (Aum)

a.k.a. Aum Shinrikyō, Aleph

Description

A cult established in 1987 by Shoko Asahara, the Aum aimed to take over Japan and then the world. Approved as a religious entity in 1989 under Japanese law, the group ran candidates in a Japanese parliamentary election in 1990. Over time, the cult began to emphasize the imminence of the end of the world and stated that the United States would initiate Armageddon by starting World War III with Japan. The Japanese government revoked its recognition of the Aum as a religious organization in October 1995, but in 1997, a government panel decided not to invoke the Anti-Subversive Law against the group, which would have outlawed the cult. A 1999 law gave the Japanese government authorization to continue police surveillance of the group due to concerns that the Aum might launch future terrorist attacks. Under the leadership of Fumihiro Joyu, the Aum changed its name to Aleph in January 2000 and claimed to have rejected the violent and apocalyptic teachings of its founder. First designated in October 1997.

Activities

On 20 March 1995, Aum members simultaneously released the chemical nerve agent sarin on several Tokyo subway trains, killing 12 persons and injuring up to 6,000. The group was responsible for other mysterious chemical accidents in Japan in 1994. Its efforts to conduct attacks using biological agents have been unsuccessful. Japanese police arrested Asahara in May 1995. Asahara was sentenced in February 2004 and received the death sentence for his role in the attacks of 1995. Since 1997, the cult continued to recruit new members, engage in commercial enterprise, and acquire property, although it scaled back these activities significantly in 2001 in response to public outcry. The cult maintains an Internet home page. In July 2001, Russian authorities arrested a group of Russian Aum followers who had planned to set off bombs near the Imperial Palace in Tokyo as part of an operation to free Asahara from jail and then smuggle him to Russia.

Basque Fatherland and Liberty (ETA)

a.k.a. Euzkadi Ta Askatasuna, Batasuna

Description

Founded in 1959 with the aim of establishing an independent homeland based on Marxist principles encompassing the Spanish Basque provinces of Vizcaya, Guipuzcoa, and Alava, as well as the autonomous region of Navarra and the southwestern French Departments of Labourd, Basse-Navarra, and Soule. Recent Spanish counterterrorism initiatives are hampering the group's operational capabilities. Spanish police arrested 125 ETA members and accomplices in 2003; French authorities arrested 46, including the group's top leadership; several other members were arrested in Latin America, Germany, and the Netherlands. In March 2003, a Spanish Supreme Court ruling banned ETA's political wing, Batasuna. Spain currently holds 572 ETA members in prison, while France holds 124. First designated in October 1997.

Activities

Primarily involved in bombings and assassinations of Spanish government officials, security and military forces, politicians, and judicial figures. During the summer of 2003, ETA targeted Spanish tourist areas. In 2003, ETA killed three persons, a similar figure to 2002s death toll of five, and wounded dozens more. The group has killed more than 850 persons and injured hundreds of others since it began lethal attacks in the early 1960s. ETA finances its activities primarily through extortion and robbery.

Cambodian Freedom Fighters (CFF)

a.k.a. Cholana Kangtoap Serei Cheat Kampouchea

Description

The Cambodian Freedom Fighters (CFF) emerged in November 1998 in the wake of political violence that saw many influential Cambodian leaders flee and the Cambodian People's Party assume power. With an avowed aim of overthrowing the government, the U.S.-based group is led by a Cambodian-American, a former member of the opposition Sam Rainsy Party. The CFF's membership reportedly includes Cambodian-Americans based in Thailand and the United States and former soldiers from the Khmer Rouge, Royal Cambodian Armed Forces, and various political factions.

Activities

The Cambodian government arrested seven CFF members who were reportedly planning an unspecified terrorist attack in southwestern Cambodia in late 2003, but there were no successful CFF attacks in 2003. Cambodian courts in February and March 2002 prosecuted 38 CFF members suspected of staging an attack in Cambodia in 2000. The courts convicted 19 members, including one U.S. citizen, of "terrorism" and/or "membership in an armed group" and sentenced them to terms of five years to life imprisonment. The group claimed responsibility for an attack in late November 2000 on several government installations that killed at least eight persons and wounded more than a dozen. In April 1999, five CFF members were arrested for plotting to blow up a fuel depot outside Phnom Penh with antitank weapons.

Covenant, Sword and the
Arm of the Lord

Description

Founded in 1971 by former San Antonio fundamentalist minister James Ellison, The Covenant,
the Sword, and the Arm of the Lord (CSA) was a
paramilitary survivalist group which operated an
Identity-oriented communal settlement near the
Arkansas-Missouri border. It is linked with the
Christian Patriots Defense League and other Christian Identity movement entities, whose adherents
include the likes of Timothy McVeigh—the man responsible for the deadly 1995 bombing in Oklahoma City.

Activities

At one point, this group had amassed one of the
largest private arms caches ever uncovered in
American history on its 224-acre base, Zarepath-
Horeb, consisting of a 30-gallon oil drum of arsenic, at least one improvised armored vehicle,
facilities for retooling machine guns out of semiautomatic weapons, grenades, RPGs, silencers, and
thousands of rounds of ammunition. In September
1985, CSA leaders James Ellison and Kerry Noble
and four other CSA activists—Gary Stone, Timothy Russell, Rudy Loewen, and David Giles—were
sentenced to lengthy federal prison terms on racketeering and illegal weapons charges. CSA member
Stephen Scott pleaded guilty in an Arkansas federal
court to charges he dynamited a natural gas
pipeline near Fulton, Arkansas, in 1983. Ex-CSA
member Kent Yates also pleaded guilty to a charge
of conspiring to make and transfer automatic
weapons silencers. Several members of CSA are
still at large, but the group is no longer considered
a major threat.

Communist Party of Nepal
(Maoist)/United People's
Front

Description

The Communist Party of Nepal (Maoist) insurgency grew out of the increasing radicalization and
fragmentation of leftwing parties following the
emergence of democracy in 1990. The United
People's Front—a coalition of leftwing parties—
participated in the elections of 1991, but the
Maoist wing failed to win the minimum 3 percent

of the vote leading to their exclusion from voter lists in the elections of 1994. In response, they abandoned electoral politics and in 1996 launched the insurgency. The Maoists' ultimate objective is the takeover of the government and the transformation of society, probably including the elimination of the present elite, nationalization of the private sector, and collectivization of agriculture. In 2003, the United States designated Nepal's Maoists under Executive Order (EO) 13224 as a supporter of terrorist activity.

Activities

The Maoists have utilized traditional guerrilla war tactics aimed at ultimately overthrowing the Nepalese government in favor of a single-party Communist state. In line with these efforts, the Maoists continue to use murder, torture, arson, sabotage, extortion, child conscription, kidnapping, threats of physical violence, bombings, and assassinations to intimidate and coerce the populace. In 2002, Maoists claimed responsibility for assassinating two Nepalese U.S. embassy guards, citing anti-Maoist spying, and in a press statement threatened foreign embassy missions—including the U.S. mission—to deter foreign support for the Nepalese government.

Communist Party of Philippines/New People's Army (CPP/NPA)

Description

The military wing of the Communist Party of the Philippines (CPP), the NPA is a Maoist group formed in March 1969 with the aim of overthrowing the government through protracted guerrilla warfare. The chairman of the CPP's Central Committee and the NPA's founder, Jose Maria Sison, reportedly directs CPP and NPA activity from the Netherlands, where he lives in self-imposed exile. Fellow Central Committee member and director of the CPP's overt political wing, the National Democratic Front (NDF), Luis Jalandoni also lives in the Netherlands and has become a Dutch citizen. Although primarily a rural-based guerrilla group, the NPA has an active urban infrastructure to conduct terrorism and uses city-based assassination squads.

Derives most of its funding from contributions of supporters in the Philippines, Europe, and elsewhere and from so-called revolutionary taxes extorted from local businesses and politicians. First designated in August 2002. Designations by the United States and the European Union may have had an impact on funding.

Activities

The NPA primarily targets Philippine security forces, politicians, judges, government informers, former rebels who wish to leave the NPA, rival splinter groups, and alleged criminals. Opposes any U.S. military presence in the Philippines and attacked U.S. military interests, killing several U.S. service personnel, before the U.S. base closures in 1992. Press reports in 1999 and in late 2001 indicated that the NPA is again targeting U.S. troops participating in joint military exercises as well as U.S. embassy personnel. The NPA claimed responsibility for the assassination of two congressmen from Quezon in May 2001 and Cagayan in June 2001 and many other killings. In January 2002, the NPA publicly expressed its intent to target U.S. personnel if discovered in NPA operating areas.

Continuity Irish Republican Army (CIRA)

Description

Terrorist splinter group formed in 1994 as the clandestine armed wing of Republican Sinn Fein (RSF), which split from Sinn Fein in 1986. "Continuity" refers to the group's belief that it is carrying on the original IRA goal of forcing the British out of Northern Ireland. Cooperates with the larger Real IRA. Designated under Executive Order 13224 in December 2001.

Activities

CIRA has been active in Belfast and the border areas of Northern Ireland where it has carried out bombings, assassinations, kidnappings, hijackings, extortion, and robberies. On occasion, it has provided advance warning to police of its attacks. Targets include British military, Northern Ireland security targets, and loyalist paramilitary groups.

Unlike the Provisional IRA, CIRA is not observing a cease-fire. CIRA continued its bombing campaign in 2003 with a string of low-level improvised explosive device attacks. A senior CIRA member was arrested, and two powerful RIRA bombs were seized in a June 2003 raid.

Eastern Turkistan Islamic Movement (ETIM)

Description

The Eastern Turkistan Islamic Movement (ETIM), a small Islamic extremist group based in China's western Xinjiang Province, is the most militant of the ethnic Uighur separatist groups pursuing an independent "Eastern Turkistan," an area that would include Turkey, Kazakhstan, Kyrgyzstan, Uzbekistan, Pakistan, Afghanistan, and Xinjiang. ETIM is linked to al Qaeda and the international mujahideen movement. Designated under EO 13224 in September 2002.

Activities

ETIM militants fought alongside al Qaeda and Taliban forces in Afghanistan during Operation Enduring Freedom. In October 2003, Pakistani soldiers killed ETIM leader Hassan Makhsum during raids on al Qaeda–associated compounds in western Pakistan. U.S. and Chinese government information suggests ETIM is responsible for various terrorist acts inside and outside China. In May 2002, two ETIM members were deported to China from Kyrgyzstan for plotting to attack the U.S. embassy in Kyrgyzstan as well as other U.S. interests abroad.

First of October Antifascist Resistance Group (GRAPO)/Grupo de Resistencia Anti-Fascista Primero de Octubre

Description

Formed in 1975 as the armed wing of the illegal Communist Party of Spain during the Franco era. Advocates the overthrow of the Spanish government and its replacement with a Marxist-Leninist regime. GRAPO is vehemently anti–United States, seeks the removal of all U.S. military forces from Spanish territory, and has conducted and attempted several attacks against U.S. targets since 1977. The group issued a communique following the attacks of 11 September in the United States, expressing its satisfaction that "symbols of imperialist power" were decimated and affirming that "the war" has only just begun. Designated under EO 13224 in December 2001.

Activities

GRAPO did not mount a successful terrorist attack in 2003, marking the second consecutive year without an attack. The group suffered several major setbacks as well. In March, the group's political wing—the Reconstituted Communist Party of Spain (PCE/R)—was outlawed, marking the first time in the organization's 28-year history that the Spanish judicial system ruled that GRAPO and the PCE/R comprised a single organization. In June, seven GRAPO members—including four leaders—were sentenced to various prison terms in France. Early in 2003, GRAPO committed a series of bank robberies, ostensibly to fund its operations. GRAPO has killed more than 90 persons and injured more than 200 since its formation. The group's operations traditionally have been designed to cause material damage and gain publicity rather than inflict casualties, but the terrorists have conducted lethal bombings and close range assassinations. In May 2000, the group killed two security guards during a botched armed robbery attempt of an armored truck carrying an estimated $2 million, and in November 2000, members assassinated a Spanish policeman in a possible reprisal for the arrest that month of several GRAPO leaders in France.

Great East Islamic Raiders—Front (IBDA-C)

Description

The Islamic Great Eastern Raiders—Front (IBDA—C) is a Sunni Salafist group that supports Islamic rule in Turkey and believes that Turkey's present secular leadership is "illegal." It has been known to cooperate with various opposition elements in Turkey in attempts to destabilize the country's political structure. The group supports the establishment of a "pure Islamic" state, to replace the present "corrupt" Turkish regime that is cooperating with the West. Its primary goal is the establishment of the Federative Islamic State, a goal backed by armed terrorist attacks primarily against civilian targets. It has been active since the mid-1970s.

Activities

The IBDA—C has engaged in activities that minimize personal risk, such as bombings, throwing Molotov cocktails, and sabotage. The group has announced its actions and targets in publications to its members, who are free to launch independent attacks. The IBDA—C typically has attacked civilian targets, including churches, charities, minority-affiliated targets, television transmitters, newspapers, prosecular journalists, Ataturk statues, taverns, banks, clubs, and tobacco shops. One of the IBDA—C's more renowned attacks was the killing of 37 people in a firebomb attack in July 1993 on a hotel in Sivas. The group claimed responsibility for a quadruple bomb attack in Istanbul in February 2002. In 1994, the IBDA—C was tied to an attempt to assassinate a Jewish businessman and an attack on the Greek Orthodox Church in Istanbul. In 1992, the group had unconfirmed involvement in an attack on an Istanbul synagogue. Turkish police believe that the IBDA—C has also claimed responsibilities for attacks carried out by other groups to elevate its image.

HAMAS

a.k.a. Islamic Resistance Movement

Description

Formed in late 1987 as an outgrowth of the Palestinian branch of the Muslim Brotherhood. Various HAMAS elements have used both violent and political means—including terrorism—to pursue the goal of establishing an Islamic Palestinian state in Israel. Loosely structured, with some elements working clandestinely and others openly through mosques and social service institutions to recruit members, raise money, organize activities, and distribute propaganda. HAMAS's strength is concentrated in the Gaza Strip and the West Bank. First designated in October 1997.

Activities

HAMAS terrorists, especially those in the Izz al-Din al-Qassam Brigades, have conducted many attacks—including large-scale suicide bombings—

against Israeli civilian and military targets. HAMAS maintained the pace of its operational activity during 2002–03, claiming numerous attacks against Israeli interests. HAMAS has not yet directly targeted U.S. interests, although the group makes little or no effort to avoid targets frequented by foreigners. HAMAS continues to confine its attacks to Israel and the territories.

Harakat ul-Jihad-i-Islami (HUJI)

(Movement of Islamic Holy War)

Description

HUJI, a Sunni extremist group that follows the Deobandi tradition of Islam, was founded in 1980 in Afghanistan to fight in the jihad against the Soviets. It also is affliated with the Jamiat Ulema-i-Islam Fazlur Rehman Jalili faction (JUI-F) and the Deobandi school of Sunni Islam. The group, led by Qari Saifullah Akhtar and chief commander Amin Rabbani, is made up primarily of Pakistanis and foreign Islamists who are fighting for the liberation of Jammu and Kashmir and its accession to Pakistan.

Activities

Has conducted a number of operations against Indian military targets in Jammu and Kashmir. Linked to the Kashmiri militant group al-Faran that kidnapped five Western tourists in Jammu and Kashmir in July 1995; one was killed in August 1995, and the other four reportedly were killed in December of the same year.

Harakat ul-Jihad-i-Islami/Bangladesh (HUJI-B)

(Movement of Islamic Holy War)

Description

The mission of HUJI-B, led by Shauqat Osman, is to establish Islamic rule in Bangladesh. HUJI-B has connections to the Pakistani militant groups Harakat ul-Jihadi-Islami (HUJI) and Harakat ul-Mujahidin (HUM), who advocate similar objectives in Pakistan and Jammu and Kashmir.

Activities

HUJI-B was accused of stabbing a senior Bangladeshi journalist in November 2000 for making a documentary on the plight of Hindus in Bangladesh. HUJI-B was suspected in the assassination attempt in July 2000 of Bangladeshi Prime Minister Sheikh Hasina.

Harakat ul-Mujahidin (HUM)

(Movement of Warriors)

Description

The HUM is an Islamic militant group based in Pakistan that operates primarily in Holy Kashmir. It is politically aligned with the radical political party, Jamiat Ulema-i-Islam Fazlur Rehman faction (JUI-F). Longtime leader of the group, Fazlur Rehman Khalil, stepped down in mid-February 2000 as HUM emir, turning the reins over to the popular Kashmiri commander and his second in command, Farooq Kashmiri. Khalil, who has been linked to Osama bin Laden and signed his *fatwa* in February 1998 calling for attacks on U.S. and Western interests, assumed the position of HUM Secretary-General. HUM operated terrorist training camps in eastern Afghanistan until Coalition airstrikes destroyed them during fall 2001. In 2003, HUM began using the name Jamiat ul-Ansar (JUA), and Pakistan banned the successor JUA in November 2003. First designated in October 1997.

Activities

Has conducted a number of operations against Indian troops and civilian targets in Kashmir. Linked to the Kashmiri militant group al-Faran that kidnapped five Western tourists in Kashmir in July 1995; one was killed in August 1995, and the other four reportedly were killed in December of the same year. The HUM is responsible for the hijacking of an Indian airliner on 24 December 1999, which resulted in the release of Masood Azhar—an important leader in the former Harakat ul-Ansar imprisoned by the Indians in 1994—and Ahmed Omar Sheik, who was convicted of the abduction/murder in January–February 2002 of U.S. journalist Daniel Pearl.

Hizballah/Hezbollah (Party of God)

a.k.a. Islamic Jihad, Revolutionary Justice Organization, Organization of the Oppressed on Earth, and Islamic Jihad for the Liberation of Palestine

Description

Also known as Lebanese Hizballah, this group was formed in 1982 in response to the Israeli invasion of Lebanon, this Lebanon-based radical Shi'a group takes its ideological inspiration from the Iranian revolution and the teachings of the late Ayatollah Khomeini. The *Majlis al-Shura*, or Consultative Council, is the group's highest governing body and is led by Secretary-General Hassan Nasrallah. Hizballah is dedicated to liberating Jerusalem and eliminating Israel and has formally advocated ultimate establishment of Islamic rule in Lebanon. Nonetheless, Hizballah has actively participated in Lebanon's political system since 1992. Hizballah is closely allied with, and often directed by, Iran but has the capability and willingness to act alone. Although Hizballah does not share the Syrian regime's secular orientation, the group has been a strong ally in helping Syria advance its political objectives in the region. First designated in October 1997.

Activities

Known or suspected to have been involved in numerous anti-U.S. and anti-Israeli terrorist attacks, including the suicide truck bombings of the U.S. Embassy and U.S. Marine barracks in Beirut in 1983 and the U.S. Embassy annex in Beirut in September 1984. Three members of Hizballah—'Imad Mughniyah, Hasan Izz-al-Din, and Ali Atwa—are on the FBI's list of 22 Most-Wanted Terrorists for the hijacking in 1985 of TWA Flight 847 during which a U.S. Navy diver was murdered. Elements of the group were responsible for the kidnapping and detention of U.S. and other Westerners in Lebanon in the 1980s. Hizballah also attacked the Israeli Embassy in Argentina in 1992 and the Israeli cultural center in Buenos Aires in 1994. In fall 2000, Hizballah operatives captured three Israeli soldiers in the Shab'a Farms and kidnapped an Israeli noncombatant whom may have been lured to Lebanon under false pretenses.

In 2003, Hizballah appeared to have established a presence in Iraq, but for the moment its activities there are limited. Hizballah Secretary-General Hassan Nasrallah stated in speeches that "we are heading . . . toward the end and elimination of Israel from the region" and that the group's "slogan is and will continue to be death to America." Hizballah's television station, al-Manar, continued to use inflammatory images and reporting in an effort to encourage the *Intifada* and promote Palestinian suicide operations.

Hizb-I Islami Gulbuddin
(HIG)

Description

Gulbuddin Hekmatyar founded Hizb-I Islami
Gulbuddin (HIG) as a faction of the Hizb-I Islami party in 1977, and it was one of the major
mujahideen groups in the war against the Soviets. HIG has long-established ties with Osama
bin Laden. In the early 1990s, Hekmatyar ran
several terrorist training camps in Afghanistan
and was a pioneer in sending mercenary fighters
to other Islamic conflicts. Hekmatyar offered to
shelter bin Laden after the latter fled Sudan in
1996.

Activities

HIG has staged small attacks in its attempt to
force U.S. troops to withdraw from Afghanistan,
overthrow the Afghan Transitional Administration,
and establish a fundamentalist state.

Hizbul-Mujahidin (HM)

Description

Hizb ul-Mujahidin, the largest Kashmiri militant
group, was founded in 1989 and officially supports
the liberation of Jammu and Kashmir and its accession to Pakistan, although some cadres are pro-
independence. The group is the militant wing of
Pakistan's largest Islamic political party, the
Jamaat-i-Islami. It currently is focused on Indian
security forces and politicians in Jammu and Kashmir and has conducted operations jointly with
other Kashmiri militants. It reportedly operated in
Afghanistan through the mid-1990s and trained
alongside the Afghan Hizb-I-Islami Gulbuddin
(HIG) in Afghanistan until the Taliban takeover.
The group, led by Syed Salahuddin, is made up
primarily of ethnic Kashmiris.

Activities

Has conducted a number of operations against Indian military targets in Jammu and Kashmir. The
group also occasionally strikes at civilian targets in
Jammu and Kashmir but has not engaged in terrorist acts elsewhere.

Islamic Movement of
Uzbekistan (IMU)

Description

Coalition of Islamic militants from Uzbekistan and
other Central Asian states. The IMU is closely affiliated with al Qaeda and, under the leadership of
Tohir Yoldashev, has embraced Osama bin Laden's
anti-U.S. anti-Western agenda. The IMU also remains committed to its original goals of overthrowing Uzbekistani President Islom Karimov and
establishing an Islamic state in Uzbekistan. First
designated in September 2000.

Activities

The IMU in recent years has participated in attacks
on U.S. and Coalition soldiers in Afghanistan and
plotted attacks on U.S. diplomatic facilities in Central Asia. In May 2003, Kyrgyzstani security forces
disrupted an IMU cell that was seeking to bomb
the U.S. Embassy and a nearby hotel in Bishkek,
Kyrgyzstan. The IMU primarily targeted Uzbekistani interests before October 2001 and is believed
to have been responsible for five car bombs in
Tashkent in February 1999. Militants also took
foreigners hostage in 1999 and 2000, including
four U.S. citizens who were mountain climbing in
August 2000 and four Japanese geologists and
eight Kyrgyzstani soldiers in August 1999.

Irish National Liberation
Army (INLA)

Description

Terrorist group formed in 1975 as the military
wing of the Irish Republican Socialist Party (IRSP),
which split from the Official IRA (OIRA) because
of OIRA's cease-fire in 1972. Responsible for some
of the most notorious killings of "the Troubles,"
including the bombing of a Ballykelly pub that
killed 17 people in 1982, bloody internal feuding
has repeatedly torn the INLA. The INLA announced a cease-fire in August 1998 but continues
to carry out occasional attacks and punishment
beatings.

Activities

The INLA has been active in Belfast and the border areas of Northern Ireland where it has carried
out bombings, assassinations, kidnappings, hijack-

ings, extortion, and robberies. On occasion, it has provided advance warning to police of its attacks. Targets include British military, Northern Ireland security targets, and loyalist paramilitary groups. The INLA continues to observe a cease-fire as—in the words of its leadership in 2003—a return to the armed struggle is "not a viable option at this time."

Irish Republican Army (IRA)

a.k.a. Provisional Irish Republican Army (PIRA), the Provos (sometimes referred to as the PIRA to distinguish it from RIRA and CIRA)

Description

Dissension within the IRA over support for the Northern Ireland peace process resulted in the formation of two more radical splinter groups: Continuity IRA in 1995 and the Real IRA in 1997. Until its cease-fire in July 1997, the Provisional IRA had sought to remove British forces from Northern Ireland and unify Ireland by force. In July 2002, the IRA reiterated its commitment to the peace process and apologized to the families of what it called "noncombatants" who had been killed or injured by the IRA. The IRA is organized into small, tightly knit cells under the leadership of the Army Council.

Activities

IRA traditional activities have included bombings, assassinations, kidnappings, punishment beatings, extortion, smuggling, and robberies. Before the cease-fire in 1997, bombing campaigns had been conducted on various targets in Northern Ireland and Great Britain and included senior British Government officials, civilians, police, and British military targets. In October 2003, the IRA conducted a third act of arms decommissioning that the Independent International Commission on Decommissioning (IICD) called "considerably larger" than the previous IRA move. The group disposed of light, medium, and heavy weapons, ammunition, and explosives. The IRA retains the ability to conduct paramilitary operations. The IRA's extensive criminal activities reportedly provide the organizations with millions of dollars each year.

Islamic Army of Aden (IAA)

a.k.a. Aden-Abyan Islamic Army (AAIA)

Description

The Islamic Army of Aden (IAA) emerged publicly in mid-1998 when the group released a series of communiques that expressed support for Osama bin Laden, appealed for the overthrow of the Yemeni government, and called for operations against U.S. and other Western interests in Yemen. Designated under EO 13224 in September 2001.

Activities

Engages in bombings and kidnappings to promote its goals. The group reportedly was behind an attack in June 2003 against a medical assistance convoy in the Abyan Governorate. Yemeni authorities responded with a raid on a suspected IAA facility, killing several individuals and capturing others, including Khalid al-Nabi al-Yazidi, the group's leader.

Before that attack, the group had not conducted operations since the bombing of the British Embassy in Sanaa in October 2000. In 2001, Sanaa found an IAA member and three associates responsible for that attack. In December 1998, the group kidnapped 16 British, American, and Australian tourists near Mudiyah in southern Yemen.

Although Yemeni officials previously have claimed that the group is operationally defunct, their recent attribution of the attack in 2003 against the medical convoy and reports that al-Yazidi was released from prison in mid-October 2003 suggest that the IAA, or at least elements of the group, have resumed activity.

Islamic International Peacekeeping Brigade (IIPB)

Description

One of three terrorist groups affiliated with Chechen guerrillas that furnished personnel to carry out the seizure of the Dubrovka Theater in Moscow on 23 October 2002. The suicide attackers took more than 800 hostages, whom they threatened to kill if the Russian government did not meet their demands, including the withdrawal of Russian forces from Chechnya. Chechen extremist leader Shamil Basayev—who claimed responsibility for ordering the seizure—established the IIPB in 1998, which he led with Saudi-born mujahideen leader Ibn al-Khattab until the latter's death in March 2002. Arab mujahideen leader Abu al-Walid has since taken over Khattab's leadership role in the IIPB, which consists of Chechens, Arabs, and other foreign fighters.

Activities

Primarily guerrilla operations against Russian forces.

Jaish-e-Mohammed (JEM) (Army of Mohammed)

a.k.a. Tehrik ul-Furqaah, Khuddam-ul-Islam

Description

The Jaish-e-Mohammed is an Islamic extremist group based in Pakistan that was formed by Masood Azhar upon his release from prison in India in early 2000. The group's aim is to unite Kashmir with Pakistan. It is politically aligned with the radical political party, Jamiat Ulema-i-Islam Fazlur Rehman faction (JUI-F). The United States announced the addition of JEM to the U.S. Treasury Department's Office of Foreign Asset Control (OFAC) list—which includes organizations that are believed to support terrorist groups and have assets in U.S. jurisdiction that can be frozen or controlled—in October 2001 and the Foreign Terrorist Organization list in December 2001. By 2003, JEM had splintered into Khuddam ul-Islam (KUI) and Jamaat ul-Furqan (JUF). Pakistan banned KUA and JUF in November 2003. First designated in December 2001.

Activities

The JEM's leader, Masood Azhar, was released from Indian imprisonment in December 1999 in exchange for 155 hijacked Indian Airlines hostages. The HUA kidnappings by Omar Sheik of U.S. and British nationals in 1994 in New Delhi and the HUA/al-Faran kidnappings in July 1995 of Westerners in Kashmir were two of several previous HUA efforts to free Azhar. On 1 October 2001 the JEM claimed responsibility for a suicide attack on the Jammu and Kashmir legislative assembly building in Srinagar that killed at least 31 persons, but the group later denied the claim. The Indian government has publicly implicated the JEM—along with Lashkar-e-Taiba—for the attack on 13 December 2001 on the Indian Parliament that killed 9 and injured 18. Pakistani authorities suspect that perpetrators of fatal anti-Christian attacks in Islamabad, Murree, and Taxila during 2002 were affiliated with the JEM.

Jamiat ul-Mujahidin (JUM)

Description

Small pro-Pakistan militant group formed in Jammu and Kashmir in 1990. Followers are mostly Kashmiris, but the group includes some Pakistanis.

Activities

Has conducted a number of operations against Indian military targets in Jammu and Kashmir.

Japanese Red Army (JRA)

a.k.a. Anti-Imperialist International Brigade

Description

An international terrorist group formed around 1970 after breaking away from the Japanese Communist League–Red Army Faction. The JRA's historical goal has been to overthrow the Japanese government and monarchy and to help foment world revolution. JRA's leader, Fusako Shigenobu, claimed that the forefront of the battle against international imperialism was in Palestine, so in the early 1970s, she led her small group to the Middle East to support the Palestinian struggle against Israel and the West. After her arrest in November 2000, Shigenobu announced she intended to pursue her goals using a legitimate political party rather than revolutionary violence, and the group announced it would disband in April 2001.

Activities

During the 1970s, JRA carried out a series of attacks around the world, including the massacre in 1972 at Lod Airport in Israel, two Japanese airliner hijackings, and an attempted takeover of the U.S. Embassy in Kuala Lumpur. During the late 1980s, JRA began to single out American targets and used car bombs and rockets in attempted attacks on U.S. embassies in Jakarta, Rome, and Madrid. In April 1988, JRA operative Yu Kikumura was arrested with explosives on the New Jersey Turnpike, apparently planning an attack to co-incide with the bombing of a USO club in Naples, a suspected JRA operation that killed five, including a U.S. servicewoman. He was convicted of the charges and is serving a lengthy prison sentence in the United States. Tsutomu Shirosaki, captured in 1996, is also jailed in the United States. In 2000, Lebanon deported to Japan four members it arrested in 1997 but granted a fifth operative, Kozo Okamoto, political asylum. Longtime leader Shigenobu was arrested in November 2000 and faces charges of terrorism and passport fraud.

Jemaah Islamiyah (JI)

Description

Jemaah Islamiyah is a Southeast Asian—based terrorist network with links to al Qaeda. The network recruited and trained extremists in the late 1990s, following the stated goal of creating an Islamic state comprising Brunei, Indonesia, Malaysia, Singapore, the southern Philippines, and southern Thailand. First designated in October 2002.

Activities

JI was responsible for the bombing of the J. W. Marriott Hotel in Jakarta on 5 August 2003, the Bali bombings on 12 October 2002, and an attack against the Philippine Ambassador to Indonesia in August 2000. The Bali plot, which left more than 200 dead, was reportedly the final outcome of meetings in early 2002 in Thailand, where attacks against Singapore and soft targets such as tourist spots in the region were also considered. In December 2001, Singapore authorities uncovered a JI plot to attack the U.S. and Israeli embassies and British and Australian diplomatic buildings in Singapore, and in June 2003, Thai authorities disrupted a JI plan to attack several Western embassies and tourist sites there. Investigations also linked the JI to bombings in December 2000 where dozens of bombs were detonated in Indonesia and the Philippines, killing 22 in the Philippines and 15 in Indonesia.

The capture in August of Indonesian Riduan bin Isomoddin (a.k.a. Hambali), JI leader and al

Qaeda Southeast Asia operations chief, damaged the JI, but the group maintains its ability to target Western interests in the region and to recruit new members through a network of radical Islamic schools based primarily in Indonesia.

Kahane Chai

a.k.a. Kach

Description

Stated goal is to restore the biblical state of Israel. Kach (founded by radical Israeli-American rabbi Meir Kahane) and its offshoot Kahane Chai, which means "Kahane Lives," (founded by Meir Kahane's son Binyamin following his father's assassination in the United States) were declared terrorist organizations in March 1994 by the Israeli Cabinet under the 1948 Terrorism Law. This followed the groups' statements in support of Dr. Baruch Goldstein's attack in February 1994 on the al-Ibrahimi Mosque—Goldstein was affiliated with Kach—and their verbal attacks on the Israeli Government. Palestinian gunmen killed Binyamin Kahane and his wife in a drive-by shooting in December 2000 in the West Bank. Kahane Chai and Kach were first designated separately in October 1997.

Activities

The group has organized protests against the Israeli government. Kach has harassed and threatened Arabs, Palestinians, and Israeli government officials. Has vowed revenge for the deaths of Binyamin Kahane and his wife. Suspected of involvement in a number of low-level attacks since the start of the al-Aqsa *intifada*.

Kongra-Gel (KGK) (Kurdistan Workers' Party, PKK, KADEK)

a.k.a. Kurdistan People's Congress, Kurdistan Freedom and Democracy Congress (KADEK), Freedom and Democracy Congress of Kurdistan

Description

Founded in 1978 as a Marxist-Leninist insurgent group primarily composed of Turkish Kurds. The group's goal has been to establish an independent, democratic Kurdish state in the Middle East. In the early 1990s, the PKK moved beyond rural-based insurgent activities to include urban terrorism. Turkish authorities captured Chairman Abdullah Ocalan in Kenya in early 1999; the Turkish State Security Court subsequently sentenced him to death. In August 1999, Ocalan announced a "peace initiative," ordering members to refrain from violence and requesting dialogue with Ankara on Kurdish issues. At a PKK Congress in January 2000, members supported Ocalan's initiative and claimed the group now would use only political means to achieve its public goal of improved rights for Kurds in Turkey. In April 2002 at its 8th Party Congress, the PKK changed its name to the Kurdistan Freedom and Democracy Congress (KADEK) and proclaimed a commitment to nonviolent activities in support of Kurdish rights. Despite this pledge, a PKK/KADEK spokesman stated that its armed wing, The People's Defense Force, would not disband or surrender its weapons for reasons of self-defense. In late 2003, the group sought to engineer another political face-lift, renaming the group Kongra-Gel (KGK) and brandishing its "peaceful" intentions, while continuing to commit attacks and refuse disarmament. First designated in October 1997.

Activities

Primary targets have been Turkish government security forces in Turkey, local Turkish officials, and villagers who oppose the organization in Turkey. Conducted attacks on Turkish diplomatic and commercial facilities in dozens of West European cities in 1993 and again in spring 1995. In an attempt to damage Turkey's tourist industry, the then PKK bombed tourist sites and hotels and kidnapped foreign tourists in the early to mid-1990s. KGK continued to engage in violent acts—including at least one terrorist attack—against the Turkish state in 2003. Several members were arrested in Istanbul in late 2003 in possession of explosive materials.

Kumpulan Mujahidin Malaysia (KMM)

Description

Kumpulan Mujahidin Malaysia (KMM) favors the overthrow of the Malaysian government and the creation of an Islamic state comprising Malaysia, Indonesia, and the southern Philippines. Malaysian authorities believe an extremist wing of the KMM has engaged in terrorist acts and has close ties to the regional terrorist organization Jemaah Islamiyah (JI). Key JI leaders, including the group's spiritual head, Abu Bakar Ba'asyir and JI operational leader Hambali, reportedly had great influence over KMM members. The government of Singapore asserts that a Singapore JI member assisted the KMM in buying a boat to support jihad activities in Indonesia.

Activities

Malaysia is holding scores of KMM members under the Internal Security Act (ISA) for activities deemed threatening to Malaysia's national security, including planning to wage jihad, possession of weaponry, bombings and robberies, the murder of a former state assemblyman, and planning attacks on foreigners—including U.S. citizens. The alleged leader of KMM, Nik Adli Nik Abdul Aziz, had his detention under the ISA extended for another two years in September 2003. A number of those detained are also believed to be members of JI. Several of the arrested KMM militants have reportedly undergone military training in Afghanistan, and some fought with the Afghan mujahideen during the war against the former Soviet Union, as did a significant number of JI members. Some members are alleged to have ties to Islamic extremist organizations in Indonesia and the Philippines.

Lashkar-e-Taiba (LT) (Army of the Righteous)

Description

The LT is the armed wing of the Pakistan-based religious organization, Markaz-ud-Dawa-wal-Irshad (MDI)—a Sunni anti-U.S. missionary organization formed in 1989. The LT is led by Hafiz Muhammad Saeed and is one of the three largest and best-trained groups fighting in Kashmir against India; it is not connected to a political party. The United States in October 2001 announced the addition of the LT to the U.S. Treasury Department's Office of Foreign Asset Control (OFAC) list—which includes organizations that are believed to support terrorist groups and have assets in U.S. jurisdiction that can be frozen or controlled. The group was banned, and the Pakistani government froze its assets in January 2002. The LT is also known by the name of its associated organization, Jamaat ud-Dawa (JUD). Musharraf placed JUD on a watchlist in November 2003. First designated in December 2001.

Activities

The LT has conducted a number of operations against Indian troops and civilian targets in Jammu and Kashmir since 1993. The LT claimed responsibility for numerous attacks in 2001, including an attack in January on Srinagar airport that killed five Indians along with six militants; an attack on a police station in Srinagar that killed at least eight officers and wounded several others; and an attack in April against Indian border-security forces that left at least four dead. The Indian government publicly implicated the LT— along with JEM—for the attack on 13 December 2001 on the Indian Parliament building, although concrete evidence is lacking. The LT is also suspected of involvement in the attack on 14 May 2002 on an Indian Army base in Kaluchak that left 36 dead. Senior al Qaeda lieutenant Abu Zubaydah was captured at an LT safehouse in Faisalabad in March 2002, suggesting some members are facilitating the movement of al Qaeda members in Pakistan.

Lashkar-i-Jhangvi (LJ)
(Army of Jhangvi)

Description

Lashkar I Jhangvi (LJ) is the militant offshoot of the Sunni sectarian group Sipah-i-Sahaba Pakistan (SSP). The group focuses primarily on anti-Shia attacks and was banned by Pakistani President Musharraf in August 2001 as part of an effort to rein in sectarian violence. Many of its members then sought refuge with the Taliban in Afghanistan, with whom they had existing ties. After the collapse of the Taliban, LJ members became active in aiding other terrorists with safehouses, false identities, and protection in Pakistani cities, including Karachi, Peshawar, and Rawalpindi. In January 2003, the United States added LJ to the list of Foreign Terrorist Organizations. First designated in January 2003.

Activities

LJ specializes in armed attacks and bombings. The group attempted to assassinate former Prime Minister Nawaz Sharif and his brother Shabaz Sharif, Chief Minister of Punjab Province, in January 1999. Pakistani authorities have publicly linked LJ members to the kidnap and murder of U.S. journalist Daniel Pearl in early 2002. Police officials initially suspected LJ members were involved in the two suicide car bombings in Karachi in 2002—against a French shuttle bus in May and the U.S. Consulate in June—but their subsequent investigations have not led to any LJ members being charged in the attacks. Similarly, press reports have linked LJ to attacks on Christian targets in Pakistan, including a grenade assault on the Protestant International Church in Islamabad in March 2002 that killed two U.S. citizens, but no formal charges have been filed against the group. Pakistani authorities believe LJ was responsible for the bombing in July 2003 of a Shiite mosque in Quetta, Pakistan.

Liberation Tigers of Tamil Eelam (LTTE)

Other known front organizations: World Tamil Association (WTA), World Tamil Movement (WTM), the Federation of Associations of Canadian Tamils (FACT), the Ellalan Force, and the Sangilian Force.

Description

Founded in 1976, the LTTE is the most powerful Tamil group in Sri Lanka and uses overt and illegal methods to raise funds, acquire weapons, and publicize its cause of establishing an independent Tamil state. The LTTE began its armed conflict with the Sri Lankan government in 1983 and has relied on a guerrilla strategy that includes the use of terrorist tactics. The LTTE is currently observing a cease-fire agreement with the Sri Lankan government. First designated in October 1997.

Activities

The Tigers have integrated a battlefield insurgent strategy with a terrorist program that targets not only key personnel in the countryside but also senior Sri Lankan political and military leaders in Colombo and other urban centers. The Tigers are most notorious for their cadre of suicide bombers, the Black Tigers. Political assassinations and bombings are commonplace.

Libyan Islamic Fighting Group (LIFG)

a.k.a. Al-Jam'a al-Islamiyyah al-Muqatilah, Fighting Islamic Group, Libyan Fighting Group, Libyan Islamic Group

Description

Emerged in 1995 among Libyans who had fought against Soviet forces in Afghanistan. Declared the government of Libyan leader Muammar Qadhafi un-Islamic and pledged to overthrow it. Some members maintain a strictly anti-Qadhafi focus and organize against Libyan government interests, but others are aligned with Osama bin Laden's al Qaeda organization or are active in the international mujahideen network. The group was designated for asset freeze under EO 13224 and UNSCR 1333 in September 2001.

Activities

Libyans associated with the LIFG are part of the support network of the broader international jihadist movement. LIFG is one of the groups believed to be involved in planning the Casablanca suicide bombings of May 2003. Claimed responsibility for a failed assassination attempt against Qadhafi in 1996 and engaged Libyan security forces in armed clashes during the mid-to-late 1990s. Continues to target Libyan interests and may engage in sporadic clashes with Libyan security forces.

Lord's Resistance Army (LRA)

Description

The LRA was founded in 1986 as the successor to the ethnic Acholi-dominated Holy Spirit Movement. LRA leader Joseph Kony has called for the overthrow of the Ugandan government and its replacement with a regime run on the basis of the Ten Commandments. More frequently, however, he has spoken of the liberation and honor of the Acholi people who he sees as oppressed by the "foreign" government of Ugandan President Museveni. Kony is the LRA's undisputed leader. He claims to have supernatural powers and to receive messages from spirits, which he uses to formulate the LRA's strategy.

Activities

Since the early 1990's, the LRA has kidnapped 20,000 Ugandan children, mostly ethnic Acholi, to replenish its ranks. Kony despises Acholi elders for having given up the fight against Museveni and relies on abducted children who can be manipulated to fight for the LRA cause. The LRA forces kidnapped children and adult civilians to become soldiers, porters, and "wives" for LRA leaders. The LRA prefers to attack internally displaced persons camps and other civilian targets, avoiding direct engagement with the Ugandan military. Victims of LRA attacks sometimes have their hands, fingers, ears, noses, or other extremities cut off. LRA has stepped up its activities since early 2002 when the Ugandan army, with the Sudanese government's permission, attacked LRA positions inside Sudan. Since then, the number of internally displaced has doubled to 1.4 million, and the LRA has pushed deep into non-Acholi areas where it had never previously operated.

Loyalist Volunteer Force (LVF)

Description

An extreme loyalist group formed in 1996 as a faction of the loyalist Ulster Volunteer Force (UVF) but did not emerge publicly until 1997. Composed largely of UVF hard-liners who have sought to prevent a political settlement with Irish nationalists in Northern Ireland by attacking Catholic politicians, civilians, and Protestant politicians who endorse the Northern Ireland peace process. LVF occasionally uses the Red Hand Defenders as a cover name for its actions but in February called for the group's disbandment. In October 2001, the British government ruled that the LVF had broken the cease-fire it declared in 1998 after linking the group to the murder of a journalist. According to the Independent International Commission on Decommissioning, the LVF decommissioned a small amount of weapons in December 1998, but it has not repeated this gesture. Designated under EO 13224 in December 2001.

Activities

Bombings, kidnappings, and close-quarter shooting attacks. Finances its activities with drug money and other criminal activities. LVF bombs often have contained Powergel commercial explosives, typical of many loyalist groups. LVF attacks have been particularly vicious: the group has murdered numerous Catholic civilians with no political or paramilitary affiliations, including an 18-year-old Catholic girl, in July 1997, because she had a Protestant boyfriend. The terrorists also have conducted successful attacks against Irish targets in Irish border towns. From 2000 to 2003, the LVF has been engaged in a violent feud with other loyalists, which has left several men dead. In February 2003, the LVF was the chief suspect behind a bomb attack against a Catholic home in Northern Ireland; no injuries occurred in this attack.

Maoist Communist Center of India (MCCI)

a.k.a. the Maoist Communist Center [MCC] and Naxalites

Description

MCCI was founded in the early 1970s in Bahragora (now part of Jharkhand), near the borders of West Bengal and Orissa. Its "Naxalite" goals are peasant revolution, abolition of class hierarchies, and expansion of "liberated zones." Like its ideological partner, the People's War, the MCCI has significant numbers of women cadre. The MCCI frequently restructures its organization and leadership portfolios to complicate police action against it. Pramod Mishra is now believed to head the MCCI, and other important leaders are Uma Shankar and P.N.G. (alias Nathu Mistry, arrested by Jharkhand police in 2003).

Activities

The MCCI runs a virtual parallel government in remote areas where state and central government control are weak. It collects "tax" from the villagers and, in turn, completes small projects such as building hospitals, schools, and hand water pumps. It also runs a parallel court system wherein allegedly corrupt block development officials have been punished by amputation and even death. Landlords are a frequent MCCI target, and they are believed to kill an average of 100 civilians a year.

Moro Islamic Liberation Front

Description

The Moro Islamic Liberation Front is an Islamic liberation movement based in the Bangsamoro region in Mindanao and the neighboring islands. It is currently the largest Islamic separatist group in the Philippines, with an estimated 15,000 members. The MILF seeks to establish an independent Islamic state comprising Mindanao island (the second largest of the Philippine islands) Palawan, Basilan, the Sulu archipelago, and the neighboring islands. In support of this aim, the organization has carried out a campaign of attacks against civilian and military targets throughout the southern Philippines.

Activities

In the early 1990s the MILF launched a wave of terrorist attacks in the southern Philippines, leading former Philippines president Joseph Estrada to pursue an "all-out war" against the organization. However, by the late 1990s, the Moro Islamic Liberation Front claimed to have 120,000 fighters and many more supporters. In May 2000, the Philippine army launched a major assault upon the MILF military headquarters at Camp Abubakar, capturing the camp. This did not significantly harm the group's military capabilities, as most of its senior leaders had been evacuated before the camp fell. In response to the military offensive, the MILF countered with a series of bombings in Manila. A splinter group also claimed responsibility for a bomb attack against the Philippine ambassador to Indonesia, and a series of bombs that exploded in the capital. The majority of the MILF's forces are deployed in four provinces of Mindanao: Lanao del Norte, Lanao del Sur, Maguindanao, and North Cotabato.

Moroccan Islamic Combatant Group (GICM)

Description

The goals of the Moroccan Islamic Combatant Group (GICM) include establishing an Islamic State in Morocco and supporting al Qaeda's jihad against the West. The group appears to have emerged in the late 1990s and comprises Moroccan recruits who trained in armed camps in Afghanistan. GICM members interact with other North African extremists, particularly in Europe. On 22 November 2002, the United States designated the GICM for asset freeze under EO 13224 following the group's submission to the UNSCR 1267 Sanctions Committee. Designated under EO 13224 in November 2002.

Activities

Moroccans associated with the GICM are part of the support network of the broader international jihadist movement. GICM is one of the groups believed to be involved in planning the Casablanca suicide bombings in May 2003. Members work with other North African extremists engaging in trafficking falsified documents and possibly arms smuggling. The group in the past has issued communiques and statements against the Moroccan government.

Mujahedin-e Khalq Organization (MEK or MKO)

a.k.a. The National Liberation Army of Iran (NLA, the militant wing of the MEK), the People's Mujahedin of Iran (PMOI), National Council of Resistance (NCR), the National Council of Resistance of Iran (NCRI), Muslim Iranian Student's Society (front organization used to garner financial support)

Description

The MEK philosophy mixes Marxism and Islam. Formed in the 1960s, the organization was expelled from Iran after the Islamic Revolution in 1979, and its primary support came from the former Iraqi regime of Saddam Hussein since the late 1980s. The MEK's history is filled with anti-Western attacks as well as terrorist attacks on the interests of the clerical regime in Iran and abroad. The MEK now advocates the overthrow of the Iranian regime and its replacement with the group's own leadership. First designated in October 1997.

Activities

The group's worldwide campaign against the Iranian Government stresses propaganda and occasionally uses terrorism. During the 1970s, the MEK killed U.S. military personnel and U.S. civilians working on defense projects in Tehran and supported the takeover in 1979 of the U.S. embassy in Tehran. In 1981, the MEK detonated bombs in the head office of the Islamic Republic Party and the premier's office, killing some 70 high-ranking Iranian officials, including chief Justice Ayatollah Mohammad Beheshti, President Mohammad-Ali Rajaei, and Premier Mohammad-Javad Bahonar. Near the end of the war with Iran during 1980–88, Baghdad armed the MEK with military equipment and sent it into action against Iranian forces. In 1991, it assisted the government of Iraq in suppressing the Shia and Kurdish uprisings in southern Iraq and the Kurdish uprisings in the north. In April 1992, the MEK conducted near-simultaneous attacks on Iranian embassies and installations in 13 countries, demonstrating the group's ability to mount large-scale operations overseas. In April 1999, the MEK targeted key military officers and assassinated the deputy chief of the Armed Forces General Staff. In April 2000, the MEK attempted to assassinate the commander of the Nasr Headquarters—Tehran's interagency board responsible for coordinating policies on Iraq. The normal pace of anti-Iranian operations increased during the "Operation Great Bahman" in February 2000, when the group launched a dozen attacks against Iran. In 2000 and 2001, the MEK was involved regularly in mortar attacks and hit-and-run raids on Iranian military and law-enforcement units and government buildings near the Iran-Iraq border, although MEK terrorism in Iran declined throughout the remainder of 2001. In February 2000, for example, the MEK launched a mortar attack against the leadership complex in Tehran that houses the offices of the Supreme Leader and the President. Coalition aircraft bombed MEK bases during Operation Iraqi Freedom, and the Coalition forced the MEK forces to surrender in May 2003. The future of the MEK forces remains undetermined with Coalition forces.

National Liberation Army (ELN)—Colombia

Description

Marxist insurgent group formed in 1965 by urban intellectuals inspired by Fidel Castro and Che Guevara. In October 2003, the Colombian government released top ELN leader Felipe Torres from prison, hoping to spur the ELN to accept government demands to declare a cease-fire and come back to the negotiating table, but by year's end peace talks had not commenced. First designated in October 1997.

Activities

Kidnapping, hijacking, bombing, and extortion. Minimal conventional military capability. Annually conducts hundreds of kidnappings for ransom, often targeting foreign employees of large corporations, especially in the petroleum industry. Derives some revenue from taxation of the illegal narcotics industry. Frequently assaults energy infrastructure and has inflicted major damage on pipelines and the electric distribution network. In September, the ELN kidnapped eight foreign tourists, but they have all since either escaped or been released.

New Red Brigades/Communist Combatant Party (BR/PCC)

a.k.a. Brigate Rosse/Partito Comunista Combattente

Description

This Marxist-Leninist group is a successor to the Red Brigades, active in the 1970s and 1980s. In addition to ideology, both groups share the same symbol, a five-pointed star inside a circle. The group is opposed to Italy's foreign and labor policies and NATO.

Activities

In 2003, Italian authorities captured at least seven members of the BR/PCC, one in March and six in October, dealing the terrorist group a severe blow to its future operational effectiveness. Some of those arrested are suspects in the assassination in 1999 of Labor Ministry advisor Massimo D'Antona, and authorities are hoping to link them to the assassination in 2002 of Labor Ministry advisor Marco Biagi. The arrests in October came on the heels of a clash in March 2003 involving Italian Railway Police and two BR/PCC members, which resulted in the death of one of the members of the group and the death of an Italian security officer. Italian officials believe they have netted key BR/PCC operatives. Remaining BR/PCC members may conduct a retaliatory attack at some point, if only to prove their continued viability. Has financed its activities through armed robberies.

The Palestine Islamic Jihad (PIJ)

Description

Originated among militant Palestinians in the Gaza Strip during the 1970s. Committed to the creation of an Islamic Palestinian state and the destruction of Israel through holy war. Also opposes moderate Arab governments that it believes have been tainted by Western secularism. First designated in October 1997.

Activities

PIJ activists have conducted many attacks including large-scale suicide bombings against Israeli civilian and military targets. The group decreased its operational activity in 2003 but still claimed numerous attacks against Israeli interests. The group has not yet targeted U.S. interests and continues to confine its attacks to Israelis inside Israel and the territories. U.S. citizens have died in attacks mounted by the PIJ.

Palestine Liberation Front (PLF)

Description

Broke away from the PFLP-GC in the late 1970s. Later, split again into pro-PLO, pro-Syrian, and pro-Libyan factions. Pro-PLO faction led by Muhammad Abbas (a.k.a. Abu Abbas) had been based in Baghdad. Abbas himself was detained by Coalition Forces in April 2003 and subsequently died in custody of natural causes in March 2004. First designated in October 1997.

Activities

The Abu Abbas—led faction is known for aerial attacks against Israel. Abbas's group also was responsible for the attack in 1985 on the Italian cruise ship *Achille Lauro* and the murder of U.S. citizen Leon Klinghoffer. Has become more active since the start of the al Aqsa *intifada*, and several PLF members have been arrested by Israeli authorities for planning attacks in Israel and the West Bank.

People Against Gangsterism and Drugs (PAGAD)

Description

PAGAD and its ally Qibla view the South African government as a threat to Islamic values. The two groups work to promote a greater political voice for

South African Muslims. PAGAD sometime uses front names such as Muslims Against Global Oppression and Muslims Against Illegitimate Leaders when launching anti-Western protests and campaigns.

Activities

PAGAD's activities have been severely curtailed since 2001 by law-enforcement and prosecutorial efforts against leading members of the organization. Between 1996 and 2000, however, they conducted a total of 189 bomb attacks, including nine bombings in the Western Cape that caused serious injuries. PAGAD's previous bombing targets have included South African authorities, moderate Muslims, synagogues, gay nightclubs, tourist attractions, and Western-associated restaurants. PAGAD is believed to have masterminded the bombing on 25 August 1998 of the Cape Town Planet Hollywood.

Peoples War

a.k.a. Peoples War Group (PWG) and Naxalites

Description

Kondapally Sitaramaiah (a.k.a. Kondapalli Seetharamiah) founded the Andhra Pradesh branch of the PWG in 1980 with the aim of creating an independent "Maoist" state stretching from rural Andhra Pradesh through Orissa and Bihar. Sitaramaiah cited the need for land reform as cause to rebel. Local press often refer to PWG cadres as "Naxalites" after the West Bengal village thought to have originally spawned the organization.

Activities

Peoples War continues a low-intensity insurgency that local police report kills about a dozen police officers, 60 PWG rebels, and as many innocent civilians each year. PWG activities have included attempted (but failed) political assassination, theft of weapons from police stations, kidnapping police officers, assaulting civilians, extorting money from construction firms, and vandalizing the property of multinational corporations. On 1 October 2003, the PWG ambushed the motorcade of Andhra Pradesh Chief Minister Naidu using several roadside improvised explosive devices. The attack killed no one but injured a senior state government official.

Popular Front for the Liberation of Palestine (PFLP)

Description

Marxist-Leninist group founded in 1967 by George Habash—as a member of the PLO—when it broke away from the Arab Nationalist Movement. The PFLP does not view the Palestinian struggle as a religious one, seeing it instead as a broader revolution against Western imperialism. The group earned a reputation for spectacular international attacks, including airline hijackings that have killed at least 20 U.S. citizens. The PFLP is opposed to the Oslo process. First designated in October 1997.

Activities

Committed numerous international terrorist attacks during the 1970s. Since 1978 has conducted attacks against Israeli or moderate Arab targets, including killing a settler and her son in December 1996. The PFLP has stepped up its operational activity since the start of the current *intifada* highlighted by its assassination of the Israeli Tourism Minster in October 2001 to avenge Israel's killing of the PFLP Secretary-General earlier that year.

Popular Front for the Liberation of Palestine—General Command (PFLP-GC)

Description

Split from the PFLP in 1968, claiming it wanted to focus more on fighting and less on politics. Violently opposed to Arafat's PLO. Led by Ahmad Jabril, a former captain in the Syrian Army. Jabril's son, Jihad, was killed by a car bomb in May 2002. Closely tied to both Syria and Iran. First designated in October 1997.

Activities

Carried out dozens of attacks in Europe and the Middle East during the 1970s and 1980s. Known for cross-border terrorist attacks into Israel using unusual means, such as hot air balloons and motorized hang gliders. Primary focus now on guerrilla operations in southern Lebanon and small-scale attacks in Israel, West Bank, and Gaza Strip.

Posse Comitatus

Description

Posse Comitatus is a loosely-knit survivalist movement which grew out of the teachings of Col. William Potter Gale in California. Survivalists believe the collapse of society is imminent, and thus they collect weapons and conduct field exercises in armed self-defense and reconnaissance. Some survivalists store large quantities of grains, dried foods, canned goods, water, and vitamins in anticipation of long-projected economic or political collapse and racial rioting. Many have moved to isolated rural areas. *Posse Comitatus* is Latin for "power of the county"—but more accurately transliterated as "to empower the citizenry"—and is a legal term that means the right to deputize citizens to carry out law enforcement functions; it also is the basis of a federal law preventing the use of federal troops in civilian law enforcement without the express consent of the President. Members of the Posse Comitatus, however, promote an unsubstantiated belief that the Constitution does not authorize any law enforcement powers above the level of county sheriff, and that state and federal officials above the county level are part of a gigantic conspiracy to deny average citizens their rights.

Activities

The group was particularly responsible for spreading the tenets of the Christian Identity movement during the 1980s. Posse activity has been reported in states such as California, Colorado, Idaho, Illinois, Iowa, Kansas, Minnesota, Missouri, Montana, Nebraska, North Dakota, Oregon, Pennsylvania, South Dakota, Texas, Washington, Wisconsin, and Wyoming. The most violent Posse confrontation involved the mishandled attempt to serve legal papers on Posse activist Gordon Kahl. Two U.S. Marshals were killed and several persons wounded. Kahl fled underground and was later killed in another mishandled attempt to flush him from a fortified bunker. Kahl and other white supremacists killed or jailed by the government have become martyrs to Posse adherents and other racists. After the Gordon Kahl incident, many Posse and Christian Identity members decided to carry out activities in secret or through front groups.

Real IRA (RIRA)

a.k.a. 32-County Sovereignty Committee

Description

Formed in early 1998 as the clandestine armed wing of the 32-County Sovereignty Movement, a "political pressure group" dedicated to removing British forces from Northern Ireland and unifying Ireland. RIRA also seeks to disrupt the Northern Ireland peace process. The 32-County Sovereignty Movement opposed Sinn Fein's adoption in September 1997 of the Mitchell principles of democracy and nonviolence and opposed the amendment in December 1999 of Articles 2 and 3 of the Irish Constitution, which laid claim to Northern Ireland. Despite internal rifts and calls by some jailed members—including the group's founder Michael "Mickey" McKevitt—for a cease-fire and the group's disbandment, the group pledged additional violence in October 2002 and continued to conduct attacks. First designated in May 2001.

Activities

Bombings, assassinations, and robberies. Many Real IRA members are former Provisional IRA members who left that organization following the Provisional IRA cease-fire and bring to RIRA a wealth of experience in terrorist tactics and bombmaking. Targets have included civilians (most notoriously in the Omagh bombing in August 1998), the British military, the police in Northern Ireland, and Northern Ireland Protestant communities. Since October 1999, RIRA has carried out more than 80 terrorist attacks. RIRA's most recent fatal attack was in August 2002 at a London Army Base that killed a construction worker. In June 2003 raids, Irish national police interdicted two large-scale vehicle-born improvised explosive devices, each weighing more than 1,000 pounds. Five RIRA members and a senior Continuity Irish Republican Army member (CIRA) also were arrested during the raids.

Red Hand Defenders
(RHD)

Description

Extremist terrorist group formed in 1998 and composed largely of Protestant hardliners from loyalist groups observing a cease-fire. RHD seeks to prevent a political settlement with Irish nationalists by attacking Catholic civilian interests in Northern Ireland. In January 2002, the group announced all staff at Catholic schools in Belfast and Catholic postal workers were legitimate targets. Despite calls in February 2002 by the Ulster Defense Association (UDA), Ulster Freedom Fighters (UFF), and Loyalist Volunteer Force (LVF) to announce its disbandment, RHD continued to make threats and issue claims of responsibility. RHD is a cover name often used by elements of the banned UDA and LVF. Designated under EO 13224 in December 2001.

Activities

In early 2003, the RHD claimed responsibility for killing two UDA members as a result of what is described as loyalist internecine warfare. They also claimed responsibility for a bomb that was left in the offices of Republican Sinn Fein in West Belfast, though the device was defused and no one was injured. In recent years, the group has carried out numerous pipe bombings and arson attacks against "soft" civilian targets such as homes, churches, and private businesses. In January 2002, the group bombed the home of a prison official in North Belfast. Twice in 2002 the group claimed responsibility for attacks—the murder of a Catholic postman and Catholic teenager—that were later claimed by the UDA-UFF, further blurring distinctions between the groups. In 2001, RHD claimed responsibility for killing five persons.

Revolutionary Armed
Forces of Colombia
(FARC)

Description

Growing out of the turmoil and fighting in the 1950s between liberal and conservative militias, the FARC was established in 1964 by the Colombian Communist Party to defend what were then autonomous Communist-controlled rural areas. The FARC is Latin America's oldest, largest, most

capable, and best-equipped insurgency of Marxist
origin. Although only nominally fighting in support
of Marxist goals today, the FARC is governed by a
general-secretariat led by longtime leader Manuel
Marulanda (a.k.a. "Tirofi jo") and six others, including senior military commander Jorge Briceno
(a.k.a. "Mono Jojoy"). It is organized along military lines and includes several units that operate
mostly in key urban areas such as Bogotá. In
2003, the FARC conducted several high profile terrorist attacks, including a February car bombing of
a Bogotá nightclub that killed more than 30 persons and wounded more than 160, as well as a
November grenade attack in Bogotá's restaurant
district that wounded three Americans. First designated in October 1997.

Activities

Bombings, murder, mortar attacks, narcotrafficking, kidnapping, extortion, hijacking, as well as
guerrilla and conventional military action against
Colombian political, military, and economic targets. In March 1999, the FARC executed three
U.S. Indian rights activists on Venezuelan territory
after it kidnapped them in Colombia. In February
2003, the FARC captured and continues to hold
three U.S. contractors and killed one other American and a Colombian when their plane crashed in
Florencia. Foreign citizens often are targets of
FARC kidnapping for ransom. The FARC has well-
documented ties to the full range of narcotics trafficking activities, including taxation, cultivation,
and distribution.

Revolutionary Nuclei (RN)

a.k.a. Revolutionary Cells

Description

Revolutionary Nuclei (RN) emerged from a broad
range of antiestablishment and anti-U.S./NATO/
EU leftist groups active in Greece between 1995
and 1998. The group is believed to be the successor to or offshoot of Greece's most prolific terrorist
group, Revolutionary People's Struggle (ELA),
which has not claimed an attack since January
1995. Indeed, RN appeared to fill the void left by
ELA, particularly as lesser groups faded from the

scene. RN's few communiques show strong similarities in rhetoric, tone, and theme to ELA proclamations. RN has not claimed an attack since November 2000 nor has it announced its disbandment. First designated in October 1997.

Activities

Since it began operations in January 1995, the group has claimed responsibility for some two dozen arson attacks and low-level bombings targeting a range of U.S., Greek, and other European targets in Greece. In its most infamous and lethal attack to date, the group claimed responsibility for a bomb it detonated at the Intercontinental Hotel in April 1999 that resulted in the death of a Greek woman and injured a Greek man. Its modus operandi includes warning calls of impending attacks, attacks targeting property, use of rudimentary timing devices, and strikes during the late evening to early morning hours. RN may have been responsible for two attacks in July against a U.S. insurance company and a local bank in Athens. RN's last confirmed attack against U.S. interests in Greece was in November 2000 with two separate bombings against the Athens offices of Citigroup and the studio of a Greek/American sculptor. Greek targets have included judicial and other government office buildings, private vehicles, and the offices of Greek firms involved in NATO-related defense contracts in Greece. Similarly, the group has attacked European interests in Athens, including Barclays Bank in December 1998 and November 2000.

Revolutionary Organization 17 November

a.k.a. 17 November

Description

Radical leftist group established in 1975 and named for the student uprising in Greece in November 1973 that protested the ruling military junta. Anti-Greek establishment, anti-United States, anti-Turkey, and anti-NATO group that seeks the ouster of U.S. bases from Greece, the removal of Turkish military forces from Cyprus, and the severing of Greece's ties to NATO and the European Union (EU). First designated in October 1997.

Activities

Initially conducted assassinations of senior U.S. officials and Greek public figures. Added bombings in the 1980s. Since 1990 has expanded its targets to include EU facilities and foreign firms investing in Greece and has added improvised rocket attacks to its methods. Supports itself largely through bank robberies. A failed 17 November bombing attempt in June 2002 at the Port of Piraeus in Athens coupled with robust detective work led to the first-ever arrests of this group. In December 2003, a Greek court convicted 15 members—five of whom were given multiple life terms—of hundreds of crimes. Four other alleged members were acquitted because of a lack of evidence.

Revolutionary People's Liberation Party/Front (DHKP/C)

a.k.a. Devrimci Sol, Revolutionary Left, Dev Sol

Description

Originally formed in 1978 as Devrimci Sol, or Dev Sol, a splinter faction of Dev Genc (Revolutionary Youth). Renamed in 1994 after factional infighting; "Party" refers to the group's political activities, while "Front" is a reference to the group's militant operations. The group espouses a Marxist-Leninist ideology and is virulently anti-U.S., anti-NATO, and anti-Turkish establishment. It finances its activities chiefly through donations and extortion. First designated in October 1997.

Activities

Since the late 1980s, the group has targeted primarily current and retired Turkish security and military officials. It began a new campaign against foreign interests in 1990, which included attacks against U.S. military and diplomatic personnel and facilities. To protest perceived U.S. imperialism during the Gulf war, the DHKP/C assassinated two U.S. military contractors, wounded an Air Force officer, and bombed more than 20 U.S. and NATO military, commercial, and cultural facilities. In its first significant terrorist act as DHKP/C in 1996, it assassinated a prominent Turkish businessman and two others. DHKP/C added suicide bombings to its repertoire in 2001, with successful attacks against Turkish police in January and September. Security operations in Turkey and elsewhere have weakened the group, however. DHKP/C did not conduct any major terrorist attacks in 2003, although a DHKP/C operative prematurely detonated her explosive belt in May.

Revolutionary Proletarian Initiative Nuclei (NIPR)

Description

Clandestine leftist extremist group that appeared in Rome in 2000. Adopted the logo of the Red Brigades of the 1970s and 1980s—an encircled five-point star—for its declarations. Opposes Italy's foreign and labor polices. Has targeted property interests rather than personnel in its attacks.

Activities

Did not claim responsibility for any attacks in 2002. Claimed responsibility for bomb attack in April 2001 on building housing a U.S.-Italian relations association and an international affairs institute in Rome's historic center. Claimed to have carried out explosion in May 2000 in Rome at oversight committee facility for implementation of the law on strikes in public services. Claimed responsibility for explosion in February 2002 on Via Palermo adjacent to Interior Ministry in Rome.

Riyadus-Salikhin Reconnaissance and Sabotage Battalion of Chechen Martyrs (RSRSBCM)

Description

One of three terrorist groups affiliated with Chechen guerrillas that furnished personnel to carry out the seizure of the Dubrovka Theater in Moscow on 23 October 2002. The suicide attackers took more than 800 hostages, whom they threatened to kill if the Russian government did not meet their demands, including the withdrawal of Russian forces from Chechnya. The RSRSBCM—whose name translates into English as "Requirements for Getting into Paradise"—was not known to Western observers before the seizure. Chechen extremist leader Shamil Basayev, who claimed responsibility for ordering the seizure, continues to lead the RSRSBCM. Designated under EO 13224 in February 2003.

Activities

Primarily guerrilla operations against Russian forces.

Salafist Group for Call and Combat (GSPC)

Description

The Salafist Group for Call and Combat (GSPC), an outgrowth of the GIA, appears to have eclipsed the GIA since approximately 1998 and is currently the most effective armed group inside Algeria. In contrast to the GIA, the GSPC has gained some popular support through its pledge to avoid civilian attacks inside Algeria. Its adherents abroad appear to have largely co-opted the external networks of the GIA and are particularly active throughout Europe, Africa, and the Middle East. First designated in March 2002.

Activities

The GSPC continues to conduct operations aimed at government and military targets, primarily in rural areas, although civilians are sometimes killed. A faction within the GSPC held 31 European tourists hostage in 2003 to collect ransom for their release. According to press reporting, some GSPC members in Europe maintain contacts with other North African extremists sympathetic to al Qaeda. In late 2003, the new GSPC leader issued a communique declaring the group's allegiance to a number of jihadist causes and movements, including al Qaeda.

Sendero Luminoso (Shining Path or SL)

Description

Former university professor Abimael Guzman formed SL in Peru in the late 1960s, and his teachings created the foundation of SL's militant Maoist doctrine. In the 1980s, SL became one of the most ruthless terrorist groups in the Western Hemisphere approximately 30,000 persons have died since Shining Path took up arms in 1980. The Peruvian Government made dramatic gains against SL during the 1990s, but reports of recent SL involvement in narcotrafficking and kidnapping for ransom indicate it may have a new source of funding with which to sustain a resurgence. Its stated goal is to destroy existing Peruvian institutions and replace them with a communist peasant revolutionary regime. It also opposes any influence by foreign governments. In January 2003, Peruvian courts granted approximately 1,900 members the right to request retrials in a civilian court, including the imprisoned top leadership. Counterterrorist operations targeted pockets of terrorist activity in the Upper Huallaga River Valley and the Apurimac/Ene River Valley, where SL columns continued to conduct periodic attacks. Peruvian authorities captured several SL members in 2003. First designated in October 1997.

Activities

Conducted indiscriminate bombing campaigns and selective assassinations. In June 2003, an SL column kidnapped 71 Peruvian and foreign employees working on the Camisea gas line in Ayacucho Department.

Sipah-i-Sahaba/Pakistan (SSP)

Description

The Sipah-I-Sahaba/Pakistan (SSP) is a Sunni sectarian group that follows the Deobandi school. Violently anti-Shia, the SSP emerged in central Punjab in the mid-1980s as a response to the Iranian Revolution. Pakistani President Musharraf banned the SSP in January 2002. In August 2002, the SSP renamed itself Millat-i-Islami, and Musharraf re-banned the group in November 2003.

Activities

The group's activities range from organizing political rallies calling for Shia to be declared non-Muslims to assassinating prominent Shia leaders.

Special Purpose Islamic Regiment (SPIR)

Description

One of three terrorist groups affiliated with Chechen guerrillas that furnished personnel to carry out the seizure of the Dubrovka Theater in Moscow on 23 October 2002. The suicide attackers took more than 800 hostages, whom they threatened to kill if the Russian government did not meet their demands, including the withdrawal of Russian forces from Chechnya. Movzar Barayev commanded the SPIR until he was killed in the October seizure, which he led. The SPIR has continued to carry out guerrilla operations in Chechnya under the leadership of another Chechen leader, Khamzat, whose true identity is not known. Designated under EO 13224 in February 2003.

Activities

Primarily guerrilla operations against Russian forces. Has also been involved in various hostage and ransom operations, as well as the execution of ethnic Chechens who have collaborated with Russian authorities.

The Tunisian Combatant Group (TCG)

Description

The Tunisian Combatant Group (TCG), also known as the Jama'a Combattante Tunisienne, seeks to establish an Islamic regime in Tunisia and has targeted U.S. and Western interests. Founded around 2000 by Tarek Maaroufi and Saifallah Ben Hassine, the loosely organized group is associated with al Qaeda and North African extremist networks implicated in terrorist plots during the past two years. The group was designated for sanctions under UNSCR 1333 in December 2000. Belgian authorities sentenced Maaroufi to six years in 2003. Designated under EO 13224 in October 2002.

Activities

Tunisians associated with the TCG are part of the support network of the broader international jihadist movement. According to European press reports, TCG members or affiliates in the past have engaged in trafficking falsified documents and recruiting for terror training camps in Afghanistan. Some TCG associates are suspected of planning an attack against the U.S., Algerian, and Tunisian diplomatic missions in Rome in April 2001. Some members reportedly maintain ties to the Algerian Salafist Group for Preaching and Combat.

Tupac Amaru Revolution-
ary Movement (MRTA)

Description

Traditional Marxist-Leninist revolutionary movement formed in 1983 from remnants of the Movement of the Revolutionary Left, a Peruvian
insurgent group active in the 1960s. Aims to establish a Marxist regime and to rid Peru of all imperialist elements (primarily U.S. and Japanese
influence). Peru's counterterrorist program has diminished the group's ability to carry out terrorist
attacks, and the MRTA has suffered from infighting, the imprisonment or deaths of senior leaders,
and loss of leftist support. In 2003, several MRTA
members remained imprisoned in Bolivia.

Activities

Previously conducted bombings, kidnappings, ambushes, and assassinations, but recent activity has
fallen drastically. In December 1996, 14 MRTA
members occupied the Japanese Ambassador's residence in Lima and held 72 hostages for more than
four months. Peruvian forces stormed the residence
in April 1997 rescuing all but one of the remaining
hostages and killing all 14 group members, including the remaining leaders. The group has not conducted a significant terrorist operation since and
appears more focused on obtaining the release of
imprisoned MRTA members.

Turkish Hizballah

Description

Turkish Hizballah is a Kurdish Islamic (Sunni) extremist organization that arose in the early 1980s
in response to Kurdistan Workers' Party (PKK)
atrocities against Muslims in southeastern Turkey,
where Turkish Hizballah seeks to establish an independent Islamic state.

Activities

Beginning in the mid-1990s, Turkish Hizballah,
which is unrelated to Lebanese Hizballah, expanded its target base and modus operandi from
killing PKK militants to conducting low-level
bombings against liquor stores, bordellos, and
other establishments that the organization considered "anti-Islamic." In January 2000, Turkish secu-

rity forces killed Huseyin Velioglu, the leader of Turkish Hizballah, in a shootout at a safehouse in Istanbul. The incident sparked a year-long series of counterterrorist operations against the group that resulted in the detention of some 2,000 individuals; authorities arrested several hundred of those on criminal charges. At the same time, police recovered nearly 70 bodies of Turkish and Kurdish businessmen and journalists that Turkish Hizballah had tortured and brutally murdered during the mid-to-late 1990s. The group began targeting official Turkish interests in January 2001, when its operatives assassinated the Diyarbakir police chief in the group's most sophisticated operation to date. Turkish Hizballah did not conduct a major operation in 2003 but is probably attempting to reorganize.

Ulster Defense Association/Ulster Freedom Fighters (UDA/UFF)

Description

The Ulster Defense Association (UDA), the largest loyalist paramilitary group in Northern Ireland, was formed in 1971 as an umbrella organization for loyalist paramilitary groups such as the Ulster Freedom Fighters (UFF). Today, the UFF constitutes almost the entire UDA membership. The UDA/UFF declared a series of cease-fires between 1994 and 1998. In September 2001, the UDA/UFF's Inner Council withdrew its support for Northern Ireland's Good Friday Agreement. The following month, after a series of murders, bombings, and street violence, the British Government ruled the UDA/UFF's cease-fire defunct. The dissolution of the organization's political wing, the Ulster Democratic Party, soon followed. In January 2002, however, the UDA created the Ulster Political Research Group to serve in a similar capacity. Designated under EO 13224 in December 2001.

Activities

The UDA/UFF has evolved into a criminal organization involved in drug trafficking and other moneymaking criminal activities. In February of 2003, the UDA/UFF declared a 12-month cease-fire but refused to decommission its weapons arsenal until Republican groups did likewise and emphasized its continued disagreement with the Good Friday accords. Even though numerous attacks on Catholics were blamed on the group, the UDA/UFF did not claim credit for any attacks and in August reiterated its intention to remain militarily inactive. The group has been involved in an internecine war with other loyalist groups for the past several years, which has lead to the deaths of numerous members of the organization. In January 2002, the UDA/UFF called for an end to sectarian violence; in the preceding months, the UDA had been blamed for more than 300 bombings and shootings against Catholics in Belfast. Nevertheless, the UDA/UFF continued its attacks against Catholics, as well as those seen as a threat to its criminal enterprises. The UDA/UFF admitted responsibility for the murder of a Catholic postman in January 2002, an attack also claimed by the Red Hand Defenders, a group used as a cover name by some UDA/UFF elements. The UDA also was blamed for a drive-by shooting that wounded three Catholics in September. Johnny Adair, the only person ever convicted of directing terrorism in Northern Ireland, was a leading UDA member until September 2002 when he was expelled from the group because of his growing ties to the LVF.

Ulster Volunteer Force (UVF)

Description

Loyalist terrorist group formed in 1966 to oppose liberal reforms in Northern Ireland that members feared would lead to unification of Ireland. The group adopted the name of an earlier organization formed in 1912 to combat Home Rule for Ireland. The UVF's goal is to maintain Northern Ireland's status as part of the United Kingdom; to that end it has killed some 550 persons since 1966. The UVF and its offshoots have been responsible for some of the most vicious attacks of "the Troubles" including horrific sectarian killings like those perpetrated in the 1970s by the UVF-affiliated "Shankill Butchers." In October 1994, the Combined Loyalist Military Command, which included the UVF, declared a cease-fire, and the UVF's political wing—the Progressive Unionist Party—has played an active role in the peace process. Despite the cease-fire, the organization has been involved in a series of bloody feuds with other Loyalist paramilitary organizations.

Activities

The UVF has been active in Belfast and the border areas of Northern Ireland where it has carried out bombings, assassinations, kidnappings, hijackings, extortion, and robberies. On occasion, it has provided advance warning to police of its attacks. Targets include nationalist civilians, republican paramilitary groups and, on occasion, rival loyalist paramilitary groups. The UVF continues to observe a cease-fire.

United Self-Defense Forces/Group of Colombia

a.k.a. AUC—Autodefensas Unidas de Colombia

Description

The AUC—commonly referred to as the paramilitaries—is a loose umbrella organization formed in April 1997 to consolidate most local and regional self-defense groups each with the mission to protect economic interests and combat FARC and ELN insurgents locally. The AUC is supported by economic elites, drug traffickers, and local communities lacking effective government security and claims its primary objective is to protect its sponsors from insurgents. Some elements under the AUC umbrella, under its former political leader Carlos Castano's influence, have voluntarily agreed to a unilateral cease-fire though violations of the cease-fire do occur. Parts of the AUC loyal to Castano currently are in negotiations with the government of Colombia to demobilize. To date, approximately 1,000 AUC fighters have demobilized. Note: Carlos Castaño was captured on 16 April 2004.

Activities

AUC operations vary from assassinating suspected insurgent supporters to engaging FARC and ELN combat units. Castano has publicly claimed that 70 percent of the AUC's operational costs are financed with drug-related earnings, the rest from "donations" from its sponsors. The AUC generally avoids actions against U.S. personnel or interests.

APPENDIX B

Al Qaeda Declarations of War

(1). 1996 Declaration of War

The following text is a *fatwa*, or declaration of war, by Osama bin Laden first published in *al Quds al Arabi*, a London-based newspaper, in August, 1996.

"Declaration of War against the Americans Occupying the Land of the Two Holy Places."

Praise be to Allah, we seek His help and ask for his pardon. We take refuge in Allah from our wrongs and bad deeds. Who ever has been guided by Allah will not be misled, and who ever has been misled, he will never be guided. I bear witness that there is no God except Allah—no associates with Him—and I bear witness that Muhammad is His slave and messenger.

{O you who believe! be careful of your duty to Allah with the proper care which is due to Him, and do not die unless you are Muslim} (Imraan 3:102), {O people be careful of your duty to your Lord, Who created you from a single being and created its mate of the same kind and spread from these two, many men and women; and be careful of your duty to Allah, by whom you demand one of another your rights, and (be careful) to the ties of kinship; surely Allah ever watches over you} (An-Nisa 4:1), {O you who believe! be careful of your duty to Allah and speak the right word; He will put your deeds into a right state for you, and forgive you your faults; and who ever obeys Allah and his Apostle, he indeed achieve a mighty success} (Al-Ahzab 33:70–71).

Praise be to Allah, reporting the saying of the prophet Shu'aib: {I desire nothing but reform so far as I am able, and with none but Allah is the direction of my affair to the right and successful path; on him do I rely and to him do I turn} (Hud 11:88).

Praise be to Allah, saying: {You are the best of the nations raised up for the benefit of men; you enjoin what is right and forbid the wrong and believe in Allah} (Aal-Imraan 3:110). Allah's blessing and salutations on His slave and messenger who said: (The people are close to an all-encompassing punishment from Allah if they see the oppressor and fail to restrain him.)

It should not be hidden from you that the people of Islam had suffered from aggression, iniquity, and injustice imposed on them by the Zionist-Crusaders alliance and their collaborators; to the extent that the Muslims' blood became the cheapest and their wealth as loot in the hands of the enemies. Their blood was spilled in Palestine and Iraq. The horrifying pictures of the massacre of Qana, in Lebanon are still fresh in our memory. Massacres in Tajakestan, Burma, Cashmere, Assam, Philippines, Fatani, Ogadin, Somalia, Erithria, Chechnya, and in Bosnia-Herzegovina took place, massacres that send shivers in the body and shake the conscience. All of this and the world watched and heard, and not only didn't respond to these atrocities, but also with a clear conspiracy between the USA and its allies and under the cover of the iniquitous United Nations, the dispossessed people were even prevented from obtaining arms to defend themselves.

The people of Islam awakened and realized that they are the main target for the aggression of the Zionist-Crusaders alliance. All false claims and propaganda about "Human Rights" were hammered down and exposed by the massacres that took place against the Muslims in every part of the world.

The latest and the greatest of these aggressions, incurred by the Muslims since the death of the Prophet (ALLAH'S BLESSING AND SALUTATIONS ON HIM) is the occupation of the land of the two Holy Places—the foundation of the house of Islam, the place of the revelation, the source of the message and the place of the noble Ka'ba, the Qiblah of all Muslims—by the armies of the American Crusaders and their allies. (We bemoan this and can only say: "No power and power acquiring except through Allah.")

Under the present circumstances, and under the banner of the blessed awakening which is sweeping the world in general and the Islamic world in particular, I meet with you today. And after a long absence, imposed on the scholars (*ulama*) and callers (Da'ees) of Islam by the iniquitous crusaders movement under the leadership of the USA; who fears that they, the scholars and callers of Islam, will instigate the Ummah of Islam against its enemies as their ancestor scholars—may Allah be pleased with them—like Ibn Taymiyyah and Al'iz Ibn Abdes-Salaam did. And therefore the Zionist-Crusader alliance resorted to killing and arresting the truthful Ulama and the working Da'ees. (We are not praising or sanctifying them; Allah sanctify whom He pleased.) They killed the Mujahid Sheikh Abdullah Azzaam, and they arrested the Mujahid Sheikh Ahmad Yaseen and the Mujahid Sheikh Omar Abdur Rahman (in America).

By orders from the USA they also arrested a large number of scholars, Da'ees and young people—in the land of the two Holy Places—among them the prominent Sheikh Salman Al-Oud'a and Sheikh Safar Al-Hawali and their brothers; (we bemoan this and can only say: "No power and power acquiring except through Allah"). We, myself and my group, have suffered some of this injustice ourselves; we have been prevented from addressing the Muslims. We have been pursued in Pakistan, Sudan, and Afghanistan, hence this long absence on my part. But by the Grace of Allah, a safe base is now available in the high Hindukush mountains in Khurasan; where—by the Grace of Allah—the largest infidel military force of the world was destroyed. And the myth of the super power was withered in front of the Mujahideen cries of Allahu Akbar (God is greater). Today we work from the same mountains to lift the iniquity that had been imposed on the Ummah by the Zionist-Crusader alliance, particularly after they have occupied the blessed land around Jerusalem, route of the journey of the Prophet (ALLAH'S BLESSING AND SALUTATIONS ON HIM) and the land of the two Holy Places. We ask Allah to bestow us with victory, He is our Patron and He is the Most Capable.

From here, today we begin the work, talking and discussing the ways of correcting what had happened to the Islamic world in general, and the Land of the two Holy Places in particular. We wish to study the means that we could follow to return the situation to its normal path. And to return to the people their own rights, particularly after the large damages and the great aggression on the life and the religion of the people. An injustice that had affected every section and group of the people; the civilians, military, and security men, government officials and merchants, the young and the old people as well as schools and university students. Hundred of thousands of the unemployed graduates, who became the widest section of the society, were also affected.

Injustice had affected the people of the industry and agriculture. It affected the people of the rural and urban areas. And almost everybody complained about something. The situation at the land of the two Holy Places became like a huge volcano at the verge of eruption that would destroy the Kufr and the corruption and its sources. The explosion at Riyadh and Al-Khobar is a warning of this volcanic eruption emerging as a result of the sever oppression, suffering, excessive iniquity, humiliation, and poverty.

People are fully concerned about their everyday livings; everybody talks about the deterioration of the economy, inflation, ever increasing debts, and jails full of prisoners. Government employees with limited income talk about debts of ten thousands and hundred thousands of Saudi Riyals. They complain that the value of the Riyal is greatly and continuously deteriorating among most of the main currencies. Great merchants and contractors speak about hundreds and thousands of million Riyals owed to them by the government. More than 340 billion Riyal owed by the government to the people in addition to the daily accumulated interest, let alone the foreign debt. People wonder whether we are the largest oil exporting country?! They even believe that this situation is a curse put on them by Allah for not objecting to the oppressive and illegitimate behavior and measures of the ruling regime: Ignoring the divine Sharia law; depriving people of their legitimate rights; allowing the American to occupy the land of the two Holy Places; imprisonment, unjustly, of the sincere scholars. The honorable *ulama* and scholars as well as merchants, economists, and eminent people of the country were all alerted by this disastrous situation.

Quick efforts were made by each group to contain and to correct the situation. All agreed that the country is heading toward a great catastrophe, the depth of which is not known except by Allah. One big merchant commented: "The king is leading the state into 'sixty-six' folded disaster." (We bemoan this and can only say: "No power and power acquiring except through Allah.") Numerous princes share with the people their feelings, privately expressing their concerns and objecting to the corruption, repression, and the intimidation taking place in the country. But the competition between influential princes for personal gains and interest had destroyed the country. Through its course of actions the regime has torn off its legitimacy:

1. Suspension of the Islamic Sharia law and exchanging it with man-made civil law. The regime entered into a bloody confrontation with the truthful Ulama and the righteous youths (we sanctify nobody; Allah sanctify Whom He pleaseth).

2. The inability of the regime to protect the country, and allowing the enemy of the Ummah—the American crusader forces—to occupy the land for the longest of years. The crusader forces became the main cause of our disastrous condition, particularly in the economical aspect of it due to the unjustified heavy spending on these forces. As a result of the policy imposed on the country, especially in the field of oil industry where production is restricted or expanded and prices are fixed to suit the American economy ignoring the economy of the country. Expensive deals were imposed on the country to purchase arms. People asking what is the justification for the very existence of the regime then?

Quick efforts were made by individuals and by different groups of the society to contain the situation and to prevent the danger. They advised the government both privately and openly; they sent letters and poems, reports after reports, reminders after reminders, they explored every avenue and enlist every influential man in their movement of reform and correction.

They wrote with style of passion, diplomacy, and wisdom asking for corrective measures and repentance from the "great wrong doings and corruption" that had engulfed even the basic principles of the religion and the legitimate rights of the people.

But—to our deepest regret—the regime refused to listen to the people ac-

cusing them of being ridiculous and imbecile. The matter got worse as previous wrongdoings were followed by mischief's of greater magnitudes. All of
this taking place in the land of the two Holy Places! It is no longer possible
to be quiet. It is not acceptable to give a blind eye to this matter.

As the extent of these infringements reached the highest of levels and turned
into demolishing forces threatening the very existence of the Islamic principles, a group of scholars—who could take no more—supported by hundreds
of retired officials, merchants, and prominent and educated people wrote to
the King asking for implementation of the corrective measures. In 1411 A.H.
(May 1991), at the time of the Gulf war, a letter, the famous letter of
Shawwaal, with over 400 signatures, was send to the king demanding the lift
of oppression and the implementation of corrective actions. The king humiliated those people and choose to ignore the content of their letter, and the
very bad situation of the country became even worse.

People, however, tried again and sent more letters and petitions. One particular report, the glorious Memorandum Of Advice, was handed over to the
king on Muharram, 1413 A.H. (July 1992), which tackled the problem,
pointed out the illness, and prescribed the medicine in an original, righteous,
and scientific style. It described the gaps and the shortcoming in the philosophy of the regime and suggested the required course of action and remedy.
The report gave a description of:

1. The intimidation and harassment suffered by the leaders of the society, the
   scholars, heads of tribes, merchants, academic teachers and other eminent
   individuals;

2. The situation of the law within the country and the arbitrary declaration
   of what is Halal and Haram (lawful and unlawful) regardless of the Sharia
   as instituted by Allah;

3. The state of the press and the media which became a tool of truth-hiding
   and misinformation; the media carried out the plan of the enemy of idolizing cult of certain personalities and spreading scandals among the believers
   to repel the people away from their religion, as Allah, the Exalted said:
   {surely as for those who love that scandal should circulate between the believers, they shall have a grievous chastisement in this world and in the here
   after} (An-Noor 24:19);

4. Abuse and confiscation of human rights;

5. The financial and the economical situation of the country and the frightening future in the view of the enormous amount of debts and interest
   owed by the government; this is at the time when the wealth of the Ummah
   is being wasted to satisfy personal desires of certain individuals!! while
   imposing more custom duties and taxes on the nation. (The prophet said
   about the woman who committed adultery: "She repented in such a way
   sufficient to bring forgiveness to a custom collector!!");

6. The miserable situation of the social services and infrastructure especially the water service and supply, the basic requirement of life;

7. The state of the ill-trained and ill-prepared army and the impotence of its commander-in-chief despite the incredible amount of money that has been spent on the army. The Gulf war clearly exposed the situation;

8. Sharia law was suspended and man-made law was used instead;

9. And as far as the foreign policy is concerned the report exposed not only how this policy has disregarded the Islamic issues and ignored the Muslims, but also how help and support were provided to the enemy against the Muslims; the cases of Gaza-Ariha and the communist in the south of Yemen are still fresh in the memory, and more can be said.

As stated by the people of knowledge, it is not a secret that to use man-made law instead of the Sharia and to support the infidels against the Muslims is one of the 10 "voiders" that would strip a person from his Islamic status (turn a Muslim into a Mushrik, nonbeliever status). The All Mighty said: {and whoever did not judge by what Allah revealed, those are the unbelievers} (Al-Ma'ida 5:44), and {but no! by your Lord! they do not believe (in reality) until they make you a judge of that which has become a matter of disagreement among them, and then do not find the slightest misgiving in their hearts as to what you have decided and submit with entire submission} (An-Nissa 4:65).

In spite of the fact that the report was written with soft words and very diplomatic style, reminding of Allah, giving truthful sincere advice, and despite of the importance of advice in Islam—being absolutely essential for those in charge of the people—and the large number who signed this document as well as their supporters, all of that was not an intercession for the Memorandum. Its content was rejected and those who signed it and their sympathisers were ridiculed, prevented from travel, punished, and even jailed.

Therefore it is very clear that the advocates of correction and reform movement were very keen on using peaceful means in order to protect the unity of the country and to prevent bloodshed. Why is it then the regime closed all peaceful routes and pushed the people toward armed actions which is the only choice left for them to implement righteousness and justice?!! To whose benefit do Prince Sultan and Prince Nayeff push the country into a civil war that will destroy everything, and why consulting those who ignite internal feuds, playing the people against each other and instigate the policemen, the sons of the nation, to abort the reform movement, while leaving in peace and security such traitors who implement the policy of the enemy in order to bleed the financial and the human resources of the Ummah, and leaving the main enemy in the area-the American Zionist alliance enjoy peace and security?!

The advisor (Zaki Badr, the Egyptian ex-minister of the interior) to Prince Nayeff, Minister of Interior, was not acceptable even to his own country; he was sacked from his position there due to the filthy attitude and the aggression he exercised on his own people, yet he was warmly welcomed by Prince Nayeff to assist in sins and aggressions. He unjustly filled the prisons with the best sons of this Umma and caused miseries to their mothers. Does the regime want to play the civilians against their military personnel and vice versa, like what had happened in some of the neighbouring countries?!! No doubt this is the policy of the American-Israeli alliance as they are the first to benefit from this situation.

But with the grace of Allah, the majority of the nation, both civilians and military individuals are aware of the wicked plan. They refused to be played against each other and to be used by the regime as a tool to carry out the policy of the American-Israeli alliance through their agent in our country: the Saudi regime.

Therefore everyone agreed that the situation can not be rectified (the shadow cannot be straighten when its source, the rod, is not straight either) unless the root of the problem is tackled. Hence it is essential to hit the main enemy who divided the Ummah into small and little countries and pushed it, for the last few decades, into a state of confusion. The Zionist-Crusader alliance moves quickly to contain and abort any "corrective movement" appearing in the Islamic countries. Different means and methods are used to achieve their target; on occasion the "movement" is dragged into an armed struggle at a predetermined unfavorable time and place. Sometime officials from the Ministry of Interior, who are also graduates of the colleges of the Sharia, are leased out to mislead and confuse the nation and the Ummah (by wrong *fatwas*) and to circulate false information about the movement. At other occasions some righteous people were tricked into a war of words against the *ulama* and the leaders of the movement, wasting the energy of the nation in discussing minor issues and ignoring the main one that is the unification of the people under the divine law of Allah.

In the shadow of these discussions and arguments truthfulness is covered by the falsehood and personal feuds and partisanship created among the people increasing the division and the weakness of the Ummah; priorities of the Islamic work are lost while the blasphemy and polytheism continue its grip and control over the Ummah. We should be alert to these atrocious plans carried out by the Ministry of Interior. The right answer is to follow what have been decided by the people of knowledge, as was said by Ibn Taymiyyah (Allah's mercy upon him): "People of Islam should join forces and support each other to get rid of the main 'Kufr' who is controlling the countries of the Islamic world, even to bear the lesser damage to get rid of the major one, that is the great Kufr."

If there is more than one duty to be carried out, then the most important one should receive priority. Clearly after Belief (Imaan) there is no more important duty than pushing the American enemy out of the holy land. No other priority, except Belief, could be considered before it; the people of knowledge, Ibn Taymiyyah, stated: "To fight in defence of religion and Belief is a collective duty; there is no other duty after Belief than fighting the enemy who is corrupting the life and the religion. There are no preconditions for this duty and the enemy should be fought with one best abilities. If it is not possible to push back the enemy except by the collective movement of the Muslim people, then there is a duty on the Muslims to ignore the minor differences among themselves; the ill effect of ignoring these differences, at a given period of time, is much less than the ill effect of the occupation of the Muslims' land by the main Kufr. Ibn Taymiyyah had explained this issue and emphasised the importance of dealing with the major threat on the expense of the minor one. He described the situation of the Muslims and the Mujahideen and stated that even the military personnel who are not practicing Islam are not exempted from the duty of Jihad against the enemy.

Ibn Taymiyyah, after mentioning the Moguls (Tatar) and their behavior in changing the law of Allah, stated that the ultimate aim of pleasing Allah, raising His word, instituting His religion and obeying His messenger (ALLAH'S BLESSING AND SALUTATIONS ON HIM) is to fight the enemy, in every aspects and in a complete manner; if the danger to the religion from not fighting is greater than that of fighting, then it is a duty to fight them even if the intention of some of the fighters is not pure, i.e., fighting for the sake of leadership (personal gain) or if they do not observe some of the rules and commandments of Islam. To repel the greatest of the two dangers on the expense of the lesser one is an Islamic principle which should be observed. It was the tradition of the people of the Sunnah (Ahlul-Sunnah) to join and invade— fight—with the righteous and nonrighteous men. Allah may support this religion by righteous and nonrighteous people as told by the prophet (ALLAH'S BLESSING AND SALUTATIONS ON HIM). If it is not possible to fight except with the help of nonrighteous military personnel and commanders, then there are two possibilities: either fighting will be ignored and the others, who are the great danger to this life and religion, will take control; or to fight with the help of nonrighteous rulers and therefore repelling the greatest of the two dangers and implementing most, though not all, of the Islamic laws. The latter option is the right duty to be carried out in these circumstances and in many other similar situations. In fact many of the fights and conquests that took place after the time of Rashidoon, the guided Imams, were of this type (majmoo' al Fatawa, 26/506).

No one, not even a blind or a deaf person, can deny the presence of the widely spread mischiefs or the prevalence of the great sins that had reached the grievous iniquity of polytheism and to share with Allah in His sole right of sovereignty and making of the law. The All Mighty stated: {And when Luqman said to his son while he admonish him: O my son! do not associate ought with Allah; most surely polytheism is a grievous iniquity} (Luqman 31:13). Man-fabricated laws were put forward permitting what has been forbidden by Allah such as usury (Riba) and other matters. Banks dealing in usury are competing, for lands, with the two Holy Places and declaring war against Allah by disobeying His order {Allah has allowed trading and forbidden usury} (Baqarah 2:275). All this taking place at the vicinity of the Holy Mosque in the Holy Land! Allah (SWT) stated in His Holy Book a unique promise (that had not been promised to any other sinner) to the Muslims who deals in usury: {O you who believe! Be careful of your duty to Allah and relinquish what remains (due) from usury, if you are believers. But if you do (it) not, then be appraised of WAR from Allah and His Apostle} (Baqarah 2:278–279). This is for the "Muslim" who deals in usury (believing that it is a sin), what is it then to the person who make himself a partner and equal to Allah, legalizing usury and other sins that have been forbidden by Allah. Despite of all of the above we see the government misled and dragged some of the righteous *ulama* and Da'ees away from the issue of objecting to the greatest of sins and Kufr. (We bemoan this and can only say: "No power and power acquiring except through Allah.")

Under such circumstances, to push the enemy—the greatest Kufr—out of the country is a prime duty. No other duty after Belief is more important than the duty of haddith. Utmost effort should be made to prepare and instigate the Umma against the enemy, the American-Israeli alliance, occupying the country of the two Holy Places and the route of the Apostle (Allah's Blessings and Salutations may be on him) to the Furthest Mosque (al-Aqsa Mosque); also to remind the Muslims not to be engaged in an internal war among themselves, as that will have grieve consequences namely:

1. consumption of the Muslims human resources as most casualties and fatalities will be among the Muslims people.
2. Exhaustion of the economic and financial resources.
3. Destruction of the country's infrastructures.
4. Dissociation of the society.
5. Destruction of the oil industries: The presence of the USA Crusader military forces on land, sea, and air of the states of the Islamic Gulf is the greatest danger threatening the largest oil reserve in the world. The existence of these forces in the area will provoke the people of the country and induces aggression on their religion, feelings, and prides and push them to take up armed struggle against the invaders occupying the land; therefore spread of the fighting in the region will expose the oil wealth to the danger of being burned up. The economic interests of the States of the Gulf and the land of the two Holy Places will be damaged and even a greater damage will be caused to the economy of the world. I would like here to alert my brothers, the Mujahideen, the sons of the nation, to protect this (oil) wealth and not to include it in the battle as it is a great Islamic wealth and a large economical power essential for the soon to be established Islamic state, by Allah's Permission and Grace. We also warn

the aggressors, the USA, against burning this Islamic wealth (a crime which they may commit in order to prevent it, at the end of the war, from falling in the hands of its legitimate owners and to cause economic damages to the competitors of the USA in Europe or the Far East, particularly Japan which is the major consumer of the oil of the region).

6. Division of the land of the two Holy Places, and annexing of the northerly part of it by Israel: Dividing the land of the two Holy Places is an essential demand of the Zionist-Crusader alliance. The existence of such a large country with its huge resources under the leadership of the forthcoming Islamic State, by Allah's Grace, represent a serious danger to the very existence of the Zionist state in Palestine. The Nobel Ka'ba—the Qiblah of all Muslims—makes the land of the two Holy Places a symbol for the unity of the Islamic world. Moreover, the presence of the world's largest oil reserve makes the land of the two Holy Places an important economical power in the Islamic world. The sons of the two Holy Places are directly related to the life style (Seerah) of their forefathers, the companions, may Allah be pleased with them. They consider the Seerah of their forefathers as a source and an example for re-establishing the greatness of this Ummah and to raise the word of Allah again. Furthermore, the presence of a population of fighters in the south of Yemen, fighting in the cause of Allah, is a strategic threat to the Zionist-Crusader alliance in the area. The Prophet (ALLAH'S BLESSING AND SALUTATIONS ON HIM) said: (around 12 thousand will emerge from Aden/Abian helping the cause of Allah and His messenger, they are the best, in the time, between me and them) narrated by Ahmad with a correct trustworthy reference.

7. An internal war is a great mistake, no matter what reasons are there for it. The presence of the occupier—the USA—forces will control the outcome of the battle for the benefit of the international Kufr.

I address now my brothers of the security and military forces and the national guards; may Allah preserve you hoard for Islam and the Muslims people:

O you protectors of unity and guardians of Faith; O you descendent of the ancestors who carried the light (torch) of guidance and spread it all over the world. O you grandsons of Sa'd Ibn Abi Waqqaas, Almothanna Ibn Haritha Ash-Shaybani, Alga'ga' Ibn Amroo Al-Tameemi, and those pious companions who fought Jihad alongside them; you competed to join the army and the guard forces with the intention to carry out Jihad in the cause of Allah—raising His word—and to defend the faith of Islam and the land of the two Holy Places against the invaders and the occupying forces. That is the ultimate level of believing in this religion "Deen." But the regime had reversed these principles and their understanding, humiliating the Ummah and disobeying Allah. Half a century ago the rulers promised the Ummah to regain the first Qiblah, but 50 years later new generation arrived and the promises have been changed; al-Aqsa Mosque handed over to the Zionists and the wounds of the Ummah still bleeding there. At the time when the Ummah has not regained the first Qiblah and the rout of the journey of the Prophet (Allah's Blessings and Salutations may be on him), and despite of all of the above, the Saudi regime had stunt the Ummah in the remaining sanctities, the Holy city of Mecca and the mosque of the Prophet (Al-Masjid An-Nabawy), by calling the Christians army to defend the regime. The crusaders were permitted to be in the land of the two Holy Places. Not surprisingly though, the King himself wore the cross on his chest. The country was widely opened from the north to the south and from east to the west for the crusaders. The land was filled with the military bases of the USA and the allies. The regime became unable to keep control without the help of these bases. You know more than any body else about the size, intention and the danger of the presence of the USA military bases in the area. The regime betrayed the Ummah and joined the Kufr, assisting and helping them against the Muslims. It is well known that this is one of the 10 "voiders" of Islam, deeds of de-Islamisation. By opening the Arab peninsula to the crusaders the regime disobeyed and acted against what has been enjoined by the messenger of Allah (Allah's Blessings and Salutations may be on him), while he was at the bed of his death: (Expel the polytheists out of the Arab Peninsula); (narrated by Al-Bukhari) and: (If I survive, Allah willing, I'll expel the Jews and the Christians out of the Arab Peninsula); saheeh Aljame' As-Sagheer.

It is out of date and no longer acceptable to claim that the presence of the crusaders is necessity and only a temporary measures to protect the land of the two Holy Places.

Especially when the civil and the military infrastructures of Iraq were savagely destroyed showing the depth of the Zionist-Crusaders' hatred to the Muslims and their children, and the rejection of the idea of replacing the crusaders' forces by an Islamic force composed of the sons of the country and other Muslim people. Moreover the foundations of the claim and the claim itself were demolished and wiped out by the sequence of speeches given by the leaders of the Kuffar in America. The latest of these speeches was the one given by William Perry, the Defense Secretary, after the explosion in Al-Khobar saying that the presence of the American solders there is to protect the interest of the USA. The imprisoned Sheikh Safar Al-Hawali, may Allah hasten his release, wrote a book of 70 pages; in it he presented evidence and proof that the presence of the Americans in the Arab Peninsula is a pre-planned military occupation. The regime wants to deceive the Muslim people in the same manner when the Palestinian fighters, Mujahideen, were deceived causing the loss of al-Aqsa Mosque. In 1304 A.H. (A.D. 1936) the awakened Muslim nation of Palestine started their great struggle, Jihad, against the British occupying forces. Britain was impotent to stop the Mujahideen and their Jihad, but their devil inspired that there is no way to stop the armed struggle in Palestine unless through their agent King Abdul Azeez, who managed to deceive the Mujahideen. King Abdul Azeez carried out his duty to his British masters. He sent his two sons to meet the Mujahideen leaders and to inform them that King Abdul Azeez would guarantee the promises made by the British government in leaving the area and responding positively to the demands of the Mujahideen if the latter stopped their Jihad. And so King Abdul Azeez caused the loss of the first Qiblah of the Muslims people. The King joined the crusaders against the Muslims and, instead of supporting the Mujahideen in the cause of Allah to liberate the al-Aqsa Mosque, he disappointed and humiliated them.

Today, his son, King Fahd, trying to deceive the Muslims for the second time so as to loose what is left of the sanctities. When the Islamic world resented the arrival of the crusader forces to the land of the two Holy Places, the king told lies to the *ulama* (who issued *fatwas* about the arrival of the Americans) and to the gathering of the Islamic leaders at the conference of Rabitah which was held in the Holy City of Mecca. The King said that "the issue is simple, the American and the alliance forces will leave the area in few months." Today it is seven years since their arrival and the regime is not able to move them out of the country. The regime made no confession about its inability and carried on lying to the people claiming that the American will leave. But never never again; a believer will not be bitten twice from the same hole or snake! Happy is the one who takes note of the sad experience of the others!!

Instead of motivating the army, the guards, and the security men to oppose the occupiers, the regime used these men to protect the invaders, further deepening the humiliation and the betrayal. (We bemoan this and can only say: "No power and power acquiring except through Allah.") To those little groups of men within the army, police, and security forces, who have been tricked and pressured by the regime to attack the Muslims and spill their blood, we would like to remind them of the narration: (I promise war against those who take my friends as their enemy) narrated by al-Bukhari. And his saying (Allah's Blessings and Salutations may be on him) saying of: (In the day of judgement a man comes holding another and complaining being slain by him. Allah, blessed be His Names, asks: Why did you slay him?! The accused replies: I did so that all exaltation may be Yours. Allah, blessed be His Names, says: All exaltation is indeed mine! Another man comes holding a fourth with a similar complaint. Allah, blessed be His Names, asks: Why did you kill him?! The accused replies: I did so that exaltation may be for Mr. X! Allah, blessed be His Names, says: exaltation is mine, not for Mr. X, carry all the slain man's sins (and proceed to the Hell fire)!). In another wording of An-Nasa'i: "The accused says: for strengthening the rule or kingdom of Mr. X."

Today your brothers and sons, the sons of the two Holy Places, have started their Jihad in the cause of Allah, to expel the occupying enemy from of the country of the two Holy Places. And there is no doubt you would like to carry out this mission too, in order to re-establish the greatness of this Ummah and to liberate its occupied sanctities. Nevertheless, it must be obvious to you that, due to the imbalance of power between our armed forces and the enemy forces, a suitable means of fighting must be adopted, i.e., using fast-moving light forces that work under complete secrecy. In other word to initiate a guerrilla warfare, were the sons of the nation, and not the military forces, take part in it. And as you know, it is wise, in the present circumstances, for the armed military forces not to be engaged in a conventional fighting with the forces of the crusader enemy (the exceptions are the bold and the forceful operations carried out by the members of the armed forces individually, that is, without the movement of the formal forces in its conventional shape and hence the responses will not be directed, strongly, against the army) unless a big advantage is likely to be achieved; and great losses induced on the enemy side (that would shaken and destroy its foundations and infrastructures) that will help to expel the defeated enemy from the country.

The Mujahideen, your brothers and sons, requesting that you support them in every possible way by supplying them with the necessary information, materials and arms. Security men are especially asked to cover up for the Mujahideen and to assist them as much as possible against the occupying enemy, and to spread rumours, fear and discouragement among the members of the enemy forces.

We bring to your attention that the regime, in order to create a friction and feud between the Mujahideen and yourselves, might resort to take a deliberate action against personnel of the security, guards and military forces and blame the Mujahideen for these actions. The regime should not be allowed to have such opportunity.

The regime is fully responsible for what had been incurred by the country and the nation; however the occupying American enemy is the principle and the main cause of the situation. Therefore efforts should be concentrated on destroying, fighting and killing the enemy until, by the Grace of Allah, it is completely defeated. The time will come—by the Permission of Allah—when you'll perform your decisive role so that the word of Allah will be supreme and the word of the infidels (Kaferoon) will be the inferior. You will hit with iron fist against the aggressors. You'll re-establish the normal course and give the people their rights and carry out your truly Islamic duty. Allah willing, I'll have a separate talk about these issues.

My Muslim Brothers (particularly those of the Arab Peninsula): The money you pay to buy American goods will be transformed into bullets and used against our brothers in Palestine and tomorrow (future) against our sons in the land of the two Holy Places. By buying these goods we are strengthening their economy while our dispossession and poverty increases.

Muslims Brothers of land of the two Holy Places:

It is incredible that our country is the world's largest buyer of arms from the USA and the area biggest commercial partners of the Americans who are assisting their Zionist brothers in occupying Palestine and in evicting and killing the Muslims there, by providing arms, men and financial supports.

To deny these occupiers the enormous revenues of their trading with our country is a very important help for our Jihad against them. To express our anger and hate to them is a very important moral gesture. By doing so we would have taken part in (the process of) cleansing our sanctities from the crusaders and the Zionists and forcing them, by the Permission of Allah, to leave disappointed and defeated.

We expect the woman of the land of the two Holy Places and other countries to carry out their role in boycotting the American goods.

If economical boycotting is intertwined with the military operations of the Mujahideen, then defeating the enemy will be even nearer, by the Permission of Allah. However if Muslims don't co-operate and support their Mujahideen brothers then, in effect, they are supplying the army of the enemy with financial help and extending the war and increasing the suffering of the Muslims.

The security and the intelligence services of the entire world cannot force a single citizen to buy the goods of his/her enemy. Economical boycotting of the American goods is a very effective weapon of hitting and weakening the enemy, and it is not under the control of the security forces of the regime.

Before closing my talk, I have a very important message to the youths of Islam, men of the brilliant future of the Ummah of Muhammad (ALLAH'S BLESSING AND SALUTATIONS ON HIM). Our talk with the youths about their duty in this difficult period in the history of our Ummah. A period in which the youths and no one else came forward to carry out the variable and different duties. While some of the well-known individuals had hesitated in their duty of defending Islam and saving themselves and their wealth from the injustice, aggression and terror—exercised by the government—the youths (may Allah protect them) were forthcoming and raised the banner of Jihad against the American-Zionist alliance occupying the sanctities of Islam. Others who have been tricked into loving this materialistic world, and those who have been terrorized by the government choose to give legitimacy to the greatest betrayal, the occupation of the land of the two Holy Places. (We bemoan this and can only say: "No power and power acquiring except through Allah.") We are not surprised from the action of our youths. The youths were the companions of Muhammad (Allah's Blessings and Salutations may be on him), and was it not the youths themselves who killed Aba-Jahl, the Pharaoh of this Ummah? Our youths are the best descendent of the best ancestors.

Abdul-Rahman Ibn Awf—may Allah be pleased with him—said: (I was at Badr where I noticed two youths, one to my right and the other to my left. One of them asked me quietly (so not to be heard by the other): O uncle point out Aba-Jahl to me. What do you want him for? said Abdul Rahman. The boy answered: I have been informed that he—Aba-Jahl—abused the Messenger of Allah, I swear by Allah, who have my soul in His hand, that if I see Aba-Jahl I'll not let my shadow depart his shadow till one of us is dead. I was astonished, said Abdul Rahman; then the other youth said the same thing as the first one. Subsequently I saw Aba-Jahl among the people; I said to the boys do you see? This is the man you are asking me about. The two youths hit Aba-Jahl with their swords till he was dead. Allah is the greatest, Praise be to Him: Two youths of young age but with great perseverance, enthusiasm, courage and pride for the religion of Allah, each one of them asking about the most important act of killing that should be induced on the enemy. That is the killing of the pharaoh of this Ummah—Aba-Jahl—the leader of the unbelievers (Mushrikeen) at the battle of Badr.

The role of Abdul Rahman Ibn Awf, may Allah be pleased with him, was to direct the two youths toward Aba-Jahl. That was the perseverance and the enthusiasm of the youths of that time and that was the perseverance and the enthusiasm of their fathers. It is this role that is now required from the people who have the expertise and knowledge in fighting the enemy. They should guide their brothers and sons in this matter; once that has been done, then our youths will repeat what their forefathers had said before: "I swear by Allah if I see him I'll not let my shadow to departs from his shadow till one of us is dead."

And the story of Abdur-Rahman Ibn Awf about Ummayyah Ibn Khalaf shows the extent of Bilal's (may Allah be pleased with him) persistence in killing the head of the Kufr: "The head of Kufr is Ummayyah Ibn Khalaf. . . . I shall live not if he survives" said Bilal.

Few days ago the news agencies had reported that the Defense Secretary of the Crusading Americans had said that "the explosion at Riyadh and Al-Khobar had taught him one lesson: that is not to withdraw when attacked by coward terrorists."

We say to the Defense Secretary that his talk can induce a grieving mother to laughter and shows the fears that had enshrined you all. Where was this false courage of yours when the explosion in Beirut took place on A.D. 1983 (1403 A.H.). You were turned into scattered pits and pieces at that time; 241 mainly marines were killed. And where was this courage of yours when two explosions made you to leave Aden in less than 24 hours!

But your most disgraceful case was in Somalia; where—after vigorous propaganda about the power of the USA and its post–cold war leadership of the new world order—you moved tens of thousands of international forces, including 28 thousand American soldiers into Somalia. However, when tens of your soldiers were killed in minor battles and one American pilot was dragged in the streets of Mogadishu you left the area carrying disappointment, humiliation, defeat and your dead with you. Clinton appeared in front of the whole world threatening and promising revenge, but these threats were merely a preparation for withdrawal. You have been disgraced by Allah and you withdrew; the extent of your impotence and weaknesses became very clear. It was a pleasure for the "heart" of every Muslim and a remedy to the "chests" of believing nations to see you defeated in the three Islamic cities of Beirut, Aden and Mogadishu.

I say to Secretary of Defense: The sons of the land of the two Holy Places had come out to fight against the Russian in Afghanistan, the Serb in Bosnia-Herzegovina and today they are fighting in Chechnya and—by the Permission of Allah—they have been made victorious over your partner, the Russians. By the command of Allah, they are also fighting in Tajakistan.

I say: Since the sons of the land of the two Holy Places feel and strongly believe that fighting (Jihad) against the Kuffar in every part of the world is absolutely essential; then they would be even more enthusiastic, more powerful and larger in number upon fighting on their own land—the place of their births—defending the greatest of their sanctities, the noble Ka'ba (the Qiblah of all Muslims). They know that the Muslims of the world will assist and help them to victory. To liberate their sanctities is the greatest of issues concerning all Muslims; it is the duty of every Muslims in this world.

I say to you William (Defense Secretary) that these youths love death as you love life. They inherit dignity, pride, courage, generosity, truthfulness and sacrifice from father to father. They are most delivering and steadfast at war. They inherit these values from their ancestors (even from the time of the Jaheliyyah, before Islam). These values were approved and completed by the arriving Islam as stated by the messenger of Allah (Allah's Blessings and Salutations may be on him): "I have been send to perfecting the good values" (Saheeh Al-Jame' As-Sagheer).

When the pagan King Amroo Ibn Hind tried to humiliate the pagan Amroo Ibn Kulthoom, the latter cut the head of the King with his sword rejecting aggression, humiliation and indignation.

If the king oppresses the people excessively, we reject submitting to humiliation.

By which legitimacy (or command) O Amroo bin Hind you want us to be degraded?!

By which legitimacy (or command) O Amroo bin Hind you listen to our foes and disrespect us?!

Our toughness has, O Amroo, tired the enemies before you, never giving in!

Our youths believe in paradise after death. They believe that taking part in fighting will not bring their day nearer; and staying behind will not postpone their day either. Exalted be to Allah who said: {And a soul will not die but with the permission of Allah, the term is fixed} (Aal Imraan 3:145). Our youths believe in the saying of the messenger of Allah (Allah's Blessings and Salutations may be on him): "O boy, I teach a few words; guard (guard the cause of, keep the commandments of) Allah, then He guards you, guard (the cause of) Allah, then He will be with you; if you ask (for your need) ask Allah, if you seek assistance, seek Allah's; and know definitely that if the Whole World gathered to (bestow) profit on you they will not profit you ex-

cept with what was determined for you by Allah, and if they gathered to
harm you they will not harm you except with what has been determined for
you by Allah; Pen lifted, papers dried, it is fixed nothing in these truths can
be changed" Saheeh Al-Jame' As-Sagheer. Our youths took note of the meaning of the poetic verse:

"If death is a predetermined must, then it is a shame to die cowardly."

and the other poet saying:

*"Who do not die by the sword will die by other reason; many causes are
there but one death."*

These youths believe in what has been told by Allah and His messenger
(Allah's Blessings and Salutations may be on him) about the greatness of the
reward for the Mujahideen and Martyrs; Allah, the most exalted said: {and—
so far—those who are slain in the way of Allah, He will by no means allow
their deeds to perish. He will guide them and improve their condition and
cause them to enter the garden—paradise—which He has made known to
them}. (Muhammad 47:4–6). Allah the Exalted also said: {and do not speak
of those who are slain in Allah's way as dead; nay they are alive, but you do
not perceive} (Bagarah 2:154). His messenger (Allah's Blessings and Salutations may be on him) said, "For those who strive in His cause Allah prepared
hundred degrees (levels) in paradise; in-between two degrees as the in-
between heaven and earth" Saheeh Al-Jame' As-Sagheer. He (Allah's Blessings and Salutations may be on him) also said, "The best of the martyrs are
those who do NOT turn their faces away from the battle till they are killed.
They are in the high level of Jannah (paradise). Their Lord laughs to them
(in pleasure) and when your Lord laughs to a slave of His, He will not hold
him to an account" narrated by Ahmad with correct and trustworthy reference. And: "A martyr will not feel the pain of death except like how you feel
when you are pinched" Saheeh Al-Jame' As-Sagheer. He also said, "A martyr's privileges are guaranteed by Allah; forgiveness with the first gush of his
blood, he will be shown his seat in paradise, he will be decorated with the
jewels of belief (Imaan), married off to the beautiful ones, protected from the
test in the grave, assured security in the day of judgement, crowned with the
crown of dignity, a ruby of which is better than this whole world (Duniah)
and its entire content, wedded to 72 of the pure Houries (beautiful ones of
Paradise) and his intercession on the behalf of 70 of his relatives will be accepted" narrated by Ahmad and At-Tirmithi (with the correct and trustworthy reference).

Those youths know that their rewards in fighting you, the USA, is double
their rewards in fighting someone else not from the people of the book. They
have no intention except to enter paradise by killing you. An infidel, and

enemy of God like you, cannot be in the same hell with his righteous executioner.

Our youths chanting and reciting the word of Allah, the most exalted: {fight them; Allah will punish them by your hands and bring them to disgrace, and assist you against them and heal the heart of a believing people} (At-Taubah 9:14) and the words of the Prophet (ALLAH'S BLESSING AND SALUTATIONS ON HIM): "I swear by Him, who has my soul in His hand, that no man get killed fighting them today, patiently attacking and not retreating, surely Allah will let him into paradise." And His (Allah's Blessings and Salutations may be on him) saying to them: "Get up to a paradise as wide as heaven and earth."

The youths also reciting the All Mighty words of: "so when you meet in battle those who disbelieve, then smite the necks . . ." (Muhammad 47:19). Those youths will not ask you (William Perry) for explanations, they will tell you singing there is nothing between us need to be explained, there is only killing and neck-smiting.

And they will say to you what their grandfather, Haroon Ar-Rasheed, Ameer-ul-Mu'meneen, replied to your grandfather, Nagfoor, the Byzantine emperor, when he threatened the Muslims: "From Haroon Ar-Rasheed, Ameer-ul-Mu'meneen, to Nagfoor, the dog of the Romans; the answer is what you will see not what you hear." Haroon El-Rasheed led the armies of Islam to the battle and handed Nagfoor a devastating defeat.

The youths you called cowards are competing among themselves for fighting and killing you. reciting what one of them said:

The crusader army became dust when we detonated al-Khobar.
With courageous youth of Islam fearing no danger.
If (they are) threatened: The tyrants will kill you, they reply my death is a victory.
I did not betray that king, he did betray our Qiblah.
And he permitted in the holy country the most filthy sort of humans.
I have made an oath by Allah, the Great, to fight who ever rejected the faith.

For more than a decade, they carried arms on their shoulders in Afghanistan and they have made vows to Allah that as long as they are alive, they will continue to carry arms against you until you are—Allah willing—expelled, defeated and humiliated, they will carry on as long as they live saying:

O William, tomorrow you will know which young man is confronting your misguided brethren!
A youth fighting in smile, returning with the spear colored red.
May Allah keep me close to knights, humans in peace, demons in war.

Lions in Jungle but their teeth are spears and Indian swords.
The horses witness that I push them hard forwarded in the fire of battle.
The dust of the battle bears witnesses for me, so also the fighting itself, the
pens and the books!

So to abuse the grandsons of the companions, may Allah be pleased with them, by calling them cowards and challenging them by refusing to leave the land of the two Holy Places shows the insanity and the imbalance you are suffering from. Its appropriate "remedy," however, is in the hands of the youths of Islam, as the poet said:

I am willing to sacrifice self and wealth for knights who never disappointed
me.
Knights who are never fed up or deterred by death, even if the mill of war
turns.
In the heat of battle they do not care, and cure the insanity of the enemy
by their "insane" courage.

Terrorizing you, while you are carrying arms on our land, is a legitimate and morally demanded duty. It is a legitimate right well-known to all humans and other creatures. Your example and our example is like a snake which entered into a house of a man and got killed by him. The coward is the one who lets you walk, while carrying arms, freely on his land and provides you with peace and security.

Those youths are different from your soldiers. Your problem will be how to convince your troops to fight, while our problem will be how to restrain our youths to wait for their turn in fighting and in operations. These youths are commendation and praiseworthy.

They stood up tall to defend the religion; at the time when the government misled the prominent scholars and tricked them into issuing *fatwas* (that have no basis neither in the book of Allah, nor in the Sunnah of His prophet (Allah's Blessings and Salutations may be on him)) of opening the land of the two Holy Places for the Christian armies and handing the al-Aqsa Mosque to the Zionists. Twisting the meanings of the holy text will not change this fact at all. They deserve the praise of the poet:

I rejected all the critics, who chose the wrong way;
I rejected those who enjoy fireplaces in clubs discussing eternally;
I rejected those, who inspite being lost, think they are at the goal;
I respect those who carried on not asking or bothering about the difficulties;
Never letting up from their goals, in spite all hardships of the road;
Whose blood is the oil for the flame guiding in the darkness of confusion;
I feel still the pain of (the loss) al-Quds in my internal organs;

That loss is like a burning fire in my intestines;
I did not betray my covenant with God, when even states did betray it! As
their grandfather Assim Bin Thabit said rejecting a surrender offer of the
pagans:
What for an excuse I had to surrender, while I am still able, having arrows
and my bow having a tough string?!
Death is truth and ultimate destiny, and life will end any way. If I do not
fight you, then my mother must be insane!

The youths hold you responsible for all of the killings and evictions of the
Muslims and the violation of the sanctities, carried out by your Zionist brothers in Lebanon; you openly supplied them with arms and finance. More than
600,000 Iraqi children have died due to lack of food and medicine and as a
result of the unjustifiable aggression (sanction) imposed on Iraq and its nation. The children of Iraq are our children. You, the USA, together with the
Saudi regime, are responsible for the shedding of the blood of these innocent
children. Due to all of that, whatever treaty you have with our country is
now null and void.

The treaty of Hudaybiyyah was cancelled by the messenger of Allah
(Allah's Blessings and Salutations may be on him) once Quraysh had assisted
Bani Bakr against Khusa'ah, the allies of the Prophet (Allah's Blessings and
Salutations may be on him). The prophet (Allah's Blessings and Salutations
may be on him) fought Quraysh and concurred Makka. He (Allah's Blessings
and Salutations may be on him) considered the treaty with Bani Qainuqa'
void because one of their Jews publicly hurt one Muslim woman, one single
woman, at the market. Let alone then, the killing you caused to hundred of
thousands Muslims and occupying their sanctities. It is now clear that those
who claim that the blood of the American soldiers (the enemy occupying the
land of the Muslims) should be protected are merely repeating what is imposed on them by the regime; fearing the aggression and interested in saving
themselves. It is a duty now on every tribe in the Arab Peninsula to fight,
Jihad, in the cause of Allah and to cleanse the land from those occupiers.
Allah knows that their blood is permitted (to be spilled) and their wealth is
a booty; their wealth is a booty to those who kill them. The most Exalted
said in the verse of As-Sayef, The Sword: "So when the sacred months have
passed away, then slay the idolaters where ever you find them, and take them
captives and besiege them and lie in wait for them in every ambush" (At-
Tauba 9:5). Our youths knew that the humiliation suffered by the Muslims
as a result of the occupation of their sanctities can not be kicked and removed
except by explosions and Jihad. As the poet said:

The walls of oppression and humiliation cannot be demolished except in a
rain of bullets.
The freeman does not surrender leadership to infidels and sinners.

Without shedding blood no degradation and branding can be removed from the forehead.

I remind the youths of the Islamic world, who fought in Afghanistan and Bosnia-Herzegovina with their wealth, pens, tongues and themselves that the battle had not finished yet. I remind them about the talk between Jibreel (Gabriel) and the messenger of Allah (Allah's Blessings and Salutations may be on both of them) after the battle of Ahzab when the messenger of Allah (Allah's Blessings and Salutations may be on him) returned to Medina and before putting his sword aside; when Jibreel (Allah's Blessings and Salutations may be on him) descended saying: "Are you putting your sword aside? By Allah the angels haven't dropped their arms yet; march with your companions to Bani Quraydah, I am (going) ahead of you to throw fears in their hearts and to shake their fortresses on them." Jibreel marched with the angels (Allah's Blessings and Salutations may be on them all), followed by the messenger of Allah (Allah's Blessings and Salutations may be on him) marching with the immigrants, Muhajeroon, and supporters, Ansar (narrated by Al-Bukhary).

These youths know that if one is not to be killed one will die (anyway) and the most honorable death is to be killed in the way of Allah. They are even more determined after the martyrdom of the four heroes who bombed the Americans in Riyadh. Those youths who raised high the head of the Ummah and humiliated the Americans—the occupier—by their operation in Riyadh. They remember the poetry of Ja'far, the second commander in the battle of Mu'tah, in which 3,000 Muslims faced over 100,000 Romans:

How good is the Paradise and its nearness, good with cool drink But the Romans are promised punishment (in Hell), if I meet them.
I will fight them.

And the poetry of Abdullah Bin Rawaha, the third commander in the battle of Mu'tah, after the martyrdom of Ja'far, when he felt some hesitation:

O my soul if you do not get killed, you are going to die, anyway.
This is death pool in front of you!
You are getting what you have wished for (martyrdom) before, and you follow the example of the two previous commanders you are rightly guided!

As for our daughters, wives, sisters and mothers they should take prime example from the prophet (Allah's Blessings and Salutations may be on him) pious female companions, may Allah be pleased with them; they should adopt the life style (Seerah) of the female companions of courage, sacrifice and generosity in the cause of the supremacy of Allah's religion.

They should remember the courage and the personality of Fatima, daughter of Khatab, when she accepted Islam and stood up in front of her brother, Omar Ibn Al-Khatab and challenged him (before he became a Muslim) saying: "O Omar, what will you do if the truth is not in your religion?!" And to remember the stand of Asma', daughter of Abu Bakr, on the day of Hijra, when she attended the Messenger and his companion in the cave and split her belt in two pieces for them. And to remember the stand of Naseeba Bent Ka'b striving to defend the messenger of Allah (Allah's Blessings and Salutations may be on him) on the day of Uhud, in which she suffered 12 injuries, one of which was so deep leaving a deep lifelong scar! They should remember the generosity of the early woman of Islam who raised finance for the Muslims army by selling their jewelery.

Our women had set a tremendous example of generosity in the cause of Allah; they motivated and encouraged their sons, brothers and husbands to fight—in the cause of Allah—in Afghanistan, Bosnia-Herzegovina, Chechnya and in other countries. We ask Allah to accept from them these deeds, and may He help their fathers, brothers, husbands and sons. May Allah strengthen the belief—Imaan—of our women in the way of generosity and sacrifice for the supremacy of the word of Allah. Our women weep not, except over men who fight in the cause of Allah; our women instigate their brothers to fight in the cause of Allah.

Our women bemoan only fighters in the cause of Allah, as said:

Do not moan on any one except a lion in the woods, courageous in the burning wars. Let me die dignified in wars, honorable death is better than my current life.

Our women encourage Jihad saying:

Prepare yourself like a struggler, the matter is bigger than words!

Are you going to leave us else for the wolves of Kufr eating our wings?!

The wolves of Kufr are mobilising all evil persons from everywhere!

Where are the freemen defending free women by the arms?!

Death is better than life in humiliation! Some scandals and shames will never be otherwise eradicated.

My Muslim Brothers of The World:

Your brothers in Palestine and in the land of the two Holy Places are calling upon your help and asking you to take part in fighting against the enemy—your enemy and their enemy—the Americans and the Israelis. They are asking you to do whatever you can, with one's own means and ability, to expel the enemy, humiliated and defeated, out of the sanctities of Islam. Exalted be to Allah said in His book: {and if they ask your support, because they are oppressed in their faith, then support them} (Anfaal 8:72)!

O you horses (soldiers) of Allah ride and march on. This is the time of hardship so be tough. And know that your gathering and co-operation in order to liberate the sanctities of Islam is the right step toward unifying the word of the Ummah under the banner of "No God but Allah.")

From our place we raise our palms humbly to Allah asking Him to bestow on us His guide in every aspects of this issue.

Our Lord, we ask you to secure the release of the truthful scholars, *ulama*, of Islam and pious youths of the Ummah from their imprisonment. O Allah, strengthen them and help their families.

Our Lord, the people of the cross had come with their horses (soldiers) and occupied the land of the two Holy Places. And the Zionist Jews fiddling as they wish with the al-Aqsa Mosque, the route of the ascendance of the messenger of Allah (ALLAH'S BLESSING AND SALUTATIONS ON HIM). Our Lord, shatter their gathering, divide them among themselves, shake the earth under their feet and give us control over them; Our Lord, we take refuge in you from their deeds and take you as a shield between us and them

Our Lord, show us a black day in them!

Our Lord, show us the wonderment of your ability in them!

Our Lord, You are the Revealer of the book, Director of the clouds, You defeated the allies (Ahzab); defeat them and make us victorious over them.

Our Lord, You are the one who help us and You are the one who assist us, with Your Power we move and by Your Power we fight. On You we rely and You are our cause.

Our Lord, those youths got together to make Your religion victorious and raise Your banner. Our Lord, send them Your help and strengthen their hearts.

Our Lord, make the youths of Islam steadfast and descend patience on them and guide their shots!

Our Lord, unify the Muslims and bestow love among their hearts!

O Lord pour down upon us patience, and make our steps firm and assist us against the unbelieving people!

Our Lord, do not lay on us a burden as Thou didst lay on those before us; Our Lord, do not impose upon us that which we have no strength to bear; and pardon us and grant us protection and have mercy on us; Thou art our patron, so help us against the unbelieving people.

Our Lord, guide this Ummah, and make the right conditions (by which) the people of your obedience will be in dignity and the people of disobedience in humiliation, and by which the good deeds are enjoined and the bad deeds are forebode.

Our Lord, bless Muhammad, Your slave and messenger, his family and descendants, and companions and salute him with a (becoming) salutation.

And our last supplication is: All praise is due to Allah.

(2). 1998 Declaration of War

The following statement from Usama bin Laden and his associates purports to be a religious ruling (fatwa) requiring the killing of Americans, both civilian and military. This document is part of the evidence that links the bin Laden network to the September 11 terrorist attacks on New York and Washington.

Jihad Against Jews and Crusaders
World Islamic Front Statement

23 February 1998

(Signatories)

Shaykh Usamah Bin-Muhammad Bin-Ladin

Ayman al-Zawahiri, amir of the Jihad Group in Egypt

Abu-Yasir Rifa'i Ahmad Taha, Egyptian Islamic Group

Shaykh Mir Hamzah, secretary of the Jamiat-ul-Ulema-e-Pakistan

Fazlur Rahman, amir of the Jihad Movement in Bangladesh

Praise be to Allah, who revealed the Book, controls the clouds, defeats factionalism, and says in His Book: "But when the forbidden months are past, then fight and slay the pagans wherever ye find them, seize them, beleaguer them, and lie in wait for them in every stratagem (of war)"; and peace be upon our Prophet, Muhammad Bin-'Abdallah, who said: I have been sent with the sword between my hands to ensure that no one but Allah is worshipped, Allah who put my livelihood under the shadow of my spear and who inflicts humiliation and scorn on those who disobey my orders.

The Arabian Peninsula has never—since Allah made it flat, created its desert, and encircled it with seas—been stormed by any forces like the crusader armies spreading in it like locusts, eating its riches and wiping out its plantations. All this is happening at a time in which nations are attacking Muslims like people fighting over a plate of food. In the light of the grave situation and the lack of support, we and you are obliged to discuss current events, and we should all agree on how to settle the matter.

No one argues today about three facts that are known to everyone; we will list them, in order to remind everyone:

First, for over seven years the United States has been occupying the lands of Islam in the holiest of places, the Arabian Peninsula, plundering its riches, dictating to its rulers, humiliating its people, terrorizing its neighbors, and turning its bases in the Peninsula into a spearhead through which to fight the neighboring Muslim peoples.

If some people have in the past argued about the fact of the occupation, all the people of the Peninsula have now acknowledged it. The best proof of this is the Americans' continuing aggression against the Iraqi people using the Peninsula as a staging post, even though all its rulers are against their territories being used to that end, but they are helpless.

Second, despite the great devastation inflicted on the Iraqi people by the crusader-Zionist alliance, and despite the huge number of those killed, which has exceeded 1 million . . . despite all this, the Americans are once against trying to repeat the horrific massacres, as though they are not content with the protracted blockade imposed after the ferocious war or the fragmentation and devastation.

So here they come to annihilate what is left of this people and to humiliate their Muslim neighbors.

Third, if the Americans' aims behind these wars are religious and economic, the aim is also to serve the Jews' petty state and divert attention from its occupation of Jerusalem and murder of Muslims there. The best proof of this is their eagerness to destroy Iraq, the strongest neighboring Arab state, and their endeavor to fragment all the states of the region such as Iraq, Saudi Arabia, Egypt, and Sudan into paper statelets and through their disunion and weakness to guarantee Israel's survival and the continuation of the brutal crusade occupation of the Peninsula.

All these crimes and sins committed by the Americans are a clear declaration of war on Allah, his messenger, and Muslims. And *ulama* have throughout Islamic history unanimously agreed that the jihad is an individual duty if the enemy destroys the Muslim countries. This was revealed by Imam Bin-Qadamah in "Al- Mughni," Imam al-Kisa'i in "Al-Bada'i," al-Qurtubi in his interpretation, and the shaykh of al-Islam in his books, where he said: "As for the fighting to repulse [an enemy], it is aimed at defending sanctity and religion, and it is a duty as agreed [by the *ulama*]. Nothing is more sacred than belief except repulsing an enemy who is attacking religion and life."

On that basis, and in compliance with Allah's order, we issue the following *fatwa* to all Muslims:

The ruling to kill the Americans and their allies—civilians and military— is an individual duty for every Muslim who can do it in any country in which it is possible to do it, in order to liberate the al-Aqsa Mosque and the holy mosque [Mecca] from their grip, and in order for their armies to move out of all the lands of Islam, defeated and unable to threaten any Muslim. This is in accordance with the words of Almighty Allah, "and fight the pagans all together as they fight you all together," and "fight them until there is no more tumult or oppression, and there prevail justice and faith in Allah."

This is in addition to the words of Almighty Allah: "And why should ye not fight in the cause of Allah and of those who, being weak, are ill-treated (and oppressed)?—women and children, whose cry is: 'Our Lord, rescue us from this town, whose people are oppressors; and raise for us from thee one who will help!' "

We—with Allah's help—call on every Muslim who believes in Allah and wishes to be rewarded to comply with Allah's order to kill the Americans and plunder their money wherever and whenever they find it. We also call on Muslim *ulama*, leaders, youths, and soldiers to launch the raid on Satan's U.S. troops and the devil's supporters allying with them, and to displace those who are behind them so that they may learn a lesson.

Almighty Allah said: "O ye who believe, give your response to Allah and His Apostle, when He calleth you to that which will give you life. And know that Allah cometh between a man and his heart, and that it is He to whom ye shall all be gathered."

Almighty Allah also says: "O ye who believe, what is the matter with you, that when ye are asked to go forth in the cause of Allah, ye cling so heavily to the earth! Do ye prefer the life of this world to the hereafter? But little is the comfort of this life, as compared with the hereafter. Unless ye go forth, He will punish you with a grievous penalty, and put others in your place; but Him ye would not harm in the least. For Allah hath power over all things."

Almighty Allah also says: "So lose no heart, nor fall into despair. For ye must gain mastery if ye are true in faith."

Notes

Editor's Note

1. Mark Juergensmeyer, *Terror in the Mind of God: The Global Rise of Religious Violence* (Berkeley, CA: University of California Press, 2000).

2. For more on definitions of terrorism, see Raphael Perl, "Terrorism and National Security: Issues and Trends," CRS Issue Brief for Congress, 21 December 2004 (Washington, DC: Congressional Research Service, Library of Congress).

3. See Jerrold Post, "Terrorist Psycho-logic: Terrorist Behavior as a Product of Psychological Forces," in *Origins of Terrorism: Psychologies, Ideologies, Theologies, States of Mind*, edited by Walter Reich (Baltimore, MD: Woodrow Wilson Center Press, 1998); also, for a discussion of moral disengagement, see Albert Bandura, "Mechanisms of Moral Disengagement," in *Origins of Terrorism: Psychologies, Ideologies, Theologies, States of Mind*, edited by Walter Reich (Baltimore, MD: Woodrow Wilson Center Press, 1998).

Preface

1. For more on this global problem, please see Peter W. Singer, *Children At War* (New York: Pantheon, 2005).

2. Jamie Tarabay, "Islamic Militants Gain Influence through Philanthropic Work," Associated Press, 2 March 2001.

3. "Waco, Oklahoma City Mark Anniversary of Tragedies," CNN, 19 April 1998, online at http://edition.cnn.com/US/9804/19/okc.waco.

4. Please see the chapter by J. P. Larsson in this volume.

5. Please see the chapter by Rohan Gunaratna and Arabinda Acharya in Volume 2 of this publication.

Chapter 1: Exploring the Recruitment of Terrorists

1. Dana R. Dillon, "Southeast Asia and the Brotherhood of Terrorism," Heritage Lecture No. 860 (Washington, DC: Heritage Foundation, 19 November 2004).

2. Michael Taarnby, "Recruitment of Islamist Terrorists in Europe: Trends and Perspectives," Research Report funded by the Danish Ministry of Justice, 14 January 2005, p. 5.

3. Ibid.

4. Karen Armstrong, *The Battle for God* (New York: Alfred A. Knopf, 2000).

5. For example, see John L. Esposito, "Overview: The Significance of Religion for Global Order," in *Religion and Global Order*, edited by John L. Esposito and Michael Watson (Cardiff: University of Wales Press, 2000), pp. 17–37; and John L. Esposito, *Unholy War: Terror in the Name of Islam* (New York: Oxford University Press, 2002).

6. Daniel Benjamin and Steven Simon, *The Age of Sacred Terror* (New York: Random House, 2002).

7. Ibid.

8. Mark Juergensmeyer, *Terror in the Mind of God: The Global Rise of Religious Violence* (Berkeley: University of California Press, 2000). In particular, see pages 19–36 and 60–83.

9. See David C. Rapoport, "Fear and Trembling: Terrorism in Three Religious Traditions," *American Political Science Review* 78, no. 3 (September 1984): 658–77; and David C. Rapoport, "Sacred Terror: A Contemporary Example from Islam," in *Origins of Terrorism: Psychologies, Ideologies, Theologies, States of Mind*, edited by Walter Reich (Baltimore, MD: Woodrow Wilson Center Press, 1998), pp. 103–30.

10. See Donatella della Porta, *Social Movements, Political Violence and the State: A Comparative Analysis of Italy and Germany* (Cambridge University Press, 1995); and Konrad Kellen, "Ideology and Rebellion: Terrorism in Western Germany," in *Origins of Terrorism: Psychologies, Ideologies, Theologies, States of Mind*, edited by Walter Reich (Baltimore, MD: Woodrow Wilson Center Press, 1998), pp. 43–58.

11. For example, see Peter Heehs, *The Bomb in Bengal: The Rise of Revolutionary Terrorism in India, 1900–1910* (New York: Oxford University Press, 1996); and Rohan Gunaratna, *Sri Lanka's Ethnic Crisis and National Security* (Colombo: South Asian Network on Conflict Research, 1998).

12. John Darby, "The Historical Background," in *Northern Ireland: The Background to the Conflict* (Belfast, Northern Ireland: Appletree Press, 1983), pp. 13–31; Marianne Elliott, "A Resentful Belonging: Catholic Identity in the Twentieth Century," in *The Catholics of Ulster: A History* (New York: Basic Books, 2002), pp. 431–82; and J. Bowyer Bell, *The IRA, 1968–2000: Analysis of a Secret Army* (London: Frank Cass, 2000).

13. See Robert J. Lifton, *Thought Reform and the Psychology of Totalism: A Study of "Brainwashing" in China* (Chapel Hill: University of North Carolina Uni-

versity Press, 1989); and Robert J. Lifton, *The Future of Immortality and Other Essays for a Nuclear Age* (New York: Basic Books, 1987).

14. Ibid.

15. Jerrold M. Post, "Terrorist Psycho-logic: Terrorist Behavior as a Product of Psychological Forces," in *Origins of Terrorism: Psychologies, Ideologies, Theologies, States of Mind*, edited by Walter Reich (Baltimore, MD: Woodrow Wilson Center Press, 1998), pp. 25–40. Also see Jerrold Post's chapter in Volume 2 of this publication.

16. Albert Bandura, "Mechanisms of Moral Disengagement," in *Origins of Terrorism: Psychologies, Ideologies, Theologies, States of Mind*, edited by Walter Reich (Cambridge: Cambridge University Press, 1990), pp. 161–91. Also see the chapter by Albert Bandura in Volume 2 of this publication.

17. Anthony Stahelski, "Terrorists are Made, not Born: Creating Terrorists Using Social Psychological Conditioning," *Journal of Homeland Security* (March 2004), online at http://www.homelandsecurity.org/journal/Articles/stahelski.html.

18. Martha Crenshaw, "The Logic of Terrorism: Terrorist Behavior as a Product of Strategic Choice," in *Origins of Terrorism: Psychologies, Ideologies, Theologies, States of Mind*, edited by Walter Reich (Baltimore, MD: Woodrow Wilson Center Press, 1998), pp. 7–24.

19. Marc Sageman, *Understanding Terror Networks* (Philadelphia: University of Pennsylvania Press, 2004), p. 178.

20. AIVD, "Recruitment for the Jihad in the Netherlands: From Incident to Trend" (The Hague: Buro van Bergenhenogouwen, December 2000), available online at http://www.aivd.nl, p. 5.

21. Michael Taarnby, "Recruitment," p. 5.

22. Marc Sageman, *Understanding Terror Networks*.

23. See "Controversial Cleric of UK Mosque," CNN, 1 April 2003, online at http://www.cnn.com/2003/WORLD/europe/01/20/uk.hamzaprofile.

24. For the ongoing news reports on this story, see http://www.arabnews.com, http://www.bbc.com, and http://abu-hamza-news.newslib.com.

25. See "Abu Hamza: Controversial Muslim Figure," CNN, 27 May 2004, http://www.cnn.com/2004/WORLD/europe/05/27/uk.hamza.profile.

26. Peter Finn, "Hamburg's Cauldron of Terror," *Washington Post*, 11 September 2002, p. A1. Also see *The 9/11 Commission Report* (New York: W. W. Norton, 2004).

27. Founded by Mohammed ibn Abd Wahhab in the 1740s, Wahhabism seeks to purge what are viewed as corrupting influences in Islam and return it to original orthodoxy. Non-Wahhabis are considered infidels, and failure to adhere to the faith's tenets draws severe punishment.

28. See, for example, Peter W. Singer, "Pakistan's Madrassahs: Ensuring a System of Education, not Jihad," Brookings Institution Analysis Paper #14 (Washington, DC: Brookings Institution, November 2001).

29. See Zachary Abuza, *Militant Islam in Southeast Asia: Crucible of Terror* (Boulder, CO: Lynne Rienner, 2003); see also International Crisis Group (ICG), *Al-*

Qaeda in Southeast Asia: The Case of the Ngruki Network (Brussels, 8 August 2002), p. 7.

30. Peter W. Singer, "Pakistan's Madrassahs," 2001.

31. Mary Anne Weaver, "A Land of Madrassahs," *APF Report* 20 (Washington, DC: Alicia Patterson Foundation, 2002), available online at www.aliciapatterson. org/APF2002/Weaver.

32. See the testimony of Mr. John Pistole, Assistant Director of Counterterrorism, Federal Bureau of Investigation. Terrorist Recruitment and Infiltration in the United States: Prisons and Military as an Operational Base, *United States Senate Committee on the Judiciary*, 14 October 2003; Kevin Flynn and Gary Gerhardt, *The Silent Brotherhood: Inside America's Racist Underground* (New York: Free Press, 1989); Anti-Defamation League, 2002, *Dangerous Convictions: An Introduction to Extremist Activities in Prison,* available online at http://www.adl.org/ learn/Ext_Terr/dangerous_convictions.pdf.

33. See U.S. Department of Justice, "A Review of the Bureau of Prisons' Selection of Muslim Religious Services Providers" (April 2004), http://www.usdoj. gov/oig/special/0404.

34. Ian M. Cuthbertson, "Prisons and the Education of Terrorists," *World Policy Journal* 21, no. 3 (Fall 2004): 15–22.

35. Ibid., p. 19.

36. Thomas M. Sanderson, "Transnational Terror and Organized Crime: Blurring the Lines," *SAIS Review* 24, no. 1 (Winter 2004): 56.

37. Ibid.

Chapter 2: Innovative Recruitment and Indoctrination Tactics

1. www.geocities.com/wu_renegade1948/downloads.html (last accessed 13 November 2004).

2. Video can be downloaded from many sites on the web, including at www. sharealike.org (last accessed 13 November 2004).

3. Soldiers of Allah dissolved in February 2004. The SOA site was replaced by a chat board (www.trustislam.com) operated by one of the former band members.

4. Lyrics to "Staring Into Kafir's Eyes" can still be found on several websites, including www.soldiersofallah.com/kafirseye.doc (last accessed 13 November 2004).

5. "Sleeping Giant" can be downloaded at www.afghanhits.com (last accessed 13 November 2004).

6. www.nasrproductions.i-p.com (last accessed 13 November 2004).

7. Cynthia G. Wagner, "Aggression and Violent Media," *The Futurist* 38, no. 4 (July/August 2004): 16.

8. See www.specialforce.net (last accessed 13 November 2004).

9. Kenneth Nguyen, "Outrage over Hezbollah Game," *The Age* (Australia), 29 May 2003.

Chapter 3: Prisons as Terrorist Breeding Grounds

1. J. Bowyer Bell, *The Secret Army: The IRA, 1916–1979* (Cambridge, MA: MIT Press, 1983), p. 400.

2. U.S. Congress, House of Representatives, Committee on Internal Security, Hearing of 29 March and 1 May 1973, "Revolutionary Activities Directed Toward the Administration of Penal or Correctional Systems," 93rd Cong., 1st sess., part 1, testimony of Russell G. Oswald, p. 84.

3. Ibid.

4. Ibid., p. 85.

5. Ibid.

6. Ibid.

7. Ibid., p. 86. The full text of the letter appears in Appendix 2 of the hearing.

8. Ibid.

9. U.S. Congress, House, "Revolutionary Activities," testimony of Thomas Henry Hughes, p. 114.

10. U.S. Congress, Senate Judiciary Committee, Subcommittee on Terrorism, Technology and Homeland Security. Hearing of 14 October 2003. "Terrorist Recruitment and Infiltration in the United States: Prisons and Military as an Operational Base," 108th Cong., 1st sess. The transcript of this testimony is available online at http://judiciary.senate.gov/hearing.cfm?id=960 and also online at http://www.centerforsecuritypolicy.org/index.jsp?section=static&page=judhrgs03.

11. *Moneysworth Magazine* (September 1975).

12. Michael Ratner, as guest with this author on CNN *Crossfire*, 1987; reported in print by J. Michael Waller, "Alive and Kicking," *Insight on the News*, 28 January 2002, online at http://www.insightmag.com/main.cfm/include/detail/storyid/170071.html.

13. Susie Day, "Counter-Intelligent: The Surveillance and Indictment of Lynne Stewart," *Monthly Review* 54, no. 6 (November 2002), online at http://www.monthlyreview.org/1102day.htm. Note: On 10 February, 2005, Lynne Stewart was convicted of conspiracy to aid and abet terrorism.

14. Andrew Rice, "Kunstler Protege Stanley Cohen Brings American Rights to Hamas," *The New York Observer*, 1 October 2001.

15. See the Aryan Nations Resource Unit at www.aryannations.org. That and other sites serve as portals to Nazi, white supremacist, and skinhead websites and chat rooms in the United States, Latin America, Europe, and Russia.

16. Richard Scutari, former Head of Security of The Order, undated interview posted on freetheorder.net, online at http://www.freetheorder.net/RS_part_2.html

17. See Aryan Nations website: http://www.aryannations.org/leaderless.html. The Leaderless Resistance concept is similar to that of information-age terrorist networks such as Al Qaeda. RAND Corporation scholars John Arquilla and David Ronfeldt developed a theoretical construct to describe this phenomenon, which they call "netwar." See John Arquilla and David Ronfeldt, eds., *Networks and Netwars: The Future of Crime, Terror and Militancy* (RAND Corporation, 2001).

18. However, as noted in several chapters of this publication, the tenets of Islam expressly forbid suicide. Islamic militants' willingness to become suicide bombers is generally attributed more to the political interpretations of Islamic texts by terrorist leaders like Osama bin Laden and Abu Musab al-Zarqawi. For more on suicide terrorism, please see the chapter in this volume by Ami Pedahzur and Arie Perliger, and the chapter in Volume 2 by Adam Dolnik.

19. This author and others have conducted research in recent years with worried Muslims, who provided information about how the Islamists have penetrated their mosques, centers, and communities, politicized the faith, and sought to use it as a tool of political warfare against the both United States and against the traditional practice of Islam. We would not know what we already know without the active collaboration of Muslims from many countries and currents who fear the political Islamists, and it is clear that federal terrorism fighters and the nation at large have benefited likewise. Many Islamists, however, try to prevent sincere discussion of the issue with false denunciations of bigotry and Islamophobia. For more on the ideology of political Islam, please see the chapters in this volume by J. P. Larsson, Jarret Brachman, and Maha Azzam.

20. U.S. Congress, House, Committee on Internal Security, *Revolutionary Target: The American Penal System*, 93rd Cong., 1st sess., 18 December 1973, pp. 65–66.

21. U.S. Congress, House, "Revolutionary Activities," Oswald testimony, p. 99.

22. Sebastian Rotella, "Al Qaeda's Stealth Weapons," *Los Angeles Times*, 20 September 2003.

23. Definition furnished by Paul E. Rogers, President, American Correctional Chaplains Association.

24. U.S. Congress, Senate, "Terrorist Recruitment and Infiltration."

25. Ibid.

26. Ibid.

27. Ibid.

28. J. Michael Waller, "A Resounding Voice in Traditional Islam: Sheik Muhammad Hisham Kabbani Is a Vocal Opponent of Saudi Extremist Wahhabi Islam, which He Says Has Infected Many Muslim Institutions in the United States," *Insight on the News*, 1 October 2002, online at http://www.insightmag.com/main.cfm?include=detail&storyid=273232.

29. For more on Wahhabism, see the chapter by Maha Azzam in Volume 3 of this publication.

30. J. Michael Waller, "A Resounding Voice."

31. Ibid.

32. Ibid.

33. U.S. Congress, House, "Revolutionary Activities," Oswald testimony, p. 89.

34. Ibid.

35. U.S. Congress, House, *Revolutionary Target: The American Penal System*, p. 66.

36. U.S. Congress, Senate, "Terrorist Recruitment and Infiltration," testimony of J. Michael Waller.

38. Ron Scherer and Alexandra Marks, "Gangs, Prison: Al Qaeda Breeding Grounds?" *Christian Science Monitor*, 14 June 2002, online at http://www.csmonitor.com/2002/0614/p02s01-usju.html.

39. Siraj Islam Mufti, "Islam in American Prisons," *IslamOnline*, 31 August 2001.

40. Ibid.

41. Jerry Seper, "Terrorists Recruited from U.S. Seen as a Rising Threat," *Washington Times*, 18 June 2002.

42. Theodore Dalrymple, "I See Richard Reids in Jail Every Day," *Daily Telegraph* (London), 30 December 2001, online at http://www.telegraph.co.uk/core/Content/displayPrintable.jhtml?xml=/opinion/2001/12/30/do3001.xml&site=15.

43. U.S. Congress, House, "Revolutionary Activities."

44. Jerry Markon, "Muslim Activist Sentenced to 23 Years for Libya Contacts," *Washington Post*, 16 October 2004, p. A17.

45. Paul M. Barrett, "How a Muslim Chaplain Spread Extremism to an Inmate Flock," *Wall Street Journal*, 5 February 2003, p. A1.

46. Ibid.

47. Ibid.

48. Ibid.

49. U.S. Congress, House, "Revolutionary Activities," part 1, testimony of Thomas Henry Hughes, p. 115.

50. Susie Day, "Counter–Intelligent: The Surveillance and Indictment of Lynne Stewart." *Monthly Review* 54 no. 6 (November 2002) online at http://www.monthlyreview.org/1102day.htm.

51. Ibid.

52. For more on suicide terrorism, please see the chapter in this volume by Ami Pedahzur and Arie Perliger, and the chapter in Volume 2 by Adam Dolnik.

Chapter 4: Communication and Recruitment

1. Jerry Rubin, *Do It* (New York: Ballentine Books, 1970), p. 106.

2. Donatella della Porta, "Left-Wing Terrorism in Italy," in *Terrorism in Context*, edited by Martha Crenshaw (University Park: The Pennsylvania State University Press, 1995), pp. 105–59.

3. Anthony Pratkanis and Elliott Aronson, *Age of Propaganda: The Everyday Use and Abuse of Persuasion* (New York: W. H. Freeman and Company, 1999), pp. 5, 6.

4. "The Time of Killing," *Harper's Magazine*, July 2004, pp. 22–25.

5. "Earth Liberation Member Gets 3 1/2 Years for Arsons," *New York Times* (Long Island Section), 1 August 2004, p. 5.

6. Patrick E. Tyler and Don Van Natta Jr., "Militants in Europe Openly Call for Jihad and the Rule of Islam," *New York Times*, 26 April 2004, p. 1.

7. Daphne Burdman, "Education, Indoctrination, and Incitement: Palestinian Children on Their Way to Martyrdom," *Terrorism and Political Violence* 15, no. 1 (Spring 2003): 102.

8. Ibid., p. 105.

9. From a presentation by Dr. Iyad Zaqout at the International Assembly on Managing Fear and Terror, Austin, Texas, 19–21 August 2004.

10. Quote is taken from "Anarchy at the Turn of the Century," University Libraries, Pan-American Exposition Exhibit Group, University of Buffalo, http://ublib. buffalo.edu/libraries/exhibits/panam/copyright.html, retrieved 27 March 2003.

11. Portions of Carlos Marighella's book *The Liberation of Brazil* were widely translated and employed by Latin American and European terrorists. See Christopher Dobson and Ronald Payne, *The Terrorists, Their Weapons, Leaders and Tactics* (New York: Facts on File Publications, 1982), pp. 12–13; also see Major David E. Smith USMC, "The Training of Terrorist Organizations" (CSC Report, 1995), p. 6, available online at http://www.globalsecurity.org/military/report/1995/SDE.htm.

12. Simon Reeve, *The New Jackals* (Boston: Northeastern University Press, 1999), p. 265.

13. "In Their Own Words: Ahmed and a Protégé," *New York Times*, 12 June 2004, p. 9; and Elaine Sciolino, "Terror Suspect in Italy Linked to More Plots," *New York Times*, 12 June 2004, p. 9.

14. Ayla Schbley, "Religious Terrorism, the Media, and International Islamization Terrorism: Justifying the Unjustifiable," *Studies in Conflict & Terrorism* 27, no. 3 (May–June 2004): 213.

15. Avi Jorisch, "Al-Manar: Hizbullah TV, 24/7," *The Middle East Quarterly* 11 (Winter 2004).

16. Ibid., p. 217.

17. Ibid.

18. MEMRI TV Project Special Report: "Arab and Iranian TV Clips in Support of Suicide Bombing," 1 September 2004.

19. Ibid.

Chapter 5: Terrorist Dot Com

1. "Terrorists Rely on Tech Tools," *PCWorld*, 7 July 2004, at http://www. pcworld.com/news/article/0,aid,116822,tk,dn070804X,00.asp.

2. This chapter is based on a research project funded by the United States Institute of Peace, Washington, DC, where the author was a Senior Fellow in 2003–2004.

3. Bruce Hoffman, "Redefining Counterterrorism: The Terrorist Leader as CEO," *Rand Review* (Spring 2004): 1.

4. Marc Sageman, *Understanding Terror Networks* (Philadelphia: University of Pennsylvania Press, 2004).

5. Bruce Hoffman, *Al Qaeda, Trends in Terrorism and Future Potentialities: An Assessment* (Washington, DC: RAND, 2003); Bruce Hoffman, "Redefining Counterterrorism."

6. Joseph Von Hammer-Purgstall, *The History of Assassins* (New York: Burt Franklin, 1968); and Bernard Lewis, *The Assassins: A Radical Sect in Islam* (New York: Basic Books, 2002).

7. Marc Sageman, *Terror Networks*, p. 64.

8. Ibid., p. 65.

9. Adam Gadahn, "Becoming Muslim" (2004), online at http://www.usc.edu/dept/MSA/newmuslims/yahiye.html.

10. Paul M. Rodriguez, "Iranian Group Seeks Recruits for 'Martyrdom Operations,' " *Insight Online*, 8 June 2004, online at http://www.insightmag.com/global_user_elements/printpage.cfm?storyid=684918.

11. J. M. Berger, "Online Videos Shows Children Training for Jihad; Young Son of Osama bin Laden Reads Statement," *Intelwire* (2004), online at http://www.intelwire.com/2004_10_13_exclusives.html.

12. Yariv Tzfati and Gabriel Weimann, "WWW.terrorism.com: Terror on the Internet," *Studies in Conflict and Terrorism* 25, no. 5 (2002): 317–32; and Gabriel Weimann, *WWW.Terror.Net: How Modern Terrorism Uses the Internet*, Special Report (Washington, DC: United States Institute of Peace, 2004).

13. Weimann, *WWW.Terror.Net*, 2004.

14. Available online at http://www.state.gov.

15. Michelle Zanini and Sean J. A. Edwards, "The Networking of Terror in the Information Age," in *Networks and Netwars*, edited by Jon Arquilla and David Ronfeldt (Santa Monica: RAND Corporation, 2001), pp. 43–44.

16. Cited by Lawrence Wright, "The Terror Web," *New Yorker*, 2 August 2004.

17. "Army: GI Wanted To Help Al Qaeda," *CBS News*, 13 February 2004, at http://www.cbsnews.com/stories/2004/02/12/national/main599982.shtml.

18. Michelle Malkin, "Trailing Attempted Espionage," *National Review Online*, 13 February 2004, at http://www.nationalreview.com/comment/malkin200402130909.asp.

19. Niles Lathem, "Al-Qaeda Terror.com," *New York Post* (16 September 2003), p. A12.

20. See SITE at http://www.siteinstitute.org/.

21. Cited in Laura Rozen, "Forums Point the Way to Jihad," *Wired New* (2003), at http://www.wired.com/news/conflict/0,2100,59897,00.html.

22. Ibid.

23. This exchange is cited by Niles Lathem, "Al Qaeda Trolls Net," *New York Post*, 15 September 2003.

24. Etgar Lefkovitz, "Three Arabs Held in Jerusalem Cafe Poisoning Plot," *The Jerusalem Post*, 10 September 2002, online at http://www.jpost.com/.

25. Translated and published online at http://www.arabianews.org/english/article.cfm?qid=19&sid=6&printme=1 (last accessed August 2004).

26. The picture and the text translated to English are included in the report *Educating Children for Hatred and Terrorism: Encouragement for Suicide Bombing Attacks and Hatred for Israel and the Jews Spread via the Internet on Hamas' Online Children's Magazine (Al-Fateh)* posted at www.intelligence.org.il/eng/sib/11_04/edu.htm.

27. The text is included in the report *Educating Children for Hatred and Terrorism*, ibid.

28. See http://www.worldnetdaily.com/news/article.asp?ARTICLE_ID=31323.

29. Ibid.

Chapter 6: Education and Radicalization

1. International Crisis Group (ICG), "Jemaah Islamiyah in Southeast Asia: Damaged But Still Dangerous," 26 August 2003; and ICG, "Indonesia Backgrounder: Jihad in Central Sulawesi," 3 February 2004. For more on the history of JI see Zachary Abuza, *Militant Islam in Southeast Asia: Crucible of Terror* (Boulder, CO: Lynne Rienner, 2003).

2. Wong Chun Wai and Lourdes Charles, "More than 100 Marriages Involve Key JI Members," *The Star* (Malaysia), 7 September 2004.

3. For more on this phenomenon see chapters 9–16 in this volume. Also see Rex Hudson, *The Sociology and Psychology of Terrorism* (Washington, DC: Library of Congress Federal Research Division, 2000), pp. 20–55 (available online at http://www.loc.gov/rr/frd/Sociology-Psychology%20of%20Terrorism.htm); and Scott Atran, "Mishandling Suicide Terrorism," *The Washington Quarterly* 27, no. 3 (Summer 2004): 67–90.

4. For more on Jemaah Islamiyah, see Abuza, *Militant Islam in Southeast Asia*, or "Terrorism: The War on Terror in Southeast Asia," in Richard J. Ellings, Aaron L. Freidberg, and Michael Wills, eds., *Strategic Asia: Fragility and Crisis* (Seattle, WA: National Bureau of Asian Research, 2003), pp. 321–64; and the superb studies by Sidney Jones of the International Crisis Group, *How the Jemaah Islamiyah Terrorist Network Operates*, Asia Report no. 43 (11 December 2002); *Jemaah Islamiyah in Southeast Asia: Damaged But Still Dangerous* (26 August 2003); and *Indonesia Backgrounder: Jihad in Central Sulawesi* (3 February 2004).

5. Ronald A. Lukens-Bull, "Two Sides of the Same Coin: Modernity and Tradition in Islamic Education," *Anthropology and Education Quarterly* 32, no. 3 (2001): 353.

6. Ibid., 354.

7. Cited in Michael Richardson, "Asians Take a Closer Look at Islamic Schools," *International Herald Tribune*, 12 February 2002.

8. For more on Al Mukmin, see Bina Bektiati, Imron Rosyid, and L. N. Idayanie, "Exclusive and Secretive," *Tempo* no. 21 (29 January–4 February 2002).

9. International Crisis Group (ICG), *Al-Qaeda in Southeast Asia: The Case of the Ngruki Network* (Brussels, 8 August 2002), p. 7.

10. Baraja was also a part-time textile trader. He was related to Ba'asyir by marriage. Arrested in 1979, he was sentenced to 5 years in prison. In March 1985 he was again arrested for his role in the Borobudur bombing and sentenced to 15 years in prison. He was released in 1999 and became a senior leader of the Majelis Muhajidin Indonesia (MMI), (the Indonesian Mujahidin Council) heading its Fatwah Division.

11. Their escape and resettlement was arranged by Abdul Wahid Kadungga, a radical Muslim who had fled to Europe in 1971 and formed the Muslim Youth As-

sociation of Europe, which put him into close contact with Muslim leaders from around the world, and especially the Muslim Brotherhood. The preachers lived in a small town on the Malacca Strait that had ferry service to Indonesia and heavy flows of traffic between the two states. The two served as a way station for Indonesians and Malaysians who were on their way to Afghanistan and Pakistan to study and fight the Soviets or train in one of the forty al Qaeda camps that were established in the late 1990s. Sungkar traveled to Pakistan and the Afghan border region in the early 1990s where he met bin Laden and other senior al Qaeda members and where he pledged *bayat*, effectively absorbing his movement into al Qaeda.

12. Interview with a senior Indonesian National Police intelligence official, Jakarta, 10 March 2003.

13. Interview with NU leader, Jakarta, July 2004.

14. For more on Om al-Qura, see Zachary Abuza, *Funding Terrorism in Southeast Asia: The Financial Network of Al Qaeda and Jemaah Islamiya*, NBR Analysis 14, no. 5 (2003).

15. Robert W. Hefner, "Global Violence and Indonesian Muslim Politics," *American Anthropologist* 104, no. 3 (September 2002): 756.

16. Ibid., pp. 756–57.

17. Zachary Abuza, *Funding Terrorism in Southeast Asia.*

18. Per conversation with author, 2001.

19. John McBeth, "The Danger Within," *Far Eastern Economic Review* (27 September 2001): 21.

20. "KL to Require Students Going Abroad to Register," *Singapore Times*, 13 October 2001.

21. Private conversation with author, 2002.

22. Only thirty-five of the 1,600 madrasas were integrated into the national educational system with government oversight. Beginning in June 2002, the Arroyo administration has begun to integrate the madrasas into the national curriculum.

23. Kean Wong, "A Malaysian Vision in Cairo," *New Straits Times*, 7 November 2001; and "12 Malaysian Students Arrested in Yemen," *Singapore Times*, 28 February 2002.

24. Dore Gold, *Hatred's Kingdom* (Washington, DC: Regency, 2003), p. 90. One of IUM's trustees was none other than Mawlana Abu ala Mawdudi, the radical Pakistani cleric.

25. The law requires madrasas to register with the government, disclose their sources of funding, and register foreign students. It also encourages the voluntary integration of mathematics and sciences into the madrasa curriculum. The government promised that those madrasas that did expand their course offerings would receive state aid, additional teachers, and textbooks. Most madrasas have rejected the law and have refused to comply. The government has not dedicated the resources to fully implement the law, leading to charges of "cosmetic changes" to appease the Bush administration. See John Lancaster, "Room for Reform," *Washington Post Weekly*, 22–28 July 2002, p. 16; and Douglas Jehl, "Pakistan to Expel Foreign Religious Students," *New York Times*, 9 March 2002, p. A8.

26. This is a very important point. Contacts between JI and the LET keep appearing in the course of research on JI. The LET has emerged from an ethnonationalist group, to a group much more committed to the cause of international Islamic terrorism. In many ways, security experts warn that the LET is poised to replace al Qaeda as a truly global organization. This truly needs more study. Not only were members of the Al Ghuraba cell studying in LET madrasas, but several fought with the Kashmiri militant group, and were trained in their camps, or in al Qaeda camps in Afghanistan with other LET cadres.

27. Singapore Government Press Statement on the Detention of 2 Singaporean Members of the Jemaah Islamiyah Karachi Cell, 18 December 2003.

28. A Central Jakarta District Court has postponed the trial of terror suspect Rusman "Gun Gun" Gunawan due to the absence of key witnesses. He is charged with being an accessory to the August 2003 bombing of Jakarta's J. W. Marriott hotel that killed 12 people and injured 150 others. Three others—Mohammad Syaifudin, Ilham Sofyandi, and Furqon Abdullah—were subsequently charged with terrorism, while two were released due a lack of evidence; see http://www.laksamana.net/vnews.cfm?ncat=45&news_id=7394.

29. Ellen Nakashima, "Indonesian Militants 'Keep Regenerating,' " *Washington Post*, 25 March 2004.

30. Ministry of Home Affairs, "Singapore Government Press Statement on the Detention of 2 Singaporean Members of the Jemaah Islamiyah Karachi Cell," 18 December 2003.

31. Ellen Nakashima, "Indonesian Militants 'Keep Regenerating,' " *Washington Post*, 25 March 2004. *Ulamas* are generally described as learned or knowledgeable religious leaders in the Islamic world.

32. Hudson, *The Psychology and Sociology of Terrorism.*

33. *Pedoman Umum Perjuangan al-Jama'ah al-Islamiyyah* (*The General Guidebook for the Struggle of Jema'ah Islamiyyah*), was issued by The Council of Qiyadah Markaziyah Jemaah Islamiyah in 1996.

34. This can be found at http://www.usdoj.gov.

35. The PUPJI does talk about how operations should be conducted in the *General Manual for Operations*. It emphasizes planning and that "the operation should be planned and carried out according to plan." It also outlines a schema for guerilla war: "View, analyze and explore all aspects of life in the enemy's body and in the environment"; "View carefully and honestly all our potential strengths and effective powers we possess"; and "Determine points of target at the enemy and the environment to be handled in relation with our goals." The document calls for four stages of operations: 1) planning, 2) execution, 3) reporting, and 4) evaluation. Emphasis is placed on education, meticulous planning, and learning from past acts (including mistakes). Later the document discusses how members should focus on Intelligence Operations, Strength Building Operations, Strength Utilization Operations, and Fighting Operations. Almost all emphasis is placed on Strength Building Operations, which is defined as a lengthy process that includes spiritual and physical strengthening. The goals of this educational period include enlightenment,

discipline, instilling a sense of loyalty, physical readiness and skills to use weapons, tactical and strategic thinking, and leadership development.

36. Kean Wong, "A Malaysian Vision in Cairo," *New Straits Times,* 7 November 2001; and "12 Malaysian Students Arrested in Yemen," *Singapore Times,* 28 February 2002.

37. Republic of Singapore, Ministry of Home Affairs, *White Paper: The Jemaah Islamiyah Arrests and the Threat of Terrorism* (Singapore, 2003).

38. Scot Atran, "Who Wants to Be a Martyr," *New York Times,* 5 May 2003, p. A23.

39. Atran, "Mishandling Suicide Terrorism," p. 75.

40. Republic of Singapore, *White Paper.*

41. Lawrence Wright, "The Terror Web," *The New Yorker,* 2 August 2004.

42. Cited in Wright, "The Terror Web." For more on terrorist use of the internet, please see Gabriel Weimann's chapter in this volume.

43. Gary Becker, "Crime and Punishment: An Economic Approach," *Political Economy* 76 (1968): 169–217.

44. Atran, "Mishandling Suicide Terrorism," pp. 76–77.

45. David Brown, *The State and Ethnic Politics in Southeast Asia* (London: Routledge, 1994), pp. 250–51; also see Chandra Muzaffar, *Islamic Resurgence in Malaysia* (Selangor: Penerbit Fajar Bakti, 1987), pp. 24, 56.

46. KAMMI has been an active group in demonstrations against the United States and was active in drumming up popular support for the jihad in the Malukus. Wicksono and Endri Kurniawati, "Following Up on Fuad," *Tempo,* 21 April 2003, pp. 34–35.

47. Wicksono and Kurniawati, "Following Up on Fuad," pp. 34–35.

48. Hefner, "Global Violence and Indonesian Muslim Politics," p. 762.

49. Interview with a senior Indonesian National Police intelligence official, Jakarta, 10 March 2003.

50. The Justice Party was renamed, which allowed it to slip through a loophole in the electoral law that prevented parties who received less than 2 percent of the vote in 1999 from standing in the 2004 election.

51. Saiful Mujani and R. William Liddle, "Politics, Islam and Public Opinion," *Journal of Democracy* 15 no. 1 (January 2004): 118.

52. Jane Perlez, "Asia Letter: Indonesian Islamist Party Is Quietly Gaining Ground," *International Herald Tribune,* 7 April 2004.

53. Ibid.

Chapter 7: Recruitment in the Philippines

1. The term Communist Terrorist Movement (CTM) is the latest name used by the Armed Forces of the Philippines and other Philippine government agencies for what has been called—and is still widely referred to—as the Local Communist Movement consisting of the Communist People's Party of the Philippines (CPP) and its armed wing, the New Peoples Army (NPA). Many references to the ongoing

communist insurgency will use CPP–NPA or LCM. This chapter uses the term CTM for consistency and to avoid confusion.

2. This introduction refers to Ted Robert Gurr's classic 1970 work *Why Men Rebel* (Princeton, NJ: Princeton University Press, 1970).

3. Donald Horowitz's seminal 1985 book, *Ethnic Groups in Conflict* (Berkeley: University of California Press, 1985) stresses that *how* ethnic groups become ranked in society is important and impacts grievance formation.

4. See Barbara Walter, "Does Conflict Beget Conflict? Explaining Recurring Civil War," *Journal of Peace Research* 4, no. 3 (2004): 374. Walter calls the condition where the status quo is worse than the perceived risk of death in combat "misery," and this combined with the absence of alternative legal drives individuals to join rebel groups.

5. Paul Collier and Anke Hoeffler are the scholars credited with articulating this theory. Their research shows a high correlation between civil war risk and countries that depend on primary commodity exports and have large amounts of "lootable" resources within their borders. See Paul Collier and Anke Hoeffler, "Greed and Grievance in Civil War," World Bank Policy Research Paper 2355 (Washington: The World Bank, 2000).

6. See John Mueller, "Policing the Remnants of War," *Journal of Peace Research* 40, no. 5 (2003): 507–18.

7. James Fearon and David Laitin, "Ethnicity, Insurgency, and Civil War," *American Political Science Review* 97, no. 1 (2003): 91–106.

8. Ibid.

9. See Nicholas Sambanis, "Expanding Economic Models of Civil War Using Case Studies" (unpublished paper, Yale University Department of Political Science, 2003).

10. This supports the Fearon–Laitin 2003 study, but emphasizes that many states experiencing rebellion and civil war have the capacity to suppress these threats more effectively but do not employ it.

11. This "theory" refers to classic international relations maxims outlined by Kenneth Waltz's *Theory of International Politics* (Reading, MA: Addison-Wesley, 1979). I am suggesting here that selection forces driving states to maximize their security and position in the international system should be expected to result in optimal internal security practices as well.

12. Of course rebels can "even the playing field" and shift the balance of forces towards their favor at the incident level by leveraging advantages afforded by factors such as familiarity with the terrain, support of the local populace, and by exercising the initiative to choose the time and place to mass their limited combat resources against government forces. These same advantages, however, can be generated by government forces in response to rebel aggression.

13. The Philippines is no stranger to insurgency and terrorism, having dealt with the ongoing communist insurgency for over 35 years. Along with this classic Maoist peoples' war instigated around the country, Filipino Muslims continue to wage a concurrent separatist struggle on the southern island of Mindanao. The Moro Na-

tional Liberation Front championed this armed struggle from the early 1970s until peace was brokered in 1996 and an autonomy arrangement agreed upon. Rebels from the Moro Islamic Liberation Front refused to disarm and have continued the separatist struggle punctuated by several cease fires through negotiated efforts to resolve the conflict. Lawless elements and criminal groups are also active throughout the Philippines. The notorious Abu Sayyef Group known to have linkages with international terrorist groups, including al Qaeda, has been active in kidnap for ransom and other illegal and terrorist activities since the mid-1990s.

14. Data for this brief history and select statistics was obtained from internal reference material maintained by the Combat Research Division Library, Armed Forces of the Philippines (AFP) Office of the Deputy Chief of Staff for Operations (J3).

15. The point man for this U.S. assistance was Lt. Col. Edwin Landsdale who coordinated it through the Philippine Defense Minister and future President Ramon Magsaysay. Landsdale went on to earn notoriety in Vietnam and is widely considered to be the inspiration for "Colonel Hillandale," one of the protagonists in *The Ugly American*, as well as the idealistic Alden Pyle in Graham Greene's *The Quiet American*.

16. Reasons for the steep decline in CPP–NPA include the 1986 People Power Revolution that ousted the corrupt dictatorship of Ferdinand Marcos, the fall of the Soviet Union in 1989, and the implementation of Lambat Bitag, a progressive counterinsurgency campaign plan that used an holistic interagency approach to addressing the roots as well as the symptoms of the insurgency with a "Clear–Hold–Consolidate–Develop" methodology to gradually constrict the CTM. Interestingly, the plan was developed by then Lt. Col. Victor Corpus who had defected to the CPP–NPA as a young Army Lieutenant, fought for several years against the government, surrendered and spent 10 years in jail until he was pardoned by President Cory Aquino after Marcos was deposed. Another reason the CTM strength was reduced was the CPP–NPA party leadership's major purges of its ranks during the mid-1980s, killing unknown hundreds suspected of being disloyal.

17. A resurgence in Muslim separatist violence by the Moro Islamic Liberation Front in the late-1990s forced the armed forces to shift resources to meet this threat, which further diluted its capacity to aggressively meet the communist insurgency threat at the same time.

18. This quote is from the text of the Second Rectification Campaign and is used in official manuals maintained at the Combat Research Division of the AFP Office of the Deputy Chief of Staff for Operations (J3), Camp Aguinaldo, Quezon City, Philippines.

19. Order-of-battle data on CTM strength and affected villages was obtained through the generous cooperation of the Office of the Deputy Chief of Staff for Intelligence (J2) of the Armed Forces of the Philippines. The latest data used was recorded in August 2004.

20. See the CPP's official website at www.philippinerevolution.org for a great example of cyber propaganda at work!

21. This description of how the communist insurgents recruit members and ex-

pand their mass base is developed from interviews with senior intelligence officers in the AFP Office of the Deputy Chief of Staff for Intelligence (J2) on 4–5 August 2004, an extensive recorded interview with General (Ret.) Raul S. Urgello, former Commanding General of the Philippine Army, on 10 August 2004, and from documents maintained by the Office of the Assistant Chief of Staff for Intelligence (G2) of the Philippine Army.

22. This quote is cited in an Raul S. Uregello's internally distributed and undated document, *Aspects of Insurgency*, maintained by the Philippine Army Doctrine Office, Fort Andres Bonifacio, Makati City, Philippines. This study attributes the quote originally to Ying-Mao Kao in *Urban and Rural Strategies in the Chinese Communist Revolution*. Bibliographic data for this source was not available.

23. According to a senior officer assigned to the AFP Office of the Deputy Chief of Staff for Intelligence, individuals selected to make initial contact with a targeted village are selected because they are "very very good at it (recruiting support). . . . [E]ven though they may be elementary graduates they are good in talking." Tape recorded interview, AFP General Headquarters, Quezon City, 5 August 2004.

24. The term Semi-Legal Team is given to them because they enter the village "semi-legally" carrying only concealed pistols and without explicitly violating any laws.

25. The SYP further breaks down the landowners in the Reactionary Class into subcategories: Big Landlord—50 Hectares and up; Middle Landlord—10–49 Hectares and up; Small Landlord—1–9 Hectares.

26. These four steps are discussed by Lt. Gen. (Ret.) Raul Urgello in his internally distributed manual, *Aspects of Insurgency*, with additional details provided by AFP J2 officers and Gen. Urgello himself during tape recorded interviews in Manila, 10 August 2004.

27. As the organization process continues, militia members are provided opportunities to join mobile guerrilla units at the provincial and regional levels.

28. The author is indebted to Col. Aurelio Baladad, Chief Armed Forces of the Philippines Special Operations Team Center, for his tremendous cooperation and support while conducting field research July–August 2004. Col. Baladad's staff provided access to the raw data from the field interrogation reports of the 767 rebel returnees as well as the initial compilation and analysis of the 30 percent sample used here. The staff at the AFP SOT Center provided copies of unpublished briefings and the text of official reports as well as clarification of all uncertain terms and programs.

29. Admittedly, the profile of the "typical new recruit" belongs more specifically to the subclass of rebels who eventually surrender to the government. Important differences likely exist among the populations of rebels who are persuaded to surrender and those who do not. On 19 August 2004 the author arranged to have prison authorities at the Philippine National Prison at Mutinlupa interview two former rebels who were arrested and jailed–who had not surrendered voluntarily. The responses to questions on recruitment were focused more on grievances over land and abuses by the military, not the propaganda efforts of the organizing cadre.

30. Information on the KALAHI program was obtained from interviews with Under Secretary Susan Abaya of the National Anti-Poverty Commission and from

unpublished internally distributed literature she provided. Additional insights were gained from attending a KALAHI coordinating meeting held in Butuan City, Augusan Del Norte, on the southern island of Mindanao, 17–18 August 2004.

31. An OLS regression testing predictors of Communist Terrorist Movement Incidents in the fifteen geographic regions of the Philippines from 1998–2003 demonstrates that the number of hectares of timberland in a region is a statistically and substantively significant predictor of CTM activities controlling for GDP, land area, population, and unemployment level. Illegal logging is a major source of criminal predation in the Philippines, and the hectares of timberland in an area is a reasonable proxy for this illegal activity. Also, incident reports received by the Armed Forces of the Philippines Joint Operations Center from military units deployed in the field frequently identify theft, arson, murder, and other criminal activities as being committed by known members of the CTM.

32. Particular details and goals of both these plans are omitted due to security classification concerns of those individuals who provided them.

33. Philippine military intelligence officers identify 108 active CTM Guerrilla Fronts organized around multiple affected villages. This data is current as of August 2004.

34. Following intensified U.S.-assisted military efforts to track down and kill terrorists from another rebel organization in the Philippines, the Abu Sayyef Group, one officer reported the parents of an ASG member actually turned their son in because they feared that he would be killed by government troops if he remained with the group and this was worse than going to jail. Interview with a senior officer from the office of the Philippine Army, Assistant Chief of Staff for Operations (G3) Fort Bonifacio, Makati City, Philippines, 20 July 2004.

35. Military officers and representatives of government-sponsored development agencies both mention the difficulty in coordinating military clearing efforts with government development. This issue was a topic of discussion at a KALAHI coordinating meeting held in Butuan City, Augusan Del Norte, on 17 August 2004. The local army brigade commander and senior representative for the National Anti-Poverty Commission identified the importance of coordination and timing of military and development efforts and its affect on maintaining control of villages at risk of falling into insurgent control.

36. The conditions Fearon and Laitin mention include financially, organizationally, and politically weak central governments, the presence of rural base areas, rough inaccessible terrain, and rebels with superior local knowledge, and external support. The state's police and military capabilities and the government's reach into far-flung areas are mentioned explicitly in this study.

37. A briefing from a military intelligence officer acknowledged that "usually the police do not exist in the far-flung *barangay* (village). There may be a policeman from that place but he will stay at the *poblacion* (more-populated area) during the week and only return on Saturday or Sunday" (Taped interview, 6 August 2004).

38. The Clear-Hold-Support methodology is defined in Oplan Bantay Laya, the current Philippines internal security operations plan. It is similar to the Clear-Hold-Consolidate-Develop approach outlined in earlier plans.

39. CAFGUs (territorial militia) are deployed in remote areas with little support. With inferior training and equipment, the CTM target them as easier prey. An analysis of combat operations from 2001–2003 shows that CAFGUs were nearly twice as likely to die per combat incident than their comrades in regular units. The author thanks the AFP Joint Operations Center and Combat Research Division of the J3 for access to this raw data for analysis.

40. For those not familiar with the latest U.S. Army recruiting campaign, this is a play on its slogan "An Army of One."

41. Roger Petersen's work, for example, assesses variation in support for rebellion at the individual and community level, using a model he calls "the spectrum of individual roles during rebellion" that includes the triggering mechanisms that can move individuals across the scale from compliance with the government to neutrality to armed rebellion against the government. This is measured on a 7-point scale ranging from −3 to +3 and includes possible activities of individuals at each point on the scale. See Roger Petersen, *Resistance and Rebellion* (Cambridge, MA: MIT Press, 1991).

42. Mancur Olsen describes the powerful effect that selective incentives can have on mobilizing collective action in *The Logic of Collective Action* (Cambridge, MA: Harvard University Press, 1960).

43. The ability of the rebels to provide private rewards for rebel participation has a powerful motivational effect and impacts the commitment level of those recruited. Low-commitment individuals may need immediate payoffs while higher-commitment individuals are willing to support the rebels based on rewards promised in the distant future. The Philippines military intelligence operatives call these "low-commitment" individuals the "lie-lows" who tend to avoid fighting and are more prone to surrender. See Jeremy Weinstein, "Resources and the Information Problem in Rebel Recruitment" (unpublished paper, Stanford University, 2003).

44. Mancur Olsen discusses the motivating effect of social incentives such as the desire for *prestige, respect, and friendship* in *The Logic of Collective Action*, p. 60.

45. An excellent first hand account is Victor Corpus's *Silent War* (Quezon City, Philipines: VNC Enterprises, 1989).

46. A difficult challenge facing the central government of the Philippines is the ability to follow through with its sophisticated poverty reduction and counterinsurgency programs at local levels. Scarce resources devoted to such efforts get even scarcer when diluted by graft and corruption. The payoffs generated by communist insurgency and efforts to reduce it provide perverse incentives to some individuals and organizations to insure it continues.

Chapter 8: New Children of Terror

1. Jack Kelley, "The Sickening World of Suicide Terrorists," *USA Today*, 26 June 2001.

2. For more on this global problem, please see Peter W. Singer, *Children At War* (New York: Pantheon, 2005).

3. "National Roundup," *Miami Herald*, 23 April 2003; Human Rights Watch, "U.S. Guantanamo Kids at Risk," 24 April 2003; Bruce Auster and Kevin Whitelaw, "Terror's Cellblock," *U.S. News and World Report*, 12 May 2003; and Michelle Faul, "U.S. Defends Detaining Teens," Associated Press, 28 June 2003. The ages of the young detainees are 13, 14, 15, and 16. There is an unknown added number between 16 and 18 that the United States has held in the general adult population, contrary to both U.S. and international law on how children should be treated by the law.

4. Hancy Gibbs, "Inside 'The Wire.'" *Time*, 8 December 2003.

5. Interviews with U.S. Army officer, March 2004; and Keith Richburg, "Taliban Maintains Grip Rooted in Fear," *Washington Post*, 9 August 2004, p. 9.

6. P. W. Singer, "Facing Saddam's Child Soldiers," Brookings Iraq Memo #8, January 2003.

7. Matthew Cox, "War Even Uglier When a Child is the Enemy," *USA Today*, 8 April 2003; "Report: Marines Wounded in Fighting Late Wednesday in Iraq," Associated Press, 27 March 2003; and Alex Perry, "When Kids Are in the Cross Hairs," *Time*, 21 April 2003.

8. Martin Bentham, "Fedayeen Use Children as Shields," *The Telegraph*, London, 4 April 2003.

9. Mary Beth Sheridan, "For Help in Rebuilding Mosul, U.S. Turns to Its Former Foes," *Washington Post*, 25 April 2003.

10. "Enemy Tactics, Techniques, and Procedures (TTP) and Recommendations," Third Corps Support Command briefing document, LSA Anaconda, Iraq, September 2003; Joseph Galloway, "Hurt Still Arriving at Army Hospital," *Charlotte Observer*, 3 November 2003; interviews with U.S. Army officers, November–December 2003.

11. As quoted in "Child Soldiers Square Up to U.S. Tanks," *London Daily Telegraph*, 23 August 2004.

12. Ibid.

13. Neil Mackay, "Iraq's Child Prisoners," *Sunday Herald*, Glasgow, Scotland, 1 August 2004; and Richard Sisk, "Teen Held, U.S. Admits Juveniles in Abu Ghraib," *New York Daily News*, 15 July 2004.

14. U.S. Army Lt. Col. Barry Johnson, quoted in Richard Sisk, "Teen Held, U.S. Admits Juveniles in Abu Ghraib."

15. "Palestinian Teen Stopped with Bomb Vest," CNN, 25 March 2004.

16. Gul Luft, "The Palestinian H-Bomb," *Foreign Affairs* (July 2002): 5; Coalition to Stop the Use of Child Soldiers (CSC), *1379 Report* (www.child-soldiers.org), 2002, p. 54; Suzanne Goldenberg, "A Mission to Murder," *The Guardian* (London), 11 June 2003; and Johanna McGeary, "Inside Hamas," *Time*, 28 March 2004.

17. Interview with U.S. Security agency official, December 2003.

18. "Enemy Tactics, Techniques, and Procedures (TTP) and Recommendations," Third Corps Support Command briefing document, LSA Anaconda, Iraq, September 2003.

19. "Teenage Boys Trained by Paramilitary Group," *Guardian Weekly*, 29 November 2000.

20. U.S. State Department, *Report on Human Rights*, 1997, Colombia section. UNICEF-Columbia, Situation Report, 22 April 2003.

21. Rohan Gunaratna, "LTTE Child Combatants," *Jane's Intelligence Review*, July 1998.

22. "Teenage Boys Trained by Paramilitary Group," *Guardian Weekly*.

23. Jack Kelley, "Street Clashes Now Deliberate Warfare," *USA Today*, 23 October 2000; Herb Keinon, "Israel to the UN: Keep Palestinians from Using Kids as Shields," *Jerusalem Post*, 8 November 2000; and D. Kuttab, "A Profile of the Stone Throwers," *Journal of Palestine Studies* 17 (1988): 14–23.

24. Nasra Hassan, "An Arsenal of Believers," *The New Yorker*, 19 November 2001.

25. Gehud Auda, *Palestinian Suicide Bombing: Description and Evaluation*, Ahram Strategic Papers, no. 114 (Cairo, Egypt: Al-Ahram Center for Political and Strategic Studies, 2002); and Hassan, "Arsenal of Believers."

26. Daniel Williams, "Bomber Unleashed Secret Rage," *Washington Post*, 14 April 2002.

27. Quoted in "Child Soldiers Square Up to U.S. Tanks," *London Daily Telegraph*, 23 August 2004.

28. Samir Kouta, as quoted in the weekly financial news magazine, *Al Alam al Yom*, 24 January 1995.

29. "The Appeal of Suicide Bombers Grows," Associated Press, 28 April 2002.

30. Krueger and Maleckova have argued the opposite in a highly cited study. Alan Krueger and Jitka Maleckova, "Education, Poverty, Political Violence and Terrorism: Is There a Causal Connection?" NBER Working Paper No. w9074, July 2002, http://papers.nber.org/papers/W9074. However, many analysts believe that the study was highly limited in its purview, only looking at one case that was suboptimal in selection, and thus flawed in its methodology. Omer Tapsinar, "Promoting Educational and Economic Opportunity in the Islamic World," *Brookings Monograph*, 2003.

31. Jessica Stern, "Islamic Extremists: How do they Mobilize Support?" *USIP Presentation*, 17 April 2002.

32. Ibid.

33. Jessica Stern, *Terror in the Name of God* (New York: HarperCollins, 2003), p. 51; "The Appeal of Suicide Bombers Grows," Associated Press, 28 April 2002.

34. Jessica Stern, *Terror in the Name of God*, p. 219.

35. Amy Waldman, "Sri Lanka's Young Are Forced to Fill Ranks of Endless Rebellion," *New York Times*, 6 January 2003.

36. *South Asia Intelligence Review*, 2 August 2002.

37. Jack Kelley, "The Sickening World of Suicide Terrorists."

38. David Pryce Jones, "Priests of Killing," *National Review*, 22 April 2002, pp. 19–20.

39. "PA Mufti of Jerusalem and Palestine Discusses the Intifada," *al-Ahram al-Arabi*, 28 October 2000, via MEMRI, 8 November 2000.

40. John F. Burns, "Palestinian Summer Camp Offers the Games of War," *New York Times*, 3 August 2000.

41. Peter W. Singer, "Facing Saddam's Child Soldiers."

42. Franz Fanon, *The Wretched of the Earth* (New York: Grove Press, 1963), p. 93.

43. Colin Nickerson, "A Boy's Journey from Canada to Al Qaeda," *Boston Globe*, 9 March 2003; and Joseph Farah, "Family of Canadian Teen Has Extensive Al Qaeda Ties," *World Net Daily*, 6 September 2002.

44. Colin Nickerson, "A Boy's Journey."

45. Johanna McGeary, "Inside Hamas," *Time*, 28 March 2004.

46. James Garabino, "A Note on Children and Youth in Dangerous Environments: The Palestinian Situation as a Case Study," *The Erickson Institute*, Chicago, undated.

47. Hassan, "Arsenal of Believers."

48. For example, one in al-Istiqlal, the Palestinian Authority's newspaper, read "With great pride, The Palestinian Islamic Jihad marries the member of its military wing . . . the martyr and hero Yasser-Adhami, to the black-eyed [virgins]." From Yotam Feldner, "72 Black-eyed Virgins': A Muslim Debate on the Rewards of Martyrs," MEMRI paper, 2002, http://www.memri.org.

49. Hassan, "Arsenal of Believers."

50. Quoted in Jessica Stern, *Terror in the Name of God*, p. 221.

51. Chris Hedges, "The Glamour of Martyrdom," *New York Times*, 29 October 2000; and *Al Hayat-Al Jadida*, 27 October 2000, from Palestinian Media Watch, Jerusalem.

52. David Kupelian, "Trouble in the Holy Land: Jerusalem Cleric Praises Child 'Sacrifices,' " *WorldNetDaily.com*, 10 November 2000.

53. Emily Wax, "Outrage Spreads in Arab World," *Washington Post*, 30 March 2003, p. 19.

54. Walter Laqueur, *No End to War*, p. 91.

55. "Profile of a Suicide Bomber." CNN.com, 15 December 2001.

56. Haim Malka, "Must Innocents Die? The Islamic Debate on Suicide Attacks," *Middle East Quarterly* (Spring 2003).

57. David Van Biema, "Why the Bombers Keep Coming," *Time*, 17 December 2001; David Pryce Jones, "Priests of Killing," *National Review*, 22 April 2002, pp. 19–20; and Hamza Hendawi, "Gaza's Children Worship Martyrdom," Associated Press, 14 May 2002.

58. Huda Al-Husseini, an Arab journalist with the London-based daily, *al-Sharq al-Awsat*, as quoted in Kupelian, "Trouble in the Holy Land."

59. Its first human bomber, Ala'a al Kahlout, even wore shorts, a T-shirt, a cap, and dark glasses before climbing aboard a bus in 1993 and blowing it up (Hassan, "Arsenal of Believers").

60. Auda, Palestinian Suicide Bombing, *al-Sharq al-Awsat*, 8 August 2001.

61. Martin Cohn, "The Teen Soldiers Who Refused to Die," *Toronto Star*, 18 January 2002.

62. Hassan, "Arsenal of Believers."

63. Jessica Stern, *Terror in the Name of God*, p. 51.

64. Walter Laquer, *No End to War*, p. 83.

65. Amos Harel, "Portrait of the Terrorist as a Young Man," *Ha'aretz Daily*, 23 April 2002.

66. Dewayne Wickham, "Root Out the Seeds of Terrorism in Sub-Saharan Countries," Associated Press, 14 April 2003.

67. Jessica Stern, *Terror in the Name of God*.

68. "The Appeal of Suicide Bombers Grows," Associated Press, 28 April 2002.

Chapter 9: Hamas Social Welfare

1. This chapter is adapted from the author's winter 2004 article in *Middle East Quarterly* 9, no. 1, entitled "Hamas from Cradle to Grave." Julie Sawyer, Research Assistant at the Washington Institute for Near East Policy, provided much research and editorial support for this piece.

2. World Bank Reform for West Bank and Gaza, Proposed Public Financial Management Trust Fund, 1.

3. United Nations Development Program, *Arab Human Development Report 2003* (New York: United Nations Publications, 2003), p. 25.

4. Ibid.

5. Steve Franklin, "Health Plight Rises for Palestinian Kids," *Chicago Tribune*, 28 June 2001.

6. Ghassan Charbel, "The Khaled Mishaal Interview (2 of 7)," *al Hayat*, 15 December 2003, available online (in English) at http://english.daralhayat.com/Spec/12-2003/Article-20031215-7a215ab8-c0a8-01ed-0015-c5ece4bc1b17/story.html (accessed 13 January 2005).

7. Ibid.

8. Khaled Hroub, *Hamas: Political Thought and Practice* (Washington, DC: Institute for Palestine Studies, 2000), p. 35.

9. Shaul Mishal and Avraham Sela, *The Palestinian Hamas: Vision, Violence, and Coexistence* (New York: Columbia University Press, 2000), p. 19.

10. FBI summary of translated transcripts of Philadelphia meeting, marked "typed version of Bates 203–287," Entry for 2 October 1993, Tape 6—Conference Room, p. 35 (author's personal files).

11. FBI summary of translated transcripts of Philadelphia meeting.

12. Reuters, 27 May 1998.

13. "A May 2002 Interview with the Hamas Commander of the Al-Qassam Brigades, Salah Shehadeh," Middle East Media Research Institute, 25 July 2002, http://www.memri.de/uebersetzungen_analysen/themen/islamistische_ideologie/isl_shehadeh_25_07_02.pdf (accessed 13 January 2005).

14. Reuters, 31 July 2001, cited in John Pistole, testimony before House Committee on Financial Services, Subcommittee on Oversight and Investigations, 24 September 2003.

15. "Hamas-Related Associations Raising Funds throughout Europe, the U.S. and the Arab World," Israel Defense Forces Spokesperson's Unit, available online at

http://www.idf.il/english/announcements/2002/july/hamas.stm (accessed 13 January 2005).

16. Ibid.

17. Jessica Stern, *Terror in the Name of God: Why Religious Militants Kill* (New York: HarperCollins, 2003), p. 48.

18. Dale L. Watson, assistant director for counterterrorism, FBI, "Holy Land Foundation for Relief and Development, International Emergency Economic Powers Act, Action Memorandum," memorandum to R. Richard Newcomb, director of the Office of Foreign Assets Control, U.S. Department of the Treasury, 5 November 2001.

19. U.S. Treasury Department, "U.S. Designates Five Charities Funding Hamas and Six Senior Hamas Leaders as Terrorist Entities," Office of Public Affairs, Department of the Treasury, 22 August 2003, at http://www.ustreas.gov/press/releases/js672.htm.

20. "Erased in a Moment: Suicide Bombing Attacks against Israeli Civilians," Human Rights Watch, October 2002, p. 63, at http://www.hrw.org/reports/2002/isrl-pa/ (accessed 13 January 2005).

21. Michael Getler, "The Language of Terrorism," *Washington Post*, 21 September 2003, p. B06.

22. Christine Chinlund, "The Ombudsman: Who Should Wear the Terrorist Label?" *Boston Globe*, 8 September 2003, p. A15.

23. U.S. Congress, House, Committee on Financial Services, Subcommittee on Oversight and Investigations, David Aufhauser testimony, 108th Cong., 1st sess., 24 September 2003, at http://www.treas.gov/press/releases/js758.htm (accessed 13 January 2005).

24. Watson memo, "Holy Land Foundation."

25. Ian Fisher, "A Sudden, Violent End for a Promising Youth," *New York Times*, 13 June 2003.

26. "Unmasking Hamas' Hydra of Terror," Simon Wiesenthal Center Snider Social Action Institute Report, August 2003, at http://www.wiesenthal.com/social/pdf/index.cfm?ItemID=7993 (accessed 13 January 2005).

27. Jerrold M. Post, Ehud Srpinzak, and Laurita M. Denny, "The Terrorists in Their Own Words: Interviews with 35 Incarcerated Middle Eastern Terrorists," *Journal of Terrorism and Political Violence* 15, no. 1 (Spring 2003): 171–84.

28. Jessica Stern, *Terror in the Name of God*, pp. 50–51.

29. "Subject: Transcriptions of the Police Interviews with Salah Arouri," Israeli Police Document recording Arouri's 27 January 1993 interview (author's personal files).

30. All examples from Watson memo, "Holy Land Foundation."

31. "Terrorists Misuse of Medical Services to Further Terrorist Activity," Israel Foreign Ministry, 26 August 2002, available at http://www.israel-mfa.gov.il/mfa/go.asp?MFAH0md20. The FBI has described al-Ghazi Hospital as Hamas-affiliated; see also Watson memo, "Holy Land Foundation."

32. "The Use of Ambulances and Medical Material for Terror—Background In-

formation," Israeli Foreign Ministry Website, 22 December 2003, available online at http://www.mfa.gov.il/mfa/go.asp?MFAH0o3b0 (accessed 13 January 2005).

33. Watson memo, "Holy Land Foundation."

34. "The Use of Ambulances and Medical Material for Terror"; and Margot Dudkevitch, "Chemist Supplies Hamas," *Jerusalem Post*, 11 December 2003.

35. Saud Abu Ramadan, "Police Arrest Hamas Leader's Bodyguard," UPI, 5 March 2000.

36. Mohammed Daragmeh, "After Israel's Warning, Militants Shave Off Beards, Ditch Cellphones to Escape Intensified Manhunt," Associated Press, 27 August 2003.

37. "Transcript of Interview with Sufian Abu Samara on 14 January, 1991," Israeli police document, 21 August 1995 (author's personal files).

38. Shimon Peres, address to the Knesset, 26 February 1996 at http://www.mfa.gov.il/mfa/mfaarchive/1990_1999/1996/2/pm+peres+knesset+speech+on+jerusalem+and+ashkelon.htm (accessed 13 January 2005).

39. "Suicide Bomber: The Planning of the Bloodiest Suicide Bombing Campaign in Israel's History," *CBS 60 Minutes*, 5 October 1997.

40. Ibid.; and "Details Released on Hamas Bombing Supporters," Israel Ministry of Foreign Affairs, 9 May 1996, at http://www.mfa.gov.il/mfa/mfaarchive/1990_1999/1996/5/details+released+on+hamas+bombing+supporters+-+09-.htm (accessed 13 January 2005).

41. U.S. District Court for the District of Columbia, *Susan Weinstein, et al., Plaintiffs v. The Islamic Republic of Iran, et al., Defendants*, Civil Action No. 00-2601 (RCL); and United States District Court for the District of Columbia, *Leonard I. Eisenfeld, et al., Plaintiffs, v. The Islamic Republic of Iran, et al., Defendants*, Civil Action No. 98-1945 (RCL).

42. "The Involvement of Female Palestinians in Terror," Government of Israel, available online at http://www.idf.il/newsite/engligh/0218-5.stm (accessed 13 January 2005).

43. Daragmeh, "Militants Shave Off Beards."

44. Watson memo, "Holy Land Foundation."

45. Ibid.

46. "The Financial Sources of the Hamas Terror Organization," Israel Foreign Ministry, 30 July 2003, available at http://www.mfa.gov.il/mfa/mfaarchive/2000_2009/2003/7/the+financial+sources+of+the+hamas+terror+organiza.htm (accessed 13 January 2005).

47. Catherine Hours, "Charity and Bombings: Hamas Gains Ground with Desperate Palestinians," *Agence France-Presse*, 15 August 2001.

48. Jamie Tarabay, "Islamic Militants Gain Influence through Philanthropic Work," Associated Press, 2 March 2001.

49. Amos Harel, " 'The PA Steals from Me, Hamas Takes Care of Me,' " *Ha'aretz*, 27 June 2002.

50. *Filastin al-Muslima* (London), January 1998, quoted in Watson memo, "Holy Land Foundation."

51. Lee Hockstader, "Palestinians Find Heroes in Hamas; Popularity Surges for Once-Marginal Sponsor of Suicide Bombings," *Washington Post*, 11 August 2001, p. A01.

52. Watson memo, "Holy Land Foundation."

53. Ibid.

54. "Hamas's Use of Charitable Societies to Fund and Support Terror," Israel Government Press Office, 22 September 2003, available at http://www.mfa.gov.il/mfa/go.asp?MFAH0nt70 (accessed 13 January 2005).

55. Watson memo, "Holy Land Foundation."

56. Ibid.

57. Colin L. Powell interview by Tony Snow, *Fox News Sunday with Tony Snow*, Washington, DC, 30 June 2002, available at http://usembassy.state.gov/tokyo/wwwhse1499.html (accessed 13 January 2005).

58. Meir Litvak, *The Islamization of Palestinian Identity: The Case of Hamas*, The Moshe Dayan Center for Middle Eastern Studies, Tel Aviv University, available at http://www.dayan.org/d&a-hamas-litvak.htm (accessed 13 January 2005).

59. "Participation of Children and Teenagers in Terrorist Activity During the Al Aqsa Intifada," Government of Israel, available online at http://www.mfa.gov.il/mfa/go.asp?MFAH0n100.

60. "Incitement to Terror and Hatred," Intelligence and Terrorism Information Center at the Center for Special Studies, Special Information Bulletin, Tel Aviv, June 2003, http://www.intelligence.org.il/eng/var/h_sch/hs_inc.htm (accessed 13 January 2005).

61. Ibid.

62. Neil MacFarquhar, "Portrait of a Suicide Bomber: Devout, Apolitical and Angry," *New York Times*, 18 March 1996, p. A1.

63. "The Martyrdom and Suicide Culture in Palestinian Universities—An-Najah University in Nablus as a Case Study," Special Information Bulletin, Intelligence and Terrorism Information Center at the Center for Special Studies, May 2003, http://www.intelligence.org.il/eng/bu/sib_mb/university.htm (accessed 13 January 2005).

64. Khaled Abu Toameh, "Hamas Wins Student Election Race on Israeli Body-count Ticket," *Jerusalem Post*, 11 December 2003.

65. "Participation of Children and Teenagers in Terrorist Activity during the Al Aqsa Intifada."

66. *Ha'aretz*, 24 October 2003.

67. Ibid.

68. Majeda El-Batsh, "Parents Fear Their Children Could Take on Suicide Missions," *Agence France-Presse*, 8 July 2003.

69. Neil MacFarquhar, "Portrait of a Suicide Bomber: Devout, Apolitical and Angry."

70. Jamie Tarabay, "Islamic Militants Gain Influence through Philanthropic Work."

71. "Hamas Penetration into the PA Ministry of Education and Its Growing In-

fluence over Palestinian Youth," Intelligence and Terrorism Information Center, Center for Special Studies, Tel Aviv, at http://www.intelligence.org.il/eng/bu/hamas/education.htm (accessed 13 January 2005).

72. "U.S. Berates Europe for Ambiguous Stand on Hamas," Reuters, 27 November 2002.

73. Ibid.

74. U.S. Congress, House Committee on Financial Services, "The Hamas Asset Freeze and Other Government Efforts to Stop Terrorist Financing," 108th Cong., 1st sess., E. Anthony Wayne testimony, 24 September 2003, at http://www.state.gov/e/eb/rls/rm/2003/24622.htm (accessed 13 January 2005).

75. "President Bush, European Leaders Act to Fight Global Terror," remarks by President Bush, Prime Minister Simitis, and President Prodi, White House news release, 25 June 2003, available at http://www.whitehouse.gov/news/releases/2003/06/20030625-12.html (accessed 13 January 2005).

76. Press Gaggle by Claire Buchan, Crawford Middle School, Crawford, Texas, 12 August 2003, available at http://www.whitehouse.gov/news/releases/2003/08/2000812-2.html (accessed 13 January 2005).

77. Secretary of State Colin L. Powell on Egypt's Nile Television with Mohammed El Setohi, 12 August 2003, Washington, DC, available at http://www.useu.be/Categories/GlobalAffairs/Middle_East/Aug1203Palestinians.html (accessed 13 January 2005).

78. FBI summary of translated transcripts of Philadelphia meeting, marked "typed version of Bates 203–287," entry for 5 October 1993, p. 10.

79. Ibid., p. 11.

Chapter 10: Terrorism, Gender, and Ideology

1. Jean Bethke Elshtain, *Women and War* (Chicago: University of Chicago Press, 1995), pp. 178–79 [original emphasis].

2. CNN, "Russia's 'Black Widows' Wreak Terror," CNN.com (3 September 2004), online at http://www.cnn.com/2004/WORLD/europe/09/01/russia.widows

3. Ricardo Vargas Meza, "The FARC, the War, and the Crisis of the State," *NACLA Report on the Americas* 31, no. 5 (March/April 1998): 22.

4. Dennis M. Rempe, "Guerrillas, Bandits, and Independent Republics: U.S. Counter-insurgency Efforts in Colombia 1959–1965," *Small Wars and Insurgencies* 6, no. 3 (Winter 1995): 312.

5. FARC, "38 Years of the FARC-EP," online at http://six.swix.ch/farcep/Nuestra_historia/38_aniversario_de_las_FARC-EP.html.

6. FARC, "Esbozo histórico" (Sendero Luminoso, Comisión Internacional, 1998), p. 18.

7. FARC, "Revolutionary Armed Forces of Colombia-People's Army: History," online at http://www.farcep.org/pagina_ingles.

8. FARC, "Proposed Agenda of the FARC, May 6, 1999," online at http://www.ciponline.org/colombia/farc.htm.

9. Ramón D. Ortiz, "Insurgent Strategies in the Post-Cold War: The Case of the Revolutionary Armed Forces of Colombia," *Studies in Conflict & Terrorism* 25, no. 2 (March–April 2002): 130.

10. FARC, "Women in Active Resistance" (FARC, undated), online at http://www.farcep.org/mujer/articulos/resistencia.php.

11. Karl Penhaul, "Colombia's Communist Guerrillas Take on Feminine Face," *Boston Globe*, 7 January 2001, p. 6A.

12. FARC, "Women: May 2004" (FARC, 2004), online at http://www.farcep.org/mujer/09demayo/madres2004.php.

13. FARC, "Women and their Battles—Disadvantaged Situation" (FARC, 2004), online at http://www.farcep.org/mujer/09demayo/mayo2004.php.

14. Juan Guillermo Ferro Medina and Graciela Uribe Ramón, *The Order of the War: The FARC-EP Between the Organization and the Politics* (Bogotá: CEJA, 2002), p. 67.

15. Credible human rights organizations and media outlets routinely report instances of FARC and other armed groups employing coercion or force to enlist civilians. While this illegal and deplorable tactic must be recognized and addressed, it is beyond the scope of this chapter. All the women interviewed for this chapter reported to have voluntarily joined the movement. For example, see Save the Children UK, "Angie walks on stilts to escape fear" (30 September 2002).

16. As agreed before each interview, pseudonyms are used instead of the women's actual names. The interviews described in this chapter were conducted by this author in Bogotá, Colombia, 16–21 January 2004.

17. Laura, interview by author, Bogotá, Colombia, 16 January 2004.

18. Human Rights Watch, *You'll Learn Not to Cry* (New York: Human Rights Watch, 2003), p. 10.

19. Laura, interview by author.

20. Ibid.

21. See Claire Marshall, "The Battle for Colombia's Children," BBC News, 1 October 2003; and Howard LaFranchi, "When War Veterans are Children," *Christian Science Monitor*, 20 March 2000, p. 1.

22. Maria Clara, interview by author, Bogotá, Colombia, 21 January 2004.

23. Ibid.

24. Jeremy McDermott briefly touches on the FARC's adventurous mystic as an attraction to young girls in his article, "Colombia's Female Fighting Force," BBC News, January 2002, online at http://news.bbc.co.uk/2/hi/americas/1742217.stm.

25. Laura, interview by author.

26. Ibid.

27. Serena, interview by author, Bogotá, Colombia, 16 January 2004.

28. Ibid.

29. María Clara, interview by author.

30. Jeremy McDermott quotes an 11-year veteran of the FARC, Commandante Mariana Perez, "Women are not treated differently, we do not cut them any slack

during training operations," in "Colombia's Female Fighting Force," BBC News, 4 January 2002.

31. Serena, interview by author.

32. Jeremy McDermott, "Female Fighting Force," 4 January 2002.

33. Quoted in Arturo Alape, "Women in the FARC Guerrilla," online at http://www.farcep.org/pagina_ingles.

34. See Patricia Lara, *Mujeres en la Guerra*, 2nd ed. (Bogotá: Planeta, 2000), pp. 79–132; Jeremy McDermott, "Colombia's Female Fighting Force"; and Karl Penhaul, "Colombia's Communist Guerrillas Take on a Feminine Face," *Boston Globe*, 7 January 2001, p. 6A.

35. Laura, interview by author.

36. Arturo Alape, "Women in the FARC Guerrilla."

37. Ibid.

38. Ibid.

39. Sandra Jordan, "Girls Go to War as Colombia's Frontline Killers," *The Observer*, London, 14 July 2002, online at http://www.observer.co.uk/Print/0,3855,4461189,00.html.

40. The UN High Commissioner for Human Rights notes that their office has received reports of sexual abuse of girls in the FARC and other terrorist movements, generally by middle-ranking officers. Report of the UN High Commissioner for Human Rights on the Human Rights Situation in Colombia, E/CN.4/2001/15, 2 August 2001, no. 109.

41. Human Rights Watch, p. 10.

42. Ibid.

43. Ibid.

44. Human Rights Watch, p. 58.

45. Ibid.

46. Ibid.

47. Ibid.

48. Ibid., p. 59.

49. Ibid.

Chapter 11: Making of Suicide Bombers

1. Yoram Schweitzer, "Suicide Bombings—The Ultimate Weapon?" (Herzlia: ICT, 2001), http://www.ict.org.il/articles/articledet.cfm?articleid=373.

2. Boaz Ganor, "Suicide Terrorism: An Overview," in *Countering Suicide Terrorism* (Herzlia: ICT, 2000).

3. Ibid.

4. *Chechnya Weekly*, 11 February 2004, www.jamestown.org/images/pdf/chw_005_006.pdf+suicide+bomber+chechnay+filetype:pdf&hl=iw.

5. Amira Hes, "Floating to Paradise," *Ha'aretz Daily Newspaper*, 4 April 2003 (Hebrew).

6. http://www.hagada.org.il; http://www.intelligence.org.il/sp/4_04/women.htm;

Vered Levi Brazilay, "Ticking Bomb," *Ha'aretz Daily Newspaper*, 17 October 2003 (Hebrew).

7. Thomas L. Friedman, "Boy Says Lebanese Recruited Him a Car Bomber," *The New York Times*, 14 April 1985, Sunday, Late City Final Edition; and Edward Walsh, "16-Year-Old, Among Shiites Demanded by Hijackers, Describes Growing Up in Lebanon," *The Washington Post*, 18 June 1985, Tuesday, Final Edition, Washington Post Foreign Service.

8. Rohan Gunaratna, *Inside Al-Qaeda—Global Network of Terror* (New York: Columbia University Press, 2002), p. 75.

9. Marc Sageman, "Statement to the National Commission on Terrorist Attacks Upon USA" (9 July 2003), http://www.globalsecurity.org/security/library/congress/9-11_commission/030709-sageman.htm; "Recruitment for the Jihad in the Netherlands, from Incident to Trend," paper published by the Dutch Ministry of Interior and Kingdom Relations, pp. 11–14, http://www.aivd.nl/contents/pages/2285/recruitmentbw.pdf.

10. Marc Sageman, "Statement to the National Commission."

11. Faramarzi Scheherezade, "Girl Who Drove Car Bomb First Sent Mother Present," Associated Press, 7 April 1986, Monday, PM cycle; and Rima Salameh, "Lebanon's Militia Women Fight and Become Suicide Bomb 'Martyrs,'" *World News Tonight, ABC*, 10 April 1985.

12. Rohan Gunaranta, *Terrorism in the Asia Pacific: Threat and Response* (Singapore: International Specialized Book Services, 2003).

13. Audrey Kurth Cronin, "Terrorism and Suicide Attack," *CRS Report for Congress*, 28 August 2003.

14. Shaul Shay, *The Shahids: Islam and Suicide Attacks* (Herzlia: ICT, 2003), p. 43 (Hebrew); and Assaf Moghadam, "Palestinian Suicide Terrorism in the Second Intifada: Motivation and Organization Aspects," *Studies in Conflict and Terrorism* 26 (2003): 84.

15. Shaul Shay, *The Shahids*, p. 44 (Hebrew).

16. Lawrence Uzzell, "Profile of Female Suicide Bomber," *Terrorism Monitor 5*, no. 6 (11 April 2004).

17. Kim Murphy, "The Black Widows of Chechnya: Suicide Bombers who Stalk Russia," *Los Angeles Times*, 4 February 2004.

18. "The Karbala Connection: Where Bombs, Heroin and Islam Meet," ONASA News Agency, 23 March 2004.

19. "Raided Base is Breeding Place for Fanatics," Associated Press, 3 June 1994.

20. Sanjay Sonawani, *On the Brink of Death* (New York: Pushpaparakashan, 2001), p. 281.

21. Ibid.

22. See http://www.mfa.gov.tr/grupe/eh/terror/greecebk/annex8.htm.

23. "Profiling the Islamic Suicide Terrorist," A Research Report for the Danish Ministry of Justice, 27 November 2003, p. 36 and p. 29, http://www.jm.dk/image.asp?page=image&objno=71157.

24. Rohan Gunaratna, *Inside Al-Qaeda: Global Network of Terror* (New York: Columbia University Press, 2002), p. 73.

25. Yoram Schweitzer, "Suicide Terrorism and the September 11th Attacks," *ICT* (www.ict.org.il, 20 October 2002); "Translation of the Letter Left by Hijackers," *ICT* (www.ict.org.il, 29 September 2001). See also the al-Qaeda manual, lesson 2, on www.usdoj.gov.

26. Zachary Abuza, "Tentacles of Terror: Al-Qaeda's Southeast Asian Network," *Contemporary Southeast Asia* 24, no. 3 (December 2002): 427–66.

27. For more information on the use of the Internet by terrorist organizations, please see the chapters in this volume by Gruen, Nacos and Weimann.

28. Martin Kramer, "Sacrifice and 'Self-Martyrdom' in Shiite Lebanon," *Terrorism and Political Violence* 3, no. 3 (Autumn 1991): 30–47.

29. "Shiites Posthumously Honour Teenager as Suicide Bomber," Associated Press, 19 December 1985.

30. "Hezbollah Commemorates Suicide Bombers," Associated Press, 12 November 1989.

31. Martin Kramer, "Sacrifice and 'Self-Martyrdom' in Shiite Lebanon."

32. Ibid.

Chapter 12: Unresolved Trauma

1. WordNet ® 1.6, © 1997 Princeton University. References include "Vengeance is mine; I will repay, saith the Lord"—Rom. 12:19; "For vengeance I would do nothing. This nation is too great to look for mere revenge"—James Garfield; "He swore vengeance on the man who betrayed him"; "the swiftness of divine retribution."

2. Several studies in this area were conducted by this author at the Human Relations Institute and Clinics in Washington, DC, 1984. For more information on his consultations in clinical and forensic psychology, please contact Dr. Raymond Hamden, Post Office Box 11806, Dubai, United Arab Emirates.

3. Corrie Ten Boom, *The Hiding Place* (Old Tappan, NJ: Revell, 1971).

4. Robert D. Enright, *Forgiveness Is A Choice* (Washington, DC: American Psychological Association, 2001).

5. American Psychiatric Association, *Diagnostic and Statistical Manual of Mental Disorders*, 4th ed., Text Revised, 309.81 (Washington, DC: American Psychiatric Association, 2000).

6. Suzanne C. Kobasa, Salvatore R. Maddi, and Stephen Khan, "Hardiness and Health: A Perspective Study," *Journal of Personality and Social Psychology* 42 (1982): 168–77; and Richard S. Lazarus, James R. Avrill, and Edward M. Opton, Jr., "The Psychology of Coping: Issues of Research and Assessment," in *Coping and Adaptation*, edited by George V. Coehlo, David A. Hamburg, and John E. Adams (New York: Basic Books, 1974), pp. 249–315.

7. George E. Vaillant, *Ego Mechanisms of Defense: A Guide for Clinicians and Researchers* (Washington, DC: American Psychiatric Association, 1992), pp. 3–4.

8. For a discussion of how membership in groups alters an individual's behav-

ior, please see the chapters by Jerrold Post, Arthur Deikman, and Marc Galanter and James Forest in Volume 2 of this publication.

9. The following story of Hanadi Jaradat is borrowed from the chapter by Ami Pedahzur and Arie Perliger in this volume.

10. http://www.hagada.org.il; http://www.intelligence.org.il/sp/4_04/women.htm; Vered Levi Brazilay, "Ticking Bomb," *Ha'aretz Daily Newspaper*, 17 October 2003 (Hebrew).

11. "Waco, Oklahoma City Mark Anniversary of Tragedies," CNN, 19 April 1998, online at http://edition.cnn.com/US/9804/19/okc.waco.

Chapter 13: Political and Revolutionary Ideologies

1. J. L. Talmon, *The Origins of Totalitarian Democracy* (London: Secker and Warburg, 1952), p. 3.

2. David Apter, "Ideology and Discontent," in *Ideology and Discontent* (Glencoe, IL: Free Press, 1964), p. 16.

3. Neil Smelser, *Theory of Collective Behavior* (New York: Free Press, 1962), pp. 16–17.

4. Albert Bandura, "Mechanisms of Moral Disengagement," in *Origins of Terrorism*, edited by Walter Reich (New York: Cambridge University Press, 1990), pp. 161–91. Also see Bandura's chapter in Volume 2 of this publication.

5. Robert Paxton, *The Anatomy of Fascism* (New York: Alfred A. Knopf, 2003), pp. 24–54.

6. Philip Pomper, "Russian Revolutionary Terrorism," in *Terrorism in Context*, edited by Martha Crenshaw (University Park: Pennsylvania State University Press, 1995), pp. 82–85.

7. Sergei Nechaev, "Catechism of the Revolutionist," in *The Terrorism Reader: A Historical Anthology,* edited by Walter Laqueur (New York: New American Library, 1978), pp. 71–72.

8. Anna Geifman, *Thou Shalt Kill* (Princeton, NJ: Princeton University Press, 1993), pp. 45–48.

9. Christopher Hewitt, *Understanding Terrorism in America* (New York: Routledge, 2003), pp. 62–65.

10. Walter Laqueur, *Terrorism* (Boston, MA: Little Brown, 1977), pp. 24–71.

11. Phillip Pomper, "Russian Revolutionary Terrorism," pp. 63–101.

12. Maureen Perrie, "Political and Economic Terror in the Tactics of the Russian Social Revolutionary Party Before 1914," in *Social Protest, Violence and Terror in Nineteenth and Twentieth Century Europe*, edited by Wolgang Mommsen and Gerhard Hirschfeld (New York: St. Martin's Press, 1982), pp. 65–66.

13. V. I. Lenin, "Revolutionary Adventurism," in *Voices of Terror*, edited by Walter Laqueur (New York: Reed Press, 2004), pp. 196–99.

14. Leon Trotsky, "The Collapse of Terrorism," in *Voices of Terror*, pp. 200–202.

15. Richard Jensen, "Daggers, Rifles and Dynamite: Anarchist Terrorism in Nineteenth Century Europe," *Terrorism and Political Violence* 16, no. 1 (2004): 134.

16. Karl Heinzen, "Murder," in *Voices of Terror*, p. 59.

17. Pyotr Kropotkin, "The Spirit of Revolt," in *Voices of Terror*, p. 94.

18. David Scott Palmer, "The Revolutionary Terrorism of Peru's Shining Path," in *Terrorism in Context*, p. 281.

19. Carlos Marighella, *The Manual of the Urban Guerrilla* (Chapel Hill, NC: Documentary Publications, 1985).

20. Ibid., pp. 84–85.

21. Leonard Weinberg and William Eubank, *The Rise and Fall of Italian Terrorism* (Boulder, CO: Westview Press, 1987), p. 8.

22. Walter Laqueur, *Terrorism*, p. 207.

23. Zeev Sternhell, *The Birth of Fascist Ideology* (Princeton, NJ: Princeton University Press, 1994).

24. Zeev Sternhell, "Fascist Ideology," in *The Fascism Reader*, edited by Walter Laqueur (Berkeley: University of California Press, 1976), pp. 315–76.

25. Sidney Tarrow, *Democracy and Disorder: Protest and Politics in Italy, 1965–1975* (New York: Oxford University Press, 1989), pp. 143–93.

26. Franco Ferraresi, *Threats to Democracy* (Princeton, NJ: Princeton University Press, 1996), pp. 43–50.

27. James Coates, *Armed and Dangerous* (New York: Hill and Wang, 1995).

28. Jeffrey Kaplan, "Right-Wing Violence in North America," in *Terror from the Extreme Right*, edited by Tore Bjorgo (London: Frank Cass, 1995), pp. 44–95.

29. Kevin Flynn and Gary Gerhardt, *The Silent Brotherhood* (New York: Signet, 1990); and Michael Barkun, *Religion and the Racist Right* (Chapel Hill: University of North Carolina Press, 1994), pp. 225–33.

Chapter 14: Role of Religious Ideology

1. Aref M. Al-Khattar, *Religion and Terrorism; An Interfaith Perspective* (Westport, CT: Praeger, 2003), p. 45.

2. J. P. Larsson, *Understanding Religious Violence; Thinking Outside the Box on Terrorism* (Aldershot, UK, and Burlington, VT: Ashgate, 2004), p. 106.

3. Andrew Sinclair, *An Anatomy of Terror; A History of Terrorism* (London: Macmillan, 2003).

4. For example, see J. P. Larsson, *Understanding Religious Terrorism*; Mark Juergensmeyer, *Terror in the Mind of God: The Global Rise of Religious Violence* (Berkeley: University of California Press, 2000); Dawn Perlmutter, *Investigating Religious Terrorism and Ritualistic Crimes* (Boca Raton, FL: CRC Press, 2004); Aref M. Al-Khattar. *Religion and Terrorism.*

5. Dawn Perlmutter, *Investigating Religious Terrorism*, p. 45ff, 181ff; Mark Juergensmeyer, *Terror in the Mind of God*, p. 19ff.

6. Dawn Perlmutter, *Investigating Religious Terrorism*, p. 317.

7. See, for example, Ian Reader, *Religious Violence in Contemporary Japan; The Case of Aum Shinrikyō* (Richmond, UK: Curzon, 2000).

8. Dawn Perlmutter, *Investigating Religious Terrorism*, p. 312.

9. Ibid., p. 311.

10. Mark Juergensmeyer, *Terror in the Mind of God*, p. 189; Dawn Perlmutter, *Investigating Religious Terrorism*, p. 313.

11. Dawn Perlmutter, *Investigating Religious Terrorism*, p. 312ff.

12. See, for example, Walter Reich, ed., *Origins of Terrorism; Psychologies, Ideologies, Theologies, States of Mind* (Washington, DC: Woodrow Wilson Center Press, 1998).

13. Mark Juergensmeyer, *Terror in the Mind of God*, pp. 195–207.

14. Jerrold M. Post, "Terrorist Psycho-Logic," in Walter Reich, ed., *Origins of Terrorism*, p. 35.

15. J. P. Larsson, *Understanding Religious Violence*, p. 111.

16. Mark Juergensmeyer, *Terror in the Mind of God*, p. 146.

17. J. P. Larsson, *Understanding Religious Violence*, p. 107.

18. Ibid., p. 111.

19. Mark Juergensmeyer, *Terror in the Mind of God*, p. 145ff.

20. J. P. Larsson, *Understanding Religious Violence*, p. 116; Mark Juergensmeyer, *Terror in the Mind of God*, p. 165.

21. J. P. Larsson, *Understanding Religious Violence*, p. 116.

22. Ibid., p. 126ff.

23. Mark Juergensmeyer, *Terror in the Mind of God*, p. 60ff.

24. Aref M. Al-Khattar, *Religion and Terrorism*, p. 85.

25. Ian Reader, *Religious Violence in Contemporary Japan*, p. 193.

26. Dawn Perlmutter, *Investigating Religious Terrorism*, p. 314; Mark Juergensmeyer, *Terror in the Mind of God*, p. 187ff.

27. J. P. Larsson, *Understanding Religious Violence*, pp. 107, 119–20.

28. J. P. Larsson, *Understanding Religious Violence*, pp. 12, 107–8; Mark Juergensmeyer, *Terror in the Mind of God*, p. 175.

29. Mark Juergensmeyer, *Terror in the Mind of God*, p. 167.

30. Jerrold M. Post, "Terrorist Psycho-Logic," in Walter Reich, ed., *Origins of Terrorism*, p. 35.

31. Aref M. Al-Khattar, *Religion and Terrorism*, p. 26; J. P. Larsson, *Understanding Religious Violence*, ch. 6.

32. Dawn Perlmutter, *Investigating Religious Terrorism*, pp. 312–13; J. P. Larsson, *Understanding Religious Violence*, ch. 6.

33. See, for example, Dawn Perlmutter, *Investigating Religious Terrorism*, ch. 3.

34. J. P. Larsson, *Understanding Religious Violence*, pp. 47, 128.

35. Ibid., pp. 124, 129.

36. Mark Juergensmeyer, *Terror in the Mind of God*, pp. 32, 33, 78.

37. Ian Reader, *Religious Violence in Contemporary Japan*, p. 75ff.

38. For a discussion of charismatic leaders, please see the chapter in Volume 2 by Arthur Deikman.

39. Dawn Perlmutter, *Investigating Religious Terrorism*, p. 315.

Chapter 15: Christian Fundamentalism

1. Norman Cohn, *The Pursuit of the Millennium* (New York: Oxford University Press, 1970).

2. Roger Griffin, "Fascism," in *Encyclopedia of Fundamentalism*, edited by Brenda Brasher (New York: Routledge, 2001), p. 172.

3. Sara Diamond, *Roads to Dominion: Right-Wing Movements and Political Power in the United States* (New York: Guilford Press, 1995).

4. Michael Barkun, *Religion and the Racist Right: The Origins of the Christian Identity Movement* (Chapel Hill: University of North Carolina Press, 1994).

5. James Aho, *The Politics of Righteousness* (Seattle: University of Washington Press, 1990), pp. 138–46.

6. Robert Nisbet, *The Quest for Community* (New York: Harper and Brothers, 1953), p. 34.

7. Betty Dobratz and Stephanie Shanks-Meile, *"White Power, White Pride!" The White Separatist Movement in the United States* (New York: Twayne Publishers, 1997), pp. 256–94.

8. Seymour M. Lipset and Earl Raab, *The Politics of Unreason* (New York: Harper and Row, 1970).

9. James Aho, *The Politics of Righteousness*, pp. 164–84.

10. Charles Glock and Rodney Stark, *Christian Beliefs and Anti-Semitism* (New York: Harper and Row, 1966).

11. Jack Glazier, "Anti-Semitism," in *Encyclopedia of Fundamentalism* (New York: Routledge, 2001), p. 23.

12. Theodor Adorno et al., *The Authoritarian Personality* (New York: W. W. Norton, 1969 [1950]), p. 6.

13. Kathleen Blee, *Inside Organized Racism: Women in the Movement* (Berkeley: University of California Press, 2002).

14. Rosabeth Moss-Kanter, *Commitment and Community: Communes and Utopias in Sociological Perspective* (Cambridge, MA: Harvard University Press, 1972).

15. Kevin Flynn and Gary Gerhardt, *The Silent Brotherhood: Inside America's Racist Underground* (New York: Free Press, 1989).

16. Kathleen Blee, *Inside Organized Racism*.

Chapter 16: Political Islam

1. Ahmad al-Katib, *Al-Fikr al-Siyasi al-Wahhabi* [Wahhabi Political Thought] (Dar al-Shura Lidirasat wal I'lam, 2003).

2. "Strengthening Education in the Muslim World," USAID Issue Paper #2 (June 2003).

3. William E. Shepard, *Sayyid Qutb and Islamic Activism* (Boston: E. J. Brill, 1996).

4. For an alternative view that emphasises the Wahhabi connection of al Qaeda,

see Stephen Schwartz, *The Two Faces of Islam: The House of Saud from Tradition to Terror* (New York: Doubleday, 2002).

5. Rudolph Peters, *Jihad in Classical and Modern Islam* (Princeton, NJ: Markus Wiener Publishers 1996), pp. 43–55.

6. See Maha Azzam, "Al-Qaeda: The Misunderstood Wahhabi Connection and the Ideology of Violence," Royal Institute of International Affairs, Briefing Paper No. 1 (February 2003), p. 3.

7. The financial network is discussed in Roland Jacquard, *In the Name of Osama bin Laden* (Durham, NC: Duke University Press, 2002), pp. 126–35.

8. The full title is *Shifa' Sudur al-Mu'minin: Risala 'an ba'd ma'ani al-jihad fi 'amaliyyat Islam Abad* [The Cure for Believers Hearts: A Treatise Regarding Some of the Meanings of Jihad in the Operation of Islamabad]. Published as publication No. 11 of the series of the publications of al-Mujahideen in Egypt (March 1996).

9. A radical Egyptian Islamist group which declared the wider Egyptian society to be Kafir (nonbelieving) and called on its members to separate themselves from it through internal Hijra (immigration) to isolated communities of like-minded believers.

10. *Al-Quds al-Arabi* newspaper, London, 20 January 2002, p. 13. See also a discussion of "Under the Prophet's Banner" by al-Zawahri in G. Kepel, *The War for Muslim Minds* (Cambridge, MA: The Belknap Press of Harvard University Press, 2004), pp. 89–108.

Chapter 17: Jihad Doctrine and Radical Islam

1. Bin Laden audio tape broadcast on al-Jazeera on 11 February 2003. Translated and published on BBC, 12 February 2003, http://news.bbc.co.uk/2/hi/middle_east/2751019.stm.

2. Mr. Rafiq Ahmed Hayat, National President, Ahmadiyya Muslim Association UK, press release 26 July 2004, www.alislam.org/jalsa/uk/2004/press-release2004.pdf.

3. The framing of that interaction between globalizing and localizing forces was popularized by Benjamin Barber in his book *Jihad vs. McWorld* (New York: Times Books, 1995). For more on this, please see Professor Barber's chapter in Volume 3 of this publication.

4. "Is the Sultan the Caliph?" *New York Times*, 10 July 1877, p. A1.

5. Please see the chapter by Maha Azzam in this volume for a discussion of political Islam and its association with violence, particularly by adherents by the Wahhabi interpretation of Islamic principles.

6. Surah al-Hajj, verses 39–40.

7. Ibid., verse 78.

8. Surah al-Baqarat, verses 190–93.

9. I am indebted to William McCants for sharing this among numerous other insights with me.

10. "Declaration of War Against the Americans Occupying the Land of the Two

Holy Places," 23 August 1996, http://www.terrorismfiles.org/individuals/declaration_of_jihad1.html.

11. The United Nations General Assembly passed United Nations Resolution 37/37 on 29 November 1983, which stated that the Soviet Union forces should withdraw from Afghanistan.

12. Ronald Reagan, President of the United States, Proclamation 4908—*Afghanistan Day*, 10 March 1982, http://www.reagan.utexas.edu/resource/speeches/1982/31082c.htm.

13. Please see the chapter by Rohan Gunaratna and Arabinda Acharya in Volume 2 of this publication.

14. Please see the chapter by Evan Kohlmann in Volume 2 of this publication.

15. Jozias van Aartsen, parliamentary speaker for the nationalist People's Party for Freedom and Democracy (VVD), the second-largest party in the government of Prime Minister Jan Peter Balkenende. Anthony Deutsche, "Netherlands braces for 'jihad,' " *Washington Times*, 6 November 2004, http://www.washtimes.com/world/20041105-111203-2758r.htm.

16. Ella Landau-Tasseron, "Jihad," in *Encyclopaedia of the Qur'an*, Volume 3 (Leiden-Boston: Brill, 2003), p. 35.

17. For more on the social and psychological dimensions of group cohesion in the terrorist world, please see the chapters by Jerrold Post and by Marc Galanter and James Forest in Volume 2 of this publication.

18. Peter Finn, "Qaeda-linked Group Claims It Was behind Tunisian Blast," *International Herald Tribune*, 17 April 2002, http://www.iht.com/articles/54962.html.

19. Taipei Times, AFP, Indonesia, 17 July 2003, http://www.taipeitimes.com/News/world/archives/2003/07/17/2003059747.

20. "Evidence Growing that al-Qaeda Sponsored Kenya Attacks," *USA Today*, 2 December 2002, http://www.usatoday.com/news/world/2002-12-02-kenya-attacks_x.htm.

21. "Attacks May Signal Shift in al Qaeda's Strategy. Terrorist Group Seems Ready to Challenge Saudi Monarchy," 11 November 2003, CNN World, http://www.cnn.com/2003/WORLD/meast/11/10/al.qaeda.saudi/.

22. *Straits Times* (Singapore), "Finger Pointed at JI Militants," 6 August 2003; and "Warning to Megawati, Message to U.S.," 6 August 2003.

23. BBC News, al-Qaeda statement, Full text, 17 November 2003, http://news.bbc.co.uk/1/hi/world/3276859.stm.

24. BBC News, 12 February 2003, "Bin Laden tape: Text," http://news.bbc.co.uk/2/hi/middle_east/2751019.stm.

25. News 24, "Al Qaeda Group Claims Blast," 22 April 2004, http://www.news24.com/News24/World/News/0,2-10-1462_1516119,00.html.

26. *Sunday Observer* (UK), "Sinai Resort Bombings: Al-Qaeda-linked Group Claims Responsibility," 10 October 2004, http://www.sundayobserver.lk/2004/10/10/wor02.html.

Chapter 18: Zionism and the Pursuit of West Bank Settlements

1. See Michael Karpin and Ina Friedman, *Murder in the Name of God, The Plot to Kill Yitzhak Rabin* (London: Granta Books, 1998), pp. 4–5.

2. Ibid., pp. 8–9.

3. See Allan C. Brownfeld, "Religious Zionism: A Growing Impediment To Middle East Peace," *Washington Report on Middle East Affairs* 21, no. 9 (December 2002): 71.

4. Ibid.

5. Ibid.

6. For more on the Basel meeting, see David Mendelsson, "From the First Zionist Congress (1897) to the Twelfth (1921)," online at the Jewish Virtual Library website http://www.jewishvirtuallibrary.org/jsource/Zionism/firstcong.html.

7. Ibid. Also, see Allan C. Brownfeld, "Religious Zionism"; and Michael Karpin and Ina Friedman, *Murder in the Name of God*.

8. Ibid.

9. Milton Viorst, *What Shall I do with This People? The Jews and the Fractious Politics of Judaism* (New York: Free Press, 2002), p. 10.

10. Ibid., p. 11.

11. Ibid.

12. Ibid., p. 13.

13. Ibid., p. 44.

14. Yehoshafat Harkabi, *The Bar Kokhba Syndrome: Risk and Realism in International Politics* (New York: S.P.I. Books, 1983).

15. Ibid.

16. See Donald Neff, "Settlements in U.S. Policy," *Journal of Palestine Studies* 23, no. 3 (Spring 1994): 53–69; also see Mark Rosenblit, "International Law And Jewish Settlement In The Land Of Israel," online at http://www.rosenblit.com/Law.htm.

17. See Allan C. Brownfeld, "Are Jewish Intolerance and Extremism the Real Threat?" *Issues* (Winter 2003), available online at http://www.acjna.org/article_view.asp?article_id=271.

18. Allan C. Brownfeld, "Is Israel Prepared to Confront Increasingly Widespread Jewish Intolerance?" *Washington Report on Middle East Affairs* (January/February 2000): 67–68; also see Michael Karpin and Ina Friedman, *Murder in the Name of God*.

19. *New York Times* (28 February 1994): 1.

20. Allan C. Brownfeld, "Growing Intolerance Threatens the Humane Jewish Tradition," *Washington Report on Middle East Affairs* (March 1999): 84–85, 89.

21. Donald Neff, "Jewish Defense League Unleashes Campaign of Violence in America," *Washington Report on Middle East Affairs* (July–August 1999): 81.

22. U.S. Department of Justice, Federal Bureau of Investigation, Terrorist Research and Analytical Center, Terrorism Section, Criminal Investigative Division,

FBI Analysis of Terrorist Incidents and Terrorist-Related Activities in the United States (1985).

23. Department of Energy, *Terrorism in the United States and the Potential Threat to Nuclear Facilities*, R-3351-DOE, January 1986, pp. 11–16.

24. Donald Neff, "Jewish Defense League," p. 2.

25. Yair Kotler, *Heil Kahane* (New York: Adama Books, 1986), p. 153; also see pp. 198–212. Also see http://www.ihr.org/books/ztn/ztn.shtml.

26. Ehud Sprinzak, *The Ascendance of Israel's Radical Right* (New York: Oxford University Press, 1991), p. 239.

27. Ehud Sprinzak, *Brother against Brother: Violence and Extremism in Israeli Politics From Altalena to the Rabin Assassination* (New York: Free Press, 1999), p. 145.

28. Ehud Sprinzak, *Brother against Brother*, p. 147.

29. For more on this, see Haggai Segal, "Clear Away the Abomination!" in *Dear Brothers: The West Bank Jewish Underground* (Woodmere, NY: Beit Shamai Publications, 1988), pp. 52–60.

30. Ehud Sprinzak, *The Ascendance of Israel's Radical Right* (New York: Oxford University Press, 1991), p. 258.

31. Yair Kotler, *Heil Kahane*, p. 198.

32. Allan C. Brownfeld, "Rhetorical Violence and Religious Extremism," *Issues* (Fall 1995), available online at http://acnja.org/article_view.asp?article_id=54.

33. Ehud Sprinzak, *Brother against Brother*, p. 245.

34. See Karpin and Friedman, *Murder in the Name of God*, pp. 83–85.

35. Robert Friedman, "The Rabbi Who Sentenced Yitzhak Rabin to Death," *New York Times*, 9 October 1995.

36. Ehud Sprinzak, *Brother against Brother*, pp. 259–60.

37. Steven Simon, "The New Terrorism and the Peace Process," Madeleine Feher European Scholar Lecture, Begin Sadat Center for Strategic Studies, 1999, online at http://www.biu.ac.il/SOC/besa/publications.

38. Eric Silver, *Begin* (London: Weidenfeld and Nicolson, 1984), p. 88.

39. David Shipler, *Arab and Jew: Wounded Spirits in a Promised Land* (New York: Times Books, 1986), pp. 37–38.

40. For more on the story of Kfar Kassem, see http://www.jewishvirtuallibrary.org/jsource/History/Kassem.html and http://www.jerusalemites.org/crimes/massacres/2.htm.

41. Mark Juergensmeyer, *Terror in the Mind of God: The Global Rise of Religious Violence* (Berkeley: University of California Press, 2000), pp. 46–47.

42. Ibid., pp. 54–55.

43. Gil Sedan, "Settlers Stage Militant Protests in Land-for-Peace Battle," *Jewish Telegraphic Agency*, 23 June 2000.

44. Joseph Aaron, "The Bogeyman Phenomenon," *The Jerusalem Post*, 3 July 2000.

45. Ibid.

46. Gil Sedan, "Settlers Stage Militant Protests."

47. David Horovitz, cited in the *New York Times*, 30 June 2000.

48. Barbara Sofer, *Jerusalem Post*, International Edition, 30 June 2000.

49. "Masorti Synagogue Firebombed," *Pluralist* (Israel Religious Action Center Monthly Newsletter), 25 June 2000, p. 2.

50. Ibid., pp. 2–3.

51. Ibid.

52. Avi Machlis, "Conservative Synagogue Torched in Jerusalem," *Jerusalem Post*, International Edition, 7 July 2000.

53. Ehud Sprinzak, *Brother against Brother*, pp. 46–47.

54. "Assassination Worries in Israel," CBS News, 22 October 2004, online at http://www.cbsnews.com/stories/2004/10/22/world/main650780.shtml.

55. "Rebel Forces Set to Disrupt Final Withdrawal Vote," *Sunday Herald*, 24 October 2004, online at http://www.sundayherald.com/45603.

56. "Dichter Warns of Rise in Extremist Jews," *Newsmax Wires*, 5 July 2004, online at http://www.newsmax.com/archives/articles/2004/7/4/172029.shtml.

57. Allan C. Brownfeld, "Fear of Ultra-Orthodox Violence Threatens Israeli Political Process, Withdrawal Prospects," *Washington Report on Middle East Affairs*, 21 October 2004, pp. 73–74.

58. Yossi Alpher, "The Specter of Another Murder," *The Forward*, 16 July 2004, available online at www.forward.com/main/article.php?ref=alpher 20040715-1201.

59. Ibid.

60. Jeffrey Goldberg, "Among the Settlers," *The New Yorker*, 31 May 2004. Available online at http://www.newyorker.com/fact/content/?040531fa_fact2_a.

61. Ibid.

62. Ibid.

63. Ibid.

64. Chris McGreal, "Jewish Settlers threaten Sharon's Life, Shin Bet Says," *The Guardian* (UK), 7 July 2004.

65. Gil Sedan, "Tales of the Temple Mount: Talk of Plots Prompts a Debate about Motives of Accusers and Extremists," *Jewish Telegraphic Agency*, 24 July 2004.

66. *Washington Jewish Week*, 29 July 2004.

67. *The Jerusalem Report*, 9 August 2004.

68. Mark Juergensmeyer, *Terror in the Mind of God*, p. 4.

69. Ibid.

70. Allan C. Brownfeld, "Extremism in Israel is Fueled by a Growing Ultra-Orthodox Movement in the U.S.," *Washington Report on Middle East Affairs* (January–February 2001): 71–72.

71. Steven Simon, "The New Terrorism."

72. Ehud Sprinzak, "The Israeli Radical Right: History, Culture and Politics," in *Encounters with the Contemporary Radical Right*, edited by Peter Merkl and Leonard Weinberg (Boulder, CO: Westview Press, 1993).

73. Steven Simon, "The New Terrorism."

74. Ibid.

75. Reuven Firestone, "The War is About Religion," *Sh'ma* (December 2000), available online at http://www.shma.com/decol/firestone.phtml.

76. Ibid.

77. Ibid.

Select Bibliography and Resources for Further Reading

Printed Resources

Abou El Fadl, Khaled. *Rebellion & Violence in Islamic Law*. New York: Cambridge University Press, 2001.

Abu Amr, Ziad. *Islamic Fundamentalism in the West Bank and Gaza*. Bloomington: Indiana University Press, 1994.

Abuza, Zachary. *Militant Islam in Southeast Asia: Crucible of Terror*. Boulder, CO: Lynne Rienner, 2003.

Abuza, Zachary. *Muslims, Politics and Violence in Indonesia: An Emerging Jihadist–Islamist*. National Bureau of Asian Research, 2004.

Adorno, Theodor, et al. *The Authoritarian Personality*. New York: W. W. Norton, 1969 (1950).

Aho, James. *The Politics of Righteousness*. Seattle: University of Washington Press, 1990.

Al-Khattar, Aref M. *Religion and Terrorism; An Interfaith Perspective*. Westport, CT: Praeger, 2003.

Alape, Arturo. "Women in the FARC Guerrilla." Undated. Available online at http://www.farcep.org/pagina_ingles.

Algar, Hamid. *Wahhabism: A Critical Essay*. Oneonta, NY: Islamic Publications International, 2002.

American Psychiatric Association. *Diagnostic and Statistical Manual of Mental Disorders*, 4th ed., Text Revised, 309.81. Washington, DC: APA, 2000.

Anderson, C. A., et al. *The Influence of Media Violence on Youth*. Washington, DC: Psychological Science in the Public Interest, 2003.

Anti-Defamation League. *Racist Groups Using Computer Gaming to Promote Violence Against Blacks, Latinos, and Jews*. Anti-Defamation League website: http://www.adl.org.

Apter, David, ed. *Ideology and Discontent*. Glencoe, IL: Free Press, 1964.

Armstrong, Karen. *The Battle for God*. New York: Alfred A. Knopf, 2000.

Atran, Scott. "Genesis of Suicide Terrorism." *Science* 299 (2003): 1534–39.

Auda, Gehud. *Palestinian Suicide Bombing: Description and Evaluation*. Ahram Strategic Papers, no. 114. Cairo, Egypt: Al-Ahram Center for Political and Strategic Studies, 2002.

Azzam, Maha. "Al-Qaeda: The Misunderstood Wahhabi Connection and the Ideology of Violence." Briefing Paper No. 1, Royal Institute of International Affairs (February 2003).

Bandura, Albert. "Mechanisms of Moral Disengagement." In *Origins of Terrorism: Psychologies, Ideologies, Theologies, States of Mind*. Edited by Walter Reich, pp. 161–91. Cambridge: Cambridge University Press, 1990.

Baran, Zeyno, ed. *The Challenge of Hizb ut-Tahrir: Deciphering and Combating Radical Islamist Ideology*. Conference Report, The Nixon Center, September 2004.

Barkun, Michael. *Religion and the Racist Right*. Chapel Hill, NC: University of North Carolina Press, 1994.

Begin, Menachem. *The Revolt: Story of the Irgun*. New York: Henry Schuman, Inc., 1951.

Bell, J. Bowyer. *The IRA, 1968–2000: Analysis of a Secret Army*. London: Frank Cass, 2000.

Bell, J. Bowyer. *The Secret Army: The IRA, 1916–1979*. Cambridge, MA: MIT Press, 1980.

Bell, J. Bowyer. *Terror Out of Zion: Irgun Zvai Leumi, LEHI, and the Palestine Underground, 1929–1949*. New York: St. Martin's Press, 1977.

Benjamin, Daniel, and Steven Simon. *The Age of Sacred Terror*. New York: Random House, 2002.

Berger, J. M. "Online Videos Shows Children Training for Jihad; Young Son of Osama bin Laden Reads Statement." *Intelwire* (2004). Online at http://www.intelwire.com/2004_10_13_exclusives.html and by subscription at http://intelwire.egoplex.com.

Blee, Kathleen. *Inside Organized Racism: Women in the Movement*. Berkeley: University of California Press, 2002.

Bloom, Mia M. *Dying to Kill: The Allure of Suicide Terror*. New York: Columbia University Press, 2005.

Bloom, Mia M. "Palestinian Suicide Bombing: Public Support, Market Share and Outbidding." *Political Science Quarterly* 119, no. 1 (Spring 2004): 61–88.

Burdman, Daphne. "Education, Indoctrination, and Incitement: Palestinian Children on Their Way to Martyrdom." *Terrorism and Political Violence* 15, no. 1 (Spring 2003).

Charbel, Ghassan. "The Khaled Mishaal Interview (2 of 7)." *al Hayat*, 15 December 2003. Available online (in English) at http://english.daralhayat.com/Spec/12-2003/Article-20031215-7a215ab8-c0a8-01ed-0015-c5ece4bc1b17/story.html.

Cialdini, Robert. *Influence: The Psychology of Persuasion*. New York: Harper-Collins, 1993.

CNN. "Russia's 'black widows' wreak terror." CNN.com. 3 September 2004, http://www.cnn.com/2004/WORLD/europe/09/01/russia.widows.

Coates, James. *Armed and Dangerous*. New York: Hill and Wang, 1995.

Cohn, Norman. *The Pursuit of the Millennium*. New York: Oxford University Press, 1970.

Collier, Paul. "Rebellion as a Quasi-Criminal Activity." *Journal of Conflict Resolution* 44, no. 6 (2000): 838–52.

Collier, Paul, and Anke Hoeffler. "Greed and Grievance in Civil War." World Bank Policy Research Paper 2355. Washington, DC: The World Bank, 2000.

Combs, Cindy C. "The Media: A Weapon for Both Sides?" In *Terrorism in the Twenty-First Century*. Edited by Cindy Combs, pp. 120–48. Saddle River, NJ: Prentice Hall, 1997.

Crenshaw, Martha. *Terrorism in Context*. University Park: The Pennsylvania State University Press, 1995.

Cuthbertson, Ian M. "Prisons and the Education of Terrorists." *World Policy Journal* 21, no. 3 (Fall 2004).

Darby, John, ed. *Northern Ireland: The Background to the Conflict*. Belfast, Northern Ireland: Appletree Press, 1983.

Day, Susie. "Counter-Intelligent: The Surveillance and Indictment of Lynne Stewart." *Monthly Review* 54, no. 6 (November 2002). Online at http://www.monthlyreview.org/1102day.htm.

della Porta, Donatella. *Social Movements, Political Violence and the State: A Comparative Analysis of Italy and Germany*. Cambridge: Cambridge University Press, 1995.

Diamond, Sara. *Roads to Dominion: Right-Wing Movements and Political Power in the United States*. New York: Guilford Press, 1995.

Dobratz, Betty, and Stephanie Shanks-Meile. *"White Power, White Pride!" The White Separatist Movement in the United States*. New York: Twayne Publishers, 1997.

Elliott, Marianne. *The Catholics of Ulster: A History*. New York: Basic Books, 2002.

Elshtain, Jean Bethke. *Women and War*. Chicago: University of Chicago Press, 1995.

Enright, Robert D. *Forgiveness Is A Choice*. American Psychological Association. Washington, DC: American Psychiatric Association, 2001.

Esposito, John L. *Unholy War: Terror in the Name of Islam*. New York: Oxford University Press, 2002.

Esposito, John L., and Michael Watson, eds. *Religion and Global Order*. Cardiff: University of Wales Press, 2000.

FARC. *Esbozo Histórico*. Comisión Internacional, 1998 (self-published propaganda booklet).

FARC. "Proposed Agenda of the FARC, May 6, 1999." Available online at http://www.ciponline.org/colombia/farc.htm.

FARC. "Revolutionary Armed Forces of Colombia-People's Army: History." Available online at http://www.farcep.org/pagina_ingles (restricted access).

FARC. "38 Years of the FARC-EP." Available online at http://six.swix.ch/farcep/Nuestra_historia/38_aniversario_de_las_FARC-EP.html.

FARC. "Women: May 2004." FARC, 2004. Available online at http://www.farcep.org/mujer/09demayo/madres2004.php (restricted access).

FARC. "Women and their Battles—Disadvantaged Situation." FARC, 2004. Available online at http://www.farcep.org/mujer/09demayo/mayo2004.php (restricted access).

FARC. "Women in Active Resistance." FARC, undated. Available online at http://www.farcep.org/mujer/articulos/resistencia.php (restricted access).

Fearon, James, and David Laitin. "Insurgency and Civil War." *American Political Science Review* 97, no. 1 (2003): 91–106.

Fergosi, Paul. *Jihad in the West: Muslim Conquest from the 7th to the 21st Centuries.* Amherst, MA: Prometheus Books, 1998.

Ferraresi, Franco. *Threats to Democracy.* Princeton, NJ: Princeton University Press, 1996.

Flynn, Kevin, and Gary Gerhardt. *The Silent Brotherhood: Inside America's Racist Underground.* New York: Signet, 1990.

Friedman, Robert I. *The False Prophet: Rabbi Meir Kahane: From FBI Informant to Knesset Member.* Chicago: Lawrence Hill Books, 1990.

Ganor, Boaz. "Suicide Attacks in Isreal." In *Countering Suicide Terrorism.* Herzliya: International Policy Institute for Counter-Terrorism, 2000.

Gartenstein-Ross, Daveed. "Jihadi Rap." *Front Page Magazine* (FrontPage Magazine.com), 10 November 2004.

Geifman, Anna. *Thou Shalt Kill.* Princeton, NJ: Princeton University Press, 1993.

Glazier, Jack. "Anti-Semitism." In *Encyclopedia of Fundamentalism.* Edited by Brenda Brasher, pp. 21–24. New York: Routledge, 2001.

Glock, Charles, and Rodney Stark. *Christian Beliefs and Anti-Semitism.* New York: Harper and Row, 1966.

Gordon, Harvey. "The 'Suicide' Bomber: Is it a Psychiatric Phenomenon?" *Psychiatric Bulletin* 26, no. 8 (2002): 285–87.

Griffin, Roger. "Fascism." In *Encyclopedia of Fundamentalism.* Edited by Brenda Brasher, pp. 171–78. New York: Routledge, 2001.

Griffith, Lee. *The War on Terrorism and the Terror of God.* Grand Rapids, MI: William B. Eerdmans, 2002.

Gunaratna, Rohan. *Inside Al Qaeda: Global Network of Terror.* New York: Columbia University Press, 2002.

Gunaratna, Rohan. *Sri Lanka's Ethnic Crisis and National Security.* Colombo: South Asian Network on Conflict Research, 1998.

Gurr, Ted Robert. *Why Men Rebel.* Princeton, NJ: Princeton University Press, 1970.

Hamden, Raymond H. "The Retributional Terrorist—Type 4." In *The Psychology of Terrorism.* Edited by Chris E. Stout. Westport, CT: Praeger, 2002.

Hatina, Meir. *Islam and Salvation in Palestine*. Dayan Center Papers #127. Tel Aviv: The Moshe Dayan Center for Middle Eastern and African Studies, Tel Aviv University, 2001.

Heehs, Peter. *The Bomb in Bengal: The Rise of Revolutionary Terrorism in India, 1900–1910*. New York: Oxford University Press, 1996.

Hefner, Robert W. *Civil Islam: Muslims and Democratization in Indonesia*. Princeton, NJ: Princeton University Press, 2000.

Hefner, Robert W. "Global Violence and Indonesian Muslim Politics." *American Anthropologist* 104, no. 3 (September 2002): 756.

Heilman, Samuel C. "Guides of the Faithful: Contemporary Religious Zionist Rabbis." In *Spokesman for the Despised: Fundamentalist Leaders of the Middle East*. Edited by R. Scott Appleby, pp. 328–62. Chicago: University of Chicago Press, 1997.

Heinzen, Karl. "Murder." In *Voices of Terror*. Edited by Walter Laqueur. New York: New American Library, 1978.

Hertzberg, Arthur. "Rabbi Abraham Isaac Kook, 1865–1935." In *The Zionist Idea: A Historical Analysis and Reader*, pp. 417–25. New York: Atheneum, 1977.

Hewitt, Christopher. *Understanding Terrorism in America*. New York: Routledge, 2003.

Hoffman, Bruce. *Al Qaeda, Trends in Terrorism and Future Potentialities: An Assessment*. Washington, DC: RAND, 2003.

Hoffman, Bruce. "The Logic of Suicide Terrorism," *Atlantic Monthly* 291, no. 5 (2003): 40–47.

Hoffman, Bruce, and Gordon H. McCormick. "Terrorism, Signaling, and Suicide Attack." *Studies in Conflict and Terrorism* 27, no. 4 (July–August 2004): 243–81.

Horowitz, Donald. *Ethnic and Religious Groups in Conflict*. Berkeley, CA: University of California Press, 1985 (Updated edition with new preface, 2001).

Hroub, Khaled. *Hamas: Political Thought and Practice*. Washington, DC: Institute for Palestine Studies, 2000.

Human Rights Watch. *You'll Learn Not to Cry*. New York: Human Rights Watch, 2003.

Intelligence.org Center for Special Studies. "The Martyrdom and Suicide Culture in Palestinian Universities—An-Najah University in Nablus as a Case Study." Special Information Bulletin, Intelligence and Terrorism Information Center at the Center for Special Studies, May 2003, http://www.intelligence.org.il/eng/bu/sib_mb/university.htm (accessed 13 January 2005).

International Crisis Group (ICG). "Indonesia Backgrounder: Jihad in Central Sulawesi." Report No. 74. Jakarta and Brussels: ICG, 3 February 2004.

International Crisis Group (ICG). "Islamic Social Welfare Activism in the Occupied Palestinian Territories: A Legitimate Target?" ICG Middle East. Report No. 13, International Crisis Group, 2 April 2003, http://www.intl-crisis-group.org/projects/showreport.cfm?reportid=933.

International Crisis Group (ICG). "Jemaah Islamiyah in Southeast Asia: Damaged But Still Dangerous." Report No. 63. Jakarta and Brussels: ICG, 26 August 2004.

Jacquard, Roland. *In the Name of Osama bin Laden*. Durham, NC: Duke University Press, 2002.

Jensen, Richard. "Daggers, Rifles and Dynamite: Anarchist Terrorism in Nineteenth Century Europe." *Terrorism and Political Violence* 16, no. 1 (2004).

Jones, Sidney. *Indonesia Backgrounder: Jihad in Central Sulawesi*. London and Jakarta: International Crisis Group, 2004.

Jones, Sidney. *Jemaah Islamiyah in Southeast Asia: Damaged But Still Dangerous*. London and Jakarta: International Crisis Group, 2003.

Jordan, Sandra. "Girls Go to War as Colombia's Frontline Killers." *The Observer* (London) (14 July 2002).

Jorisch, Avi. "Al-Manar: Hizballah TV, 24/7." *The Middle East Quarterly* 11 (Winter 2004).

Juergensmeyer, Mark. *Terror in the Mind of God: The Global Rise of Religious Violence*. Berkeley, CA: University of California Press, 2000.

Kaplan, Jeffrey. "Right-Wing Violence in North America." In *Terror from the Extreme Right*. Edited by Tore Bjorgo. London: Frank Cass, 1995.

Karpin, Michael, and Ina Friedman. *Murder in the Name of God: The Plot to Kill Yitzhak Rabin*. London: Granta Books, 1998.

Kepel, Gilles. *The War for Muslim Minds*. Translated by Pascale Ghazale. Cambridge, MA: The Belknap Press of Harvard University Press, 2004.

Kobasa, Suzanne C., Salvatore R. Maddi, and Stephen Khan. "Hardiness and Health: A Perspective Study." *Journal of Personality and Social Psychology* 42 (1982): 168–77.

Kotler, Yair. *Heil Kahane*. New York: Adama Books, 1986.

Kropotkin, Pyotr. "The Spirit of Revolt." In *Voices of Terror*. Edited by Walter Laqueur. New York: Reed Press, 1978.

Kurz, Anat, and Nahman Tal. *Hamas: Radical Islam in a National Struggle*. Memorandum #48. Tel Aviv: Jaffee Center for Strategic Studies, Tel Aviv University, 1997.

Kushner, Harvey W. "Suicide Bombers: Business as Usual." *Studies in Conflict and Terrorism* 19, no. 4 (October–December 1996): 329–37.

Lachkar, Joan. "The Psychological Make-Up of the Suicide Bomber." *Journal of Psychohistory* 20 (Spring 2002): 349–67.

LaFranchi, Howard. "When War Veterans are Children." *Christian Science Monitor*. 20 March 2000, p. 1.

Landau-Tasseron, Ella. "Jihad." In *Encyclopaedia of the Qur'an*, Volume 3. Leiden-Boston: Brill, 2003.

Laqueur, Walter. *No End to War*. New York: Continuum, 2003.

Laqueur, Walter. *Terrorism*. Boston, MA: Little, Brown & Co., 1977.

Lara, Patricia. *Mujeres en la Guerra*. 2nd ed. Bogotá: Planeta, 2000.

Larsson, J. P. *Understanding Religious Violence: Thinking Outside the Box on Terrorism*. Aldershot (UK) and Burlington, VT: Ashgate, 2004.

Lathem, Niles. "Al-Qaeda Terror.com." *New York Post*, 16 September 2003, p. A12.

Lawrence, Bruce B. *Shattering the Myth: Islam Beyond Violence.* Princeton: Princeton University Press, 1998.

Lazarus, Richard S., James R. Averill, and Edward M. Opton, Jr. "The Psychology of Coping: Issues of Research and Assessment." In *Coping and Adaptation.* Edited by George V. Coehlo, David A. Hamburg, and John E. Adams, pp. 249–315. New York: Basic Books, 1974.

Lenin, V. I. "Revolutionary Adventurism." In *Voices of Terror.* Edited by Walter Laqueur. New York: Reed Press, 1978.

Lester, David, Bijou Yang, and Mark Lindsay. "Suicide Bombers: Are Psychological Profiles Possible?" *Studies in Conflict and Terrorism* 27, no. 4 (2004): 283–95.

Levitt, Matthew A. "Ban Hamas in Europe." *Peacewatch #430.* Washington Institute for Near East Policy. 4 September 2003 (with Jeff Cary).

Levitt, Matthew A. *Exposing Hamas: Funding Terror Under the Cover of Charity.* New Haven: Yale University Press, forthcoming 2006.

Levitt, Matthew A. "Hamas Blood Money: Mixing Good Works and Terror is No Formula for Peace." *Peacewatch # 418.* Washington Institute for Near East Policy. 5 May 2003.

Levitt, Matthew A. "Hamas's Political Wing: Terror by Other Means." *Peacewatch #440.* Washington Institute for Near East Policy. 6 January 2004.

Levitt, Matthew A. "Hamas: Toward a Lebanese-Style War of Attrition?" *Peacewatch #367.* Washington Institute for Near East Policy. 26 February 2002.

Levitt, Matthew A. "Hamas from Cradle to Grave." *Middle East Quarterly* 9, no. 1 (Winter 2004).

Levitt, Matthew A. "Indicting Hamas: By Disrupting its Operations, Does the West Become a Target?" *Peacewatch #471.* Washington Institute for Near East Policy. 26 August 2004.

Levitt, Matthew A. "The Politics of Terrorist Financing in the Middle East." *The Middle East Review of International Affairs (MERIA) Journal* 6, no. 4 (December 2002).

Levitt, Matthew A. "Shaykh Yassin and Hamas Terror." *Peacewatch #448.* Washington Institute for Near East Policy. 23 March 2004.

Levitt, Matthew A. "Untangling the Terror Web: Identifying and Counteracting the Phenomenon of Crossover between Terrorist Groups." *SAIS Review* 24, no. 1 (Winter–Spring 2004).

Lewis, Bernard. *The Assassins: A Radical Sect in Islam.* New York: Basic Books, 2002.

Lipset, Seymour M., and Earl Raab. *The Politics of Unreason.* New York: Harper and Row, 1970.

Litvak, Meir. *The Islamization of Palestinian Identity: The Case of Hamas.* Data and Analysis Paper. Tel Aviv: The Moshe Dayan Center for Middle Eastern and African Studies, Tel Aviv University, 1996.

Lukens-Bull, Ronald A. "Two Sides of the Same Coin: Modernity and Tradition in Islamic Education." *Anthropology and Education Quarterly* 32, no. 3 (2001): 353.

Marighella, Carlos. *The Manual of the Urban Guerrilla*. Chapel Hill, NC: Documentary Publications, 1985.

Marshall, Claire. "The Battle for Colombia's Children." *BBC News*. 1 October 2003.

Mayer, Ann Elizabeth. "War and Peace in the Islamic Law Tradition and International Law." In *Just War and Jihad*. Edited by James Turner Johnson and John Kelsay. New York: Greenwood, 1991.

Medina, Juan Guillermo Ferro, and Graciela Uribe Ramón. *The Order of the War: The FARC-EP Between the Organization and the Politics*. Bogotá: CEJA, 2002.

Merari, Ariel. "The Readiness to Kill and Die: Suicidal Terrorism in the Middle East." In *Origins of Terrorism: Psychologies, Ideologies, Theologies, State of Mind*. Edited by Walter Reich. New York: Woodrow Wilson International Center for Scholars and Cambridge University Press, 1990, pp. 192–210.

Meza Vargas, Ricardo. "The FARC, the War and the Crisis of the State." *NACLA Report on the Americas* 31 (1998): 220–27.

Mir, Mustansir. "Jihad in Islam." In *The Jihad and Its Times*. Edited by Hadia Dajani-Shakeel and Ronald Messier. Ann Arbor: University of Michigan, 1991.

Mishal, Shaul, and Avraham Sela. *The Palestinian Hamas: Vision, Violence, and Coexistence*. New York: Columbia University Press, 2000.

Moser, Caroline O. N., and Fiona C. Clark, eds. *Victims, Perpetrators or Actors*. London: Zed Books, 2001.

Moss-Kanter, Rosabeth. *Commitment and Community: Communes and Utopias in Sociological Perspective*. Cambridge, MA: Harvard University Press, 1972.

Nacos, Brigitte L. *Terrorism and the Media: From the Iran Hostage Crisis to the World Trade Center Bombing*. New York: Columbia University Press, 1994.

Nechaev, Sergey. "Catechism of the Revolutionist." In *The Terrorism Reader*. Edited by Walter Laqueur. New York: New American Library, 1987.

Nisbet, Robert. *The Quest for Community*. New York: Harper and Brothers, 1953.

Ortiz, Ramón D. "Insurgent Strategies in the Post-Cold War: The Case of the Revolutionary Armed Forces of Colombia." *Studies in Conflict & Terrorism* 25, no. 2 (March/April 2002): 127–43.

Pape, Robert A. "The Strategic Logic of Suicide Terrorism." *American Political Science Review* 97, no. 3 (2003): 343–61.

Paxton, Robert. *The Anatomy of Fascism*. New York: Alfred A. Knopf, 2003.

Penhaul, Karl. "Colombia's Communist Guerrillas Take on Feminine Face." *Boston Globe*, 7 January 2001, p. 6A.

Perlmutter, Dawn. *Investigating Religious Terrorism and Ritualistic Crimes*. Boca Raton, FL: CRC Press, 2004.

Perrie, Maureen. "Political and Economic Terror in the Tactics of the Russian Social Revolutionary Party before 1914." In *Social Protest, Violence and Terror in Nineteenth and Twentieth Century Europe.* Edited by Wolgang Mommsen and Gerhard Hirschfeld. New York: St. Martin's Press, 1982.

Peters, Rudolph. *Jihad in Classical and Modern Islam.* Princeton, NJ: Markus Wiener Publishers, 1996.

Pew Research Center for People and the Press. Online at http://people.press.org.

Pomper, Philip. "Russian Revolutionary Terrorism." In *Terrorism in Context.* Edited by Martha Crenshaw. University Park: Pennsylvania State University Press, 1995.

Post, Jerrold M. "Terrorist Psycho-logic: Terrorist Behavior as a Product of Psychological Forces." In *Origins of Terrorism: Psychologies, Ideologies, Theologies, States of Mind.* Edited by Walter Reich, pp. 25–40. Baltimore, MD: Woodrow Wilson Center Press, 1998.

Post, Jerrold M., Ehud Sprinzak, and Laurita M. Denny. "The Terrorists in Their Own Words: Interviews with 35 Incarcerated Middle Eastern Terrorists." *Journal of Terrorism and Political Violence* 15, no. 1 (Spring 2003): 171–84.

Pratkanis, Anthony, and Elliott Aronson. *Age of Propaganda: The Everyday Use and Abuse of Persuasion.* New York: W. H. Freeman and Company, 1999.

Rapoport, David C. "Fear and Trembling: Terrorism in Three Religious Traditions." *American Political Science Review* 78, no. 3 (September 1984): 658–77.

Reader, Ian. *Religious Violence in Contemporary Japan; The Case of Aum Shinrikyō.* Richmond (UK): Curzon, 2000.

Reeve, Simon. *The New Jackals.* Boston: Northeastern University Press, 1999.

Reich, Walter, ed. *Origins of Terrorism: Psychologies, Ideologies, Theologies, States of Mind.* Washington, DC: Woodrow Wilson Center Press, 1998.

Rempe, Dennis M. "Guerrillas, Bandits, and Independent Republics: U.S. Counterinsurgency Efforts in Colombia 1959–1965." *Small Wars and Insurgencies* 6, no. 3 (Winter 1995): 304–27.

Rodgers, Peter. "Israel and the Palestinians: Endless Blood and Retribution?" Research Paper no. 8, Australian Information Research Services. Canberra, Australia: Department of the Parliamentary Library, 2002. Online at: http://www.aph.gov.au/library/pubs/rp/2001-02/02RP08.pdf.

Rosenberger, John. "Discerning the Behavior of the Suicide Bomber: The Role of Vengeance." *Journal of Religion and Health* 42, no. 1 (2003): 13–20.

Roy, Olivier. *Globalized Islam.* New York: Columbia University Press, 2004.

Rozen, Laura. "Forums Point the Way to Jihad." *Wired News,* 2003. Online at http://www.wired.com/news/conflict/0,2100,59897,00.html.

Sageman, Marc. *Understanding Terror Networks.* Philadelphia: University of Pennsylvania Press, 2004.

Salib, Emad. "Suicide Terrorism: A Case of Folie à Plusieurs?" *British Journal of Psychiatry* 182, no. 6 (2003): 475–76.

Sanderson, Thomas M. "Transnational Terror and Organized Crime: Blurring the Lines." *SAIS Review* 24, no. 1 (Winter 2004).

Save the Children UK. "Angie walks on stilts to escape fear." 20 September 2002.

Schbley, Ayla. "Religious Terrorism, the Media, and International Islamization Terrorism: Justifying the Unjustifiable." *Studies in Conflict & Terrorism* 27, no. 3 (May–June 2004).

[Scherer, Michael]. Through Our Enemies Eyes: Osama bin Laden, Radical Islam, and the Future of America. Washington, DC: Brassey's, Inc., 2002.

Scherer, Ron, and Alexandra Marks. "Gangs, Prison: Al Qaeda Breeding Grounds?" *Christian Science Monitor*, 14 June 2002. Online at http://www.csmonitor.com/2002/0614/p02s01-usju.html.

Schoch, Bernd. *The Islamic Movement: A Challenge for Palestinian State-Building*. Jerusalem: Palestinian Academic Society for the Study of International Affairs (PASSIA), 1999.

Schwartz, Stephen. *The Two Faces of Islam: The House of Saud from Tradition to Terror*. New York: Doubleday, 2002.

Segal, Haggai. *Dear Brothers: The West Bank Jewish Underground*. Woodmere, NY: Beit Shamai Publications, 1988.

Shepard, William E. *Sayyid Qutb and Islamic Activism*. Boston: E. J. Brill, 1996.

Shipler, David. *Arab and Jew: Wounded Spirits in a Promised Land*. New York: Times Books, 1986.

Simon, Steve, and Jonathan Stevenson. "Confronting Hamas." *The National Interest* no. 74 (Winter 2003).

Sinclair, Andrew. *An Anatomy of Terror: A History of Terrorism*. London: Macmillan, 2003.

Singer, Peter W. *Children At War*. New York: Pantheon, 2005.

Singer, Peter W. "Pakistan's Madrassahs: Ensuring a System of Education, not Jihad." Brookings Institution Analysis Paper #14. Washington, DC: Brookings Institution, November 2001.

Singer, Peter W. "Western Militaries Confront Child Soldiers Threat." *Jane's Intelligence Review* (January 2005).

Smelser, Neil. *Theory of Collective Behavior*. New York: Free Press, 1962.

Sprinzak, Ehud. *The Ascendance of Israel's Radical Right*. New York: Oxford University Press, 1991.

Sprinzak, Ehud. *Brother against Brother: Violence and Extremism in Israeli Politics From Altalena to the Rabin Assassination*. New York: Free Press, 1999.

Sprinzak, Ehud. "The Israeli Radical Right: History, Culture and Politics." In *Encounters with the Contemporary Radical Right*. Edited by Peter Merkl and Leonard Weinberg. Boulder, CO: Westview Press, 1993.

Sprinzak, Ehud. "Rational Fanatics." *Foreign Policy*, 120 (2000): 66–73.

Stern, Jessica. "The Protean Enemy." *Foreign Affairs*. August 2003, p. 3.

Stern, Jessica. *Terror in the Name of God: Why Religious Militants Kill*. New York: HarperCollins, 2003.

Sternhell, Zeev. *The Birth of Fascist Ideology*. Princeton, NJ: Princeton University Press, 1994.

Sternhell, Zeev. "Fascist Ideology." In *The Fascism Reader*. Edited by Walter Laqueur. Berkeley: University of California Press, 1994.

Taarnby, Michael. "Recruitment of Islamist Terrorists in Europe: Trends and Perspectives." Center for Cultural Research (University of Aarhus, Denmark) on behalf of the Danish Ministry of Justice. 14 January 2005.

Tapsinar, Omer. "Promoting Educational and Economic Opportunity in the Islamic World." *Brookings Monograph*. Washington, DC: Brookings Institution, 2003.

Tarrow, Sidney. *Democracy and Disorder: Protest and Politics in Italy 1965–1975*. New York: Oxford University Press, 1989.

Trotsky, Leon. "The Collapse of Terrorism." In *Voices of Terror*. Edited by Walter Laqueur. New York: Reed Press, 1978.

Tzfati, Yariv, and Gabriel Weimann. "Terror on the Internet." *Politika* 4 (1999): 45–64 (in Hebrew).

Tzfati, Yariv, and Gabriel Weimann. "WWW.terrorism.com: Terror on the Internet." *Studies in Conflict and Terrorism* 25, no. 5 (2002): 317–32.

UN High Commissioner for Human Rights. Report of the UN High Commissioner for Human Rights on the Human Rights Situation in Colombia. E/CN. 4/2001/15 (8 August 2001), no. 109.

United Nations Development Program. *Arab Human Development Report*. New York: United Nations, 2003.

U. S. Congress. House. Committee on Internal Security. Hearings of March 29 and May 1, 1973. "Revolutionary Activities Directed Toward the Administration of Penal or Correctional Systems." Part I.

U. S. Congress. House. Committee on Internal Security. *Revolutionary Target: The American Penal System*. 93rd Cong., 1st sess. Committee Report, 18 December 1973.

U.S. Congress. Senate. Judiciary Committee, Subcommittee on Terrorism, Technology and Homeland Security. Hearing of 14 October 2003. "Terrorist Recruitment and Infiltration in the United States: Prisons and Military as an Operational Base." 108th Cong., 1st sess. The transcript of this testimony is available online at: http://judiciary.senate.gov/hearing.cfm?id=960.

U.S. Treasury Department. "Treasury Designates al-Aqsa International Foundation as Financier of Terror: Charity Linked to Funding of the Hamas Terrorist Organization." Department of the Treasury, Office of Public Affairs. http://www.treas.gov/press/releases/js439.htm.

U.S. Treasury Department. "U.S. Designates Five Charities Funding Hamas and Six Senior Hamas Leaders as Terrorist Entities." Office of Public Affairs, Department of the Treasury, 22 August 2003. http://www.ustreas.gov/press/releases/js672.htm.

Vaillant, George E. *Ego Mechanisms of Defense: A Guide for Clinicians and Researchers*. Washington, DC: American Psychiatric Association, 1992.

Verton, Dan. *Black Ice: The Invisible Threat of Cyber-Terrorism.* New York: McGraw-Hill Osborne Media, 2003.

Weimann, Gabriel. *WWW.Terror.Net: How Modern Terrorism Uses the Internet*, Special Report #116. Washington DC: United States Institute of Peace, 2004. Available online at http://www.usip.org

Weinberg, Leonard, and William Eubank. *The Rise and Fall of Italian Terrorism.* Boulder, CO: Westview Press, 1987.

Wright, Lawrence. "The Terror Web." *New Yorker.* 2 August 2004.

Zanini, Michele, and Sean J. A. Edwards. "The Networking of Terror in the Information Age." In *Networks and Netwars.* Edited by Jon Arquilla and David Ronfeldt, pp. 29–60. Santa Monica: RAND Corporation, 2001.

Websites

http://www.hizb-ut-tahrir.org

http://www.khilafah.com.pk

http://www.1924.org

http://www.hizbuttahrir.org

http://www.pewinternet.org

http://www.muslimhiphop.com

Index

About the Editor and Contributors

JAMES J. F. FOREST, Ph.D., is Director of Terrorism Studies and Assistant Professor of Political Science at the U.S. Military Academy, where he teaches undergraduate courses in a range of subjects and directs research initiatives for the Combating Terrorism Center. Recent publications include *Homeland Security and Terrorism* (with Russell Howard and Joanne Moore, 2005); *Teaching Terror: Knowledge Transfer in the Terrorist World* (2005); a 200-page *Annotated Bibliography of Terrorism and Counterterrorism* (2004), available online at the Center's website (http://ctc.usma.edu); and *Terrorism and Oil in the New Gulf* (with Matt Sousa, forthcoming). His research has also appeared in the *Cambridge Review of International Affairs*, the *Journal of Political Science Education*, and the *Encyclopedia of Intelligence and Counterintelligence* (2005). Dr. Forest received his graduate degrees from Stanford University and Boston College and undergraduate degrees from Georgetown University and De Anza College.

ZACHARY ABUZA, Ph.D., is a Senior Fellow at the U.S. Institute of Peace and Associate Professor of Political Science and International Relations at Simmons College. He is the author of *Militant Islam in Southeast Asia* (2003) and several studies of Jemaah Islamiyah published by the National Bureau of Asian Research.

JAMES AHO, Ph.D., is Professor of Sociology at Idaho State University, Pocatello. He researches and writes about the connections between religion and violence, the body, and wealth. His published works include *This Thing of Darkness: A Sociology of the Enemy* (1994) and *The Politics of Righteousness* (1995).

MAHA AZZAM, Ph.D., is an Associate Fellow of the Middle East Program at the Royal Institute of International Affairs, London. She is the author of several book chapters, articles, and conference presentations on ideology and Islamic movements, and completed her doctoral thesis (at Oxford University) on the Muslim Brotherhood.

JARRET BRACHMAN is an Assistant Professor in the Department of Social Sciences and a Senior Associate in the Combating Terrorism Center at the United States Military Academy. His research interests include terrorism, counterterrorism policy, and militant Islamic ideology.

ALLAN C. BROWNFELD, J. D., is a nationally syndicated columnist and serves as Associate Editor of *The Lincoln Review* and editor of *Issues*, the quarterly journal of the American Council for Judaism. The author of five books, including *The Revolution Lobby* (with J. Michael Waller, 1985), and has served on the staff of the U.S. Senate, House of Representatives, and the Office of the Vice President.

JOSEPH FELTER, Ph.D., a Lieutenant Colonel in the U.S. Army and a career Special Forces and Foreign Area Officer, recently completed his doctorate in political science at Stanford University and joined the faculty of the Department of Social Sciences at the United States Military Academy in the fall of 2005. As a military attaché in Manila, he planned and coordinated combined efforts to develop the counterterrorist capabilities of the Armed Forces of the Philippines.

MADELEINE GRUEN is an intelligence analyst at the New York City Police Department's Counter Terrorism Division. She has done extensive research on radicalizing agents and terrorism on the Internet. Her articles on terrorist use of the Internet to recruit, indoctrinate, and raise funds have been published in journals and collected editions.

RAYMOND H. HAMDEN, Ph.D., is an American clinical and forensic psychologist practicing in Dubai, United Arab Emirates, where he consults in clinical psychology, crisis intervention, trauma, and domestic relations. In 1986, Dr. Hamden was a Visiting Fellow at the University of Maryland's Center for International Development and Conflict Management, where he coined the term "the retributional terrorist—type 4."

J. P. LARSSON, Ph.D., currently works for the British Government putting theoretical knowledge into practical use. He is author of *Understanding Religious Violence: Thinking Outside the Box on Terrorism* (2003) among other publications. His doctoral research on religious violence was conducted at the University of Wales Aberystwyth, where still teaches courses on terrorism, religion, and war.

MATTHEW A. LEVITT, Ph.D., is the Director of the Terrorism Studies Program at the Washington Institute for Near East Policy and a former FBI counterterrorism intelligence analyst. Dr. Levitt is an adjunct professor at the Paul H. Nitze School of Advanced International Studies (SAIS) at Johns Hopkins University and is the author of *Targeting Terror: U.S. Policy Toward Middle Eastern Terrorist Groups and State Sponsors in the War on Terror* (2002) and *Exposing Hamas: Funding Terror Under the Cover of Charity* (forthcoming).

BRIGITTE L. NACOS, Ph.D., a long-time U.S. correspondent for publications in Germany, is an adjunct professor of political science at Columbia University. Her published works include *Terrorism and the Media: From the Iran Hostage Crisis to the World Trade Center Bombing* (1994) and *Mass-Mediated Terrorism: The Central Role of the Media in Terrorism and Counterterrorism* (2002).

AMI PEDAHZUR, Ph.D., is a senior lecturer at the School of Political Science at the University of Haifa Israel and a Harrington Fellow at the University of Texas, Austin. He has written extensively on terrorism, right-wing extremism and the democratic response to extremism and violence. His published works include *The Israeli Response to Jewish Extremism and Violence: Defending Democracy* (2002) and *Political Parties and Terrorist Groups* (with Leonard Weinberg, 2003).

ARIE PERLIGER, Ph.D., is Instructor at the School of Political Science at the University of Haifa, Israel, and Assistant Fellow at The National Security Study Center, University of Haifa. His published works include "Altruism and Fatalism: The Characteristic of Palestinian Suicide Terrorists" (with Ami Pedahzur and Leonard Weinberg) in *Deviant Behavior* (July–August, 2003).

P. W. SINGER is National Security Fellow at the Brookings Institution and Director of the Brookings Project on U.S. Policy Towards the Islamic World. He is the author of *Children at War* (2005), from which his chapter in this publication is derived.

KEITH STANSKI is currently an independent consultant working with NGOs in Afghanistan and this fall will be pursuing graduate studies in International Relations, with a special focus on the language of terrorism. Keith earned a B.A. with honors in International Relations from Brown University, where he was Editor-in-Chief of the *Brown Journal of World*

Affairs. He has received several research and travel grants to study the armed conflict in Colombia, and has published widely on the topic.

J. MICHAEL WALLER, Ph.D., is the Walter and Leonore Annenberg Professor of International Communication at the Institute of World Politics in Washington, DC. He directs the Institute's graduate program on the study of public diplomacy and political warfare and has served as a consultant to the U.S. Information Agency, the Senate Foreign Relations Committee, the U.S. Agency for International Development, and the Office of the Secretary of Defense.

GABRIEL WEIMANN, Ph.D., is a professor of communication at the University of Haifa, Israel. His published works include *Communicating Unreality* (2000), *The Influentials: People Who Influence People* (1995), *The Theater of Terror* (1994), *Hate on Trial* (1986), and *The Singaporean Enigma* (2001). His chapter in this volume is based on a research project funded by the United States Institute of Peace, Washington, DC, where the author was a Senior Fellow in 2003–2004.

LEONARD WEINBERG, Ph.D., is Foundation Professor of Political Science at the University of Nevada. Over the course of his career he has been a Fulbright Senior Research Fellow for Italy, a Visiting Fellow at the National Security Studies Center (University of Haifa), and a consultant to the United Nations Office for the Prevention of Terrorism (Agency for Crime Control and Drug Prevention). His published works include *Political Parties and Terrorist Groups* (with Ami Pedahzur, 2003) and *Right-Wing Extremism in the Twenty-First Century* (with Peter Merk, 2003), and *Religious Fundamentalism and Political Extremism* (with Ami Pedahzur, 2003).